MW01631942

STRATEGIC ANTISUBMARINE WARFARE AND NAVAL STRATEGY

Tom Stefanick

Institute for Defense & Disarmament Studies

Lexington Books
D.C. Heath and Company/Lexington, Massachusetts/Toronto

Library of Congress Cataloging-in-Publication Data

Stefanick, Tom.
Strategic antisubmarine warfare and naval strategy.

Includes index.
1. Anti-submarine warfare. 2. Fleet ballistic missile weapons systems. 3. Naval strategy. 4. Nuclear warfare. 5. Nuclear disarmament. 6. Underwater acoustics. I. Title.
V214.S74 1987 359.4'3 86-45596
ISBN 0-669-14015-5 (alk. paper)

Published simultaneously in Canada
Printed in the United States of America
Casebound International Standard Book Number: 0-669-14015-5
Library of Congress Catalog Card Number: 86-45596

The paper used in this publication meets the minimum requirements of American National Standard for Information Sciences—Permanence of Paper for Printed Library Materials, ANSI Z39.48-1984.
∞ ™

89 90 91 8 7 6 5 4

You have seen a 688 class submarine. It is a mean looking machine. They are paranoid about that big black submarine.

Adm. Kinnaird McKee
Congressional testimony
May 1984

The Soviet Union will not allow any disruption of the present military-strategic balance in peacetime, and in a war it will always be ready to take crushing retaliatory action against any aggressor.

G. M. Sturua
"Strategic ASW: American Views and Policies"
February 1985

It will come,
Humanity must perforce prey on itself,
Like monsters of the deep.

William Shakespeare
King Lear
First performed in 1606

to my mother and father

Contents

List of Figures

List of Tables

List of Symbols

A	Surface area of a submarine
a	Approximately half the length of a submarine (App. 3)
a	Mutual kill probability (Chp. 2)
B	Processor bandwidth (A7.2)
B	Hull shape coefficient (A1.3)
b	Probability of clean blue kill (Chp. 2)
C	Speed of sound in seawater
c	Speed of light
C_f	Surface friction coefficient
D	Submarine hull diameter (A1.3; A3.1)
D	Detector threshold level (App. 7)
d	Hydrophone separation
E	Exchange ratio
f_c	Center frequency of narrowband
$\hat{f}$	Nearfield wave shape function
g	Acceleration of gravity
H	Separation of sonar arrays for triangulation
h	Depth of submarine centerline
I	Acoustic intensity
$\mathcal{J}$	Threshold for detection

K	Constant in propulsion equation
k_0	Wavenumber
L	Length of submarine (App. 1)
L	Length of sonar array (App. 5)
L_{wave}	Length of submarine-generated waves
M	Difference between two intensities in decibels
N	Number of hydrophones in an array
$\tilde{N}$	Average noise power per Hz
n	Integer number (A3.4)
n	Geometric spreading factor ($n = 2$ is spherical) (App. 5)
$n(t)$	Noise signal
P_s	Maximum propeller shaft horsepower
$p(x, t)$	Instantaneous pressure
p_{det}	Probability of detection
p_{fa}	Probability of false alarm
p_{max}	Maximum pressure
p_{rms}	Root mean squared pressure
Q_{1-2}	Correlation coefficient
R	Sound transmission range
r_0	Correlation distance
r	Probability of clean red kill
$S(t)$	Signal from hydrophone
$\tilde{S}$	Average signal power per Hz
$s(t)$	Signature of target
T_{avg}	Processor averaging time
T_{BV}	Brunt-Väisälä period
T_{wave}	Wave period
T_{rt}	Round-trip travel time of laser pulse between ocean surface and submarine

t	Time
U	Speed of submarine
$\tilde{U}$	Average total signal power per Hz
$u(t)$	Total signal
$W(U,D,h)$	Nearfield wave scaling function
x	Distance

Greek Symbols

α	Acoustic attenuation coefficient
$\zeta_{N,T}(x,0)$	Nearfield surface elevation on centerline
$\zeta_{F,T}(x,0)$	Farfield surface elevation on centerline
η	Propeller efficiency
θ	Angle
λ	Acoustic wavelength
π	3.14159 . . .
ρ	Density of seawater
σ_N^2	Noise variance
σ_{N+S}^2	Variance of signature plus noise
ψ^2	Average power per Hz

Foreword

Randall Forsberg
Executive Director
Institute for Defense & Disarmament Studies

Tom Stefanick has performed an exceptionally useful service for all concerned with the issues of peace and arms control: He has identified the major differences between the United States and the Soviet Union in the vulnerability of strategic submarines (SSBNs) and in strategy and forces for conducting strategic antisubmarine warfare (ASW).

For too long, Western analysts have tended to assume, without hard evidence, that Soviet SSBNs, like their US counterparts, were virtually invulnerable to detection. The first detailed, unclassified study to investigate this critical assumption, Stefanick's work shows that throughout the past 30 years, Soviet SSBNs have been much more vulnerable to detection than US SSBNs. Stefanick's study also shows that threatening Soviet strategic submarines has been a deliberate part of US naval strategy. Among other things, there are plans to send US attack or "hunter-killer" submarines, which are quieter than their Soviet quarry, into areas near Soviet SSBN ports. There they can, in theory, detect, trail, and destroy exiting submarines of all types, ignoring the risks that would be involved in attacking SSBNs. Alternatively, they could be directed to discriminate by sound signature between strategic and nonstrategic submarines and limit their attacks to the latter, although this would be very difficult in practice.

The vulnerability of Soviet SSBNs has undoubtedly had a profound impact on other aspects of Soviet policy. It has certainly increased Soviet reliance on land-based ICBMs. It has probably made the Soviet Union reluctant to accept fully symmetrical quantitative limits on strategic forces. Together with other factors, it may have influenced the size and composition of the Soviet general purpose Navy, which is designed in part to provide defensive barriers around SSBN deployment regions. (The US Navy has no counterpart to this mission.)

For years, the goal of arms control has been to increase crisis stability—making the use of nuclear weapons in a war or crisis extremely unlikely—while the goal of US nuclear policy has been to make escalation to acts of nuclear warfighting plausible, in order to help deter an East-West conventional war.

Strategic ASW is just one of the varied means of implementing the long-standing US policy of extended deterrence. Perhaps more than any other feature of US nuclear-warfighting capability, however, strategic ASW tends to erode the firebreak between nuclear and conventional war. For clandestinely destroying a strategic submarine carrying up to 200 nuclear warheads, using a conventional torpedo fired from an attack submarine, blurs the sharp line that we typically draw in our imaginations between nuclear and conventional war.

Given the risk that strategic ASW might lead to a general nuclear war, it is reassuring to learn from Stefanick's study that the vulnerability of Soviet SSBNs is declining. For some time it has been widely known that Soviet SSBNs became somewhat less vulnerable to detection in the 1970s, when long-range missiles allowed them to begin operating in shallow northern seas, instead of mid-ocean areas, where the deep sound channel can carry submarine noise for hundreds of miles. The new evidence assembled by Stefanick indicates that Soviet SSBNs have become even less vulnerable in the 1980s, and are likely to continue the trend in the 1990s. This is due to increased Soviet emphasis on submarine quieting, and diminishing returns to the US submarine quieting and sonar programs, as they approach the physical limits of achievement.

Stefanick concludes with several recommendations for US policymakers. He proposes that the US Congress mandate a study of the control of strategic ASW. He argues that the United States should stop contemplating threats to Soviet strategic submarines as an indirect means of forcing the USSR to end a conventional war. He observes that although in the near future Soviet general-purpose naval forces, especially new, quiet submarines, may be tied down defending SSBNs, this is unlikely to be so in the next century, given steady improvements in Soviet SSBNs. He concludes that such "tie down" should not be assumed in planning future US naval forces. Stefanick also points out that in order to strengthen US ASW capabilities against the increasingly quiet Soviet submarines of both types (strategic and general purpose), greater emphasis must be given to "distributed" airborne and fixed systems. Such systems will do much more to improve tactical ASW, aimed at defending the sea lanes across the Atlantic and the Pacific, than to strengthen capabilities for strategic ASW.

Stefanick's concluding recommendations stress technical developments and policy changes that tend to improve US military or naval efficiency while reducing the far forward ASW operations that threaten strategic submarines. Similarly, Stefanick's analysis of potential bilateral arms control measures to reduce or prevent strategic ASW stresses incentives for the US Navy to agree. He argues, for example, that limiting the ratio of each side's SSNs relative to the opponent's SSBNs might be "in US interest" because the United States "will be facing a decline in its technical advantage" over Soviet SSNs; and he dismisses SSBN sanctuaries on the grounds that they would release Soviet general purpose forces for other uses and would not benefit the already secure US SSBNs.

A basic point raised by Stefanick's study is whether the conduct of strategic ASW in a time of severe crisis or conventional war will increase the risk of a general nuclear war. Although concerned about this possibility, Stefanick concludes that US attacks with conventional weaponry on Soviet strategic submarines are not likely to provoke the use of nuclear weapons by the USSR, for several reasons: large-scale Soviet nuclear attacks on US cities would be suicidal; Soviet nuclear attacks on US aircraft carriers carrying nuclear weapons would not be necessary to sink or disable the carriers; and use of Soviet nuclear weapons against US attack submarines or other naval forces might start a tactical nuclear war near Soviet territory.

These points are plausible. The firebreak between conventional and nuclear war *may* hold, even if many Soviet strategic submarines are sunk by US forces in a war, because Soviet use of nuclear weapons is not a rational response. However, in a time of war or crisis, control and information will be in short supply, and responses may not be fully rational. Thus, in assessing the impact of strategic ASW, it is important to ask not only whether it will make the use of nuclear weapons *likely,* but also whether it will make the use of nuclear weapons *more likely* than if threats to Soviet strategic submarines were assiduously and explicitly avoided. Even if we accept Stefanick's view that US strategic ASW during a conventional war will not make Soviet use of nuclear weapons *likely,* we must allow that it may make Soviet use of nuclear weapons *more likely* than it would be otherwise. In fact, US attacks on the Soviet strategic nuclear reserve, in the heat of battle and with incomplete information, are almost certain to increase tension, confrontation, fear, suspicion, and hostility in a way that will pull the Soviet nuclear tripwire tighter than it might be otherwise.

Since US wartime conduct of strategic ASW will almost certainly increase the risk of a general nuclear war—even if it does not make a general nuclear war likely—policy recommendations in this area should look beyond the narrow "interest" of the United States as defined by pre-nuclear military standards to the broader global, US, and even post-nuclear military interest in avoiding a nuclear war. The standard of minimizing the risk of nuclear war—which should be the bottom line of every policy in the nuclear age—suggests that the United States, the Soviet Union, and the international community should all support stringent bilateral limits on the SSN-SSBN ratio—preferably less than one, certainly no more than one—and should adopt peacetime practices and wartime rules of engagement that provide SSBN sanctuaries in areas contiguous to SSBN ports.

These strategic ASW arms control measures may conflict with other interests of the United States, NATO, the US Navy, and, indeed, of the Soviet Union. And they may raise problems in regard to implementation (e.g., whether to count allied SSNs in the ratio) and enforcement (what to do if an agreed sanctuary area is violated). But the conflicting interests and the practical problems can and should be subordinated to the general interest in minimizing the risk of nuclear war. In force design, in warplans, and in peacetime deployments, threats to the opponent's strategic submarines should be strictly avoided. The US Navy should be directed to follow this policy by the US civilian leadership; and the international community should press the US civilian leadership to adopt the policy.

This difference on concluding policy recommendations concerns an important but small part of Stefanick's impressive study. The appendixes cover a truly extraordinary range of relevant technical material, which they digest and explicate clearly for the nonexpert. The analytical chapters of the main text clarify many poorly understood connections not only between strategic and tactical ASW, but also between nuclear and conventional war, between naval and land warfare, and between offensively oriented and defensively oriented naval forces. In sum, Stefanick's work represents a major advance in the unclassified literature on nuclear policy, on naval strategy, and on antisubmarine warfare.

Perhaps most important for the Institute for Defense and Disarmament Studies, Stefanick's study provides an essential piece of the technical foundation, previously lacking, needed to develop sound alternative defense policies. One component of such policies must be to dismantle the huge, dangerous panoply of US and Soviet nuclear-warfighting forces, built up over the past 30 years, cutting back to small, stable minimum or finite deterrent forces. Because strategic submarines are less vulnerable than other nuclear forces, they are the preferred candidate for carrying the residual force, after other nuclear systems are abolished. Whether or not they are adequately invulnerable to comprise the only remaining nuclear forces, on both sides, and for how long are important questions that Stefanick's thorough, meticulous study will help answer.

Acknowledgments

I am very grateful to Josie Stein for her help and encouragement. Her technical and editorial skills were extremely helpful in turning this project from a "study" into a manuscript.

Dr. Robert Urick spent many hours answering my questions about underwater acoustics and reviewing appendixes. Don Daniel very kindly shared an early draft of his book on strategic ASW, which provided the foundation for much of my thinking. Michael MccGwire took several afternoons out to discuss Soviet naval and military objectives, and guided me to many valuable references. Robert Herrick furnished me with very detailed analyses of Soviet views regarding the employment of their Navy. James McConnell proposed an alternative viewpoint, and outlined his own approach to the Soviet naval literature. Dr. Theodore Postol passed on some invaluable perspectives on the relationship of planning to political decisionmaking. Dr. James Tritten and others in the Net Assessment Office of the Office of the Secretary of Defense offered probing and valuable comments on an earlier draft. James Westwood reviewed the first printing very thoroughly and made useful suggestions for the second.

Charles Glaser, Peter Hayes, Robert Aldridge, and Frank von Hippel reviewed parts of the manuscript at an early stage, and all raised points which found their way into the final version. Capt. James Bush offered useful insight on submarine operations. Jan Breemer shared data from his files on submarines. The responsibility of the final result rests with me alone, and the views expressed herein do not necessarily reflect those of any institution or individual.

Work on this project was conducted at the Institute for Defense and Disarmament Studies from 1981 through 1985. I gratefully acknowledge the support of many foundations and individuals whose unrestricted grants to the Institute during that period made the work possible: The CS Fund, the Max and Anna Levinson Foundation, the Rockefeller Family Fund, Alan Kay, Hayward Alker, Jr., Stewart Rawlings Mott, several major individual donors who wish to remain anonymous, and many smaller contributors. I also thank Randall Forsberg for initially suggesting the project, and for supporting it through several major revisions of scope and definition.

The Federation of American Scientists supported the project in 1986, during the final stages of editing and preparing the book for publication. I am grateful to Jeremy Stone for generously allowing me the time to complete the work. We were both surprised at how long the "finishing touches" took.

Computer support at IDDS was provided by Bart Wright and Peter Steven. Word processing and in-house editing were performed by Deb Mapes, Nancy Piore, Amy Lustig, and Sarah Leinbach.

1
Strategic Antisubmarine Warfare

Introduction

In the United States, missiles on submarines at sea are considered the most survivable strategic nuclear force, and submarines carry about as many nuclear warheads as ICBMs and bombers combined. Soviet submarines are considered to be more vulnerable, and for geographical, technical, and bureaucratic reasons submarines carry a smaller portion of Soviet strategic warheads.

A concept from arms control theory closely associated with survivability is that of crisis stability: the reluctance of each side to launch strategic weapons in a crisis when it is clear that the opponent will retain enough nuclear weapons to retaliate with an intolerable blow, in the perception of the side that might have to bear the retaliation. This form of stability increases with the survivability of the weapons on both sides. The quintessentially unstable situation is one in which all strategic nuclear weapons on each side are vulnerable to rapid and total destruction. As long as leaders on each side believe that some portion of their own and the opponent's forces are invulnerable, some measure of crisis stability is preserved. This is the context in which the question of submarine vulnerability is usually posed: "Can enough strategic submarines survive a preemptive attack to deter the use of *any* strategic nuclear weapons in a preemptive first strike?"

The requirements of a sudden, totally disarming strike against missile submarines (SSBNs) are extremely stringent. Such a strike must be coordinated with attacks on land-based missiles and bombers; virtually all submarines must be destroyed, since the nuclear warheads on just a few submarines could destroy many targets on the homeland; and the entire attack must be very rapid. Moreover, the planning and preparation for such an attack must be covert. These requirements place a huge demand on command and control systems and on general purpose naval forces, which would have to be diverted from other missions to this one. The coordination requirement alone rules out such an attack, since the time needed for one side's ICBMs to attack the other's is just 30 minutes, while the time needed for one side's antisubmarine forces to detect, localize, trail, and destroy the other's submarines could be on the order of days or weeks. The time allowed for this process can be reduced—but then the likelihood of finding and destroying *all* of the opponent's submarines diminishes.

A disarming or damage-limiting strike becomes more plausible, however, if attacks on strategic submarines are carried out in an extended campaign of attrition prior to attacks against land-based forces. Moreover, the likelihood that World War III would begin as a conventional war introduces a period during which such an attrition campaign could be waged. In scenarios involving a protracted conventional war, for example, in east Asia or Europe, US naval forces would attack a wide range of targets, including bomber bases, shipyards, surface ships, aircraft, submarines, and their bases. In the course of such attacks, missile submarines at sea and in their hardened bases could be attacked by mines, torpedoes, and missiles.

The Soviet Navy is extremely unlikely to find even one US strategic submarine at sea. The US Navy, in contrast, has a good chance of finding at least a few Soviet missile submarines, and given time perhaps more than a few. The US Navy plans to take advantage of this capability by trailing some Soviet SSBNs in peacetime, and destroying them immediately upon the outbreak of conventional war. In addition, some Soviet SSBNs would probably be destroyed by US mines or by US attack submarines operating "far forward," engaged in a random search for Soviet submarines.

This raises several important questions: How much capability does the United States have to destroy Soviet strategic submarines? How much would it cost in general purpose naval forces for the US Navy to achieve various levels of attrition of Soviet ballistic missile submarines? What might the United States gain from destroying some Soviet missile submarines if it cannot destroy all? Related questions concern possible Soviet responses to attacks on their strategic submarines: How many missile submarines might the Soviet military command be willing to lose? What portion of the general purpose naval forces might they be willing to invest in defending the missile submarines?

There are four interlocking objectives that might be achieved by a partial US strike (or threatened strike) against Soviet missile submarines. The first is significantly limiting damage to the United States—that is, eliminating at least some of the weapons that can strike the United States. Without nearly complete elimination of the Soviet submarines and all other strategic forces, however, an attempt to limit damage is of questionable value for protecting population in an era of massive overkill.

A second potential objective is to help win a conventional war by means of a strategy of "horizontal escalation," in which a stalemate or US disadvantage in one theater of war is offset by a deliberate shift and escalation to strategic antisubmarine warfare. We know that the Soviet Navy places a very high priority on the ability to launch submarine-based missiles against the United

States. If the forces needed to carry out that mission are deliberately threatened by the United States in response to Soviet actions elsewhere, implying that continued hostilities will lead to the loss of more and more submarines, this may create pressure to end hostilities or to concede some other political objective. History suggests, however, that the calculated responses, risks, and benefits of such an indirect strategy are highly uncertain, and that horizontal escalation can backfire in many ways.[1]

A third potential objective of threatening partial destruction of the Soviet strategic submarine fleet is to provide the US Navy with conventional advantage at sea. Given the high priority of the strategic reserve mission in the Soviet Navy, the threat to destroy strategic submarines or their actual destruction may reasonably be expected to elicit a defensive response. Uncertain as to the magnitude of the threat, the Soviet leaders, some US planners believe, would tend to overestimate it and would allocate a disproportionately large part of their general-purpose naval forces to defend their strategic submarines. The basic principle is that an unknown threat to a highly valued asset can produce a magnified response because of uncertainty, a principle loosely referred to as leverage. In the words of Adm. Kinnaird R. McKee, director of the Nuclear Propulsion Program:

> In a crisis, fear of our attack submarines ties up Soviet naval and air forces that might otherwise be used against our NATO resupply, in support of a land campaign in Europe, or against our own supply lines. What we would most like to do is insert such uncertainty into Soviet estimates that they will be deterred from executing their war plans in the first place.[2]

The major concern of the US Navy in confrontations between US and Soviet general-purpose forces is the large Soviet fleet of attack submarines armed with torpedoes or cruise missiles. The Navy hopes to "tie up" many of these vessels, so as to lessen the potential threat to US aircraft carriers—a threat that is growing as Soviet attack submarines are built with quieter propulsion machinery. At the same time, reducing the number of Soviet attack submarines in the North Atlantic and North Pacific eases the burden of protecting the wartime sea lines of communication to Europe and Japan.

The aim of "tying up" the Soviet fleet during conventional war is to gain sufficient use of the sea, so that the Soviet leadership will be unlikely to be able to stop the resupply of allies (these scenarios assume a long conventional war). According to Navy officials this prospect is expected to inhibit the Soviet Union from going to war in the first place and from directly interfering with the United States in regions of competing interests.

The fourth objective of threatening Soviet SSBNs is to apply leverage at the strategic nuclear level. The Soviet leadership is sufficiently concerned about the survivability of its sea-based strategic forces that it has dedicated an entire branch of the Soviet armed forces to a primary mission of defending them. US nuclear policy is partly driven by the view that if Soviet leaders perceive *all* their strategic forces to be theoretically vulnerable, then they will not be willing to risk any confrontation with the United States for fear that the escalation from such a conflict will lead them into a level of warfighting in which they believe themselves to be inferior. Thus, the sum of the attrition threat from strategic antisubmarine warfare (ASW)—which would occur during a conventional war—plus the threat from a disarming strike against land-based weapons is becoming an explicit part of the US foreign policy of deterring direct Soviet interference with the United States. This is another version of the third objective.[3]

This study addresses strategic antisubmarine warfare in two basic contexts: the threat of a preemptive disarming first strike by either side against the other, and the US capability to conduct limited strikes against Soviet strategic submarines versus the Soviet capability to defend these submarines. The bulk of the analysis and discussion is on the US threat to Soviet strategic submarines, not because that question is more important, but because the nearly unanimous opinion of experts, as well as the results of the analysis in this study, show US strategic submarines to be more survivable for the foreseeable future. In addition, there has been relatively little analysis in the open literature on the vulnerability of Soviet submarines.

The remainder of chapter 1 outlines the various means of attacking strategic submarines, with particular emphasis on detection, and identifies probable limits to improvements in detection capabilities. The chapter concludes with a discussion of the vulnerability of submarines to underwater explosions as background for later discussions of barrage attack. Chapter 2 applies the general principles of chapter 1 to the case of US strategic antisubmarine warfare against Soviet SSBNs, ending with a discussion of Soviet defense against US attack submarines. Chapter 3 is an introduction to open ocean Soviet ASW threats to US strategic submarines. Unfortunately, the lack of time and resources prevented a more extended discussion of US submarines and Soviet ASW.[4] Chapter 4 contains an analysis of US naval strategy for fighting a conventional war with the Soviet Union and describes the potential role of strategic ASW in US attempts to contain the Soviet Navy. Chapter 5 discusses US policies (or lack of policies) regarding strategic ASW as a damage-limiting capability and the more recent thoughts regarding strategic ASW as a means of pressuring the Soviet Union to terminate hostilities if war begins. Chapter 6 summarizes the main conclusions.

Submarine Detection and Destruction

There are several essential tasks involved in destroying a submarine: detection, classification, localization to a small area, and destruction. Detection may provide very little information or a great deal, depending on the circumstances under which it is made. At one extreme, if the detection information is, say, that a submarine has passed through a strait from one sea to another, antisubmarine warfare forces may still face a formidable task in localizing it. At the other extreme, if a submarine enters an area fully monitored by a network of detection devices, it may be detected and tracked continuously. If the initial detection is made using a few long-range sensors that give only a rough indication of where the submarine is located, then additional effort will be needed to pinpoint it. If a detection system comprising many widely distributed, short-range sensors is used, then the detection and localization will be simultaneous. At some point in the process of detecting and localizing a submarine, it is usual to classify it by country, type, and class.

Once a submarine is located and sufficient information about it has been gathered, it may be attacked. If the localization is very precise and if the submarine can be attacked promptly, a small weapon such as a torpedo may have a high probability of destroying it. If the location of the submarine will be less certain by the time the weapon arrives, then the attacking forces must use several weapons, or a far more powerful weapon, or a weapon that can seek out the target. Modern navies take all three approaches: Soviet surface ships use short-range, rocket-propelled conventional depth charges in barrages; both the United States and the Soviet Union have nuclear-tipped ship- and submarine-launched weapons; and both sides use homing torpedoes of various types.

The location of the target may be uncertain by the time the weapon arrives because of a time lag, the "time late," between the launching of the weapon and its arrival at the point where the target was at launch time. Between launch and arrival, the submarine may have moved in any direction. Thus, the area of uncertainty is a circle whose radius is the product of the speed of the target submarine and the time late. Ballistic missiles suffer from a time late problem because their targeting information cannot be updated. A system such as a cruise missile or a terminally guided warhead, which can receive updated information in flight, or a homing torpedo or aircraft, which can generate its own updated information from on-board sensors, can compensate for the time late to some extent.

There are five potential operational schemes for conducting antisubmarine warfare against strategic submarines or SSBNs:

1. **Area search and destroy:** With no prior knowledge of the location of individual SSBNs, ASW platforms (aircraft, ships, or submarines) may systematically search large ocean areas believed to contain them. Using their own sensors and weapons, these ASW systems can attack SSBNs as soon as they are detected and localized.

2. **Barrage:** Again, with little or no prior knowledge of the location of SSBNs, one side can barrage an area with weapons, hoping to destroy all SSBNs that

may be in the area. To have high confidence of being effective, this would require a regularly spaced pattern of nuclear bombing over large parts of the ocean.

Alternatively, with *some* prior knowledge of SSBN locations, a more limited barrage attack can be launched to offset localization error and time late. Limited barrage relies heavily on area surveillance, tracking, and the availability of large numbers of very fast delivery systems—specifically, ballistic missiles.

3. **Area surveillance:** This is sometimes referred to as tracking. It may be continuous or sporadic, and it need not be continuous to threaten SSBNs. While surveillance does not include the destruction of submarines, it can support all phases leading up to the actual attack. Surveillance can be conducted by long-range sensors placed on the the periphery of a particular ocean area, or even beyond it, where they are arguably less vulnerable. Alternatively, there are "distributed" surveillance systems—fields of short-range sensors that rely on great numbers to scan a large area and to provide redundancy in case of sabotage. Contemporary US surveillance systems are based on acoustic detection, but there is considerable interest in nonacoustic surveillance techniques.[5] The status and potential of these techniques, particularly space-based remote surveillance, is the subject of ongoing debate both within and outside of the US government. Several such techniques are being investigated in the West as well as in the Soviet Union.

Area surveillance systems may be used to pass localization information to those controlling weapons—ballistic missiles in particular—for targeting a limited barrage. Information from area surveillance systems may also be sent to ASW platforms such as aircraft to indicate where they should begin to search for the submarine. This cooperation between stationary surveillance and mobile ASW units, called vectored intercept, is the key to US ASW barrier operations in the Greenland-Iceland-United Kingdom (GIUK) gap and elsewhere. The US Orion P-3 antisubmarine aircraft is considered at its most effective when operating with information provided by the US fixed Sound Ocean Surveillance System (SOSUS).

Surveillance systems that function with great effectiveness in peacetime may be quickly destroyed in wartime. Fixed systems based near the opponent's home waters, such as the US SOSUS surveillance system, are particularly vulnerable and are expected to be destroyed "probably before conflict starts by either sabotage or some other manner."[6] The United States has attempted to compensate for this vulnerability by building a fleet of special ships to tow long surveillance arrays, called Surveillance Towed Array System (SURTASS), through the areas covered by SOSUS. In addition to SURTASS, the US Navy has been developing a Rapidly Deployable Surveillance System (RDSS) that can be deployed by air if SOSUS is destroyed.

4. **Trailing:** Strategic submarines can be trailed as they leave their ports and begin their patrols or while they are on patrol. Quiet nuclear-powered attack

submarines (SSNs) are the best platform for trailing SSBNs because they are relatively hidden and invulnerable, can go anywhere an SSBN goes, and have comparable endurance. Attack submarines can trail overtly using active ("pinging") sonar, which broadcasts their own position. Alternatively, they can trail covertly, albeit less reliably, with passive (listening) sonar. Either way, trailing requires some area surveillance or area search to acquire a target SSBN initially.

5. **Bastion attack and antisubmarine barriers:** The notion of *active defense* of SSBNs within ocean bastions—completely alien to US strategic submarine policy—is central to Soviet naval policy. A large-scale attack on Soviet SSBNs within heavily defended waters could be carried out only by US attack submarines, and it would require some surveillance, some area search, and some trailing. To enter or leave defended bastions and to operate within them, US attack submarines would have to avoid or defeat several potential threats: Soviet mine barriers around the periphery of the bastions and within them; Soviet diesel-electric submarines; Soviet nuclear-powered attack submarines escorting SSBNs or patrolling barriers; area surveillance; and the considerable self-defense capability of Soviet SSBNs themselves.

Acoustic and nonacoustic detection methods that are too costly for ocean-wide surveillance may prove useful and feasible in the limited role of guarding the periphery of a bastion. Since they would support the Soviet Navy's primary mission of defending SSBNs, developments in Soviet acoustic and nonacoustic detection systems are expected to play a role in bastion defense long before they gain more offensive, wide-ranging applications.

A special vulnerability arises when an SSBN fires its ballistic missiles, for it emits powerful signals that broadcast its position. Ejecting the missile from a tube using gas or steam under very high pressure generates a loud noise. In addition, the infrared signature of the missile's exhaust is detectable from air or space, and the missile itself can be detected by radar. If the submarine were to fire all its missiles in sequence, it would have to do so in a time shorter than the time required for hostile ASW forces to detect, localize, and attack it. If the submarine were to participate in a limited nuclear attack, it is important that the launch of a few missiles not significantly reduce the ability of that submarine to fire missiles at a later time.

Still another potential vulnerability of SSBNs is that the communication systems that send submarines their instructions may be attacked in an attempt to prevent submarines from receiving a launch order. Most primary transmitters are very large because they must broadcast at very low radio frequencies to penetrate seawater, and these large installations are difficult to harden. The US Navy, however, provides many wartime backup systems to supplement its primary communication channels, and US strategic submarines can technically fire their missiles without any instructions or codes from the National Command Authorities. The Soviet Union also maintains redundant communications systems and may have the ability to launch without a code from higher authorities.

Other methods of minimizing SSBN threats include destroying navigation support and interception of missiles during the various phases of their flights.

Potentials and Limits of Passive Acoustic Detection

Systems that detect the sound radiated by submarine machinery and propellers are called passive sonars; those that emit a sound that reflects back from a target submarine hull are called active sonars. In the past, passive detection offered longer detection range against noisy targets in deep water because active sonar could not emit sufficient power for very long round-trip propagation, and it was hampered by reverberation of the emitted pulse off the ocean bottom, the surface, and particles and organisms in the sea. In addition, a submarine using passive sonar could detect a submarine using active sonar several times farther away than the user of the active sonar could detect it. Recently, however, as submarines have become extremely quiet, the relative importance of active sonar is beginning to grow. The most recently developed classes of US strategic and attack submarines are so quiet that they are detectable at longer ranges with active sonar than with passive sonar. Nonetheless, the use of active sonar remains unattractive because it entails a high risk of detection and counter-attack. Drawing on material in several of the appendixes, this section summarizes the potential capability of passive detection, with emphasis on prospects for technical breakthroughs. The emphasis on passive detection, especially in the context of submarines' hunting other submarines, reflects the fact that submarines are the best mobile antisubmarine system, and that passive detection is now and will remain the preferred US Navy tactic for conducting antisubmarine warfare from another submarine.

There are two basic parameters needed to describe sound: the *intensity* of the sound, and its distribution among various *frequencies*. The standard measure of intensity is the decibel (dB), which is ten times the logarithm (base ten) of the intensity of a given sound relative to a standard reference intensity: for example, a sound that is 10 times louder than the reference is 10 dB higher; a sound 100 times louder is 20 dB higher. Frequency is measured in cycles per second, or hertz (Hz). The frequency range of interest in ASW is roughly in the range audible to humans: 10–20,000 Hz. Frequencies below a few hundred hertz are considered "low"; those between a few hundred and a few thousand hertz are "medium" frequencies.

Most sounds contain a spectrum of frequencies of different intensities. The spectrum may contain a continuous distribution of sound energy over a broad band of frequencies: this will sound like a hiss. Rapidly turning propellers create small bubbles that generate such a noise, called cavitation noise. A sound may also be composed of several distinct tones at several discrete frequencies. A musical chord is such a sound, containing three or more individual tones that combine to make a pleasing sound. Rotating machinery on submarines generates sounds that lie in narrow frequency bands. Nuclear submarines within a particular class, equipped with the same machinery, generally share a similar narrowband frequency spectrum. With this information passive sonar operators can sometimes identify the nationality and class of an unknown submarine. Unique machinery noises may even permit identification of a particular submarine.

Submarines make different kinds and levels of sound at different speeds. When a nuclear-powered submarine is stopped, it must continue to run reactor cooling pumps, generators, and air conditioning. These generate narrowband spectra that are relatively independent of speed. As the submarine begins to move slowly, narrowband turbine and gear sounds in the propulsion system are generated, some of which are speed dependent. In addition, the individual blades on the slowly moving propeller (less than 60 rpm), act as a low-level sound source as they rotate through the nonuniform flow behind the submarine. At speeds of 5–8 knots (9.3–14.7 km/hr), US and Soviet submarines produce sufficiently low levels of noise to permit the use of their own passive sonar systems. At higher speeds, turbulence near the passive arrays as well as the submarine's own noise begin to reduce the effectiveness of that submarine's passive sonars. Finally, at speeds in excess of 25 knots (46 km/hr) or so, at moderate depths, cavitation noise may set in, rendering the passive systems useless. At the "quiet" speeds of up to 8 knots (14.7 km/hr), the US submarines are much quieter than Soviet submarines. On the other hand, a US submarine running at high speeds at shallow depths will produce about the same cavitation noise as a Soviet submarine operating under the same conditions. However, at moderate depths and high speeds US submarines probably do not cavitate, whereas Soviet submarines may, giving the United States an acoustic advantage during "sprints."[7] From a tactical standpoint, the relative sound output at quiet speed is probably more important, since that is the speed at which US and Soviet attack submarines hunt.

Passive sonar systems have advantages over active ones in that they emit no energy and are covert; they can in some circumstances provide information on the type of submarine being detected through its particular sound signature (in the way that people have a characteristic voice signature); and they can detect loud sounds at very long ranges. Their disadvantages are that they must use long arrays of underwater microphones (hydrophones), such long arrays must be fixed on the sea floor or towed slowly on long cables behind submarines or ships, and from a single measurement, most passive sonars yield information only on the direction to the target. The latter is important because both distance and direction to the target is necessary to launch torpedoes or other ASW weapons. The size of the array is very important because to receive low frequencies (below 100 Hz) efficiently requires the use of line arrays longer than

50 feet (15 meters), and for 10 Hz sounds the length should exceed 500 feet (150 meters). Active sonars are much smaller.

In this chapter I discuss only the sensitivity of passive sonars, that is, the maximum detection range against quiet submarines. This discussion is in the context of long surveillance arrays like the US SOSUS, which is planted between Greenland, Iceland, and the United Kingdom, or long arrays towed behind submarines or surface ships. From a tactical standpoint, an equally important question is how efficiently a passive sonar system can localize its target, that is, determine the direction and distance. This is discussed later in the context of submarine versus submarine tactics.

The sensitivity of passive sonar systems can be improved in three ways: by increasing the amount of time over which they accumulate or integrate a sample of signal embedded in noise; by decreasing the frequency bandwidth over which they process narrowband signatures; and by discriminating against ambient noise arriving at the array from directions other than the direction of the target. These parameters cannot be improved without limit, however. The internal and surface motions of the sea and its spatial variability conspire to impose restrictions on sonar improvements that are extremely difficult to overcome.

The goal of signal processing is to enable the sensor operator to discriminate between incoming data that indicate the absence of a submarine (ambient noise) and data that indicate the presence of a submarine (ambient noise plus signal).[8] The smaller the "signal-to-noise" ratio (that is, the quieter the submarine or the louder the ambient noise), the more difficult it will be to discriminate reliably between cases where the submarine is present and those where it is not. The most basic model of passive sonar signal detection can be imagined as a sound threshold that is set at some increment above the average noise level. If the addition of sound from a submarine drives the total sound level over the threshold, a signal interpreted as a submarine sound is "detected" by the processor. The smaller the increment between the average ambient noise level and the detection threshold, the smaller the signal that can be detected.

Both background noise and submarine-generated signals are random variables, however, and both vary around a mean. As a result, there is a chance that background noise will exceed the threshold and trigger a false alarm. For any given setting of the detection threshold, the probability of this happening depends on how much variance there is in the noise: more variance means more chance of noise alone exceeding the threshold and causing a false alarm. This leads to a basic trade-off in signal processing. If the threshold is high, the probability of a false alarm will be low, but the chance of detecting a faint submarine sound will also be low. If the threshold is low, this will offer a better probability of detecting a quiet sound, but it will increase the chance of false alarms. Ordinarily, there is no way to avoid this trade-off: the sonar operator must set the threshold by comparing the value of ensuring detection with the value of avoiding false alarms. The "hunter's" situation can be improved by reducing the variance in the signal processor's estimate of the ambient noise level. This can be done by simply taking a larger sample of the noise: that is, using a longer time period over which data are averaged. With less variance in the noise estimate, it is possible to set the threshold lower without increasing the false alarm probability. Doubling the averaging time of a sonar processor would yield a 40 percent (1.5 dB) decrease in the detectable signal-to-noise ratio if the statistics of the signal and ambient noise remained constant.

Fluctuations in the signal are introduced, however, as the target submarine moves through the nonhomogeneous sea. In addition, the sea's internal waves and currents cause fluctuations in the transmission of both signal and noise. As a result, some measurements have indicated that the detection capability of a sonar system does not improve consistently with longer averaging times: a 1.5 dB decrease in the detection threshold has been observed as averaging time doubles up to 0.5 seconds, but increases in averaging time between 0.5 and 120 seconds have in some circumstances had little further effect on the threshold. Although it is not clear how general this result is, it does suggest one fundamental physical constraint on improvements in passive sonar signal processing.[9]

This effect of the nonhomogeneous sound transmission medium of the ocean can be partially circumvented by accumulating samples of the signal in the computer for a series of short periods and then representing successive estimates of the spectra of those samples on a visual display where a human operator averages them visually. In one type of display, a few seconds of data are averaged, and then across an electronic screen on which frequency is displayed horizontally, a black mark is made if the threshold is exceeded at a given frequency. Successive observations of the frequency spectrum of the ocean noise are displayed one below the other. When a target is just on the threshold of detectability, its signature may be just high enough to appear for a brief moment and then fade, so in looking down the screen, there may be places where the submarine sound is apparent, below which there may be nothing. A human operator can recognize such a pattern and ignore the blank spots where the signal fades, whereas a system that integrates a long period of "no signal" together with brief periods of "signal present" might well miss the signal. The method of using human operators as part of the processing seems to yield some improvement over purely automated detection systems.

A second limit on integration time is tactical: the time available for a decision may not be sufficiently long to permit extended integration. As the target submarine moves, it may lose the tracker or move beyond range of attack.

A third limit on integration time is that longer integration times degrade the gain of a listening array. As integration time lengthens, the ocean appears to be a less coherent transmission medium, and array gain depends on signal coherence. Under Arctic and shallow water ice, where much of the hunt for

Soviet SSBNs would occur, the ambient noise is generally different from that found in open seas. The cracking of ice due to temperature changes and the banging and rubbing of ice floes generate ambient noise, which, though similar to open ocean noise in intensity, may not share its statistical properties. The ordinary model for determining whether or not a signal is present on top of noise assumes that both signal and noise have bell-shaped probability distributions around the mean. A specific bell-shaped distribution called the Gaussian distribution is assumed. By using detection-decision criteria that rely on the impulsive, non-Gaussian character of underice noise, the performance of a sonar may be improved (that is, the detection threshold lowered) by a few to as many as 12 dB.[10] This does not mean, however, that detection conditions under ice are always better than in the open sea.

Sonar capability can also be improved by processing the sound in narrow frequency bands, matching the widths of the individual tones (called *tonals* in the jargon) of the source. For example, if there is a 1-Hz-wide submarine tonal embedded in broadband noise, then a matching filter that is 1 Hz wide will admit all of the signal energy but only a small fraction of the noise energy, thereby maximizing the signal-to-noise ratio. Narrower filters would reduce the signal at the same rate as they reduced the noise, leaving the signal-to-noise ratio constant. Wider filters would admit more of the broadband noise, while leaving the signal energy constant, reducing the signal-to-noise ratio. Since the cost in terms of processing time and complexity increases as the filter bandwidth decreases, the optimum bandwidth is that which just matches the narrowest tonal width.

If the submarine generates a fixed amount of acoustic energy in a tonal at a particular frequency, then the narrower that tonal, the narrower the filter bandwidth that can be used to match it, and therefore the higher the signal-to-noise ratio. Many of the rotational machines on submarines have very high inertia and rotate at nearly constant speeds. As a result, the vibrations they emit lie in very narrow frequency bands. However, as these signals propagate through the ocean, their energy becomes smeared over wider bandwidths, partially due to interactions with internal waves and partially due to reflections off the moving sea surface. Minimum transmission bandwidths may vary from 0.01 Hz to 1 Hz, depending on ocean conditions and interactions with the sea surface.[11] By spreading the submarine noise energy over wider frequency bands, the sea imposes a limit on improving the signal-to-noise ratio through narrower filtering.

One way to make a submarine hard to detect is to shift constantly the speed of main machinery so as to cause the emitted tonals to drift in frequency somewhat. A drift of just a few hertz on a signal of several hundred hertz would oblige ASW sonar operators to use wide processing filters to capture all of the energy within one band, or, if very narrow bands were used, would spread the energy over several of them, preventing an accumulation of averaging time in any one of them. Either way, the signal-to-noise ratio (and therefore the detectability) is reduced, even though the submarine is not actually quieter.

A third way to improve sonar detection capability is to increase the spatial discrimination of the receiving array. To the extent that an array can accept signals and noise from a particular direction while rejecting noise from all other directions, it can improve discrimination of signal against noise compared with a nondirectional receiver. Under the idealized conditions of perfectly coherent signals in an isotropic noise medium (with noise arriving in equal measure from all directions), this improvement, called the array gain, is proportional to the ratio between the array length and the acoustic wavelength. This means that, in theory, array gain might increase without limit. The spatial coherence of any signal—that is, its statistical correlation from one point to the next—is limited, however. Similarly, noise is never perfectly isotropic. As a result, potential array gain is limited.

Evidence available in the unclassified literature suggests that the maximum array gain achievable under most circumstances, for long-range, low-frequency detection with an arbitrarily long array, is about 20 dB. In cases when there are many alternate transmission paths through the ocean between source and receiver, the figure is probably lower. For small arrays—those associated with sonobuoys, the Rapidly Deployable Surveillance System, and small, distributed surveillance systems—the array gain at low frequencies is much lower.

This limit on improvements in array performance is partly responsible for the shift in emphasis by the US Defense Advanced Research Projects Agency (DARPA) in the early 1980s away from very long arrays for acoustic surveillance to distributed systems with many short-range sensors.[12] Cost-effectiveness considerations probably also played a role in this shift. The cost of a passive sonar surveillance system is roughly proportional to its array length, and the limits the ocean imposes on increased gain with increasing length depress the ratio of effectiveness to cost.

There is no known computational method for completely overcoming the limits on improving the signal-to-noise ratio that are imposed by the complexity and variability of the ocean medium. Modern advances in signal processing generally provide gains measured in no more than fractions of decibels. Moreover, "there are few processing tricks remaining that might lower the threshold signal-to-noise ratio for detection faster than the rate at which the world's submarines are getting quieter."[13] Special computer processing of the arrays themselves (as a part of signal processing) can adapt their functioning to the statistics and spatial characteristics of the signal and noise fields. The principal gain of adaptive processing, however, lies in discriminating between two sound sources that are close together, both exhibiting high signal-to-noise ratios; but in ASW surveillance, the main problem is detecting very low signals buried in high levels of background noise. Thus, adaptive processing is not likely to offer greatly improved long-range surveillance of increasingly quiet submarines.

In the 1970s, the DARPA Acoustic Research Center (ARC) was responsible for state-of-the-art research in long-range surveillance, using SOSUS in conjunction with supercomputers such as the Illiac IV. The conclusion of the ARC research effort is that the potential for acoustic detection has "nearly been met and any additional significant advances can be expected to be expensive and difficult to implement."[14]

Since the limits on improvements in array gain are related to the scrambling of the signal over the transmission path through the ocean, there is reason to believe that detailed knowledge of the transmission path might permit a reversal of the scrambling process, thereby improving array performance. There are two strategies for obtaining this information: to take "point" acoustic measurements throughout the ocean at a sufficiently fine scale, or to take "slice" acoustic measurements crisscrossing throughout the ocean, again at a sufficiently fine scale. Since it appears that internal waves generally dominate the oceanic influences on signal coherence (and therefore array performance),[15] they determine the required scale of resolution. At the peak of the internal wave spectrum, the horizontal scales of internal waves are on the order of 2.7 nm (5 km),[16] so the resolution should be on the order of 1 nm (2 km). This means that to obtain information on the perturbations of the ocean transmission path caused by internal waves in an ocean area 540 nm (1,000 km) by 540 nm (1,000 km), a quarter of million "point" measurements would be required!

The alternative, called acoustic ocean tomography, involves taking a set of transmission samples that slice through the area of interest from one part of the periphery to another, and from the transmission properties of such slices, to infer the structure of the interior.[17] In order to attain the required degree of resolution, the spacing of the sensors on the periphery must be 2 km. With this method, the total number of sampling stations is reduced from 250,000 to 2,000. However, at this density of deployment, it is more cost-effective to install sonar arrays for detecting submarines directly than to use tomographic arrays to analyze the acoustic field and then add sonar arrays to detect submarines. The real value of acoustic tomography lies in its usefulness as a technique for mapping large-scale oceanographic structures such as fronts and eddies. Distributed systems involving many short-range 2.7–8 nm (5–15 km) sensors scattered throughout a surveillance area would require fewer sensors than a tomography system and would, in addition, detect the high-frequency components in the submarine spectrum, which are not transmitted long distances due to absorption. These high-frequency components aid in the process of target classification.

Taking into account the various limitations on passive sonar, I have estimated the minimum detection threshold to be in the neighborhood of −16 dB—that is, a tone can be detected if the noise is at most 40 times louder.[18] Maximum array gain at low frequencies is estimated to be about 20 dB; in other words, by shutting out noise from many different directions, an array can improve the signal-to-noise ratio by a factor of 100 at most. These figures should be considered the best that can be attained at low frequencies over long ranges in deep water with idealized sonar array and processing systems. Under most circumstances, in shallow water, for example, or on smaller systems, the array gain will be lower and the detection threshold higher. For instance, it is reported that the array gain associated with sonobuoys is on the order of 5 dB.

These figures are used in appendix 8 as the basis for estimating the detection range of a surveillance system in the Arctic Ocean and surrounding seas. Separate estimates are given for the detection range of a passive sonar, detecting a single, narrow-band signal of specified intensity, under the best and worst expected conditions for detection. Since optimistic estimates are used for the sonar system parameters, both the maximum and minimum detection ranges should be overestimates most of the time. The most striking feature of the detection range estimates is the large variance between the calculated minimum and maximum. In most cases, the maximum range is greater than the minimum by at least a factor of three; in some cases, it is greater by a factor of ten.

There are occasional public reports of sonar detection range, but they are more misleading than instructive because they offer little or no information about the conditions in which detections were made. Some reports have claimed, for example, that submarines were detected at ranges of 3,000 to 6,000 miles (6520–11,040 km), and were localized to circular areas with radii of 8 to 45 miles (14.7–83 km).[19] One author asserts that "SOSUS can spot a sub anywhere in the ocean when conditions are favorable and pinpoint it within a sixty-mile radius."[20] The analysis in appendixes 4–8 strongly suggests that while such detection ranges may have been possible, they are extreme cases that are associated with only the noisiest submarines. Some modern submarines have become quiet enough to avoid detection at ranges of tens of miles, even with relatively good conditions for detection in the deep ocean.

Potentials and Limits of Nonacoustic Detection

Since most nonacoustic detection techniques involve the emission and detection of electromagnetic radiation, it is helpful to begin by reviewing the electromagnetic spectrum. Figure 1–1 shows the spectrum of frequencies in cycles per second, or hertz (Hz), and wavelength (in meters), and the different kinds of radiation in various regions of the spectrum.

The ability of electromagnetic radiation to penetrate seawater is a complicated function of frequency. Frequencies that can penetrate deeper than a few meters are those below 100 Hz and those above 10^{19} Hz. The lowest end of the radio wave band, around 60 Hz (called extremely low frequency [ELF]), is used for submarine communication. Between very high and very low frequencies,

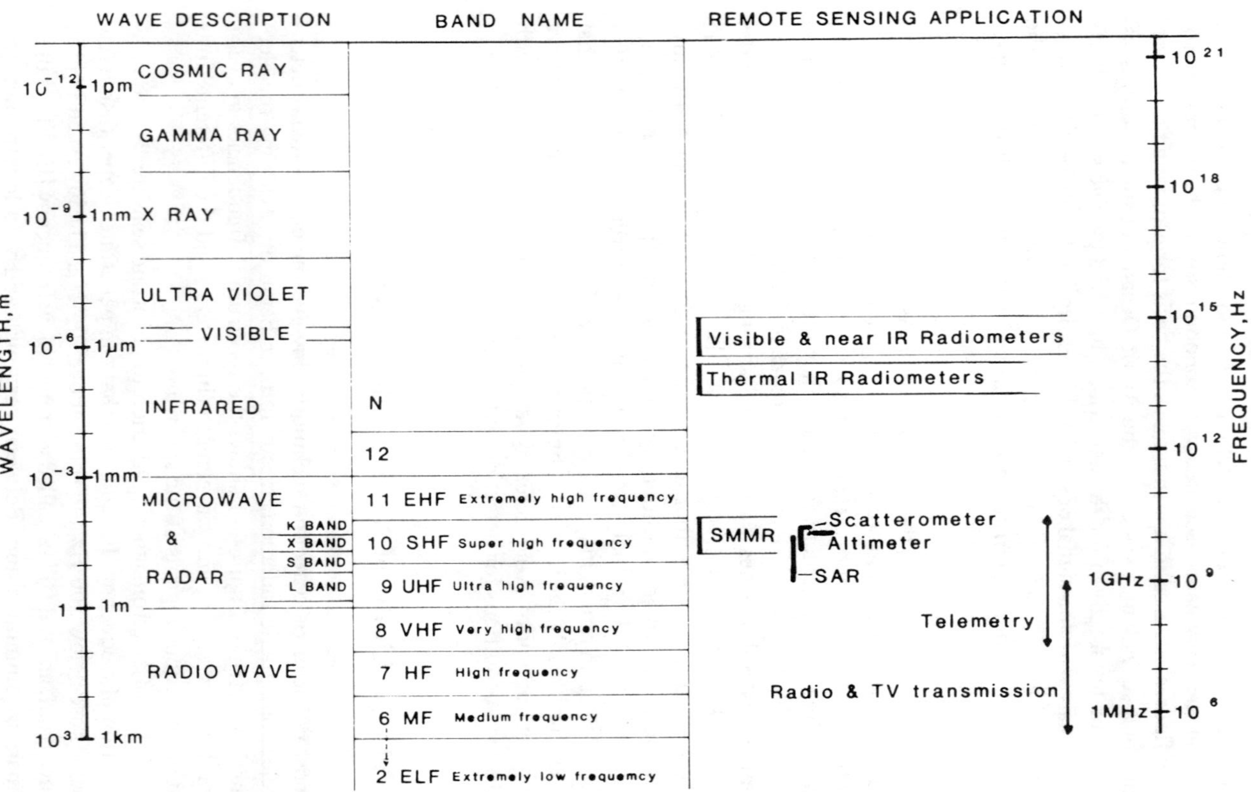

Figure 1–1. The electromagnetic spectrum.

Source: I. S. Robinson, *Satellite Oceanography* (New York: John Wiley & Sons, 1985), fig. 2.11, p. 42.

water is very nearly opaque to electromagnetic radiation except for a very narrow band in the blue to blue-green portion of the visible spectrum.

At present it appears unlikely that any nonacoustic detection technology will allow large-scale remote surveillance and localization of SSBNs on patrol in the next 15 years. However, several phenomena and the technologies associated with detecting them, particularly those associated with internal waves, are not sufficiently well understood to be ruled out as irrelevant to the problem of submarine detection. There are other potential uses for these technologies that may be on the horizon: preventing the intrusion of hostile SSNs into SSBN patrol areas; conducting limited surveillance at chokepoints for tactical ASW; and permitting submarine-to-shore or submarine-to-submarine communication.

All nonacoustic detection technologies still have major technological and financial hurdles to overcome between the drawing board and an operational surveillance system. Perhaps the most important problem is that all these systems can be incapacitated relatively easily by countermeasures: false targets, jamming, or direct attack. In general, the chief technical difficulty is not their lack of sensitivity, but the very low signal-to-noise ratio, which cannot be offset by increased sensitivity. If a submarine is cooperating, any of these systems can be shown to work, but the single most effective countermeasure to all of them is the target submarine's operating elusively, so as to avoid them. As with acoustic detection, a poorly operated submarine can be easy to find, and one that is operated well is extremely difficult to find.

The following sections survey briefly the most prominently discussed nonacoustic technologies relevant to submarine detection. Where appropriate, I have included statements made by the technical director of the US SSBN Security Program, Dr. Edward Y. Harper, who reviewed the state of nonacoustic detection technology for the Senate Armed Services Committee in 1984. A more complete analysis of the nonacoustic detection technologies is given in appendix 3.

Magnetic Detection

The main obstacle to detecting the magnetic field associated with a submarine is the low signal-to-noise ratio. As the sensitivity of magnetic sensors increases,[21] their sensitivity to the spatial and temporal fluctuations in the earth's magnetic field also increases. Some of this can be filtered, but not the part of the noise that lies in the same frequency range as expected target signals. Therefore, the signal-to-noise ratio, which is the most important measure of detectability, will remain approximately the same. A second technical problem is that signal strength decreases with the cube of range. As a result, a hundredfold increase in sensitivity provides less than a fivefold increase in range. Current ranges in quiet environments are on the order of a few thousand feet. This is useful for localization, but is much too short for large-area surveillance. Countermeasures to magnetic detection are free-swimming electromagnets to generate false targets, demagnetization of the hull, and use of nonmagnetic materials. The United States currently employs false targets and demagnetization. It is not known whether the Soviet Union uses false targets, but since the technique is simple, they probably do. In addition, it is known that the USSR uses nonmagnetic materials in some of their submarines.

Magnetic detection devices, called magnetic anomaly detectors, or MAD, are deployed on ASW aircraft for final localization. In the future, magnetic surveillance across relatively shallow barriers may prove feasible for limited surveillance. On the sea floor, moored on cables, on the sea surface, or on the ice, magnetic sensors can provide a passive backup to acoustic sensors. Since magnetometers have a short range, large numbers must be deployed even for a limited surveillance system. This makes low unit cost an important prerequisite.

Bioluminescence Detection

Once submarines are submerged beyond a hundred meters, there is very little chance that there will be a strong turbulent disturbance at the surface, effectively ruling out surface bioluminescence, or, the light emitted by living organisms. In addition, powerful bioluminescent activity at submarine diving depth is not known to be a widespread phenomenon, and any bioluminescent light originating at these depths is strongly attenuated by the overlying water. Even at night and with high densities of bioluminescent organisms, the signal-to-noise ratio measured at the sea surface is so small that detection is precluded. Soviet strategic submarine patrol areas do not appear to include regions that have high levels of bioluminescence, but there is very little data available. There would appear to be little need for special countermeasures to avoid detection of bioluminescent disturbance, the most effective being simply to remain at depths below one hundred meters or so, in order to avoid disturbing the surface.

The one concern about bioluminescence is that it can degrade a blue-green laser communication system by generating "noise" in the submarine's laser receiver. That is, turbulent water flowing over the submarine's laser receiver may contain luminescent organisms that could flash directly into it. These flashes may be relatively powerful compared with the weak communication signal that must pass through the atmosphere and part of the ocean before being received. The Navy's continued interest in bioluminescence may have as much to do with submarine communications as it does with ASW.

Submarine-generated Surface Waves

Two types of surface wave are generated by submarines: the near-field wave or Bernoulli hump, which exists directly over the submarine and a few hundred meters behind it; and the far-field or Kelvin-type wave, which may persist for thousands or tens of thousands of meters behind. The far-field wave is equivalent to the wave pattern that is visible behind a moving surface ship, except that behind a submerged submarine, the wave field is much weaker. Under normal patrol conditions, the near-field wave is on the order of a millimeter high, and the far-field wave is not apparent. Edward Harper said about the near-field wave, "that miniscule displacement at the surface is completely swamped by the wave action at the surface."[22]

The moving submarine generates an underwater pressure disturbance that is associated with the surface near-field wave. Very low frequency pressure or acoustic sensors could be used to detect this signal, but only at very short range. Some underwater mines use this signal as a triggering mechanism.

Submarine-generated Internal Waves

As a submarine moves through the stratified water of the thermocline, it creates an unstable cylindrical wake that collapses and produces internal waves. Unlike surface waves, internal waves are oscillations of internal temperature layers, and they cannot be seen on the surface directly as variations in the surface height. They can, however, affect the radar-reflecting properties of the surface by modulating surface ripples. Internal waves can generate surface currents, which, in turn, can change the characteristic wavelengths of capillary waves or very short (on the order of 10 cm) gravity waves. These surface currents can also cause the naturally occurring film of organic matter and oil to thicken into bands that alter the surface tension and the thermal and microwave emissivity of the surface. The change in the surface tension can alter the characteristics of the capillary waves, thereby altering the radar-scattering properties of the surface. To give an example, according to Harper, the SEASAT A satellite passed over US missile submarines four times during its period in orbit, including once over a submarine traveling at 5.5 knots (10 km/hr) at the very shallow keel depth of about 58 feet (18 meters). In no case was the submarines' presence apparent in the radar data presented to Congress—a result consistent with the US Navy's theoretical analysis, according to Harper.[23] In addition, naturally occurring forces can modulate surface ripples, generating noise and even false targets.[24] According to some Navy officials, recent tests from the space shuttle confirm the judgment that surface effects due to submarine-generated internal waves cannot be reliably detected.

It would seem from official US Navy statements that detection of internal waves from their surface effects could not provide even a partially effective system for area surveillance or even barrier detection. However, some Soviet statements have been interpreted as hints of a "breakthrough" in this area, and some "leaked" US reports suggest this possibility. Currently the weight of available evidence does not support a Soviet "breakthrough." A striking feature of the evidence regarding synthetic aperture radar (SAR) detection of internal wave effects is the contrast between the technical literature and the official statements of the Navy. The former imply that many of the physical processes relevant to the problem are still poorly understood. The official Navy position, on the other hand, is explicit on the subject of the infeasibility of the technology, implying that the level of scientific understanding is high. This cannot be easily explained by the fact that the Navy has access to classified information, since the uncertainty arises at the level of basic science, much of which is unclassified.

Temperature Change at the Surface

There are several mechanisms by which a submarine can change the apparent temperature of the sea surface, and it is useful to separate them in order to avoid confusion. The submarine may mix deeper, colder water up to the surface, or heat the water with its reactor cooling system, both of which processes actually change the water temperature. Submarine-generated wakes, vortices, or internal waves may cause surface currents, which in turn sweep organic and oil surface films into thicker or thinner layers. These layers of film change the apparent temperature of the surface by altering the emissivity of the surface, in either the infrared or microwave regions of the spectrum. These phenomena are therefore hydrodynamically induced changes in the apparent temperature. Actual changes in surface water temperature are caused by turbulent transport of water from the submarine wake.

The turbulent wake of a submarine traveling below 165 feet (50 meters) is unlikely ever to reach the surface for two main reasons. First, it can be shown that the diameter of the turbulent wake generated by a submarine grows very slowly with distance behind the submarine. The diameter grows as the fourth root of distance, measured in hull diameters. At a distance of one hull diameter, the diameter of the wake is about equal to the hull diameter, 36 feet (11 meters). At a thousand times that distance (over a kilometer), the diameter of the wake is theoretically only 204 feet (62 meters). This means that it extends only 50 feet (15 meters) over the top of the submarine sail, the large structure on top of the submarine. At 6 miles (11 km), the wake theoretically extends only 132 feet (40 meters) above the top of the sail.

The waste heat from the reactor raises the temperature of the surrounding water, causing the wake to become buoyant. As the wake expands and pulls in more cold water, however, its temperature decreases rapidly to a few hundredths of a degree centigrade above the ambient temperature. In ocean waters as far north as the Norwegian Sea, solar heating of water near the surface ensures that as the slightly heated wake rises, it will encounter an equal temperature in the ambient water, causing its buoyancy force to disappear. As a result, the buoyancy introduced by reactor heating probably does not significantly affect the growth of the wake.

The second main reason that the submarine wake does not reach the surface is that within a few miles behind the submarine, the wake collapses. Because the wake contains a mixture of cooler water entrained from below and warmer water from above, its temperature is slightly warmer than the water below it, and slightly cooler than the water above it. (In this context, the reactor heating effect is negligible.) This creates an upward force on the bottom of the wake and a downward force on the top, which collapse it. The rate of change in ambient temperature with depth determines how far behind the submarine the wake will collapse. In waters where the temperature changes with depth, such as the North Atlantic, it may occur just a few hundred meters behind the submarine; in waters closer to the Arctic, where the water temperature is more nearly uniform, it may occur several kilometers behind.

An important caveat is that the influence of reactor heating can be neglected only if the submarine is moving at more than a few knots, so that the water it heats is quickly diluted. A stationary submarine in the Arctic, where the water is cold uniformly throughout its depth during the winter, can easily cause a measurable temperature rise at the surface. If a stationary submarine remains under relatively thin ice for long, it may leave a persistent temperature scar on the surface of the ice.

For these reasons, submarines moving at patrol speeds in areas where there is some solar heating are very unlikely to cause temperature anomalies at the surface.[25] Since temperature anomalies can be detected remotely only if they appear on the surface, it follows that wake or temperature anomaly detection holds very little promise as a means of detecting submarines. Harper described experiments in which detectable surface wakes were deliberately generated by submarines, but indicated that under normal operating conditions, this was not a problem for SSBN security.[26] In a discussion of wake detection before a closed session of the House Armed Services Committee, Adm. Nils Thunman (Deputy Chief of Naval Operations for Submarine Warfare) stated that "if you operate the submarine properly, [the Navy has] found no evidence of any system that can detect [deleted]."[27]

Lidar

Lidar is a means of detecting an object by reflecting laser light off of it. If a laser in the atmosphere or in outer space fires a short pulse into the water, light may be returned because of three processes: (1) backscattering from clouds and airborne particles, (2) reflection from the sea surface, and (3) reflection from a submerged submarine or from the much larger submarine wake. Of the three, backscattering gives the most powerful return; surface reflection is one or two orders of magnitude below that; and the reflection off a submarine at 330 feet (100 meters) depth is further reduced by many orders of magnitude, because of the high attenuation of light in water and the low reflectivity of the flat black surface of the submarine. A submarine at relatively shallow depth may, on the other hand, reflect less light than the natural backscattering processes in the ocean. In such a case, lidar would attempt to detect a dark spot in the ocean, rather than an anomalously high reflection. The signal processing problems involved in distinguishing either a dark spot or a light spot from the ocean and atmospheric backscatter and reflection are very similar, however.

In order to differentiate the very weak submarine reflection or absorption from the much more intense sea surface reflection, the laser pulse duration must be shorter than 0.1 microsecond, which is approximately the round-trip travel time of light between the water surface and a submerged submarine. Longer pulses will cause the powerful surface reflection to interfere with the weaker submarine reflection or absorption. In the atmosphere, however, even with the thinnest of clouds, backscattering will cause such short pulses to spread several microseconds. This phenomenon can be overcome only by firing the laser from well below the clouds, which at any given time cover about 60 percent of the ocean's surface. As a result, this method of detection may be useful for barrier patrol, but it would be very impractical for large area surveillance unless some way is found to overcome the inherently low signal-to-noise ratio of such a system when it must operate through clouds.[28] Sufficiently high laser pulse power is already available to allow airborne detection of moderately deep (less than 330 feet [100 meters]) submarines in the absence of clouds. Therefore, like magnetic anomaly detection, lidar may provide a means of short-range detection or localization of submarines that are not very deep.

Detection of Submarine Missile Launch

When an SSBN fires a missile, it emits a powerful acoustic signal from the escaping gases in the water, and nonacoustic signals in the form of heat from the engine, radar reflectance of the missile, and a visual vapor trail from the missile exhaust. Although these signals are transient phenomena, they may be powerful enough to point ASW forces to their source. For the case in which an SSBN is firing all missiles in a short time period, the most important parameters are the time required to fire all the missiles and the time required for hostile ASW forces to react and attack the SSBN.

US Poseidon submarines can launch missiles as rapidly as one every 57 seconds, which would allow launch of all 16 missiles in 15 minutes. At the same rate, the Ohio class submarine could launch its 24 missiles in less than 23 minutes. In reality, however, improved fire control systems are said to permit all 24 Trident I missiles to be launched in just 6 minutes.[29]

No information is available regarding the time required for Soviet SSBNs to launch all their missiles; but in one test, two SS-N-20 missiles were launched within 15 seconds.[30] It seems reasonable to assume that launch times for Soviet SSBNs are comparable to those of US SSBNs. With such short firing times, it is unlikely that either US or Soviet submarines could be located, targeted, and attacked by a remotely launched weapon in time to catch and destroy them.

If the SSBN is supposed to participate in limited nuclear strikes, it must be able to fire a few weapons and then move far enough away to escape detection and attack. This may be one of the few circumstances in which high speed is useful to an SSBN. Command and control problems may well be the limiting factors in the ability of SSBNs to conduct limited strikes, retargeting, and follow-on attacks.

Platforms for Nonacoustic Sensors

A basic question in using nonacoustic sensors for surveillance is where to put them. The choices are to put them on aircraft or satellites or to fix them in the ocean itself. Aircraft have the advantages of low altitude and flexible maneuvering. Low altitudes give short-range sensors relatively high spatial resolution and avoid cloud cover—an important factor for sensors in the visible and infrared bands. In addition, on aircraft sensitive equipment such as laser components and short-lived power supplies can easily be replaced. The disadvantages of aircraft are that they cannot operate over hostile territory; their search time is limited; and, most important, for a given time period, the area they can survey at lower altitudes is much smaller than the area that can be surveyed by satellites at higher altitudes.[31]

When a satellite's circular orbital period (which is determined by altitude) is the same as the period of the earth's rotation, the satellite will remain above a fixed location on the earth's surface. As one author points out, however, such geostationary satellites "are too high [40,000 km] for the effective use of most ocean surveillance sensors, which are usually found on satellites whose orbits do not exceed 1000 km."[32] Satellites in low orbits spend less time over a particular region of the earth so that many satellites would be needed to provide coverage of SSBN patrol areas.

As an example, consider the characteristics of the SEASAT A synthetic aperture radar (SAR). During its brief life, it operated at an altitude of 432 nm (800 km) and had a swath width on the surface of 54 nm (100 km). At that altitude, a satellite in a circular polar orbit would circle the earth every 100 minutes. During one orbit, the earth would rotate through 25 degrees of longitude.

Soviet SSBN patrol areas in the Arctic are probably limited to regions north of 70 degrees north latitude, an area that covers the entire Arctic and about half the Norwegian and Greenland seas. At that latitude, the swath width of the SAR would cover about 2.5 degrees of longitude. Therefore, in order to cover the entire region every 100 minutes, about 70 satellites, each carrying one radar, would be needed. The number of satellites could be reduced in a number of ways: more radars could be mounted on each satellite; the radars could be designed with a higher swath width; or less frequent coverage could be accepted.

The inherent intermittency and predictability of satellite coverage is a major factor in the assessment of spaceborne ASW surveillance. Continuous, real time tracking of targets has obvious value in an ASW campaign, while the utility of sporadic and uncertain surveillance is more difficult to measure. It is important to recognize that the value of sporadic tracking is not negligible. Any process that can shift a campaign from a random search over a large area to a series of random searches over several much smaller areas is the first step to increasing the rate at which ASW forces engage submarines. The surveillance information must be transmitted through command and control networks and must be received by submarines and aircraft on patrol.

The persistence of submarine-generated surface phenomena could contribute to satellite surveillance since they might yield information about the direction of a target, making the task of correlating successive observations more efficient.

Many nonacoustic detection methods work best under the same conditions: when a submarine is moving at high speed in a shallow depth in some combination of calm seas, clear skies, clear water, and perhaps darkness. Such methods include infrared sensing, lidar, and other optical methods. Conversely, when conditions are unfavorable for one of these nonacoustic sensors, they are unfavorable for the others. Simply operating the submarine at deep levels, below 330 feet (100 meters), drives the signal-to-noise ratio to extremely low levels. Additional security can be gained by a relatively small increase in depth. As an expert on the Navy's SSBN Security Program has testified, "essentially all nonacoustic phenomena are attenuated by water."[33] The analysis presented in this study largely supports this statement, particularly in the cases of lidar detection, detection of surface waves, detection of actual temperature changes in the surface layers, bioluminescence imaging, and magnetic anomaly detection. The analysis in this study provides much less support for this statement in the specific context of detection of submarine-generated internal waves and their surface effects.

The Soviet interest in nonacoustic detection is usually described in terms of a hypothetical threat to US SSBNs. Given the Soviet Navy's shift in 1960 from anti-carrier defense to anti-Polaris defense, the emphasis on nonacoustic detection of SSBNs may have been the Soviet priority in the 1960s.[34]

According to Michael MccGwire, a Soviet shift in doctrine in late 1966 put as the top Soviet military objective "avoiding the nuclear devastation of Russia."[35] With this objective came the requirement of maintaining and protecting the Soviet SSBN fleet as a form of "insurance" lest US technological developments put the Soviet land-based nuclear forces at risk.[36] By the late 1960s, the US had already made significant strides in making attack submarines quiet and difficult to detect by acoustic means.[37] Nonacoustic methods of submarine detection would probably have been seen as a way of contributing to the survivability of Soviet SSBNs, and therefore an important technological means of supporting the main Soviet military objective.

Since most emerging nonacoustic detection technologies are most easily implemented on a small scale in limited areas, it seems likely that on the Soviet side these technologies will initially be used with the greatest effectiveness for detecting US attack submarines in and around Soviet Arctic and Pacific home waters. Such systems could supplement Soviet acoustic surveillance, which is likely to be well developed. This would not only help protect Soviet SSBNs, but would also provide vital practice and evaluation prior to any attempted large-scale implementation. For these reasons, developments in nonacoustic or acoustic technology should be observed in Soviet barrier operations against US SSNs before they can employ it effectively in large-area surveillance, searching for US SSBNs in millions of square miles of ocean.

Destruction of Submarines

Once a submarine is localized, the likelihood of destroying it will depend on the time late of the weapon, the destructive radius of the weapon, and the possible means of countering it.[38] The ASW weapons in the US and Soviet arsenals fall into two general categories: conventionally armed torpedoes that compensate for time late by seeking out the target, and nuclear depth charges that compensate for time late with a large destructive radius.[39] The standard heavy US ASW torpedo, the Mk 48, has a maximum range of about 21 nm (38 km), a maximum speed of 55 knots (100 km/hr), and a maximum depth of 3016 feet (914 meters). Almost no information is available regarding capabilities of Soviet ASW torpedoes. The Submarine Rocket (SUBROC) rocket-propelled nuclear depth charges fired from US submarines can reach 10 to 15 miles (19 to 28 km), and various reports say that its successor, the ASW Standoff Weapon (ASW/SOW), may reach 35 to 100 miles (64 to 184 km).[40]

Torpedoes using active sonar to home on a submarine can be deceived by mechanisms that generate loud broadband noise to mask the echoes or that return false echoes; those using passive sonar can also be jammed or else deceived by mechanisms that simulate submarine noises at some distance from any actual submarine. Nuclear depth charges cannot be countered, but their destructiveness requires that if they are launched from a ship or submarine, they must be boosted over a considerable distance, and this increases the time late. This disadvantage to the attacker can be avoided by dropping nuclear depth charges from the very ASW aircraft that localizes the submarine.

Barrage is another method of compensating for uncertainty in localizing or detecting submarines. In analyzing barrage requirements, there is a basic trade-off between the numbers of weapons used and their yields (and, thus, destructive radii). Most discussions of ASW barrage concern the potential destruction of submarines throughout whole seas and involve calculations of the use of very large numbers of high-yield nuclear weapons.

There are three main ways in which a large underwater explosion can render a strategic submarine incapable of performing its mission: hull rupture; shock damage to systems controlling depth, life-support, or sensitive instruments relating to its ballistic missiles or to the missiles themselves; and wave overturning. So little is known about these mechanisms that the US Navy's Mk 45 nuclear-tipped torpedo became unpopular with submarine operators, who were never sure whether its detonation would damage their own submarines.[41]

The hulls of US submarines are designed to fail at the depth where the pressure hull yields to static pressure. I assume that if the peak overpressure imparted by a nuclear explosion raises the static pressure on the submerged submarine hull beyond its yield pressure, the submarine hull will be ruptured. This may not be as good an assumption for some Soviet double-hulled submarines, which may have a few feet of water between the two hulls. Experiments using high explosive charges at relatively close ranges have suggested that the peak overpressure incident on the inner pressure hull of a double-hulled submarine may be as low as half of the pressure that would be imparted to a single-hulled vessel.[42] On the other hand, theory suggests that the approximately planar pressure wave from a relatively distant nuclear explosion would be transmitted through an outer hull with little attenuation.[43] It is also possible that deformation of frames or even rupture of internal seawater systems, such as cooling loops, might be a mechanism for hull rupture, although there is not enough information in the open literature to evaluate such potential effects.

In a study on shock testing of submarines performed in the early 1960s, it was found that "in some cases disabling [submarine] casualties have occurred at shock factors only a fraction of those required to cause hull splitting or even of those which would probably cause serious personnel casualties." Most of these failures were caused by installation errors or poor housekeeping; only 10 percent were due to inadequacy of properly tested components.[44] Thus, it is likely that unpredictable effects may determine the actual "kill" radius of a nuclear weapon, which may be considerably greater than the theoretical hull-rupture range.[45]

Another important class of damage is that to internal systems of the missiles and their fire control systems. The gyroscopes in the ship's inertial navigation system or in the missiles' guidance systems can be damaged by shock, which would render the missiles useless. Separation joints between missile stages are weak spots, and the solid propellant casting is sensitive to cracking and crumbling.

From the viewpoint of the attacker, however, planning to rupture hulls probably offers the highest confidence of incapacitating all the submarines in a given area. I therefore adopt this conservative assumption. In addition, lacking more detailed information on Soviet submarines, I assume that what is true of US submarines is also true on the Soviet side. It should be noted, however, that features such as double hulls may suggest greater emphasis on shock survivability in Soviet submarine design.

According to one Soviet study of US sources, the collapse depth of the Thresher and Ethan Allen classes was about 1,650 feet (500 meters).[46] Standard Western sources such as *Janes Fighting Ships* give 990 feet (300 meters) as the maximum operating depth of US submarines. Allowing a factor of 1.5 as a safety margin, this implies a collapse depth of 1,485 feet (450 meters).[47] For the purpose of evaluating barrage requirements, I estimate conservatively that in general submarine hulls will rupture under the pressure created by about 1,650 feet (500 meters) of seawater. For a submarine at 330 feet (100 meters), the additional static overpressure that must be applied to rupture the hull is 590 pounds per square inch (psi). Table 1-1 shows the ranges at which nuclear explosions of various yields will produce such overpressure.

The surface waves generated by a nuclear explosion are high, particularly the first wave, which propagates outward; but they are not higher than the waves generated by a prolonged, severe storm. A 1 MT bomb detonated in water as deep as the Barents Sea or the northern Sea of Okhotsk (typically 660–1,320 feet [200–400 meters]) will generate a wave with a height of about 20–30 feet (6–9 meters) at a distance of 4 miles (7.4 km) from the explosion. This wave has a period of about 38 seconds[48] and is not breaking.[49]

The length of the wave will be about 4,800 feet (1,475 meters),[50] and the slope of the water surface along the wave will be about 1 degree. Given such a wave, a submarine submerged at 330 feet (100 meters) would probably be unaware of the tilt. The maximum horizontal acceleration would be about 0.02 g's at that depth—hardly perceptible. The entire submarine would move gently with the underwater motion. Even at the surface, the entire submarine would simply rise and fall, without tilting, in a slow elliptical motion.[51]

In sum, it is clear that at a range of, say, 4 nm (7.4 km) from a 1 MT explosion, the shock and hull rupture effects will dominate the wave effect.

Table 1–1
Yield-range combinations for achieving 590 psi overpressure underwater

	Range for 590 psi		
Yield	*(meters)*	*(yards)*	*(nm)*
200 kT	4,550	5,000	<1
1 MT	7,280	8,000	4
5 MT	12,700	14,000	7

Source: Samuel Glasstone and Phillip J. Dolan, *The Effect of Nuclear Weapons* (Washington, D.C.: US Government Printing Office, 1977), p. 271; read from figure 6.115.

Explosion waves must shoal into very shallow water before they become steep enough to topple a submarine.

Several sources have given estimates of the kill radius of a 1 MT weapon against submarines. Daniel reviews statements by former US Secretary of Defense Harold Brown and former US Director of Defense Research William Perry which suggested radii of 5 nm (9.2 km) and 3.5 nm (6.4 km), respectively.[52] Another author quotes a "DoD source" in giving an estimate of 4 nm (7.4 km).[53] Shallow water bursts deliver less energy to water than deep water bursts, according to Glasstone and Dolan,[54] but it is unclear how much less. Sidney Drell has calculated that a 1 MT weapon detonated near the bottom can destroy a submarine at a range of 1.5 nm (2.8 km), but he assumes "very conservative damage criteria."[55] One report claims that a 10 kT bomb can destroy a submarine at 495 feet (150 meters) depth out to a range of 1.2 nm (2.2 km).[56] A Soviet analysis of "foreign sources" from the late 1950s gives the destructive radius of a 2.5 kT bomb (explosion depth 100 feet [30 meters], submarine depth 200 feet [60 meters]) as 1,980 feet (600 meters), and that of a 10 kT weapon as 5,280–5,610 feet (1,600–1,700 meters).[57]

In one major 1955 experiment called Operation Wigwam, a 20 kiloton underwater nuclear weapon was detonated at a depth of 2000 feet in deep water near some submerged scale models of World War II vintage SS 567 class submarines in order "to determine the lethal range for an atomic depth charge against a submarine target."[58] Results from that test and others suggested that peak total pressure required to rupture the hull was 1.5–1.9 times the maximum static pressure resistance of the submarine. The pressure had to remain high for at least 4 milliseconds in order to cause damage, and the orientation of the submarine to the explosion was not an important factor in the vulnerability of the hull to the pressure wave.[59] It was also shown that the vulnerability of the hull was not sensitive to the presence of heavy internal masses, such as heavy machinery.[60]

Operation Wigwam provided data on the relationship between target depth and lethal range from a nuclear weapon. Hull collapse pressure of the targets was 655 pounds per square inch. For the 20 kiloton weapon against targets at various depths, the lethal ranges were as follows: 100 feet, 0.8 nm; 200 feet, 1.0 nm; 400 feet, 1.3 nm; 600 feet, 1.6 nm; 800 feet, 2.1 nm. Since lethal range scales with the square root of weapon yield, the lethal range of a 1 megaton bomb can be calculated as follows: 100 feet, 5.7 nm; 200 feet, 7.1 nm; 400 feet, 9.2 nm; 600 feet, 11.3 nm; 800 feet, 15 nm. The Wigwam test also showed that an increase in weapon depth from 500 to 2,000 feet increases the lethal range by about 20 percent.[61] Against modern submarines, the lethal ranges should be shorter, since the Wigwam targets were made of HTS steel, with a yield strength of 47,000 psi, and modern submarines are made with HY-80 steel, with a minimum yield strength of 80,000 psi. This suggests that the kill radius against modern submarines is about half the figures given above, where the kill mechanism is hull rupture.

McCue has pointed out that the area over which a given overpressure is achieved scales with yield and numbers in the same way as the formula for aggregating yields into equivalent megatons (EMT).[62] As a result, the area that can be covered in a barrage by weapons of varying yield is a simple function of total EMT, specifically, the product of total EMT and the area within the destructive radius of a 1 MT bomb. Taking account of the need to cover gaps between the circles of lethal radius and to allow for warhead accuracy of 1,220 feet (370 meters) circular error probable (CEP), the number of weapons that must be used to barrage a given area increases by 35 percent.[63]

Comparing the various estimates, it seems that 4 nm is a reasonable estimate for the kill radius of a 1 MT weapon in water as deep as the typical Soviet SSBN patrol areas or deeper. The uncertainty in this or any other estimate is very large, however, and any result based on it should be viewed as approximate. The actual destructive radius depends on the depth of the burst, the water depth, the depth of the submarine, and other factors. This result is considered to be conservative (a low estimate of the destructive radius) and will be used in the discussion of threats to US and Soviet SSBN fleets. It will be shown that neither the United States nor the USSR has sufficient EMT to barrage large areas if the kill radius is 4 miles, so if the true radius of kill is lower, the conclusion that area barrage is impractical is unchanged. On the other hand, there is no evidence that a very reliable kill mechanism exists much beyond 4 miles, so that an attempt to barrage using wider spacing may not be likely to result in destroying the great majority of SSBNs with high confidence.

Notes

1. *See* Robert Perry, Mark A. Lorell, and Kevin N. Lewis, *Second Area Operations: A Strategy Option* (Santa Monica, Cal.: RAND), R-2992–USDP, May 1984.

2. Department of Defense Authorization for Appropriations for Fiscal Year 1985, Hearings before the Committee on Armed Services, United States Senate, part 7, p. 3692. Hereafter, such citations from annual hearings on the Defense Department authorizations and appropriations are given in the following form: SASC, FY 1985, part 7, p. 3692. House Armed Services Committee is abbreviated HASC, Senate Appropriations Committee is SAC, and HAC is House Appropriations Committee. HAC and SAC hearings are before the defense subcommittees.

3. An excellent summary of the debate over the Maritime Strategy can be found in the Fall 1986 issue of *International Security*. John J. Mearsheimer presents the opposing views in "A Strategic Misstep: The Maritime Strategy and Deterrence in Europe," and Linton F. Brooks argues in support of the strategy in "Naval Power and National Security: The Case for the Maritime Strategy."

4. For a more lengthy treatment of the subject, the reader is referred to *Antisubmarine Warfare and Superpower Strategic Stability,* by Donald C. Daniel (Urbana, Ill.: University of Illinois Press, 1986).

5. For more information, see appendix 3, "Nonacoustic Means of Submarine Detection."

6. Adm. James D. Watkins, Chief of Naval Operations, HAC, FY 1986, part 2, p. 913.

7. Rear Adm. John Butts, SASC, FY 1986, part 8, p. 4350. The Navy has told Congress that the new generation US attack submarine, the SSN-21, will have a quiet speed of 20 knots.

8. *See* appendix 7, "Detection of Submarine Signatures in Noise."

9. Ibid.

10. Roger F. Dwyer, "A Technique for Improving Detection and Estimation of Signals Contaminated by Under Ice Noise," *Journal of the Acoustical Society of America* (hereafter *JASA*) 74:1, July 1983, pp. 124–130.

11. Under a solid Arctic ice cover, where there is relatively little surface motion, the frequency spreading may be relatively low. No direct evidence for this was found in the unclassified literature, however.

12. Another advantage of using many short-range sensors is that since high-frequency components of submarine noise are absorbed by the ocean over long ranges, short-range sensors will also pick up more high-frequency data, which aids in identifying submarines by class and even individually.

13. Lt. Comdr. Ralph E. Chatham, USN, "A Quiet Revolution," *US Naval Institute Proceedings* 110:1, January 1984, pp. 41–46.

14. Robert Fossum, *DARPA Summary Statement by the Director, FY 1982,* p. II-1.

15. Stanley M. Flatté et al., eds., *Sound Transmission through a Fluctuating Ocean* (New York: Cambridge University Press, 1979).

16. Ibid., p. 47.

17. A. J. Rockmore, "A Tomographic Approach to Multiarray Ocean Surveillance," *IEEE Journal of Oceanic Engineering,* OE–7:2, April 1982, pp. 83–89. See also Walter Munk and Carl Wunsch, "Ocean Acoustic Tomography: A Scheme for Large Scale Monitoring," *Deep Sea Research* 26A, 1979, pp. 123–161; V. M. Bukhshtaber et al., "Acoustic Tomography of the Ocean," *Izvestiya, Atmospheric and Oceanic Physics* 20:7, 1984, pp. 571–577.

18. For an analysis of this result see appendix 7, "Detection of Submarine Signatures in Noise."

19. Jeffrey Richelson, "Technical Collection and Arms Control," in *Verification and Arms Control,* ed. William C. Potter (Lexington, Mass.: Lexington Books, 1985), p. 190.

20. Robert Aldridge, *First Strike!* (Boston: South End Press, 1983), p. 166.

21. Superconducting magnetometers may be as sensitive as 10^{-5} gammas in a 1 Hz band. Donald G. Polvani, "Current and Future Underwater Magnetic Sensing," Marine Technology Society and Institute of Electrical and Electronics Engineers, *Oceans 81 Conference Record* (Boston, MA: Sept. 1981) vol. 1, pp. 442–446.

22. SASC, FY 1985, part 7, p. 3409.

23. The height of the *surface wave* generated over the submarine in this case of shallow depth is calculated to be about 4 centimeters (*see* appendix 3, equation A3.1).

This is a very large disturbance, and while it is not related to internal wave detection, it raises the question of whether some other system, such as a high-resolution laser altimeter could have detected such a disturbance.

24. SASC, FY 1985, part 7, p. 3414.

25. During the summer, even Arctic surface waters are heated sufficiently to stem the rise of a slightly buoyant wake.

26. SASC, FY 1985, part 7, pp. 3410–3412. One publicized account described a test in which a submarine wake was detected from the air. However, the submarine was traveling at "high speed and unusually shallow depth" (Melinda Beck and David C. Martin, "The War beneath the Seas," *Newsweek*, 8 February 1982, p. 36).

27. HASC, FY 1986, part 3, p. 167.

28. When DARPA found that lidar was "more complex and costly than anticipated," it shifted the technology to the Strategic Laser Communications Program (Robert Fossum, *DARPA Summary Statement by the Director, FY 1982,* p. V-2).

29. D. Douglas Dalgleish and Larry Schweikart, *Trident* (Carbondale: Southern Illinois University Press, 1984), p. 28. The Trident II missiles will probably require more than 6 minutes to launch, but the time will still be sufficiently fast for the submarine to escape detection. Some submarine commanders have assumed that they would surface if they ever had to fire all their missiles. They would thus avoid the need to re-balance the submarine after each individual missile was launched.

30. *Aviation Week and Space Technology,* 25 October 1982, p. 17.

31. A calculation of the time required by aircraft, ships, and submarines to search entire US and Soviet SSBN patrol areas is given in appendix 2, "ASW Forces of the United States and the Soviet Union."

32. Daniel, *Anti-Submarine Warfare,* p. 62.

33. Commodore Theodore E. Lewin, HASC, FY 1986, part 3, p. 169.

34. Michael MccGwire, "The Rationale for the Development of Soviet Seapower," *US Naval Institute Proceedings* 106:5, May 1980, pp. 155–183.

35. Michael MccGwire, "Contingency Plans for World War" in *The Soviet and Other Communist Navies—The View from the Mid-1980s,* James L. George, ed. (Annapolis: Naval Institute Press, 1986), pp. 61–81.

36. Ibid., pp. 64, 65.

37. *See* appendix 6, figure A6–5.

38. A more strict definition of localization is the determination of the position of a target to within an area equal to the effective area of a weapon.

39. The Soviet Navy also makes extensive use of short-range ship-launched conventional depth charges.

40. Randolph Steer, "Understanding Anti-Submarine Warfare Technology," chap. 8 in *Review of US Military Research and Development, 1984,* eds. Kosta Tsipis and Penny Janeway (Elmsford, N.Y.: Pergamon-Brassey's, 1984), p. 141. This author reports a range for the Mk-48 of 10 or 12 nm, and for high confidence, a range of 5–6 miles (*see* p. 151).

41. The Mk 45 was also unpopular because it had to be guided and detonated by wire, while the attacking submarine used active sonar. Norman Friedman, *Submarine Design and Development* (Annapolis: Naval Institute Press, 1984), p. 157.

42. A.H. Keil, "The Response of Ships to Underwater Explosions," *Naval Engineers Journal* 69, 1961, pp. 366–399; discussion, pp. 399–410.

43. G. Chertock et al., *Lethal Range of Wigwam Targets Based on Hull Response and*

Applied Pressure Measurements (Washington, D.C.: David Taylor Model Basin, 1956), AD-361 916/0, p. 61.

44. Capt. W. D. Roseborough, USN, responding to Keil, *Naval Engineers Journal* 69, 1961, p. 405.

45. The response of a submarine's interior machinery and systems to an underwater explosion is a function of the "shock factor," a measure of the hull velocity caused by the impact of a shock wave, and which is proportional to the square root of the energy imparted to the hull. According to an article entitled "Submarine Resistance to Noncontact Explosions" by Vice Adm. Robert Gooding USN (Ret.) in the January 1986 *Submarine Review* (pp. 24–31), Navy specifications require machinery to survive shock factors of 0.47. A TNT charge of 150 pounds detonated at a distance of 12 feet from a submarine hull will cause a local shock factor of 1.02, and the same charge detonated within 6 feet gives rise to a shock factor of 2.04. A charge of 750 pounds at 12 feet yields a shock factor of 2.28, and at 6 feet the same charge creates a shock factor of 4.56. Since the high velocities associated with these shock factors probably cause significant disruption to machinery near the explosion, it is likely that the large spacing between the hulls of Soviet double-hulled submarines protects the interior to some extent, but does not neutralize the effects of large torpedo warheads.

46. V. M. Bukalov and A. A. Narusbayev, *Atomic-powered Submarine Design* (Leningrad: Shipbuilding Publishing House, 1964), p. 82.

47. Friedman, *Submarine Design,* p. 118.

48. Samuel Glasstone and Phillip J. Dolan, *The Effects of Nuclear Weapons* (Washington, DC: US Government Printing Office, 1977), pp. 272–273.

49. Bernard LeMehaute, "Theory of Explosion-generated Water Waves," in *Advances in Hydroscience,* Vol. 7, ed. Ven Te Chow, (Orlando, Fla.: Academic Press, 1971), p. 39, figure 15.

50. US Army Corps of Engineers, *Shore Protection Manual,* vol. 3 (1975), table C-1, pp. C-5 to C-17. This estimate is based on linear wave theory, which, given the characteristics of this wave, is considered generally valid.

51. A Soviet study states that this is true for any wavelength greater than four times the length of the submarine, which will be the case for explosion-generated waves. Bukalov and Narusbayev, *Atomic-powered Submarine Design,* p. 57.

52. Donald C. Daniel, *Anti-submarine Warfare,* p. 21.

53. Brian McCue, "The Threat to the SSBN" (Master's thesis, MIT, 1980), pp. 83–84.

54. Glasstone and Dolan, *Effects of Nuclear Weapons,* p. 273.

55. Sidney Drell, "SUM," *Arms Control Today* 9:8, September 1979, p. 4.

56. Dr. Milan Vego, "Soviet Mine Warfare: Doctrine and Capabilities," *Navy International* 11, November 1982, pp. 1414–1420.

57. Bukalov and Narusbayev, *Atomic-powered Submarine Design,* p. 229.

58. Chertock, "Lethal Range," p. 11.

59. Ibid., pp. 15–17.

60. Ibid.

61. Ibid., p. 74.

62. McCue, "The Threat to the SSBN," p. 86.

63. Ibid., p. 88.

2
US ASW Threats to Soviet SSBNs

This chapter discusses the prospects for the United States to find and destroy Soviet SSBNs by means of the various ASW tactics and technologies outlined in chapter 1. Within each section of this chapter, the ASW problem is analyzed in the context of actual operating areas and force levels. Where the text draws on a more detailed appendix, it gives only the main outline and conclusions. Intended as a general framework for policy analysis, the chapter devotes little space to particular new research and development projects, which are regularly described in detail in other sources.[1]

Soviet SSBN Operating Policy

Soviet SSBNs carrying the 4,200 nm-range SS-N-8 and SS-N-18 missiles can target most of the continental United States from ocean areas within a few hundred miles from their ports in Murmansk in the Arctic and in Petropavlovsk in the Pacific.[2] Figure A8-1 in appendix 8 shows the coverage of these missiles from near their ports, and it is apparent that parts of the continental United States are not covered. With the SS-NX-23 missile, which will to some extent replace the SS-N-18, Soviet SSBNs will be able to target the entire United States from port.[3] In practice, Soviet SSBNs can travel in the shallow ice-covered waters of the Soviet Arctic continental shelf, which is about 500 miles wide and thousands of miles long. They can travel in the central Arctic under the ice pack, and they can travel (at greater risk) in the North Atlantic and North Pacific.

The Soviet Navy maintains an average of about 15–25 percent of its SSBN fleet at sea at any given time, a figure that has remained fairly constant over the past 10 years, though it may be increasing.[4] There are a number of reasons for this rate, which is low compared to the 50–66 percent at-sea rate of US submarines. The Soviet SSBN force (other than those forward deployed such as the Yankee and the occasional Delta) may be more narrowly assigned to the mission of providing a surviving strategic reserve force than is the US fleet. A strategic reserve is intended to ride out an entire war, including a general nuclear war, and be prepared to provide a capability to strike the United States during the war or after the war is over, no matter what happens. The central rationales may be to deter all-out attacks against society during the course of a limited nuclear war, and to provide a force for influencing the course and outcome of postwar negotiations. Given this mission, and the general belief that World War III and certainly general nuclear war will be preceded by a significant period of crisis and warning, there may be no great incentive for keeping a large portion of the SSBN fleet at sea all the time. Soviet submarines in port can be put to sea in what is called a surge. The US Navy has "watched [the Soviet Navy] surge their SSBNs and SSNs many times" and believes that the Soviet surge capability is "excellent." The Soviet Navy can put a large portion of its SSBNs (and SSNs) to sea within 24 to 48 hours.[5] This is a reasonable alternative to keeping a larger fraction of submarines at sea at all times.

The Soviet Navy has developed hardened shelters for SSBNs to protect them from attack while they are in port.[6] This might allow them a means of surviving attack by conventional weapons without surging. It is difficult to see how such shelters could help in a nuclear attack, however, when the rubble in the bomb craters would very possibly cover the openings to the shelters. The Soviet investment in this kind of protection for SSBNs may reflect some belief that SSBNs may only need to last throughout a conventional war, or it may constitute an additional measure to provide "combat stability" to those submarines (SSBNs and others) that may need to be in port during a war for refitting.

Logistical and bureaucratic factors may also explain the relatively low at-sea rate. One analyst points out that "the Soviet shipyards and repair sites are located in the worst possible environment for ship repair."[7] All yards involved with nuclear submarines are located in extremely cold climates, in which most work can be performed only in covered and heated facilities and buildings. In addition, the Soviet Ministry of Shipbuilding is separate from the Navy, and is responsible for repairs to submarines as well as for building ships. The bureaucratic pressure to produce ships is greater than the incentives to repair older ones, leading to a bias in the allocation of resources toward turning out new ships as opposed to keeping the Navy's existing ones in good repair. As the same analyst put it, "The Soviet Ministry [of Shipbuilding] does not want to be in the ship repair business, especially the most difficult of all ship repairs, nuclear submarine work."[8] Together with the large numbers of highly trained specialists needed to operate a large fleet of nuclear submarines, the technical complexity of the systems, the demand for civilian nuclear reactor specialists, and related problems, there are abundant reasons for the Soviet Navy to opt for a lower at-sea rate.

The price the Soviet Navy pays for such low at-sea rates is great, nonetheless:

> Soviet crews decry the fact they don't get enough at-sea training time. They bitch about it in the documents and we see the results. In the last ten years, they have had over 200 submarine accidents, some of which have been very serious. They have lost submarines, had fires, had real problems.[9]

As for the relative levels of training between US and Soviet submarine crews, the nearly three-fold advantage in US at-sea time has led to a situation in which there is "no contest in terms of crew proficiency," which gives the United States an incalculable edge in the quality of an individual submarine as a fighting unit.[10] In terms of the actual number of Soviet SSBNs at sea, using the figure of 15 percent translates to about 10 submarines at sea worldwide. Presumably some of those, namely the Yankees with their shorter-range missiles, are not always in range of the United States and therefore are not always on alert. Since only a couple of Yankees patrol off the US coast, perhaps 8 submarines at sea are on alert with 2 Yankees in transit, on the average. Using the figure of 25 percent at sea translates to about 17 submarines at sea at any time. The US Navy claims, however, that at any given time 28 Soviet SSBNs are on alert,[11] which means that about 11 to 20 of them must be on alert status while in their ports, near their hardened "bunkers." These numbers should be accepted as approximate, however.

While Soviet submarines are at sea, there are a number of ways of making them more secure, one of these being to accompany the SSBN with an SSN, a common practice in the Soviet Navy, using the Victor III.[12] Other defensive means will be discussed in detail later.

Area Search for Soviet SSBNs

Area search is the most easily visualized threat to SSBNs, yet it is one of the least efficient and least realistic approaches. Although US attack submarines search for SSBNs in Soviet home waters, there is little support within the US Navy for sending surface ships or aircraft into the SSBN patrol areas contiguous to major Soviet naval bases.[13] For this reason and others, it is extremely doubtful that the main US threat to Soviet SSBNs is the threat of a brute-force search of the entire Barents Sea and Sea of Okhotsk. What is more plausible is a hybrid of operations involving area surveillance, trailing, and mining. Nonetheless, it is useful to begin by discussing area search alone as a first-order approach to operations analysis, since it clarifies the time scale for strategic antisubmarine warfare.

To give a general idea of the vulnerability of Soviet SSBNs, this analysis uses simple assumptions that favor the ASW forces (not the SSBNs). The detection range of each individual US surface ship and submarine equipped with low-frequency sonar is assumed to be on the order of 30 nm (55 km)—a very high estimate.[14] For carrier battle groups including one aircraft carrier each, plus destroyers, cruisers, and SSNs, the detection range is assumed to be 150 nm (280 km). Quoted estimates of modern active sonar systems are on the order of 10 nm (18 km) or out to 30 nm (55 km) with convergence zones, although convergence zones would not exist in Soviet home waters. Passive sonar ranges vary widely with conditions; they are shorter in shallow water, which transmits sound much less efficiently than deep water. I use 30 nm as an optimistically long range out to which a modern sonar system might reliably detect a moderately quiet, modern class of Soviet SSBN; actual ranges may be on the order of 3 miles against extremely quiet submarines.[15] It is important to remember that since search time is inversely proportional to detection range, the results obtained here are very sensitive to this assumption. For the initial calculations, I make the highly unrealistic assumption that the Soviet SSBNs do not move to evade the search or take countermeasures, that the search patterns of the US ASW units are perfectly coordinated with no gaps and no overlap, and that the Soviet armed forces do not interfere.

Under these unrealistic circumstances and assuming that Soviet SSBNs remained entirely stationary, it would take about five hours for the US Navy frigates and carrier battle groups now based in the Atlantic to search the Barents Sea and the adjoining Kara Sea. If the same search were conducted by US attack submarines stationed in the Atlantic alone, it would take about eight hours. All US SSNs in the Atlantic could search the entire Arctic Ocean in 20 hours, while those in the Pacific would take 14 hours to search the Sea of Okhotsk.

If the Soviet SSBNs are assumed to move about randomly (not evasively) or if the search process itself is assumed to be random (search units move randomly rather than systematically through the area), then the time required to detect 95 percent of the SSBNs will be about three times the first set of estimates given.[16]

Thus, even without harassment or defense on the part of the Soviet Navy, the time needed to search comprehensively for Soviet SSBNs throughout the Arctic and the Sea of Okhotsk is on the order of two days. In realistic wartime or crisis conditions, the process would take much longer. First, the searching US forces, even if limited to SSNs, would be slowed down by Soviet minefields and groups of quiet Soviet defending submarines, both new nuclear-powered submarines and the even quieter diesel-electric types suitable for coastal defense. Second, some US attack submarines would be destroyed, further stretching out the search, and perhaps forcing the US Navy to accept losses that might be more costly than the likely gains. Finally, in real situations, real systems like sonars do not perform ideally and sometimes do not perform at all. Simple countermeasures like noisemakers and submarine simulators would slow the search process enormously. Clearly, it would make no sense to attempt a comprehensive area search for Soviet SSBNs *simultaneously with* a 30-minute strike by US ICBMs against Soviet land-based nuclear forces in a sudden, disarming first-strike scenario. The calculated search results do suggest, however, that a search campaign lasting 10–20 days might result in many encounters between US SSNs and Soviet SSBNs.

Even though the threat of attrition of Soviet SSBNs is discounted in discussions of disarming strike scenarios, it is important to recognize that the United States probably does maintain some SSNs in or near Soviet SSBN patrol waters in peacetime; and it is possible for these and other SSNs to attack any Soviet SSBNs they have under trail or can find very quickly at the outbreak of an East-West *conventional* war. If the Soviet leadership anticipates that such a war might last longer than a week, they must take very seriously the dangers of area search for and attrition of their SSBNs. The magnitude and significance of this attrition threat is the central issue of the later chapters.

Area Barrage against Soviet SSBNs

Instead of searching an area known to contain submarines, the attacker can detonate a large number of weapons in a pattern over that area—a tactic known as barrage. Taking 4 nm as the submarine kill radius for a 1 MT bomb and allowing a 35 percent increase in EMT to correct for missile inaccuracy and overlapping circles of destruction, I have made the conservative calculation of the equivalent megatons (EMT) needed to barrage selected Soviet SSBN patrol areas and give high confidence of destroying all SSBNs in them. The results are given in table 2-1 and the total EMT required is 67,100 EMT.

Table 2-1
Estimated EMT required to create 590 psi overpressure throughout Soviet SSBN patrol areas[a]

Area	*Equivalent Megatons*
Barents Sea (394,000 nm^2)	10,600
Norwegian-Greenland Sea (650,000 nm^2)	17,500
Arctic Ocean (1,000,000 nm^2)	26,900
Sea of Okhotsk (452,000 nm^2)	12,100
Total	67,100

[a]This does not include all of the Soviet Arctic marginal seas, the Bering Sea, or the Yankee/Delta patrol areas off the US coast.

In 1985, the United States had 1,272 EMT on intercontinental ballistic missiles (ICBMs), 935 EMT on submarine-launched ballistic missiles (SLBMs), and 1,663 EMT on bombers—a total of 3,870 EMT. This represents only 6 percent of what would be needed to barrage Soviet SSBN patrol areas. Clearly, the requirements for comprehensive, high-confidence area barrage are not only far beyond current US nuclear forces, but are also far beyond any foreseeable future capability.

However, if Soviet SSBNs were observed leaving port and were tracked accurately enough to reduce the total area of uncertainty to 36,000 nm^2, they could be attacked with just 1,000 EMT. The area 36,000 nm^2 is equivalent to 20 targets localized to within 24 miles (44 km) each. The tactic of a nuclear barrage would be feasible only if high-confidence, accurate surveillance were to become available.

Acoustic Surveillance of Submarines

The feasibility of acoustic surveillance of Soviet strategic submarines has been drastically reduced with the introduction of very long range missiles, which permit Soviet submarines to operate in the seas near the Asian continent. No longer do most Soviet SSBNs have to transit narrow chokepoints in order to be within striking range of the United States. Furthermore, there are few locations near the Soviet SSBN deployment areas where Western nations can install fixed, large-scale surveillance equipment. The Barents Sea and the Sea of Okhotsk are both international waters with international straits entering them, but there is an obvious logistical problem in attempting to protect large sonar arrays on the ocean floor, with cables running up to shore-based facilities, off the coast of a country whose strategic forces are threatened by these arrays. Last but not least, the physical properties of the ocean in current Soviet SSBN patrol areas make long-range detection very difficult.

From the late 1950s, when the USSR started producing submarines with ballistic missiles, until the late 1970s, when the bulk of Soviet SLBMs were those with a range of at least 4,000 nm (7360 km), the United States relied heavily on the Sound Ocean Surveillance System (SOSUS) for detecting Soviet SSBNs. SOSUS is a series of passive acoustic systems based on linear arrays of hydrophones several hundred meters long.[17] The SOSUS system is actually only one of several passive acoustic long-range surveillance systems, but the term is now used to describe all these systems since they are very similar. The SOSUS arrays are buried a few feet in the mud[18] by four specialized array-laying ships,[19] which may be assisted by the US nuclear minisub NR-1.[20]

The hydrophone arrays, designated AN/FQQ-10(V), are apparently strung out at intervals of 5–15 miles (9–28 km),[21] though the individual arrays are probably not more than a thousand meters or so long. They are connected by cable to shore stations called Naval Facilities (NAVFACS). These shore stations are located on both US coasts and on the Aleutian Islands, in Canada, Denmark, Iceland, Italy, Japan, Korea, the Philippines, Spain, Turkey, and the United Kingdom.[22] Some of the original NAVFACS on the US coasts, such as the one at Lewes, Delaware, are being phased out.[23] The older Soviet submarines are also being removed from service or converted to attack submarines (with their ballistic missiles removed), which can be effectively countered by US attack submarines.

The SOSUS arrays considered most threatening to modern Soviet SSBNs are those nearest the Kuril Islands[24] (if they exist) and elsewhere in the western Pacific,[25] and the one that runs off the northern coast of Norway from the military base at Andøya north toward Svalbard.[26] The critical technical question in terms of US strategic ASW capability is how far into the nearby Soviet patrol areas these SOSUS arrays can detect Soviet submarines, although surveillance against Soviet SSNs is probably an equally important and feasible function of undersea surveillance.

In the early 1960s, US defenses against Soviet strategic submarines were focused on the deep waters off US coasts. Large arrays, such as the Artemis and Trident systems, were used to gather data on the detectability and coherence of sound propagated in the "deep sound channel," a natural waveguide that transmits low-frequency machinery noises efficiently at very long ranges through the deep oceans.[27] During the early years of Secretary of Defense McNamara's tenure, these systems were considered an integral part of US damage-limiting capability.[28] At the same time, the US Navy recognized that Soviet submarines could be detected closer to their home ports, and surveillance was moved "forward" into the western Pacific. Nature seemed to support these efforts by placing the deep sound channel along the routes the original Soviet SSBNs had to travel to come within range of the United States. However, even with the relatively favorable acoustic environment of the deep ocean, there were still major sources of uncertainty in sound transmission and noise levels.

The other major US passive acoustic surveillance system is the Surveillance Towed Array System (SURTASS). This is a long line array (perhaps about the same length of a SOSUS array or shorter), towed from a very slow ocean-going tugboat called T-AGOS. The initial contract is for 12 ships of this type. T-AGOS and SURTASS are intended to provide a backup to SOSUS, though only in waters that are very secure and heavily defended by the United States in wartime, since T-AGOS is defenseless. SOSUS NAVFAC data collection stations and the arrays themselves are targeted by the Soviet Union and are not expected to survive the outbreak of a war, and SURTASS may provide a short-term replacement. A more plausible use of SURTASS is as a complement to SOSUS in peacetime. Since both are passive arrays and are for all practical purposes immobile, they each yield only information on the direction to a distant target. However, a SOSUS array in conjunction with a distant SURTASS array can provide two lines of direction that yield the position of the target.

There are major questions about the roles and utility of SURTASS and SOSUS. Both are very vulnerable and are not likely to survive long in forward areas in a major war. They can provide a means of keeping track of some submarines up to the time war begins, but within a few days after the surveillance systems are destroyed, the Soviet attack submarine fleet can be redistributed by over a thousand miles. In terms of surveillance against Soviet SSBNs, these systems are even less useful. The older Yankee class SSBNs used to be the major undersea threat to the United States, but they had to come close to US shores because of the short range of their missiles. They still patrol, with some Deltas, in the North Atlantic and North Pacific, which also happen to be excellent ocean areas in which to detect the loud, low-frequency tones of the Yankees. The newer Delta and Typhoon submarines carrying the vast majority of Soviet submarine-launched ballistic missile warheads, however, deploy for the most part in shallow or ice-covered waters, which are much less favorable environments for long-range acoustic detection. As a result, the range at which a surveillance system might detect Yankee submarines in the Norwegian Sea has been estimated at several hundred to over a thousand miles, while the range associated with new Soviet SSBNs (which are probably over a thousand times quieter than the Yankees) in the shallow Barents Sea is just 1–20 nm.[29] Data from US Navy tests against actual Soviet submarines appear to confirm these results, which are derived in appendixes 4–8.

As noted in chapter 1, the range at which an acoustic system can detect a submarine depends on three factors: the capability of the system, the acoustic characteristics of the ocean environment, and the intensity of the submarine's radiated noise signature. The Navy has used the SOSUS/SURTASS combination to track Soviet Yankee submarines in the eastern Pacific at ranges of between 400 and 1,000 nm (740–1840 km). The Yankee is one of the easier Soviet submarines to track, however, since it radiates sound at about the 150 dB level.[30] Using the same sonar system and assuming the same ocean characteristics as in these Navy tests, a submarine radiating only 130 dB—probably typical of the quietest Soviet Victor III SSNs[31]—could be detected at ranges of only 5-100 nm (9–184 km).[32] Against 120 dB sources, probably characteristic of slow-moving Typhoon SSBNs and the next generation of Soviet SSNs, the detection range of the same SOSUS/SURTASS system in the same conditions would be between 1 and 15 nm (2–28 km).[33] In the shallow Barents Sea, where the sound transmission characteristics are less amenable to long-range passive detection than are those of the eastern Pacific site, the detection range of a SOSUS/SURTASS system would probably be even less, assuming that such a system would survive for any length of time in Soviet waters.

The Norwegian Sea, north of the GIUK gap, resembles a deep ocean area in some sound transmission characteristics, but because of its limited depth, it exhibits some features not common in the deep oceans. Most important, in many locations the conditions for the formation of "convergence zones"—zones of especially low sound-transmission loss—generally occur only in the winter.[34] The neighboring Greenland Sea, also a possible SSBN deployment area, is covered by an ice pack during the winter and is acoustically like the deep central Arctic, discussed in the next section.

The GIUK gap is shallower than either the Norwegian Sea or the northern Atlantic Ocean, and to some extent, it acoustically isolates the two. Yet because submarines passing between Greenland and Iceland or Iceland and the United Kingdom must approach SOSUS surveillance arrays at relatively close range, the chances of detection used to be relatively high. As Soviet submarines become quiet enough to elude even passive SOSUS arrays, the GIUK gap will still afford the West an opportunity to employ active acoustic and nonacoustic surveillance. An active adjunct to SOSUS may help offset some of the recent advances in Soviet submarine quieting on the Victor III and on the Akula and its successors. An active adjunct would involve sound sources whose "ping" would reflect off transiting submarines and be received at the SOSUS arrays. A shift from passive to active SOSUS is not without precedent, since SOSUS was apparently originally an active system, converted to passive in the mid-1960s.[35]

In sum, there is today no long-range US acoustic surveillance system—or a set of systems—that can detect all or even most Soviet strategic submarines within their patrol areas. This state of affairs is unlikely to change in the future because US technology is already "approaching physical limits to sonar detection of submarines."[36] Surveillance will probably be useful only as a prewar means of accounting for the movement of Soviet SSNs and Yankee SSBNs in and out of their home waters.

Acoustic Surveillance under the Ice

Most Soviet SSBNs patrol in the central Arctic or in the shallow marginal seas above the USSR's wide northern continental shelf. Some may be deployed closer to the Canadian Arctic in the shallow waters of the Canadian archipelago. In all these ice-covered regions, many of the complex, coordinated tactics of open ocean ASW are much more difficult. Large-scale fixed surveillance systems are more difficult to implant, maintain, and monitor, and ASW aircraft are of little use, although developments in through-ice sensors may change this. Without fixed surveillance, vectored intercept using ships or submarines must rely on satellites or on covertly implanted sensors. Communication, which is essential to a coordinated ASW effort, is unusually difficult and limited.

Sound transmission in the central Arctic is particularly influenced by the continuous increase in sound speed with depth. At the surface, where sound speed is at a minimum, signals are refracted into the underside of the ice; and the character of the underice surface largely controls sound transmission. Smooth new ice, characteristic of annual freezing, will reflect low-frequency sound without much scattering or absorption. Older, ridged ice will scatter sound and propagate it poorly. The smaller the distance between ridges, the poorer will be the transmission. In the central Arctic, transmission of sounds below 100 Hz is better than free-field (spherically spreading) transmission out to ranges beyond a few hundred miles—that is, at those frequencies and ranges, the Arctic behaves like a sound channel. At frequencies of 200–500 Hz, however, the Arctic does not behave like a sound channel at ranges over 54 nm (100 km). In contrast, the deep ocean in the northeast Pacific acts as a waveguide for sound in those same frequencies beyond 540 nm (1,000 km). In terms of ambient noise, the central Arctic is a highly variable environment: noise intensity can change by several orders of magnitude over the course of a day. Due to the absence of shipping, low-frequency ambient noise rarely reaches the intensity associated with moderate shipping in the open sea. At frequencies above 100 Hz, noise levels in the central Arctic frequently fall below those of a calm open sea. At such frequencies, however, the higher Arctic transmission losses tend to offset this gain for detection.

In short, the uncertainty in predicting detection range in the central Arctic is comparable to that in deep ocean. In the central Arctic, detection ranges at frequencies below 100 Hz may *at times* be better than those in the central North Atlantic and North Pacific, due to the absence of shipping noise, whose spectrum peaks at low frequencies. This advantage for detection is offset by the sharp cutoff of high frequencies in the Arctic, which attenuates high-frequency components of submarine spectra and makes them more difficult to identify.

Between the deep central Arctic and the Soviet coast there is a continental shelf about 600 nm (1,100 km) wide and generally less than 900 feet (280 meters) deep. This area tends to be covered by ice all year, unlike the Barents Sea, which clears in summer because of the Gulf Stream. The continental shelf region, called the "marginal sea ice zone," is one of the most difficult acoustic environments in which to detect submarines. Just as in the central Arctic, the ice cover inhibits coordinated activity between ASW aircraft, ships, and fixed surveillance. In fact, as a rule these waters are accessible exclusively by submarines.

In the Pacific, the northern quarter of the Sea of Okhotsk has a depth of 600–1,200 feet (200–400 meters); and most of the remainder is deeper than 3,000 feet (900 meters). Acoustically, most of the Sea of Okhotsk probably behaves like intermediate-depth water—that is, it is too shallow to permit the formation of convergence zones except in its very deepest section, adjacent to the Kuril Islands. Since the northern Sea of Okhotsk is shallow and shares most of the acoustic properties of the Soviet marginal seas, it is not discussed separately; the general conclusions regarding detection in the shallow Arctic waters are also assumed to apply here.

In the Arctic, moving from west to east, potential deployment areas in shallow water are the Barents, Kara, Laptev, East Siberian, and Chukchi seas. Some areas along the Siberian coast are too shallow for submarines, although recent evidence suggests that Soviet submarines may be able to operate in very shallow depths. A photograph taken by the National Oceanic and Atmospheric Administration's LANDSAT 4 satellite on 28 March 1984 showed what is believed to be a Soviet strategic submarine testing equipment that breaks a hole in the ice. The test took place 50 miles north of Wrangel Island in the East Siberian Sea in less than 126 feet (40 meters) of water.[37] The test may have been related to telecommunications or emergency escape, but if Soviet submarines can in fact launch ballistic missiles in such shallow water, then larger parts of the Soviet marginal seas and the Canadian archipelago than previously expected are possible patrol areas. Submarine operations under ice in shallow marginal seas are not new. As long ago as 1960, a US nuclear attack submarine traveled 900 miles across the Bering-Chukchi shelf in 125–180 feet (40–55 meters) of water, cruising just 35 feet above the bottom.[38] Operations in shallow water also carry the danger of being lifted to the surface due to the low pressure caused by flow between the submarine deck and the surface.

A problem for the Soviets is that not all ballistic missiles can be launched from a surfaced submarine. In fact, the early Soviet SS-N-4 SLBM had to be launched at the surface. Underwater launch through a hole in the ice would require accurate maneuvering to remain under a hole, and constant reballasting.[39] Surface launch might be preferable in areas where the submarine had to break through the ice, since a missile floating upward could easily hit floating blocks of ice dislodged by the submarine, damaging both the missile and the submarine. Moreover, because submerged launch probably generates a louder acoustic signal and because the missile launch is a strong nonacoustic signal, there would be no inherent advantage to submerged launch in terms of covertness.

There is little prospect of US area acoustic surveillance of the Soviet marginal seas. The length of the Soviet Arctic coast exceeds the total length of the coastline of the continental United States. Even if US sonar arrays were successfully placed along the Soviet coast, the presence and movement of ice would restrict access from the arrays to the ocean surface for telemetry of data. Arrays can be suspended from the ice, as they usually are in Arctic acoustic experiments, but they are then within range of Soviet aircraft based in Siberia, and they are subject to dislocation or disorientation as the ice shifts. Two US programs may be partly aimed at solving the problem of surveillance under ice. One is the Ice Pick, which involves a remote sensor capable of penetrating ice. The other is Ariadne, which is a basic program to make very thin fiber-optic arrays and cables. Very thin arrays could be laid covertly by submarines.

Acoustically, shallow water is an extremely complex environment. It is generally agreed that current theory cannot provide good predictions of noise or sound propagation. This is not for lack of data; thousands of measurements exist in the *unclassified* literature, which is itself only the tip of the scientific iceberg. The Navy sends submarines through the Soviet marginal seas at least once a year with "a first priority research task" of measuring noise and sound propagation.[40] Yet understanding, particularly of propagation, "is far less than we now have for deep water."[41]

Sound propagation in shallow water is generally poor. The optimum frequency for propagation decreases with water depth, approximately linearly, from about 800 Hz at 165 feet (50 meters) depth to about 100 Hz at 660 feet (200 meters) depth. At a given depth, frequencies below the optimum are strongly attenuated due to increased loss to the bottom, while frequencies above the optimum are attenuated by absorption and scattering, which is particularly strong under ice.[42] Measurements suggest that sounds at frequencies below optimum may be reduced in intensity by 10–15 dB more than sounds at the optimum frequency.

Low-frequency sound attenuation in the Soviet marginal seas should complicate submarine detection there, particularly for quiet SSBNs. As submarine machinery becomes quieter, the focus for deep-water ASW is the 5–40 Hz tonals associated with propeller-blade beats and other extremely low frequency tonals. Since those frequencies propagate well in deep water, listening for them is the best acoustic strategy even though it requires using long towed arrays. In shallow water, ASW forces may not be able to offset machinery quieting by switching to very low detection frequencies—that is, below 20 Hz—due to the great attenuation at those frequencies. Therefore as Soviet submarines are built with quieter machinery *and* stay in shallow water, they become extremely difficult to detect and probably cut off many avenues of technical advances in US detection capability.

Another important tactical feature of shallow water is the variability of transmission characteristics, both temporally and spatially. This makes it very difficult for submarine operators to predict the range at which they might detect another submarine, or the range at which they may themselves be detected. One main source of the variability in shallow-water sound transmission is the type and topography of the ocean bottom, neither of which is well known. Bottom mapping by submarines in the western Laptev Sea has revealed highly irregular features, as the following account of a submarine survey indicates:

> While ice conditions were quite favorable in the Western Laptev Sea, they became increasingly severe (average drafts in excess of 70 feet) as the survey

> proceeded westward. Large icebergs were encountered throughout the Western Laptev Sea, and bottom conditions were discovered to be quite irregular, caused by many depressions and gouges, with the bottom shoaling up quite dramatically at times—e.g., over 50 feet in one ship length. More intriguing gouges were encountered in the East Siberian Sea as heavy deep draft ice was noted in the proximity.[43]

All in all, the shallow, ice-covered waters of the Soviet marginal seas are difficult areas in which to conduct searches for or surveillance of Soviet SSBNs. Admiral Watkins has called this region "a beautiful place to hide." He notes that it is "clearly an advantage to [the Soviets] to take their ice that is heavy most of the year around their homeland and use their forces accordingly."[44] The US Navy is putting increased emphasis on underice training in order to prepare for attacks on Soviet SSBNs there.

Remote surveillance of SSBNs under ice has received some attention. According to one report, "New Navy initiatives to develop methods of locating Soviet submarines based under the Arctic ice pack include laser techniques and sonar and other systems that could be dropped on the ice to locate any submarines under the pack."[45] It would be difficult for an airborne laser system to detect submarines under ice, since laser transmission loss through ice and snow is extremely high, and "false target" reflections off submerged ice ridges would be frequent. Sonar suspended through the ice would have some ability to detect very quiet submarines, but probably not much beyond 30 miles, so it would have to be widely distributed to provide area surveillance. DARPA's Arctic Surveillance Program "is developing specialized surveillance techniques for ice-covered regions, beginning initially with a through-the-ice acoustic sensor," called Ice Pick, which "will be tested in an air launch sequence."[46] The US P-3 Orion and other ASW aircraft, however, are turboprop planes, designed to fly for long periods at slow patrol speeds, and they have neither antiaircraft defense nor means of concealment. If US ASW aircraft attempted to fly over the marginal seas along the Soviet Arctic coast, they would be extremely vulnerable to Soviet supersonic interceptor aircraft based in Siberia.

One possible means of detection in this area is infrared sensing of temperature anomalies associated with nuclear submarines remaining stationary under holes in the ice. As noted earlier, heated water from the reactor seawater cooling loop would not mix and disperse, but would tend to rise to the surface where it could cause a detectable temperature change in open water. The remedy for this is for submarines to stay under solid ice or to keep moving. However, as a countermeasure, Soviet submarines could release oil in the water, which might reduce the emissivity of the surface.

Coordination of air and naval ASW platforms using surveillance data is of course only feasible where such data can be collected. In time of crisis or war, few if any Soviet SSBNs will be patrolling in areas where area surveillance is available to the United States.

Even in the parts of the northwest Pacific and Norwegian Sea where there are SOSUS arrays that can provide data to guide ASW aircraft to submarines, US Orion aircraft are not certain of finding and destroying them. The vulnerability of SOSUS in wartime is a key factor. The time late of the aircraft, which will range from minutes to hours, will limit the probability of localization. In probabilistic search theory, it is well known that for a target starting within a circular area and moving out at a constant speed, the probability of detection even after an *infinite* search is always less than unity. Assume, for example, that a Soviet submarine traveling at 10 knots is detected by a SOSUS array. After two and a half hours, a US Orion aircraft arrives in the vicinity to search for the submarine using sonobuoys with a detection range of 2.7 nm (5 km). If the Orion searches at a speed of, say, 250 knots, there will be at most an 80 percent chance of detecting the target, regardless of the length of the search.[47]

Trailing and Mining in Soviet Bastions

US policy regarding trailing Soviet SSBNs in peacetime is secret. As training for submarine crews, trailing a real Soviet submarine demands all the skills needed by those crews to carry out their wartime mission, and since peacetime trailing provides an excellent simulation of what might happen in wartime, there is a powerful incentive for the US Navy to engage in such activity covertly. One analyst, presumably drawing on discussions with submariners, asserted that some Soviet submarines are trailed in peacetime as they leave port but may not be followed into their most sensitive patrol areas, such as the Sea of Okhotsk.[48] On the other hand, the US does not consider the Sea of Okhotsk "off limits." It is also known that US SSNs spend a fair amount of time at sea getting close to and spying on Soviet submarines and their bases.[49] Moreover, US attack submarines reportedly trail at times within 200 yards of Soviet strategic submarines, although data passed to the USSR by the John Walker spy ring may have made the Soviet Navy "aware of the extent of their missile subs' vulnerability."[50]

Given the density of defenses near Soviet ports, US trailing tactics must be as covert as possible, and given the limited number of US SSNs based in the Atlantic (about 57) and Pacific (about 39) and given the competing demands on SSNs, the tactics must be efficient. As noted earlier, random search is relatively inefficient, particularly with the large marginal sea ice zones as Soviet SSBN deployment areas. In addition, a random search is more likely to result in encounters between US attack submarines and Soviet defenses—such as mines, conventionally powered submarines (SSs), and SSNs—than a strategy aimed at encountering only SSBNs.

Trailing is typically used to mean a tactic of waiting in an area through which Soviet SSBNs are expected to pass, often near home ports, and beginning to follow them as they pass. The process of initially picking up the trail is called acquiring an SSBN. The SSBN may be trailed for a length of time up to and including its entire patrol period. The likelihood of succeeding in putting US SSNs on station, waiting, acquiring, trailing, and finally returning to US bases, all covertly, can be treated in part as an arithmetic problem, using assumptions first about the numbers of SSNs required to wait and trail, then about the effects of defenses such as Soviet attack submarines, aircraft, mines, and surveillance.

Table 2–2 shows the number of Soviet SSBNs based in the Arctic and the estimated minimum number of US SSNs needed to keep all of them under trail. The table assumes an at-sea rate of 25 percent for Soviet SSBNs and patrol durations of 45 and 60 days for the Yankee and Delta/Typhoon classes respectively. This implies an average rotation rate of one submarine putting out to sea every 9 days. If US submarine commanders could predict the actual times when Soviet SSBNs would put to sea, US SSNs would spend little time waiting, but if Soviet SSBN departure times are random, the waiting time for US forces will be substantially increased. The calculation assumes that US

Table 2–2
Number of US attack submarines required to trail Soviet SSBNs

	Number of SSBNs Based	*Number of SSBNs at Sea*	*Time at Sea, in days*	*Rotation, in days*	*SSBN Time to Station at 25 knots, in days*	*Required SSNs*[a]	
						Trail	*Wait*[b]
Arctic:							
Delta and Typhoon	30	7	60	9	0	14	6
Yankee	12	3	45	15	3	6	
Pacific:							
Delta	12	3	60	20	0	6	6
Yankee	9	2	45	20	5	4	

Totals (SALT limits not assumed)	*SSNs* *Trail*	*Wait*
Delta and Typhoon: 42	20	12
Yankee: 21	10	

[a]These figures are for the number of vessels on station. It is assumed that two US attack submarines are needed to trail each Soviet strategic submarine and that SSNs have an at-sea rate of 33 percent. Thus, three SSNs must be maintained in the US fleet for each one required either to trail or wait. The table shows that at least 126 SSNs would be required in the fleet, of which 42 would actually be trailing or waiting at a given time.

[b]Waiting submarines are assumed to be stationed 30 nm from the SSBN port in a semicircular arc. If the gap between waiting SSNs is set at 12 nm, then 6 SSNs would be needed. If the SSNs were stationed closer to the port, fewer would be needed.

attack submarines will return to the United States after 60 days at sea, and it allows a round-trip transit time from and to US territory, traveling at 25 knots, of 12 days for SSNs that trail SSBNs coming out of Murmansk and Petropavlovsk, and 8 days for SSNs guarding the GIUK gap. This leaves the SSN 48 and 52 days, respectively, for waiting, acquiring, and trailing SSBNs at ports and at chokepoints. An obstacle to continuous trailing will arise if the SSBN remains at sea longer than the SSN, since a "hand-off" would require communication between the first and second trailers, and such communication, made covertly, would be extremely difficult if not impossible, particularly under ice. Although the United States could increase the patrol duration of its SSNs, the Soviet Union could counter with even longer patrols by its SSBNs.

The means of communicating with SSNs is similar to the means of communicating with SSBNs. If the submarine wants to remain submerged with a minimum of antenna structure above the surface, or is under ice, the main options are the floating wire antenna or the buoy, which remains submerged as it is towed along. The drawbacks of these systems are that neither can be used for transmission, only reception; the buoy is prone to entanglement on the underwater ice ridges; and in order to use a floating wire under ice, the submarine must come to a virtual stop to allow the wire to float up between ice ridges or into open water.[51] None of these limitations is crippling to those SSBNs primarily intended as strategic reserve forces—as most Soviet SSBNs probably are. These vessels are more covert if they do not transmit radio signals and are generally quieter and more difficult to find the more slowly they travel. For the SSN, however, speed is more important, the potential for a mission's changing in the course of a patrol is greater, and in the context of a campaign against SSBNs, the ability of the SSN to report back would be of tremendous value to National Command Authorities. Particularly in the context of a trailing operation, the effectiveness of SSNs would be constrained by the fact that they could not easily signal another SSN to take over the trailing of an SSBN that had been at sea beyond the SSN's endurance time.

Other important technical issues in covert trailing are the difference in passive sonar detection range between the SSN and the SSBN, and the ability of the trailer to keep track of the SSBN's course, speed, and range. The trailer must maintain a distance close enough to detect the target, yet far enough away so that the target cannot detect the trailer. Counterdetection (getting too close) is as important a problem as losing the target.

Using the estimates of submarine signal level given in Figure A6–5[52] and the estimates of detection range given in appendix 8, detection-range advantages for various pairs of US and Soviet submarine classes can be estimated. These estimates, shown in table 2–3 are based on the assumption that the entire acoustic output of the submarine occurs in a 1-Hz-wide tonal band, as no data are available regarding the actual spectrum of submarine-radiated noise. This assumption, which leads to overestimates of detection range, can be partially

Table 2-3
Detection-range advantage of US submarines over Soviet submarines

US Class	Soviet Class[a]	Acoustic Advantage (dB)	Range Advantage (nm) Deep Ocean	Central Arctic	Shallow Water
SSN Los Angeles	Akula	0–15	0–20	0–20	0–10
	Victor III	10–20	25–300	100–400	2–70
	Victor I, II	30–40	100–1,000	200–1,000	40–200
SSN Sturgeon	Victor III	0	0	0	0
	Victor I, II	10–20	400–1,000	100–500	40–100
SSN Permit	Victor III	0	0	0	0
	Victor I, II	15	500–1,000	80–400	30–70
SSBN Ohio	Victor III	35–45	30–300	50–500	10–100
	Victor I, II	50–60	500–2,500	400–1,000	10–200

[a]No direct data are available on Soviet SSBNs, except for the Yankee, which radiates at about 150 db. It has been reported, however, that the Delta I SSBN class was about as noisy as the Yankee SSBN. The Delta I and Yankee are assumed to resemble the Victor I and II, while later Delta III, Delta IV, and Typhoon classes are assumed to be equivalent to the Victor III or quieter. All the estimates use sonar parameters that approximate the best achievable. Thus, the detection ranges are probably overestimates. The lower figure is probably realistic.

justified because a small number of tonals in an actual spectrum contribute most of the radiated sound, and the error introduced by lumping them together (a few decibels) will be small compared with the errors in the estimates of signal intensity, ambient noise, and transmission loss. In general, table 2-3 like the other acoustic and nonacoustic detection analyses in this study, is meant to suggest general relationships, not precise predictions.

The table shows three important relationships. First, a wide range of variability in detection range advantage—typically a factor of 5–10—is inherent to passive detection. It is created by the environment and cannot be significantly reduced by improving the sonar system, through array gain, or through signal processing gain (lowering the detection threshold). A US planner considering a trailing operation against Soviet SSBNs would have to assume "worst-case" ambient conditions, at which the detection range advantage would be at a minimum. The actual advantage in any given case will depend on the specific classes of Soviet SSBN and US SSN involved; the detection range advantage varies from nothing to several tens of miles. There are in fact a number of older US attack submarines that can probably be detected by new Soviet SSBNs at greater ranges than the SSNs can detect the SSBNs. Having a detection advantage that will allow the trailer to remain many miles away is particularly important for long-range passive detection of low-frequency tonals. This requires the use of a very long towed array, which streams behind the trailing SSN, and to get separate lines of bearing on the target, so as to triangulate its range, the SSN needs to allow a considerable distance for maneuvering this towed array.

The second observation is that the detection-range advantage of any given US submarine class against any given Soviet submarine class is usually somewhat less in deep, ice-covered water than in deep open water, and it is always much less in shallow water than in deep water. In other words, a given acoustic advantage provides much less tactical (detection range) advantage in shallow water than in deep water. In the worst detection conditions for two submarines in deep water, the trailer might have a 100-mile (184 km) detection-range advantage over the target. In shallow, ice-covered waters, this could be reduced to 25 miles (46 km) or less. Under the latter circumstances the trailer's maneuvering room is more constrained.

The third observation is that, for any given acoustic advantage in dBs, the corresponding range advantage decreases as both target and trailer become quieter. For example, taking into account both submarine signal emission levels and sonar capabilities, the US Los Angeles (SSN-688) class attack submarine is estimated to have a 10–20 dB advantage over the Soviet Victor III attack submarine; yet because both are very quiet in shallow wate the range advantage under poor acoustic conditions may be as little as 2 miles (3.7 km). In the same environment, an estimated 10–20 dB acoustic advantage of the US Sturgeon (SSN-637) class over the even louder Victor I and II classes yields a range advantage of 40 miles (74 km). The reasons for this are clear when one considers the general shape of the transmission loss curves.[53]

This is an extremely important phenomenon, because as both US and Soviet submarines become quieter, as indicated in figure A6–5, the United States' maintaining the same relative acoustic advantage *does not preserve the tactically critical detection range advantage,* which may shrink to the point at which covert trailing, even with long, hull-mounted arrays, is extemely unreliable.[54] This has grave implications to the planning of submarine campaigns in Soviet waters, which are key elements of the US maritime strategy, particularly when Soviet SSNs of the Akula vintage are considered.

Attempts to improve US sensors for covert trailing and attack capability in the next generation of SSNs are centered on the Advanced Conformal Submarine Array System (ACSAS) and the rapid passive localization system called the Wide Aperture Array (WAA), both of which will be part of an overall Submarine Advanced Combat System (SUBACS).[55] The Navy has predicted that ACSAS will yield a 10-fold increase in detection range (*not* a 10 dB improvement in array gain).[56] This is a misleading statement, since detection range is a function not only of the sensor system but also of the transmission characteristics of the particular environment in which it is operating. For example, a 10 dB increase in array gain may yield a 10-fold increase in detection range in the north Pacific, but only a 4-fold increase in the Barents Sea. ACSAS is an attempt to merge acoustic array design with submarine hull design. It will use very thin hydrophones that conform to the shape of the outside of the submarine hull. The sensors will be made of polymers that have the property of changing their electrical characteristics in response to slight changes in pressure.[57]

By placing hydrophones along a substantial length of the submarine hull, ACSAS will take advantage of the fact that horizontal arrays realize the greatest gain. A long array integral to the submarine's hull may in some circumstances eliminate the maneuvering problems of towing a long array behind the submarine, although ACSAS may not eliminate the need for a towed array. Another advantage of ACSAS is that beamforming, i.e., direction-finding, is much easier if the geometry of the array is known precisely, and the shape of towed arrays changes as the submarine maneuvers. ACSAS does face major technical hurdles, however: isolating the array from hull vibrations and from turbulent pressure fluctuations near the hull.[58] The submarine itself, the SSN-21, "unlike earlier US boats (and even the most recent Soviet designs) . . . will have to be extraordinarily quiet across its entire speed range."[59]

Passive localization from a single array requires the array to be moved to at least one and in practice several points in order to triangulate on the target. As a rough guide, in order to localize a target this way requires a submarine about 1 minute of tracking time for every 1,000 yards to the target.[60] To localize a target near the maximum range at which US torpedoes are reliable (about 10 miles) would take about 20 minutes, during which time a target moving at 15 knots would travel 5 miles. To localize a target at 30 miles—an estimate of the range of the next generation of ASW standoff weapon—would require one hour of tracking, during which the target could move 15 miles. Clearly there is a powerful incentive to develop a rapid passive localization device that can determine distance to the target from a single measurement.

One class of passive range finding methods are the Low Ship Impact Ranging (LSIR) techniques. The towed array can determine one bearing (direction to the target) from over a thousand feet behind the submarine, while an array integral to the hull, such as the bow spherical array or hull conformal array provides the second bearing, and the triangulation is done without moving the submarine. Another LSIR method uses the fact that some sound from the target may reach the searcher via a single bounce off the bottom. If the vertical arrival angle of the bottom bounce sound is determined relative to the vertical arrival angle of the sound coming directly from the target, a simple geometrical argument yields the range to the target. This technique requires a knowledge of the sound transmission characteristics and bottom characteristics between target and searcher, but is one of several tools that can be used by submarine operators.

The Wide Aperture Array (WAA) is a Rapid Passive Localization (RAPLOC) system that makes use of the fact that as sound radiates from any source, it radiates in wave fronts that form a circle. The radius of curvature of the wave front is the radius of the circle and therefore the range to the target. Three measurements at three points on the searching submarine are sufficient to determine the range to the target using the WAA technique. A significant limitation of WAA is that it must use broadband signal processing in order to avoid ambiguous detections. Specifically, passive rangefinding requires the determination of very small time shifts in the signal as it is received at different points along the array. Since broadband processing uses more of the information contained in the signal radiated by the submarine, it should yield a better estimate of the time shifts, and therefore a better estimate of range, than narrowband processing.

The use of broadband processing severely limits its detection range capability, particularly against quiet Soviet submarines, which generate most of their sound in a few narrow bands. In addition, the processing requirements of the WAA are large, and large parallel processors must be used. Also, tiny perturbations of the wave front itself can impair the WAA. Because of these difficulties, it is not clear that WAA will be introduced operationally in the US fleet, although a smaller version is operational in the Australian fleet.[61]

It is difficult to predict whether or not hull-mounted arrays and passive range-finding systems will be able to overcome the tactical obstacles to trailing quiet Soviet submarines in shallow water. Passive *range* finding from a submarine depends a great deal on local transmission properties, which vary widely in shallow water. Even the much simpler problem of passive *direction* finding is complicated in shallow water by the fact that the apparent direction from which a sound emanates is a function of local conditions such as bottom material and water depth, and large errors can result from a failure to account accurately for such conditions. In theory, corrections can be made using data on the acoustic properties of the transmission path in conjunction with adaptive array processing, but in practice, data on the transmission path is extremely difficult to obtain. "Therefore," as one analyst stated, "application in mobile systems does not seem to be very promising."[62]

A phenomenon that occurs only in deep water can also impede trailing. Convergence zone propagation creates zones around the target, at radii of approximately 30, 60, and 90 miles (55, 110, and 165 km), within which the detectability of the *trailer* may increase sharply. Transmission loss in convergence zones may be 10–15 dB less than in water 5 miles (9 km) away. Thus, a trailer outside the convergence zone surrounding the target may be undetectable. Upon entering the zone 30 miles (55 km) from the target, the trailer would find that the strength of the target signal suddenly increased, while the target might suddenly learn that it was being trailed. Since the focus of SSBN trailing is shifting more and more to shallow and Arctic waters where there are no convergence zones, however, this phenomenon may no longer be a major concern.

Mining is another threat to SSBNs—as well as to SSNs—that could potentially play an important role in forward submarine strategies. US attack submarines of the improved SSN-688 and SSN-21 classes have the ability to mine Soviet waters. They could theoretically plant mines near Soviet ports with submarine-launched mobile mines (SLMM), which swim out of the submarine, travel on their own somewhere between 5 and 11 miles (9 and 20 km), come to rest, wait for a passing ship or submarine, and attack it like an armed torpedo. The SLMM is based on the Mk 37 torpedo. The tactical advantages of such standoff mines are that they allow the submarine to mine areas near harbors without actually entering them, and that the submarine can replenish an existing minefield in which a number of mines have exploded without having to enter it. Some mines may possibly be used under ice, including the Captor mine, which is based on the Mk-46 torpedo.[63] Submarines do not have a large capacity to lay mines, however, given the fact that they must carry torpedoes, Harpoon antiship cruise missiles, Subroc, and mines in a weapon compartment that has a limited capacity. The SSN-688 carries a total of about 25 weapons, the improved SSN-688 carries 33 weapons, and the SSN-21 is to carry about 50. The mix of weapons can be determined by the mission, but it is unlikely that enough mines could be planted by submarines to make mining over large areas effective. Mining harbors would be very effective under many conditions; even if they were swept, the mines could be set to fire only after their sensors were triggered several times, creating a potent but random threat. The psychological impact of such a threat would be great, and of course a major sinking within a narrow channel could impede traffic for many days. Many Soviet ports are kept open in winter only by means of constant icebreaker operations. This tends to channel ship traffic into narrow lanes and may hamper minesweeping operations.

Soviet Defense of Bastions

The preferred US tactic for finding Soviet strategic submarines is probably for SSNs to wait outside a port, acquire the SSBNs as they exit, and then keep them under trail. This method is more efficient than random search and is probably safer than risking random encounters with minefields and Soviet attack submarines in wartime. However, the Soviet Navy is likely to concentrate its surveillance and defensive efforts near its ports for just this reason. The farther away US attack submarines must wait, the wider will be the channel through which Soviet SSBNs can exit and the lower the chance of picking them up.

An important problem, both for the Soviet submarines defending waters near their coasts and for US SSNs attacking them, is identifying a detected submarine as friend or foe. Identification friend or foe (IFF) is of course a problem common to all branches of the military, but in submarine warfare its impact on basic tactics is unusually large. US SSNs operate individually and are assigned areas within which other friendly submarines are not permitted to enter. This allows the US submarine the maximum detection range advantage, since a vessel can be detected at a longer range than it can be classified. If all vessels detected can be presumed to be hostile, the submarine commander has more flexibility in deciding whether to avoid, approach, or attack the vessel at long range. In this way the submarine forms a kind of stationary barrier, like a minefield, which causes vessels to be sunk more or less indiscriminantly. In practice, many factors make this tactic more discriminating than a minefield, such as the political impact on rules of engagement, the aggressiveness of the commander and crew, and so forth.

The same IFF problems would be present for Soviet submarines and ASW forces in home waters, though they would probably be far more complex. In defending against US attack submarines near Soviet ports, the most effective ASW weapon the Soviets could use would be their own SSs, SSNs, and mines. They could also use ASW aircraft and surface ships. With so many submarines and ASW forces in a relatively small area trying to destroy an extremely elusive target, the IFF problem would be compounded. The Soviet Navy must seek an optimum between concentrating their ships to obtain for themselves numerical superiority at the risk of destroying some of their own vessels, and dispersing their forces in a layered defense that relies on attrition to US attack submarines at each layer.

The optimum bastion defense may be a mix of these two approaches: in addition to local defense near ports, there may be Soviet defenses around the perimeters of SSBN patrol areas, providing defense-in-depth. A major advantage to stopping hostile submarines at the periphery is that once a US attack submarine is intermingled with Soviet vessels, Soviet forces must approach and identify each contact before attacking, to avoid inadvertently destroying Soviet submarines. At a barrier on the periphery, it is possible to follow a rule that all unaccounted-for submarines are hostile. Because this simple rule of engagement would allow Soviet attack submarines to launch their torpedoes at a greater range, it gives them a tactical benefit that they sorely need against the quieter US SSNs.

Tables 2–4 and 2–5 show the width of the entrances into the Soviet SSBN patrol areas in the Barents Sea and the Sea of Okhotsk. In both areas there are hundreds of miles through which US attack submarines might pass covertly, including many passages from the central Arctic Ocean. Nonetheless, these passages can be partially defended with the use of mines, submarines, surface ships and aircraft, and underwater surveillance. The Soviet ASW forces that could contribute to this effort are described in some detail in appendix 2.

Table 2–4
Passages into the Barents Sea: The Soviet Arctic bastion perimeter

Chokepoint	*Width*
Greenland–Alaska (including Bering Strait)	2,000 nm
Svalbard–Greenland	240 nm
Svalbard–Kola	480 nm
Svalbard–Franz Josef	120 nm
Franz Josef–Northland	300 nm
Franz Josef–Novaya Zemlya	300 nm
Norwegian Sea width	720 nm
Denmark Strait	180 nm
Iceland–Norway	600 nm

Table 2–5
Passages into the Sea of Okhotsk from north to south

Island	*Width (nm)*	*Maximum Depth (feet)*
Kamchatka peninsula	10	<600
Shimushu	2	<600
Paramushira	35	1,200
Onekotan	7	<600
Harumukatan	25	<600
Yakeruma	5	600
Shasukotan	45	4,800
Matsuwa	15	1,800
Rashuwa	10	1,800
Ushishiru	15	1,800
Ketoi	10	900
Shimushira	35	7,800
Chirihoi	15	600
Uruppu	20	1,200
Etorofu	10	1,000
Kunashiri Shima	12	<600
Hokkaido	25	<600
Sakhalin		

Mines offer the Soviet Navy a potentially effective counter to US attack submarines that attempt to enter Soviet SSBN bastions. US SSNs can be destroyed upon entering a minefield, or they can be forced to avoid certain areas where SSBNs may be hidden. Soviet mining capabilities are extensive, and they are well respected by the US Navy. Given the proximity of narrow passages leading to Soviet ports, defensive mine barriers could be created very rapidly using a wide variety of ships and aircraft. Said one analyst: "Most, if not all, Soviet surface combatants and many of their long-range naval aircraft are equipped for minelaying, and according to a recent unclassified US Air Force study, all Soviet submarine classes can lay mines."[64] Table 2–6 shows the mine capacities of older Soviet classes, which would be most likely to be assigned this task.[65]

The total number of mines carried in the Arctic on these older vessels is about 2,600 on submarines, plus 2,600 on surface ships; in the Pacific, it is 2,200 on submarines and 2,300 on surface ships. Soviet light frigates—a type of small surface ship that has no counterpart in the US Navy—may have an important potential role as defensive minelayers, since they cannot travel great distances at sea or conduct effective ASW search. In addition, submarines contribute much to potential Soviet mine-laying capability, since they can lay minefields in waters not ostensibly or legally controlled by the Soviet Navy.

Table 2–6
Minelaying capacity of older classes of Soviet naval vessels[a]

		Number of Vessels in Fleet	
Class	*Mines per Vessel*	*Northern*	*Pacific*
Surface Ships (includes reserves)			
Alesha (3 minelayers)	400	2[b]	1[b]
Sverdlov[c] (cruisers)	150	2	2
Kilden[c] (destroyers)	80	0	1
Kotlin[c] (destroyers)	55	5	4
Kashin[c] (destroyers)	30	4	4
Skoryy[c] (destroyers)	50	1	3
Riga (47), Grisha (50), Koni (1), Mirka (18), Petya (40) (frigates)	26[d]	41	40
Total mine capacity		2611	2310
Submarines[e]			
November (SSN)	48	8	4
Echo I, II (SSN, SSGN)	36	14	19
Victor I, II (SSN)	32	18	5
Foxtrot (SS)	40	28	27
Romeo (SS)	22	4	3
Whiskey (50)[b] (SS)	20		
Total mine capacity		2672	2182

Source: Tables in appendix 2, and Milan Vego, "Soviet Navy: Mines and Their Platforms," *Navy International*, July 1986, pp. 431–436.

[a]Soviet aircraft can also carry mines; the Bear D, F, and G versions can hold 10–20, and the May can hold 6–12 mines.

[b]Distribution unknown.

[c]Includes all versions, some of which are modern.

[d]This is a weighted average. The Grisha, Koni, Mirka, and Petya vessels carry about 20 mines, Riga carries 40. This assumes all classes distributed in the same proportion.

[e]Yankee SSN conversions are not included, but may carry 32 mines.

Mines can be used effectively in the relatively shallow water of the Soviet continental shelf. Most of the passages into the SSBN patrol areas could be mined by Soviet ships and submarines in a matter of days or a few weeks, and aircraft could accomplish the task even faster. In the Arctic, the entrance via the Parry channel in the Canadian archipelago could be mined, as could the Bering Strait. Much of the northern perimeter of the Barents Sea could be mined in a few days during the summer by conventional and nuclear-powered submarines and by surface ships. In winter in the northern Barents Sea, ice would block mining access by surface ships, aircraft, and diesel-electric submarines (which can travel only limited distances under ice). Since most nuclear attack submarines would be assigned to missions other than mining, setting minefields in the extensive ice around Franz Josef Land would take considerably longer in winter. Diesel-electric submarines could probably not set mines here safely.

Soviet diesel-electric submarines are potentially very important in the defense of Soviet SSBN bastions. They can run on batteries for several days when moving at 4 knots or less, and when they do, they are quieter than many quiet nuclear-powered submarines. At high speeds of 18 knots the batteries will be drained after only a few hours of travel due to the rapid increase of hydrodynamic friction with speed. Diesel-electric submarines can be expected to form barriers at key chokepoints and near ports, where high speeds are not required. The US Navy is clearly concerned about the Soviet SSs defending their SSBN deployment areas. Adm. Kinnaird R. McKee expressed this when he said, "Diesel boats will get in our hair when we try to go to [the Soviets'] home-waters . . . they are a minefield."[66] Under the ice, nuclear-powered attack submarines would be employed to escort SSBNs or patrol barriers. The Victor III SSN regularly accompanies Soviet SSBNs on patrol.

As shown in table A2–3 in appendix 2, modern torpedo attack submarines of the Mike, Sierra, Alfa, Yankee, and Victor class are concentrated in the Northern Fleet, with about 36 there and 14 in the Pacific Fleet. The new Akula class SSN is only in the Pacific (as of 1986). Older SSNs of the Echo and November classes are divided evenly, with 8 in the Northern Fleet and 9 in the Pacific. Modern nuclear-powered cruise missile submarines (SSGNs), though intended primarily as antiship platforms, can fire torpedoes, use sonars, and are formidable ASW units. The Northern Fleet has 17 modern SSGNs of the Yankee, Charlie, Papa, and Oscar class, while the Pacific Fleet has 5 of these. There are 14 of the older Echo II SSGNs in the Northern Fleet and 14 in the Pacific Fleet. The modern SSs that would be most potent in ASW are the Foxtrot, Tango, and Kilo classes. There are about 43 of these in the Northern Fleet and 34 in the Pacific Fleet. Older SSs include the Whiskey and Romeo, of which there may be about 20 in the Northern Fleet and 20 in the Pacific, although the distribution is unknown. In terms of total numbers of modern nuclear and diesel-electric submarines equipped for torpedo attack, the Soviet Northern Fleet has nearly 96 and the Pacific Fleet nearly 53. Given the short transit time from Soviet submarine bases to most of the chokepoints, Soviet submarines could spend most of their at-sea time actually on patrol. A low wartime at-sea rate of, say, 50 percent would generate 18 modern SSNs plus 20 modern SSs in the North Atlantic and 8 modern SSNs plus 17 modern SSs in the Pacific.

Little information is available about the at-sea numbers to which the Soviet Navy can surge. As noted earlier in this chapter, the Soviet Navy has surged its SSNs several times in exercises and can put a substantial portion of them to sea in 24–48 hours.[67] Unlike the United States, which maintains peacetime at-sea rates of various classes of ships of 40–60 percent, the fraction of Soviet naval vessels out of port and on patrol at sea in peacetime is typically 10–20 percent. Given the Soviet Union's lack of experience in maintaining a large fraction of its ships at sea and the generic difficulties involved in surging, it is unlikely that a high surge level could be sustained for many months. Instead, a very high surge is likely to be followed by a fairly sharp decline in the number of fully functioning ships at sea within a few months. In addition, given time and basing constraints, it is highly unlikely that the Soviet Navy would attempt to move a significant number of vessels from one fleet to the other in wartime.[68]

In the event of a crisis and of a Soviet surge of ASW assets to protect SSBN bastions, a critical parameter would be the size of the bastions themselves, and especially the length of their perimeters. In the Arctic, the perimeter of the Barents Sea is about 900 miles (1,660 km), most of which is under ice during the winter. Since much of the perimeter is also shallow water, it would be difficult for the Soviet Navy to rely on acoustic surveillance for detection of US SSNs. If 18 modern Soviet SSNs in the Northern Fleet—that is, half the fleet—were assigned to patrol the northern perimeter of the Barents Sea, each submarine would have to cover a 25-mile (46-km) front, searching for US submarines that might be detected at ranges of only a few miles there under adverse sonar conditions. Even a total surge of almost 40 modern Soviet SSNs would be unable to stop a large majority of US SSNs. All US attack submarines built since the SSN-637 class have a significant acoustic advantage over all but the most recent Soviet SSNs (Mike, Sierra, and Akula), and even against these few vessels, SSN-688 submarines probably maintain some advantage. A Soviet SSN perimeter along the boundary of the central Arctic Ocean would probably yield very little benefit. As I mentioned earlier, mining that northern perimeter would depend to a large extent on season. In the winter, the edge of the solid ice pack may approach to within less than 200 miles (370 km) of the Kola peninsula, while in the summer, the edge of the solid ice may retreat into the Arctic Ocean itself. Mining the edge of the ice pack in the winter would require planting mines in the central Barents Sea, near Soviet sea lanes.

In the Pacific, the six northernmost passages into the Sea of Okhotsk (those nearest Petropavlovsk) have a combined width of 84 miles (155 km), and all but one are less than 660 feet (200 meters) deep. Since Soviet SSBNs have practiced launching missiles from ice-covered waters only 40 meters deep, there are probably few limits on where they can enter the Sea of Okhotsk. Defending this bastion might involve mining most of the passages, leaving only a few to be guarded by submarine "gatekeepers." The task of maintaining such a series of minefields over hundreds of miles during a war would not be an easy task. Many airfields on the Kurils might be subject to early attack by cruise missiles and carrier-based aircraft, and the straits themselves may have strong currents.

A possible problem of Soviet SSBN security in the Pacific is getting their SSBNs into the Sea of Okhotsk to begin with. However, even though Soviet SSBNs traveling the 150 miles (280 km) from the naval base at Petropavlovsk to a patrol area in the Sea of Okhotsk could be threatened by US SSNs waiting near the base, extremely quiet Tango class SSs could escort SSBNs, traveling on battery for the entire trip at a speed of 15 knots or less. This would create a potent, undetectable threat to any US submarine attempting to trail. The US Navy expects to move several SSNs into the Sea of Okhotsk probably just before a conflict begins, in the phase defined as "transition to war."[69] In anticipation of this, the Soviet Navy would probably try to surge their SSBNs first, enter the Sea of Okhotsk as a force, and begin heavy mining.

Soviet surface ASW would be conducted by large ASW cruisers and destroyers: the Kiev, Kirov, Kara, Kresta II, Udaloy, and Krivak classes. It is unlikely, however, that these ships would cause any significant attrition of US attack submarines, since they are noisy, which both gives away their position and degrades their sensors, and they cannot penetrate heavy, solid ice. Helicopters based on these ships cannot search wide areas and are best suited for defending the ship. There are 19 of these ships in the Northern Fleet and 17 in the Pacific.[70] Ships of smaller surface classes, with even less ASW capability, total about 40 in the Arctic and 45 in the Pacific. Finally, the Soviet Navy has a total of about 70 small coastal corvettes that can conduct some limited ASW. Their distribution between the two oceans is unknown. As escorts for Soviet SSBNs leaving port, these vessels may be useful since their high noise levels could mask the sound of an SSBN beneath.

It is not clear whether or how the operations of Soviet attack submarines are integrated with those of the surface forces. John Jordan believes that tactical coordination between SSNs and surface ships is likely, "especially in barrier operations in support of Soviet ballistic missile submarines."[71] An analysis of Soviet writings up to 1979 by Robert Herrick, however, suggests the opposite:

> The Soviet Navy's nuclear powered attack submarines, despite their potentially great capabilities for pro-SSBN ASW, still appear not to have been

> integrated tactically into the Navy's aircraft-surface ship ASW effort. This appears to be the case despite the fact that senior Soviet naval officers repeatedly have claimed in print that the US Navy sets great store in using SSNs for ASW.[72]

Arguments can be adduced for both views. On the one hand, coordination between submarines and surface ships would permit each to make the best use of its unique ASW capabilities. On the other hand, mating noisy surface ships with quiet submarines would make it easy for US SSNs to avoid the entire group, defeating the purpose of a defensive barrier.

Soviet surface ships may contribute to the defense of Soviet SSBNs by using active sonar to sweep out lanes from submarine bases to the open sea. Coordinated searches by surface ships would complicate the task of US attack submarines attempting to trail or ambush the SSBNs as they exit or enter. One tactic discussed in the Soviet literature involves using ASW surface ships to sweep out a lane prior to the exit of an SSBN, returning to the base to form a screen around the submarine and escorting it out the lane. Another tactic mentioned is the use of ships to sweep out certain areas, without the direct screening.[73] The large number of small Soviet ASW-capable ships suggests that there would be a number of options available to the Soviet Navy to protect SSBNs as they exit, particularly prior to or early in a conflict.

It has also been argued that coordination among Soviet submarines would be tactically advantageous, particularly when they are working against quieter US counterparts.[74] Various tactics might be employed by groups of submarines to offset the tactical advantage in detection range that allows US SSNs to approach and fire a torpedo without being counterdetected. For example, after a torpedo launch, ending the concealment of the US submarine, that submarine could be targeted by two or more Soviet submarines from different angles. In another scenario, a US attack submarine might turn to avoid a Soviet SSN, only to encounter a quieter conventional submarine running on battery. Even if a US attack submarine launches the first torpedo, training exercises suggest that there is only a 50 percent chance that the torpedo will hit the target.[75] Moreover, it is reported that under ice and in shallow water, the Mk-48 is "frequently ineffective."[76]

Torpedo performance seems particularly poor in the shallow, ice-covered waters of the marginal seas. The protruding ice ridges and sudden changes in depth characteristic of the Soviet marginal seas would be unavoidable hazards for a torpedo traveling with passive acoustic guidance. An active homing torpedo would have to be equipped with a sensor that detected the bottom and surface in order to avoid targeting the bottom or the ice, which is very efficient sound-reflecting material. Torpedoes could be set to search for an object moving against a stationary background, a common technique in radar.

Attrition to US Attack Submarines by Soviet Bastion Defenses

The process of trying to create an analytical model of all the factors that determine the outcome of a submarine/ASW campaign begins with theoretical or empirical models of submarine, weapon, and sensor performance and attempts to build to more complex levels of interaction. At each higher level of analysis, the problem becomes much more complex and requires simplifying measures that lump all of the lower-level considerations into a few parameters. One such parameter is called the exchange ratio.

An exchange ratio can be defined to represent the likely outcome of repeated one-on-one battles between submarines. The exchange ratio, defined here as being "US-favorable," is $E = (b + a)/(r + a)$, where b is the probability that the US submarine survives and destroys the Soviet one, r is the probability that the opposite occurs, and a is the probability that both are destroyed. The three probabilities represent the net impact of a host of important tactical parameters, including crew proficiency, sonar capability, weapon characteristics, quietness, speed, and so on, as they relate to a one-on-one engagement. Combining the individual probabilities into an exchange ratio gives a single parameter to describe the expected outcome of many engagements between submarines with those same characteristics. The US-favorable exchange ratio defines the expected ratio of Soviet losses to US losses. For example, a 10:1 exchange ratio means that for every 10 Soviet submarines destroyed, the expected US loss is one.

The actual probabilities vary with specific classes of submarine and acoustic environments, but an often cited *average* exchange ratio between US and Soviet attack submarines is about 3:1.[77] Assuming no mutual destruction, this implies a probability of 0.75 that the US SSN will be successful, and 0.25 that the Soviet SSN will be successful. US training drills, which provide the data for these figures, usually stop after one submarine has detected the other and has launched a torpedo.[78] Therefore, the exchange ratio reflects the ability of quiet US submarines to detect, approach, localize, and fire a torpedo at a Soviet submarine without being detected. Apparently, little effort has been spent determining what might happen if the torpedo fails to destroy the Soviet submarine, because of either mechanical failure or successful use of Soviet countermeasures. Henry Young has pointed out that if the first torpedo does not in fact destroy the Soviet submarine, the alerted Soviet submarine may well use active sonar, since it will have nothing to lose (already having been localized) and much to gain (instant localization of the US submarine). In an active sonar environment, the US advantage in quieting is largely eliminated and the exchange ratio approaches 1:1, with a high probability of mutual destruction. Young has demonstrated that even if the exchange ratio on the initial shot is as high as 10:1, with a torpedo miss probability of 0.5 and an exchange ratio of 1:1 on subsequent interaction (when the Soviet vessel is alerted and using active sonar), the *net* exchange ratio is only 2.4:1.[79]

The effectiveness of US nuclear-powered attack submarines against Soviet diesel-electric submarines operating on battery is considered very low. One source states that the "probability of kill" of US SSNs against Soviet SSs (presumably on battery) is 0.12–0.40, compared with 0.55 against one of the newest SSNs, the Victor III. These figures apply in the North Atlantic. In shallower water, where the US detection range advantage is generally lower, the kill probabilities may be lower. Because such numbers are generally cited without any qualification as to the specific scenario, they are not particularly useful as absolute measures, although the relative vulnerability of the Victor III compared to diesel-electric submarines is worth noting.[80] In response to Soviet SSs deployed in home waters, "the Navy's official advice to US warship and submarine captains is simply to avoid areas in which the boats are believed to operate. If that is impossible, US units are advised to move through such areas at high speed."[81] Neither of these options is available to a commander waiting to trail Soviet SSBNs.

The aggregate outcome of many one-on-one encounters has thus far been represented by its probabilistic "expected value." A more accurate conception of the outcome, however, is a probability distribution whose mean is the expected outcome, but whose "tails" show the probability that either side might do better or worse. For example, assume that the Soviet Union has 18 SSNs on patrol in the Arctic opposed by an equal number of US SSNs. With a 3:1 exchange ratio (and no mutual destruction), the expected outcome is that all Soviet SSNs would be destroyed, along with 6 US SSNs, leaving 12 US SSNs. However, there is a 7 percent chance that 7 or fewer US SSNs would survive and a 1 percent chance that fewer than 4 US SSNs would survive. If the probability of a Soviet attack submarine being destroyed is 0.6, the probability of a US attack submarine being destroyed is 0.2, and the probability of mutual destruction is 0.2, then the overall exchange ratio is 2:1. Given the encounters between 18 submarines on each side, the expected outcome is that all Soviet SSNs would be destroyed, 9 US SSNs would be destroyed, and 9 US SSNs would survive. There is a 12 percent chance, however, that fewer than 5 US SSNs will survive and a 1 percent chance that the US SSN fleet will be obliterated.

In appendix 2, the impact of mined decoys on US attack submarine attrition is analyzed in a simple case. These are basically minefields baited with acoustic transmitters that sound like Soviet SSBNs. Even with only a 1 in 10 chance of being destroyed in such a minefield, a US-favorable exchange ratio of 3:1 can be reduced to 1.6:1 if four minefields are implanted for every SSBN at sea. It is important to recognize that this result is independent of changes in Soviet or US submarine technology.

Summary of US ASW Threats to Soviet SSBNs

It is very unlikely that US SOSUS or SURTASS arrays at the periphery of the Barents Sea and Sea of Okhotsk can detect modern Soviet SSBNs on patrol at ranges beyond 75 miles. Complete SOSUS coverage of the primary Soviet SSBN patrol areas in the Barents Sea, the marginal seas of the Soviet Arctic, and the Sea of Okhotsk is not possible with current technology and is almost certainly not possible within the foreseeable future. SOSUS and other large surveillance systems remain useful in peacetime for detecting Soviet attack submarines passing through narrow straits, such as the Greenland–Iceland–United Kingdom gap, and for detecting Soviet attack submarines close to the US coast. The US coastal surveillance systems are probably also effective at detecting Yankee class SSBNs, which is a task they were designed for in the 1960s. SOSUS is not a wartime system.

US airborne ASW forces are not able to contribute to US strategic ASW in Soviet SSBN bastions while Soviet air defenses are operating. Without SOSUS to narrow down the location of Soviet submarines to some degree, the search capabilities of the US P-3 Orion aircraft are too limited to be very useful. Besides their inefficiency when not directed by SOSUS, these aircraft can do little over ice and they are highly vulnerable to Soviet tactical supersonic aircraft based on the Kuril Islands, the Kamchatka peninsula, and the Kola peninsula. The SOSUS, SURTASS, and Orion combination still represent a potent threat to Soviet Yankee class submarines coming out into the North Atlantic and North Pacific.

SOSUS, aided by SURTASS and RDSS systems, will continue to enable the US to detect Soviet attack submarines entering the Atlantic, Mediterranean, and Pacific in peacetime, but SOSUS may have to convert back to an active system since Soviet submarines are "becoming quieter faster than we can improve our detection capabilities."[82] A drawback to this approach is that it does not provide the acoustic signature information that can be used to identify a submarine's nationality and class.

The tactical advantage of US SSNs over their Soviet counterparts is also decreasing. The analysis of relative submarine noise levels in this study that indicates this is supported by the Navy's 1985 Program Objective Memorandum:

> The US submarine force cannot match the Soviets in numbers, and therefore must maintain a distinct qualitative advantage over the projected threat if an acceptable exchange ratio is to be sustained. Soviet quieting and sensor improvements will significantly narrow our acoustic advantage by the late 1980s.[83]

The only way for the United States to regain its former acoustic advantage is through quieting; improved sensors and processors will not help since "our two [US and Soviet] relative knowledges of the sea are driving us back into the background noise levels of the ocean [and] it is going to be extremely difficult to find each other no matter what kind of system we have."[84]

Analysis of passive acoustic detection suggests that even if the United States regains a large *relative* acoustic advantage by further quieting the SSN-21, the *absolute* detection range advantage, which is the important tactical measure, will continue to decline as the Soviet Union builds quieter submarines. This will interfere with potential US forward SSN operations in a couple of ways. First, the decreasing acoustic advantage will lead to more "dogfights" between SSNs, which the US Navy considers "the worst situations in submarine warfare."[85] A submarine-versus-submarine dogfight is a battle (or more accurately a melee) between two or more submarines at relatively close quarters, say several thousand yards. Active sonar is generally assumed to be in use by both sides, and each side probably knows the location of the other. Such dogfights might involve multiple and rapid torpedo launches as well as the use of torpedo countermeasures. The tactics involved in dogfights are very different from the passive tactics favored by the US. In a dogfight, the advantage shifts away from the quieter submarine and favors the one with greater firepower, resistance to damage, countermeasures, and maneuverability. It is conceivably very easy for a quiet "sneak attack" by a US SSN to turn into a dogfight if the US submarine is counterdetected. Already an SSN-688 class submarine has been detected during an exercise, though it is not clear under what conditions the detection took place.[86]

The second way in which quieter submarines on *both* sides will interfere with the US forward SSN strategy is that, with lower noise levels on both sides, the time spent searching for opponents is growing, and it will simply take longer to accomplish many objectives. This will benefit the Soviet Navy, whose main mission is to preserve intact as much of the SSBN fleet as possible over as long a period as possible. US naval strategy, as we shall see in chapters 4 and 5, is currently based on having a major impact very rapidly. The technical trends in ASW work against this.

The goal the Navy is pursuing that provides the rationale behind the SSN-21 is to build a submarine that: 1) has a high search rate, 2) is itself extremely quiet, 3) can engage and fire on targets and move on rapidly and quietly, and 4) has enough weapons to enable it to remain on station for a long time. Search rate is the product of speed and detection range, so the SSN-21 is supposed to have a high "quiet speed"—the maximum speed at which sensors are not deafened by the submarine's own noise—and improved sonar systems and arrays.[87] It is supposed to have a quiet speed of over 20 knots,[88] and at lower speeds it may have a total radiated sound level close to that of the Ohio class SSBNs, between 100 dB and 120 dB (relative to 1 micropascal at one yard).[89]

Achieving a high engagement rate is a major problem using only passive sonar. As I mentioned earlier, obtaining several lines of bearing on a moving target is time consuming, unreliable, and potentially dangerous. The SSN-21 is supposed to address this problem with improvements in a rapid passive localization system, the Wide Aperture Array. Passive range finding and localization capability at speeds in excess of 10 knots and at ranges in excess of 25 miles would be an enormous tactical advantage over an opponent that had to search using multiple bearings at lower speeds. This would allow the SSN-21 to detect a target, fire a torpedo, and continue to search. The SSN-21 is expected to be able to search half again as quickly as the improved SSN-688.[90] A major drawback in the WAA system, however, is that it uses broadband signal processing, and in order to detect and classify quieter Soviet submarines, narrowband signal processing is the best approach. Therefore, in order to use the WAA system to obtain faster localization, the designer must trade away longer-range detection and classification capability. The net result of this trade-off may be a relatively small gain in the engagement rate, which is the tactically important parameter.

The proposed weapon store of the SSN-21 is around 50 weapons of all kinds,[91] but this will include Tomahawk cruise missiles as well as mines, Harpoons, and ASW weapons. That is about double the loading of the SSN-688 and a third greater than the improved SSN-688.[92] In order to prevent an engagement from turning into a dogfight, the SSN-21 is also being fitted with a quiet torpedo launching system.[93]

The most important question that is raised here, however, is whether the United States can engage the Soviet SSBNs as they leave port—a kind of gatekeeping operation—and either trail them or sink them. If the Soviet surge of SSBNs is rapid, then the United States is faced with an area search, and as the attrition calculations suggest, the attrition rates in this scenario are very sensitive to the environmental parameters, to the dynamics of the US and Soviet surge of SSNs and SSBNs, and to Soviet choice of operating areas. In the worst case, from the US searcher's point of view, the attrition rate is very slow, and it would take months to reduce the Soviet SSBN force to a fraction of its total strength. Under the best-case conditions for the searcher, the process may require only a week or two—a rate fast enough possibly to raise concerns in Soviet leaders' minds that all SSBNs would be destroyed. Ironically, if the Soviet SSBNs are destroyed too quickly, the Soviet general-purpose navy would be left with less to defend (although the general defense of the homeland would still be a mission) and might be to some extent less tied down to home waters.

The assessment of how fast Soviet SSBNs could be sunk depends very much on whose "worst-case" planning is being used. Soviet worst-case planning might see the SSBNs in danger, while US worst-case planning might see the Soviet SSBNs relatively secure over a reasonably long time. The US worst-case planner might view sending SSNs into the Soviet marginal seas as a waste of time and resources on a target that cannot be found and whose eventual destruction may have little effect on the resolution of the war. It may well be that the forward SSN component of the maritime strategy is based on a best case for the United States and on a worst case for the Soviet Union.

Finally, even under very favorable conditions for search, Soviet use of mines and decoys could dramatically shift the exchange ratio in an ASW campaign. Higher US search speeds and engagement rates would increase the rate of engaging minefields and would serve to increase the rate of SSN attrition at unfavorable exchange ratios.

Notes

1. Many US research, development, and procurement programs for antisubmarine warfare are described in detail in *Jane's Weapon Systems,* ed. Ronald Pretty (New York: Jane's Publishing Company, annual), and in *Ships and Aircraft of the US Fleet,* ed. Norman Polmar (Annapolis: US Naval Institute Press, irregular). The best sources of information on research and development programs are found in testimony by US Navy officials and others before congressional committees. The DARPA Annual Summary Statement describes advanced naval warfare programs in general terms: it usually gives a glimpse of new technologies before they are turned over to the Navy for engineering development. A review of some sensor programs is contained in *Review of Military Research and Development,* ed. Kosta Tsipis and Penny Janeway (Elmsford, N.Y.: Pergamon-Brassey's). In particular, see "Understanding Anti-submarine Warfare Technology," by Randolph J. Steer, in the 1984 edition.

2. The actual name of the Soviet port on the Kamchatka Peninsula is Petropavlovsk-Kamchatski, to differentiate it from the town in Kazakhstan called Petropavlovsk. Used here, the name refers to the port.

3. Rear Adm. John Butts, HAC, FY 1986, part 2, p. 908.

4. According to John Collins of the Congressional Research Service, "About 25 percent of Soviet SSBNs are at sea an any given day. . . . Another 25 percent of Soviet SSBNs probably are alert in port." His footnote reads "Oral Navy comments on a draft of this study, January 1985." *See US-Soviet Military Balance 1980–1985,* John M. Collins, report no. 85-895, Congressional Research Service, Library of Congress, p. CRS-100.

5. Adm. James D. Watkins, HAC, FY 1986, part 2, p. 927.

6. Caspar W. Weinberger, *Soviet Military Power* (Washington, DC: US Government Printing Office, 1986), p. 21.

7. Commander C. C. Holcomb, "The Wartime Role of Soviet SSBNs: Controversy and Speculation," *US Naval Institute Proceedings,* July 1978, pp. 21–22.

8. Ibid. In addition to the low rate of SSBNs at sea, "the Soviets deploy even fewer SSNs and SSGNs."

9. Adm. James D. Watkins, HAC, FY 1986, part 2, p. 928.

10. Ibid.

11. Ibid., p. 927.

12. Ibid., p. 913.

13. For a discussion on this point between Secretary of the Navy John Lehman and Sen. Sam Nunn, *see* SASC, FY 1985, part 8, pp. 3871–3873.

14. This is a highly simplified assumption, that all submarines inside the detection range are detected and all beyond are not. In real systems, there is a probability of detection and a probability of false alarm associated with any range. *See* appendix 7, "Detection of Submarine Signatures in Noise."

15. From the analysis contained in appendix 8, 30 nm is the range at which a source of 140 dB can be detected most of the time, using nearly ideal sensors in most areas. Modern Soviet SSBNs are probably quieter than this, and sonar systems are not ideal.

16. For more detailed calculations, *see* appendix 2, "ASW Forces of the United States and the Soviet Union."

17. Up to 600 meters long according to one Soviet source. *See* Norman L. Stone, "ASW: The Soviet View, Part I," *Military Electronics/Countermeasures* 5:6, June 1979, p. 34.

18. Orr Kelly, "The Navy vs. Soviet Subs—A Plus for US," *US News and World Report,* 13 November 1978, p. 78.

19. The USNS *Myers, Neptune, Aeolus,* and *Zeus.* Vice Adm. J. H. Doyle, HAC, FY 1979, part 6, p. 92.

20. "The NR-1 has been used . . . to support the Navy's seafloor acoustic monitoring program." Norman Polmar, *The American Submarine* (Annapolis: Naval Institute Press, 1983), p. 168.

21. *Jane's Weapon Systems 1983/1984,* pp. 173–174.

22. Ibid.

23. Jim Bussert, "Computers Add New Effectiveness to SOSUS/CAESAR," *Defense Electronics,* October 1979, p. 59.

24. Owen Wilkes, "Strategic Anti-Submarine Warfare and Its Implications for a Counterforce First Strike," *World Armaments and Disarmaments: SIPRI Yearbook 1979* (London: Taylor and Francis, 1979), p. 429.

25. Robert S. McNamara, FY 1968 *Annual Report of the Secretary of Defense* to the Senate Appropriations Committee, declassified (formerly secret) version, pp. 68–72.

26. "SOSUS—anlegget er pa Andøya (SOSUS—The Shore Station at Andøya)," *Ikkevold* no. 7, September 1983, p. 3.

27. The deep sound channel is described in appendix 4, "The Oceans and Submarine Detection."

28. For a discussion of the history of strategic ASW *see* chapter 5.

29. *See* appendix 8, figures A8–15, A8–18, A8–19, A8–20, A8–22.

30. Adm. James D. Watkins, HAC, FY 1986, part 2, pp. 912, 913.

31. *See* figure A5–5 in appendix 5.

32. *See* figure A8–20 (appendix 8), which shows a typical transmission loss curve in the North Pacific. I assume that the frequencies detected lie between 20 and 200 Hz, and ignore convergence zone detection, which is sporadic and not reliable for continuous surveillance.

33. Ibid.

34. *See* the discussion of convergence zones in appendix 4, "The Oceans and Submarine Detection."

35. Bussert, "Computers Add New Effectiveness," p. 59.

36. Lt. Comdr. Ralph E. Chatham, USN, "A Quiet Revolution," *US Naval Institute Proceedings* 110:1, January 1984, pp. 41–46.

37. Craig Covault, "Soviet Ability to Fire through Ice Creates New SLBM Basing Mode," *Aviation Week and Space Technology* 10, December 1984, pp. 16, 17.

38. Capt. Alfred S. McLaren, USN, "Under the Ice in Submarines," *US Naval Institute Proceedings* 107:7, July 1981, pp. 105–109.

39. The weight of the Trident II missile is greater than the weight of the water in the flooded tube. However, Soviet missiles must weigh less than the water in the flooded tubes in order to float. *See* D. Douglas Dalgleish and Larry Schweikart, *Trident* (Carbondale: Southern Illinois University Press, 1984), p. 28.

40. McLaren, "Under the Ice," pp. 105–109.

41. Robert J. Urick, *Sound Propagation in the Sea* (Los Altos, Calif.: Peninsula Publishing, 1982), p. 9-1.

42. Urick, *Sound Propagation in the Sea,* p. 9-1. *See* also F. B. Jensen and W. A. Kuperman, "Optimum Frequency of Propagation in Shallow Water Environments," *Journal of the Acoustical Society of America* 73:3, March 1983, pp. 813–819.

43. McLaren, "Under the Ice," pp. 105–109.

44. George C. Wilson, "Navy Is Preparing for Submarine Warfare beneath Coastal Ice," *Washington Post,* 19 May 1983, p. A5.

45. Covault, "Soviet Ability to Fire through Ice," pp. 16, 17.

46. *DARPA Fiscal Year 1984 Research and Development Program* (Arlington, Va.: Defense Advanced Research Projects Agency), p. 8.

47. US Naval Academy Operations Analysis Group, *Naval Operations Analysis* (Annapolis: Naval Institute Press, 1979), pp. 136–137). *See* also Walter R. Nunn, *A Result in the Theory of Spiral Search,* Center for Naval Analysis, Professional Paper 274, March 1980.

48. Joel Wit, "Advances in Antisubmarine Warfare," *Scientific American* 244:2, February 1981, pp. 31–41.

49. Seymour M. Hersh, "A False Navy Report Alleged in Sub Crash," *New York Times,* 6 July 1975, p. 1; and Seymour M. Hersh, "Submarines of US Stage Spy Mission inside Soviet Waters," *New York Times,* 25 May 1975, p. 1.

50. Robert C. Toth, "Change in Soviets' Sub Tactics Tied to Spy Case," *Los Angeles Times,* 17 June 1985, p. 1.

51. *See* appendix 1, "The Design of Submarines."

52. *See* also figures A5–6 and A5–7 in appendix 6.

53. Examples of transmission loss curves for deep and shallow water, with and without ice, are given in appendix 8, "Submarine Detection in the Arctic Ocean and Northern Seas," figures A8–12, A8–13, A8–15, A8–16, A8–20.

54. Chatham, "A Quiet Revolution," pp. 41–46. Towed arrays may be too difficult to maneuver to be useful at trailing, even if they could improve the array gain.

55. Vice Adm. Nils R. Thunman, USN, SASC, FY 1983, part 6, p. 4042.

56. Ibid.

57. Steer, "Understanding Antisubmarine Warfare Technology," p. 168.

58. *DARPA FY83 Research and Development Program,* p. 28.

59. Adm. Kinnaird R. McKee, USN, HASC, Subcommittee on Procurement and Military Nuclear Systems, 22 February 1985, p. 7.

60. Steer, "Understanding Antisubmarine Warfare Technology," p. 199.

61. Ibid., p. 204.

62. Richard Klemm, "The Influence of Unknown Bottom Parameters on Bearing Estimation in Shallow Water," in *Bottom Interacting Ocean Acoustics*, ed. W. A. Kuperman and F. B. Jensen (New York: Plenum Press, 1980), pp. 691–700.

63. The evidence for Captor underice capability is scant. HAC, FY 1986, part 4, p. 285.

64. Norman L. Stone, "Soviets on Mine Warfare," *Military Electronics/Countermeasures* 6:5, May 1980, p. 58.

65. Dr. Milan Vego, "Soviet Mine Warfare: Doctrine and Capabilities," and "Mine Warfare: Threat and Counterthreat," *Navy International*, November 1982, pp. 1414–1420.

66. HASC, FY 1986, part 3, pp. 211, 212.

67. Adm. James D. Watkins, HAC, FY 1986, part 2, p. 927. In April 1977, the Soviet Navy surged 89 submarines to sea. *See* "Soviets Hold Massive Submarine Exercise," *Washington Post*, 29 July 1977.

68. Patrick Duffy, *NATO ASW: Strategy, Requirements, and the Need for Cooperation*, NATO Military Committee, Subcommittee on Defense Cooperation, October 1981, p. 3.

69. SASC, FY 1985, part 8, pp. 3874, 4164.

70. Since no SSBNs are deployed in the Baltic or Black seas, Soviet ASW forces in those areas are not considered.

71. John Jordan, "Soviet Torpedo Attack Submarines—Part 3," *Jane's Defence Weekly*, 20 October 1984, pp. 686–689.

72. Robert W. Herrick, *The SSBN-Protection Mission, Part II, Final Report, Soviet Naval Mission Assignments*, Ketron Study KFR 234-279 (Arlington, Va.: Ketron, July 1979) p. v.

73. Dr. Milan Vego, "Combat Support of Submarines, Part 1: Theory and Combat Intentions," *Navy International* 89, August 1984, pp. 492–499.

74. Richard Pariseau, "How Silent the Silent Service?" *US Naval Institute Proceedings* 109, July 1983, pp. 40–44.

75. Ibid.

76. Richard Barnard, "Soviets Plan Nine New Classes of Attack and Ballistic Subs," *Defense Week*, 23 July 1984, p. 1.

77. Senator William S. Cohen, SASC, FY 1985, part 8, p. 4165.

78. Pariseau, "How Silent the Silent Service?" pp. 40–44.

79. Henry Young, Comment on "How Silent the Silent Service?" *US Naval Institute Proceedings* 109, December 1983, p. 97.

80. Richard Barnard, "Navy Has No Counter against Half of Soviet Attack Subs," *Defense Week*, 23 July 1984, p. 17.

81. Ibid.

82. Chatham, "A Quiet Revolution," pp. 41–46.

83. Dave Griffiths, "New Attack Submarines: 30 Boats for $36 Billion," *Defense Week*, 5 July 1983, p. 1.

84. Ibid., quoting a statement made by Admiral Watkins made in March 1983.

85. Adm. Nils R. Thunman, SASC, FY 1985, part 8, pp. 4167–4168.

86. Anthony Battista, HASC, FY 1986, part 4, p. 786. In another incident, a US attack submarine of the Los Angeles class hit an undetected Soviet submarine while attempting to evade a second Soviet submarine that was trailing the US vessel. This is an example of the difficulty of engaging small groups of quiet submarines. (Jim Miklaszewski, *NBC Nightly News,* 13 November 1986).

87. Gerald Cann, HASC, FY 1986, part 4, p. 784.

88. Adm. James D. Watkins, HAC, FY 1986, part 2, p. 919.

89. *See* figure A6–5 in appendix 6.

90. SASC, FY 1986, part 8, p. 4590.

91. Gerald Cann, SASC, FY 1986, part 8, p. 4693.

92. SASC, FY 1986, part 8, p. 4590.

93. Captain James A. Carney, HASC, FY 1986, part 3, p. 232.

3
Soviet ASW Threats to US SSBNs

The possibility of attrition of US strategic submarines has long been a concern among members of the US arms control community, Congress, and the military. Each year since the first Polaris submarine went to sea in 1960, congressional committees have asked the Navy to evaluate the prospect of US submarines' becoming vulnerable to Soviet ASW. Each year, the Navy has said that there is no threat in the foreseeable future. So far, this prediction has proved to be correct.

The danger of losing a few US strategic submarines should be distinguished from the threat of large-scale destruction of most or all US SSBNs at sea. The Navy often says—and apparently the Congress likes to hear—that the US SSBN fleet is *completely* secure: that not one US submarine has been detected while on patrol, and that this is likely to continue to be true at least a decade into the future. One wonders what the political impact would be if just one Poseidon submarine were detected and trailed, however briefly, and the fact were publicized. Such an event might not change the assessment that the SSBN fleet is a largely invulnerable force,[1] but it would undoubtedly help those seeking to build more land-based missiles and to develop ballistic missile defense. In this sense, "submarine survivability" is as much a political issue as a technical problem for the United States.

The most economical way to begin an assessment of the potential Soviet ASW threats to US submarines is by analogy with the techniques and tactics already described in detail for US ASW threats to Soviet submarines in the previous chapter. This approach has the disadvantage of posing the Soviet strategic ASW problem as a mirror image of the approach taken by the US Navy, which it is not. On the other hand, addressing the problem of defense against US ballistic missile submarines in this way helps identify some of the very reasons why Soviet strategic ASW might have different emphases than US strategic ASW. There are three broad categories for comparison: geography, technology, and military policy.

1. Geography. Of all the advantages US SSBNs have in remaining undetectable and survivable, geography may be the most important. Soviet SSBN bases are close to US territory or to the territory of US allies, where there are forward staging areas for US ASW operations. In the northwest Pacific, the US Aleutian Islands serve as bases for intelligence collection, ASW aircraft, and undersea surveillance shore facilities. Japanese territory supports similar operations in the Sea of Japan and in and around the Sea of Okhotsk.

In contrast, the US base for Ohio class SSBNs in the state of Washington is thousands of miles from the nearest Soviet port or ally. In the Atlantic, Cuba provides the closest potential base for surveillance of US strategic submarines leaving from South Carolina and Georgia. The Bahamas lie between Cuba and the US bases, and block the acoustic path. However, and even under ideal detection conditions, US Lafayette class submarines are unlikely to be detected beyond a few tens of miles, while Ohio class submarines are unlikely to be detected beyond a few miles. There is no evidence that Cuba provides a support base for large scale, prolonged SOSUS-type surveillance or for trailing by nuclear-powered submarines.

Soviet SSBN patrol waters in the Barents Sea, the Sea of Okhotsk, and the northwestern Pacific are largely within range of US, Japanese, or British ASW aircraft. US SSBNs, in contrast, remain beyond the range of all but very few Soviet Bear F ASW aircraft. The proximity of Soviet patrol waters to US-allied bases allows the US to install surveillance arrays to aid ASW aircraft, particularly at chokepoints, while there are no convenient bases for Soviet surveillance of US patrol areas.

2. Technology. The key technical comparison lies in the area of acoustic detection and quieting. US attack submarines have maintained an acoustic advantage over most Soviet SSBNs, which has allowed the United States to conduct covert trailing operations against them. The fact that the Delta I and II SSBN classes did not incorporate significant quieting advances over the Yankee class means that this will remain true for at least several years. The Yankees radiate sound at about 150 dB as do the Delta I's, whereas the Delta II may be somewhat quieter.[2] However, Delta I and II class SSBNs may become quieter during overhauls, and only the most recent US SSN classes are likely to maintain a significant acoustic advantage. Figure A6–6 in appendix 6 shows an estimate of the long-term trends in the quietness of US and Soviet nuclear-powered submarines. By the early 1960s, US strategic submarines appear to have established a solid 30–40 dB advantage over Soviet attack submarines of the same vintage, an estimate that is supported by US claims that its SSBNs have never been trailed. The Ohio (SSBN-726) class is so quiet that one of those submarines, with the most modern sonar equipment, cannot detect another beyond a few miles under good detection conditions. Because they are noisier, Soviet SSNs could not trail a US SSBN covertly if they happened across one because the US target submarine would hear them well beforehand and could take evasive action.

US attack submarines have in the past maintained a 20–30 dB advantage in quietness over Soviet SSNs of the same vintage. The US attack submarines built in the 1960s and 1970s are reportedly being matched in quietness by the most recent Soviet classes of strategic and attack submarines. These recent Soviet vessels are quieter than expected, sometimes as much as 10 dB quieter.[3] The Soviet Akula class submarine may be approaching to within around 10 dB of the latest Los Angeles class submarines in total radiated sound, and it would appear to require the US to make a major technological leap to recover the acoustic advantages that it held in the 1960s and 1970s.

The other important part of US acoustic advantage lies in sonar detection capability, which is better because there is less self-generated noise to interfere with the sonar and because US signal-processing computers on submarines are better.[4] Most potential signal processing gain, however, can be obtained through relatively basic processing schemes, and current improvements in US sonar systems are oriented more toward tracking multiple targets, passive localization, and increased automation in the fire control system than toward improving sensitivity (that is, detecting signals with smaller signal-to-noise ratios).

3. Military Policy. Because of the acoustic advantage of US attack submarines and Soviet interest in the "combat stability" of their SSBNs, Soviet SSBN security is supported in defensive operations by general-purpose naval forces, probably including fixed undersea surveillance in SSBN patrol areas. This makes SSBN survivability one of several competing demands on the Soviet Navy. In contrast, by custom, US SSBNs are independent of almost all other components of the US Navy. To an extent, SSBN vulnerabilities on the two sides are inversely related, since the greater the US threat to Soviet strategic submarines, the more likely it is that Soviet SSNs will be engaged in defending them and not free to search for US strategic submarines. However, the corollary to this is that the Soviet Union may be able to respond to an unexpected threat to its SSBNs more effectively than can the United States. Finally, as is the case for most components of the armed forces on the two sides, crew effectiveness is much greater for US submarines (both strategic and attack) than for their Soviet counterparts. US crews spend more time at sea and get more hands-on training.[5]

Having approached the question of US missile submarine vulnerability relative to Soviet SSBN vulnerability, it is useful to examine some of the operational problems involved in a set of hypothetical threats to US SSBNs. Following the organization of earlier chapters, these threats are categorized as area search, area barrage, nonacoustic surveillance, long-range acoustic surveillance, and covert trailing.

Area Search, Trailing, and Surveillance against US Submarines

Calculations of the time required for Soviet ASW forces to search for stationary US strategic submarines are given in appendix 2, "ASW Forces of the United States and the Soviet Union." In brief, if *all* Arctic-based Soviet ships and submarines are used to search the area of the North Atlantic within Poseidon and Trident I range of Moscow, assuming detection ranges on about an order of magnitude larger than would be expected, with no opposition from forces of either the US or of NATO allies, it would take 60 hours assuming a search speed of about 20 knots. Soviet ASW aircraft would contribute relatively little to this effort. In the Pacific, about 150 hours would be required to search the area between the Aleutians, Hawaii, and the Soviet Union with the surface and subsurface forces currently available and given the same unrealistic assumptions. Allowing for the effects of random target motion and seeking 95 percent detection probability increases these times by a factor of three.

It is unlikely that in a wartime context, Soviet surface ships would last long south of the GIUK gap or in the northwest Pacific. Thus, a more appropriate measure of Soviet strategic ASW capability might be the search times for submarines alone. In the Atlantic, it would take about 13 days for unopposed Soviet submarines to search the entire patrol area described above, and in the Pacific, about a month. A reexamination of the assumptions reveals the actual magnitude of the problems the Soviets would face in trying to search for US SSBNs.

The assumed detection range of 30 miles is undoubtedly too high as an average figure, since it is based on submarines much noisier than US SSBNs. As noted earlier, the new US Ohio class submarine, which is an ideal sensor platform because it is so quiet, cannot detect one of its own kind beyond a few miles at most. The range at which a Soviet attack submarine might detect an Ohio class submarine may under many circumstances be less than a mile, and usually less than a few miles.[6] In addition, the search speed of about 20 knots is unrealistically high. Towed arrays would probably not function, and Soviet submarines would make so much noise that they would deafen themselves. Typical search speeds of Soviet submarines are around 5–8 knots. Accounting for the probable overestimates of search speed and detection range, more realistic search times against the Ohio fleet would be on the order of 50 times longer than the figures given above, and that still assumes that the US does not interfere in any way! When one considers the fact that many Soviet submarines would never make it into the north Atlantic or north Pacific because they would be caught or would be defending SSBNs, the times redouble. Perhaps most important, US SSBNs will constantly evade the noisier Soviet submarines. Thus, it is unlikely that the USSR can efficiently conduct strategic ASW through area search.

Covert trailing against US SSBNs would pose a threat similar to one of the possible threats to Soviet SSBNs from US attack submarines. Soviet SSNs have patrolled off the US coasts since 1966, particularly around important ports. Today, most of these patrols are conducted by Victor III SSNs. The Navy has testified that these "do not pose a major threat to US Naval forces,"[7] and presumably this includes US ballistic missile submarines.

The most recent designs of Soviet attack submarines, the Akula, Mike, and Sierra classes, may be approaching the US Lafayette class SSBNs in total radiated sound level. The detection range advantage of the US SSBNs over the newest Soviet SSNs would decrease and may perhaps disappear before the Lafayette class SSBNs reach the end of their service lives in the mid- to late 1990s. Under such circumstances it would be much more difficult for a US missile submarine to evade a Soviet attack submarine that came across its path. Soviet SSNs are still far from having a capability to trail covertly US Lafayette SSBNs, which would require a substantial Soviet acoustic advantage over the US vessels. In addition, it would be only a relatively small fraction of the Soviet submarine fleet that might achieve this acoustic equivalence.

As for large area acoustic surveillance, even if the Soviet Union had territory on which to base large acoustic arrays, there is not likely to be a passive array or an associated processing system that could produce the signal gain needed to hear Ohio class submarines beyond a few miles. Further complicating acoustic surveillance in the North Atlantic is the fact that in peacetime, there are typically about 3,000 cargo vessels in transit across the ocean,[8] each radiating about 10 million times as much acoustic power as an Ohio class submarine. During wartime, the shipping levels might drop by about half,[9] which would reduce the noise level by only 3 dB. Analysis also suggests that at low frequencies on the order of 50 Hz, wind noise at high latitudes may be a significant source of ambient noise at lower latitudes in the deep sound channel.[10]

There is no *technical* reason why the Soviet Union could not attempt to undertake trailing of US SSBNs in peacetime with active sonar. The main considerations are political and military: what would the USSR stand to gain or lose by such a policy? An unprecedented, overt threat to US SSBNs might be viewed as a message of the most threatening kind. In military terms, it would be similar to the Soviet practice of trailing US surface ships with their own combat ships—a means of keeping track of and potentially threatening the US vessel at the cost of putting a Soviet vessel at direct risk. Over a hundred US warheads might be threatened by a single Soviet SSN, and that SSN would be simultaneously held hostage. In terms of damage limitation, such a trade might seem favorable.

A major interest in damage limitation on the part of the Soviet Union should be accompanied by a response against the United States SSBNs, which carry about half of the US long-range nuclear arsenal. There is no unclassified evidence that active trailing has been attempted off US missile submarine ports, however. This may be because such activity does not occur, or because when it occurs, it is not made public, although the latter seems somewhat unlikely. Given the fact that there have been a number of instances in which US submarines trailing Soviet SSBNs and collecting intelligence in Soviet territorial waters have been reported in the press, it would seem probable that news of at least one successful Soviet active trailing attempt would have reached the press. It seems improbable that a major trailing attempt against US SSBNs has been mounted using active sonar, although some effort may be ongoing.

Area Barrage against US SSBNs

While the United States has only about 6 percent of the megatonnage needed for complete barrage of Soviet SSBN patrol areas, the Soviet capability for area barrage against the much larger US SSBN patrol areas is nil without a wide area surveillance system. The Soviets could barrage less than 1 percent of these ocean spaces. Given the uncertainty of the assumptions regarding the kill radius of a 1 megaton bomb, the estimate of four miles remains conservative (that is, in giving high confidence of kill) for deep water. The wave effects in deep water are not significantly different from those in the Barents Sea, although the overpressure at a given range from an explosion may be somewhat higher. The total area in which US submarines may patrol, including those regions a few days' transit from launch points, is almost an order of magnitude larger than the Soviet SSBN bastions. Therefore, an area barrage seems like a very inefficient approach for Soviet strategic ASW. To the extent that nonacoustic surveillance could localize US missile submarines, however, the barrage area could be decreased.

Nonacoustic Surveillance of Submarines

The physical limits on nonacoustic surveillance apply in the same way to US and Soviet submarines. Earlier, it was suggested that the most plausible immediate use for Soviet nonacoustic surveillance was to detect US attack submarines crossing the periphery of Soviet SSBN patrol waters, or actually within them. Since most of the evidence regarding nonacoustic submarine observables and detection comes from the US Navy's SSBN Security Office, it is most applicable to conditions present in US patrol areas. Testimony from that office strongly supports the conclusion that no known nonacoustic phenomenon can be used with confidence of detecting US submarines in the deep oceans of the Atlantic and Pacific.

For most of the phenomena examined in this study, the most effective countermeasure available is simply to increase submarine operating depth, which lowers the signal-to-noise ratio by a very large factor.

It has been suggested that US strategic submarines might be detected by detecting communications antennae. US SSBNs receive communications continuously while on alert (that is, on station and ready to fire missiles) and periodically while on "mod-alert" (in transit or on special exercises).[11] Since a floating wire antenna is a principal means of receiving these communications,[12] there has been much speculation about detection of these floating wires. The Navy does "not feel that they represent a serious threat" to the covertness of US strategic submarines.[13] On the same point, the director of the SSBN Security Program, Dr. Edward Harper, has "no concerns about detectability of antennas, either floating wire antenna or buoy" today. "The concern is not airborne or aircraft systems. They probably cannot pose a forcewide threat to the submarines because of the large patrol areas."[14] He also stated that while satellites are possible future concerns in SSBN security, "there is no imminent breakthrough on the horizon" and that "it is almost certain . . . that if such a breakthrough were made, that sensor would be counterable by patrolling deeper and slower."[15] A similar prognosis regarding Soviet satellite nonacoustic ASW was advanced by the director of the Navy's Strategic Submarine Division: "There is no indication that the Soviets are doing more than basic research, as we are, in the satellite ASW system. . . . There is no breakthrough that we see in the foreseeable future to affect the ASW survivability of our submarines."[16]

It has already been noted, however, that the relationships between submarine motions, generation of internal waves, and modifications to the surface due to internal waves are not well understood. Definitive statements regarding the application of synthetic aperture radar or sea surface emissivity sensors to submarine detection probably cannot be made with confidence. Yet after looking at four SEASAT radar images over submerged US submarines, one Navy official testified "that the notion that you can find a submerged submarine with side-looking radar from space is wrong."[17]

It is important to bear in mind two essential facts in the assessment of nonacoustic ASW, one technological and one political. The physical effects caused by a submarine's presence and movement through the ocean are complex and not completely understood. Although the analysis in appendix 3, "Nonacoustic Means of Submarine Detection," fails to reveal a mechanism for the detection of submarines in midlatitudes, there is a considerable uncertainty in some of the results, particularly in the areas of internal wave generation and of detection of internal waves at the surface via radar or microwave radiometry. In addition, there are a number of potential submarine observables that have not been discussed in this chapter, but are the subject of active research. These include electromagnetic disturbances, wake effects on salinity, biological disturbances of marine life, chemical and radiochemical effluents, erosion and corrosion products, and the disturbance of organic films on the water surface.

The Navy has so many missions, and organizations to support these missions, that inevitably some internal incentives come into conflict. Part of the Navy's goal is to maintain the ability to attack the Soviet Union with nuclear weapons. The Navy has been seen as providing a highly survivable soft target capability and with Trident II will provide a highly survivable hard target capability. Strategic nuclear capability and targeting roles have been perceived as important bureaucratic bargaining levers in interservice negotiations, and the Navy has little incentive to advertise a degradation in its major strategic asset—survivability.

At the same time, antisubmarine warfare is an extremely important mission (or set of missions) for the US Navy, and the importance of developing nonacoustic means of detecting submarines will increase as the Soviet attack submarines become quieter. A basic nonacoustic research program (without large development programs) can be justified by saying that it is a means of avoiding technological surprise. Any attempt to fund major nonacoustic sensor development programs, however, will have to show some real progress in detecting submarines. This is likely to raise the question "If we can do it, why can't the Soviets do it?" and introduce some doubts about US SSBN survivability. These conflicting incentives may tend to inhibit nonacoustic ASW development programs.

The threat to US ballistic missile submarines at sea appears to be very low and is unlikely to grow rapidly in the next 10–15 years. The major sources of uncertainty in this statement appear to be the complexity and potential for detection of submarine generated internal waves, and a possible bias within the Navy to make public only that data that reflects positively on SSBN security.

To the extent that the Soviet Union would attempt to limit damage to the homeland from US SSBNs, it would have to use very different approaches. One would be active trailing outside of ports, and, as we have seen, there is no unclassified evidence that the Soviets are doing this. Another defense would be to attack US SSBNs in port, either with sea-launched cruise missiles or special forces, although the Soviet leaders would have to assume that in a crisis a very large fraction of US SSBNs would be at sea.

Notes

1. "CIA Study Investigates Vulnerability of Submarine Fleet," *Boston Globe,* 6 June 1985, p. 25.

2. See figure A6–5 in appendix 6 and accompanying notes, particularly note 5.

3. Richard Barnard, "Soviets Plan Nine New Classes of Attack and Ballistic Subs," *Defense Week,* 23 July 1984, p. 1.

4. The United States is solidly ahead in computers, software, and signal processing, according to the *DoD Program for Research, Development, and Acquisition, FY86,* p. II-4. The erosion of the US lead in submarine detection is mostly due to Soviet quieting programs.

5. The US Navy has even observed that US strategic submarine crews are more capable than US attack submarine crews, as a result of the more intense training of the SSBN crews. *See* Capt. James H. Patton, Jr., USN, "The Good, the Bad, and the Best," *US Naval Institute Proceedings,* July 1982, pp. 105–107.

6. Convergence zones may yield intermittent detection at ranges on the orders of 30 miles, but not a consistent capability to do so.

7. Rear Adm. John L. Butts, SASC, FY 1986, part 8, p. 4402.

8. Didier Brenot, "Antisubmarine Warfare: Historical and Prospective Considerations," *Defense Nationale,* June 1977, pp. 55–70.

9. Ibid.

10. R.W. Bannister, "Deep Sound Channel Noise from High Latitude Winds," *Journal of the Acoustical Society of America* 79, January 1986, pp. 41–48.

11. Vice Adm. Gordon R. Nagler, USN, Director, Command and Control, SASC, FY 1984, part 5, pp. 2504–2507.

12. See appendix 1, "The Design of Submarines," for a more detailed description of submarine communications systems.

13. Commodore Roger Bacon, Director, Strategic and Theater Nuclear Warfare Division, Office of the Chief of Naval Operations, SASC, FY 1985, part 7, p. 3402. The technical argument about detection of floating wires is closely related to the political argument surrounding the land-based ELF communication system.

14. SASC, FY 1986, part 7, p. 3854.

15. Ibid.

16. Rear Adm. (Lower Half) Theodore E. Lewin, before the Senate Appropriations Defense Subcommittee. Quoted in *Aerospace Daily,* 7 April, 1986, p. 33.

17. Adm. Kinnaird R. McKee, *The 600-Ship Navy and the Maritime Strategy,* HASC Hearings before the Seapower and Strategic and Critical Materials Subcommittee (Washington, DC: US Government Printing Office, 1986), p. 164.

4
Attacks on Soviet SSBNs to Tie Up Soviet Naval Forces

By attacking Soviet SSBNs during the initial stage of a US-Soviet war, the United States expects to tie up Soviet attack submarines and prevent many of them from challenging US control of the sea. This chapter describes US naval strategy for fighting the Soviet Union for control of the seas, and the role of strategic ASW in that strategy. The next chapter views attacks on SSBNs in light of their impact on the strategic balance.

While many of the official statements cited in this and other chapters are recent, many of the ideas they express have a long history. Defense against missile submarines, or strategic ASW, appeared as a naval mission as soon as submarines that could launch nuclear weapons against shore targets appeared.

The context and intent of official Navy statements regarding maritime strategy are important and sometimes unclear. No statements of this kind, even those made by the secretary of the Navy or the chief of naval operations, are war plans, nor are war plans articulated in public. The nature and purposes of official utterances of strategy were discussed by the chief of naval operations, Adm. James D. Watkins, in the introduction of his *Maritime Strategy*, published in January 1986:

> The Maritime Strategy recognizes that the unified and specified commanders fight the wars, under the direction of the President and the Secretary of Defense, and this does not purport to be a detailed warplan with firm timelines, tactical doctrine, or specific target sets. Instead it offers a global perspective to operational commanders and provides a foundation for advice to the National Command Authorities. The strategy has become a key element on shaping Navy programmatic decisions. It is of equal value as a vehicle for shaping and disseminating a professional consensus on warfighting where it matters—at sea.[1]

In this passage, Admiral Watkins has taken some pains to be clear that he is not making statements about how to fight battles, and that he is leaving the war plans to the commanders in chief. The intentions of strategy statements of this kind appear to fall into three categories, two of which he mentions. First, such a statement can be an attempt to build a consensus within the Navy on warfighting at sea. Second, the strategy statement is to be used as a programming guide, so that research, operations, maintenance, and procurement decisions can be fit into a larger framework. This can be used for decision making and advocacy within the Navy, at the level of the secretary of defense, and before Congress.

The third category of possible intents of the statement is as a political signal. The fact that such a statement was made by the chief of naval operations gives it weight in the eyes of allies and potential opponents. As it applies to the Soviet Union, it may be intended to function partly as a deterrent statement, a way of backing up potential US military capability with statements that attempt to increase the credibility of the threat actually to use that capability. In the deterrent role, such statements try to influence the perceptions of Soviet leaders, and it is of course difficult to determine the impact of statements.

An article that attempts to do all three things must balance some competing requirements. It must contain enough detail to serve as a programming guide in order to provide clear hooks on which to hang specific programs, and it must remain broad enough to provide a platform on which a consensus can be built. It must talk about war with enough specificity to really guide planning and perhaps make a deterrent statement to the Soviet Union, while at the same time it must avoid the appearance of a war plan.[2] It is probably impossible to satisfy fully all these conditions.

The main features of US naval strategy as it has been articulated are forward attacks near Soviet territory and horizontal escalation into theaters where the US Navy holds an advantage, with both moves to be made as rapidly as possible. These elements are bound together by the overarching objective of containing the Soviet Navy, both to deny the use of the seas to the Soviet Union and to permit the United States to use the seas freely. By demonstrating a capability to control the seas, US planners hope to deter the Soviet Union from going to war in the first place. This undermines Soviet attempts to interfere with US foreign policy on a military level, and it is expected to deter conventional war. The following section presents some official views on US naval strategy and on how its components relate to strategic antisubmarine warfare.

US Naval Strategy

The general wartime naval strategy of the United States has been outlined by the chief of naval operations, Adm. James D. Watkins. In war, the US Navy will take the fighting "as far forward—in the direction of the aggressor—as possible."[3] "By confining and destroying air, surface and subsurface threats to the transoceanic sea lanes well forward, we control the initiative and capitalize on geographical advantages, thereby maximizing the effectiveness of our forces."[4] This forward element in US naval strategy may take several forms, which are, in increasing order of "forwardness": (1) attacks on ships coming through chokepoints; (2) forward air control using aircraft carriers; (3) submarine attacks and mining in the farthest forward areas where the USSR controls the air and surface; and finally, (4) bringing the war home to the Soviet motherland with air or missile strikes against Soviet naval bases. Wartime conditions will determine the degree of emphasis placed on each of these options and will generally influence the "forwardness" of the operations. The perception of likely Soviet response to an attack on their homeland will—or at least should—weigh heavily in any US decision to strike the Soviet Union.

There is a good deal of debate at the highest levels of the US Navy about how closely to Soviet bases to operate aircraft carriers, their aircraft, and their escorts.[5] There has thus far been less debate about limits on forward operations of attack submarines. It is clear that the US Navy is counting on Britain and other NATO submarine fleets to conduct ASW in the Greenland-Iceland-United Kingdom (GIUK) gap, while US SSNs go north into the northern Norwegian and Barents seas. According to the US secretary of the Navy, John Lehman: "US dependence on allied submarines [nuclear or conventional] beyond their coastal and chokepoint reaches is minimal."[6] This does not exclude the possibility that some US submarines would be used at chokepoints. Of the 40–45 US SSNs that might be available in the Atlantic, about a dozen might be assigned to carrier battle groups, nine or ten to the GIUK gap,[7] and perhaps up to twenty or more could be assigned to forward areas.

The main strategy is to go as far forward as is deemed "prudent": for example, to send attack submarines into the Barents Sea and aircraft carriers into the Norwegian Sea. A potential weakness of this strategy is that it puts the most valuable and capable US ships up against the densest concentration of Soviet naval forces. The Soviet Union can send aircraft, submarines, and ships in repeated sorties against US forward-deployed ships, which would themselves be far from bases and highly dependent on resupply for fuel and ammunition. The USSR has many small ships and diesel-electric submarines suitable for use in and around the Barents Sea. These warships, though much less capable than US ships and submarines, would complicate the problems of US surface forces, especially if the Soviet ships conducted a coordinated cruise missile strike against US surface ships. In addition, all ships in the Soviet Navy have the advantage of being able to return more easily to bases for ammunition and supplies. As a result, over the course of a long engagement,[8] Soviet ships might have the opportunity to expend many missiles without being constrained by lack of resupply. US strategy therefore calls for creating a barrier very near the base with a combination of submarines and mines, or else blowing up the bases themselves. Adm. Stansfield Turner calls this part of the strategy "sortie control":

> Bottling up an opponent in his ports or on his bases . . . , today's blockade seeks destruction of individual units as they sortie. If we assume an opponent will be in control of the air near his ports, sortie control tactics must depend primarily on submarines and mines . . . a most economical means of cutting off a nation's use of the seas or ability to interfere.[9]

The idea that destroying bases is a vital task in the sea control strategy is not new. In the mid-1950s, Henry Kissinger reported that "our naval strategy proposes to defeat the submarine menace by destroying the opponent's port facilities and base installations. The chief of naval operations has said that an attack on enemy bases is the primary task of antisubmarine warfare."[10] More recently a deputy chief of naval operations for surface warfare, Vice Adm. J. H. Doyle, confirmed that this is still an option: "Sea control entails the use of naval forces for a variety of tasks including . . . strikes against enemy bases."[11]

Which weapons would be used to attack Soviet bases? The Tomahawk nuclear land-attack cruise missile (TLAM-N) has been a candidate since it "would provide an enhanced maritime capability to inflict major damage on Soviet shore-based naval infrastructure."[12] Such an attack would invite a response in kind. Since conventionally armed Tomahawks can destroy buildings and airfields, the conventional version is much more likely to be used in a conventional war. The Soviet Navy may have been practicing defense against a simulated SLCM attack when one of its sea-launched cruise missiles went off course in January 1985 and flew over Norway and Finland, 120 miles west of the main Soviet naval complex near Murmansk. This Soviet cruise missile was launched from the Barents Sea, and the Soviet Navy is probably concerned about possible submarine-launched cruise missile attacks from that area.[13] On the other hand, the test might simply have been an exercise for using Soviet cruise missiles against targets in Scandinavia and the Baltic.

Destroying Soviet bases is not the only way to provide for sortie control. According to Secretary of Defense Weinberger, "Nuclear-powered attack submarines remain a key element in our ASW defense-in-depth strategy, especially in antisubmarine operations. Early in a wartime scenario, our undersea forces must be capable of moving into far forward positions, including waters where Soviet naval forces would operate in large numbers."[14] He goes on to list a number of improvements to the current attack submarines (Los Angeles class) that will enable them better to carry out their ASW and sea control mission: larger cruise missile magazines, noise reduction, underice capability, and minelaying capability. Offensive minelaying capability was reemphasized in fiscal year 1985,[15] after having been dropped as an SSN mission priority in the mid-1970s.[16] New Los Angeles class attack submarines are being constructed with minelaying capability, and existing vessels of that class are being backfitted with mines.[17]

Another major feature of current US naval strategy is preparation for horizontal escalation—that is, expanding or shifting the theater of naval conflict to regions where the United States holds an advantage. Admiral Watkins places the possible responses of the US Navy to Soviet aggression into four categories, saying that the United States could: "(1) attempt to meet force with like force at the point of attack; (2) increase the intensity of the conflict; (3) alter the geographic breadth of the conflict; or (4) control the duration of the fighting."[18] According to Watkins, the first option is undesirable because it "leads to long wars of attrition and does not by itself generate pressure to end the war." How could the United States generate such pressure? Escalation in the level of violence—that is, vertical escalation—is one possibility. But in the nuclear age, the higher levels of violence can quickly and easily get out of hand, and vertical "escalation is an option fraught with the most serious and frightening risks."[19] By default, the preferred naval strategy is to expand the war into theaters where the USSR is at a disadvantage: "Maritime superiority enables us to deny the enemy any advantage through expansion and permits us, if we choose, to take the conflict to a geographic area where the enemy does not want to fight."[20]

Horizontal escalation is also considered a means of forcing the USSR to spread its forces over many fronts:

> The inherent flexibility of seapower which permits us to outflank a foe has a series of benefits. We can force the Soviets to spread forces around their perimeter, requiring a considerable commitment in personnel and material resources to the defense of otherwise secure flanks in the Baltic, the Kola Peninsula, the Black Sea littoral, and the Soviet Far East.[21]
>
> It is the Soviets who must be prepared to defend their territory "anywhere" on their perimeter. The option to define what "anywhere" means in terms of conducting offensive operations remains with us.[22]

The forwardness of the strategy and its geographic breadth are integrated into a "Tight Squeeze" around the Soviet periphery, from the Sea of Japan and the Kamchatka peninsula in the Northwest Pacific to the Mediterranean and Black seas, the Baltic, and finally the Barents Sea.

Common to both arms of the "Tight Squeeze" strategy—forwardness and geographic breadth—is a heavy emphasis on initiative and speed. If a war is about to start or has just started, the US Navy is to move far forward on all fronts quickly. As Navy Secretary Lehman put it, "The Navy has a very clear, simple strategy—and that is to take the initiative very early on to ensure that we establish control of the vital sea areas we need."[23] In part, the rapid forward advance is expected to keep the Soviet Navy from increasing deployment of

SSNs to the North Atlantic, where they normally keep only three or four attack submarines in peacetime.[24]

The containment objective has been described by British naval historian Geoffrey Till as "a major Western preoccupation."[25] Although the Reagan administration's concept of containing the USSR is certainly not new, there are some ways in which the emphases in naval strategy have changed from those of the Nixon, Ford, and Carter administrations.[26] The first difference is the stress given to simultaneous rather than sequential carrier operations. This justifies an increase in carrier battle groups. It is not simply a budget ploy, however; it is a direct result of the Navy's demand for rapid and simultaneous escalation around the USSR, especially in the Northwest Pacific. A former commander in chief of the US Pacific Fleet, Adm. William J. Crowe, Jr., has testified that the Navy's buildup to 600 ships, based around 15 carrier battle groups, "goes to the heart of [the Pacific Command's] needs" because he expects "intense and immediate air and sea engagements in the Northwest Pacific if global hostilities break out."[27] The chief of naval operations, however, remains guarded on the prospect of truly simultaneous operations on the Soviet periphery and believes the US Navy "may have to sequence [its] operations among theaters,"[28] in accordance with the National Security Design Document 32 (NSDD-32) of May 1982. Other statements by Navy officials suggest that NSDD-32 calls for sequential operations "within a particular theater."[29] It is not clear what, if any, distinction is being made, however.

A second change in emphasis is the planned use of aircraft carriers to attack naval bases and other land targets. According to Robert Komer, the "US Navy has long had contingency plans for multicarrier nonnuclear strikes against Soviet naval bases, but clearly these are now being more heavily stressed."[30]

In sum, the current statements of maritime strategy are drawn largely from concepts that have appeared in the past. Some of the language used to describe these elements is more specific and tends to emphasize the offensive character of naval warfare. These elements are: the rapid initial escalation of US naval deployments during a crisis, the early movement of naval forces toward the Soviet Union during such a crisis, and an effort to broaden the geographic scope of the war at sea to the maximum extent feasible as early as possible. US attack submarines, because of their stealth, form the most forward salient of the US Navy, and they can begin to use torpedoes, cruise missiles, and mines in Soviet home waters and against bases very early in a conflict. To this end, they are being refitted for offensive minelaying and for launching conventional and nuclear cruise missiles capable of attacking naval bases and airfields. Aircraft carriers, much more vulnerable than attack submarines, must remain farther from the main concentration of Soviet naval forces.

Soviet Naval Strategy

The Soviet naval experience in World War II largely involved supporting ground forces and defending crucial ports, such as Murmansk.[31] After the war, in which most Soviet shipbuilding facilities were destroyed, Stalin approved a large naval buildup as a response to the perceived threat of invasion by the United States and Britain, which had both sent huge armies overseas during World War II and had intervened in the USSR during the revolution.[32] Khrushchev downgraded the perceived threat of invasion in the mid-1950s and appointed Adm. Sergei Gorshkov as head of the Navy. Gorshkov directed a building program that emphasized short- and medium-range defenses against carrier-based nuclear attack aircraft, relying mainly on submarines and small surface ships armed with cruise missiles. By the time he came into power, the United States was on the way to developing a large nuclear strike force based on bombers launched from carriers.

As soon as World War II ended, the US Navy began expanding its capability to bomb Soviet territory. The carrier-based, nuclear-capable A-2 Savage attack aircraft was approved for production in 1946. By 1949 the Navy had six A-2s, along with 12 experimental P2V-1 Neptunes, which were modified to carry nuclear weapons from the carrier *Midway*.[33] By 1953, there were about 240 nuclear-capable US naval aircraft, mostly A-1 Skyraiders and P2V-5 Neptunes. By 1960, the US Navy had well over 500 nuclear-capable attack aircraft, mainly A-3 Skywarriors and A-4 Skyhawks.[34] When the US Navy wanted to increase quickly its carrier-based nuclear strike capabilities during the late 1950s and early 1960s, it deployed one extra carrier to the Sixth Fleet and another to the Seventh Fleet, each equipped solely with nuclear-capable attack aircraft.[35] From the Soviet point of view, these nuclear strike carriers were potentially devastating threats—and were therefore very important targets.

In the late 1950s, the Soviet Navy responded to the US carriers with nuclear-armed aircraft by designating strikes against such vessels as the primary naval mission. Initially, ship-launched antiship missiles were the main Soviet anticarrier weapons—when the ranges of US strike aircraft were still sufficiently short to permit Soviet ships to operate against carriers under the cover of Soviet land-based tactical aircraft. As longer-range aircraft were deployed on US aircraft carriers, however, the Soviet Navy emphasized cruise missile and ballistic missile submarines as the main anticarrier platforms.[36] Thus, the early Soviet interest in shore-, air-, ship-, and submarine-launched guided missiles stems directly from the effort to counter a very powerful, immediate, and otherwise unanswerable threat of nuclear strikes originating from US carriers.

The early 1960s saw the official birth—at least in Soviet writings—of an entirely new mission for Soviet general-purpose naval forces: the maintenance of secure SSBN fleets.[37] There is no evidence that Hotel, Golf, Zulu, and Yankee SSBNs were accompanied while on patrol during the 1960s, however. A major technological requirement of this maintenance task is to ensure that SSBNs cannot be destroyed. This requirement consumes naval resources, and SSBNs do not provide any unique contribution to traditional sea control or denial missions. Even if they were aimed at naval bases, they would duplicate a function of ICBMs. Therefore, the decision to build and protect SSBNs was also a decision to shift the emphasis of the entire Navy toward the strategic strike mission.

While the United States Navy, favored by geography and by a superior technical establishment, has been able to isolate its extremely quiet SSBNs from other naval operations, the Soviet Navy has not opted for such a means of fulfilling its tasks.

There is much support within the Soviet Navy for the idea that the submarine-launched strategic strike, as well as defense against SSBNs capable of striking the homeland, have become foremost missions of superpower navies.[38] The two Soviet objectives that spring from the belief that nuclear strikes are a dominant mission of both the United States and the Soviet Union are (1) ensuring Soviet nuclear striking power and (2) blunting the nuclear strike potential of the United States, Britain, France, and other potential enemies. But in the mid-1960s, when US SLBM ranges increased, US missile submarine patrol areas increased, and the submarines got quieter, making them more difficult to find. This created an operational environment in which Soviet ASW forces, originally designed and built to search for US SSBNs, were becoming more effective at detecting US attack submarines searching for Soviet submarines near Soviet territory. It appears that Soviet interest in strategic ASW was then redirected toward "unconventional" means, such as nonacoustics.

The ability of the Soviet Union to conduct ASW against British, French, and Chinese SSBNs is not addressed in this study, but it is important to consider the possible impacts of a threat to the nuclear systems of those countries. In the heat of a threat of escalation to nuclear war in Europe, attrition to French sea-based forces would erode a major portion of French retaliatory capability.

A plausible explanation of the shift of Soviet antisubmarine warfare objectives and tactics away from seeking to attack US SSBNs and toward defense of Soviet SSBNs is offered by Michael MccGwire. As noted in chapter 1, MccGwire argues that in late 1966, the Soviet Union adopted as its main military objective avoiding the "nuclear devastation of Russia."[39] The new objective shifted the emphasis toward not allowing a nuclear exchange to occur in the first place. Thus, it made sense for the Soviets to apply ASW to nuclear deterrence, that is, to protecting SSBNs as a short-term solution for preventing strikes on the Soviet Union. According to one analyst, by the late 1970s it was clear that strategic ASW was a "secondary" task of the Soviet navy.[40] The prominence of defending the Arctic was recently emphasized by the commander in chief of the Soviet Northern Fleet, Adm. A. Mikhaylovskiy: "Nuclear-powered submarines with ballistic missiles on board are the main striking force. . . . An enormous responsibility for insuring the reliable defense of the polar perimeters of the Homeland rests on the naval personnel of the Red Banner Northern Fleet."[41]

Vice Adm. K. Stalbo, one of the Soviet Navy's chief theorists, wrote in this regard: "The relative importance is constantly increasing of strategic naval armaments and of the forces for their protection of the strategic-forces balance."[42]

The commitment of the Soviets to SSBNs as a strategic force can also be seen in the amount of money they put into them, compared with the investment in ICBMs and bombers. Between 1975 and 1985, the investment value of deployed SSBNs and SLBMs accounted for about 75 percent of the total Soviet investment in deployed strategic weapons, with ICBMs taking about 15 percent and bombers 10 percent. The share going to submarines and their missiles is now closer to 80 percent. This is much larger than the fraction of Soviet strategic warheads based on submarines, which is only about a quarter, and suggests that the Soviet Union is willing to pay heavily to put strategic forces at sea. In contrast, the United States has about 50 percent of its investment in strategic forces in SSBNs and SLBMs at any given time, which is roughly the same as the fraction of US warheads on submarine-launched missiles.[43]

There is no absolute need for the Soviet Navy to "stay home" to defend SSBNs. There is evidence that they have a commitment to moving some vessels, particularly submarines, out of home waters in the event of a war. Cruise missile submarines, such as the large Oscar class may be used more effectively outside home waters. Providing US undersea surveillance has been disrupted early in a war, some Soviet SSBNs could attempt to enter the Atlantic and disperse. James McConnell has noted that Soviet naval writings in the early 1980s contain two related themes: the possibility of a development in nonacoustic ASW and increased discussion about interdicting US sea lines of communication to Europe.[44] The expectation of an improvement in the ability to detect US attack submarines in the waters near the Soviet Union would be an incentive to consider more roles for the Soviet general-purpose naval forces beyond sea control near the homeland. Soviet attack submarines, which are known to support directly SSBNs on patrol, would be prime candidates for entering the North Atlantic after SOSUS had been destroyed.

The Interaction of US and Soviet Naval Strategy

A simple model of the interaction between US and Soviet naval strategy can be proposed. The preceding discussion shows that Soviet Navy missions include the important mission of protecting the strategic reserve, plus participation in some initial strikes at coastal targets. Since forces for strategic reserve, postwar bargaining, or intrawar deterrence[45] are the guarantors of the ultimate wartime option of annihilating the enemy—deterring the enemy from annihilating the homeland—SSBNs have a high value. This is reflected in the proportion of total strategic forces investment that the Soviets put into SSBNs and SLBMs.

The value of SSBNs derives from the perception of how the *entire* Soviet intercontinental nuclear arsenal might survive a war. Soviet general-purpose naval forces, including land-based aircraft, surface ships, mines, and submarines, are important instruments, though not the only ones, by which SSBNs can be preserved throughout the course of the war. The degree to which the Soviet Navy will be obliged to defend the SSBNs close to home will be an increasing function of two key variables: the vulnerability of the SSBNs and the importance of the SSBNs to Soviet objectives.

If Soviet naval leaders feel confident, for example, that a subset of the general-purpose naval forces would ensure that the SSBNs in bastions can perform their missions on time at an acceptable price (in their determination of acceptable) against the worst US strategic ASW threat, then the rest of the Soviet Navy might be free to undertake other tasks. In other words, Soviet leaders would probably accept some attrition of SSBNs if they felt there were enough remaining SSBNs to carry out their primary mission, and if the general-purpose forces that could be released could do something of greater value than protecting SSBNs. The trade-off for the USSR is the value of the extra options created by releasing general-purpose forces from protecting SSBNs versus the value of the expected number of SSBNs lost because of that weakened defense. If the defense were deemed inadequate to ensure the ability of SSBNs to carry out their primary mission, then the Soviet Navy would have to pull back from lower priority operations.

Metaphorically, the wartime Soviet Navy resembles an organism that, if prodded in its underbelly, will retreat; if kicked really hard, it might even curl up into a tight, armored ball, armadillo-like. Of course this analysis assumes that the organism will always make a "rational" cost-benefit calculation and respond proportionately. If this were true, then the behavior of the organism might be predictable. Much of the published thinking by US Navy officials on this subject, however, is founded on the assumption that, given uncertainty about the actual threat to Soviet SSBNs in the minds of Soviet planners, the Soviet Navy will overreact.

Since the Soviet Navy is probably committed to protecting SSBNs, the obvious point of attack for maximum effect is those vessels. In particular, it is the Soviet attack submarine fleet that the United States is most concerned about, particularly now that the Akula and other classes have approached and surpassed some US attack submarines in capabilities. Soviet attack submarines are a greater concern than are Soviet aircraft or surface ships.[46]

The other variable that determines Soviet sensitivity to SSBN attrition in defended home waters is the number of SSBNs needed to carry out the mission of the reserve. If Soviet leaders believed that they would lose a fundamentally important strategic warfighting option if they lost just one SSBN, then they would increase defense of SSBNs, without any change in the perceived threat to them. If the threat to land-based forces rises, all other things being equal, the value of sea-based systems will also rise. This is a little recognized yet very important likely impact of the planned US Trident II missile. When members of the Soviet military see their silos threatened, they may place a greater value on protecting SSBNs in wartime and allocate more attack submarines to their defense—which would mean fewer attack submarines to oppose the US Navy. In effect, Trident II may shift the open-ocean conventional naval balance in favor of the United States. This in turn must provide an additional incentive for the Soviet Union to develop survivable land-based systems such as the mobile versions of the SS-24 and SS-25 missiles.

To carry the hypothetical strategy of attrition to Soviet SSBNs further, it is helpful to see how well it fits into the broader US naval strategy, characterized by being forward, horizontal, and rapid. As articulated by Admiral Watkins, the underlying assumption of the strategy is that the United States must put the Soviet Navy on the defensive in places that the US chooses[47]—the flanks of the Soviet Union. The two most vital of these also happen to be the main SSBN patrol areas. Already, Watkins claims, "the current allocation of Soviet resources to homeland and home water defense indicates that they consider our threat to their flanks to be highly credible."[48] The Soviet Union may be concerned not only about SSBN attrition on their flanks, but also about strikes against land targets, amphibious landings, or complete containment of their fleet.

Operationally, attacks on Soviet SSBNs during the initial phase of a conventional war are virtually unavoidable given a far forward strategy. Barry Posen has addressed the problem of "inadvertent" destruction of Soviet ballistic missile submarines by forces defending forward-based US aircraft carriers.[49] The carriers are not the most forward platform, however; that role goes to US attack submarines, which, according to the chief of naval operations, are also the main vehicle for the forward "Tight Squeeze" strategy:

> The employment of SSNs, both prior to conflict and in conflict, is probably one of the most sensitive and significant areas of our maritime strategy. Without going into great detail I can say it is probably the most significant part of the strategy. The rapid surge of SSNs is absolutely key as an option for the movement of SSNs as a tool in the National Command Authority to try to deter conflict or, if unsuccessful, to win on terms favorable to us.[50]

US SSNs operating covertly and independently in the vicinity of Soviet naval bases and under the ice are by far the greatest threat to Soviet SSBNs at sea. Admiral Watkins's statement is entirely consistent with other views about the crucial role of attack submarines in the forward strategy. A more specific statement was made by the head of the submarine warfare branch of the US Navy, Vice Adm. Nils R. Thunman:

> Attack submarines are central to effective execution of our forward naval strategy. This was clearly stated by the Secretary of the Navy when he recently

> wrote: "Particularly in submarine warfare, unless a forward strategy is employed at once to force the Soviet submarines to protect their strategic missile forces and the approaches to their home waters, Soviet superiority in numbers could well determine the outcome of the war." Our attack submarine force is capable of fighting and winning against today's threat. But our qualitative edge is eroding and we face a serious challenge to the undersea superiority we have enjoyed for the past three decades.[51]

Admiral Thunman believes this early attack by US SSNs is "the most important function of our attack submarine forces."[52] Thunman's successor, Vice Adm. Bruce DeMars, has emphasized submarine warfare as the "underpinning" of the US maritime strategy. "If [US] submarines don't go up there in the Soviets' back yard and clean up on the Soviet submarines early in a war, then our current view of the maritime strategy is invalid. It is as simple as that."[53]

Adm. Kinnaird R. McKee has emphasized the role of uncertainty in "tying up" Soviet naval forces in defense of their SSBNs:

> Lots of people don't understand . . . that a handful of submarines operating in the other guy's back yard are going to tie up forces far out of proportion. As long as there is one guy . . . mobile enough to look like more than one, he creates a terrible situation. The principal element of that leverage is certainty and uncertainty in the minds of the enemy; certainty because he knows what this submarine can do and terrible uncertainty because he doesn't know what it will do and how we will use it.
>
> Uncertainty is the most damaging element in the planner's book. It just drives them nuts. In submarine warfare, we bring uncertainty to the table like nothing else.[54]

These statements are made by some of the highest ranking current and former decision makers in the US Navy (Watkins and Lehman), the head of the Submarine Warfare branch (Thunman), and the head of the Nuclear Propulsion Program (McKee). All four agree that a central component of US naval strategy for *conventional* war is threatening Soviet SSBNs in waters near the Soviet Union. A key requirement of this threat is that it occur immediately upon the beginning of hostilities.

The timing of SSN movements into the Soviet SSBN patrol areas is a matter of great import to the US Navy. During peacetime, there are probably a few US attack submarines engaged in intelligence operations or trailing Soviet SSBNs. Occasionally these operations are reported.[55] If a crisis were to intensify, the SSN operations near the Soviet Union could probably be stepped up somewhat within the normal 40-plus percent SSN at-sea rate. The next stage would be a surge of US SSNs into Soviet home waters.

According to the US chief of naval operations, "the normal scenario in the North Atlantic-Norwegian Sea is characterized by aggressiveness. . . . [It] is very well planned, in my opinion, with SSNs being up there before the conflict starts."[56] The US Navy conducted a worldwide surge of SSNs in 1984 as practice for this strategy. It was the first time SSNs were surged on that scale in 30 years.[57] The suggestion of the chief of naval operations is to surge SSNs out of all ports "30 days or so, 10 days before the conflict starts." This plan assumes that the president would not be inhibited from doing so because such a move is not considered "provocative."[58]

Three questions immediately come to mind: First, why does Admiral Watkins call for an SSN surge 10–30 days *before* a war? Second, how does the president know when World War III is 10–30 days off? And third, what makes naval leaders think that a sudden surge of SSNs aimed at Soviet strategic submarines will not be "provocative"? Indeed, the US Navy expects the threat to Soviet SSBNs to be provocative enough to warrant the allocation of major Soviet naval resources to defend them. Admiral Watkins himself raised the question of the dangers of provocation during the early phases of superpower conflict, a question that is constantly raised during major naval war games: "There is great consternation during the game on the part of the players about whether we are sending more of a deterrent signal by moving forces, or whether we are actually tearing down deterrence and encouraging adventurism."[59]

It is clear that there is no consensus on the third question; even the US Navy is split, and there is no indication of how the civilian leadership might respond. As for the second question, common estimates of war warning used in NATO planning are between 10 and 30 days, which is consistent with the Navy's statement.

The first question does have a plausible answer. The prewar surge is expected to force the Soviet Navy into its defensive posture so early that it would not surge its own SSNs into the North Atlantic. According to Admiral Watkins, "The Soviets expect us on warning [of an approaching war] to surge SSN's. They know we are going to the bastions. They know we can get inside their knickers before they can find us and they don't like it."[60] Furthermore, "Aggressive forward movement of anti-submarine warfare forces, both submarines and maritime patrol aircraft, will force Soviet submarines to retreat into defensive bastions to protect their ballistic missile submarines. This both denies the Soviets the option of a massive, early attempt to interdict our sea-lanes of communication and counters such operations against them that the Soviets undertake."[61]

However, while the Navy argues that the rapid forward surge of most US attack submarines will force the Soviet Navy onto the defensive in home waters early on, it also argues that, in any case, the Soviet Navy would probably stay in home waters in the defensive role, at the beginning of a war. As Admiral Watkins put it, "Roles such as interdicting sea lines of communication or supporting the Soviet Army, while important, will probably be secondary, at least at the war's start. This view of the Soviet Navy's role in overall Soviet strategy suggests that initially the bulk of Soviet naval forces will deploy in areas near the Soviet Union, with only a small fraction deployed forward."[62] There seem to be two different views of Soviet intentions for the beginning of the war: 1) that the US must "force" them onto the defensive "at once" or else face "superiority in numbers" of Soviet submarines, and 2) that the Soviet Navy would probably only send out a "small fraction" of its forces beyond home waters early on, given their strategy.

If the objective of an SSN surge is to threaten Soviet SSBNs in their patrol areas at the outbreak of war, then the SSNs would have to go to sea at least a week ahead of time to allow for transit. However, those SSNs have a limited endurance, two or perhaps three months, so if the surge is too early, the US attack submarines will begin to run out of supplies when the war begins. Surging a month ahead of time allows for at least one and possibly two months of time at sea during a conflict.

The early phase of the submarine war in the Arctic is seen as "a very carefully planned and coordinated rollback operation with heavy SSN to SSN combat in the upper Norwegian Sea."[63] The level of coordination would have to be high in order to avoid having US SSNs attack each other in these very stressful situations. Hypothetical US SSN operations in the Northwest Pacific during the early phase of war are illustrated by figure 4–1. This diagram, submitted to Congress by the secretary of the Navy, shows US attack submarines in the Sea of Japan and off the Kamchatka peninsula, where the three main Soviet Pacific naval bases are situated: Vladivostok and Sovetskaya Gavan' in the Sea of Japan, and Petropavlovsk on the Kamchatka peninsula. The diagram also shows attack submarines moving through the Kuril Islands and into the northern part of the Sea of Okhotsk, where there is a base for "submarines and light forces" at Magadan.[64] The northern Sea of Okhotsk is also a natural area for the Soviet Navy to hide SSBNs in because the water is shallow and covered with ice from December through April, which makes detection difficult.[65] It seems more likely that if the US attack submarines were deployed in the Sea of Okhotsk, it would be to threaten Soviet SSBNs there, rather than to attack a secondary naval base.

It is important to note that these hypothetical US attack submarine movements are expected to take place during a phase beginning before the initiation of conflict. The US Navy calls this period "transition to war" and considers it "perhaps the most crucial of all."[66] Attack submarine deployments may, as Admiral Watkins suggested, deepen political crises between the superpowers in a period when war is threatening to engulf them both.

The number of US attack submarines allocated to various missions in the early phase is unknown but is a key parameter of the strategy that may have to be decided beforehand. Too many US SSNs too close to the Soviet home waters may shoot at each other, or may leave other areas inadequately defended, whereas too few may not cause enough damage rapidly enough. Admiral McKee suggested above that "a handful" of submarines can tie up a disproportionately large part of the Soviet Navy in home waters due to the uncertainty of

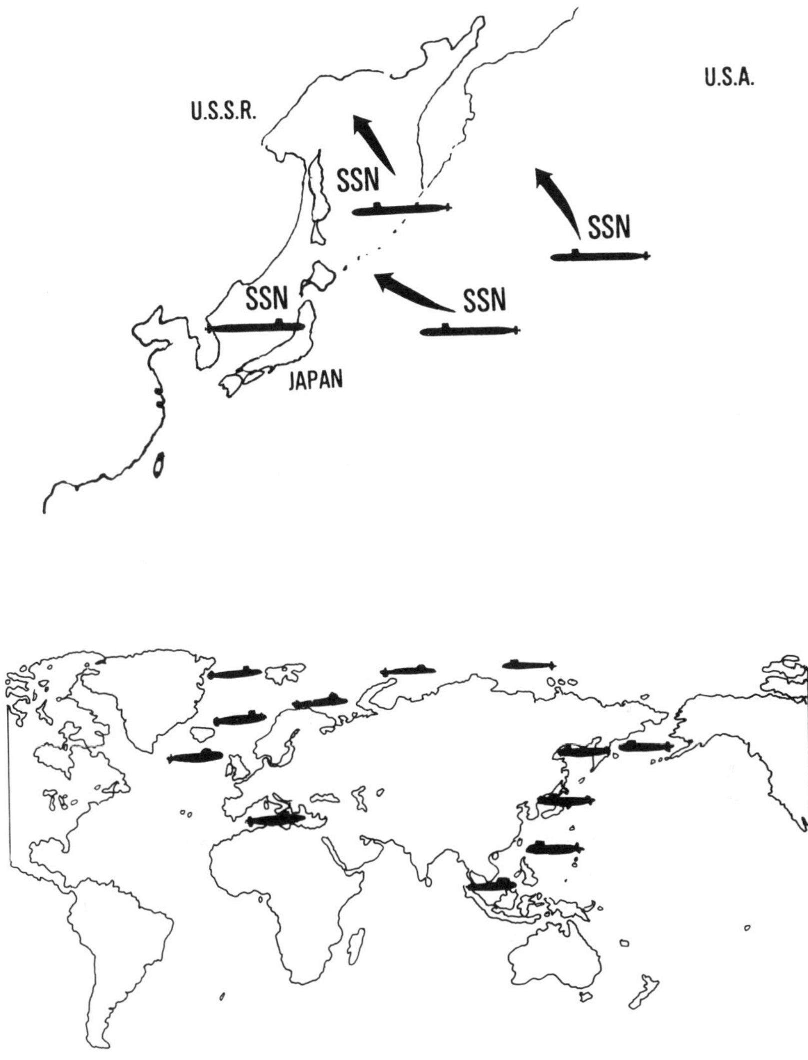

Figure 4–1. US attack submarine movements in forward areas.

Source: Department of Defense Authorization for Appropriations for Fiscal Year 1985, Senate Armed Service Committee, part 8, pp. 3874, 4164.

the threat.[67] On the other hand, the chief of naval operations has said that "the majority of our SSNs would be involved with this forward effort. The rest would be supporting our carrier battle groups as they perform their offensive operations worldwide."[68] While area commanders would decide how to move forces in a crisis, the strategy of putting the Soviet Navy on the defensive is best served by official statements that suggest the maximum US threat.

The timing of later phases of a submarine war would be highly uncertain. According to John Lehman, "One can't easily determine . . . how long it will take . . . to nullify the submarine force in the Norwegian Sea. That is a tough area to operate in. It may take a week or it may take a month or three months."[69]

Even if the rapid forward deployment of US SSNs were only intended for mining and for attacks on Soviet ships and attack submarines early in a war, the US SSNs would probably destroy some Soviet SSBNs anyway. The modern attack submarine is "designed to fight in the enemy's backyard."[70] and the submarine-launched mobile mine (SLMM), a stand-off weapon, is intended for use in enemy harbors.[71] In these "backyard" operations, there would be SSBNs either coming into or leaving the harbor, and were a US attack submarine to run across a Soviet SSBN, the US SSN "would not be in a position of differentiating their attack submarines from their SSBNs."[72] Said Vice Adm. Robert Kaufman, "In a conventional war all submarines are submarines, they are all fair game."[73] Nor is it likely that the SLMM could reliably distinguish between SSBNs and SSNs, particularly in shallow water near harbors where the noise signatures of submarines are masked by loud background noises. All SSBNs are potential threats to the SSNs because they are armed with torpedoes and sonars. Many submarine operators think that a policy of avoiding SSBNs in the dangerous conditions of Soviet home waters would be infeasible, even if accurate classification of detected submarines were possible. Also, the emphasis on the rapidity of forward operations would make an "avoid SSBNs" rule of engagement more difficult, since it would require closing in to check on every detection to identify it and taking a long circuitous route to avoid SSBNs. However, if one accepts the stated strategy, the US Navy sees no reason to avoid Soviet SSBNs. According to the assumptions that seem to underlie current strategy, a few SSBNs destroyed at the outbreak of hostilities would make very real the threat on which US naval strategy so crucially depends.

All of these statements strongly suggest that Soviet strategic submarines would be attacked "in the first five minutes of the war," which is exactly what John Lehman said in an off-the-record session in April 1985.[74] This is also exactly what happens when the US Navy runs its large-scale war games at the Naval War College. In fact, the training of Navy submarine commanders and strategists in conventional war games has never excluded SSBNs from the target list of attack submarines. As a result, destroying Soviet SSBNs may become part of the "tactical culture" of the attack submarine fleet. As one former member of the chief of naval operations staff put it: "One of the ridiculous and alarming features of the Navy war-gaming studies of non-nuclear conflicts at sea has always been the lack of any recognition that [SSBN] sanctuaries must be provided, lest the threat to survival of nuclear deterrent forces rapidly escalate the conflict."[75]

In short, the declared US forward naval strategy, with its emphasis on attacking the Soviet Navy in its "backyard" and making it defend SSBN bastions, has generated a set of very powerful arguments and incentives to use attack submarines against defended Soviet SSBNs very early in a war. Exactly how these ideas find their way into war plans cannot be known in the unclassified realm, and if they do, no one knows if such plans would be executed.

It is possible that the United States may consider stepped-up attacks on Soviet SSBNs during wartime as a form of horizontal escalation, to apply pressure for particular US war aims. One could imagine, for example, a situation in which Soviet SSBNs might be attacked in response to a Soviet Army move toward the Middle East, or in response to a stalemate or an impending NATO setback, or as an attempt to limit or terminate hostilities in some other context.

Using strategic ASW as a form of horizontal escalation by shifting the "correlation of forces" is a highly uncertain plan. Soviet concepts of the "correlation of forces" include, but are much broader than, calculations of military capability. Also, as noted in chapter 1, the record of actual applications of horizontal escalation is marked by inconclusive or counterproductive results.

Antisubmarine warfare itself is a probabilistic process characterized by a large degree of uncertainty. The rate of attrition to Soviet SSBNs at sea depends on a large number of random variables with large variances. If the United States were to increase its ASW efforts in the bastions as a form of escalation, it is not clear that the results would be immediately evident, in terms of the attrition rate as well as the rate at which the Soviet leadership became aware of the attrition.

The preceding discussion has deliberately ignored the question of the feasibility of a strategic ASW campaign and the risk to US attack submarines in highly defended Soviet waters. As the analysis in appendix 2 shows, however, such a campaign might not be very rapid, and might be very costly in military terms. The ability of Soviet SSBNs to hide under ice or near the ice edge, coupled with their increasing quietness would make them very difficult to find. The attrition rate to the Soviet SSBNs would probably be slow and therefore might have little impact on a rapidly developing political and military situation on land. If events on land unfold slowly—which seems less likely—then the slow attrition rate of Soviet SSBNs might have some impact. However, in order to effect this attrition, US attack submarines must be tied down in the Arctic, at the very time when they could be directly protecting shipping in the Atlantic.

Tying down US attack submarines in the Arctic in this way during a long war can help keep the sea-lanes open if many Soviet attack submarines are tied down also. The Soviet home waters filled with many Soviet attack submarines is one of the most dangerous places in the world for US attack submarines, even very quiet ones. The one-on-one combat exchange ratio in shallow Soviet home waters is less favorable to the United States than the exchange ratio between submarines in open water. This is due to the advantages of coordinated Soviet ASW defenses in aircraft, nuclear and conventionally powered submarines, command and control, and fixed undersea surveillance. Acoustic and perhaps magnetic detectors in Soviet home waters could provide accurate localization data for all Soviet ASW forces. The exchange ratio is also influenced by the fact that for a given acoustic advantage, the detection range advantage in deep water may be several times greater than the detection range advantage in shallow water.

A strategic ASW campaign may cost the United States a large number of attack submarines, and it may happen that such a campaign ties down a larger portion of the US submarine fleet than it does the Soviet submarine fleet. This would run counter to the objective of shifting the balance of submarine forces in favor of the United States, although it has been argued by some that strategic ASW would support another major objective of the declared maritime strategy, which is to induce the Soviet Union to terminate hostilites during a major war by sinking its SSBNs. This is the subject of the next chapter.

Notes

1. Adm. James D. Watkins, CNO, *The Maritime Strategy* (Annapolis: US Naval Institute Press, 1986), p. 4.

2. John Lehman, interview in *Armed Forces Journal International,* November 1983, p. 72.

3. Adm. James D. Watkins, HASC, FY 1985, part 1, p. 575.

4. Adm. James D. Watkins, HAC, FY 1984, part 2, pp. 429–430.

5. As far as sailing aircraft carriers into Soviet home waters is concerned, Adm. Stansfield Turner as of 1982 had "yet to find an Admiral who believes that the US Navy would even attempt it" (*Foreign Affairs* 61:2, Winter 1982–1983, p. 457).

6. John Lehman, HAC, FY 1984, part 2, p. 642.

7. Richard Barnard, "Captor Capsized; Funding Sinks," *Defense Week,* 30 July 1984, p. 12.

8. The likelihood of a prolonged conventional war is unknown. In spite of doctrinal shifts on both sides toward limiting war to the use of conventional weapons, the nuclearization of naval forces on both sides continues apace. For a study of the Soviet shift, *see* James McConnell, *The Soviet Shift in Emphasis from Nuclear to Conventional,* Vols. I and II, CRC 490. (Alexandria, Va.: Center for Naval Analyses, June 1983). The US Navy's desire to terminate war "without the use of nuclear weapons" is summarized by Admiral Watkins, SASC, FY 1985, part 8, p. 3893. The best recent study on the expansion of nuclear capability at sea is William Arkir et al., *Nuclearization of the Oceans,* Background Paper for the symposium on the Denuclearization of the Oceans, Norrtalje, Sweden, 11–14 May 1984, Institute for Policy Studies, Washington, DC.

9. Quoted in Geoffrey Till, *Maritime Strategy in the Nuclear Age* (New York: St. Martin's, 1984), p. 187.

10. Henry Kissinger, *Nuclear Weapons and Foreign Policy* (Garden City, N.Y.: Doubleday, 1957), pp. 138–139.

11. SAC, FY 1979, part 4, p. 356.

12. Joint Chiefs of Staff, *Statement on US Military Posture for Fiscal Year 1982* (hereafter, JCS Posture Statement FY 1982), p. 78. It is interesting to note that subsequent posture statements (FY 1983, FY 1984, and FY 1985) drop the explicit reference to shore bombardment when mentioning TLAM-N—but do not exclude the mission. This is the period of internal US Navy debate regarding the role of the Tomahawk. (*See*, for example, Lt. Paul G. Johnson, USN, "Tomahawk: The Implications of a Strategic-Tactical Mix," *US Naval Institute Proceedings*, April 1982.) The controversy seems to have been resolved by removing Tomahawks from the SIOP, the Single Integrated Operational Plan for the use of strategic nuclear weapons by all services (Rear Adm. Frank B. Kelso, Director of Strategic Submarine Division, SASC, FY 1983, part 7, p. 4517).

13. "Soviet Cruise Missile Said to Stray Across Norway and into Finland," *New York Times*, 3 January 1985, p. 1.

14. Caspar W. Weinberger, *Annual Report of the Secretary of Defense for Fiscal Year 1985*, p. 148.

15. Ibid., p. 149.

16. Adm. Thomas Hayward, Chief of Naval Operations, SASC, FY 1981, part 2, p. 867.

17. Vice Adm. Nils R. Thunman, SASC, FY 1985, part 8, p. 4161.

18. Adm. James D. Watkins, HASC, FY 1985, part 1, p. 575.

19. Ibid.

20. Ibid., pp. 575–576.

21. Ibid., p. 576.

22. Adm. James D. Watkins, SASC, FY 1985, part 2, p. 922.

23. Lehman, interview in *Armed Forces Journal International*, p. 72.

24. Patrick Duffy, *NATO ASW: Strategy, Requirements, and the Need for Co-Operation*, NAA Military Committee, Subcommittee on Defense Cooperation, October 1981, pp. 3, 9.

25. Till, *Maritime Strategy in the Nuclear Age*, p. 187.

26. Robert W. Komer, *Maritime Strategy or Coalition Defense*? (Cambridge, Mass.: Abt Books, 1984), pp. 60–61.

27. Adm. William J. Crowe, Jr., SASC, FY 1985, part 2, p. 1198.

28. Adm. James D. Watkins, SASC, FY 1985, part 2, pp. 920–921.

29. Linton F. Brooks, "Naval Power and National Security," *International Security* II, Fall 1986, p. 66. *See also* SASC, FY 1985, part 8, p. 3854.

30. Komer, *Maritime Strategy*, p. 60.

31. Frederich Ruge, *The Soviets as Naval Opponents*: 1942–1945 (Annapolis: Naval Institute Press, 1979).

32. Michael MccGwire, "The Rationale for the Development of Soviet Seapower," *US Naval Institute Proceedings*, May 1980, pp. 155–182.

33. Capt. Dominic A. Paolucci, USN, Ret., "The Development of Navy Strategic Offensive and Defensive Systems," *US Naval Institute Proceedings* 96, May 1970, pp. 205–223.

34. Data from US Navy, *Allowances and Location of Navy Aircraft*, OPNAV Notice PO3110.

35. Adm. Arleigh Burke, Chief of Naval Operations, HASC, FY 1962, p. 953.

36. MccGwire, "Rationale," pp. 155–182.

37. Robert Herrick, *The SSBN-Protection Mission, Final Report, Soviet Naval Mission Assignments*, KFR 234–79 (Arlington, Va.: Ketron, Inc., 1979).

38. Bryan Ranft and Geoffrey Till, *The Sea in Soviet Strategy* (Annapolis: Naval Institute Press, 1983), p. 170. One illustration is that of Soviet investment in major warships between 1965 and 1975, when over 40 percent was allotted to strategic submarines. *See* James M. McConnell, "Strategy and Missions of the Soviet Navy in the Year 2000," in *Problems of Seapower as We Approach the Twenty-First Century*, ed. James L. George, (Washington, DC: American Enterprise Institute, 1978), p. 43.

39. Michael MccGwire, "Contingency Plans for World War," in *The Soviet and other Communist Navies—A View from the Mid-1980s*, ed. James L. George (Annapolis, Md.: Naval Institute Presss, 1986), pp. 61–81.

40. McConnell, "Strategy and Missions," p. 48. The mission of destroying US missile submarines has not altogether vanished, however; it is one goal of a continuing acoustic and nonacoustic detection research and development program.

41. Adm. A. Mikhaylovskiy, "Vsegda v Gotovnosti (Always in Readiness)," *Krasnaya Zvezda*, 1 June 1983, cited in an early 1984 study by Robert Herrick, as reported in a private communication. The Soviet Military Encyclopedia includes the entire area north of the GIUK gap and the Bering Sea in its definition of the Arctic Ocean.

42. Doctor of Naval Science, Vice Adm. K. Stalbo, "The Anti-Soviet Myth and Aggressive Designs," *Krasnaya Zvezda*, 20 September 1980.

43. James Wade, Jr., *The FY 1986 DoD Program for Research, Development, and Acquisition*, in HASC FY 1986, part 4, p. 122.

44. James M. McConnell, *The Soviet Shift in Emphasis from Nuclear to Conventional*, vol. 2, (Alexandria, Va.: Center for Naval Analyses, 1983), CRC-490, pp. 32, 33, 38.

45. Not all Soviet SSBNs are necessarily assigned the reserve role; those deployed forward near the United States may have other roles.

46. Drew Middleton, "Soviet Reacts to New US War-Game Policy," *New York Times*, 30 September 1982. Probably the second-ranked Soviet naval threat is the Backfire bomber. However, its bases are not hardened, only revetted, and are considered "lucrative" targets for US carrier-based aircraft and, in the Pacific, even for land-based aircraft (John Lehman, SASC, FY 1985, part 8, p. 3875).

47. Adm. James D. Watkins, SASC, FY 1985, part 2, p. 922.

48. Ibid., p. 921.

49. Barry Posen, "Inadvertent Nuclear War?" *International Security*, Fall 1982, pp. 28–54.

50. Adm. James D. Watkins, SASC, FY 1985, part 2, p. 902.

51. HASC, FY 1985, part 3, pp. 128–129.

52. HASC, FY 1986, part 3, p. 161.

53. James O'Shea, "U.S. to Sink Billions into New Attack Sub," *Chicago Tribune*, 20 July 1986, p. 1.

54. Adm. Kinnaird R. McKee, SASC, FY 1985, part 7, p. 3681.

55. Seymour M. Hersh, "A False Navy Report Alleged in Sub Crash," *New York Times*, 6 July 1975, p. 1; and Seymour M. Hersh, "Submarines of US Stage Spy Missions inside Soviet Waters," *New York Times*, 25 May 1975, p. 1.

56. Adm. James D. Watkins, SASC, FY 1985, part 8, p. 3888.

57. Ibid.

58. Ibid.

59. SASC, FY 1985, part 8, p. 3864.

60. Adm. James D. Watkins, HAC FY 1986, part 2, p. 927.

61. Adm. James D. Watkins, "The Maritime Strategy", a special supplement to the *US Naval Institute Proceedings*, January 1986, p. 9.

62. Ibid., p. 7.

63. Adm. James D. Watkins, SASC, FY 1985, part 8, p. 3887.

64. Norman Polmar, *Guide to the Soviet Navy* (Annapolis: Naval Institute Press, 1983), p. 392.

65. *Marine Geography of the Sea of Okhotsk*, US Navy Hydrographic Office, Washington, DC, HO pub. no. 758, March 1965.

66. John Lehman, SASC, FY 1985, part 8, p. 3864.

67. SASC, FY 1985, part 7, p. 3681.

68. HASC, FY 1986, part 3, p. 144.

69. John Lehman, SASC, FY 1985, part 8, p. 3877.

70. Vice Adm. Nils R. Thunman, HASC, FY 1985, part 3, p. 131.

71. Adm. Baciocco, HASC, FY 1985, part 4, p. 779.

72. Daniel Murphy, former director of ASW and Ocean Surveillance, SASC, FY 1977, part 4, p. 1972, quoted in Bruce Blair, "Arms Control Implications of Anti-Submarine Warfare Programs," in *Evaluation of Fiscal Year 1979 Arms Control Impact Statements* (Washington, DC: US Government Printing Office, 1979), p. 115.

73. Vice Adm. Robert Kaufman, Navy Director of Command, Control and Communications, SASC, FY 1978, p. 6699, quoted in Blair, "Arms Control Implications," p. 115.

74. Melissa Healy, "Lehman: We'll Sink Their Subs," *Defense Week*, 13 May 1985.

75. Stuart B. Baker, letter to the Editor, *Washington Post*, 13 January 1973.

5
Attacks on Soviet SSBNs for Damage Limitation and War Termination

Deterrence based narrowly on mutual assured destruction (MAD) has never been the official military strategy of the United States[1] nor of the Soviet Union.[2] US military planning has stressed the need for "flexible options" to destroy selected military targets in order to make the use of nuclear weapons a plausible response to lower levels of conflict, mainly conventional war. In scenarios for fighting nuclear wars, the possibility of destroying society looms as the ultimate threat. At any point in a war among nuclear powers, the side that perceives that it is losing can threaten the softest target set of all: the people, the political apparatus, and the industrial infrastructure that *are* the opponent. To deter such a threat by the opponent, some nuclear weapons must be held back from warfighting uses to threaten assured destruction of the opponent's society. The requirements for a force to deter such an attack *during* a war are essentially the same as the requirements for a minimum deterrent *before* war breaks out: sufficient force and survivability.

The only real differences lie in the context. First, while MAD-type deterrence of nuclear attack must function in a prenuclear-war world (peacetime or conventional war), the intrawar nuclear deterrent must function in a world in which some nuclear weapons may have been used and millions of people, perhaps even tens of millions, may have been killed. This raises the question of whether a different size or type of force is needed to deter leaders in the midst of a war, as opposed to in peacetime. Second, the survivability of the intrawar deterrent depends on the amount of damage that has already been done to the retaliatory force or its defenses, and on the changing threats to it. Given these factors, the intrawar deterrent or strategic reserve force is not static; rather, it will change throughout a war as forces and perceptions change.

The Roles of Strategic Submarines

Both US and Soviet nuclear strategies provide for a strategic nuclear reserve to deter large-scale destruction, and on both sides, strategies of minimum deterrence and warfighting coexist. This is particularly relevant to strategic submarines because the minimum deterrent role, which requires less flexible command and control but greater survivability, is likely to be assigned to submarines. This does not mean, however, that submarines will necessarily be excluded from the initial strikes of a nuclear attack.

Withholding strategic reserve forces has been part of US nuclear war strategy at least since the early 1960s.[3] When counterforce targeting was publicly announced in the early 1970s, withholding strategic forces also emerged as part of the official policy, as would be expected. National Security Decision Memorandum 242 (NSDM-242), an elaboration of existing policy signed by President Richard Nixon in January 1974, introduced the notion of "withholds": targets that would be preserved from destruction. Some of these, particularly population as such, are said to be exempt from targeting; others, such as centers of political leadership and control, are exempt from initial strikes, but targeted by strategic reserve forces for intrawar deterrence and "eventual destruction if necessary."[4] Distinctions between political leadership and population are illusory, however, since "large-scale attacks on Soviet leadership would be virtually indistinguishable from counter-city attacks."[5] In his fiscal year 1975 Annual Report, Secretary of Defense James R. Schlesinger wrote: "No one who has thought much about these questions disagrees with the need, at a minimum, to maintain a conservatively designed reserve for the ultimate threat of large-scale destruction."[6]

The list of principal features proposed by Schlesinger "to maintain and improve [US] strategic posture" begins with "the ability to withhold an assured destruction reserve for an extended period of time,"[7] to be aimed at "urban-industrial targets." In August 1977, the Carter administration issued Presidential Directive PD-18, which "prompted defense policymakers to focus on the possibilities of protracted nuclear war" and included an order to study the secure reserve force and the command and control associated with it.[8] The requirement for maintaining "a survivable and enduring retaliatory capability to devastate the industry and cities of the Soviet Union"[9] has persisted.

At the beginning of SSBN deployment, the US Navy made it clear that it would not settle for only a strategic reserve role.[10] There is very little information in the unclassified literature regarding the evolution of US planning for strategic reserve forces. This may be partly due to the fact that the concept of a strategic reserve arises only out of a declaratory doctrine of warfighting. Until relatively recently, US officials have been reluctant to discuss the topic of fighting nuclear wars.

As Soviet ICBMs have become more capable of destroying US missile silos, it is likely that the emphasis for strategic reserves has shifted toward submarines. In particular, submarines carrying Poseidon missiles, which have the least counterforce capability, may have been assigned a strategic reserve role. Trident I warheads on submarines (3,264 warheads on 21 submarines by

1989) can destroy targets that have some hardening,[11] so these weapons might be included in plans for initial strikes against lightly hardened targets. Sea-launched cruise missiles are also likely to be assigned a reserve role.

The roles of Soviet SSBNs have evolved very differently from their US counterparts. The Soviet Union built the first SSBNs in the mid-1950s from converted attack submarines, and then watched as the United States developed a highly sophisticated, survivable ballistic missile fleet in the early 1960s, on top of an already potent nuclear strike force on aircraft carriers. In response to US first-use policy and overwhelming nuclear superiority, Soviet military doctrine from the late 1950s to mid-1960s held that any East-West war would inevitably escalate to nuclear war. This produced immense pressure for the Soviets to create survivable strategic nuclear forces. Until such forces were in place, however, the Soviet leadership may have planned for a "spasm attack" by all nuclear forces at the outbreak of any war, because they faced certain defeat if they waited and the United States launched its vastly superior forces first.

In this context, some analysts believe that an attack on a Soviet SSBN would possibly have triggered an intercontinental nuclear war involving the launch of all missiles.[12] During that period some officials within the US Navy also assumed that "undoubtedly Soviet missile armed submarines would participate in the initial phase of a nuclear war."[13] In the latter part of the 1960s, the Soviet Navy began deploying Yankee class SSBNs, which significantly increased their strategic nuclear forces at sea, and which may have also been intended for tactical naval warfare. However, these vessels were still relatively vulnerable to NATO ASW forces, largely because of the existence of fixed acoustic surveillance systems in the Norwegian Sea region. If Yankees were to be withheld in home waters until after an initial nuclear exchange that included strikes against those surveillance systems, they would have been more capable of launching attacks on the United States.

As previously noted, it appears that in late 1966 a new doctrine was adopted in the Soviet Union which held that an East-West war need *not* escalate to an intercontinental exchange. The new doctrine, to be implemented by an ICBM deterrence force and a survivable SLBM insurance force, stressed the objective of "avoiding the nuclear devastation of Russia."[14] The SSBN insurance force was needed to ride out any attacks during a conventional war, for if the war did escalate to an intercontinental nuclear exchange in spite of the ICBM deterrent force, the undersea insurance force would become the strategic reserve.

The Soviet Navy began writing about the mission of protecting SSBNs in the early 1960s,[15] and seems to have maintained it operationally during the 1970s and up to the present. When the long-range SS-N-8 missile was introduced on the Delta class SSBN in the early 1970s, the concept of protected bastions near Soviet coasts became a logical extension of the mission of defending SSBNs. This helped bolster the "insurance" that would deter nuclear strikes on the USSR or, if nuclear war occurred, maintain a reserve.

Strategic ASW and Damage Limitation

Strategic antisubmarine warfare lies in an area of overlap between conventional and strategic nuclear policy. Thus far, the discussion regarding US strikes against Soviet SSBNs and the policy pronouncements of US Navy officials have been in the context of a *conventional* East-West war. However, it is the potential impact of US strategic ASW on the outcome of a *nuclear* war which drives the Soviet Union to assign its general-purpose navy the task of protecting SSBNs.

In the United States, strategic ASW has also been connected with an overall program of seeking a disarming or damage-limiting attack capability. When the US Congressional Joint Atomic Energy Committee studied Soviet SSBNs in 1958, the Undersea Warfare Advisory Panel found that the Soviet Union would "soon have a few, then many" SLBMs that could launch "devastating nuclear warhead" attacks from the sea by the early 1960s, and that existing US defenses could not prevent this. We know now that they were wrong about the magnitude of that threat: the early Soviet SSBNs "posed little threat to the continental US."[16] Nevertheless, strategic ASW was given a boost. The panel recommended doubling ASW R and D funding, more basic research into ASW, particularly oceanography, and accelerated testing of nuclear ASW weapons. The panel went so far as to say that of all ASW missions (protecting convoys, and so on), the primary one was to destroy Soviet SSBNs.[17] In 1963, Secretary of the Navy Paul Nitze requested Navy participation in a study to begin the following year in the office of Dr. Harold Brown, Director of Defense Research and Engineering, on the strategic offensive and defensive systems of the United States and Soviet Union. In support of this, Nitze set up the ad hoc "Great Circle Group" under Rear Adm. George Miller to study "Naval Contributions to Damage Limiting." One of the main concerns of the group was US strategic ASW.[18]

In 1963 and 1964, the services, Joint Chiefs of Staff, and other groups participated in a series of studies of US capabilities for limiting damage from Soviet strategic forces. A summary of those studies concluded that "for about $14 billion allocated to ASW, the major part of the SLBM threat from a Soviet Polaris-type operation [could] be negated and that this figure is somewhat independent of Soviet force size."[19] The fiscal year 1963 expenditures for continental air and missile defense forces in 1963 dollars was about $2 billion, for strategic retaliatory forces about $8.5 billion, and for the Navy general purpose forces, about $18 billion.[20] The defense against the projected 1970s Soviet SSBN threat would have been seen as extremely costly, particularly if deterrence through "assured destruction" were seen as an existing and sufficient condition for preventing an attack.

Declassified "secret" versions of the annual report of the secretary of defense from the early 1960s show that the secretary included strategic ASW as a top priority for strategic defense:

> Second only in importance to defense against ICBM attack is the problem of defense against submarine-launched missiles. The solution to this problem entails three different types of capabilities:
> —The detection and tracking of enemy submarines.
> —The destruction of these submarines before they have an opportunity to launch their missiles.
> —The detection, tracking and destruction of the missiles once they have been launched.[21]

The report went on to describe Caesar, Artemis, and Trident, three parts of the experimental and operational system for long-range strategic submarine detection, and the forerunners of the current SOSUS system. However, beginning in 1965 (FY 1966), even the secret version of the defense secretary's annual report no longer mentioned strategic ASW under the heading "Strategic Defense." Instead, it was shifted to the "General Purpose Naval Forces" section. Around this time, the declaratory emphasis on damage limiting was starting to wane in the Office of the Secretary of Defense. This did not stop the push for antisubmarine forces, however. In the FY 1968 Annual Report, McNamara called for an "extension of the SOSUS system into the central and far Pacific."[22] Defense against Soviet SSBNs continued to be a matter of public record, but in a very low-key way. Paul Nitze gave the topic only one passing line in his 1967 statement before the Defense Subcommittee of the House Appropriations Committee: "To assist in defense against submarine-launched ballistic missiles we are working on expanding the potential effectiveness of our antisubmarine warfare forces in that role."[23]

Strategic ASW resurfaced during 1968 as Congress debated funding of new attack submarine designs. Central to the discussion was the mission of using attack submarines to attack the most recent class of Soviet SSBN, the Yankee I, and its successors.[24]

In 1968 Adm. Thomas B. Moorer, Chief of Naval Operations, testified that United States war plans "should certainly include targets which contain forces which can attack the United States. Also . . . damage limiting is achieved two ways: one by attacking enemy weapons before they can be launched; and two, by destroying them once they are in the air."[25] Throughout the early 1970s, the quiet Los Angeles class SSN was so heavily sold on the basis of countering an expected acoustic improvement in the next class of Soviet SSBNs (presumably one of the targets) that when the new Delta class turned out to be nearly as loud as the Yankee class, some US military officials were considerably embarrassed.[26]

The next planned US attack submarine class, the SSN-21, is also being justified by the Navy on the basis of its ability to attack Soviet strategic submarines. There has been particular interest in the ability of the new submarine to carry out strategic ASW under the Arctic ice pack, since that is where most Soviet SSBNs are expected to hide. In congressional testimony, Chief of Naval Operations Watkins even went as far as to say that the new SSN-21, due for initial deployment in 1995, "has all the capability which is our Star Wars equivalent for the year 2000."[27] This is of course an explicit reference to the damage-limiting strike mission of the SSNs.

The comparison of the SSN-21 with Star Wars should be examined in the light of other US Navy statements. It could be interpreted as meaning that Admiral Watkins expects the SSN-21 to have the ability to neutralize virtually all the Soviet SSBNs at sea, as President Reagan expects Star Wars weaponry to be able to neutralize virtually all Soviet warheads in space. Such an interpretation would not square with other Navy testimony, however:

> The United States does not have the capability, or the prospect of acquiring the capability, to successfully conduct a simultaneous attack on all Soviet SSBNs at sea. Any US attempt at a first strike would necessarily fail in that Soviet strategic missile submarines capable of inflicting unacceptable damage in the United States, would survive to retaliate.[28]

This assessment was made in response to a question that raised concern over the destabilizing effects of the Trident II missiles's hard target kill capability, while Admiral Watkins's statement could be an attempt to justify the new SSNs, each of which will cost over $1 billion. In any case, at first glance the two assessments appear to be contradictory. On closer examination, however, they may be consistent. That SSBNs at sea are virtually impossible to attack simultaneously is readily demonstrable.[29] Strategic ASW is a process of attrition. Thus, if a "first strike" is defined in the usual way, as a sudden, simultaneous attack on all strategic forces, it would, in US Navy terms, "necessarily fail." The important issue is not simultaneity; it is whether the United States can disarm the Soviet Union without the Soviet Union's inflicting intolerable damage on the United States. If a preemptive disarming attack is divided into two phases—early SSBN attrition using SSN-21s and later attacks on land-based forces in a counterforce missile strike—then strategic ASW undertaken during conventional war makes a powerful contribution to an overall damage-limiting or disarming strike. Star Wars is of course intended for the same basic purpose: to destroy Soviet strategic weapons before they hit US territory.

The first phase of an East-West war probably would not involve the use of nuclear weapons—a conclusion that both the United States and the Soviet Union seem to accept, although the duration of this phase is highly uncertain.

The US Navy has stated that during the first phase of a (presumably conventional) East-West war, it will attempt to destroy Soviet SSBNs at sea. It will probably try to destroy SSBNs in port also. The longer the first phase, the fewer the Soviet SSBNs at sea that should be expected to survive a committed US strategic ASW campaign, as long as the attrition rate to US attack submarines does not exceed tolerable bounds. As we have seen, this is a very important qualification.

In terms of hardware, US developments would support a two-phase attack, though they were not procured with it in mind. At the outbreak of an East-West war, during the first phase (only conventional weapons in use), carrier-based strike aircraft and conventionally armed Tomahawk sea-launched cruise missiles could attack Soviet SSBNs in port. It is not clear how effective these weapons would be, however, since Soviet SSBNs are in hardened shelters. A hallmark of US naval policy during the early and mid-1980s has been increased emphasis on carrier-launched air strikes against Soviet bases, with no suggestion that SSBN bases would be exempt. At the same time, the proposed new SSN-21 attack submarine and the renewed interest in forward mining might increase the capability of the United States to exact attrition of Soviet SSBNs in protected seas, although the analysis of search and detection in Soviet patrol areas casts doubt on the potential effectiveness of the SSN-21 in that role. Finally, forces suitable for the second phase of a counterforce attack—a rapid, massive strike on land-based weapons and command centers—are being built and deployed: the Trident II missile, the MX missile, and the Pershing II missile. Thus, the assumption that a damage-limiting or disarming attack can be conducted *only* in the form of a rapid strike against both land- and submarine-based strategic forces is false.

Strategic ASW and War Termination

With the developments in counterforce capability, a war will confront the Soviet leadership with these choices: whether to escalate the war to the use of tactical nuclear weapons, whether to ignore the threat to SSBNs, whether to launch strategic weapons under attack on SSBNs, or whether to back down and either try to defend the bastions or stop fighting. Only by assuming that under pressure Soviet leaders will back down can there be a case for attempting the attrition phase of a damage-limiting or disarming attack.

The US Navy, in its official statement of the maritime strategy, has made this assumption and supports it with the following arguments:

> The Soviets place great weight on the nuclear correlation of forces, even during the time before nuclear weapons have been used. Maritime forces can

> influence that correlation, both by destroying Soviet ballistic missile submarines and by improving our own nuclear posture, through the deployment of carriers and Tomahawk platforms around the periphery of the Soviet Union. Some argue that such steps will lead to immediate escalation, but escalation solely as a result of actions at sea seems improbable, given the Soviet land orientation. Escalation in response to maritime pressure serves no useful purpose for the Soviets since their reserve forces would be degraded and the United States' retaliatory posture would be enhanced. Neither we nor the Soviets can rule out the possibility that escalation will occur, but aggressive use of maritime power can make escalation a less attractive option to the Soviets with the passing of every day.
>
> The real issue, however, is not how the Maritime Strategy is influenced by nuclear weapons, but the reverse: how maritime power can alter the nuclear equation. As our maritime campaign progresses, and as the nuclear option becomes less attractive, prolonging the war also becomes unattractive, since the Soviets cannot decouple Europe from the United States and the risk of escalation is always present. Maritime forces thus provide strong pressure for war termination that can come from nowhere else.[30]

Admiral Watkins's arguments contain four important assumptions. The first, is that the Soviet leadership will not be driven to escalation *solely* by events at sea. It is their emphasis on the conduct of warfare on land and on land-based nuclear systems that will make them unwilling to escalate in response to sea-based counterforce attacks from US attack submarines. The second, is that the Soviet leadership will respond to the "correlation of forces" in such a way that the faster the United States sinks Soviet SSBNs, the less likely the Soviets would be to escalate. In addition, the more sea-launched theater nuclear weapons the United States moves into range, the lower the ratio of Soviet to US theater weapons, and the less likely that the Soviets would escalate. The third assumption is that the Navy can put unique pressures on the Soviet Union to stop fighting a war by sinking SSBNs, and deploying some more theater nuclear weapons into range. The risk of escalation and the coupling between the United States and Europe are independent of naval operations. The fourth is that the US threat is feasible and not excessively costly.

The first assumption may be a reasonable one, especially in light of the development of mobile land-based missiles and submarine-launched nuclear cruise missiles that may carry some of the burden of the strategic reserve mission. Why escalate if the essential mission of the SSBN is preserved by land-based systems? *To the extent that this argument has any weight, however, it undercuts the major military rationale behind the forward SSN strategy, which is to make the Soviet leadership so concerned about their SSBNs that it would use its Navy to defend them.* The Soviet leadership, given its "land orientation," might well prefer to have Soviet attack submarines interfering with NATO resupply and amphibious operations rather than protecting SSBNs.

The second assumption rests on the balance of two opposing risks. On one hand, the longer the Soviet Union waits, the more it loses, so it is implicitly assumed that there is some kind of "use it or lose it" decision to be made. On the other hand, the jump into the use of nuclear weapons is the clearest "firebreak" in the jungle of escalation. The Soviet Union must choose between losing some SSBNs and taking a clearly defined step that definitely moves both sides toward general nuclear war. This is true whether the Soviet Union considers the use of tactical nuclear weapons or SLBMs. The latter choice probably drives both sides directly into major nuclear war. In the balance, it seems that a definite move into nuclear war is a high price to pay for losing a few more SSBNs, which might well not be needed anyway if the war does *not* go nuclear.

We cannot know for certain, however, that the option of escalation, either tactical or even strategic, will seem so obviously counterproductive to the Soviet decision maker in a confused, rapidly changing environment. What is the risk of widespread escalation from the use of several "small" Soviet nuclear ASW weapons against US attack submarines in the Soviet Arctic? What would the US response be to such a specific use of nuclear weapons, in such a specific geographic area far from the US homeland or allied countries, against a specific US threat? This use of nuclear weapons may be perceived as being sufficiently far from the "brink" of general nuclear war that it could be considered if it yielded some military advantage. In shallow Arctic waters, tactical nuclear ASW depth charges, rather than torpedoes, may yield the higher probability of destroying a US SSN, and may contribute more to defending SSBNs.

The third assumption is that the US Navy has a unique role to play by shifting the nuclear balance through sinking SSBNs and through moving SLCMs and aircraft into range of potential nuclear targets near the coasts of the USSR. These combat operations are assumed to be useful because, according to Adm. Watkins, they "provide strong pressure for war termination that can come from nowhere else." It is certainly true that some kind of pressure would be applied, but the key question remains: How strong would it be? The movement of carriers and SLCMs into the northern Norwegian Sea does increase the number of nuclear weapons, but only in that theater of military operations. It is not clear what impact a change in the nuclear correlation of forces in one theater might have on the overall conduct of a war. It is difficult to know even the broad outlines of Soviet doctrine. Given our lack of understanding, the forward strategic ASW policy derives at most weak support from the argument that it will contribute to war termination. Finally, it is true that the forward strategy contributes the unique element of strategic counterforce capability early in a conventional war,[31] but the credibility of that threat is inversely related to the risk to the US attack submarines operating far forward in Soviet waters, and that risk is great.

The US Navy puts a premium on terminating war "without the use of nuclear weapons" as an end result of naval strategy. According to Admiral

Watkins, "A large portion of this derives from our maritime strategy which says there is an opportunity to provide the President with a nonnuclear option to put at risk their nuclear force. Whether you use it, under what circumstances, how you play that game, all is another matter."[32] For the SSBN attrition campaign to play such a large role in forcing the Soviet Union to turn around and stop fighting a global war all along its periphery, the Soviet Union would have to consider SSBN attrition on the same level as the war aims that were keeping it in World War III to begin with.

It is very difficult to imagine how the Soviet leadership would weigh continental war objectives against the attrition to SSBNs, and at what point the Soviet Union would give up its continental war aims as a result of the loss of those weapons. It would appear that SSBN attrition would have to be quite dramatic in order to have a strong impact in the face of the Soviet Union's more immediate war aims. For the technical reasons advanced in earlier chapters, it appears more likely that the attrition process against defended Soviet SSBNs would be slow.

In summary, it appears that the Navy is probably correct in assuming that the destruction of Soviet SSBNs will probably not generate immediate pressures for the launch of sea-based strategic weapons. It is much less clear how the Soviet political leadership would feel about the use of tactical nuclear ASW weapons against US attack submarines in the Arctic to help preserve the "nuclear correlation of forces." A key question is how the United States would respond to such a use of nuclear weapons.

The amount of pressure that would be applied to the Soviet Union for war termination as a result of the loss of SSBNs appears to be small. Paradoxically, in the course of a conventional war, the Soviet leadership may calculate that tying down US forces in the hunt for Soviet SSBNs may shift the *conventional* correlation of forces in their favor, perhaps reducing their incentive to terminate hostilities.

Notes

1. William W. Kaufmann, *The 1985 Defense Budget* (Washington, DC: Brookings Institution, 1984), p. 9.
2. David Holloway, *The Soviet Union and the Arms Race*, 2d ed. (New Haven: Yale University Press, 1984), p. 54.
3. Desmond Ball, *Targeting for Strategic Deterrence*, Adelphi Paper 185 (London: International Institute for Strategic Studies, 1983), p. 35.
4. Ibid., pp. 18–19.
5. Ibid., p. 32.
6. James R. Schlesinger, *Department of Defense Annual Report for Fiscal Year 1975*, (Washington, DC: US Government Printing Office, 1974), p. 37.
7. Ibid., p. 44.

8. Leon Sloss and Marc Dean Millot, "US Nuclear Strategy in Evolution," *Strategic Review*, Winter 1984, p. 24.

9. Harold Brown, *Development of Defense Annual Report for Fiscal Year 1981* (Washington, DC: US Government Printing Office, 1980), p. 65.

10. In 1961, Chief of Naval Operations Arleigh Burke asserted that "when we get a good number of ballistic missiles, all fixed targets in known locations in the enemy territory can be initially struck with ballistic missiles" (SASC, FY 1962, p. 954). In a bid to acquire that initial strike role for Polaris, Burke testified that "the reliability and accuracy of this missile is better, we believe, than any other ballistic missile in existence" (SAC, FY 1962, p. 118).

11. Trident I CEP has been reported as 300 meters over a 4,000 nm course (William M. Arkin, "Sleight of Hand with Trident II," *Bulletin of the Atomic Scientists* 40:10, December 1984, pp. 5–6). With its 100-kiloton warhead, the weapon has a theoretical single-shot kill probability of 0.9 against a target hardened to 160 pounds per square inch (psi). The Minuteman Mk 12A warhead has the same kill probability against a 400 psi target.

12. James M. McConnell, *The Interacting Evolution of Soviet and American Military Doctrine*, Center for Naval Analyses, Alexandria, Va, Memo 8-1313.00, September 1980, pp. 27–28.

13. Chief of Naval Operations Arleigh Burke, HASC, FY 1962, p. 896.

14. Michael MccGwire, "Contingency Plans for World War," in *The Soviet and Other Communist Navies—A View from the Mid-1980s*, ed. James L. George (Annapolis, Md.: Naval Institute Press, 1986), pp. 61–81.

15. Robert Herrick, *The SSBN Protection Mission: Final Report* (Arlington, Va.: Ketron Inc., July 1979), p. 10.

16. Office of the Chief of Naval Operations, *Understanding Soviet Naval Developments*, 3d ed. (Washington, DC: US Government Printing Office, 1978), p. 17.

17. *Report of the Undersea Warfare Advisory Panel to the Subcommittee on Military Applications of the Joint Committee on Atomic Energy*, August 1958, Sen. Henry M. Jackson, Chairman, Military Applications Subcommittee.

18. Capt. Dominic A. Paolucci, USN, Ret., "The Development of Navy Offensive and Defensive Systems," *US Naval Institute Proceedings* 96, May 1970, pp. 205–223.

19. Director of Defense Research and Engineering Study Group, *A Summary Study of Strategic Offensive and Defensive Forces of the US and USSR*, 8 September 1964, p. 79.

20. HAC, FY 1964, part 1, p. 212.

21. Robert McNamara, *Annual Report of the Secretary of Defense*, SAC, FY 1965, p. 70, declassifed secret version.

22. Robert McNamara, *Annual Report of the Secretary of Defense*, SAC, FY 1968, p. 120, declassified secret version.

23. Paul Nitze, HAC, FY 1968, part 2, p. 858.

24. *Nuclear Submarines of Advanced Design*, Hearings before the Joint Committee on Atomic Energy, part 2 (Washington, DC: U.S. Government Printing Office, 25 July 1968), pp. 172, 201.

25. SASC, Preparedness Investigation Subcommittee, "Status of US Strategic Power," April–May 1968, p. 325.

26. Gerald A. Cann, Principal Deputy Assistant Secretary of the Navy (Research, Engineering, and Systems), HAC, FY 1985, part 5, p. 204.

27. HAC, FY 1985, part 2, p. 701.

28. Rear Adm. Daniel L. Cooper, HAC, FY 1985, part 6, p. 111.

29. Chapter 2 deals with the technical aspects of ASW.

30. Adm. James D. Watkins, "The Maritime Strategy," a special supplement to the US Naval Institute *Proceedings,* January 1986, p. 14. A powerful critique of the maritime strategy in the context of deterrence of war in central Europe can be found in John J. Mearsheimer, "A Strategic Misstep: The Maritime Strategy and Deterrence in Europe," *International Security* 11, Fall 1986, pp. 3–57.

31. There is the possibility that other nonnuclear systems could be developed that can attack strategic systems, but they do not represent current capabilities. *See* Carl H. Builder, *The Prospects and Implications of Non-nuclear Means for Strategic Conflict,* Adelphi Paper No. 200 (London: International Institute for Strategic Studies, 1985).

32. Adm. James D. Watkins, SASC, FY 1985, part 8, p. 3893.

6
Summary and Recommendations

The conclusions that have been reached can be categorized as pertaining primarily to technology or primarily to policy and strategy.

Technology

Prospects for Advances in Acoustic Detection and Quieting

In passive sonar, there are three basic means of improving detection capability: (1) reducing the range from the target to the sensor; (2) reducing the signal-to-noise ratio that can be detected at a given probability of false alarm by signal processing; and (3) increasing the gain of the sensor array. Available evidence strongly suggests that the spatial and temporal variability in the ocean imposes fundamental limits on signal processing and array gain associated with long-range passive detection, particularly in shallow water.

In the area of passive acoustic detection, the ability to detect a small signal in noise under test conditions will probably not increase by very much. The ability of US passive sonar to discriminate submarine sounds from ambient noise is probably unable to keep up with the trend in Soviet submarine quieting. As a result, the range at which US submarines are likely to detect Soviet submarines of the same vintage is likely to decrease. The SOSUS fixed acoustic array system, besides being vulnerable at the beginning of a conflict, is probably becoming less effective in peacetime tracking. The maximum coverage of the SOSUS array off the North Cape of Norway into the Barents Sea is probably less than 75 miles against recent classes of Soviet SSBNs.

An example of the kind of limits acoustic technology is facing is passive acoustic localization using the Wide Aperture Array (WAA). The WAA functions best if the signal processing is broadband, and since the dominant sounds of a quiet submarine are narrowband, the WAA must accept a lower signal-to-noise ratio, and therefore a lower detection range. The gains in search and engagement rate afforded by the rapid localization capability are partially offset by the loss of detection range. Thus, this advance may supplement rather than replace the "bearing-only" passive array. Other improvements are likely to come in the areas of tracking many targets simultaneously, and connecting sensors with weapon systems to shorten the time between locating the target and launching a weapon.

The trends in Soviet attack submarine quieting can be divided into two periods: the first, from the early 1960s to the mid-1970s, is characterized by a relatively slow rate of quieting of 7–10 dB every 10 years; the second, from the late 1970s to the mid-1980s, is characterized by an increased rate of quieting to 15–20 dB every 10 years.

The trends in US submarine (attack and ballistic missile) quieting appear to show early rapid quieting, on the order of 20 dB, during the early 1960s, and a sustained quieting rate averaging 12–18 dB every 10 years since then.

During the period between 1960 and 1975, the US attack submarine fleet enjoyed a large and steadily growing margin of advantage in quieting over Soviet attack submarines. Vintage 1958 US attack submarines might have been nearly equaled by Soviet attack submarines built in the mid-1970s, and US submarines built in the mid-1970s might be as much as 35 dB quieter than Soviet submarines built 15 years before. On a fleetwide average (comparing each vessel on one side with all of those on the other side), however, the US advantage in quieting among nuclear submarines was on the order of 20–25 dB throughout this period.

Because of the large number of submarines in the fleets and their longevity, the fleetwide average acoustic advantage changes relatively slowly. As a result, a rapid change in the radiated sound levels of submarines will not be reflected significantly in the fleetwide average for a period of at least 10 years, assuming a fairly constant rate of shipbuilding. However, the introduction of even a few substantially quieter submarines can open the possibility of executing specific missions that require greater stealth, albeit on a limited scale. Such missions might include various kinds of intelligence gathering near the adversary's ports.

It is also important to note that by 1980, the United States had been heavily emphasizing quieting in nuclear submarine design for over 20 years, and it is to be expected that diminishing returns to investment in quieting would be observed.

During the period between the late 1970s and the mid-1980s, the rate of Soviet submarine quieting seems to be accelerating. This quieting trend is probably not due to any kind of technical breakthrough, but rather to an increased emphasis on quieting—an emphasis that the United States has maintained from the beginning. The recent rates of quieting in Soviet attack submarines do not appear to be much different from the rates of US submarine quieting in the early 1960s.

As Soviet submarines become quieter, the ability to distinguish SSBNs from SSNs in combat decreases, probably substantially. Vice Adm. Lee Baggett, Jr., USN, Director of Naval Warfare said:

> I think [requiring US attack submarines to distinguish between Soviet SSBNs and SSNs] would be a stricture that would be very, very onerous from the standpoint of ASW. I don't believe you could make a distinction in a combat environment—even prehostilities—with certainty to distinguish between SSBNs and attack submarines. It is going to get worse in the future with the quieting trends that I depicted, regardless of our capabilities. I think you would not be able, with any certainty, to make that distinction.[1]

A rule of engagement that would require US attack submarines to determine the class of a hostile sonar contact would force the US vessel to give up some of its precious—and diminishing—detection range advantage.

Acoustic surveillance technology will have to shift to distributed systems of many inexpensive sensors and to arrays that can be implanted covertly in hostile waters and under ice. These will require thin, inexpensive data cables. The Ariadne program is an attempt to develop such cables and links. Arctic submarine warfare also places a higher premium on sensor and communications buoys that can penetrate ice. Several US programs are addressing these problems.

Prospects for Nonacoustic Detection

The nonacoustic observables associated with the passage of a submarine through the sea can be sensed at different spatial scales. At small scales, on the order of a meter or less, the presence of a submarine would be indicated by a local change in whatever is being measured. At scales on the order of hundreds or thousands of meters, the presence of the submarine would be indicated by a change in the variable being measured, but that change might occur in a coherent pattern.

The ability to detect coherent patterns of change in the sea permits the detection of a smaller signal than does the detection of small-scale variations.

Nonacoustic means of areawide detection and surveillance, if they should appear, would appear slowly and probably in the form of large satellite programs. For the Soviet Union, the dual imperative of defending its own SSBNs and preventing the United States from using its SSBNs means that nonacoustic ASW developments would probably be used for both. To the extent that it is easier to implement a smaller-scale system to detect US attack submarines near Soviet home waters, it is probable that a Soviet development in nonacoustic ASW would be applied to those areas initially.

The space-based nonacoustic detection technologies examined in this study fall into two groups: those that seem to be infeasible in the face of basic analysis of the physical principles involved, and those for which the physical principles do not appear to be well enough understood to judge their feasibility. In all cases it must be assumed that the submarine is operating so as to minimize its detectability. In particular it is assumed that the submarine operates at a depth in excess of 100 meters, at a speed of less than 5 knots.

Space-based nonacoustic means that appear infeasible at midlatitudes are: the detection of surface disturbances caused directly by the submarine (the Bernoulli hump and Kelvin waves); the detection of reflected or absorbed laser light; the detection of bioluminescent wakes; detection of changes in surface water temperature caused by the submarine; and detection of changes in the earth's magnetic field. At Arctic latitudes, the detection of a warm, buoyant plume from a very slow-moving submarine may be possible, even through thin ice. This may have an impact on Soviet SSBN operations.

It is much more difficult to assess the potential for the detection of submarine-related effects using synthetic aperture radar or radiometers that measure the emissivity of the surface. The processes governing the generation and propagation of internal waves by submarines do not appear to be well understood. Nor do the processes that couple the energy of internal waves to the ocean's surface in the form of surface currents. The influence of surface currents on the capillary waves and on surface organic and oil films that affect the surface emissivity might be detected by spaceborne synthetic aperture radar or radiometers, respectively. The conclusion of this study is that there is not sufficient data to rule out the possibility of such a means of detection.

Soviet SSBN Vulnerability

Soviet submarines are partially vulnerable to US ASW forces, and both sides know it. A recent major study of Soviet perceptions of US ASW concluded "the gross US/NATO ASW capability . . . is perceived as a formidable threat, one against which the mission-completion capabilities of Soviet submarines, including the SSBNs, are anything but assured."[2] The main threat to these submarines is no longer SOSUS, but the Los Angeles class attack submarines with torpedoes and mines operating in forward areas in the opening minutes of a war. The same study found that "the Soviets perceive the losses by enemy SSNs and mines as unlikely to grow to an unacceptable level in view of the Soviet Navy's already great and steadily improving capabilities for protecting its SSBNs in home waters."[3] In order to protect them, the Soviet Navy must forgo opportunities to move antisubmarine ships, aircraft, and most importantly, attack submarines out of home waters. This may interfere with the ability of the Soviet Navy to interdict US sea lines of communications.

For the next 10 years, the only plausible form of attacking Soviet SSBNs at sea, other than mining their harbors, is to put US attack submarines off their ports, wait for the SSBNs, trail them at least a short distance out to sea and then sink them with torpedoes. Establishing a trail on all Soviet SSBNs requires many more attack submarines than the United States is likely to acquire in the near future, although the United States has long maintained the ability to trail some SSBNs for periods of time. Even with assumptions very favorable to the trailing submarines, well over 100 SSN trailers would be needed for that single mission. US trailing attempts may be defeated by accompanying SSBNs to sea with quiet SSNs or SSs, by using mobile submarine simulators to send the trailer off after a false target, and by other countermeasures.

The US forward strategy contains an important signal that can trigger the Soviet defensive effort: the worldwide surge of US attack submarines. This will indicate to the Soviet Union that the United States believes war is imminent. With that information, the Soviet Navy can initiate a surge of its own SSNs as well as its SSBNs. In addition, the Soviet Union can begin to mine many of the geographic chokepoints through which US submarines would have to pass. Within these minefields, or others, the Soviet Navy could install moored submarine simulators set to emit characteristic submarine sounds at random intervals, and lure US SSNs into the mines.

Crucial factors in the ability of US submarines to catch Soviet SSBNs leaving port is the timing of the movement of US SSNs into Soviet home waters, the timing of a surge of US SSNs, and on the Soviet side, the timing of their surge of SSNs, ASW forces, mining forces, and SSBNs. All of these will be influenced by and will influence the perceptions on each side of when the actual fighting will begin. The outcome of an SSBN attrition campaign is very sensitive to whether Soviet SSBNs can surge within a few days of the US SSN surge, in order to disperse.

If Soviet SSBNs have had reasonable warning of hostilities and have gone to sea with defensive forces, the ability of US attack submarines to destroy most of them within a few weeks is not great. Over a longer period of time, the attrition to Soviet SSBNs would continue, but so would the attrition to US attack submarines. With fewer vessels, the frequency of engagement between US submarines and Soviet SSBNs would probably decline, but the frequency at which the US vessels encounter Soviet mines might increase, as the Soviet Navy has a chance to emplace them. Soviet mines, diesel-electric submarines, quieter attack submarines, ASW aircraft, command and control links, and surveillance would exact a heavy toll on US attack submarines in the Soviet arctic seas and in the Sea of Okhotsk. The advantage that US submarines and their superior crews have over Soviet submarines in one-on-one combat in the open ocean would be severely eroded in Soviet home waters.

US SSBN Vulnerability

US Ohio class ballistic missile submarines have probably become quiet enough to be undetectable using passive acoustic detection beyond a few miles. The threat of covert trailing by Soviet submarines is probably very small. Lafayette class SSBNs probably retain a major acoustic advantage over most Soviet attack submarines. The most recent class of Soviet attack submarine, the Akula, may be approaching the Lafayette in quietness, but this does not yield a reliable covert trailing capability. In the first place, there are very few Soviet attack submarines of the most recent vintage, and in the second place, the Soviet vessels lack a significant acoustic advantage over the US SSBNs.

The US can continue to rely on SSBNs as a survivable basing mode for weapons of minimum deterrence well into the next century. The only conceivable immediate threat to US missile submarines is the possibility of Soviet attack submarines' trailing them at close range using active sonar. If the Soviet Union were to attempt this on a large scale in peacetime, however, it would be a major political gamble and would be plausible only in extreme circumstances. Hostile submarines using active sonar near the US coast would be easily detected by US attack submarines and coastal surveillance systems operating in conjunction with US ASW aircraft. The intruding submarines could then be distracted or attacked, depending on the circumstances.

The threat to smaller SSBN fleets from Soviet ASW may be greater than it is in the United States. Although such threats have not been considered in this study, they would be crucially important to British, French, or Chinese perceptions of their nuclear retaliatory capability. French submarines are considered somewhat louder and therefore more vulnerable than the same vintage of US SSBNs, and the small fleet would be more vulnerable as a whole to covert trailing by the most recent classes of Soviet attack submarines.

Strategic ASW Policy

Given the degree to which the US maritime strategy is formulated around Western assumptions regarding Soviet strategy, it is crucial that those assumptions be scrutinized. The Western theory that the Soviet general purpose Navy would be primarily dedicated to defending SSBNs in specific geographic areas is based largely on Soviet writings that tend to be very general and theoretical. One expert on the Soviet Navy, Jan Breemer, has pointed out that the body of Soviet statements upon which this bastion theory is based do not explicitly acknowledge such a strategy.[4] In addition, knowledge of peacetime deployment practices provides circumstantial evidence in support of a bastion theory, but also provides contradictory data. Why is the Typhoon so large if it is to be defended in a bastion, for example? It is important to consider the sensitivity of US military objectives to these assumptions.

The two most prominent military objectives that the Navy has identified with the submarine warfare component of the maritime strategy are 1) tying up Soviet attack submarines and other naval forces in the defense of SSBNs, and 2) applying pressure on the Soviet leadership to terminate hostilities through significant attrition of their SSBN fleet. A fundamental distinction between these objectives is that the first requires an implicit threat to Soviet SSBNs, but does not necessarily require a large-scale campaign against them. The second objective requires that the US commit a substantial portion of its attack submarine fleet and perhaps other forces in an attack on the Soviet forces that would be tied up defending the SSBNs.

The United States poses a sufficiently potent threat to Soviet SSBNs to force the Soviet Navy to actively defend them, and the first objective is probably attainable. Sending a few attack submarines into Soviet waters to attack SSBNs would reinforce the sense of threat to the Soviet leadership, and they may even overestimate the threat to their SSBNs. It is very unlikely that a small-scale campaign would result in the rapid destruction of SSBNs, however.

The second objective, that of applying significant pressure for war termination, is not likely to be met. A large-scale campaign against Soviet SSBNs and defensive forces may cause a significant attrition to the SSBN fleet, but the attrition may well not be very rapid. If a US-Soviet conflict were protracted, the importance of cutting US supplies to Europe would increase for the Soviet Union and the importance of defending them would increase for the US. The Soviet leadership may weigh the tying-up of a large portion of US attack submarines in the Arctic campaign as a benefit, partially undermining the US objective in attacking the SSBNs to begin with.

The Navy's maritime strategy is a guide for using forces in the present and for buying forces for the future. As Soviet SSBNs become less reliant on "bastion"-type defenses and rely more on stealth, and as the Soviet Union diversifies its strategic reserve forces into land-based mobile missiles, both of the objectives mentioned above become less attainable. This is particularly important with regard to the first objective, because it would lead to an expanded flexibility in thc Soviet naval mission structure. This added flexibility, coupled with the increasing sophistication and stealth of Soviet attack submarines, would complicate the US ASW problem at many levels.

Technical improvements in US attack submarines, particularly those envisioned for the SSN-21, are not likely to change the assessment that Soviet SSBNs will be more capable of secure, independent patrols in the future. The SSN-21 will be more secure in Soviet home waters than will the SSN-688-class submarines, but by the time that a large fleet of SSN-21s is built, the future generations of Soviet SSBNs will probably be less detectable to the SSN-21 than the current generations of Soviet SSBNs are to the SSN-688s. In addition, decoys and mines will be no less confusing and dangerous to the commander of an SSN-21.

Soviet Responses to US Strategic ASW: The Risk of Escalation

There are many ways in which a strategic ASW campaign might induce the Soviet Union to use nuclear weapons. Four such nuclear responses can be considered representative: (1) launching SLBMs against targets in the United States, (2) attacking US aircraft carriers, (3) attacking US attack submarines in home waters using nuclear depth charges, and (4) using nuclear weapons to mask acoustically the sounds of Soviet SSBNs.

Launching missiles against the United States in the course of a conventional war as a response to attacks on Soviet SSBNs seems very unlikely. The SSBNs seem to be at least partially secure and will eventually be supplemented in the reserve role by land-based mobile missiles. The very purpose of the strategic reserve forces is to deter major attacks throughout a conflict, and the Soviet leadership would have to assume that the launch of submarine missiles would invite such attacks. The behavior of a Soviet submarine captain in an SSBN under attack is more difficult to predict, since for him and his crew the war is over.

Soviet nuclear attacks on aircraft carriers *as a response to the loss of SSBNs* also seems very unlikely, even though such attacks would not involve direct nuclear attacks on US territory and are less escalatory than SLBM attacks. There is probably little direct threat to SSBNs at sea from carrier-based ASW aircraft, and those in port might be protected in tunnels. Nor is there likely to be a significant threat from other ASW forces defended by carriers, such as destroyers or Orion P-3 aircraft. Aircraft carriers would already be very important targets because of their abilities to strike surface ships, land targets, and aircraft in areas not dominated by Soviet forces, and the carriers' potential contribution to strategic ASW probably would not significantly increase their value as targets. In addition, the relative effectiveness of nuclear weapons against carriers may be decreasing as quieting improvements in Soviet attack submarines increases their chances of attacking carriers from under the sea using conventional weapons.

The use of nuclear ASW weapons against US attack submarines in Soviet home waters seems to be a plausible nuclear response to the strategic ASW campaign. Such a use would be near the Soviet Union, far from the United States or allies, and a direct response to the US campaign against Soviet SSBNs. There are strong tactical arguments for using nuclear weapons against a quiet US submarine detected in those waters, since conventional torpedoes are probably less reliable in shallow, ice-covered waters. Because the US forces would be operating in forward areas, a US tactical nuclear counterresponse might be relatively close to the Soviet Union or another country. The Soviet leadership would have to take this into consideration.

It has been suggested that the Soviet Navy could detonate a series of nuclear weapons near its home waters to create so much noise at the low frequencies used by passive sonars for long-range detection that US sensors would be useless. There are several reasons why this peculiar kind of nuclear use seems unlikely. To use nuclear weapons at all is a major political step, and it would seem that the Soviet Union would not use them unless there seemed to be major advantage to doing so. Underwater nuclear explosions create high levels of low-frequency noise, but as the analysis shows, in shallow water low-frequency noise is attenuated rapidly and probably would not last longer than a few hours. Noise is also directional, so that while an explosion creates a great deal of noise in one direction, there may be relatively little in another. Since, in general, US submarines will approach Soviet SSBNs from seaward, such explosions would have to occur between the SSNs and the SSBNs, near Soviet sea-lanes.

The decision to use nuclear weapons in response to a threat to or attack on Soviet SSBNs would assume a grave risk, even if it were to take place in Soviet home waters. The highest political leaders would probably wish to have the final say on any such decision, since it would have to be weighed in the broadest military and political context.[5] Given the available options for nonnuclear defense of the Soviet SSBN fleet, the *early* use of tactical nuclear ASW weapons appears unlikely. As the Soviet Union develops more survivable basing modes on land, nuclear defense of SSBNs may become still less likely early in a conflict. However, over the course of an extended war, tactical nuclear ASW would be a plausible route into nuclear use as a result of forward submarine operations.

The Soviet Union is in the process of moving about a fourth of its strategic warheads onto land-based mobile missiles by the mid-1990s. As survivable systems, these will relieve some of the pressure on the Soviet Union to use its naval forces to defend its SSBNs. In addition, the Soviet Union is building 6–8 quiet attack submarines per year. This, together with the fact that US attack submarines are losing their tactical advantage in the Arctic, means that by the mid-1990s, it probably will be less likely that the Soviet Navy will respond in the initial phase of a war by withdrawing most of its submarines and ASW forces to protect SSBNs: the Soviet Navy will have begun the process of decoupling the mission of maintaining a strategic reserve from the mission of competing with the US Navy for control of the seas. This process can begin as a limited bastion defense strategy and evolve into an SSBN deployment strategy that involves large surges of SSBNs into the shallow continental seas north of the Soviet Union, selective mining of entrances to the Arctic, and a greater reliance on stealth for SSBN security. The US Navy is already prepared for and expecting some movement of Soviet general purpose naval forces far beyond home waters. According to Adm. Watkins,

> We are ready to deal with what we would call the leakage of Soviet forces southward in the North Atlantic. Frankly, that is somewhat simpler in some ways for us to handle rather than in their own backyard where they have heavy and massive air cover and the like. We are ready to go both ways, but we can match their strategy as it changes.[6]

Nuclear Arms Control and ASW

There are some useful perspectives to keep in mind when considering alternatives for submarine policy:

1. **Strategic ASW policy is highly secretive:** Policies are discussed very little in public, and ASW capabilities are among the most closely guarded secrets.
2. **Submarines and strategic ASW operations are covert:** The unique quality of the submarine as a naval vessel is its undetectability, which also makes agreements relating to submarine movements extremely difficult to monitor.
3. **Strategic ASW is seen as a means of gaining conventional leverage:** In order to obtain the benefits of this leverage early in a wartime situation, the US Navy must create at least the illusion of threat. By publicly renouncing this threat, the US Navy gives up a perceived advantage.

Limits on deployments of fixed sensors outside home waters are largely irrelevant, because fixed sensors no longer contribute very much to strategic ASW. Limits on submarine sonars would be impossible to verify without close inspection of the submarines themselves. In any case, sonar systems are vital in every other attack submarine mission, including defensive ones.

Imposing ratios on the number of each side's SSNs to the other's SSBNs might be in the interest of the United States, which will be facing a decline in its technical advantage over the Soviet SSN fleet. The current ratio of US SSNs to Soviet SSBNs is 1.5:1, and of Victor and later classes of Soviet SSNs (not including cruise missile submarines [SSGNs]) to US SSBNs is 1.4:1. Including modern Soviet SSGNs built primarily for antiship attack, the ratio increases to 1.9:1. At these ratios, neither side would have the ability to trail simultaneously all the opponent's SSBNs. However, as SSNs improve, their ASW capability increases, and a constant ratio would not ensure a constant measure of SSBN security over a long period. In addition, a reduction in SSBNs on one side would trigger a reduction in SSNs on the other.

Monitoring an SSBN sanctuary would be extremely difficult without the political will to overcome technical obstacles through cooperation. Requiring attack submarines at sea to account for themselves on a random basis may help in peacetime but would certainly break down in time of crisis, which would be the only time it would be perceived as highly relevant. It might discourage peacetime trailing and intelligence gathering, making wartime operations against SSBNs more difficult for the lack of data and experience. A peacetime sanctuary would also alleviate fears that the adversary was planting surveillance arrays covertly. However, given the increasingly short detection ranges that are likely to be realized, the large number of arrays that would be needed, the difficulty of collecting data in wartime, and the difficulty of using the data for real-time targeting, the "covert-array" threat is probably small relative to the SSN threat.

A US declaratory (and real) commitment to treating Soviet SSBN patrol areas as sanctuaries would yield tactical advantages to the Soviet Navy without significantly decreasing the risk of nuclear escalation. A threat to Soviet SSBNs exists regardless of whether they are attacked in a major campaign, and this threat will tie up some Soviet forces. In the absence of such a threat, the Soviet nuclear attack submarine fleet in particular would appear to gain a significant degree of flexibility in terms of how it might be used in a conflict. Even some of the strongest critics of the Navy's maritime strategy accept that this is useful leverage and that "the Navy should always maintain a powerful attack submarine force with offensive potential."[7] On the other hand, potential for widespread nuclear escalation generated specifically by a threat to Soviet SSBNs does not appear to be significant, for the reasons given earlier. In addition, there would be little for the United States to gain by a sanctuary agreement for its secure SSBN force.

In the future, the United States may have greater incentives to consider some kind of SSBN sanctuaries. Soviet SSBNs will be quieter, more difficult to detect even by new US acoustic sensors, and therefore easier to defend. The fraction of the Soviet Navy tied down in their defense may well decrease, and the US incentive for posing even a threat to Soviet SSBNs would therefore decrease. At the same time, it is possible in the United States that future developments in nonacoustic submarine detection might raise some questions about the survivability of its own SSBN fleet. A sanctuary agreement which included some limitations on particular types of satellite operations might increase US SSBN security. The United States would then have less to lose and more to gain from a sanctuary agreement.

Recommendations

There is no wartime experience of undersea combat between submarine fleets, and there are very large uncertainties in any prediction of outcomes of such combat. In addition, more than most aspects of modern conventional warfare, strategic ASW is an immediate step into a gray area between nonnuclear and nuclear warfighting. Plans and policies should account for the likelihood that these two factors would be extremely important to political decision makers during a conflict.

1. The Congress should request a study of the command and control issues inherent in forward strategic ASW operations. In all phases of a conflict with the Soviet Union, and particularly in the early stages, the National Command Authorities would be best served by a set of military options which contained possibilities for crisis management and control along with warfighting effectiveness. One of the declared objectives of the forward ASW strategy is war termination, and it is very possible that at some point in a conflict, *cessation* of strategic ASW operations may serve that purpose more effectively than their continuation. It is therefore entirely consistent with the maritime strategy to seek an optimum balance between warfighting capability and crisis management capability, rather than to simply maximize the former at the expense of the latter.

   Since strategic ASW is a gray area between conventional and nuclear war, US political leaders would undoubtedly feel the need for a substantial amount of control over forward ASW. Consideration of the technical and operational constraints of submarine warfare near the Soviet Union have raised some of the following questions: How many submarines would have to be sent forward early in a conflict? How much time would there be for the National Command Authorities to consider such a decision? How well could US attack submarines communicate with national authorities? Is it practical for attack submarine commanders to be required to distinguish SSBNs from other submarines? Is it plausible that US attack submarines in Soviet waters would be targets for tactical nuclear ASW weapons? What might the US response be to such a use of nuclear weapons? These are some of the questions that might be addressed by a Congressional study.
2. The United States should place little reliance on strategic ASW as a means toward war termination, both as a current strategy and as a strategy for procuring future forces. For a marginal investment in US strategic ASW capability, the marginal cost of countermeasures is lower, probably by a considerable amount.
3. The United States should expect that, in the near term, some Soviet naval forces will be tied down defending SSBNs during a conflict. Those defensive

forces should include a sizable portion of the quietest, most capable Soviet attack submarines.

4. The United States should not plan future forces (that is, those operating well into the next century) on the assumption that a strategic threat from the next generation of ASW forces will tie up a significant portion of Soviet naval forces, particularly quiet SSNs. Future forces will have to deal more directly with Soviet submarines rather than relying on indirect "leverage."
5. Development of a new class of attack submarine for the next century should continue. Detailed recommendations regarding the design and specifications of such a submarine are beyond the scope of this study. In general terms, designs should not weight the far forward ASW mission heavily, although it should be recognized that the technical requirements associated with most submarine missions overlap to a large extent.
6. The US Navy will probably have to rely more on distributed systems of acoustic and nonacoustic sensors to direct attack submarines and other ASW platforms to increasingly stealthy Soviet submarines outside Soviet home waters. Airborne and fixed systems are likely to contribute more to US abilities to defend sea-lanes than they would to the strategic ASW capabilities of the United States.

Notes

1. SASC, FY 1986, part 8, p. 4399.
2. Robert W. Herrick, Lois S. Lembo, and Mark A. Hainline, *Soviet Perceptions of US Antisubmarine Warfare Capabilities,* vol. 1 (Arlington, Va.: Ketron, Inc., 1981), p. S-28.
3. Ibid., p. S-27.
4. Jan S. Breemer, "The Soviet Navy's SSBN Bastions: Evidence, Inference, and Alternative Scenarios," *Journal of the Royal United Services Institute,* March 1985, pp. 18–26.
5. Cmdr. James J. Tritten, *Declaratory Policy for the Strategic Employment of the Soviet Navy,* RAND/P-7005 (Santa Monica: Rand Corporation, 1984), p. 210.
6. Adm. James D. Watkins, SASC, FY 1986, part 2, p. 989.
7. John J. Mearsheimer, "A Strategic Misstep: The Maritime Strategy and Deterrence In Europe," *International Security* 11, Fall 1986, p. 43.

Appendixes

Appendix 1
The Design of Submarines

As an example of an attack submarine, consider the layout of the Los Angeles (SSN-688) class submarine shown in figure A1–1.[1] The exterior hull of the submarine is essentially a cylinder with elliptical ends. Modern submarines generally have a blunt, rounded bow, the smooth lines of a body that is symmetric around its center axis, and a gently tapering stern. The ratio of length to diameter is between 9 and 12. Deviations in the hull away from the symmetric body may reflect constraints imposed by internal systems. In the case of the Soviet Delta III submarine, the length of the SS-N-18 missile (47 feet) makes it necessary to extend the missile housing on the deck to cover them. This is a design feature of Soviet Delta II, Delta I, and Yankee SSBNs also.[2] US designs deviate less from the shape of a symmetric cigar-shape, because US SLBMs are short enough to fit within a cylindrical hull (the Trident I missile is only 34 feet long).

The pressure hull of a submarine is in general not the same as the external hull, although US submarines do have a single hull over most of their length. The nuclear power plant, the propulsion systems, sonar electronics, parts of the weapon systems, and most other systems are inside the pressure hull, while the main ballast system, towed and fixed sonar hydrophones, and the propeller shaft are located between the pressure hull and the outer hull.[3] Soviet submarines are generally double-hulled over most of their length.

The buoyancy of a submarine is controlled by ballast tanks, which can be flooded with water or filled with pressurized air. Main ballast tanks in the bow and stern maintain the overall buoyancy as well as the trim angle of the submarine. In order to dive, valves on top of the tanks are opened, allowing water to enter openings on the bottom of the tanks. Particular trim adjustments may be desirable for certain maneuvers, to compensate for compartment flooding, or to compensate for weapon launch. There may be ballast tanks amidships, as in the SSN-637 class and older classes.[4] Some high-pressure trim tanks are located inside the pressure hull.

Large circular "wing" bulkheads connect the pressure hull to the outer hull, and the rest of the space between the hulls is filled with external pressure

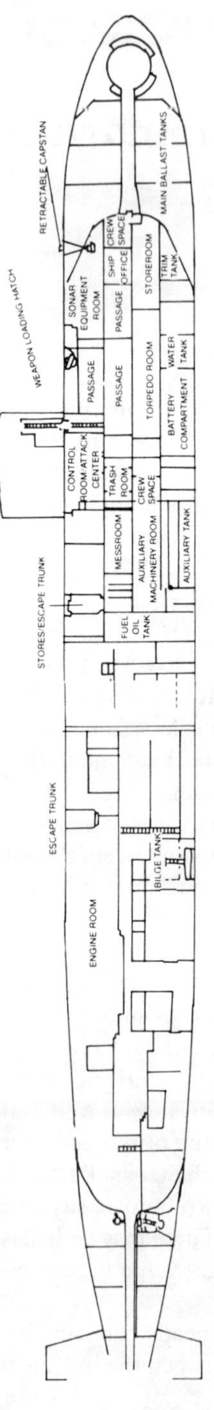

Figure A1–1. Interior layout of a US Los Angeles (SSN-688) class submarine.

Source: from *Submarine Design and Development* by Norman Friedman. Copyright © 1984, Norman Friedman.

hull frames, hydrophones, and water.[5] The hydrophones are placed inside the sound-transparent outer hull, in order to isolate them better from turbulent pressure fluctuations and noise generated in the fluid layer immediately adjacent to the hull. The submarine sail is a flooded nonpressure structure and may contain hydrophone arrays. Many older Soviet submarines have visible hydrophone windows on the bow and sail, which are made of sound transparent material. The entire bow of modern US submarines is made of acoustically transparent material, which need only support the hydrodynamic forces induced by the submarine's movement and no hydrostatic force.

The Trident missile submarine uses a glass-reinforced plastic sonar dome, and earlier US missile and attack submarine classes used mild steel domes. Glass-reinforced plastic improves the sonar performance and minimizes the hydrodynamic noise entering the sonar.[6]

The static pressure on freely flooding compartments is the same on the outside as on the inside, and there is no net collapsing force. As the vessel moves, the dynamic pressure of the water pushing against the structure can create a net collapsing force. Retractable towed array sonars can be stored in the stern flooded area or in sleeves along the hull.

Pressure Hull and Outer Hull

The two-hull construction of military submarines arises from the fact that the optimal shape for a deep-diving pressure hull and the optimal shape for a high-speed hull are different. The outer hull does not support the external water pressure; since the space between the pressure hull and the outer hull is flooded, the outer hull provides a hydrodynamically smooth surface over the main ballast tanks, hull-mounted hydrophone arrays, and external frames. US submarines have two hulls in the bow, stern, and over the missile tubes, and a single hull along the rest of the ship.

Soviet SSBNs appear to have a purely double-hull construction, which is revealed by rows of flooding holes along the side of the hull that allow water to drain from the space between the hulls. It has been suggested that the Typhoon has a separation of 6 feet between the outer and inner hulls around the sides.[7] A double hull would protect the inner pressure hull from the initial high, peak overpressure of an underwater explosion, although it would not attenuate the aftershocks associated with such an explosion.[8] The advantage of a double hull is that less space is used for structural support in the cramped pressure hull, and that "considerable eccentricity or non-circularity of the hull can be tolerated," whereas single hulls must be very nearly circular to withstand high pressures.[9] This would allow a greater margin for error in Soviet construction techniques without sacrificing submarine safety at great depths.

The pressure hull is a combination of cylindrical, conical, and ellipsoidal sections,[10] whose cross sections are perfect circles for maximum strength. The pressure hull is partly supported by closely spaced ring frames, which are essentially circular "I" beams that ring it. These frames are internal in the sections that have only one hull and are external in those sections where the pressure hull is surrounded by an outer hull.[11] The rest of the structural support comes from bulkheads, which are flat plates that extend across the entire cross section of the pressure hull. The end caps are either hemispheres or ellipsoids.

There are three basic failure modes of submarine hulls under pressure: accordianlike *buckling* of the hull between ring frames, without deformation of the circular frames; *general collapse* of the hull and ring frames between bulkheads, resulting in a general deformation of the hull; and *yielding* of the pressure hull metal itself due to deformation under compression, particularly at points where stress is concentrated, such as joints and welds.[12]

Yielding is caused by the failure of the hull metal at a particular point to stand high stress, whereas buckling and general collapse are failures of the hull/frame structure. Ring frames are usually spaced 0.1–0.2 hull diameters apart to prevent buckling, and bulkheads are spaced at 1–2 diameters to prevent general collapse. In areas where bulkheads are impractical, an external wing bulkhead can be used for support if there is a double hull. If there is only a single hull, an extra heavy ring frame can be used internally.[13]

The yield strength of the hull material is, by design, the main factor that determines the static pressure strength of a US submarine hull.[14] This means that if a metal with a higher yield strength is used to build a thinner hull, the submarine will be lighter and can still withstand the same pressure. "Indeed, several comparative designs have been prepared all of which show that the pressure hull weights are essentially inversely proportional to yield strengths" at a given maximum design pressure.[15] Table A1–1 shows that about 40 percent of the submarine's weight is in the hull, so that using a stronger hull material can significantly reduce the overall weight of the submarine. So, for example, a shift from HY-80 (which is now used) to HY-100 steel would result in a 10 percent reduction in total weight for a given design depth. A lighter submarine can have a smaller volume and still float, and therefore the surface area of the submarine can be smaller. A submarine with a lower surface area has less water resistance and will have a higher speed for a given propulsion power. There are of course other trade-offs to be made in reducing the volume, such as reduced space for quieting measures, electronic systems, crew spaces, and weapons.

Diving Depth

The diving depth of a military submarine depends on the structural strength of:

1. The pressure hull and frames
2. The fittings that penetrate the pressure hull, such as
    a. The main propulsion seawater cooling loop

Table A1–1
Weight loads for early nuclear submarines as percent of normal displacement

Item	*Percent of Normal Displacement* SSN	SSBN
Hull (shell, frames, & bulkheads)	38–44	40–45
Systems & installed equipment	16–24	18–24
Machinery	22–28	15–17
Arms & ammunition	3–4	10–12
Fuel, feedwater, & lubrication	3–4	2.5–3
Crew, provisions, & fresh water	2.5–3	1–2
Reserve displacement	2–2.5	2–2.5
Solid ballast	1.5–2.5	2–2.5

Source: V. M. Bukalov and A. A. Narusbayev, *Atomic-powered Submarine Design* (Leningrad: Shipbuilding Publishing House, 1964), p. 52.

Weight and volume distribution by function in modern US submarines

	Los Angeles (SSN–688)		*Ohio (SSBN–726)*	
Function	*Weight*	*Volume*	*Weight*	*Volume*
Weapons and weapons control	4	10	14	36
Command and control	4	10	6	20
Machinery (reactor, engines, and so forth)	33	50	22	28
Configuration (hull, tanks, ballast, and so forth)	59	30	58	16

Source: Capt. Harry A. Jackson, USN, notes from MIT summer course on submarine design, 1974.

b. The emergency reactor seawater cooling loop
c. The brine overboard discharge
d. The garbage disposal
e. The seawater ballasting (some trimming tanks are inside the pressure hull, though most are outside)
f. The escape hatches
g. The propeller shaft and periscope shaft
h. The torpedo tubes

3. The strength of internal systems that are at ambient pressure, such as the seawater condenser in the propulsion system[16]

The weakest of these sets the depth limit, and so rational submarine design provides that all of the mechanical systems will fail at the same depth. This is called the limiting, or design depth. Uncertainties in the strengths of materials and assembly procedures set the maximum operating depth to which the commander is allowed to take the submarine, which is somewhat less than the design depth. In the US Navy, the operating depth has been two-thirds of the design depth.[17] There is an element of subjectivity in this operating-to-limiting-depth ratio, since it depends upon the degree of risk that one is willing to accept under uncertainty. Comparisons of "maximum depth" between different submarines must account for possible differences in this safety factor.[18] The limiting depth for the German Type XXI (which provided a model for the Soviet Whiskey class) was 891 feet (270 meters), while the limiting depth of the Thresher and Ethan Allen classes are between 1,485 and 1,780 feet (450 and 540 meters).[19] According to some reports the "diving depth" of the Soviet Alfa class SSN is over 1,980 feet (600 meters).[20]

Another safety criterion that determines the allowable operating depth of a submarine is how deep the submarine goes at full speed at an angle of 30 degrees down in a specified time. For example, if a control accident occurs and the submarine dives at an angle of 30 degrees at a speed of 30 knots, in 30 seconds the submarine will have gone 760 feet deeper. If 30 seconds is the time that can be allotted for a crew to react and correct the error, then one option is to set the maximum operating depth at 760 feet shallower than the design depth. According to one Navy spokesman, "the judgment of the Navy [is] that the proper depth for a submarine is that which permits you to operate the submarine safely. And the safety issue is related to how fast you can go at a certain depth without having a stern plane failure driving the submarine below its maximum allowed depth."[21]

Submarine Lifetime and Shock Resistance

There is no single parameter that firmly limits a submarine's lifetime, and it is common for major ships of all kinds to receive "service life extensions" of a number of years over their original lifetimes. Older submarines might be retired from particular missions because their design, radiated noise levels, and installed systems are no longer suitable for performing them, while being retained for roles that may not require the most modern equipment. Questions have arisen from time to time regarding lifetime limits imposed by hull corrosion and metal fatigue. However, these factors are generally not limiting ones.

The pressure hull is subject to corrosion, which slowly decreases its thickness. On early classes of US submarines the hull thickness was designed at about 5 centimeters for pressure and was then increased by 3.2 millimeters to account for corrosion over 20 years.[22] Since this is only a small percent of the total thickness of the hull, and since modern anticorrosive coatings may have lessened the rate of decrease in thickness, this effect need not limit the lifetime of submarines. Submarine hull materials are generally required to have only a "modest resistance to corrosion."[23]

The hull and frames are fatigued by the normal compression-decompression cycle of submarine operations. It has been estimated that nuclear submarines may undergo 10,000 to 30,000 such cycles in the course of a 20-year lifetime.[24] The design criteria for older nuclear submarines was 25,000 cycles.[25] This corresponds to an average of about 7 depth cycles per day for a 50 percent at-sea rate over 20 years. Newer submarines with longer lifetimes may be designed for more cycles. Cycling causes metal fatigue and decreases the yield strength of the hull, particularly in spots where geometric discontinuities in the hull cause stress concentrations. Stress concentrations may occur at welds, fittings, and joints between sections. The intense heat of welding also induces local stresses in metal.

The lifetime of a submarine hull is determined by the integrity of the weakest portions, which is influenced by the number of cycles the submarine has undergone. Fatigue weakening of submarine hulls may be spotted long before the hull actually springs a leak due to the fact that the metal does 80–100 percent of its cracking just on the surface before actually breaking all the way through.[26] By checking the likely areas of stress concentration with X rays and other means, the ship repair yards can detect a potential failure long before it becomes dangerous. Older submarines with weakened hulls can be used beyond their design life by restricting the maximum operating depth, restricting the number of depth cycles, or by accepting a higher risk.

For example, the service life of the 31 Lafayette-class SSBNs was "extended" to 30 years from their previous service life of 25 years after the Navy conducted "an extensive hull monitoring program [and] concluded hull corrosion and fatigue are not limiting considerations for extending the life of Poseidon SSBNs." In addition, the Navy is "able to repair defects during each examination at very low cost."[27]

The most common material used for submarine pressure hulls is high-carbon steel alloyed with manganese and other metals to increase its yield strength. High-yield (HY) steel is rated by its yield strength in pounds per square inch (psi): HY-80 is rated at 80,000–100,000 psi, and HY-100 is rated at 100,000–120,000 psi. Titanium can also be used as a pressure hull material and has the advantages of being about half as dense (4.5 gm/cm^3) as steel and nonmagnetic. Pure titanium is not particularly strong, but in alloys of 6–8 percent aluminum and a few percent other elements, it rivals HY-150 steel for strength.[28] The disadvantages of titanium alloys are: inadequate resistance to brittle fracture, especially at the lower temperatures found in the deep ocean; the requirement of special gas welding techniques; and high cost, which in 1979 was estimated at $33,000 per ton in the United States for 2-inch-thick plates. Most of the world reserves of titanium are in India (65.9 percent), Brazil (21.7 percent), Australia (5.4 percent), and the United States (3.5 percent). Titanium reserves in the Soviet Union are negligible, although the Soviet Union is one of the world's largest producers of this metal.[29] The Soviet Union built its first titanium-hulled submarine, the *Alfa,* in the late 1960s. The prototype submarine was tested and then scrapped in the early 1970s,[30] but entered slow series production in the late 1970s.

A related aspect of design that is crucial for military submarines is their resistance to shock. The two ways in which shock can destroy a submarine are by rupturing the hull or by disrupting the internal systems, disabling the vessel without necessarily breaking the hull. Relatively small charges are designed to do the former, and large explosions such as bottom mines and nuclear weapons, the latter.[31] Since the 1950s, the shock reliability of internal components and systems in the US submarines have not improved as quickly as the shock strength of the hull. If vital controls are damaged by the shock of a weapon, the submarine could exceed crush depth. Equipment damage that forces the submarine to surface is almost as dangerous during a war. In some tests, submarines have been "disabled" by explosions much smaller than those required to split the hull or even to cause serious injury to crewmen.[32] In these early tests, the main causes of submarine failure in explosions were: installation errors, including installation of new components that had not been shock tested, inadequate clearance between components, and loose objects flying into equipment and causing damage. In extrapolating to conditions on modern submarines, great care must be used in interpreting these results.

Reactor, Steam, and Cooling Systems

Between one-third and one-half of the volume within the pressure hull of a nuclear submarine is taken up by the power plant, cooling systems, turbines, generators, power systems, and auxiliary equipment.[33] Of this, the reactor core itself is only a small portion, while the radiation shielding, cooling systems, and high-pressure machinery associated with the reactor add a great deal of weight to the system. Figure A1–2 is a schematic diagram of the main power plant and propulsion system of a nuclear submarine. Marine reactors are usually pressurized water reactors, so called because the primary coolant is light water in the liquid phase under pressure. Heat generated in the reactor core is picked up by the pressurized water, which circulates through the core and reactor vessel. The water (light water is used in these reactors) is also the neutron moderator. This water is pressurized to over 2,000 psi[34] in order to keep it from boiling in the core, which reaches 315 degrees centigrade.[35] The water enters the steam generator, where it gives up some of its heat to the water of the secondary system without mixing. The secondary system water is converted to steam since it is at less than 1,000 psi. The primary water is pumped out of the steam generator, and some is shunted through a demineralizing filter (not shown), which removes most of the radioactive minerals that have accumulated in the water. These filters are changed several times per year, and since they are

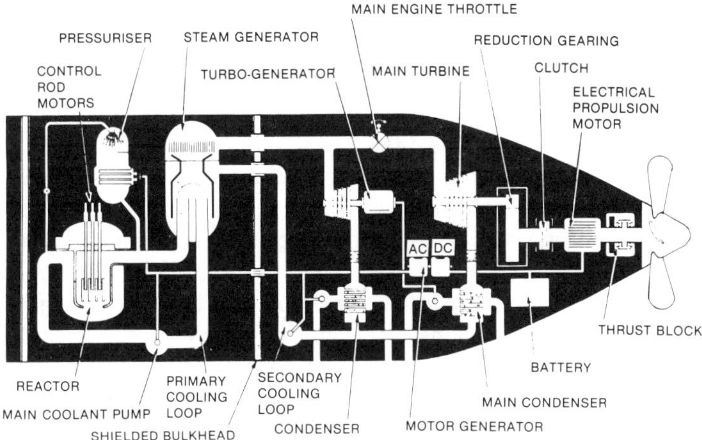

Figure A1–2. Schematic diagram of a typical current naval pressurized water reactor and propulsion system.

Source: from *Submarine Design and Development* by Norman Friedman. Copyright © 1984, Norman Friedman.

radioactive, they are buried when the submarine arrives at port.[36] The primary water reenters the reactor vessel to begin the cycle once more.

The Ohio-class missile submarine is reported to have a quiet natural circulating cooling loop, which makes use of the density change in the circulating water to generate a self-driving flow.[37] It is important to quiet or eliminate the main circulating pumps since they must connect to the reactor via high-pressure piping, which causes a noise path to the reactor vessel and then to the hull.

The secondary system is a steam–water cycle. Heated steam from the steam generator drives one or more turbines and converts some of its heat to work by expanding. In order to return this steam to liquid water, it is passed through a seawater condenser. Water from the condenser is then pumped back to the heat exchanger where it is converted to steam again.

In the seawater cooling loop, cold water is drawn from the sea, pumped through the condenser where it is heated but does not boil, and then returned to the sea. In order to prevent the cooling seawater from boiling, it must be passed through the condenser at a sufficiently high-volume flow rate to carry off the heat without its reaching the boiling point. Since the seawater cooling loop is at ambient pressure, everything in contact with it must be secure against the pressure of design depth, including the condenser tube bundle, pumps, and pipe joints. If two reactors are used, they may share the primary heat exchanger or have separate heat exchangers and share a turbine, or have a completely redundant set of machinery and cooling systems.[38]

Molten sodium metal can also be used as the primary coolant of a submarine nuclear reactor. Sodium is less of a moderator of fast neutrons than water, but its main advantages are its excellent heat transfer characteristics and its high boiling point, which means that sodium-cooled reactors can be compact and maintain the primary cooling loop at near atmospheric pressures, eliminating the need for some high-pressure equipment. Sodium reacts explosively with water and becomes radioactive in the core, which necessitates the use of an intermediary liquid metal cooling loop to circulate a less chemically active and radioactive potassium-sodium coolant. The second US nuclear submarine, the *Seawolf,* used a sodium-cooled, beryllium-moderated reactor. The *Seawolf* was launched in 1955 with the sodium reactor and about a year later developed steam leaks, which were probably caused by the corrosive sodium.[39] Between the danger of explosion, the extra shielding required by the radioactive sodium, the cost of beryllium, the problems involved in keeping the sodium molten when the reactor is shut down, and above all, the desire to get many nuclear submarines to sea quickly, it was decided that the S5W and its variants would be given priority. By the end of 1961, 52 of them had been built.[40] Submarine reactors run on uranium enriched to a high percentage of uranium-235. This uranium used to go into US reactors in the form of rectangular slabs, or "sandwiches." The inner part of the sandwich was an alloy of enriched uranium and zirconium. This was completely surrounded by a cladding made of a zirconium alloy.[41] The fuel elements were held in cassettes that could be easily installed in the reactor core without the use of heavy lift equipment or even removing the cover of the reactor. The process of changing the fuel cassettes would require a few days or weeks,[42] but the additional shielding that must be removed along with the fuel requires opening the pressure hull, a very expensive and time-consuming process. Modern reactor fuel elements are in the form of rods.

The core life of submarine reactors typically extends 4–10 years but depends on the rate at which uranium-235 atoms undergo fission and the density of U-235 in the core. The fuel density is a function of the degree of enrichment, the mix of uranium in the fuel alloy. Modern reactor fuel is enriched to 97.3 percent U-235. Decreasing the power output of a reactor also increases the core life. The core life of the S5W reactor was between 4.5 and 6 years. The core lives of recently designed naval nuclear reactors is 10–13 years.[43]

Closely related to the problems of powering a nuclear submarine are the problems of making it quiet. At high speeds, the principal noise source is the propeller, and at lower speeds, it is rotational machinery in the propulsion plant: circulating pumps, propulsion turbines, turbo-generators, and reduction gears. The major design task is to eliminate vibration "short-circuits" leading from the machinery to the hull. A major step in isolating machinery vibration on US submarines was taken in the SSBN-608 class submarines (launched in

1960), which had their main machinery mounted on a "bed plate," or raft, which was itself acoustically isolated from the hull.[44] British submarines used the same system, only the raft in their first nuclear submarine, the *Valiant,* had to be locked into place—and therefore short-circuited to the hull—when high power was used. The follow-on Swiftsure class did not require this locking procedure.[45] Although strength problems were encountered in the fabrication of the machinery raft of the Swiftsure, since it had to carry the gears, turbines, condensers, and turbogenerators, in the end the submarine was quieter than it was designed to be.[46] Further improvements in the quieting of the vessel generally took the form of noise isolation, rather than quieting the machinery itself. Noise isolation mountings require more space but are generally the more cost-effective solution.[47]

Propeller noise is being reduced by a design that is new to US submarines and will be introduced into the SSN-21 class. The propulsor is a cross between a pump and a propeller, using a propeller that rotates slowly against a second stationary propellerlike "stator" within a duct. Recent British submarines and the US Mk 48 torpedo use this design, which is called a pump-jet.[48] Theoretically, a hydrodynamic jet is a less efficient generator of acoustic energy than a propeller, and by isolating the propeller within the pump-jet, some degree of quieting may be attained.[49] By isolating the propeller from the asymmetric hull wake, it may be possible to reduce the blade rate tonals induced by the fluctuating thrust.

Propulsion System

The propulsion system is all the machinery that converts the energy of steam generated by the reactor to propeller thrust. About 20 percent of the power from the reactor is delivered to the propeller shaft. The speed of the submarine is then determined by the balance between the propeller thrust and the resistance of the hull.

The resistance on the hull is broken down into a form drag component and a skin friction component. Form drag is caused by the difference in water pressure between bow and stern and is minimized by streamlining, but contributes only about 5 percent of the total resistance of a submarine-shaped body,[50] and will be neglected. Skin friction arises because the entire surface of the submarine must drag along a thin layer of turbulent water. The surface area of the submarine is the sum of the areas of the bare hull and the appendages (planes, rudders, and sail).[51] For simple calculations, the different components of surface resistance can be lumped into the following equation for the surface friction resistance force:

$$F = \frac{1}{2} \rho C_f U^2 A \tag{A1.1}$$

where ρ is the density of seawater, C_f is the surface friction coefficient for the submarine as a whole, U is the speed of the submarine, and A is the total surface area. Setting the maximum propulsive power equal to the resistance power yields an expression for the maximum speed of the submarine:

$$U = \left[\frac{550\eta P_s}{\frac{1}{2}\rho C_f A} \right]^{\frac{1}{3}} \tag{A1.2}$$

where the numerical factor of 550 is a unit conversion factor from foot-pounds per second to horsepower, P_s is the maximum propeller shaft horsepower, and η is the ratio of the power delivered to the water to the propeller shaft power, or the propeller efficiency. The latter is always less than unity, since some of the propeller power goes into generating noise, heat, and turbulence, which do not contribute to forward motion. The friction coefficient is a very weak function of submarine speed and length and is essentially constant. For modern military submarines at speeds from 25–40 knots, the value of the roughness coefficient C_f is about 0.002.[52] The variation of the roughness coefficient between hulls is only about 10 percent. The roughness of the hull may increase slightly with age between hull cleanings, thereby lowering the maximum speed of "dirty" hulls.[53]

The surface area of a submarine depends on its exact shape, but an approximate expression can be derived from available data on surface area versus gross dimensions. The ratio of length to diameter is a measure of the slenderness of the submarine. The relationship between length, L, diameter, D, and surface area is approximately

$$A = BLD \tag{A1.3}$$

The parameter B equals 2.8 for 1960s vintage submarines and is probably similar or slightly higher for modern submarines.[54] This coefficient approaches the value of 3.14 for slender cylindrical hulls and decreases for less slender hulls. The factor of 2.8 accounts for the surface area of the appendages as well as the bare hull.

The propulsive efficiency, η, depends on the propeller shape and the structure of the submarine wake. A single propeller on the axis of a body of revolution is the most efficient geometry for propulsion, and efficiency increases for larger propellers, with more blades, at lower turning speeds. US submarines are designed in this way, while many older Soviet submarines use a less efficient two-shaft design. The maximum possible propeller efficiency is about 0.9, while actual efficiencies are about 0.8 for single propellers, and 0.68 for two propellers.[55]

Taking these values and using equation A1.3 in equation A1.2 yields

$$U = K\left(\frac{P_s}{LD}\right)^{\frac{1}{3}} \tag{A1.4}$$

This equation relates the length (feet), diameter (feet), and shaft horsepower to maximum submerged speed (knots) of a single-propeller submarine.[56] The coefficient K is 25 for single-propeller submarines and 24 for double-propeller submarines. If the quantity in brackets is increased, by making the submarine smaller or more powerful or both, the speed is increased by only a small amount. For instance, a doubling of the term in brackets leads to only a 26 percent increase in speed. In order to get that small increase, a very large price must be paid in terms of space within the submarine for weapons and sensors, since more power generally involves a larger power plant. Higher speeds also increase the noise generated by the submarine, which simultaneously blinds its own sensors and makes it more detectable to the enemy.

Table A1-2 shows some calculations of the maximum speed of various US, British, and Soviet submarines using equation A1.4. The computed speeds show reasonable agreement with the quoted speeds from published data in

Table A1-2
Unclassified speed estimates and predicted speed from equation A1.4

Submarine	*Length (feet)*	*Diameter (feet)*	*No. of Shafts*	*Shaft Horsepower*	*Stated Speed (knots)*	*Predicted Speed from Equation (knots)*
Nuclear:						
Soviet						
Delta	492	36	2	30,000	24	29
Yankee	425	30	2	30,000	30	32
Hotel III	377	28	2	30,000	26	34
Alfa	260	29	1	40,000	42+	44
Victor	341	28	1	30,000	30	37
British						
Resolution	425	31	1	15,000	25	26
Swiftsure	272	30	1	15,000	30+	31
US						
Ohio	560	40	1	60,000		35
Los Angeles	360	33	1	35,000	30+	36
Skipjack	251	30	1	15,000	30+	31
Thresher	279	30	1	15,000+	30+	30
Diesel-Electric:						
Soviet						
Kilo	230	~26	~3	~6,000		24
Tango	302	27	3	6,000	16	22
Foxtrot	300	24	3	6,000	16	23

Jane's Fighting Ships, except for the Soviet diesel-electric submarines.[57] The Skipjack, which is one of the earliest SSNs in the US Navy, has 15,000 shaft horsepower (shp) and has a maximum speed of 31 knots according to equation A1.4. The newest Soviet Alfa class submarine has 40,000 shp, is smaller than the Skipjack, and, according to equation A1.4, can travel at 44 knots. Norman Polmar, in *Guide to the Soviet Navy,* rates the Alfa's power plant at only 24,000 shp, but this would not drive the submarine over 40 knots. Some people have pointed to this discrepancy as evidence that the Soviet Union is using special chemicals to decrease the roughness coefficient and the turbulent friction forces that slow the submarine. It is more likely to be due to inconsistencies in various intelligence estimates.[58]

The gear-turbine system is a transmission system that reduces the high-speed turbine shaft rotation to low-speed high-torque propeller shaft rotation. The efficiency of this system is high, but the reduction gears emit a strong, well-defined noise signature that may be transmitted through the hull to the water. Turbine-electric drive was developed to overcome this noise problem. The turbo-generator system drives a quiet electric motor, which in turn drives the propeller, and is used in only two US submarines. This is a less efficient system for converting reactor heat to propeller power than the gear-turbine system, but it is quieter. The reason nonnuclear submarines running on batteries are quieter than most nuclear submarines is because no coolant pumps, high-speed turbines, or high-speed gears are involved, only a motor and sometimes a simple reduction gear. Recently, however, noise isolation measures have reduced the noise output from the latest US submarines to levels which approach those of most battery-driven submarines.

Submarines that are powered primarily by diesel engines must use oxygen from the atmosphere when the engines are running. These submarines must therefore travel on the surface or at a shallow depth with a snorkel above the surface to take in oxygen and expel combustion fumes. The diesel-powered submarine is highly vulnerable to detection when running on its engines, since the engines generate loud tones, the snorkel can be detected visually or by radar, and the exhaust fumes can be detected by chemical "sniffers" on aircraft. The diesel-powered submarine can also be propelled completely submerged by a battery-driven electric motor. When running on batteries, the submarine is very quiet and very difficult to detect. However, the diesel engines must be running in order to recharge the batteries. Because the submarine becomes relatively detectable when running on diesels, the ratio of diesel running time to total running time is called the indiscretion rate.

The Soviet Union maintains a large fleet of these submarines, which are only very threatening to US submarines when they are running quietly on batteries and completely submerged. The rest of the time they become quite vulnerable. Using unclassified information about current technology, we can estimate how long a diesel-electric submarine can run on batteries.

The specific capacity of modern storage batteries on German submarines (which are taken as the model) is 23 watt-hours per pound of battery weight at a discharge rate of 100 hours.[59] At a discharge rate of 10 hours, the battery capacity is about 20 percent less.[60] About 20–25 percent of the surface displacement of modern submarines is battery weight.[61]

The power drain of the batteries during submerged operations depends on which systems are being used and for what fraction of the time they are being used. Typical power requirements for older US nuclear-powered submarines were 6 kilowatts (kW) for computers and 3 kW for navigation.[62] Power for the basic life support systems may draw on the order of 50 kW. The minimum power requirement of the submarine may be around 70 kW, and a more realistic figure for modern sophisticated submarines is 100 kW. However, propulsion for the submerged submarine can easily dominate power consumption from internal systems and limit battery-powered operations.

As an example consider the Soviet Tango class submarine, which is 300 feet long and 27 feet in diameter. The surface displacement of the Tango is 3,000 tons, so its battery weight is estimated to be 1.2×10^6 pounds. Using equation A1.4, the amount of power that is needed to drive the submarine at 5 knots is 73 shaft horsepower, or 55 kW. Assuming that the conversion of electrical power to propeller shaft power via electric motor is 85 percent efficient, 64 kW of battery power are needed to drive the submarine at 5 knots. By similar reasoning, 2,100 kW of electrical power are needed to drive the submarine at 16 knots. The total power load on the batteries at 5 knots is about 164 kW, and at 16 knots it is 2,200 kW. The total energy stored in the batteries is 2.7×10^7 watt-hours. Therefore, the Tango traveling at 5 knots can run on batteries for about 160 hours (about 6 days) and has a range of 800 nautical miles. A submarine traveling at 16 knots will drain the batteries in less than 10 hours and has a range of only 150 nautical miles.

Another measure of diesel-electric submarine performance is the fraction of time at which the submarine must operate its diesel engines to recharge its batteries, called the indiscretion rate. A reasonable limit on diesel power on submarines is 1.9 kilowatts per standard ton. Extrapolating somewhat from a study on Western submarines, it is estimated that for the Tango, the indiscretion rate at 3 knots is about 5 percent, at 5 knots it is 8 percent, at 10 knots it is 25 percent, and at 13 knots it is 50 percent. Thus, at the relatively modest speed of 13 knots, the diesel-electric submarine spends half its time as an acoustic sitting duck.[63] On the other hand, at the typical patrol speed of 5 knots, 90 percent of the time a diesel-electric submarine is quiet and effective.

Submarine Communications

The command and control requirements associated with missile submarines depend foremost on their place in plans for fighting nuclear wars. If policy dictates that SSBNs are part of warfighting at its most theoretically complex level, with multiple exchanges, rapid retargeting, and so forth, then the flow of information between the national command authorities and the submarine commander must be highly reliable and secure for all times and in the most disruptive of environments. If submarines are intended to provide a strategic reserve and simply survive throughout the course of a war, maintaining a force capable of annihilating the political and industrial structure of the opponent (which largely coincides with the population centers), then the command and control requirements are considerably less stringent.

During peacetime, US missile submarines on alert (within range of their targets) are required to receive continuous communications from fixed land-based very low frequency (VLF) transmitters, which are called Verdin.[64] VLF operates at 3–30 kilohertz[65] and transmits encrypted data at 67 words per minute on several channels.[66] The two primary land-based VLF transmitters are at Cutler, Maine, and at Harold E. Holt, on the Northwest Cape of Australia, and these two transmitters alone cover all of US SSBN operating areas.[67] Additional fixed VLF systems (as of 1979) are located in Annapolis, Maryland; Jim Creek, Washington; Luoluolei, Hawaii; and Yosomi, Japan.

The fixed VLF has a primary role in the National Command Authority's World Wide Military Command and Control System (WWMCCS) and is itself backed up by 21 low frequency secondary stations.[68] A third level of backup is provided by 24 high frequency radio transmitters, at least two of which simultaneously transmit the information broadcast over Verdin VLF stations.[69] Further levels of backup are provided by ultra-high frequency (UHF) satellite communications[70] and by the Clarinet Pilgrim, which is associated with the LORAN C navigation system.[71] Clarinet Pilgrim uses the LORAN transmissions as a carrier for submarine communications.

Missile submarines rarely transmit messages while on patrol in order to minimize the possibility of detection by way of antennae or signals. They receive information constantly while on alert and periodically while on modified alert (at sea but out of target range) via a floating wire antenna or a floating buoy. The floating buoy can be used at significantly greater depths than the floating wire but must be towed at a somewhat slower speed—at about 5 knots rather than 10 knots for the floating wire.[72] In fact, the towed buoy does not appear to inhibit the diving depth of the submarine much if at all.[73] However, submarine operators are reluctant to use the buoy because it has proved unreliable[74] and because the tow wire is easily severed, leaving the buoy to bob to the surface.[75] As one former SSBN commander pointed out, SSBNs generally patrol at depths compatible with the floating wire antenna in any case to permit rapid launch of their missiles, which must be fired from depths considerably shallower than the maximum depth of the submarine.[76]

The means of communicating with submarines is expected to change radically once war begins. The National Command Authorities or their successors are supposed to survive in airborne command posts, in particular the National Emergency Airborne Command Posts (NEACPs). These command aircraft are linked to airborne VLF transmitters directly, through relay aircraft, ground stations, satellites, and even the emergency rocket communication system (ERCS) on some Minuteman II ICBMs.[77] The airborne VLF transmitters are on aircraft called TACAMO, an acronym that stands for "TAke Charge And Move Out." During a war, it is expected that the land-based VLF and LF transmitters will be destroyed, and they are therefore relegated to a support role in the Joint Chiefs' wartime Minimum Essential Emergency Communication Network.[78]

TACAMO aircraft transmit VLF signals at a power of 200 kilowatts through a pair of wires, one 30,000 feet long that hangs downward, and one 4,000 feet long that trails behind the plane as it executes a slow continuous turn. The antenna configuration resulting from this maneuver generates a signal that efficiently penetrates seawater to depths of 30–40 feet.[79] These have maintained a continuous airborne alert in the Atlantic, and beginning in 1983, in the Pacific.[80]

The airborne command and control network for missile submarine communications is shown in figure A1–3. The wartime communication links are notably different for the Atlantic and the Pacific. The main link to the Atlantic TACAMO runs from NEACP through the airborne command post of the commander in chief of the Atlantic Fleet.[81] In the Pacific, communications run from NEACP, through relay aircraft called the Post Attack Command and Control System (PACCS), to the Strategic Air Command's Looking Glass airborne command center. From there, messages can be transmitted via LF to the CINC of the Pacific Fleet or to TACAMO directly.[82] If NEACP does not survive, an Air Force general in the "Looking Glass" aircraft can send launch orders to the airborne Fleet Commanders in Chief or to TACAMO directly.[83]

Within the submarine itself, it is technically possible for a few people to initiate the process leading to missile launch without receiving an outside order and code,[84] because there is no lock on the missile system that would require a release code from the highest authorities.[85] The Navy's arguments for maintaining a procedure that increases the probability of an unauthorized launch seem to center on the point that if some part of the communication or authorization system fails, then the missiles can still be launched, although official doctrine holds that they cannot be launched without orders from outside.[86]

According to the Navy, the procedure for receiving and validating a launch order is as follows. There are always two radiomen trained in receiving such messages—although usually only one is on duty at a time. If a message comes in, the radioman on duty alerts the officer of the deck (the officer in charge on that particular watch). The officer of the deck then alerts the commanding officer and alerts the entire ship to battle stations. Two officers must enter the radio room and validate the format and content of the message by checking a

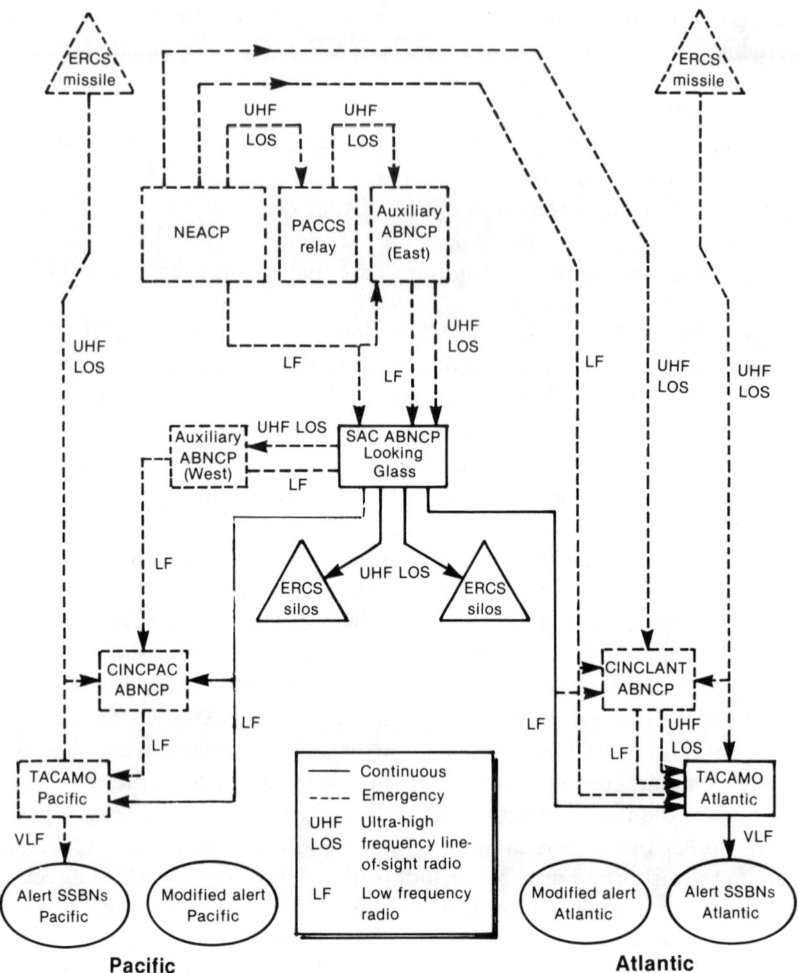

Figure A1–3. Airborne network for missile submarine communications.

Note: This figure shows the links to submerged submarines only, and excludes extremely low frequency communications. A submarine with antennas above the surface might receive high frequency and low frequency radio transmissions, sporadic ERCS transmissions, and possibly transmissions from satellites. Airborne command posts (ABNCP) of the Commanders-in-Chief of the Atlantic (CINCLANT) and Pacific (CINCPAC) may be able to transmit directly to submarines via LF radio.

Source: Bruce G. Blair, *Strategic Command and Control: Redefining the Nuclear Threat* (Washington, DC: Brookings Institution, 1985), adapted from fig. 6.1 (p. 193) and fig. 6.5 (p. 200).

received code word with codes stored in two locked safes.[87] "Then those people have to be convinced themselves, and then have to convince the commanding officer and the executive officer that the proper order has been received. That process is necessary for the appropriate keys and interlocks to be made available to be used by the rest of the crew."[88] At this point, the entire crew, which is at battle stations, is alerted that a message has been received from the National Command Authorities. This process involves validation of the launch order by as few as two or three people, although more people may examine the message, and still more must follow the orders generated by the commander in order to launch the weapons.[89] These additional people are not necessarily involved in the validation or decision-making process, however. For example, the weapons officer, launch officer, and executive officer must turn keys to enable the launch, but these are turned in response to a decision to launch and are not votes in the decision. These switches merely indicate that systems are functioning.[90]

Submarine airborne communication systems are being modernized with the procurement of the new E-6A TACAMO aircraft whose principal advantages over the current fleet of EC-130Q aircraft are greater speed (445 knots versus 335 knots) and longer endurance with refueling.[91] On the ground, the extremely low frequency (ELF) communication system is expected to supplement the Verdin ground-based VLF system and provide communications at greater depth and speed, but it is vulnerable to attack, so wartime control would still go through TACAMO.

An argument that has been put forward for ELF is that the missile submarines could operate at great depths and high speeds. While on patrol, however, SSBNs operate at low speeds to minimize their radiated noise levels as well as their disruption of the ocean in their efforts to remain undetectable, and in order to remain near missile-launch depth, submarine commanders prefer to operate at depths sufficiently shallow to use the floating wire. With a buoy, depths equivalent to the maximum ELF reception depth can be maintained,[92] and with a self-propelled buoy, such as the one suggested by Richard Garwin,[93] the submarine could be freed from its cable link to the buoy. In terms of SSBN security, the Navy does not consider the detection of floating wire antennae or towed buoys a serious threat now or into the foreseeable future.[94] The Navy makes its case for ELF mainly as a hedge against some unforeseen future ASW development that would threaten SSBNs in peacetime. The strongest case for ELF can be made in terms of communicating with attack submarines, but the Navy does not usually put forward that rationale.

Little is known about Soviet submarine communications, but their capabilities are "essentially equivalent" to those of the United States. According to a Navy space systems expert, "both use various elements of the frequency spectrum for redundant communication paths such as very low frequency transmitting sites, airborne emergency communications systems, satellites, high frequency transmitting sites, and extremely low frequency systems."[95] The Soviet Navy probably communicates with its submarines primarily via VLF, there being some 30 ground stations for that purpose in the Soviet Union, 5 of which have a power of 500 kilowatts.[96] It is likely that Soviet submarines use trailing wires and/or buoys similar to those of the United States.[97] Under the ice, however, submarines must avoid ridges that can extend a few tens of—and down to a hundred—feet below the underice surface. A portion of the floating wire antenna must be on the surface for "effective communications reception,"[98] so that the use of the floating wire antenna under the ice can be only partially effective. In order to use the trailing wire antenna, the submarine must stop, either to remain under an opening in the ice or else to permit the buoyancy of the wire to carry it around or between ice ridges that would otherwise keep it below its effective depth.[99] According to one officer, "[Received] signal strengths are also adversely affected . . . because the proximity of the magnetic North Pole creates ionic disturbances that upset the VLF signal. This latter phenomenon—known as polar-cap disturbance—can last for a week or more, though more commonly it persists for only a few days and is prevalent during periods of high sunspot activity."[100]

The towed buoy must remain within about 40 feet of the surface of the ice, which is typically 6–12 feet thick, so it must be towed at a depth of 20 feet below the underice surface. At these depths ridges could become a major obstacle to the continuous use of the towed buoy, particularly in light of the US Navy's problems with such devices in open water. One authority states that ice ridges are a "prohibitive hazard" to use of buoys.[101] Perhaps Soviet SSBN communication policy does not require constant contact, as in the United States, or these vessels must remain near gaps in the ice, although the latter tactic would be very restrictive in the winter, when fewer gaps exist. Gaps that are frozen over with a relatively thin sheet of new winter ice may be good places for the Soviet SSBNs to station themselves, since ridges would not be present, and the thin sheet of ice would hide the submarine's heated wake. During the winter, thin ice sheets several ship-lengths wide should be encountered about every 10 miles.[102] Transmission disturbances induced by solar activity would affect buoys as well as floating wire, so it would be essential for the Soviet SSBNs to maintain alternate communication channels at other frequencies.

Notes

1. *See* also Norman Polmar, "The US Navy: Attack Submarines," *US Naval Institute Proceedings,* January 1980, pp. 112, 113.

2. John Jordan, "Soviet Ballistic Missile Submarines," parts 1, 2, and 3, *Jane's Defence Weekly,* 21 January, 28 January, and 11 February 1984.

3. Capt. Harry A. Jackson, notes from MIT summer course on submarine design, 1974.

4. V. M. Bukalov and A. A. Narusbayev, *Atomic-powered Submarine Design* (Leningrad: Shipbuilding Publishing House, 1964), p. 110. Also, Jackson, notes.

5. John P. Comstock, *Principles of Naval Architecture* (New York: Society of Naval Architects and Marine Engineers, 1974), p. 206.

6. Department of the Navy supporting data for Fiscal Year 1987, budget estimates descriptive summaries, p. 256.

7. *Jane's Fighting Ships 1984/85,* p. 497. *See* also K. J. Moore, "Submarine Design and Development," review in *Submarine Review,* October 1984, pp. 96–103.

8. A. H. Keil, "The Response of Ships to Underwater Explosions," *SNAME Transactions* 69, 1961, p. 377.

9. Robert W. Peach, "Purpose and Method of Achieving a Deep Diving Submarine," *Naval Engineers Journal* 75, August 1963, pp. 575–584.

10. Capt. S. R. Heller, Ivo Fioriti, and John Vasta, "An Evaluation of HY-80 Steel as a Structural Material for Submarines—Part 1," *Naval Engineers Journal* 77, February 1965, pp. 29–44.

11. Comstock, *Principles of Naval Architecture,* p. 206.

12. Capt. E. S. Arentzen, USN, and Phillip Mandel, "Naval Architectural Aspects of Submarine Design," *SNAME Transactions* 68, 1961, pp. 622–692.

13. Comstock, *Principles of Naval Architecture,* p. 207.

14. Comdr. S. R. Heller, Jr., USN, "A Personal Philosophy of Structural Design of Submarine Pressure Hulls," *Naval Engineers Journal,* May 1962, pp. 223–233.

15. Capt. S. R. Heller, Jr., USN, Ivo Fioriti, and John Vasta, "An Evaluation of HY-80 Steel as a Structural Material for Submarines—Part 2," *Naval Engineers Journal* 77, April 1965, pp. 193–200.

16. George Sorkin, "Materials for Submarine Hard Sea Water Systems," *Naval Engineers Journal* 77, February 1965, pp. 93–100.

17. Heller, "A Personal Philosophy of Structural Design." Also, Norman Friedman, *Submarine Design and Development* (Annapolis: Naval Institute Press, 1984), p. 118.

18. E. L. Beach, "Smaller, Lighter, Faster, and Deeper Diving," *Defense Electronics* 11, August 1979, pp. 43–46, 111.

19. Bukalov and Narusbayev, *Atomic-powered Submarine Design,* p. 82.

20. *Jane's Fighting Ships 1982/83,* p. 468.

21. Gerald Cann, HASC, FY 1986, part 3, p. 233.

22. Bukalov and Narusbayev, *Atomic-powered Submarine Design,* p. 90, and Heller, "A Personal Philosophy of Structural Design."

23. Heller, Fioriti, and Vasta, "An Evaluation of HY-80 Steel—part 1," pp. 29–44.

24. Heller, "A Personal Philosophy of Structural Design." Only four World War II diesel-electric submarines exceeded 10,000 cycles in their lifetimes, which is assumed to be the lower limit. Heller uses a 100 percent at-sea rate with an average of 4 depth cycles per day to obtain the upper limit of 30,000 cycles.

25. Sorkin, "Materials for Submarine."

26. Heller, Fioriti, and Vasta, "An Evaluation of HY-80 Steel—part 2."

27. Letter from Assistant Secretary of the Navy David E. Mann to Richard Garwin, 28 March 1978, quoted by Garwin in a letter to the *Times* of London, 13 November 1982.

28. W. W. Minkler and N. Feige, "Titanium for Deep Submergence Vehicles," *Naval Engineers Journal* 77, May 1965, pp. 386–390.

29. "Titanium Ideal for Submarines," *Defense Electronics* 11, August 1979, p. 45.

30. *Jane's Fighting Ships 1982/83*, p. 468.

31. Keil, "The Response of Ships," discussion by O. H. Oakley, p. 400.

32. Keil, "The Response of Ships," discussion by Capt. W. D. Roseborough, USN, p. 404.

33. Jackson, course notes.

34. D. J. Pepper, "Experiences in the Design and Manufacture of Marine Nuclear Plant," *Naval Engineers Journal*, November 1962, pp. 741–748.

35. Joseph M. Dukert, *Nuclear Ships of the World* (New York: Coward, McCann, and Geoghegan, Inc., 1973), p. 33.

36. Ibid., p. 123.

37. Friedman, *Submarine Design*, p. 79.

38. The only US submarine with more than one reactor is the recently decommissioned Triton, which has two reactors, two propulsion turbines, and two propellers. US sources disagree about the number of reactors on Soviet submarines. The main annual sources, *Jane's Fighting Ships* and *Combat Fleets of the World*, by Jean Labayle Couhat, claim that most submarines contain two reactors, while Norman Polmar in his *Guide to the Soviet Navy* (Annapolis: Naval Institute Press, 1983) gives only one.

39. Bukalov and Narusbayev, *Atomic-powered Submarine Design*, p. 236.

40. Ibid.

41. Pepper, "Experiences in the Design and Manufacture." Also, Bukalov and Narusbayev, *Atomic-powered Submarine Design*, p. 245.

42. Bukalov and Narusbayev, *Atomic-powered Submarine Design*, p. 246.

43. HASC, DoE, FY 1979, p. 9.

44. Vice Adm. Charles H. Griffiths, Deputy Chief of Naval Operations, Submarine Warfare, HASC, FY 1981, part 3, p. 253. Also, Friedman, *Submarine Design*, p. 137.

45. Vice Adm. Sir T. Horlick, "Nuclear Submarine Propulsion in the RN," *Navy International* 87, March 1982, pp. 943–953.

46. Ibid.

47. Ibid.

48. Friedman, *Submarine Design*, p. 137.

49. Propeller noise is discussed more fully in appendix 6, "Radiated Sound from Submarines and Ambient Noise in the Ocean."

50. Comstock, *Principles of Naval Architecture*, p. 313.

51. The appendages have a total surface area of about 4,000 square feet and a roughness coefficient of about 0.006. From Jackson, course notes.

52. Comstock, *Principles of Naval Architecture*, p. 298.

53. F. Wellman, "A Survey of Hull and Propeller Roughness Data," *Naval Engineers Journal* 76, February 1964, pp. 101–103.

54. Bukalov and Narusbayev, *Atomic-powered Submarine Design*, p. 67, and *Jane's Fighting Ships 1984/85*.

55. Bukalov and Narusbayev, *Atomic-powered Submarine Design*, p. 70.

56. The conversion from feet per second to knots is 1 ft/sec = 0.59 knots.

57. It is possible that these sources use a similar equation to calculate the installed power from estimates of maximum speed, which would explain the "agreement."

58. George C. Wilson, "Reactors, Not Grease, Now Believed the Secret of Soviet Sub Speed," *Washington Post,* 5 July 1983, p. 3.

59. L. Nohse, "Conventional and Anaerobic Submarine Propulsion Systems," *Naval Forces* 3:4, 1982, pp. 56–63.

60. Norman E. Bagshaw, *Batteries on Ships* (New York: Wiley, 1982), table 3–1, p. 93.

61. Nohse, "Conventional and Anaerobic," pp. 56–63.

62. Bukalov and Narusbayev, *Atomic-powered Submarine Design,* p. 269.

63. K. M. Heggstad, "The Indiscretion Rate of Submarines," *Maritime Defence* 9:9, September 1984, pp. 340–342. The reader should note that the two analyses are inconsistent. Assuming a higher hotel load in the first analysis would bring it into the same range as the second.

64. General Accounting Office, *The Navy's Strategic Communications Systems* (unclassified version), PSAD-79-48A, May 1979, p. 2.

65. William M. Arkin and Richard Fieldhouse, "Nuclear Weapon Command, Control, and Communications," *SIPRI Yearbook 1984,* p. 458.

66. GAO, *The Navy's Strategic Communications Systems,* p. 33.

67. Ibid.

68. Ibid.

69. Ibid., p. 34.

70. Ibid.

71. William M. Arkin and Richard W. Fieldhouse, *Nuclear Battlefields* (Cambridge, Mass.: Ballinger, 1985), p. 80.

72. Robert Aldridge, *First Strike!* (Boston: South End Press, 1983), p. 238.

73. Richard Garwin made this point in Melissa Healy, "Blue-Green Scheme Leaves Navy Cold," *Defense Week,* 17 October 1983, p. 2.

74. GAO, *The Navy's Strategic Communications Systems,* p. 37.

75. Healy, "Blue-Green Scheme," p. 3.

76. Ibid.

77. GAO, *The Navy's Strategic Communications Systems,* p. 45, also Arkin and Fieldhouse, "Nuclear Weapon," pp. 466, 479.

78. GAO, *The Navy's Strategic Communications Systems,* p. 33.

79. David A. Boutacoff, "New TACAMO Aircraft Being Developed to Support Trident Missile Submarines," *Defense Electronics,* March 1985, pp. 108–111.

80. United States Arms Control and Disarmament Agency, *FY 1985 Arms Control Impact Statements* (Washington, DC: US Government Printing Office, March 1984), p. 12.

81. Bruce G. Blair, *Strategic Command and Control: Redefining the Nuclear Threat* (Washington DC: Brookings Institution, 1985), p. 199, figure on p. 200.

82. Ibid., p. 200.

83. Bruce G. Blair, "Solving the Command and Control Problem," *Arms Control Today* 15:1, January 1985, p. 8.

84. Arkin and Fieldhouse, "Nuclear Weapon," p. 468.

85. Laurence Meyer, "The Navy's Very Own Nuclear Button," *Washington Post National Weekly Edition,* 15 October 1984, pp. 6, 7.

86. Ibid.

87. Capt. James Bush, Center for Defense Information, Washington, DC, claimed

only two officers were required to validate. Personal Communication, 4 November 1986.

88. Commodore Theodore E. Lewin, Director, Strategic Submarine Division, SASC, FY 1986, part 7, p. 3858.

89. Ibid. Lewin suggests up to seven people must validate.

90. Bush, personal communication.

91. Boutacoff, "New TACAMO Aircraft," p. 109.

92. GAO, *The Navy's Strategic Communications Systems,* p. 17.

93. Richard Garwin, "Will Strategic Submarines Be Vulnerable?" *International Security* 8, Fall 1983, pp. 52–67.

94. Commodore Roger Bacon, Director, Strategic and Theater Nuclear Warfare Division, SASC, FY 1985, part 7, p. 3402.

95. SASC, FY 1986, part 7, p. 4313.

96. Capt. W. J. Ruhe, USN, Ret., "Soviet Submarine C^3," *Signal,* December 1984. Also, *see* Arkin and Fieldhouse, "Nuclear Weapon," p. 491.

97. Ruhe, "Soviet Submarine."

98. GAO, *The Navy's Strategic Communications Systems,* p. 36.

99. Capt. T. M. Le Marchand, RN, "Under Ice Operations," *Navy War College Review* 38, May–June 1985, p. 25.

100. Ibid.

101. Ibid.

102. *See* appendix 8 for more information about the Arctic ice cover.

Appendix 2
ASW Forces of the United States and the Soviet Union

Ballistic Missile Submarines

The targets of strategic antisubmarine warfare are the nuclear and conventionally powered missile submarines (SSBNs and SSBs). Soviet SSBN basing is shown in table A2–1, with the submarine-launched ballistic missile (SLBM) warhead count. Most Delta and Typhoon class SSBNs are in the Arctic, carrying about 80 percent of the long-range SS-N-8, SS-N-18, SS-N-20, and SS-N-23 warheads. These Northern Fleet SSBNs can target most of the United States from within the Barents Sea. The remaining 20 percent of the long-range SLBMs are on Pacific Fleet SSBNs and can reach the western continental United States from the protected waters of the Sea of Okhotsk and the northwest Pacific Ocean. According to table A2–1, the proportion of Delta and Typhoon submarines in the Northern Fleet is only about 70 percent, or 60 percent using DoD figures. The Yankee SSBNs with 1,600-nm-range SS-N-6 missiles can target NATO countries from the Barents Sea, and from the western Pacific they can reach China, Japan, the Aleutians, and the Philippines.

These Yankee class submarines are removed from service as the Delta IV and Typhoon classes enter sea trials, in order to comply with SALT I limits. The Soviet Union is currently constrained by the "modern" nuclear-powered submarine limit (62) and by the "modern" SLBM launcher limit (950) of SALT I. Because SALT II does not limit intercontinental ballistic missiles (ICBMs) and SLBMs under separate subtotals, it is possible to say only that the continued production of missile submarines *contributes* to three SALT II ceilings: the number of strategic nuclear delivery vehicles (MIRVed and not MIRVed), which are limited to 2,504; the number of MIRVed missile launchers and bombers, which are limited to 1,320; and the number of MIRVed missile launchers, which are limited to 1,200. The Soviet Union has reached the limit on strategic nuclear delivery vehicles, but with the retirement of Yankee submarines (which are required to remain within SALT I anyway), the total number of submarine-based strategic nuclear delivery vehicles remains relatively constant. On the other hand, the retirement of Yankee submarines with

Table A2-1
Soviet SSBN basing and warheads

	Northern		Pacific	
Class	*Submarines*	*Warheads*	*Submarines*	*Warheads*
Typhoon/SS-N-20 20 × 8 = 160	4	640 (720 max)	0	0
Delta IV/SS-NX-23 16 × 9 = 144	2	288 (320 max)	0	0
Delta III/SS-N-18 16 × 3.67 = 58.7	10	587 (1,120 max)	4	235 (448 max)
Delta II/SS-N-8 16 × 1 = 16	4	64	0	0
Delta I/SS-N-8 12 × 1 = 12	10	120	8	96
Total	30[a]	1,699 (2,344 max)	12[a]	331 (544 max)
Yankee I/SS-N-6 16 × 1 = 16	11	176	9	144
Yankee II/SS-NX-17 12 × 1 = 12	1	12	0	0
Hotel III/SS-N-8 3 × 1 = 3	1	3	0	0
Golf V/SS-N-20 1 × 9 = 9	1 (Black Sea)	9 (Black Sea)	0	0
Golf II/SS-N-5 3 × 1 = 3	6 (Baltic)	18 (Baltic)	7	21

Missile	*Warheads/Mis. (independent)*	*Range (km)*	*Yield (Mt)*	*CEP (meters)*
SS-N-5	1	1,300	1	2,800
SS-N-6 mod 3	1 (MRV)	3,000	0.35	1,900
SS-N-8 mod 1 & 2	1	7,800	0.8–1.0	1,500
SS-N-18				
mod 1	3	6,500	0.2	1,400
mod 2	1	8,000	0.45	1,400
mod 3	7	6,500	0.2	1,000
	No firm figures on deployment of each mod of SS-N-18. Assume 1/3, 1/3, 1/3 for average loading of 3.67 warheads.			
SS-N-20	6–9	8,300	0.1	1,000
SS-NX-23	8–10	9,300	0.1	1,000

Sources: Barton Wright, *Soviet Missiles* (Lexington, Mass.: Lexington Books, 1986); Caspar Weinberger, *Soviet Military Power*, 5th ed. (Washington, DC: US Government Printing Office, 1986), p. 29; Ulrich-Joachim Schulz-Torge, "The Soviet Submarine Fleet in 1985," *Military Technology*, December 1985, pp. 95–99.

[a]DoD sources in 1986 indicate that the distribution of Delta class SSBNs between the Arctic and Pacific is 22:16, respectively, while Schulz-Torge gives 26:12 as of October 1985. Other data also suggest that a larger fraction of Deltas is deploying in the Pacific.

their single warhead missile launchers does not affect the total number of sea-based systems applied against the MIRVed limits, and within a few years, the production of Delta IV and Typhoon submarines will help bring the Soviet forces up to those limits. This will leave the Soviet Union with the choice of limiting production of these systems, dismantling other fairly modern systems, or ignoring the limits.[1] The US sea-based forces are not up to the SALT I limits at all. The US, in approaching the SALT II limit on MIRVed missiles, decided to dismantle older SSBNs.

US, French, and British SSBNs operate in the North Atlantic and Mediterranean. Since the SSBN patrol areas are closely held secrets, it is not possible to assume that SSBNs are separated by nationality while on patrol. In strategic-level warfare, it must be assumed that all these SSBNs would be potential targets of Soviet ASW. Table A2–2 lists all US and other NATO SSBNs. The bulk of the SSBNs in the Atlantic are US, and all Western SSBNs in the Pacific are US.

ASW Platforms and Systems

The Soviet Navy is not directly comparable to the US and UK navies, since the evolution of naval missions has been so different since World War II. Entire

Table A2-2
NATO SSBN basing

	North Atlantic[a]		*North Pacific*	
Class	*Submarines*	*Warheads*	*Submarines*	*Warheads*
France:				
Le Redoutable/M-20 16 × 1 = 16 whs/sub	5	80	0	0
United Kingdom:				
Resolution/A-3 Chevaline 16 × 1 = 16 whs/sub	4	64	0	0
United States:				
Ohio/C-4 8 × 24 = 192 whs/sub	0	0	6	1,152
Lafayette/C-4 8 × 16 = 128 whs/sub	12	1,536	0	0
Lafayette/C-3 10 × 16 = 160 whs/sub	16	2,560	0	0
Total US	31	4,096	6	1,152
Total NATO	40	4,240	6	1,152

Missile	*Warheads/Mis. (independent)*	*Range (km)*	*Yield (Mt)*	*CEP (meters)*
M-20	1	3,000	1	?
M-4 (dev.)	1 (MRV)	4,000 +	?	?
A-3 Chevaline	1 (MRV)	4,000	0.04	?
C-3 Poseidon	10	5,900	0.04	460
C-4 Trident I	8	7,400	0.10	460

Source: Thomas Cochran et al., *US Nuclear Forces and Capabilities* (Cambridge, Mass.: Ballinger, 1984); *Jane's Weapon Systems 1984/85*.

[a]Includes Mediterranean Sea.

classes of ships exist in the US Navy that do not exist in the Soviet Navy, and vice versa, so that comparing the navies by Western category (a common exercise) is confusing and misleading. Moreover, Soviet classifications of their own ships provide at least some guidance as to their missions, although it is necessary to consider the specific weapons and sensors on individual ships.

Surface ships on their own have rather limited strategic ASW capabilities compared with modern SSNs, so that very fine distinctions between the capabilities of different classes of surface ships would not be expected to affect significantly one's assessment of overall strategic ASW capability in a navy. Surface ship capabilities can be significantly improved with stand-off weapons, low-frequency bow and towed sonar arrays, and helicopters, but even with these, SSNs have a distinct advantage in hunting SSBNs. In a surface task force, coordinated ASW from many surface ships increases the ASW capability of the task force as a whole, although US and Soviet surface-group ASW is intended primarily as a screen against hostile SSNs and not for area search against evasive targets like SSBNs. The attack submarine is the superior ASW platform as it can be very quiet, use its sonar at optimum listening depths, penetrate much closer to SSBN patrol areas covertly than can surface ships, and is the only vessel that can conduct ASW under ice.

ASW aircraft can be effective if they are given a rough localization of a target, which they can then pinpoint. ASW aircraft, however, are vulnerable to attack from land- and sea-based tactical fighter aircraft, and even from shipboard surface-to-air missiles. Land-based bomber aircraft can play a role in ASW as minelayers and with air-to-surface missile strikes against ASW surface ships. Air ASW is expected to be most effective at chokepoints that are acoustically monitored.

Soviet ASW Forces

The deployment of Soviet attack submarines is not known with certainty; for example, attack submarines from the Northern Fleet may be deployed in the Mediterranean. There are no Soviet nuclear-powered attack submarines (SSNs) or nuclear-powered cruise missile submarines (SSGNs) in either the Black Sea or the Baltic Sea fleets. An estimate of the basing of Soviet SSNs, SSGNs, and conventionally powered submarines is shown in table A2–3. It appears that the Soviet Union has tended to base its newest, most capable submarines in the Arctic rather than in the Pacific. SSGNs can operate as attack submarines, and including them the total number of nuclear-powered ASW capable submarines in the Arctic is 75. Excluding the old, very noisy November and Echo II classes brings this total down to about 53. In any likely scenario, there would be a substantial number of SSGNs assigned to antisurface strikes, so the totals above are definitely overestimates. In the Pacific, there are about 42 SSNs and

Table A2-3
Soviet attack and cruise missile submarine deployment

	Northern	*Baltic*	*Black*	*Pacific*
SSN:				
Akula	0	0	0	1[a]
Mike	1[a]	0	0	0
Sierra	1[a]	0	0	0
Alfa	6	0	0	0
Victor III	10[a]	0	0	8
Victor II	5	0	0	2
Victor I	13	0	0	3
Echo I	0	0	0	5
November	8	0	0	4
SSGN:				
Yankee	1	0	0	0
Oscar	3	0	0	0
Papa	1	0	0	0
Charlie II	4	0	0	2
Charlie I	8	0	0	3
Echo II	14	0	0	14
SSG:				
Juliet	6	4	3	3
Long Bin	0	1	0	0
SS:[b]				
Kilo	0	0	0	7[a]
Tango	15	0	3	0
Foxtrot	28	5	0	27
Romeo	4	0	3	3
Whiskey 50 (distribution unknown)				

Source: Ulrich-Joachim Schulz-Torge, "The Soviet Submarine Fleet in 1985," *Military Technology*, December 1985, pp. 95–99.

[a]Additional units building.

[b]Many Whiskey, Zulu, and Romeo SSs in reserve.

SSGNs, where only 19 of those are newer Victor and Charlie class submarines.[2] Though most US attack submarines have a detection advantage over all Soviet submarines, it is useful to make a distinction between the overwhelming US acoustic advantage against Echo/November classes, and the somewhat narrower acoustic advantage against Victor and Charlie classes. The US SSN-637 class is in fact considered equivalent to the Victor III. The three newest classes of Soviet SSNs—three vessels in all—are probably quieter than the 37 vessels of the US Sturgeon (SSN-637) class.

The conventionally powered Soviet submarine fleet is fairly large, though declining in numbers as the postwar SSs are finally retired. Diesel-electric submarines have some disadvantages relative to nuclear submarines: (1) they must refuel, either from a port or a support ship, (2) they are slow, (3) they cannot remain submerged for long periods. In fact, diesel-electric submarines are perhaps better thought of as surface ships that can submerge for limited periods. These submarines can remain submerged on batteries for about 6 days at hovering speed with a minimum of life-support and sensor gear operating. At full 16-knot speed with all systems on, however, the batteries may last less than 10 hours. The advantages of diesel-electric propulsion are lower cost relative to nuclear propulsion and quietness while on batteries. While running on batteries, SSs can be substantially quieter than older Soviet SSNs, though they are probably about as quiet as the most recent classes. Therefore, the Soviet SSs and Juliet diesel-electric cruise missile submarines (SSGs) can be employed to form stationary screens or barriers near the Soviet home waters. Acting in this role of an intelligent minefield, a barrier of Soviet SSs could pose a significant threat to US SSNs attempting to penetrate.

The Soviet surface combatant fleet can be divided into three major groups by displacement. Ships over 2,000 tons standard displacement are in the "large" group of ocean-going vessels, ships between 500 and 1,000 tons are "intermediate" ships that could be used in open ocean operations but are closer to coastal patrol ships. Finally, there are those ships less than 500 tons that are coastal and river patrol ships. Counting the "intermediate" ships among the ocean-going fleet can be misleading, since, for example, some of the largest of the "intermediate" group are run by the KGB as border patrol boats. It is interesting to note that, aside from the Coast Guard, this "intermediate" group does not exist in the US or UK navies. This is because these two major maritime nations have long been oriented toward long-range deployment for which they need larger ships with better ocean endurance. The difference is also related to fundamentally different design practices: the United States tends to build ships with much larger margins for growth and additions than does the Soviet Union. Design margins for weight, stability, and powering are about 10 percent on US ships and only 2 percent on Soviet ships. Endurance margins are up to 33 percent on US ships and zero on Soviet ships.[3] British and US frigates, for example, are more than twice the displacement of Soviet "frigates," except for the Krivak class.

Tables A2–4 and A2–5 show the distribution of Soviet large and intermediate combat ships, along with their major ASW weapons. Almost all Soviet ships have some sonar, ASW torpedoes, and depth charges. However, most of these sonars are high or medium frequency and are unsuitable for long-range detection. Soviet depth charges are propelled on rockets and can be fired out to a range of only a few kilometers, with a few reaching 6 km. These short-range weapons are matched to the short range of the sonar and are defensive systems. Modern low-frequency sonars are installed on newer ships, as is shown in table A2–4, and are generally associated with the modern, longer-range ASW weapons like the FRAS-1 and the SS-N-14. The FRAS-1 is a rocket-propelled nuclear depth bomb that has a range of 30 kilometers. Some 20 of these may be carried on a large ASW ship.[4] The SS-N-14 is a cruise missile that carries a homing torpedo or a nuclear weapon up to 45 or 55 kilometers.[5] Referring to table A2-4, it is apparent that the Soviet designation of BPK, or "large antisubmarine ship," generally agrees with my assessment, the main differences being in the Kanin and Kashin classes, which are designated BPK though they lack stand-off ASW weapons, helicopters, and low-frequency sonars. The Kiev is not designated a specifically ASW ship, but it has a strong ASW component. Of 41 large combatants in the Northern Fleet, 20 carry these ASW stand-off weapons and appropriate sensors and can be considered primary ASW ships. In the Baltic, there are 10 primary ASW ships out of 25, in the Black Sea there are 12 primary ASW ships out of 36, including 2 Moskva and 1 Kiev class ASW helicopter ships. In the Pacific, 21 out of 43 large ships are primary ASW vessels. None of the intermediate or small ship classes carries stand-off weapons or long-range sensors, though their sheer numbers would make them a significant force in very limited operations, such as acting as coastal barriers or in defense of short-range amphibious operations.

Antisubmarine warfare aircraft are generally slow, long endurance aircraft that can carry torpedoes, conventional or nuclear depth charges, expendable sonar buoys (sonobuoys), magnetic anomaly detection (MAD) gear, and some on-board processers for the acoustic data. These aircraft are not heavily armed for self-defense and are therefore vulnerable when beyond their own tactical air cover. Some of these aircraft carry antiship cruise missiles and can be a significant threat to surface ships.

ASW aircraft are in general not as effective as SSNs for area search. The MAD detection range is at most a few thousand feet, which makes it a poor search sensor, though sonobuoys can provide much longer detection ranges over wider areas on a continuous basis. The utility of sonobuoys depends largely on how many can be deployed, on how many can be monitored and processed simultaneously, and on the environment. These factors rely on miniature electronics, signal processing, and computer technology, areas in which the United States enjoys a clear and even growing superiority over the Soviet Union.[6] Even with this technical advantage, however, US ASW aircraft are generally considered most effective when vectored by an initial rough localization. In their home waters, Soviet ASW aircraft may operate using information from surveillance systems also.

Most Soviet ASW aircraft are helicopters, which have short ranges and small weapon/sensor capacities. The primary large, long-range, fixed-wing ASW aircraft are the 50–60 Bear F, which are still in production.[7] Table A2-6 shows the approximate distribution of all Soviet ASW aircraft. There are periodic deployments of ASW aircraft outside the Soviet Union[8] so the figures in table A2-6 should not be interpreted as specific basing. Table A2-7 shows some of the characteristics of Soviet ASW aircraft. The aircraft are assumed to

Table A2-4
Soviet surface ships and ASW capability

Class Type	*Year Launched*	*Standard Displacement*	*SSM Aircraft*	*ASW Helos*[e]	*Sonar*[f]	*Standoff Weapons*
Large:						
Kiev (TAKR)[a, g]	72–82	36,000	SS-N-12 12 Forger 3 Hor B	18 Hor A or Hel A	LF Bow MF VDS	FRAS-1
Moskva (PK)[a]	64–66	14,500	b	18 Hor A	LF Keel MF VDS	FRAS-1
Slava (RKR)	79–	10,000	SS-N-12 Hor B	No	LF Keel MF VDS?	
Kirov (RKR)[a]	77–	20,500	SS-N-19 2 Hor B	3 Hor A or Hel A	LF Bow LF VDS	16 SS-N-14
Kara (BPK)[a]	71–77	8,200	b	1 Hor A	LF Bow MF VDS	8 SS-N-14
Kresta I (RKR)	66–68	6,200	SS-N-3	No	MF? Keel	
Kresta II (BPK)[a]	67–76	6,200	b	1 Hor A	MF Bow	8 SS-N-14
Kynda (RKR)	62–64	4,400	SS-N-3	No	HF Keel	
Sverdlov (KR)[c]	51–55	12,900	No	No	No	
Kanin (BPK)	57–59	3,700	No	No	MF Hull	
Mod Kashin (BPK)	73–80	3,950	SS-N-2C	No	MF Keel MF VDS	
Kashin (BPK)	62–70	3,750	No	No	MF? Keel	
Kildin (BRK)	57–58	2,800	SS-N-2C	No	HF Keel	
SAM Kotlin (EM)	54–72	3,700	No	No	HF Keel	
Kotlin (EM)	53–57	2,600	No	No	HF Keel	
Sovremennyy (BRK)	78+	6,200	SS-N-22 Hor B	No	MF Bow	
Udaloy (BPK)[a]	80–	6,200	b	2 Hel A	LF Bow LF VDS	8 SS-N-14
Skoryy (EM)	50+	2,600	No	No	HF Keel	
Krivak II (SKR)[a] (ex-BPK)	75–80	3,300	b	No	MF Bow MF VDS	4 SS-N-14
Krivak I (SKR)[a] (ex-BPK)	70–81	3,300	b	No	MF Bow MF VDS	4 SS-N-14

Intermediate:					
Koni (SKR)	76	1,900	No	No	MF Keel
Riga (SKR)	51–57	1,260	No	No	HF
Grisha (MPK)	67–	950	No	No	MF Keel HF Dipping
Mirka II (SKR)	64–65	950	No	No	HF Keel Dipping
Mirka I (SKR)	63–64	950	No	No	HF Keel
Mod. Petya I/II	60–63	950	No	No	MF VDS
Petya I/II	60–63	950	No	No	HF Keel HF Dipping
Small:					
Nanucka (MRK)[c]	68–	770	SS-N-9	No	No
Pauk (MPK)	79–	480	No	No	MF Keel MF Dipping
Poti (MPK)	60–66	400	No	No	HF Keel

Sources: *Combat Fleets of the World 1984/85*; *Jane's Fighting Ships 1984/85*; John Jordan, *Soviet Warships* (Annapolis: Naval Institute Press, 1983).

[a]Primary ASW ships.

[b]SS-N-14 may have antiship capability.

[c]No torpedoes.

[d]Surface-to-air missiles may have some antiship capability.

[e]Helicopters: Hor = Hormone, Hel = Helix; A for ASW, B for targeting.

[f]LF = low frequency; MF = medium frequency; HF = high frequency; VDS = variable depth sonar.

[g]*Soviet Designations:*
TAKR = tactical aircraft cruiser
PK = antisubmarine cruiser
RKR = missile cruiser
BPK = large antisubmarine ship
KR = cruiser
BRK = large missile ship
EM = destroyer
SKR = patrol ship
MPK = small antisubmarine ship
MRK = small missile ship

Table A2–5
Soviet surface ship deployments

	Northern	*Baltic*	*Black*	*Pacific*
Large:				
Kiev[b]	1	0	1[a]	2
Moskva[b]	0	0	2	0
Kirov[b]	1	1[a]	0	1
Slava	0	0	2[a]	0
Kara[b]	0	0	3	4
Kresta I	1	1	0	2
Kresta II[b]	7	0	0	3
Kynda	0	1	1	2
Mod Sverdlov	0	0	1	1
Sverdlov SAM	0	0	1	0
Sverdlov	2	2	2	2
Kanin	5	0	0	3
Kashin (& Mod)	4	2	9	4
SAM Kotlin	2	3	1	2
Sovremennyy	3	2[a]	0	0
Udaloy[b]	3	2[a]	0	0
Kotlin/Mod Kotlin Kilden/Skoryy	4	4	7	6
Krivak I & II[b]	8	7	6	11
	41	25	36	43
Intermediate:				
Riga/Koni/Grisha/ Mirka/Petya	41	27	38	40
Small:				
Nanuchka, Tarantul	6	12	8	6
Poti, Pauk, Turya T-58, Babochka, SO-1	27	31	18	55

Source: Ulrich-Joachim Schulz-Torge, "The Soviet Navy in 1985," *Military Technology*, November 1985, pp. 120–129.

[a]Under construction.

[b]Primary ASW ships.

Table A2–6
Approximate deployment of Soviet ASW aircraft

	Northern	*Baltic*	*Black*	*Pacific*
Fixed-wing aircraft:				
Bear F (Tu-142)[a]	25	0	0	25
Mail, May (Be-12, Il-38)	45	20	25	55
Helicopters:				
Haze A, Helix A, Hormone A (Mi-14, Ka-27, Ka-25)	75[b]	30	75	65

Sources: Defense Intelligence Agency Unclassified Communist Naval Order of Battle, November 1983; *Combat Fleets of the World 1984/85*, p. 689.

[a]The distribution of 50 Bear F aircraft is an assumption.

[b]Another source gives Soviet aircraft totals in the Northern Fleet as 30 Bear F, Mail, and May fixed-wing aircraft, and a total of 100 helicopters. *See* Tomas Ries, "Defending the Far North," *International Defense Review* 17:7, 1984.

Table A2–7
Characteristics of Soviet and US ASW aircraft

Aircraft	*Weapon Load (kg)*	*Combat Radius (km)*[a]	*Max. Sea Level Speed (knots)*	*ASW Weapons*[b]	*ASW Sensors*
Soviet Systems:					
Bear F (Tu-142)	8,000	2,700	440	Torpedoes	Sonobuoys
			(810 km/h)	D/C[c]	Radar, MAD
Mail (BE-12)		1,300	240	D/C	Sonobuoys
			(440 km/h)		Radar, MAD
May (IL-38)		2,400	315	D/C	Sonobuoys
			(580 km/h)	Torpedoes	Radar, MAD
Haze A (Mi-14)		305	122	D/C	Sonobuoys
Shore-based			(220 km/h)	Torpedoes	Dipping sonar
Hormone A (Ka-25)		220	105	D/C	Sonobuoys, radar
Ship-based			(190 km/h)	Torpedoes	Dipping sonar
					MAD
Helix A (Ka-27)		300	130	D/C	Sonobuoys, radar
Ship-based			(240 km/h)	Torpedoes	Dipping sonar
					MAD
US Systems:					
Orion (P-3C)	7,700	2,760	410	D/C	87 Sonobuoys
Land-based			(750 km/h)	Torpedoes	Radar, MAD
Viking (S-3A/B)		1,800	440	D/C	60 Sonobuoys
Carrier-based			(810 km/h)	Torpedoes	
Sea King (SH-3D/H)		300	140	D/C	Radar, MAD
Carrier & Spruance			(260 km/h)	Torpedoes	Dipping sonar
Seasprite (SH-2F LAMPS I)[d]		220	140	Torpedoes	15 Sonobuoys
On surface escorts			(260 km/h)	D/C?	Radar, MAD
Seahawk (SH-60B LAMPS III)[d]		180	150	Torpedoes	25? Sonobuoys
On surface escorts			(280 km/h)	D/C?	Radar, MAD

Sources: Jean Labayle Couhat, *Combat Fleets of the World 1984/85*, pp. 690, 691. John Jordan, *Soviet Warships* (Annapolis: Naval Institute Press, 1983).

[a]Combat radius is defined here as 1/3 of maximum range.

[b]Most aircraft can carry mines.

[c]D/C = Depth charges. May be nuclear in both US and Soviet helos.

[d]LAMPS can also perform targeting mission.

remain on station for one-third of their total flight time, so the "combat radii" given here are one-third of the maximum range. There are no Soviet bases from which the shore-based helicopters and Be-12 Mail Soviet ASW aircraft can search a significant portion of NATO SSBN patrol areas. Even the Il-38 May, which is similar to the P-3, lacks the range needed to reach the central North Atlantic. Rather, these aircraft could be used for defensive ASW near Soviet submarine bases, under the cover of Soviet tactical aircraft. The Mail and May aircraft have also been used for reconnaissance.[9] The only aircraft that can reach NATO SSBN patrol areas is the Bear F, and though construction is continuing,[10] there are few of these aircraft. The large, propeller-driven Bear F is also relatively vulnerable to NATO tactical aircraft beyond the range of Soviet land-based tactical aircraft.

On the other hand, NATO ASW aircraft are vulnerable to Soviet tactical air forces. There are 19 all-weather airfields on the Kola peninsula with runways that exceed 2,000 meters and that can receive most of the several types of Soviet fighters from the Leningrad Military Districts Thirteenth Tactical Air Army.[11] In the Pacific, there are airfields on the Kamchatka peninsula and Kuril Islands.

The range of Soviet MIG-21 fighters with typical combat loads flying out of Murmansk cover the Barents Sea to Spitzbergen and only the northern Norwegian Sea, and MIG-23s reach to Southern Norway. NATO tactical aircraft can control the central Norwegian Sea and the Greenland Sea from Iceland, Norway, and aircraft carriers. Soviet ASW aircraft would operate in these areas at great risk. NATO ASW aircraft operating from Britain, Iceland, and Norway could search for submarines up to the edge of the ice in the Greenland Sea while just entering the range of Soviet fighters. Without protection, they would be vulnerable in the central Norwegian Sea and northward.

US ASW Forces

As is shown in table A2–8, there are three main classes of US attack submarines: 13 Permit class, 37 Sturgeon class, and about 40 Los Angeles class, which are still being built. As of 1986, these three large classes are about 23, 16, and 6 years old respectively. Between these main production runs there are smaller classes and individual experimental ships that were built specifically to test some new design. Attack submarines are homeported on the East Coast at Charleston, South Carolina; Groton, Connecticut; Norfolk, Virginia; and Portsmouth, New Hampshire. On the West Coast, homeports are San Diego; Pearl Harbor; Vallejo, California; Bangor, Washington; and Bremerton, Washington. From these homeports, SSNs may rotate into assignments with the various fleets as part of carrier task forces. Other assignments may include covert intelligence operations in the western Pacific or the Barents Sea as part of the

Table A2–8
Active US nuclear attack submarines (mid-1985)

Class Number	*Name*	*Years Built*	*Atlantic*	*Pacific*
575	Seawolf[a]	1955	0	1
578	Skate[a]	1957–58	0	3
585	Skipjack	1958–60	5	0
594	Permit	1961–66	5	8
597	Tullibee	1960	1	0
608	Ethan Allen	1960–62	1	1
637	Sturgeon	1967–75	23	14
671	Narwhal	1967	1	0
685	Lipscomb	1973	1	0
688	Los Angeles	1974–	20	12
Total			57	39

Source: US Navy.
[a]The Skate and Seawolf classes are no longer first-line vessels.

"Pinnacle" or "Bollard" programs,[12] or trailing Soviet submarines. US attack submarines can be armed with Mk 48 ASW torpedoes, Harpoon antiship missiles, and some with mines and SUBROC. An SSN normally has about 20 places for internal weapons, each of which can carry one of the large Mk 48 torpedoes, or 2 Harpoon antiship missiles, or 2 mines. The Los Angeles class SSNs will also get vertical launch tubes for Tomahawk land attack and antiship missiles. Most SSNs have bow spherical sonars as part of the BQQ-2 or newer BQQ-5 system. Towed linear arrays, which significantly improve the passive detection capability of submarines, are mounted in an external sleeve on the hull of Sturgeon and Los Angeles SSNs, while older SSNs may get a towed array attached externally at sea.

Unlike the Soviet Navy, the US Navy has no significant surface combatant ships smaller than 1,500 tons, as is shown in table A2–9. Virtually all major surface combatants, including frigates, are heavier than 3,000 tons and are open ocean vessels designed for global operations. All of these ships have antiair and antiship missiles. For sensors, these ships carry bow- or hull-mounted sonars that are effective for moderate detection range in medium seas and at low speeds. Tactical towed arrays (TACTASS) will be fitted to FFG-7, DD-963, DDG-51, and CG-47 classes.[13] The variable depth sonar (VDS) is a towed "fish" containing a cylindrical array that can dive below the seasonal thermocline layer and get into optimal listening layers. Towed linear arrays can do the same, and they have a greater ability to pick up low-frequency submarine sounds and are superior to VDS for long-range detection. However, towing any kind of array behind a ship limits the movement of the ship, especially if the array is to be stably oriented. Depending on the tactical situation this may or may not be an important limitation. The British Royal Navy is in the process of

Table A2–9
US surface combatants (active)

Class	*Name*	*Years Built*	*Stand. Disp.*	*ASW A/C*	*Towed Array*	*Atlantic*	*Pacific*
Aircraft Carriers:							
CVN-68	Nimitz	1972–88	81,600	18[c]	No	2	1
CVN-65	Enterprise	1960	75,700	18[c]	No	0	1
CV-63	Kitty Hawk	1960–67	60,100	18[c]	No	2	2
CV-59	Forrestal	1954–58	59,000	18[c]	No	2	1
CV-41	Midway	1945–46	52,500	18[c]	No	0	2
					Total	6	7
				Total with ASW Aircraft		6	7
Cruisers[f]:							
CGN 38	Virginia	1974–78	10,000[a]	2	No	4	0
CGN 36	California	1971–72	9,561	No	No	2	0
CGN 35	Truxtun	1964	8,200	LAMPS	No	0	1
CGN 25	Bainbridge	1961	7,600	No	No	0	1
CGN 9	Long Beach	1959	14,200	No	No	0	1
CG 47	Ticonderoga	1981–	9,600[a]	2 LAMPS[d]	TACTASS	1+	1+
CG 26	Belknap	1963–65	6,570	1 LAMPS	No	4	5
CG 16	Leahy	1961–63	5,670	No	No	3	6
					Total	14	14
				Total with ASW Aircraft		9+	5+
Destroyers[f]:							
DDG 993	Kidd	1979–80	8,500[a]	2 LAMPS	TACTASS	2	2
DDG 37	Farragut	1958–60	5,709	No	No	3	3
DDG 2	Adams	1959–63	3,370	No	No	11	12
DDG 31	Decatur	1955	4,150[a]	No	No	0	1
DD 963	Spruance	1973–83	7,810[a]	2 LAMPS[d]	TACTASS	16	15
DD 931	Sherman[b]	1955–58	2,800	No	No	3	2
DD 931	(ASW Sherman)	1955–58	3,000	No	VDS	6	2
					Total	48	34
				Total with ASW Aircraft		18	17
Frigates[f]:							
FFG 7	Perry	1976–	3,605[a]	2 LAMPS[d]	TACTASS	18+	17+
FFG 1	Brooke	1963–66	3,426[a]	1 LAMPS	No	3	3
FF 1052	Knox	1966–73	4,200[a]	1 LAMPS	VDS/TACTASS	20	22
FF 1040	Garcia	1963–65	3,403[a]	1 LAMPS	No	5	5
FF 1098	Glover	1965	3,426[a]	No	VDS	1	0
FF 1037	Bronstein	1962	2,650[a]	No	No	1	1
					Total	48+	48
				Total with ASW Aircraft		46+	47

Sources: Jane's Fighting Ships 1984/85; Jean Labayle Couhat, *Combat Fleets of the World 1984/85.*

[a]full load displacement.

[b]The Navy counts only one Sherman class DD among the active fleet.

[c]Battleships will carry four LAMPS I helicopters.

[d]LAMPS III will go on FFG 7, DD 963, and CG 47.

[e]Typical carrier ASW aircraft are 10 S-3 and 8 SH-3, though more can be carried.

[f]SQS-26 or SQS-53 sonar and ASROC on all cruisers, destroyers, and frigates.

removing VDS from some frigates because it is difficult to use and because towed linear arrays are more effective.[14]

All US ships have some ASW capability, and most compare favorably to the Soviet ASW ships. Frigates, of which there are about 100, are mostly designed as ASW escorts. Destroyers, of which there are about 82, are primarily escorts for carrier battle groups and as such have ASW defenses. Cruisers, numbering 28, are also used in conjunction with carrier battle groups. Most of these ships carry ASROC, which is a rocket-boosted torpedo (Mk 46) or kiloton nuclear depth charge with a range of about 10 kilometers. It is used on 27 cruisers, 87 destroyers, and 65 frigates in the US Navy.[15] These ships, like their Soviet counterparts, have torpedo tubes that can launch antisubmarine torpedoes directly. The Mk 46 is the standard lightweight torpedo of the US Navy. It is carried by ships and aircraft and can attack either submarines or surface ships. It has a maximum speed of 40 knots and a range of 11 kilometers, and will have its sensor and guidance systems updated in a near-term improvement program. The standard heavyweight submarine-launched torpedo is the Mk 48, which is not carried in aircraft. The Mk 48 has a maximum speed of 55 knots and a maximum range of about 38 kilometers (21 nm), although its most effective range is around half that. It can be wire-guided from the launching submarine, thereby making use of the powerful sonar systems on the submarine to provide target information over the first part of its "flight." The Mk 48 is being updated under an advanced capabilities program.

Several ASW mines also deserve mention. The Captor mine is an Mk-46 torpedo in a capsule which has a mechanism that triggers the torpedo launch when a submarine approaches. It can be sown in deep water by submarines, various surface ships, ASW aircraft, and B-52 bombers. By mid-1984, 2,116 had been produced, and the production rate was about 300 per year.[16] Production was curtailed after the fiscal year 1985 buy, because the Navy said that it could no longer afford them,[17] although the total procurement fell short of the Navy's original minimum requirement of 4,109 and does not meet the minimum requirement for the Greenland–Iceland–United Kingdom gap of 2,235.[18]

Also entering the US mine inventory is the submarine-launched mobile mine (SLMM), which is a modified Mk 37 torpedo that swims out from a submarine torpedo tube and places a mine in waters inaccessible to other minelaying craft. This would be a potent weapon near Soviet home waters. However, as of 1985, no SLMMs had been deployed because of technical difficulties encountered by the small firm that is building them. The Navy originally planned to have about 900 by the early 1990s.[19]

ASW aircraft with sonobuoys, depth charges, and torpedoes can localize a long-range detection in the vectored intercept mode. Helicopters on their own would not be able to search large areas quickly and would be most effective in groups where at least one ship or submarine would have a towed array. As table A2–9 shows, nearly all US frigates have ASW helicopters, and most of these also have either VDS or TACTASS. In the destroyer and cruiser classes, only the newest classes have helicopters. Helicopter operations are not unlimited, however, and high wind accompanied by large waves can prevent them from flying. Statistical analysis of meteorological conditions averaged over the year in the seas north of Iceland indicate that US frigates are capable of operating their ASW aircraft and sensors only 2–3 days out of ten.[20]

The primary land- and sea-based US ASW aircraft are shown in table A2–6. The Orion P-3C, the most recent version of the P-3 airframe, is considered the best ASW aircraft in the world. With its very long range and large payload, it can track submarines far from the airplane's base. P-3Cs are based in the United States at two East Coast and two West Coast bases. From these bases, squadrons of 12 flight crews and 9 aircraft rotate out to overseas US bases periodically. In addition to the US bases overseas, eight other countries operate versions of the P-3, and others operate similar aircraft, and in emergencies they could service US P-3s.

The P-3 is large enough to contain weapons, sonobuoys, and complete ASW processors for detection and classification. Ten people operate the aircraft and equipment, which makes up a complete and self-contained ASW system; it has been updated three times. The Update III, completed in January 1982, added the PROTEUS signal-processing system. This airborne acoustic system, the most advanced in existence, will improve the P-3Cs' ability to detect and track quieter Soviet submarines.[21] Update II added the Harpoon missile to the P-3C, giving these aircraft the ability to attack surface ships at long ranges, and making the P-3C a significant threat to Soviet surface ships in the Norwegian Sea.

The US operates 18 active squadrons of P-3Cs and 6 active squadrons of older P-3Bs. As new P-3Cs are produced at a rate of about 6 per year, the older P-3Bs will rotate out to the 13 reserve squadrons until the US has an all P-3C fleet by about 1990.[22]

The smaller carrier-based S-3 Viking and SH-3H Sea King, and the ship-based SH-2F light airborne multipurpose system (LAMPS) Mk I and SH-60B LAMPS Mk III cannot carry the sophisticated processing and large numbers of sonobuoys that the P-3C Orion can carry. The SH-3H Sea King is primarily used for inner zone defense within 30 miles of the carrier where its active dipping sonar, along with MAD, is considered better than sonobuoys for detecting submarines due to the high-level low-frequency ship noise there. The SH-2F LAMPS I and SH-60B LAMPS III helicopters are used for detecting submarines farther from the carrier group,[23] and therefore need sophisticated passive as well as active signal processing. The LAMPS system puts much of the heavy processing equipment on the ship, and the helicopter transmits the raw data from sonobuoys via radio to the ship and receives the results. If radio transmission is being jammed, however, the helicopter's acoustic detection capability is considerably reduced. Also, when the SH-2F LAMPS Mk I helicopter is over the horizon and near the surface using MAD, radio transmission is interrupted.[24] The SH-2F LAMPS Mk I will not be completely replaced by the newer SH-60B LAMPS Mk III because the latter is too large and heavy to land on some of the LAMPS Mk I frigates, namely the Brooke (FFG-1), Knox (FF-1052), and Garcia (FF-1040) classes. The SH-2F LAMPS Mk I is still being produced.[25]

Sonar Systems

Surface ship sonars are primarily defensive systems, providing detection and fire control information about attacking submarines and torpedoes. The sonar transducers are mounted in the hull or keel, near the middle of the ship in older classes, and in a large underwater bulb in the bow of newer ships. The bow-mounted sonars are considerably heavier than hull-mounted types but have the advantage of being far from the ship's own engine noise, which can drown out the weak submarine sounds. Many bow-mounted sonars can operate in an active or a passive mode, and feed range and bearing information directly to the fire control systems of torpedoes and other ASW weapons. Those sonars can also provide underwater acoustic links to submarines. When many ships operate in groups, passive sonar is incapacitated by the strong low-frequency sounds of the nearby ships, and active sonar is the only detection mode that can be used. Active ship sonar was used extensively by the British in the Falkland islands war, but the only result seems to have been the destruction of a large number of marine mammals that happened to reflect the sonar pulses as would a submarine.

Helicopter dunking sonar is intended for use in the midst of a fast (30 knots) carrier battle group (CVBG) where again the ambient ship's noise effectively masks any submarine sounds and hampers the use of passive sonar. Dunking sonar has the advantages of mobility and of being isolated from direct contact from heavy engine machinery. The aircraft carriers in CVBGs carry SH-3H helicopters with dunking sonar and sonobuoys, while helicopters on escort destroyers and frigates, which provide a defensive ASW screen around the carrier, launch the LAMPS helicopters in the Mk LAMPS I version (a Kaman SH-2F) and Mk LAMPS III version (a Sikorsky SH-60B), neither with dunking sonar.[26]

Sonobuoys are dropped from helicopters or aircraft traveling at up to several hundred knots and up to 10,000 or 20,000 feet. They are about three feet long and are fitted with a small drogue parachute or a rotary parachute to slow their descent. When they hit the water, they drop a weighted cable, which is attached to one or more hydrophones. A buoyant radio transmitter bobs at the surface and transmits the acoustic signals to the aircraft on one of several preselected channels. The more channels that are available, the more sonobuoys can be monitored, with some US versions allowing 99 channels for communication. The simplest sonobuoy in use is the SSQ-41B omnidirectional passive buoy, which simply picks up sounds in all directions and transmits that signal to the aircraft. A pattern of these buoys can be laid by an aircraft and can detect the presence of a submarine but cannot yield much information about its location. If, however, an explosive sound source is dropped in the water, several widely spaced SSQ-41Bs can be used to localize the submarine by measuring the difference in arrival times of the echo off the submarine. More complex are the SSQ-53 and SSQ-53A directional passive sonobuoys, which can obtain an independent bearing on a submarine. This means that only two sonobuoys are necessary to localize the submarine by simply intersecting two lines of bearing. Active sonobuoys function like active sonars, and the sophisticated SSQ-62 DICASS system (Directional Command Activated Sonobuoy System), which is just entering service, can localize a submarine with a single buoy on command from the aircraft. Hundreds of thousands of sonobuoys are needed to support ASW operations.[27]

Sonobuoys dropped from LAMPS helicopters are used to localize submarines that are trying to approach an aircraft carrier. In this mode, the helicopters are sent to the general vicinity of the intruder using initial detection information gathered by a towed array sonar. Sonobuoys can also be used to make the initial detection, and sometimes land-based P-3 or carrier-based S-3 aircraft fly ahead of CVBGs to drop a screen of sonobuoys, but due to the cost, short range, and limited supply of sonobuoys, initial detection is usually left to the ship's towed array systems.

The towed array suffers from the fact that it can only determine the angle to the target relative to the array, but there is an ambiguity as to on which side of the array the target is located. However, several towed array fixes can solve the ambiguity and provide sufficient information to send out LAMPS helicopters.

In contrast to the variety of radars and direction-finding sensors on surface ships, sonars are virtually the only sensors available on submarines besides the periscope, and great importance is given to the submarine sonar suite. Hull-mounted sonars are much more effective on submarines than they are on surface ships because of the lower hull vibration noise, remoteness from the noisy ocean surface, and the position of the submarine itself at optimal listening depths. US SSNs and SSBNs have a bow spherical sonar, a hull-mounted conformal sonar, and many have towed arrays. Attack submarines carry active as well as passive sonar, while SSBNs carry only passive sonar for defense and evasion. Another type of sonar found only on submarines is the passive range-finding sonar. This system is designed to estimate the range to a target with a single fix, rather than by using several lines of bearing obtained from different points in space.

In a class by themselves are the surveillance sonars: the principal US systems are SOSUS, SURTASS, and RDSS. The SOSUS (Sound Surveillance System) is the well-known fixed passive system that actually comprises several main subsystems, one off each coast of the United States, one in the Greenland–Iceland–United Kingdom gap, and others possibly off the Aleutians, Japan, and Norway. These systems are probably long line arrays, partly buried to prevent disruption by dragging anchors. They may be maintained by the US miniature nuclear submarine NR-1.[28] SURTASS (Surveillance Towed Array Systems) is a long line array towed at speeds of around 3 knots behind specially designed T-AGOS ships, which would be run by civilians. SURTASS is expected to provide coverage where SOSUS is unavailable, though in wartime both SOSUS and (to a lesser extent) SURTASS would be vulnerable. The rapidly deployable surveillance system (RDSS) is essentially a long-life, sophisticated, air-dropped sonobuoy that could provide surveillance in areas not covered by SOSUS or SURTASS.

Each RDSS buoy would moor itself, release hydrophone data in short bursts to an aircraft (as it is currently configured) or possibly to a satellite, and could provide lines of bearing on all submarines within a short radius. These could be rapidly dropped by aircraft like P-3s, S-3s, or even B-52s. The RDSS is based on the moored surveillance system (MSS), which was introduced in 1969 and has been in development since 1976 or 1977, when the Navy suddenly halted the MSS program and expanded the concept to the RDSS.[29] The Navy announced that it was stopping the RDSS program on 26 December 1984 because it "would not be cost effective by the time it became operational" in the early 1990s.[30] The RDSS was to have the ability to determine the direction to a sound from a single buoy using any one of a string of directional hydrophones. The amount of data generated by these sensors would require some processing in the buoy.[31] These buoys would be expected to have a relatively short range, particularly against the quiet Victor III and subsequent classes. A fundamental limitation to RDSS is that the small size of its array precludes efficient reception of low-frequency sounds from quiet submarines. In spite of this, the Navy announced in 1985 that it would revive the program.[32]

The Defense Advanced Research Projects Agency (DARPA) conducts research on Naval Tactical Technology as part of its program. The emphasis of DARPA's work in naval warfare has been and continues to be surveillance of the Soviet submarine forces.[33] To this end, DARPA has been examining methods of making fixed seabed distributed acoustic surveillance systems beyond SOSUS. At the core of the technology is the use of fiber optics to build inexpensive hydrophones and cables so that hundreds of short-range hydrophones could be laid on the ocean floor in areas where surveillance is particularly desired. This seabed distributed system avoids some of the inherent problems of long-range surveillance with long arrays by shortening the distance between the sensor and the target rather than by attempting to overcome the background ocean noise and the quietness of the target.

SSBN Attrition

Attempts to model the dynamics of strategic antisubmarine warfare at the level of a campaign must account for two processes: the search for SSBNs, and the likely outcome between individual engagements between SSBNs and the forces attacking them. The search process governs the time over which a campaign might take place, assuming that most of the time spent in ASW operations is in looking for the elusive SSBNs, while the actual battle may be relatively short. The outcome of the individual battles is determined by a large number of factors, such as quietness of the SSBN, quietness of the attacker, weapon range, weapon reliability, firing rate, presence of an ice cover, ocean conditions, and others. This level of modeling is very complex and relies on a great deal of tactical data that is either unknown or is classified. In this section and in chapter 2, some analyses are presented that reveal the basic character of strategic ASW campaigns, particularly US ASW campaigns against Soviet SSBNs. The first analysis, presented in this section, makes the simplifying assumption that all ASW forces search for SSBNs unopposed in order to examine some of the time scales involved in ASW "seek and destroy" campaigns. The analysis of trailing operations, which is fundamentally different from the search and destroy campaigns described here, is given in chapter 2.

Given the deployment of ASW forces and SSBNs, and some assumptions regarding detection range, one can calculate the time required for an ASW force to search completely an SSBN patrol area for the targets there. In order to make such a calculation without expending a huge amount of effort in modeling defenses against ASW forces, uncertainties due to the environment, sensors, weapons, and SSBN evasive tactics, the problem must be simplified to the point of being unrealistic. The benefit of such a calculation, however, is that it identifies the time scale that would govern the ideal search (ideal from the ASW point of view). One can then discuss, in a qualitative manner, the impact of more realistic assumptions on the search time.

In the idealized situation, current ASW forces in the Atlantic or Pacific mobilize simultaneously and search the opponent's SSBN patrol area completely unopposed. Each type of platform is assumed to have a constant detection range against the SSBN target and travels at a constant speed without overlapping any of the area previously covered by itself or by other ASW platforms. In the simplest case, the targets are assumed to be stationary.

The search rate in square nautical miles per hour for a given vessel is the product of its speed and twice its detection range. Detection range is defined in its simplest form as the range within which a target is detected with complete certainty, and beyond which a target cannot be detected. As appendix 7 shows, however, detection range is actually a probabilistic concept. The search rates for each vessel can be added to obtain the fleetwide search rate. This rate can then be applied to the SSBN patrol areas to obtain the time required to search—and by assumption to detect—all SSBNs in the area.

The detection ranges used in this analysis are of the order of magnitude, of 10 nautical miles. Surface ships and submarines with modern, low-frequency hulls or towed sonars were assigned ranges of about 30 nm. Vessels with medium-frequency sonars were assigned 10 nm ranges.[34] The Soviet Kiev class was assigned a 50 nm range, which is the range at which the Soviet ASW helicopters can spend 80 percent of their flying time on station. Moskva class ships are assigned a 40-mile detection range. These detection ranges, applied to US Ohio class SSBNs, are extremely overestimated, since the passive detection range against the Ohio class is on the order of a few miles or less.

US ASW assets are divided into carrier battle groups with detection ranges of 150 nm, or a total search width of 300 nm. These are the distances typically covered by a battle group,[35] and the assumption is that the SH-3H and S-3 carrier-based ASW aircraft, and the SH-2F and SH-60B helicopters, together with towed arrays detect all targets in the area. Ship and submarine search speeds are assumed to be 20 knots, which is high by at least a factor of two, since at such speeds, sensors are surrounded with too much noise to be of use.

Aircraft search areas are assumed to be equal to the product of the number of sonobuoys and the sonobuoy detection range—assumed to be 5 nm.[36] The average speed of advance of the ASW aircraft is taken to be 100 knots, about half the patrol speed. One way to visualize the aircraft search is to assume that a line of directional sonobuoys are dropped at a spacing of 5 miles, so that any two adjacent sonobuoys can localize a target. The aircraft drops the buoys at a speed of 200 knots and overflies them once, so the average speed is 100 knots. The United States has about 240 P-3 aircraft in active squadrons, and these are assumed to be divided evenly between the Atlantic and Pacific. Aircraft can also use MAD detection for open area search, but the area covered by a 1 nm sweep width in 4 hours (1/3 of total flight time) at 180 knots is much less than the area covered by sonobuoys given the assumptions.

The numbers of ASW forces in the search are based on a surge of 75 percent of major ASW ships, submarines, and long-range aircraft. Ships counted as primary ASW ships are those having low-frequency sonars and stand-off weapons to match the sonar range and those having helicopters. All modern SSNs and SSGNs are included.[37] Surface ships included in the Soviet Atlantic ASW force (including some from the Black Sea Fleet) are 2 Kiev, 2 Moskva, 2 Kirov, 2 Kara, 6 Kresta II, 2 Udaloy, 15 Krivak, and 3 Modified Kashin. In the surged Pacific Fleet are 1 Kiev, 2 Kara, 2 Kresta II, 1 Modified Kashin, and 8 Krivak. The only Soviet ASW aircraft able to cover US SSBN patrol areas are the Bear F, of which 19 are assumed available in the Atlantic and the same number in the Pacific.[38]

The Soviet Navy must search for US missile submarines in major portions of the North Atlantic and North Pacific oceans. The area of the North Atlantic that is within range of Moscow is 4 million square nautical miles. If all Soviet ships and submarines are used in this area, on the order of 60 hours is required. If only ships are used, the search time is over 200 hours, whereas if only submarines are used, the search time is about 100 hours. This emphasizes the point that submarines would provide the bulk of Soviet long-range ASW capability. ASW aircraft search time is measured by the number of search/reload cycles the entire fleet must make in order to cover the entire area. In the Atlantic, on the order of 100 cycles must be made by Soviet ASW Bear F aircraft.

In the Pacific, between Alaska, Hawaii, and the Soviet Union, the Soviet surface fleet would require over 500 hours for a search, and the nuclear submarines alone could search that area in about 200 hours. Together, these two forces could search that area in approximately 150 hours. Aircraft would require many hundreds of cycles.

The time scales for US search of Soviet SSBN patrol areas is relatively short due to the limited size of those areas and the number of modern US frigates and SSNs with low-frequency sonar systems of high quality. The sizes of primary Soviet SSBN patrol areas are as follows: Arctic 1,000,000 nm^2, Barents/Kara seas 394,000 nm^2, Norwegian/Greenland seas 650,000 nm^2, Sea of Okhotsk 452,000 nm^2. The time required by US carrier battle groups and frigates to search the Barents/Kara seas is on the order of 5 hours. Attack submarines alone require 8 hours. About 20 hours is required by the SSNs to search the Arctic Ocean, where of course surface ships cannot penetrate. The Sea of Okhotsk can be searched by the US Pacific attack submarine fleet in about 14 hours. US patrol aircraft would require a few cycles to search the Sea of Okhotsk and the Barents Sea. It is important to remember that these preliminary results are based on unrealistically long detection ranges and on total cooperation by the Soviet Navy.

Before discussing these results, it is helpful to introduce a basic idea from the theory of random search to illustrate how search time might increase if the targets move randomly. The search described above is exhaustive in the sense that as soon as the entire area is swept exactly once, all the targets are detected. This is because in the assumptions the targets do not move, so that each section that is swept can be ignored in further searching and there need be no overlap. As a probabilistic process, the exhaustive search is characterized by a linear increase over time in the probability of detecting all targets in the area. When the entire area is swept, the probability reaches unity. However, no realistic search process would have this characteristic.

If the targets move randomly, they may move into areas previously searched, which means that covering the entire area once does not guarantee that all targets are detected, and the searchers are forced to overlap. Another way to visualize this process is to see the targets as stationary, but with the searchers lacking memory of where they previously searched, and therefore overlapping randomly. The assumptions of a random search lead to the result that the probability of detecting all the targets in an area increases as unity minus a negative exponential, approaching unity asymptotically. The "time constant" of this function is the exhaustive search time, which has aleady been calculated. According to the random search model, the time required to achieve a probability of 0.95 of detecting all randomly moving targets is three times the exhaustive search time. Therefore, to account for random target motion, multiply the search times calculated above by three.

Given no prior information about the location of US SSBNs, the time required by Soviet forces to search their patrol areas is on the order of weeks, even under the extremely favorable conditions of long detection range, no SSBN evasion, and no interference from other US forces. Aircraft provide an insignificant fraction of the total ASW search capability. Under more realistic conditions it is doubtful that many Soviet surface ships could even enter the North Atlantic. Submarines would have a better chance but would suffer heavy attrition.

The time required for US forces to search Soviet SSBN deployment areas is much shorter, on the order of a day or a few days, assuming no opposition and long detection ranges. However, the level of opposition that the Soviet Navy could mount against such a search is intense, due to the proximity of Soviet SSBN patrol areas to major fleet concentrations. While aircraft can provide a significant fraction of the search capability under these highly idealized conditions, they would in fact be extremely vulnerable to Soviet tactical aircraft, as would US surface ships. In addition to human interference, the ocean itself would limit the ASW operations of surface ships. Frigates in particular are vulnerable and may be capable of conducting helicopter operations 20–30 percent of the time in northern latitudes, and even carrier-based aircraft have been "grounded" due to high winds.

The only threat that can have a major impact is that of the US attack submarines, which can penetrate the Soviet bastions and travel under the ice. However, in the presence of Soviet defenses, US SSNs in the bastions would themselves be subject to attrition, and with a sufficient density of defenses (including minefields) the attrition rate of US SSNs could be very high.

The impact of a decoy/minefield scheme on a strategic ASW search campaign can be illustrated by a simple example. Suppose that in a crisis involving the movement of US attack submarines to sea, the Soviet Navy decides to begin dispersing SSBNs and setting decoys and mines. One configuration would be a recording of an SSBN, broadcast from a submerged buoy. Surrounding the buoy at a range similar to the maximum effective range of a Mk 48 torpedo, say 10 miles, a series of mines could be set along a 60-mile circular perimeter. The mines might be set in clusters around the perimeter, with a mile-wide cluster every 10 miles. If the probability of destroying a submarine in the mine clusters is very high, then the probability of destroying a submarine that crossed the perimeter is 0.1. This assumes that the submarine is equally likely to cross the perimeter at any angle and that it exits the same way it entered. It is assumed that if the attack submarine successfully enters the mined perimeter then it can determine that the decoy is indeed a false target.

Consider a single US attack submarine searching for a single, undefended Soviet SSBN in a large area. When the two vessels engage, the expected outcome is given by the assumed kill probability. Assuming no mutual kills, the probability that the SSBN is destroyed is 0.75 and the probability that the SSN is destroyed is 0.25. In other words, the US-favorable exchange ratio is assumed to be 3:1, which is probably an overestimate against modern quiet Soviet SSBNs.

If the exchange ratio is used as a measure of the likely outcome of this one-on-one "campaign," then the impact of mines and decoys must be calculated. In the case of no decoy/minefields, the exchange ratio is simply 3:1. In the case of one decoy/minefield, if it is assumed that the SSN is as likely to encounter a decoy as an SSBN, the probability of the SSN encountering either the SSBN or the decoy is 0.5. Calculating the probabilities of the various outcomes, the probability that the US attack submarine is destroyed either by the SSBN or by the minefield is 0.288, which means that the exchange ratio drops to 2.5:1. In the case of four decoy/minefields, the exchange ratio for the ASW "campaign" reduces to 1.6:1. In terms of cost-effectiveness, this means that for every SSBN, if the Soviet Navy invests in four decoys and associated mines, the United States must invest in another attack submarine in order to achieve the same outcome.

No mention has been made of the time required for the SSN to execute such a search, but the presence of decoys that must be localized, approached, and possibly attacked clearly increases the search time. The impact of increasing the search time may not be important if the time required to search in the absence of decoys is already long. In cases where the search time is expected to be relatively short, however, the additional time required to track down decoys may give SSBN defense forces time to mobilize.

Notes

1. At the time of publication, US adherence to SALT had ceased.
2. These figures are as of late 1985.
3. Capt. James W. Kehoe, Kenneth S. Brower, and Herbert A. Meier, "US and Soviet Ship Design Practices, 1950–1980," *US Naval Institute Proceedings,* Naval Review Issue 1982, pp. 118–132.
4. John Jordan, *Soviet Warships* (Annapolis: Naval Institute Press, 1983), p. 82.
5. Jean Labayle Couhat, *Combat Fleets of the World 1982/83* (Annapolis: Naval Institute Press, 1983), p. 591.
6. *FY 1986 DoD Program for Research, Development, and Acquisition,* p. II-4.
7. Caspar Weinberger, *Soviet Military Power 1986* (Washington, DC: US Government Printing Office, 1986), p. 86.
8. US Navy, *Understanding Soviet Naval Developments* 5th ed. (Washington, DC: US Government Printing Office, 1985), pp. 49, 135.

9. In more realistic scenarios, ASW aircraft might be operating in the Indian Ocean, the eastern Mediterranean, and out of Vietnam.

10. Apparently the construction rate is yielding a very modest growth in the total number of active aircraft.

11. John M. Collins, *US-Soviet Military Balance* (New York: McGraw-Hill, 1980), pp. 333–336.

12. Seymour M. Hersh, "A False Navy Report Alleged in Sub Crash," *New York Times,* 6 July 1975, p. 1.

13. *Jane's Weapon Systems 1984/85,* p. 221.

14. Couhat, *Combat Fleets,* p. 223.

15. *Jane's Weapon Systems 1984/85,* p. 222.

16. Richard Barnard, "Captor Capsized; Funding Sinks," *Defense Week,* 30 July 1984, p. 12.

17. SASC, FY 1986, part 8, p. 4407.

18. Barnard, "Captor Capsized."

19. Steve Eisenstadt, "Firm Fouls Exotic Naval Mine; No Deliveries after Two Years," *Defense News,* 23 September 1985, p. 1.

20. Kehoe, Brower, and Meier, "US and Soviet Ship Design," pp. 118–132.

21. Vice Adm. Wesley L. McDonald, Deputy CNO, SASC, FY 1983, part 6, p. 4051.

22. Ibid.

23. These helicopters are also used for targeting distant ships beyond the horizon and guiding surface-to-surface missiles to these ships. The Soviet Navy has a separate helicopter—the Hormone B—for this purpose.

24. SASC, FY 1983, part 6, p. 4052.

25. Lt. John F. McGowan, USN, "LAMPS I: Still Glowing," *US Naval Institute Proceedings,* July 1982, pp. 108–109.

26. Norman Polmar, *The Ships and Aircraft of the U.S. Fleet* (Annapolis: Naval Institute Press, 1981), pp. 407, 414.

27. For example (to mention a few), between 1969 and 1975, 108,100 SSQ-53s were produced; between 1974 and 1981, 341,702 SSQ-53As were produced; and between 1968 and 1981, 106,308 SSQ-57As were produced. Source: *Jane's Weapon Systems, 1982/83,* pp. 754, 755.

28. Norman Polmar, *The American Submarine* (Annapolis: US Naval Institute Press, 1983), p. 168.

29. Stephen D. Biddle, "US Undersea Surveillance: An Examination of SOSUS, SURTASS, and RDSS," unpublished paper, Center for Defense Information, Washington, DC. Also, Wayne Biddle, "Navy Quietly Revives Antisubmarine Project Halted in 1984," *New York Times,* 12 January 1985, p. 5. Also, "RDSS ASW Buoy Configuration Set," *Sea Technology,* December 1981, pp. 52–53.

30. Wayne Biddle, "Navy Quietly Revives Antisubmarine Program," p. 5.

31. "RDSS ASW Buoy Configuration Set," pp. 52–53.

32. Wayne Biddle, "Navy Quietly Revives Antisubmarine Program," p. 5.

33. *FY 1984 Research and Development Program* (U), (Arlington, Va., Defense Advanced Research Projects Agency), p. 8.

34. The French DUBV 43 low-frequency towed sonar has an advertised detection range of 10–20 kilometers, so these figures represent high estimates of the detection

range. Jean Labayle Couhat, *Combat Fleets of the World 1984/85* (Annapolis: US Naval Institute Press, 1985), p. 157.

35. In the W-4 formation. Adm. James D. Watkins, SASC, FY 1985, part 8, p. 3890.

36. B. I. Rodionov, *Antisubmarine Warfare Forces and Systems in Navies* (Moscow: Voyenizdat, 1977), fig. 3.6.

37. The classes of submarines that are included are the 36 M, S, A, and V class SSNs, and the 16 O, P, and C class SSGNs in the Atlantic; and in the Pacific, 13 V class SSNs and 5 C class SSGNs. The long-range diesel-electric submarine fleet includes 43 F and T class SSs in the Atlantic, and 34 F and K class SSs in the Pacific.

38. Each Bear F aircraft is assumed to carry 87 sonobuoys, since the weapon load of a Bear F is about the same as a P-3 (7,700 kg), which carries that number. With a buoy range of 5 miles, the total area covered by the 19 aircraft is about 41,000 nm^2 (140,000 km^2) in one cycle.

Appendix 3
Nonacoustic Means of Submarine Detection

Means of detecting submarines that do not involve underwater sound (that is, sonar) are called nonacoustic detection measures. Currently, nonacoustic techniques are limited in long-range detection capability and are primarily used for short-range localization, though both the the United States and the USSR have been devoting considerable efforts to research in nonacoustic technologies that might be used to detect submerged submarines at long distances.[1]

Unofficial stories abound regarding the US Navy's interest in exotic means of detecting submarines, such as flights over the ocean with Ouija board "operators," and investigations of dowsers who claim the ability to find submarines on ocean charts. Whatever their accuracy, such stories are plausible, for the enormous military benefit that would accrue in terms of ASW capability compensates for the low probability of success. Moreover, the perceived cost of a sudden Soviet breakthrough in the ability to detect US submarines helps drive the search for new detection methods.

Observable Submarine Disturbances

Any disturbance of the physical environment caused by a submarine suggests the possibility of remote detection. The disturbance must be measurable at a distancc and must also be discriminated from the background of similar naturally occurring disturbances. Such an anomaly is frequently called an observable. To be useful, a detection system must perform both of these functions—detection and discrimination—to some degree of confidence.

The objective of this appendix is to describe the physical nature of the more prominently discussed nonacoustic submarine observables in terms of detection and discrimination. The structure of this discussion will attempt to follow roughly the logic of the system designer and will begin with the signal strength at the submarine, the transmission characteristics of the signal, the noise and false targets that must be discriminated against, and the sensors that can perform the tasks. Included are some assessments from the literature, most of which have been drawn together in a recent study by Daniel,[2] and a summary of the prospects and problems with these detection means.

The signal strength at the submarine must be defined rather broadly to include the various observables, but in general it is some measure of the degree of modification of the local environment. A related factor is the persistence of the modification. An observable that is associated only with the vessel itself presents a different detection problem from one that persists and trails behind the submarine at some distance that is large compared with the length of the submarine. A persistent observable increases the size of the target and yields information on the history of its movement. In addition to the source strength, the signal transmission or propagation loss characteristics are a major system variable. The medium of propagation is of course the sea, or the sea and air together. The atmosphere is transparent to many kinds of electromagnetic radiation, while the sea is opaque. On the other hand, the sea is a much more efficent medium for transmitting sound.

Noise and false targets are closely related and can be described generally as phenomena similar to the submarine observable, but which are caused by processes other than submarine activities. The phenomenon may be widely distributed geographically and may form an overall background against which the submarine observable must be detected, in which case it is usually referred to as noise. On the other hand, the phenomenon may be spatially discrete and as such present potential false targets. Noise and false targets can be associated with natural processes in the environment as well as with deliberate human attempts to generate them. The main questions are how strong the noise and false targets are in relation to the strength of the submarine observables, how closely they imitate the particular spatial and temporal pattern of the submarine's signal, and in the case of human attempts to create noise and false targets, how difficult it is to build and power such systems.

There is an important distinction to be made between detection of a small signal against background noise at a particular point and the detection of a pattern of disturbance against background noise.

In the former case, "detection" means that the measured signal rises above the background to a preset threshold. This method takes no account of the spatial coherence of submarine observables. The detection of a pattern involves correlating prior information about the general shape of the submarine-generated pattern with observed patterns in the ocean. The same observable might be more detectable using the additional pattern information.

The analysis contained here takes no account of the pattern of a submarine observable. Because of this, the analysis tends to underestimate the detectability of an observable that exhibits a predictable pattern. It is not clear how much more detectable the observable might be using a pattern-recognizing scheme. That would depend on the coherence of the pattern, the coherence of patterns generated by natural phenomena, knowledge of the patterns, and the ability to make the enormous number of calculations necessary to correlate assumed patterns with observed ones.

A partial list of non-acoustic submarine observables is:

Direct electromagnetic effects: galvanic currents from hull, magnetic anomaly

Biological disturbances: bioluminescence, fish and mammal behavior

Ocean surface effects: surface waves

Internal waves: electromagnetic signals generated by internal waves, modulation of surface waves

Temperature: reactor heat, disruption of the thermocline

Optical reflectivity or absorption: laser reflection or absorption

Wakes: effect of turbulent wakes on the surface, direct detection of wake

Chemical and radioactive effects: paint, corrosion, chemical effluents, radioactive elements

The following is a brief description of some of the more frequently discussed means of nonacoustic detection.[3]

Local Changes in the Earth's Magnetic Field. As a large piece of ferrous metal, the steel-hulled submarine causes a local disturbance in the earth's magnetic field. This disturbance or anomaly can be detected with a device that measures the local magnetic field. Magnetic anomaly detection (MAD) is used on US and Soviet aircraft to verify acoustic detection and localize the position of the target submarine. If a nonmagnetic hull material is used, the magnetic signature decreases but is not eliminated, since the submarine contains some ferrous parts, and the nonmagnetic shell does not shield the magnetic effects of this internal material.

Bioluminescent Detection. The sea contains bioluminescent organisms of many kinds, although it is not clear which ones are relevant to detection. These organisms can generate light when they are physically stimulated in the boundary layer of a submarine or in its wake. This phenomenon has been studied as a method for detecting submarines from the air or space.

Submarine-generated Waves on the Surface of the Ocean. Moving submarines at high speeds and shallow depths generate surface waves behind them. At reasonable depths and speeds, however, submarine-generated surface waves are negligibly small. The presence of wind-generated surface waves masks the minute submarine waves.

Submarine-generated Internal Waves. Internal waves are oscillations of the thermocline that can be caused by a solid body moving in the ocean. Internal waves in turn cause water motion at the surface that is not directly observable but that can influence preexisting wind-generated ripples and waves on the surface. These changes in the surface can in principle be detected by radar. The ocean always contains internal waves that are generated by storms, currents, tides, whales, surface ships, and submarines. Internal waves and wakes may also change the emissivity of the surface, which can be detected by passive microwave radiometry.

Submarine-related Changes in the Sea Surface Temperature. Submarine nuclear reactors generate an enormous amount of heat, which ultimately must be rejected into the surrounding seawater. Water has a very high capacity to absorb heat with a small change in temperature, however, and a moving submarine raises the water temperature by a very small amount.

A moving submarine may also change the temperature of the sea surface by mixing lower cooler water with upper water, thereby leaving a trail of cool surface water that could be detected with infrared (heat) sensors.

Laser Detection. The sea is relatively transparent to blue-green light. A burst of blue-green laser light could penetrate the sea, reflect off an object, and return to the sensor. The round-trip travel time of the laser burst indicates the depth of the object, but cannot discriminate, for example, between a large whale and a submarine. On the other hand, a black submarine may not reflect as much light as the ocean would backscatter, and the system may attempt to detect the lack of returned light. Lasers might also be used to detect changes in the internal scattering in the ocean caused by a submarine.

This consideration of nonacoustic detection methods is by no means complete, but it describes those methods that are most frequently discussed. Table A3–1 summarizes the nonacoustic effects that may be used for ASW detection.

Magnetic Anomaly Detection

Magnetic anomaly detection (MAD) devices are used to detect changes in the background magnetic induction that are associated with submarines. Terrestrial magnetism usually varies slowly over distance, but when a submarine is present, the field changes rapidly and may be detected by a low flying aircraft carrying MAD equipment.

Table A3–1
Some nonacoustic methods of submarine detection

Physical Quantity Measured	*Submarine Effect*	*Sensor*
Magnetic field strength	Perturbation of earth's magnetic field and of local fixed anomalies	Magnetic anomaly detector
Emitted light level	Excitation of light-emitting organisms	Blue-green light sensors
Sea surface elevation	Surface waves generated by moving submarine	Synthetic aperture radar
Sea surface roughness	Internal waves, which modulate sea surface roughness	Radar, or passive microwave radiometry
Sea surface temperature	Temperature anomaly due to upwelling and mixing of deep water	Infrared radiometry
Reflection or absorption of laser, backscattering	Direct reflection off (or absorption by) submarine, backscatter from internal waves	Blue-green laser (lidar)

Submarines contain a large amount of metal that becomes magnetized in the course of normal operations. The permanent magnetic field associated with the submarine remains until active measures are used to demagnetize it. The earth's magnetism induces a transient magnetic field that depends on the spatial orientation of the submarine. The total magnetic field of the submarine is the sum of the permanent and induced magnetic fields.

The strength of the magnetic field at a distance from the submarine is inversely proportional to the third power of distance. The shape of the earth's magnetic field lines are distorted by the submarine according to how far away it is. A MAD-equipped aircraft flying horizontally through such a submarine-distorted field would detect a sharp change in the magnetic induction if it passed directly over the submarine.

The earth has a strong and very complex magnetic field that varies with time and location. Typical values of the earth's magnetic induction at the surface are between 25,000 and 50,000 gammas. On a small scale the earth's magnetic field is very irregular, and small natural magnetic anomalies associated with ore deposits may be indistinguishable from submarines to MAD equipment. When searching areas in which there is a high level of geologic noise, MAD operators must set their receivers at a low sensitivity. According to a Navy study, "At these . . . settings it will be difficult, if not impossible, to see a small submarine anomaly."[4] "Parts of the Norwegian Sea," and "the seas around Iceland" are areas where geologic noise may interfere with MAD operations.[5]

The earth's magnetic field varies temporally as well as spatially. Solar storms send charged particles into space that modify the natural field. In peak years of the 12-year solar storm cycle, there are intense magnetic storms about 15 percent of the time. In quiet years, intense storm activity occurs only 3 percent of the time. Figure A3–1 shows a typical MAD signal during a moderate magnetic storm obtained from a stationary MAD device. For comparison, the box in the lower left-hand corner shows a typical signal for an aircraft passing over a submarine. The difficulties in discerning a submarine signal from the noise produced by even a moderate storm are evident. It is seldom that environmental magnet noise will produce a targetlike signal; rather, its effect is to mask signals, thereby reducing the effective range of the MAD equipment.[6] The intensity of this noise increases as one approaches the north magnetic pole.[7] In practical terms, "that means that during the same magnetic storm, aircraft flying out of Puerto Rico might see very little effect, and those flying out of Iceland would be wondering what happened to their equipment."[8]

The United States currently deploys two types of MAD equipment on its ASW aircraft, the ASQ-10A and the more recent ASQ-81. The sensitivity of the ASQ-10A is 0.2 gammas, and the sensitivity of the ASQ-81 is 0.05 gammas.[9] This fourfold increase in sensitivity yields only a 59 percent increase in detection range. These systems can detect the submarine magnetic field at a maximum range of a few thousand feet.[10]

At a range of 100 miles, the magnetic signal level from a submarine is seven orders of magnitude lower than the minimum signal that can be detected by the ASQ-81. It would be virtually impossible to identify such a small signal in the presence of noise from geologic anomalies and magnetic storms.

A more basic limitation to long-range magnetic surveillance is that a magnetic antenna would be impossible to build. Unlike sound or light, the magnetic field is not a propagating wave phenomenon. This means that it is not possible to form a passive directional beam of sensitivity, and all magnetic fields and disturbances affect the measurement of the magnetic field at a point. An extremely sensitive magnetic induction sensor that could sense the minuscule magnetic field change caused by a submarine at 100 miles would also be sensing every other minute variation in the magnetic field originating from every direction. Without directionality, such a sensor would be overcome by magnetic noise.

Area magnetic surveillance is technically feasible with a distributed system of many MAD systems. The most suitable mission would be as a barrier against

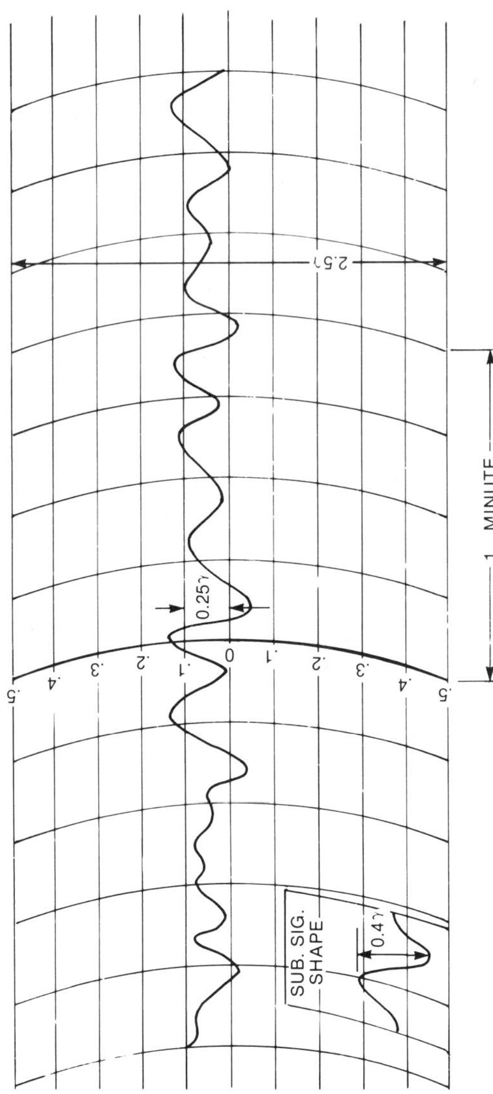

Figure A3–1. Magnetic noise in an ASQ-10 MAD system due to a moderate magnetic storm, compared with a typical submarine-generated signal.

Source: James A. Brennan and Kuno Smits, *The Effect of Geomagnetic Micropulsations on MAD Systems* (Washington, DC: Naval Oceanographic Office, Oct. 1975), TR-250, p. 12.

intruding submarines. For example, the polar ice pack north of the Barents Sea is an area in which a magnetic sensing barrier could be placed using available technology. MAD sensors placed on the ice could detect submarines passing below. Thus distributed, MAD systems might prove useful to the Soviet Navy in its efforts to defend its SSBNs.

Even if some highly sensitive MAD system were widely distributed in the ocean, simple countermeasures could render it virtually useless. Small dummy submarines could carry coils that reproduce the magnetic signature of a much larger submarine. Military submarines themselves could carry coils that neutralize their own magnetic field by imposing an equal and opposite magnetic field from the coil.

Detection of Submarine-induced Bioluminescence

The primary sources of ocean bioluminescence are certain species of dinoflagellates and some zooplankton.[11] The mechanical stimulus of a moving submarine hull and its turbulent wake will elicit luminescence from organisms disturbed or killed. The power and persistence of this light is a function of the population density, species, environmental conditions, physiological state, and submarine speed.

Luminescence is expected to be the strongest in the turbulent regions associated with a submarine—that is, the hull boundary layer and the wake. The thickness of the turbulent boundary surrounding the hull is small relative to the diameter of the hull and increases very slowly with speed. The Reynolds number, which is a measure of the turbulent forces in the wake, decreases linearly with distance behind a self-propelled body.[12] Typical length scales for surface ship luminescent wakes is several ship lengths.[13] The physical wakes of submarines may be shorter, however. Experiments on the acoustic properties of wakes from diesel-electric submarines (World War II S-class) showed that at a speed of 6 knots, the length of the acoustically detectable wake is 1,000 yards at a depth of 45 feet, 235 yards at a depth of 90 feet, and only 100 yards at a depth of 125 feet.[14] "At creeping speed (2 to 3 knots) the length of the acoustically effective wake is less than 30 yards for a fleet type submarine."[15] These submarines were smaller, had higher rpm propellers, and had more appendages than modern submarines, so these results must be used cautiously when discussing modern submarines. In addition, an acoustically effective level of turbulence may or may not be sufficient to stimulate bioluminescence. However, it has been observed that the visible manifestations of surface wakes decay before the acoustic,[16] so it is assumed that the extent of a wake that contains sufficient energy to scatter acoustic energy is equal to or greater than the extent of the wake that can stimulate bioluminescence.

The radiant flux of an individual organism varies widely among species. The dinoflagellate *noctiluca miliaris* may radiate 0.002×10^{-9} watts, while other organisms may radiate 20×10^{-9} watts or more.[17] The peak of the emission spectrum in dinoflagellates and many other organisms is in the blue to blue-green part of the visible spectrum, 0.48 microns. This is also the wavelength that is transmitted in seawater with the least attenuation. Almost all of the energy in dinoflagellate bioluminescence is radiated in a 0.17-micron-wide band between 0.42 and 0.59 microns.[18]

The population density of bioluminescent organisms varies with location and depth. At any given point, the density may also vary seasonally and diurnally. According to one study, "Under natural conditions, bioluminescence is maximum around midnight and minimum around midday. This diurnal periodicity is attributed in part to downward migration of the organisms during the day and return migration to surface waters at night."[19] Most luminescence is found between 50 and 150 meters and is associated with dense dinoflagellate populations in continental shelf areas up to 60 degrees north latitude. Maximum luminescence frequently occurs at depths where the water temperature changes relatively quickly in the vertical direction. Such layers are called thermoclines.[20] The available data on geographic distribution is sparse and heavily biased by the density of shipboard observations. In the North Atlantic from Nova Scotia to France, wintertime bioluminescent levels are low. In the summer, bioluminescent levels increase somewhat at all latitudes, but according to the little data that is available, levels in the Norwegian Sea and the GIUK gap area remain low. Wintertime bioluminescence in the Pacific is minimal, even when compared to the North Atlantic. This minimum is more pronounced at high latitudes. In the Sea of Okhotsk, bioluminescence is observed all year around, even in broken winter ice fields.[21] Population densities vary over several orders of magnitude from 10^3 cells per liter to 10^5 cells per liter.[22] It is important to note, however, that the bioluminescence is not necessarily correlated to population density.

The amount of light generated by a submarine wake can be estimated by multiplying the volume of water disturbed by the wake, the number of organisms per unit volume, and the light power emitted per organism. Since the flux of light through a unit area is the relevant measure, only the thickness of the wake need be considered, if it is assumed that the wake is very wide. This assumption will tend to overestimate the detectability of the wake. It is also assumed that the organisms emit light constantly and at their full power level. Suppose a submarine generates a wake about as thick as its diameter, 10 meters. A column through that wake generates

$$(10^5 \text{ cells/liter}) \times (10^3 \text{ liter/m}^3) \times (10^{-9} \text{ watt/cell}) \times (10 \text{ m}) = 1 \text{ watt/m}^2$$

ignoring the fact that only half this is radiated upward, and some of it is absorbed in the 10-meter water column. Since the energy is emitted in a 0.17 micron band, the spectral density of the signal is on the order of 6 watt/m^2/micron.

Measurements of ocean bioluminescence in situ suggest much lower values of the signal. Values of up to 10^{-4} watt/m^2/micron are high measurements in the ocean; typical values for the North Atlantic and North Pacific are 10^{-6} to 10^{-5} watt/m^2/micron.[23] This is four orders of magnitude lower than what is estimated by the preceding analysis, which is, incidentally, similar to the analysis used by Strand et al. Part of the reason that the analysis overestimates the output of a wake is that it assumes all organisms glow constantly, whereas dinoflagellates flash only intermittently for a duration of about 100 milliseconds, although the flash characteristics vary widely.[24]

In order to reveal the presence of a submarine, this light energy must pass through some depth of water and atmosphere and still be sufficiently strong relative to reflected and scattered sunlight or moonlight to be detected. To estimate the detectability of a wake, one must compare the bioluminescent irradiance to the sunlight and moonlight irradiance. Exponential transmission loss is assumed between the source and the surface, with an attenuation coefficient for blue-green light being a function of depth. The one-way transmission loss is given in table A3–2.[25] The geometric spreading of the light is ignored. It is important to note the sensitivity of the results to the assumption of total

Table A3–2
Optical transmission loss as a function of submarine depth
(Wavelength = 0.48 microns [blue-green])

Depth (meters)	*One-Way Loss (dB)*	*Round-Trip Loss (dB)*
50	-24	-48
75	-36	-72
100	-45	-89
150	-62	-124
200	-72	-145
250	-83	-167

Depth	*Attenuation Coefficient*
5–75 meters	0.11 m^{-1}
75–150 meters	0.08 m^{-1}
>150 meters	0.05 m^{-1}

Source: John E. Tyler, "Optical Properties of Water," in *Handbook of Optics*, ed. Walter G. Driscoll (New York: McGraw-Hill, 1978), p. 15–30.

atmospheric transmission. Attenuation of 10–40 dB over a one-way path from the earth's surface to space is common. The higher value is associated with clouds and fog, which on an oceanwide average, cover 60 percent of the surface. As oceanographer Eric Mollo-Christensen observed: "One does not realize the prevalence of cloud and fog patches before one starts looking for visible and infrared satellite data for the surface."[26]

The noise against which a bioluminescent imaging system must discriminate is scattered light from the atmosphere, reflected light from the sea surface, and scattered light from within the sea. A sensor outside the atmosphere receives about 19 percent of its light from internal sea scattering, 80 percent from atmospheric backscatter, and 1 percent from surface reflection.[27]

For the moment consider a sensor close above the water surface so that atmospheric scattering can be ignored, as can scattering from within the sea. These two assumptions reduce the predicted noise level by about a factor of 100, or 20 dB. The reflected irradiance at the sea surface is typically 4 percent of the incident irradiance.[28] Data on incident—that is, downward—irradiance is available from Priesendorfer, who indicates that under average cloud conditions, we receive on the order of 1,000 watt/m^2/micron in the bioluminescent band (0.42 to 0.59 microns) from the sun. Under the blackest of skies, this is reduced to 100 watt/m^2/micron, even at fairly low sun angles. At night, however, even a clear, full moon gives us only 10^{-2} watt/m^2/micron, and a quarter moon 10^{-3} watt/m^2/micron in the bioluminescent band.[29] There can be a six order of magnitude change in the noise level over the course of each day! Taking 4 percent of these values for the upward reflected noise detected by a downward looking sensor (and ignoring backscatter), the signal-to-noise ratio for different submarine depths at different times of the day are calculated in table A3-3. It is clear from these results that during the daytime, the

Table A3–3
Signal-to-noise ratios for bioluminescence detector at the sea surface for various sky conditions and source depths

		Upward Surface-reflected Irradiance versus Sky Condition (W/m^2/micron)			
Submarine Depth (meters)	*Surface Signal (W/m^2/micron)*	*Avg. Cloud*[a] 40	*Black Sky* 4	*Full Moon* 4×10^{-4}	*Quarter Moon* 4×10^{-5}
0	10^{-3}	-46	-36	+6	+16
50	4×10^{-6}	-71	-61	-21	-11
100	3×10^{-8}	-91	-81	-41	-31
150	6×10^{-10}	-108	-98	-58	-48

[a]Figures under sky conditions are values of upward reflected irradiance. Bioluminescent source level taken as 10^{-3} watt/m^2/micron. Typical values are 20 dB lower. Atmospheric and oceanic backscattered irradiance is omitted.

bioluminescence is lost within the surface reflection. For a sensor high in the atmosphere, the signal-to-noise ratio should degrade by an additional 20 dB due to atmospheric scattering of ambient light into the sensor's field of view. Low-level light image intensifiers can improve the absolute signal level, but not the signal-to-noise ratio. At night, disturbances on the sea surface may be detectable, according to table A3–3. However, reviewing the assumptions behind these calculations, particularly the overestimate of the bioluminescence signal and the omission of the upward noise irradiance due to scattering, it should be apparent that the signal-to-noise ratios for submarines below 50 meters may easily be less than –20 dB under practical conditions. The only other possibility for creating a surface bioluminescent disturbance is for the wake to reach the surface, but it will be shown that submarine wakes generated below 50 meters are unlikely to do so.

Before leaving the topic of bioluminescence, it is helpful to examine one publicized application of this technology. Many species of fish rise to the surface at night, to feed on plankton. As the fish disturb the water, the plankton emit light and guide fishermen to them. Low-level light image intensifiers can be used to detect these signals.[30] Referring to table A3–3, under moonlit conditions, the low surface-reflected noise results in signal-to-noise ratios of 10 dB or more, which are detectable, and under the proper conditions should be visible to the eye. In essence, it is the depth of the submarine-generated light that precludes its detection from above the surface.

Detection of Surface Waves Generated by Submarines

This section examines the physical effects and engineering problems associated with detection of submarine surface waves. Solutions are obtained for near-field and far-field waves generated by a moving body that closely approximates the hull dimensions of the Ohio class submarine. These results are then compared with typical wind-generated surface waves. It is found that the submarine wave is negligibly small relative to wind waves.

For the purposes of calculating surface effects from a submerged body the following assumptions are made:

1. The ocean is infinite in depth and extent.
2. The free surface has no surface tension.
3. The fluid has no viscosity, there are no shear stresses, only normal stresses.
4. The submarine hull is approximated as a source and a sink moving along an axis parallel to the free surface.

The first assumption is based on the fact that ocean bottom and boundaries are distant relative to the scale of the submarine. The second assumption follows from the fact that the wavelength of the surface disturbance is large relative to the wavelengths at which surface tension is important. Surface tension is effective only at wavelengths less than a few centimeters. The third assumption follows from the fact that the boundary layer on the submarine is small relative to the diameter. The fourth assumption simply follows from the fact that the body generated from such a source-sink pair, called the rankine ovoid, is geometrically a very good approximation to a modern submarine hull.[31]

The Near-Field Solution

The solution[32] for the near-field disturbance generated by a source-sink pair is given by equation A3.1. This equation predicts the sea surface disturbance, $\zeta_{N,T}$, directly over a moving submarine and is the product of two functions. The first is a scaling function that varies with speed *U*, hull diameter *D*, and depth. The second is a shape function varying over the distance from the midpoint of the hull and dependent on depth *h* and the length 2*a*, of the submarine. The *x* coordinate is zero at the midpoint of the submarine and is positive in the direction of the stern, and *g* is the acceleration due to gravity.

$$\zeta_{N,T}(x,0) = \frac{D^2U^2}{8gh^2}\left[\hat{f}\left(\frac{x+a}{h}\right) - \hat{f}\left(\frac{x-a}{h}\right)\right] \qquad \text{(A3.1)}$$

The nondimensional shape function is shown in figure A3–2 for two values of depth. Calculations of the near-field wave height are given in table A3–4 for the scaling function $W(U, D, h)$:

$$W(\mathrm{U, D, h}) = D^2U^2/8gh^2 \qquad \text{(A3.2)}$$

where a diameter *D* of 11 meters is assumed, which is about the hull diameter of the Ohio class Trident missile submarine.

The near-field disturbance of the surface appears as a hump of water (sometimes called a Bernoulli hump) over the moving submarine which dies away rapidly with distance from the submarine. The two curves plotted in figure A3–2 correspond to an Ohio class submarine at 82 meters and 164 meters depth, and have a maximum value of about 0.8. The general shape of the disturbance is not very sensitive to changes in depth. The height of the disturbance, on the other hand, increases as the square of the speed, and decreases as the square of the depth. The surface disturbance is limited in extent to a few ship-lengths.

The amplitude of the wave is shown in table A3–4 to be very small but, under certain circumstances, measurable. An Ohio class submarine running 20 knots at only 30 meters depth would generate a wave at most 0.8×19 cm = 15

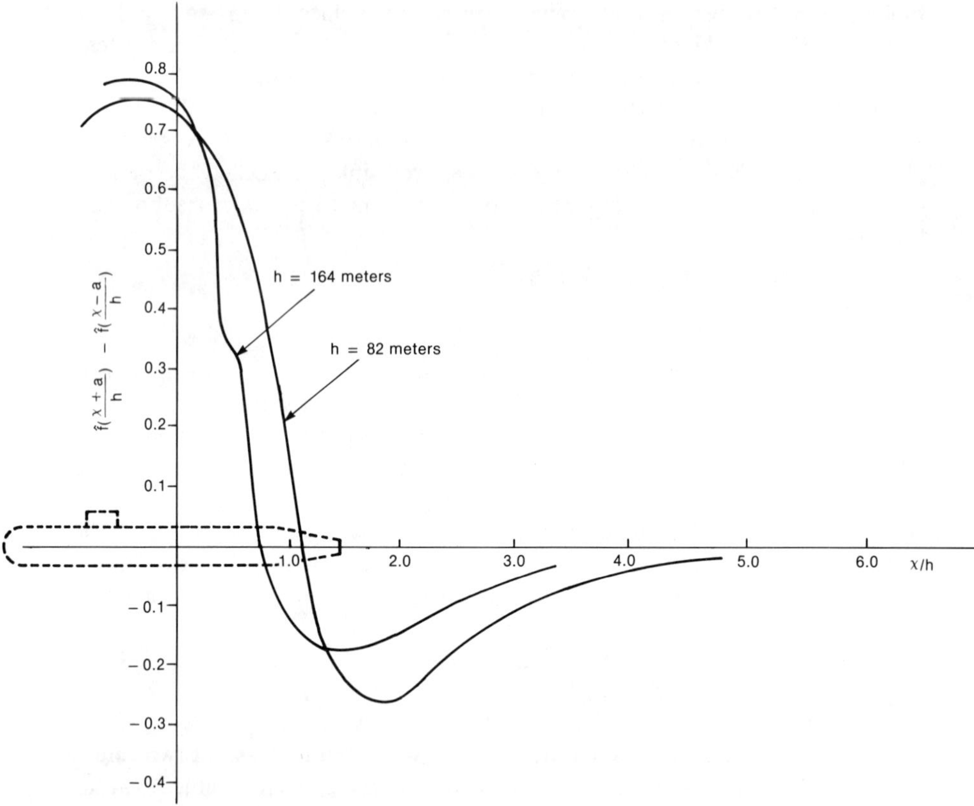

Figure A3–2. Nondimensional shape of the near field surface disturbance (Bernoulli hump) over a moving submarine (dimensions of the Ohio class).

Note: The shape is independent of speed and insensitive to depth. See table A3–4 for the height of the near field disturbance.

cm high. Under more realistic patrol conditions (5 knots at 100 meters), the wave is on the order of a millimeter.

The Far-Field Solution

The solution[33] for the far-field disturbance due to a single source contains oscillatory wave components that have a physical wavelength given by

$$L_{\text{wave}} = 6.3\ U^2/g \qquad \text{(A3.3)}$$

Table A3–4
Height of the near-field wave (Bernoulli hump)

Depth (meters)	*Speed (knots)*	*W(U, D, h) (cm)*
30	5	1.1
	12	6.5
	20	19.0
50	5	0.41
	12	2.40
	20	6.50
100	5	0.10
	12	0.59
	20	1.60
200	5	0.025
	12	0.150
	20	0.410
300	5	0.011
	12	0.065
	20	0.180

Source: Calculations of equation A3.2.

A moving source-sink pair generates a wedge-shaped Kelvin wave pattern behind it, as shown in figure A3–3. In general, both transverse and divergent waves may be present, and these are contained within an angle of 19.5 degrees to both sides of the line of motion.[34] It has been shown that for typical speeds and depths, transverse waves dominate.[35] The solution for the far-field surface transverse wave generated by a submarine is

$$\zeta_{F,T}(x,0) = -\frac{\sqrt{\pi g}}{2} D^2 \frac{1}{U} \exp\left[-\frac{gh}{U^2}\right] x^{-\frac{1}{2}} \left(1 - \frac{1}{2}\frac{a}{x}\right) \times \sin\left(k_0 x + \frac{\pi}{4}\right) \sin k_0 a \qquad \text{(A3.4)}$$

where k_0 is $2\pi/L_{\text{wave}}$. The wave height may be everywhere zero, or its maximum value according to the following criteria:

$$\text{Zero:} \quad |\sin k_0 a| = 0 \quad \frac{g}{U_{\text{zero}}} a = n\pi$$

$$\text{Maximum:} \quad |\sin k_0 a| = 1 \quad \frac{g}{U_{\text{max}}} a = \left(n + \frac{1}{2}\right)\pi$$

for $n = 0, 1, 2, \ldots$.

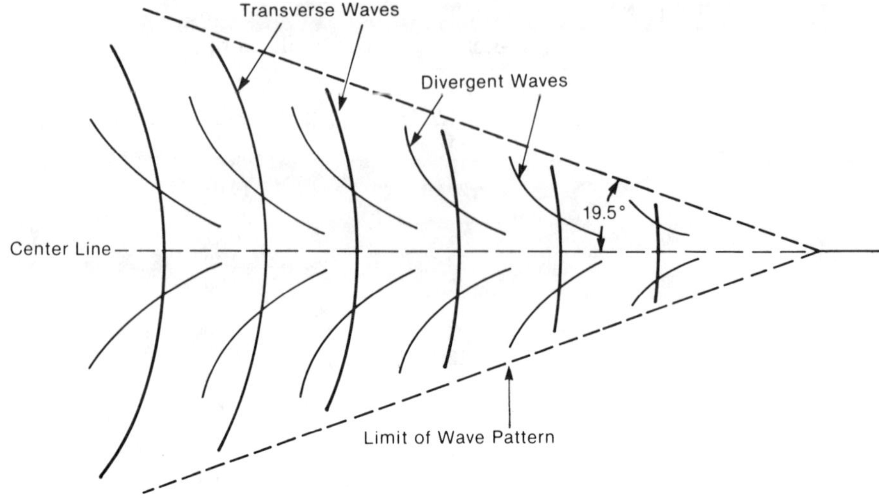

Figure A3–3. The Kelvin wave pattern.

Note: Transverse waves dominate for submerged submarines at low and moderate speeds.

The terms of equation A3.4 are grouped by independent variable to demonstrate how wave height varies with the submarine diameter, speed, depth, distance, and length. Speed and depth are the most important factors, since wave height decays exponentially with increasing depth and decreasing speed. The waves decay slowly behind the submarine, with the square root of the distance. The disturbance is sinusoidal, with wavelength L_{wave}, and has the shape of the Kelvin transverse wave pattern shown in figure A3–3.[36]

Table A3–5 shows the calculation of the maximum wave height in centimeters from equation A3.4. The table shows that even for very shallow depths and speeds up to 12 knots, the surface wave is only of the order of millimeters, and for depths greater than 100 meters, no wave is generated at reasonable speeds.

In going from the inviscid model to a real fluid with viscous effects, the conclusions are still valid, since it has been shown in model tests that the effect of the separation of the turbulent boundary layer near the stern of the submarine hull is to reduce the strength of the sink term by 10–25 percent.[37] This will not significantly change the results obtained here.

The calculations in tables A3–4 and A3–5 demonstrate that for reasonable submergence depths and speeds the near-field wave will be a few millimeters and the submarine-generated surface wave will be a few hundredths of a millimeter. The wavelengths of the submarine waves fall within the short period range of the gravity wave spectrum for deep water. These gravity waves are of the order of a meter high. Thus, the very faint submarine waves would be lost among the energetic wind-generated waves of the same wavelength.

Table A3–5
Maximum far-field wave height due to a moving submarine (equation A3.4)

$$\left(\begin{array}{c} \textit{Diameter} = 11 \textit{ meters} \\ \sin(k_0x + \pi/4)\sin(k_0a) = 1 \end{array}\right)$$

		Centerline Wave Height (cm)		
Depth (meters)	*Speed (knots)*	*Downstream Distance x = 100 m*	*Downstream Distance x = 500 m*	*Downstream Distance x = 10,000 m*
30	5	0[a]	0	0
	12	0.13	0.092	0.022
	20	12.0	8.3	2.0
50	5	0	0	0
	12	0.00074	0.00051	0.00013
	20	1.9	1.3	0.32
100	5	0	0	0
	12	0	0	0
	20	0.018	0.012	0.003

[a] A zero indicates that the predicted wave height is of the order 10^{-10} meters or less. For depths greater than 100 meters, no wave is generated.

In order to assess the possibility of detecting submarine-generated surface waves, one must consider the signal-to-noise ratio inherent in the problem. The near-field wave, or Bernoulli hump, is a single, localized perturbation a few hundred yards in extent that is three orders of magnitude below the peak of a typical wave spectrum. The prospects of detecting such a disturbance are extremely dim, irrespective of the sensitivity of a space-based system. The far-field Kelvin wave pattern covers a greater area but, as the preceding analysis shows, can only be produced at high speeds and shallow depths. With the mildest of precautions, these waves are virtually nonexistent.

Submarine-generated Turbulent Wakes and Internal Waves

As a submarine moves through the water, some of the energy of propulsion goes into generating a turbulent wake behind the hull. Figure A3–4 shows the form of the cylindrical wake and the mean velocity distribution across it.[38] The mean velocity near the centerline is directed away from the submarine, and water is drawn toward the centerline from the top and bottom of the wake. The height of the wake[39] grows as a function of $(x/D)^{0.25}$ for a submarine in an unstratified ocean, where x/D is the downstream distance in submarine diameters.[40] In general, the wake from a submarine moving in a straight line at constant speed does not persist for a long time.[41] Typical wake lengths associated with submarines below 125 feet are on the order of 100 yards at 6 knots and 30 yards at 2 to 3 knots, based on actual measurements.[42]

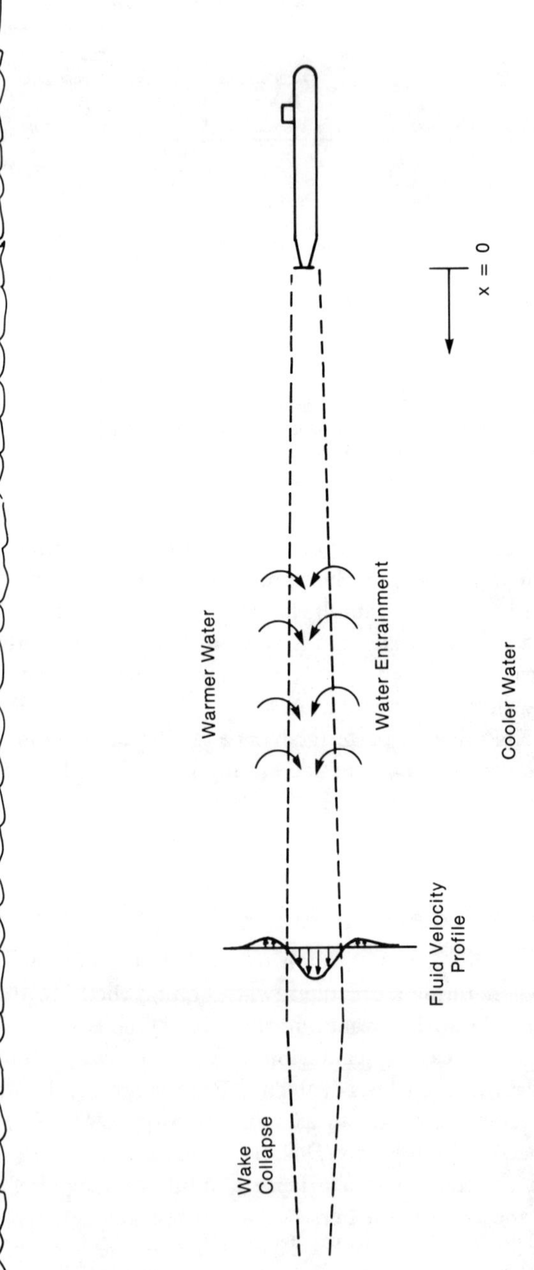

Figure A3–4. The wake behind a submarine.

In latitudes south of 60 degrees North, the water temperature decreases with depth in the upper 1,000 meters. Since this is also the operating zone of the submarine, it can be assumed that the submarine wake will disturb the temperature structure. Cooler water from below the submarine will be drawn up into the wake, and warmer water from above will be drawn downward into the wake. The mixed wake will therefore be slightly cooler than the water just above it and slightly warmer than the water just below it. Collapsing forces due to these density differences are therefore exerted on the wake from above and below. Once the wake ceases to grow or collapses vertically, it usually continues to spread horizontally.[43] In a stratified ocean, the height of the wake grows as $(x/D)^{0.25}$ until it reaches a maximum height and either stops growing or collapses.

The appropriate time scale for the wake growth is the Brunt-Väisälä period, T_{BV}, which in the ocean is on the order of 10–100 minutes, depending on the stratification of the water column.[44] This is a measure of the natural period of oscillation of the stratified layer. According to available evidence,[45] the vertical rise of the wake stops at approximately $0.2T_{BV}$. This is on the order of a few hundred seconds in typical ocean conditions. Therefore, the height of a submarine-generated wake extends a maximum of 1.3–3 hull diameters above the centerline of the wake—that is, 8–25 meters above the top of the hull. This maximum should be attained at a distance of 300–3,000 meters behind a submarine traveling at 5 knots. Beyond this point, the wake does continue to grow horizontally.

Another useful result is the rate at which the turbulent fluctuations decay behind a submarine. The root mean squared (rms) longitudinal fluctuations decay as the 0.75 power of distance (scaled in hull diameters) and increase linearly with speed. The vertical fluctuations decay linearly with distance and increase with the 1.25 power of speed.[46] The point at which the wake "ends" depends on the properties of the wake that are of interest. Acoustic measurements of actual submarine wakes show that they are detectable on the order of a few hundred meters downstream, while scale model studies suggest that the wakes may be detectable a few kilometers downstream before the turbulence decays to an undetectable level.[47]

Internal Wave Generation

When the turbulent wake collapses, it can drive an internal wave in the density-stratified layers of the ocean. Submarines also generate internal waves by the movement of the hull alone, without consideration of the wake collapse effect. This is analogous to the generation of surface Kelvin waves by submarines. Theoretical investigations have shown, however, that unlike the surface Kelvin wave, which fans out 19.5 degrees from the line of motion, these internal wave patterns associated with the hull "are sharply concentrated along" the line of motion.[48]

Internal waves cannot be seen directly as undulations of the surface. The internal wave generates horizontal currents near the surface that modulate existing surface ripples whose wavelengths are on the order of centimeters or tens of centimeters. The modulation takes the form of changes in the ripple wavelength and steepness, which in turn alters the radar scattering properties of the rippled surface. The modulation of surface waves can in principle reveal the pattern of underlying internal waves.[49]

Synthetic aperture radar (SAR)[50] can be tuned so that the radar backscatter depends on the wavelength of the short surface waves. This SAR backscatter technique has already been used to measure large ocean waves by satellite—SEASAT A. Large surface gravity waves, of the order of 100 meters long, generate horizontal surface currents that modulate the 15 centimeter waves. By detecting the pattern of modulation of the 15 cm waves, the dominant surface gravity wave can be studied.

Beyond this simple outline, it is difficult to assess the state of knowledge regarding the internal wave observable. It is known that the submarine wake will collapse fairly rapidly, within one Brunt-Väisälä period, so that the potential energy in the wake can be transferred to internal waves.[51] The energy distribution of the internal waves generated by wake collapse is not well known, but one experiment suggested that it is skewed toward higher frequencies and is peaked at about 0.8 of the Brunt-Väisälä frequency.[52] Taking this value in the ocean, the internal wave energy density spectrum associated with the collapsing wake should peak at frequencies on the order of 1 cycle per hour.[53]

On the surface of the ocean, the question of the detectability of these internal waves, in principle, appears to be open. A recent review of all the subsurface hydrodynamic mechanisms that could modulate the surface ripple field concluded that although the large surface gravity waves have a dominant effect on the surface ripples that ride upon them, "the surface wave modulations by the internal wave can still be shown observable."[54]

The surface manifestations of internal waves, or the vortices of an internal wake, may be linked to the presence of a thin film of natural organic material and oil that is commonly found on the ocean's surface. Horizontal surface currents generated directly by the submarine wake or indirectly by internal waves caused by the submarine can sweep the film into regular patterns. Relatively thick films of this floating matter can change the physical properties of the sea surface and form a pattern that might be detectable to a sensor with sufficient spatial resolution.

The surface slicks have several effects that may be detected by different sensors. They can lower the emissivity of the surface, making it appear cooler, and they can increase the reflectivity of the surface, making it appear warmer in the daytime. These effects might be detected by thermal infrared imaging or by passive microwave radiometry. The slicks also reduce the surface tension, which can affect the wave characteristics and energy dissipation in capillary waves. The variation in surface roughness may be detected using the synthetic aperture radar. Since the SEASAT radar had a theoretical spatial resolution of only 6 meters (in practice, the resolution was 25 meters), this may prove to be a possible method of satellite-based detection.[55]

Press reports, from both the United States and the Soviet Union, have suggested that internal wave detection of submarines may be a possibility. Reports from unnamed sources suggested that synthetic aperture radar was used by the USSR from aircraft and the Salyut space station to detect submerged Delta submarines in the Northwest Pacific.[56] This and other information suggested that the observable in question was the modulation of surface waves by the submarine-generated internal wave. The US Defense Department denied the report, which was supposedly based upon intelligence from the Defense Intelligence Agency, the Air Force Intelligence Agency, and the National Security Agency.[57] Of course one must be very cautious about "secret" reports of potential SSBN vulnerability, especially when the Air Force is involved and the MX missile, as it was at the time, is in political trouble. These reports do tie in, however, with a statement made in the Soviet newspaper *Izvestia* in July of 1981 by a member of the Ukrainian Academy of Sciences:

> Soon the range of electromagnetic waves exploitable for surveillance will be expanded. It is now becoming clear that, owing to satellites, we can have not only a surface but also a volumetric and depth picture of phenomena in the ocean. Internal waves are very widespread in the ocean. It is possible to register their manifestations at the surface from satellites and to judge what is taking place in that upper layer of several hundred meters which is of the utmost importance to us.[58]

The US Navy has been conducting its own research on detecting internal waves from the space shuttle. In the fall of 1984, a scientist from the Naval Underwater Systems Center tested an instrument that could detect eddies and currents in the ocean, much as the SEASAT A synthetic aperture radar had. When asked if this new technology might hasten the day when submarines could be tracked from space, the Chief of Naval Operations, Adm. James Watkins, said that the technology

> is clearly opening some doors on submarine tracking. But the question is, do you open the doors of detecting submarines faster than you close the doors on learning about the ocean depths? And the answer today is, you're still ahead of the game in the latter category. So the ability to track submarines—we don't see that as being a threat to our forces until the turn of the century or later, depending on what kind of breakthroughs we might find at the end of this decade or into the next decade.[59]

Admiral Watkins also reemphasized his judgment that as the Navy learns more about the oceans, confidence in the undetectability of submarines increases.[60]

The technical director of the Navy's SSBN Security Office, Dr. Edward Y. Harper, reported to Senate Armed Services Committee in 1984 that their "assessments are that the synthetic aperture radars cannot detect [deleted] . . . submarines."[61] There were four times that the SEASAT A radar flew over US strategic submarines on patrol and obtained radar images of the sea surface. On one of those occasions, the submarine was at a keel depth of 58 feet, which is very shallow. Nevertheless, Harper testified that no trace of the submarines was detected.[62]

This revelation by the SSBN security official is unusual in its candor. Very rarely do details of US SSBN operations come out of classified hearings. This seems motivated by the desire to make a strong public statement to the effect that synthetic aperture radar holds no promise as a means of detecting submarines. However, the analysis and brief literature review presented here suggests that the question of submarine detection by synthetic aperture radar is very much an open one.

Detection of Submarine-generated Temperature Changes

Submarines change the temperature of the water in two ways: by mixing the thermocline, and by direct heating through the reactor cooling system. These two processes may tend to cancel each other, since upwelling of cool, deep water is offset by reactor heating. The net result depends on the relative magnitudes of the heating effect and the cooling effect. If either a cool or warm temperature anomaly is present at the surface, it may in principle be detected by ASW forces.

The temperature of the ocean surface can be measured by measuring the infrared (IR) or microwave radiation emitted by the surface, using a radiometer. Infrared does not penetrate water, so only surface temperature is detectable. For this reason, only those submarine-induced temperature anomalies that reach the surface can potentially be detected. IR radiometers can actually measure a surface temperature that is about 0.5 degrees centigrade cooler than the water a millimeter below the surface. This offset is due to surface evaporation and is said to be "relatively constant," so that measurements may simply be adjusted to correct for the bias.[63] However, this surface cooling effect imposes a lower limit on the magnitude of temperature changes that can be reliably detected. For example, a 0.03° C change may be caused simply by a variation in the evaporation rate at the surface due to an oil film. A submarine-generated temperature anomaly would have to be at least on the order of 0.1° C at the surface to be distinguishable from naturally occurring variations of the surface temperature.

It has already been shown that under typical ocean conditions the maximum rise of an unheated submarine wake is at most a few tens of meters. Therefore, if the upwelled cool water is expected to dominate the wake, the submarine wake is essentially unheated and will not rise. However, if the reactor heating provides enough buoyancy to the wake to overcome the ambient density forces in the stratified ocean, then the wake may rise.

The submarine reactor generates heat that is converted into mechanical energy in the turbine. Most of the thermal energy is lost to the sea directly. Some of the mechanical energy goes to propelling the submarine and some into electricity to run the submarine systems. The electrical energy is converted back into heat in motors, transformers, heaters, and other components, and is subsequently lost to the sea. The propulsion energy is converted to turbulence in the ocean, which eventually decays away into heat. About 20 percent of the thermal energy produced by the reactor goes into propulsion. The remaining 80 percent of the energy goes directly to the sea through the condensation of steam in the seawater cooling loop, or indirectly to the sea via electrical systems that generate heat. This heat raises the temperature of the water in the submarine wake.

The thermal power of current submarine reactors is about 80–100 megawatts. Future submarines may have a higher power output, however, as new metals and reactor designs are employed. Assume a submarine power plant that delivers 50,000-shaft horsepower. This corresponds to a 190-megawatt (MW) reactor.[64] This amount of heat goes into the sea within the submarine wake. A power of 190 MW is 4.5×10^7 calories per second, or 45.4° C m^3/second. An 11-meter diameter submarine has a frontal area of about 95 m^2, so at 5 knots the submarine mixes 244 m^3/sec. of water. This increases the temperature of the water immediately behind the submarine by 0.19° C. As the wake expands downstream, however, the volume of entrained water increases and the temperature drops as $x/D^{-0.5}$. Assuming that the submarine heat is mixed into the wake 11 meters (1 diameter) behind the propeller, then at a distance of 1,100 meters downstream, the temperature in the wake is only 0.02° C higher than the surrounding water. At 10 knots the temperature 1 kilometer downstream is 0.01° C, and at 20 knots, 0.005° C. This figure is comparable to an estimate made in a Soviet study (supposedly based on data from "foreign specialists") which states that the temperature change due to a submarine is at least 0.005° C.[65] For a 100-MW reactor typical of current submarines, this corresponds to a speed of 10 knots.

The warmed water is less dense than the surrounding water and tends to rise. As the warm wake rises, however, it encounters warmer ambient water above it. In subarctic latitudes, the typical average vertical temperature gradient is about 0.005° C per meter.[66] A parcel of water in the wake at 0.02° C above ambient temperature would rise about 4 meters. At that point the wake has no more buoyancy. It will continue to rise, however, due to the effect of turbulence, but it is clear that the vertical expansion of the wake is primarily due to the turbulent forces in this case. It is interesting to point out that insofar as the buoyancy mitigates the collapse of the wake, the reactor heating may contribute somewhat to preventing internal wave generation.

Since the thermocline limits the buoyant rise of the heated wake, it is also interesting to consider what happens in the Arctic, where no thermocline exists. A heated plume of water will rise to the surface, cooling as it rises. It is more likely that a slowly moving or stationary submarine will generate a warm surface trail in the Arctic than at lower latitudes.

The possibility of detecting submarine-generated surface temperature anomalies is remote. To begin with, deep wakes in midlatitude waters do not reach the surface under most circumstances and therefore do not induce a noticeable temperature change on the ocean surface. In the constant temperature water of the Soviet Arctic, however, slowly moving or stationary submarines may produce a noticeable warm spot. The accuracy that has been obtained by IR thermometers on satellites has been about a 0.5° C error.[67] These measurements were taken by the very high resolution radiometer (VHRR) aboard the NOAA-3 and NOAA-4 satellites. Since the expected temperature anomaly from a submarine would be at least an order of magnitude smaller than this error, it could not be reliably detected. Even if some method of measuring sea surface temperature is found, it will be obscured at least half the time by clouds and fog.

Detection of reactor heat through the ice may be possible if the submarine were to remain in a single place for a long time with a fairly high thermal output. The temperature change on the surface of the ice would depend on the ice thickness, the amount of heating from below, and time. Ice conducts heat slowly, so that it could happen that the maximum temperature of the surface of the ice would be attained after the submarine had left the area. For similar reasons, the warm "scars" on the ice surface would persist for a long time, creating false targets, and reducing the tactical usefulness of detecting them.

Detection of Submarines by Laser

Lasers have been considered as an active nonacoustic detection device because of the depth to which blue-green light penetrates seawater. Such a detection system would consist of an airborne or spaceborne laser/detector, which would send short pulses into the ocean and from the return energy determine if a pulse had been either reflected off or absorbed by a subsurface object. Airborne laser systems of this type have been studied for over 15 years as a method of measuring water depth and generating the information from which bathymetric charts can be made. The first US field experiment of such a system was carried out by the Navy in 1969.[68] The Defense Mapping Agency currently uses a laser for making depth measurements in coastal waters, usually from boats. The agency is developing a system that can take measurements in 40 meters of clear water.[69] Because laser detection systems are the optical analogue of radar, they have been given the generic name of lidar. The Swedish Navy has probably used lidar in its attempts to detect Soviet submarines in its territorial waters.[70]

In order to guarantee that detectable levels of energy return from a submarine, through the overlying ocean and atmosphere to the receiver, the laser must have sufficient power to compensate for round-trip attenuation and the large reflection loss off the submarine. In addition, the laser beam will spread due to scattering off of particles and molecules along the path. Atmospheric losses can be significantly lower for a low-flying aircraft than for a satellite, although the greatest loss by far occurs in the few hundred meters of seawater through which the beam must pass.

The analysis presented here is for the problem of detecting a reflection off a submerged submarine. A system might also be designed to detect the absorption of light by the submarine. These are analogous problems, and both involve detecting an anomalous intensity of laser return (either higher or lower than average) in a particular range of depths. The same constraints that limit the "reflectance" lidar system also limit the "absorption" system.

The optimum wavelength for seawater penetration in the deep ocean is around 0.48 microns (1 micron equals 10^{-6} meter), which is blue to blue-green light. In coastal waters, green or even yellow light may propagate most efficiently, although the propagation loss in these waters is higher than in the open ocean. Attenuation in the ocean is strongly related to the density and size distribution of suspended particles, organic and inorganic, and the highest attenuation occurs in the upper 100 meters.[71] Some longer wavelengths propagate more easily through the atmosphere, but because oceanic attenuation is much greater than atmospheric, the optimum lidar wavelength is in the blue-green.

Atmospheric attenuation is caused by absorption and scattering from molecules or small particles in aerosol suspension. Scattering loss always dominates absorption loss by at least an order of magnitude. Molecular scattering loss is always of the same order of magnitude as, but less than, aerosol scattering loss.[72] Therefore, molecular and aerosol absorption are neglected, and only scattering loss is considered.

An aircraft-borne laser is attenuated through a much smaller layer of the atmosphere than is a satellite-borne laser. However, most of the scattering loss occurs in the lowest 5 kilometers, and much of it in the lowest 1 kilometer, so that from a power standpoint, there may be little difference between an aircraft and a satellite. On a round-trip through the entire atmosphere, blue-green laser suffers transmission loss of 4 dB on a clear day and 10 dB on a hazy day, as long as no clouds are encountered. An airborne lidar at 5 kilometers suffers round-trip propagation loss of 2 dB on a clear day and 8 dB on a hazy day. Moderate fog, which cannot of course be circumvented by low-flying aircraft, strongly attenuates blue-green light due to scattering. The attenuation coefficient for fog can range between 1 and 5 km^{-1},[73] and the round-trip attenuation through even a 100-meter-thick fog can be 4 dB.

Clouds cover over 75 percent of the ocean skies 6 days out of 10,[74] and in particular ocean regions, such as the GIUK gap, the figure may reach 8 days out of 10. Therefore the attenuation through cloud cover is an important system parameter. Most of the laser energy backscatters from a cloud, and the round-trip attenuation over a thick layer is on the order of 26 dB.[75] The effect of clouds on blue-green laser communications to submarines, which involve only one-way transmission, has been characterized by the head of DoD communications as a "high technical risk," so that the two-way transmission of lidar must be considered at least as uncertain.[76]

To summarize, the round-trip transmission loss of a blue-green laser over the entire atmosphere may range from as little as 4 dB over a perfectly clear path to 40 dB through clouds and fog. On an ocean-wide average, some cloud scattering is usually present. Lidar on an aircraft can avoid some of the cloud attenuation, but provides much less coverage, and is vulnerable to attack.

Oceanic attenuation coefficients are three orders of magnitude larger than atmospheric attenuation coefficients, and except for the case of very shallow targets, oceanic attenuation dominates atmospheric. The overall attenuation coefficient decreases most rapidly with depth over the upper 100 meters, becoming relatively stable below 150 meters, due to the decrease in particle concentrations over depth. Typical values in the open ocean at midlatitudes are 0.11 m^{-1} from 5–75 meters, 0.08 m^{-1} from 75–150 meters, and 0.05 m^{-1} below 150 meters.[77] Assuming constant coefficients over the three layers, the one-way and round-trip transmission losses can be calculated and are given in table A3–2. In the upper 75 meters, the round-trip transmission loss is nearly 1 dB per meter of depth, while for depths below 150 meters, the round-trip loss is approximately 0.5 dB for each additional meter. At only 75 meters, the loss is −72 dB, already much greater than the highest expected losses over the entire atmosphere. At 200 meters, well within the maximum depth of submarines, the loss is a factor of over 300 trillion.

In order to compare signal and noise levels for lidar, the bandwidth of the signal becomes a crucial parameter. The sun radiates a tremendous amount of visible energy onto the sea surface, and even with only 2–4 percent reflectance, the total upward irradiance is large, on the order of 10–50 watts/m^2/micron.[78] However, within a very narrow bandwidth, the natural irradiance is much lower. A very narrowband laser need therefore "compete" with only a tiny fraction of solar noise.

The characteristics of laser output spectra vary widely for different types and modes of operation. "For spaceborne use, the most promising candidate is the mercury-bromide laser, which radiates directly in the blue-green part of the spectrum (0.49–0.51 micron)."[79] Other lasers under investigation, and which may prove more promising, are xenon-chloride, neodymium pumped by light-emitting diodes, and copper vapor lasers.[80] Some radiate at wavelengths other than blue-green and must be frequency-shifted. Also, lasers can act as amplifiers, in which mode they can radiate very narrow lines.

The atmosphere broadens the spectral width of laser light, but this effect is negligible. For example, the frequency of blue-green light is 6.25×10^{14} Hz, and measurements of atmospheric linewidth spreading suggest smearing due to turbulent fluctuations of the refractive index of the order of 10^3 or 10^4 Hz.[81] This suggests that the atmosphere imposes a minimum linewidth of the order of 10^{-11} microns for blue-green laser light. If one could construct a laser to emit a line at this width and construct a receiver with a narrow filter of the same width, and keep it all stable, the noise could be reduced to the order of 10^{-10} watts.

There is, however, a fundamental constraint on reducing the bandwidth of a lidar system. When the laser fires into the ocean, a relatively strong reflection is returned from the ocean surface, while the reflection from a submerged submarine, even at 50 meters depth, would be quite weak, on the order of 50 dB lower than the surface-reflected intensity.[82] Since both returns are in the same frequency, the surface signal acts as an overwhelming noise source if the two returns coincide. The only way to avoid this problem is to keep the laser pulse short enough to separate the surface-return pulse from the submarine-return pulse, which must travel a slightly longer round-trip distance. For a submarine at depth h meters, the extra round-trip time for the submarine return is $T_{rt} = 2h/c$ where c is the speed of light, 3×10^8 m/sec, so the laser pulse duration must be on this order or shorter.

There is a fundamental relationship between laser pulse duration and linewidth, which is that for a pulse duration T, the linewidth must be greater than about $1/(3T)$.[83] The depth of a submarine sets an upper limit on pulse duration, and therefore a lower limit on spectral linewidth, which in turn sets an upper limit on the signal-to-noise ratio. Considering the pulse length restriction described above, the minimum linewidth for a submarine detection lidar is equal to or greater than $5 \times 10^7/h$ Hz. To resolve a target at 10 meters, a pulse duration of less than 67 nanoseconds is required, yielding a linewidth of 5×10^7 Hz, or 3.8×10^{-8} microns. For 100 meters resolution, the pulse duration must be less than 670 nanoseconds for a minimum linewidth of 3.8×10^{-9} microns.

A major environmental problem is that of pulse-stretching due to scattering in the air. On a one-way trip through the atmosphere "experimental results show that pulse widths may grow to 1 microsecond in the very thinnest clouds to over 100 microseconds in very thick ones."[84] A pulse stretched even to 1 microsecond as it travels down in virtually clear skies is too long to resolve clearly the surface from the subsurface return, particularly in view of the fact that the surface-reflected return will be stretched further on its return trip. The lidar system is thus its own noise source, analogous to the reverberation problem in active sonar. Consider the form of the return signal: because of pulse spreading, the satellite detector would first receive cloud backscatter, then the leading edge of the surface return, which would be increasing in intensity. Nanoseconds later, the much weaker (by 50 dB or more) submarine return would begin to arrive. Over a period of several thousand nanoseconds both signals would arrive together, the surface return completely burying the submarine return.

The stability of the laser output can be another limiting factor. If the output varies randomly over a range of blue-green wavelengths due to temperature and other effects, the receiver filter bandwidth must be wide enough to accept the signal despite its excursions from the mean wavelength. In any case, filter bandwidths themselves may have a lower limit, which may or may not exceed the atmospheric minimum linewidth. A filter has been developed for applications in submarine communications which has a bandwidth of only 2×10^{-4} microns, according to DARPA officials.[85]

It is important to keep in mind that in order to make these estimates, the temporary (and unrealistic) assumption is made that no pulse stretching occurs. Assume that the filter bandwidth is 10^{-5} microns—an order of magnitude narrower than DARPA's. The incoming solar energy from sea-surface reflections only (neglecting the larger atmospheric backscatter) is on the order 10^{-5} watt/m^2 assuming 10 dB atmospheric transmission loss. Against a target with 1 percent reflectance[86] at a depth of 150 meters, the laser's total round-trip transmission loss is −164 dB. In order to obtain a signal-to-noise ratio of 0 dB,[87] the laser must generate a beam with an intensity on the order of 10^{11} watt/m^2 in the same bandwidth.[88] An important parameter is the depth of the target: if it is assumed to be only 50 meters rather than 150 meters deep, the laser output need only be 4,000 watt/m^2. It is worth remembering that the sea-surface reflection detected by a sensor outside the atmosphere is only 1 percent of the total irradiance seen by that sensor.[89] Accounting for upward-scattered solar irradiance therefore decreases the signal-to-noise ratio by 20 dB.

Another calculation that can be made is to assume a lidar system whose bandwidth is limited only by the pulsewidth needed to resolve a target at 50 meters depth, which is approximately 7.6×10^{-9} microns. Assume the laser is stable and the filter is matched—that is, several thousand times narrower than the one assumed in the example above. In daylight, the surface-reflected irradiance transmitted through a clear atmosphere (10 dB attenuation) into space might be about 1 watt/m^2/micron, so the optical noise passing the filter is on the order of 10^{-8} watt/m^2. The round-trip attenuation of the space-based laser is 20 dB through the atmosphere, 48 dB through 50 meters of seawater, and 20 dB at the submarine reflection, for a total of 88 dB total loss. This would require a laser power of 10 watt/m^2 to achieve a 0 dB signal-to-noise ratio—well within current capabilities. However, at greater depths and with more realistic assumptions about submarine reflection, the power requirement can easily increase a millionfold.

The system requirements of a satellite based laser are strict. For every watt of laser power, these systems typically require 100 watts of electrical power. Solar photoelectric arrays may reasonably generate on the order of 10^4 watts of electrical power,[90] which could drive a laser at 100 watts average power. Pulsed lasers, however, can generate much higher pulsed optical power levels at the same average power. For example, a 100-nanosecond-pulse generated at a repetition rate of 500 Hz gives a ratio of pulse power to average power of 4,000. Thus, solar cells could drive a laser with a 100-nanosecond-pulse to powers of 4×10^5 watts, which for a 1-cm^2-beam is 4×10^9 watt/m^2. At these powers, reasonable signal-to-noise ratios could be achieved given a sufficiently narrow filter and moderately shallow submarine depths, *but only in the absence of atmospheric pulse stretching.*

There is an interesting alternative to detecting the light reflected from the submarine, which is to detect the *absence* of reflected light. At depths down to 100 meters, or perhaps deeper, a laser pulse should return some backscattered light as a matter of course. A submarine, painted black, may absorb the pulse and not scatter or reflect light back, leaving a kind of "hole" in the ocean. A laser detector might be set to accept a normal level of backscatter from the water, which, if interrupted, would signal the presence of a body absorbing the light. Here again, however, the same pulse length restrictions would apply, since a long pulse would be overcome by atmospheric backscatter. The tendency of the atmosphere to stretch laser pulses would interfere with the "hole detector" system in the same way as it would with the reflection detector.

The power requirements of a space-based lidar detector are severe but attainable. A 10-fold increase in laser power can be offset if a submarine dives a mere additional 20 meters, due to the high rate of attenuation in the sea. Another major problem is the lifetime of a satellite laser. Current systems that use flashlamps and corrosive vapors as the lasing medium can be used on aircraft but cannot endure long periods without maintenance. Other systems are being developed to circumvent this problem, but they in turn lack the necessary power.[91]

The determining factor, however, is the stretching of pulse length due to atmospheric scattering. Because of this stretching, the very weak submarine-reflected signal is swamped by the surface-reflected signal, which can easily be a million times more intense. The only way to defeat this effect is to fly close to the water surface, thereby severely reducing the satellite surveillance potential of lidar detection.

Lidar is not the only means by which lasers might be used to detect submarines. As noted earlier, the volume backscattering from the ocean depths is a relatively strong signal. Internal waves may alter the backscattering characteristics of the water column, and therefore be detectable by a laser system that does not suffer the same limitations as lidar. As with synthetic aperture radar, the relationship between the motion of a submarine and the generation of internal waves is a crucial factor, as is the presence of naturally occurring internal waves. Unlike synthetic aperture radar, however, the mechanisms that cause surface disturbances are probably not relevant factors. Also unlike synthetic aperture radar, the mechanism of laser backscattering is well understood.

Conclusions

The difficulties involving various nonacoustic detection technologies have three basic characteristics in common. First, they are generally problems involving a very low signal-to-noise ratio that is very difficult to overcome. Power limitations (which might be overcome) are generally not limiting factors. Second, environmental variability must be accounted for in signal-to-noise and false target considerations. Third, most of the technologies discussed here can be defeated simply by operating the submarine deeper. The signal-to-noise ratios decrease dramatically, usually by several orders of magnitude, with an increase in depth on the order of 100 meters. Operating submarines below 100 meters is probably sufficient on its own to foil most foreseeable nonacoustic detection systems. In the words of one Navy expert, "essentially all nonacoustic phenomena are attenuated by water."[92]

It is important to note that this assessment should not be applied to the detection of internal wave effects by synthetic aperture radar or by measurements of sea-surface emissivity. There does not appear to be an adequate scientific basis to rule out such a means of detection with a very high level of confidence. At the same time, there is no breakthrough in sight.

For most systems, it is likely that relatively short-range sensors on aircraft are more immediately feasible than long-range sensors on satellites.

Notes

1. Roger Speed, *Strategic Deterrence in the 1980s* (Stanford, Cal.: Hoover Institution, 1979), chap. 3.

2. Donald C. Daniel, *Anti-Submarine Warfare and Superpower Strategic Stability* (Urbana: University of Illinois Press, 1986). Summaries of the various nonacoustic technologies are contained in tables 2.1 and 3.1 of that book.

3. Many potential submarine detection methods have not been mentioned, such as neutrino flux, but the list given here seems to account for most of those observables that have been discussed and that have been the subject of extensive tests.

4. James A. Brennan and Thomas M. Davis, *The Influence of the Natural Environment on MAD Operations* (Washington, DC: Naval Oceanographic Office), NAVOCEANO TR-218, Sept. 1969, p. 30.
5. Ibid.
6. Ibid., p. 34.
7. Ibid., p. 22.
8. Ibid.
9. James A. Brennan and Kuno Smits, *The Effect of Geomagnetic Micropulsations on MAD Systems* (Washington, DC: Naval Oceanographic Office), NAVOCEANO TR-250, 1975, pp. 3, 7.
10. John Tierney, "The Invisible Force," *Science '83,* November 1983, p. 71.
11. John A. Strand, Clarence G. Pantzke, and Gordon L. Mitchell, *The Antisubmarine Warfare Potential of Bioluminescence Imaging* (Seattle, Wash.: Naval Reserve Center), ONR/NRL TAC 522 TR 80–1, 1980, p. 6.
12. H. Tennekes and J. L. Lumley, *A First Course in Turbulence* (Cambridge: MIT Press 1972), p. 127.
13. R. V. Lynch III, *The Occurrence and Distribution of Surface Bioluminescence in the Ocean during 1966 through 1977* (Washington, DC: Naval Research Lab, 1978), p. 2. Quoted in Daniel, *Anti-Submarine Warfare,* p. 42.
14. *Physics of Sound in the Sea,* (Washington, DC: Headquarters of the Naval Materiel Command, 1969), NAVMAT P-9675, originally issued as NDRC Summary Tech. Rept. Div. 6, vol. 8, part 4, "Acoustic Properties of Wakes," 1946, pp. 501, 502.
15. Ibid.
16. Ibid., p. 441.
17. Brian P. Baden and Elizabeth M. Kampa, "Bioluminescence," in *Optical Aspects of Oceanography,* ed. N. G. Jerlov and E. S. Neilsen (New York: Academic Press, 1974), p. 460.
18. Strand, Pantzke, and Mitchell, *The Antisubmarine Warfare Potential,* p. 7.
19. Ibid., p. 4.
20. Jon R. Losee and David Lapota, "Bioluminescence Measurements in the Atlantic and Pacific," in *Bioluminescence: Current Perspectives,* ed. Kenneth H. Nealson (Minneapolis: CEPCO, Burgess, 1981), pp. 143–151; also Strand, Pantzke, and Mitchell, *The Antisubmarine Warfare Potential,* p. 5.
21. R. V. Lynch III, *Patterns of Bioluminescence in the Ocean* (Washington, DC: Naval Research Laboratory) NRL-8475, April 1981.
22. Strand, Pantzke, and Mitchell, *The Antisubmarine Warfare Potential,* p. 5.
23. Losee and Lapota, "Bioluminescence Measurements," p. 143. They found that the emission spectrum was between 0.44 and 0.50 microns.
24. M. G. Kelly and P. Tett, "Bioluminescence in the Ocean," in *Bioluminescence in Action,* ed. Peter J. Herring (London: Academic Press, 1978), pp. 399–417.
25. R. W. Preisendorfer, *Hydrologic Optics* (Washington, DC: National Oceanographic and Atmospheric Administration, 1976). Also, John E. Tyler, "Optical Properties of Water," in *Handbook of Optics,* ed. Walter G. Driscoll (New York: McGraw-Hill, 1978), pp. 15–30.
26. Eric Mollo-Christensen, "Surface Wave Modulation Patterns in Radar Images," *Naval Research Reviews* 34:1, 1982, pp. 41–50.

27. B. Sturm, "The Atmospheric Correction of Remotely Sensed Data and the Quantitative Determination of Suspended Matter in Marine Water Surface Layers," in *Remote Sensing in Meteorology, Oceanography and Hydrology,* ed. A. P. Cracknel (New York: John Wiley and Sons, 1981), p. 165.

28. Strand, Pantzke, and Mitchell, *The Antisubmarine Warfare Potential,* p. 10.

29. Priesendorfer, *Hydrologic Optics,* pp. 31–33.

30. Erwin J. Bulban, "Airborne Sensor Detects Fish at Night," *Aviation Week and Space Technology,* 26 February 1979, p. 60.

31. For much of the supporting analytical material I am indebted to Laurence W. Ward of the Webb Institute of Naval Architecture. The basic sources are: L. W. Ward, "Some Observations on the Nature of the Ship-generated Wave System," *Schiffstechnik* 14:71, 1967, pp. 50–56, and J. N. Newman, *Marine Hydrodynamics* (Cambridge: MIT Press, 1977), chap. 4.

32. A. V. Hershey, *Measured versus Computed Surface Wave Trains of a Rankine Ovoid* (Dahlgren, Va.: US Naval Weapons Laboratory, 1966), p. 6.

33. For the integral solution of a single source, *see* J. K. Lunde, "On the Linearized Theory of Wave Resistance for Displacement Ships in Steady and Accelerated Motion," presented to SNAME, Washington, DC, September 1951. Integrals evaluated by National Physical Laboratory (c. 1950), Ref. Ma/16/1502. Prepared by L. Ward.

34. Newman, *Marine Hydrodynamics,* p. 273.

35. Ward, "Some Observations," p. 52.

36. It is interesting to note that the theory predicts no waves when the k_0 term satisfies the zero condition. This is due to the cancellation of the waves caused by the source by those caused by the sink. For the dimensions of the Trident submarine, there should be no waves at 10.8 knots and 10.2 knots, but maximum wave height at 10.6 knots. As this result has no meaningful interpretation outside the theory, it is ignored, and the maximum wave height condition is assumed as the worst case for SSBN security.

37. Hershey, *Measured versus Computed,* p. 27.

38. Tennekes and Lumley, *A First Course,* p. 125.

39. This analysis deals with an unheated wake.

40. Jung-Tai Lin and Yih-Ho Pao, "Wakes in Stratified Fluids," *Annual Review of Fluid Mechanics* 11, 1979, pp. 317–338; Jung-Tai Lin, Yih-Ho Pao, and S. D. Veenhuizen, "Turbulent Wake of a Propeller Driven Slender Body in Stratified and Non-Stratified Fluids," *Bulletin of the American Physical Society* 19, 1974, p. 1165.

41. Tennekes and Lumley, *A First Course,* p. 127. The one exception to this is when a submarine makes a sudden change of speed or direction and generates a localized but persistent wake. These special wake "knuckles" can reflect sound and were often detected by sonar during World War II and occasionally were attacked with depth charges.

42. *Physics of Sound in the Sea,* pp. 501, 502.

43. I. Pelech, G. G. Zipfel, and R. L. Holford, "A Wake Scattering Experiment in Thermally Stratified Water," *Journal of the Acoustical Society of America* 73:2, February 1983, pp. 528–538.

44. O. M. Phillips, *The Dynamics of the Upper Ocean* (Cambridge: Cambridge University Press, 1977), p. 209.

45. Much of this is based on Lin and Pao, "Wakes in Stratified Fluids," pp. 317–338, and J. M. Bergin, *Internal Wave Generation Caused by the Growth and Collapse of a Mixed Region* (Washington, DC: Naval Research Laboratory), NRL-G01–06, June 1973, p. 24.

46. Lin and Pao, "Wakes in Stratified Fields."

47. Pelech, Zipfel, and Holford cite echoes from a wake at a time of 5–10 T_{BV} after the passage of the model; scaling this to the values of T_{BV} in the ocean gives a wake several kilometers long.

48. J. B. Keller and W. H. Munk, "Internal Wave Wakes of a Body Moving in a Stratified Fluid," in W. H. Munk et al., *Generation and Airborne Detection of Internal Waves from an Object Moving through a Stratified Ocean* (Arlington, Va.: Institute for Defense Analyses, JASON), S-334, April 1969, p. 23. There is also some evidence that for a submarine outside the thermocline (deeply submerged) the hull-generated internal wave mechanism dominates the collapsing wake mechanism. *See* J. W. Miles, "Internal Waves Generated by a Moving Source," in Munk et al., *Generation and Airborne Detection,* p. 57.

49. Mollo-Christensen, "Surface Wave Modulation."

50. SAR is an air- or spaceborne radar that uses its motion to synthesize a longer effective antenna length and obtain improved spatial resolution.

51. J. P. Dugan, A. C. Warn-Vargas, and S. A. Piacek, *Numerical Model for Mixed Region Collapse in a Stratified Fluid,* NRL Memo Rept. 2597, 1973, p. 11.

52. Jin Wu, "Mixed Region Collapse with Internal Wave Generation in a Density-Stratified Medium," *Journal of Fluid Mechanics* 35, pt. 3, 1969, pp. 531–544.

53. Phillips, *The Dynamics of the Upper Ocean,* p. 209.

54. D. T. Chen, *Surface Effects due to Subsurface Processes,* NRL Memo Rept. 4727, 1982, p. 15.

55. I. S. Robinson, *Satellite Oceanography* (New York: Halstead Press, John Wiley and Sons, 1985), p. 373; chap. 7, 8, 10.

56. Walter Andrews, "Soviets Said Able to Target U.S. Subs from Space by Radar," *Washington Times,* 16 August 1984, p. 6A.

57. Walter Andrews, "Soviet Ability to Target Subs Is Denied," *Washington Times,* 17 August 1984, p. 12A.

58. B. Nelepo, *Izvestia,* 29 July 1981, quoted by James M. McConnell, "New Soviet Methods for Antisubmarine Warfare?" *Naval War College Review,* July/August, 1985, pp. 16–27. See also Edgar Ulsamer, "Penetrating the Sea Sanctuary," *Air Force Magazine,* September 1984, p. 29.

59. "Navy Chief Sees Gain in Space Shuttle Flight," *New York Times,* 22 March 1985, p. 19.

60. Ibid.

61. SASC, FY 1985, part 7, p. 3414.

62. Ibid.

63. Joseph Lintz, Jr., and David Simonett, *Remote Sensing of Environment* (Reading, Mass.: Addison-Wesley, 1976), p. 604.

64. The conversion factors used in this analysis are 1 MW = 1,341 hp, and 1 watt = 0.239 cal/sec. The net efficiency between the reactor and the propeller is about 0.20, although if it is assumed that all the turbulent energy decays into heat within the wake, then the total reactor power is heating the water.

65. Capt. First Rank Boris I. Rodionov, *Antisubmarine Forces and Systems in Navies* (Moscow: Military Publishing House, 1976), p. 86.

66. A. S. Monin et al., *Variability of the Oceans* (New York: Wiley-Interscience, 1977), p. 35. At polar latitudes, the water temperature is virtually constant over depth, and at temperate latitudes the gradient is typically 0.015° C per meter.

67. S. Tabata and J. F. R. Gower, "A Comparison of Ship and Satellite Measurements of Sea Surface Temperatures off the Pacific Coast of Canada," *Journal of Geophysical Research* 85: C11, November 1980, pp. 6636–6648.

68. M. B. White, "Lasers for Hydrographic Applications," *Naval Research Reviews,* Summer 1981, pp. 28–38.

69. HASC, FY 1986, part 4, p. 404.

70. "Interest in Laser Radar Grows after Sub Affair," *Svenska Dagbladet,* 17 November 1981, pp. 1, 17 (Foreign Broadcast Information Service, Nordic Affairs, 24 November 1981).

71. Tyler, "Optical Properties of Water," pp. 15–30.

72. Robert McClatchey et al., "Optical Properties of the Atmosphere" in *Handbook of Optics,* ed. Walter G. Driscoll (New York: McGraw-Hill, 1978), pp. 14-14, 14-15.

73. M. Bertolotti, "Effects of Atmosphere on the Propagation of Laser Beams," in *Lasers and Their Applications,* ed. A. Sona (New York: Gordon and Breach, 1976) p. 358.

74. See appendix on acoustic detection.

75. Lt. Comdr. William E. Wright, USN, "Blue-Green Lasers for Submarine Communications," *Naval Engineers Journal* 95, May 1983, pp. 173–177.

76. Dr. Gerald Dinneen, Asst. Secretary of Defense, C^3I, before the House Armed Services Research and Development Subcommittee, March 1979, quoted in Roland J. Starkey, Jr., "The Renaissance in Submarine Communications," *Military Electronics/Countermeasures,* May 1981, pp. 55–66.

77. Tyler, "Optical Properties of Water," pp. 15–30.

78. A. B. Meinel and M. P. Meinel, *Applied Solar Energy* (Reading, Mass.: Addison-Wesley, 1979), p. 42.

79. Phillip J. Klass, "Studies Weigh Approaches in Blue-Green Laser Use," *Aviation Week and Space Technology*, June 21, 1982, pp. 70–71.

80. Wright, "Blue-Green Lasers," pp. 173–177.

81. F. E. Goodwin, "A 3.39 Micron Infrared Optical Heterodyne Communication System," *IEEE Journal of Quantum Electronics,* November 1967, p. 530. Measurements were made of a 0.63 micron laser over an 8,000-foot turbulent path. Also, R. Meredith, "Unguided Optical Propagation in the Atmosphere and Under-Sea," in *Lasers and Their Applications* (London: Institution of Electrical Engineers, Electronics and Science Division, 1965), pp. 23-1 through 23-9.

82. This is only the round-trip attenuation in seawater. Submarine reflectivity is assumed to be similar to black paint, which is similar to the sea surface—a few percent at 0.48 microns—and so drops out of the ratio. Dr. Ove Steinvall of Sweden's Armed Forces Research Institute gave the same ratio in the context of shallow water hydrographic applications of lidar. *See* "Interest in Laser Radar Grows after Sub Affair," pp. 1, 17.

83. I am indebted to Allen Flusberg for this explanation. *See* also A. Ferrario and A. Sona, "Gaseous Laser," in *Lasers and their Applications,* ed. A. Sona (New York: Gordon and Breach, 1976), pp. 183–206.

84. This phenomenon also destroys laser phase coherence and therefore interferes with laser communication systems. W. E. Wright, "Blue-Green Lasers," p. 174.

85. Klass, "Studies Weigh Approaches," pp. 70, 71.

86. Typical reflectance of flat black nextel paint at 0.47 microns is 1 or 2 percent. J. C. McVeigh, *Sun Power* (Elmsford, N.Y.: Pergamon, 1977), p. 31.

87. This assumes incoherent processing. A coherent processor may be able to detect at lower signal-to-noise ratios, but the pulse stretching would strongly interfere.

88. The same order of magnitude intensity is required by laser weapon systems, though laser weapon pulse durations are much longer. *See* M. Callahan and K. Tsipis, *High Energy Laser Weapons* unpublished report from the Program in Science and Technology in International Security, MIT, November 1980, p. 34.

89. Sturm, "The Atmospheric Correction," p. 165.

90. Klass, "Studies Weigh Approaches," pp. 70, 71.

91. Wright, "Blue-Green Lasers."

92. HASC, FY 1986, part 3, p. 169.

Appendix 4
The Oceans and Submarine Detection

Introduction

For the foreseeable future, acoustics will remain the principal means of detecting submarines for both the United States and the USSR. This fact has a profound influence over the design and operation of ballistic missile submarines (SSBNs) and attack submarines (SSNs), particularly in view of the fact that SSNs will remain the most effective antisubmarine warfare (ASW) platform. The very tactics of submarine warfare are linked to the problems of trying to hear without being heard, and the stealthy, independent operations that characterize submarine warfare have been likened to guerrilla warfare at sea.

There are two modes of acoustic detection: active, in which a ping generated by the searcher is reflected off a target and is then detected by the searcher; and passive, in which the searcher listens to sounds that are generated by the target. The two modes of detection are associated with two somewhat different tactical environments. This discussion will be oriented toward submarine-versus-submarine operations, but some of the main ideas can be extended to surface and air ASW platforms.

When active sonar is used in the process of detecting or localizing a target, the target immediately becomes aware that a searcher is in the vicinity and knows in what direction that searcher lies, although its range is ambiguous. In practice, the target will be able to counterdetect a searcher that is using active sonar at a range of two to eight or more times the range at which the searcher can detect the target, a fact that can be of immense importance to an evasive submarine.[1] On the other hand, a detection made with active sonar yields all the information needed to launch a weapon accurately at the target: relative direction and range, as well as information about the target's motion and orientation. The target knows only the direction from which the ping is arriving, although this is sufficient information for launching a torpedo in desperation and thereby putting the searcher on the defensive. Active sonar is particularly useful when passive sonars are less effective either because the target is very quiet or the environment is very noisy. Active dunking sonar on helicopters is used for finding submarines within the inner zone of US carrier battle groups where noise from the many escort ships dominates the acoustic background. From a tactical point of view, when active sonar is used in submarine versus submarine search, the relative importance of active countermeasures, echo-reducing coatings, speed, weapon load, firing rate, and maneuverability increases. For example, once a submarine has been detected by active sonar, there is little penalty attached to its launching torpedoes, noisemakers, jamming devices, masking bubbles, or driving off in a hurry in an effort to avoid an oncoming torpedo.

Passive sonar is in a tactical sense somewhat the opposite of active sonar. Here, the searcher hopes to detect the target before being detected itself. A single passive fix only yields the direction of the target,[2] so the searcher must move around and obtain several estimates of the direction to the target from different points, triangulating to find the distance to as well as the direction of the target. This is a time-consuming process during which the target moves and complicates the geometric problem. There are systems that can determine the range to a target from a single point by estimating the curvature of the sound waves as they radiate from the target, but at long distances the waves approximate planes, and acoustic nonhomogeneities in the intervening ocean disrupt these wave fronts and degrade these passive localization systems. In passive sonar tactics, the emphasis is on quietness and sensors.

Speed is helpful for increasing sonar search rate, but only up to the point at which the sensors are deafened by the noise of the submarine or of the turbulent water. This speed is called the tactical speed of a submarine. The "maximum speed" is the fastest a submarine can travel independent of noise output. Submarine-mounted passive sonar requires acoustic decoupling of the hydrophones from the submarine's own structural vibration and noise, so that quietness not only helps the searcher approach the target inaudibly, but also improves the searcher's own detection capability. External anechoic coatings also help reduce radiated noise, but most of the quieting is done through advanced propeller design and machinery quieting and isolation.

It is impossible to say which of the two tactics is "better," since the effectiveness of each depends on the particular circumstances. US nuclear submarine tactics have been predominantly passive. Insofar as many of the wartime missions of US attack submarines would involve operations very close to the USSR where Soviet ASW forces will be dense, and insofar as the US SSN can maintain its acoustic advantage over its Soviet counterpart, this preference is likely to remain. Since the submarine fleet of the USSR is not on the whole as quiet as the US fleet and has somewhat less effective detection equipment, the Soviet fleet is less effective in passive acoustic tactics. This may partly account for the greater Soviet emphasis on active acoustics, but it may also be that active detection is the superior tactic for a submarine fleet that is defending an area from very quiet intruders. In other words, Soviet active sonars may simply give a greater detection range against US submarines than passive sonars, and if the main objective is to keep US submarines out, then the disadvantages of active sonar in the one-on-one scenario may be outweighed by advantages at the larger mission level.

In this appendix on acoustic detection, the emphasis must be limited to passive acoustics, if only because the specific application of interest here is to strategic ASW, and a covert threat to SSBNs is the more difficult to counter.

General Description of the Oceans

Water covers about 71 percent of the total area of the earth and about 60 percent of the Northern Hemisphere. Of the total ocean area, the Pacific Ocean accounts for 46 percent, the Atlantic Ocean for about 23 percent, the Indian Ocean for about 20 percent, and the rest combined for about 11 percent. The average depth of the oceans is about 4,000 meters (13,000 feet), and about 76 percent of the ocean lies between 3,000 and 6,000 meters (9,800 and 19,700 feet), with 1 percent being deeper.[3]

Ocean basins of primary significance to strategic antisubmarine warfare are in the Northern Hemisphere: the North Atlantic, the North Pacific, and the Arctic Oceans. The North Pacific Ocean is about 2,500 times as wide as it is deep, so that a scale model 200 feet in diameter would be about 1 inch deep. Similarly, an inch-deep model of the North Atlantic would be 140 feet across. Figure A4–1 shows the main features of an ocean basin with a greatly expanded vertical scale. The Atlantic Ocean has a pronounced midocean ridge, which exceeds terrestrial mountain ranges in height and angularity. The midocean ridge flattens out on both sides to regions of less dramatic topography. Areas where the deep-sea floor is quite flat for at least several thousand square miles are called the abyssal plains. Moving toward the continent, the sea floor begins to rise, first gently, then more rapidly into the continental slope. In some places, such as the North Pacific, a deep-sea trench may be encountered at the foot of the continental slope. These trenches may have depths as great as 37,950 feet. The continental slope is broken up by canyons cutting laterally into the continental shelf. The continental slope can rise as steeply as 45 degrees, although the average for all continental slopes is a mild 4 degrees 07 minutes.[4] The level continental shelf begins when the sea floor has risen to about 600 feet (180 meters) below sea level. The average slope of the shelf is only around a tenth of a degree, and the average width worldwide is 42 nautical miles (nm). The variation in the extent of the shelf is large, as is indicated by figure A4–2, ranging from 4 nm width off the US West Coast, to 100 nm off the US East Coast, to over 700 nm off the Arctic coast of the USSR. Much of the continental shelf in the high latitudes of the Northern Hemisphere was cut

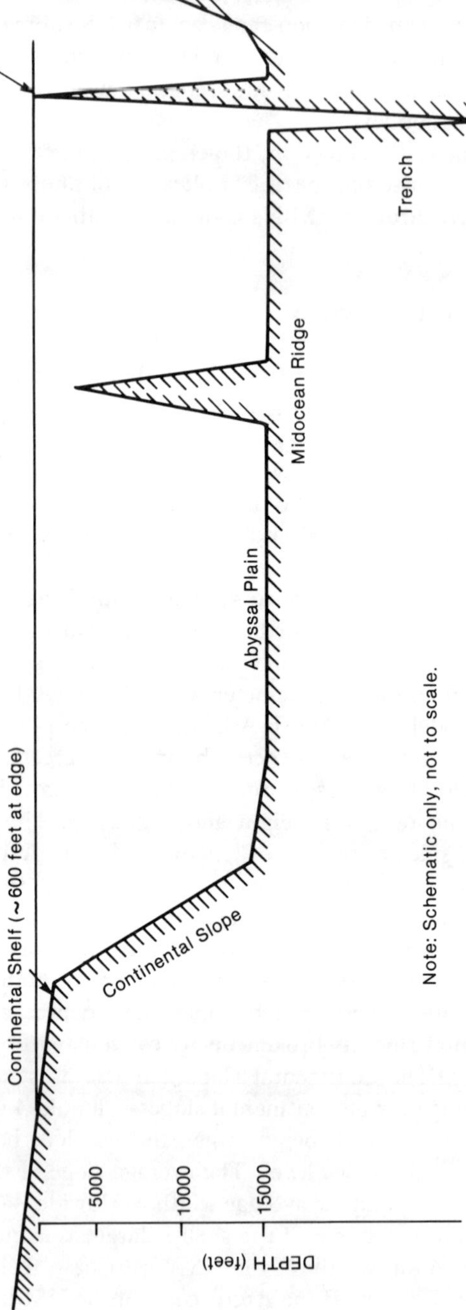

Figure A4–1. Main features of an ocean basin, with greatly expanded vertical scale.

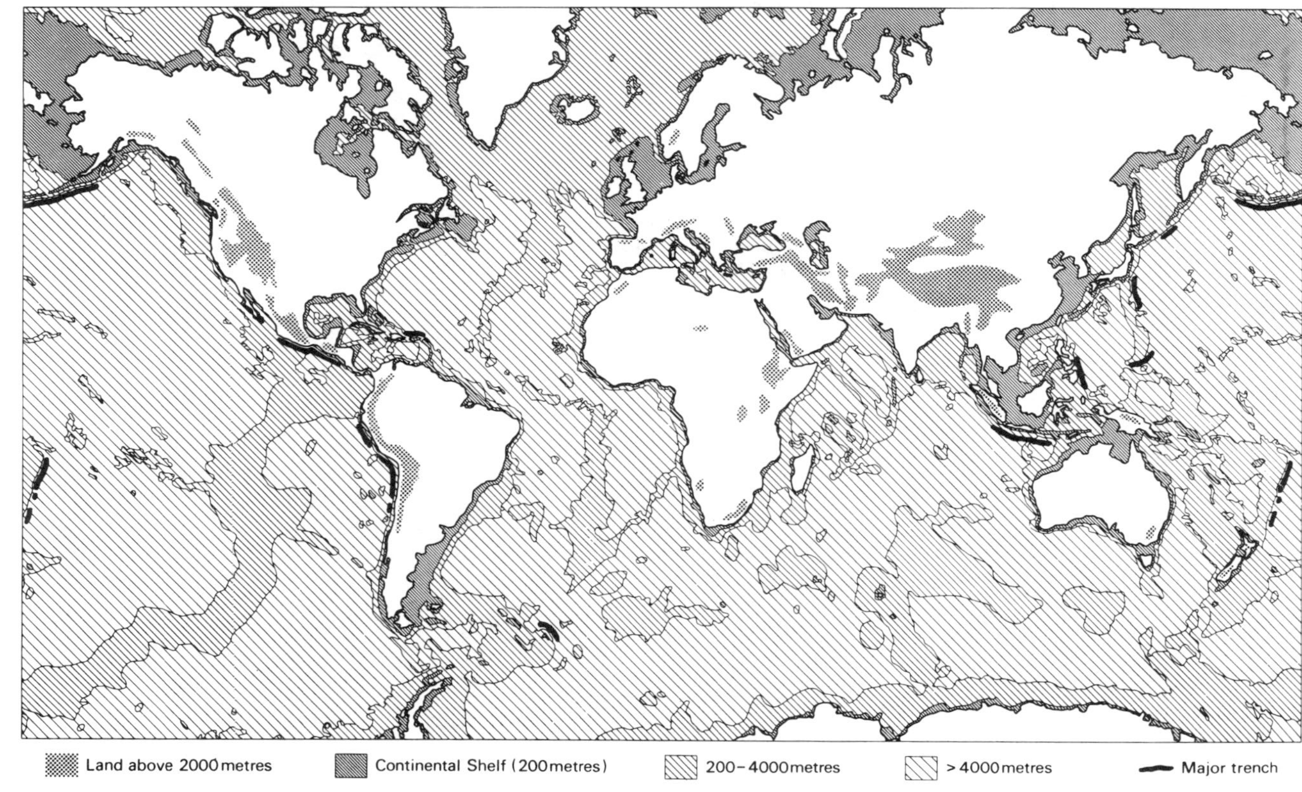

Figure A4–2. Depths of the world ocean, including the continental shelf.

Source: Neil Wells, *The Atmosphere and Ocean: A Physical Introduction* (London: Taylor and Francis, 1986), frontispiece.

and gouged by glaciers during the ice ages and has many canyons and banks. Maps showing the gross features of bathymetry for the Arctic and North Pacific oceans are shown in figures A4–3 and A4–4.

Figure A4–3. Bathymetry of the Eurasian Arctic and adjoining seas.

Source: Oceanographic Atlas of the Polar Seas, part 2, *Arctic* (NAVOCEANO pub. no. 705)

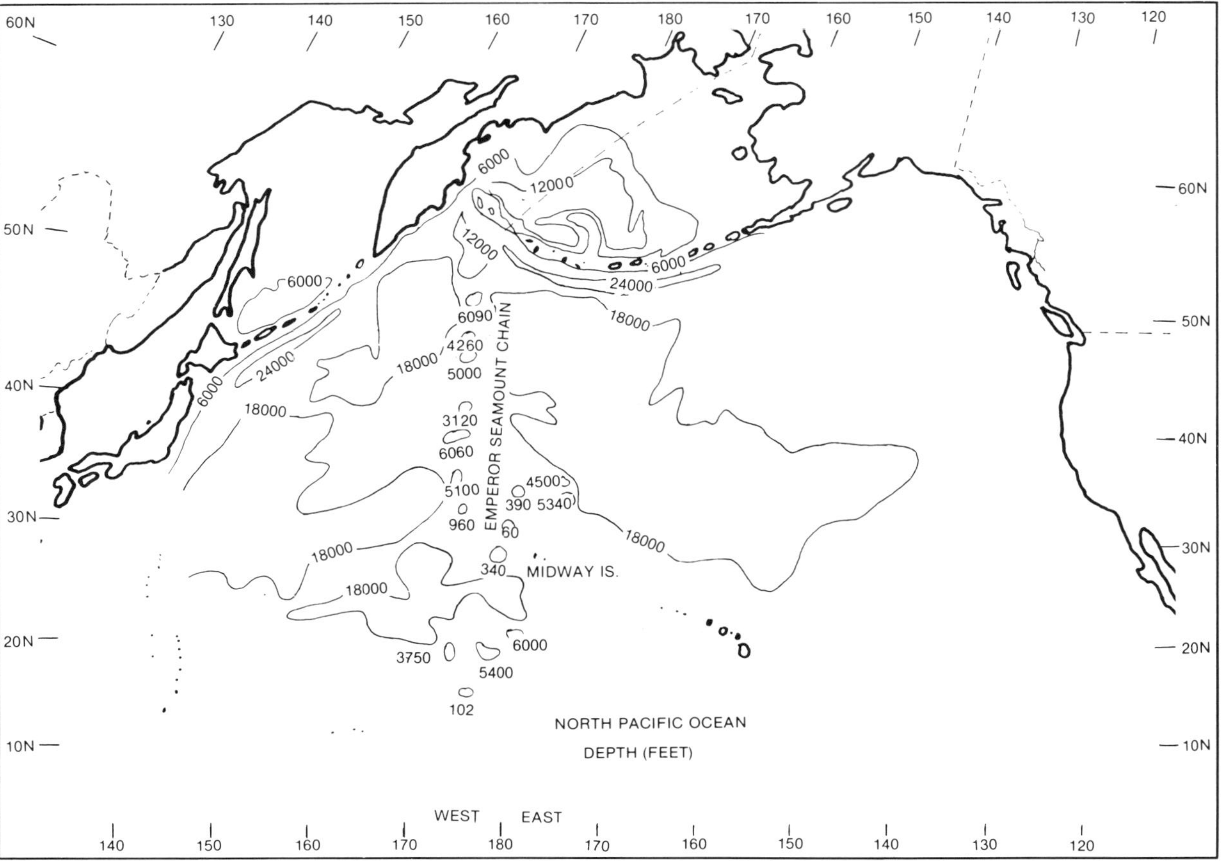

Figure A4–4. Bathymetry of the North Pacific Ocean.

Source: Bathymetric Atlas of the North Pacific Ocean, (N.O. pub. no. 1301–2–3, Naval Oceanographic Office, 1975).

Rising above the deep ocean floor are underwater mountains called seamounts. These are conically shaped underwater volcanoes that extend to within a few hundred feet of the sea surface, or actually broach it, as is the case with the island of Bermuda. Seamounts can obscure underwater sound paths and have a profound effect on underwater sound transmission.

Ocean circulation takes place on many scales and is driven by a variety of physical processes. The motions in the upper layers can influence submarine operations and submarine warfare tactics. Predictable currents may be used by submarines for drifting silently through acoustically monitored chokepoints, such as the Greenland–Iceland–United Kingdom (GIUK) gap.[5] SSBNs on patrol in the ocean are also subject to drift from ocean currents, though these currents are generally less than 10 percent of the patrol speed (5 knots) of the submarine. This drift does not cause any navigational error, however, since the ship's inertial navigation system accounts for all movements of the vessel.

The main forces that drive large-scale ocean circulation are (1) winds and (2) density forces caused by differences in temperature and salinity. The latter mechanism primarily drives the deep ocean circulation. Most of this motion occurs at depths below the maximum depth of military submarines and so is of less interest here. The large-scale upper water circulation is thought to be driven by the persistent east-to-west equatorial trade winds. Figures A4–5 and A4–6 are maps of surface water circulation in the Arctic and Pacific. The depths of these currents generally extend from the surface to a depth of 300–1,000 meters.[6] Currents are not uniform streams flowing through a quiescent ocean; rather, they may be visualized as meandering filaments moving more or less coherently in a general direction. The northward flowing currents at the western boundaries of the ocean gyres are the fastest and most well defined of the major ocean currents. These western boundary currents are driven by a dynamical force, which is driven by the earth's rotation. The Florida Current and Gulf Stream in the Atlantic, and the Kuroshio Current and Kuroshio Extension in the Pacific are examples of intensified western boundary currents.

Fluctuations and uncertainties in the acoustic transmission properties of the ocean are caused by spatial and temporal fluctuations in the speed of sound which in turn arise from temperature, pressure, and salinity fluctuations. Of these, temperature variability in time and space accounts for most of the sound velocity fluctuation.

The major internal movements of the ocean that are not categorized as currents are grouped into waves and eddies. Eddies are large (on the order of 50–100 nm) moving parcels of water that are usually spawned from a major current. The Gulf Stream, for instance, is the origin of a complex group of eddies and "rings" in the North Atlantic. Rings are identifiable by their core of water at one temperature, which is surrounded by a ring of water at a different temperature.

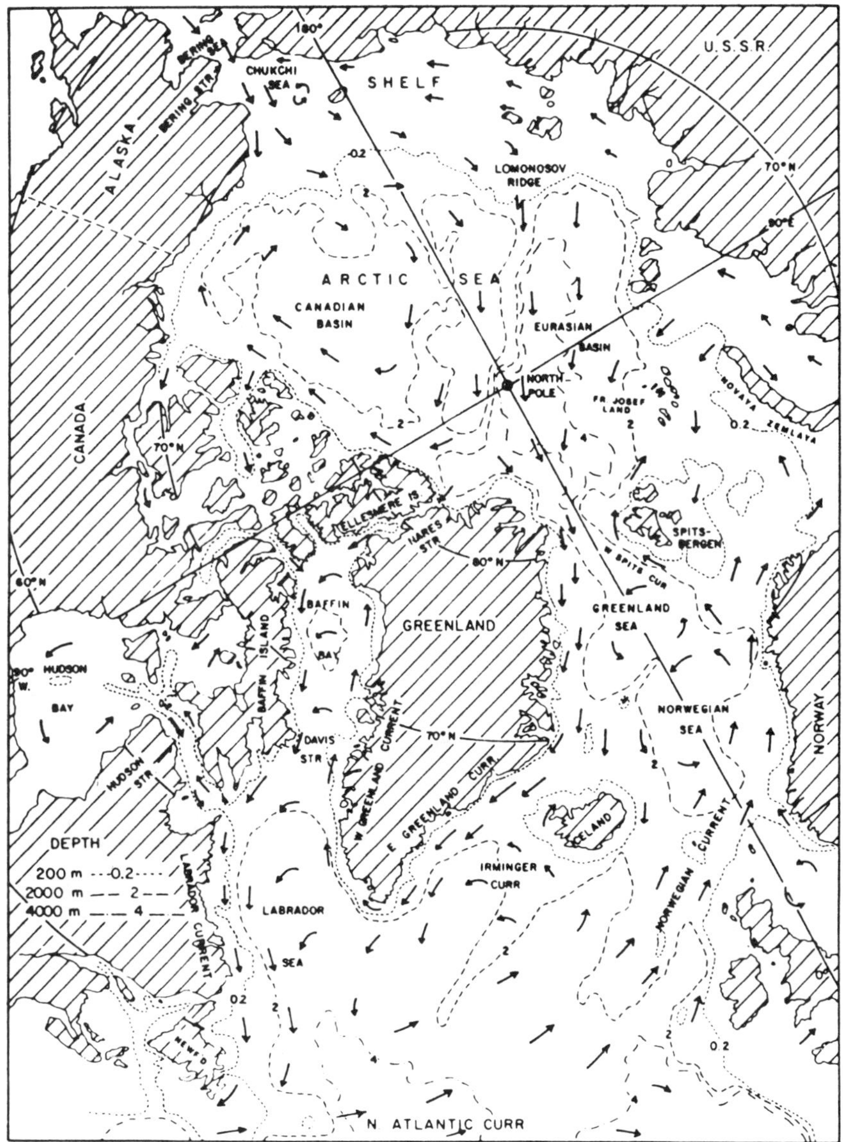

Figure A4–5. Average surface currents and bathymetry in the Arctic and adjoining seas.

Source: George L. Pickard and William J. Emery, *Descriptive Physical Oceanography,* 4th enl. ed. (New York: Pergamon, 1984), fig. 7.19, p. 169.

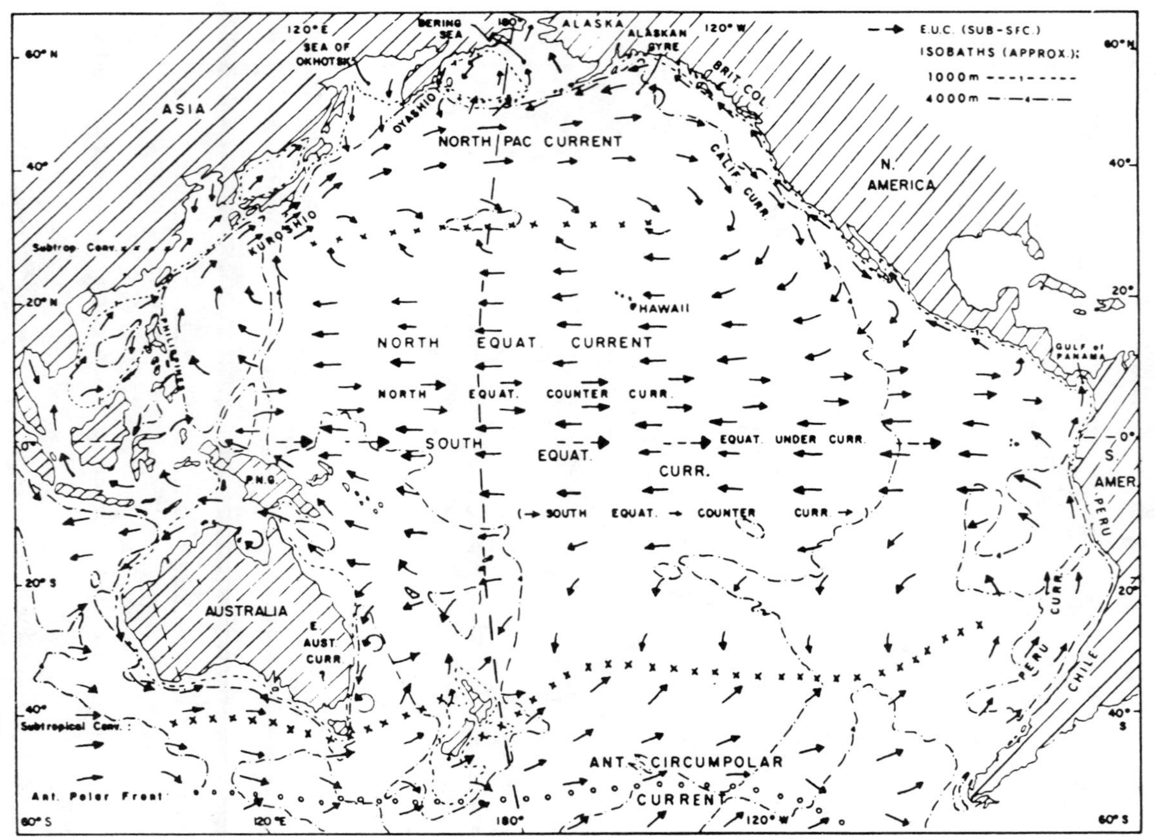

Figure A4–6. Average surface currents and bathymetry in the Pacific Ocean.

Source: George L. Pickard and William J. Emery, *Descriptive Physical Oceanography,* 4th enl. ed. (New York: Pergamon, 1984), fig. 7.24, p. 186.

Waves in the interior of the ocean are classified according to the time and length scales of their motions and (by inference) their dynamics. Slowly varying, very large scale waves that are dynamically associated with the earth's rotation introduce fluctuations on the scale of weeks or months. There are also wave motions that occur on time scales of an hour to a day. These shorter-period motions are a result of the temperature stratification of the ocean. Heated water near the surface is less dense than cooler water beneath and therefore rises toward the surface. If this stable stratification is perturbed in any way, and a warm water layer is pushed down, that layer will feel an upward restoring force from the denser water around it, and like a weight hanging from a spring, it will begin to oscillate. These oscillations of the internal thermal layers are called internal waves. The period of oscillation of an internal wave depends on water density and on the rate of change of density with depth.

Internal waves exist almost everywhere and are large near the surface but decrease rapidly with depth, and the motions have horizontal scales that are typically 10–100 times longer than the vertical scales.[7] To some extent internal waves and other random elements in the acoustic transmission characteristics of the oceans set upper bounds on the accuracy and resolution of long-range surveillance capabilities, in much the same way as atmospheric turbulence limits the potential for telescope observation of the sky.

At smaller length scales and shorter time scales, surface gravity waves and surface turbulence also have an effect on sound transmission. Sound passing through the upper layer of the ocean encounters the wave motion, which tends to shift some of the sound energy to a slightly different frequency. Turbulent fluctuations contribute to fluctuations in the received sound and may cause a wandering of the apparent bearing of a source of sound, much as atmospheric turbulence causes the twinkling of stars.

Introduction to the Theory of Sound Transmission through Water

A mathematical definition of sound is necessary in order to discuss some of the acoustic properties of the sea and how these relate to antisubmarine warfare. To begin with, assume that the ocean is completely homogeneous and that there is no spatial variation in sound transmission characteristics. If only long ranges from the source are considered, the spherical wave front can be locally approximated as a plane. The equation for the pressure of a simple sound wave is

$$p(x,t) = p_{\max} \cos \left[\frac{2\pi}{T} t - \frac{2\pi}{\lambda} x \right] \tag{A4.1}$$

where p_{max} is the maximum pressure of the wave, t is time, x is distance, λ is wavelength, and T is the period of the wave. A convenient measure of sound strength is the average rate of energy flow through a unit area or the intensity, defined as

$$I = \frac{p^2_{rms}}{\rho C} \tag{A4.2}$$

where ρ is water density, p^2_{rms} is the time-average of the squared pressure, and C is the speed of sound in seawater.

The speed of sound in seawater is a variable quantity that governs the bending, or refraction, of sound rays. Consider a wave front moving from a zone where the speed of sound is C_1 to a zone of higher sound velocity C_2. Figure A4–7 shows the wave fronts and the associated rays moving from zone 1 to a plane interface where they are transmitted into zone 2. The wave fronts bend as they pass into zone 2 as shown. The geometric relationship between successive wave fronts at the interface yields

$$\frac{C_1}{\cos\theta_1} = \frac{C_2}{\cos\theta_2} \tag{A4.3}$$

which is Snell's Law. If the speed of sound is known at all points in an ocean area, then ray paths can be constructed originating at a sound source anywhere in that area using equation A4.3 in successive small steps. An important result of Snell's Law is that a ray traveling through layers of changing sound speed always bends toward the layer of lesser sound speed. One way to remember how the law works is to think of a car traveling on a smooth road with a soft shoulder. If the right front tire drifts off the road into the dirt, that tire moves more slowly, and therefore the car is pulled to the right.

Acoustics in the Ocean

Effects of temperature, salinity, and depth on sound transmission are only relevant in that they influence the speed of sound in seawater. One equation relating sound speed to temperature, salinity, and depth is

$$\begin{aligned} C = {} & 1448.96 + 4.951\, T - 5.304 \times 10^{-2}\, T^2 + 2.374 \times 10^{-4}\, T^3 \\ & + 1.340(S-35) + 1.630 \times 10^{-2} D + 1.657 \times 10^{-7}\, D^2 \\ & - 1.025 \times 10^{-2}\, T(S-35) - 7.139 \times 10^{-13}\, TD^3 \end{aligned} \tag{A4.4}$$

where temperature T is in degrees centigrade, salinity S is in parts per thousand (ppt), depth D is in meters, and C is in meters per second.[8] Typical values

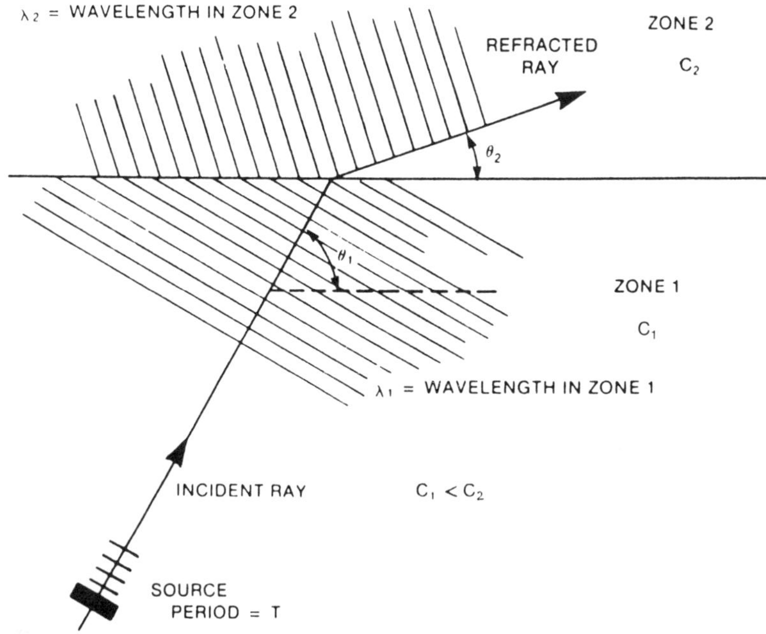

Figure A4–7. Refraction of a sound wave passing through the interface of two layers with different sound speeds.

of sound speed in the sea are 4,900 feet per second (approximately 1,500 meters per second), and although variations of more than a few percent are rare, these have a profound effect on underwater acoustics.

Oceanic temperature and salinity gradients are typically greatest in the upper 1,000 meters and are much larger in the vertical than in the horizontal direction. These vertical gradients are primarily caused by solar heating. Table A4–1 gives some values of vertical temperature and salinity gradients at middle latitudes.[9] From this data it is clear that in the upper kilometer of the ocean, temperature essentially governs the profile of sound speed with depth. The increase of sound speed due to the depth effect is smaller, and salinity effects are almost negligible, except under some special conditions near coasts, in the Mediterranean Sea, and under ice. Salinity affects the sound speed profile only if extremely large salinity gradients occur, for example, near the mouth of a major river outflow of fresh water into the sea. At depths below 1 kilometer, the solar heating and evaporation effects are negligible, so that temperature and salinity are relatively constant. About 75 percent of the total volume of the ocean has properties within the range from 0°–6° C and 34–35 ppt in salinity.[10]

Table A4–1
Average vertical temperature, salinity, and sound speed gradients in the upper 1,000 meters at middle latitude

Physical Property	*Average Gradient*	*Change in Sound Speed with Property*	*Variation in Sound Speed with Depth Due to Property*
Temperature (degrees C)	$\frac{\Delta T}{\Delta D} = \frac{-10^{0}}{1000\ m}$	$\frac{\Delta C}{\Delta T} = \frac{+4\ m/sec}{degree\ C}$	$\frac{\Delta C}{\Delta D} = \frac{-0.040\ m/sec}{meter}$
Salinity (ppt)	$\frac{\Delta S}{\Delta D} = \frac{\pm 1.5\ ppt}{1000\ m}$	$\frac{\Delta C}{\Delta S} = \frac{\pm 1.2\ m/sec}{ppt}$	$\frac{\Delta C}{\Delta D} = \frac{\pm 0.002\ m/sec}{meter}$
Depth (meters from surface)	$\frac{\Delta Z}{\Delta C} = \frac{+1000\ m}{1000\ m}$	$\frac{\Delta C}{\Delta Z} = \frac{+0.016\ m/sec}{meter}$	$\frac{\Delta C}{\Delta D} = \frac{+0.016\ m/sec}{meter}$

Source: George L. Pickard and William J. Emery, *Descriptive Physical Oceanography*, 4th ed., (New York: Pergamon, 1982), Chapter 4. Also equation A4.4.

In these lower depths, the speed of sound increases slowly with depth due to the steady increase in pressure.

The vertical temperature profile in the upper ocean is governed by the amount of solar energy absorbed by the water. A layer in which the temperature changes significantly with depth is called a thermocline. The overall temperature profile of the ocean has three components (thermoclines), which are distinguished by their temporal cycles: the steady-state profile, a seasonal variation in the upper layers, and a diurnal variation. There is a diurnal (one-day cycle) thermocline in the upper 20 meters, associated with a change of one to several degrees centigrade, depending on the latitude and season. Wave and wave mixing tend to smooth out the vertical temperature variations over the top few meters.[11] There are also longer-term seasonal variations that cycle over a year. Annual variations in temperature are typically 8 degrees Centigrade at 40 degrees north latitude. Annual variations decrease with depth and are rarely perceptible below 100–300 meters.[12] A set of seasonal temperature profiles is shown in figure A4–8. In this figure the upper 20 meters are shown as the average temperature over a day. In addition to the diurnal and seasonal thermoclines, there is a steady-state main thermocline that extends to a depth of about 1,000 meters. Figure A4–9 shows examples of the main thermocline at low, middle, and high latitudes. The observed profile is a superposition of these three thermoclines and can be very complex in detail, though it is important to note that the gross structure below 100 meters is relatively constant over time, as it is dominated by the steady-state thermocline.

The profile of sound speed over the entire depth of the ocean can be computed from the equation for sound speed as a function of temperature and depth (equation A4.4) by measuring distribution of temperature and salinity over depth (figure A4–10, part a). When this is done, a sound speed profile like

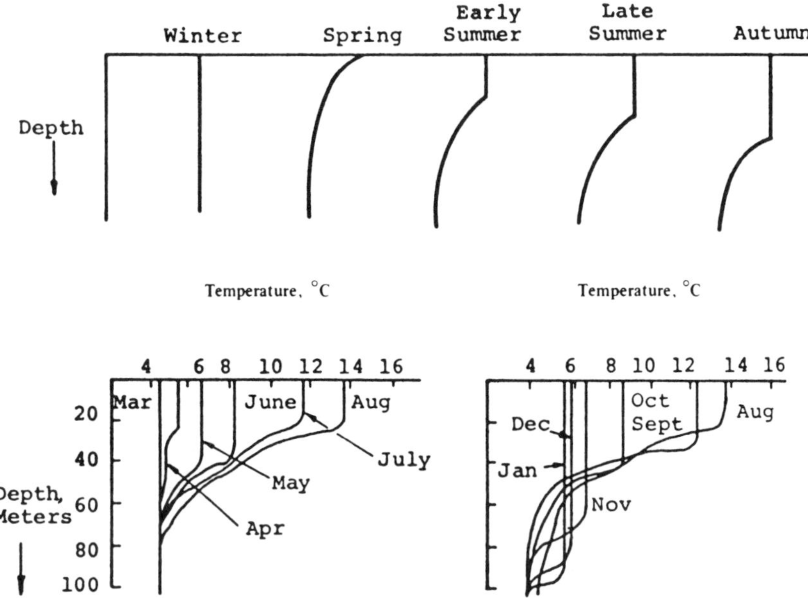

Figure A4–8. Annual cycle of the seasonal thermocline in the North Pacific.

Source: Robert J. Urick, *Sound Propation in the Sea,* (Los Altos, CA: Peninsula Publishing, 1982), p. 6–2.

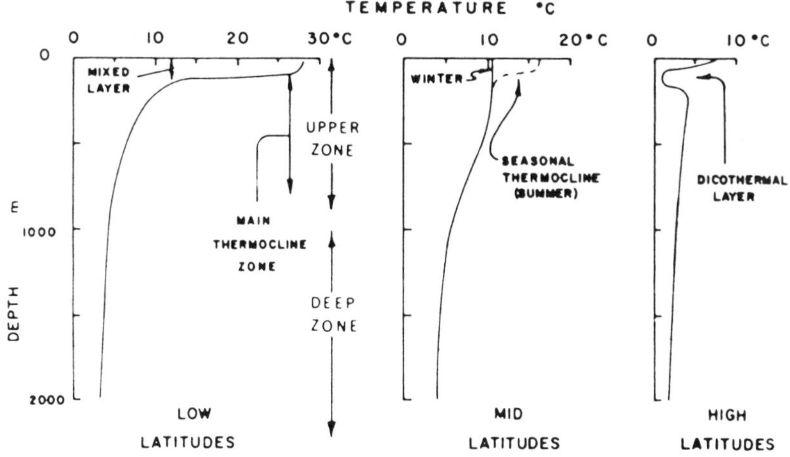

Figure A4–9. Typical mean temperature/depth profiles in the open ocean showing the main thermocline.

Source: George L. Pickard and William J. Emery, *Descriptive Physical Oceanography,* 4th enl. ed. (New York: Pergamon, 1984), fig. 4.5, p. 38.

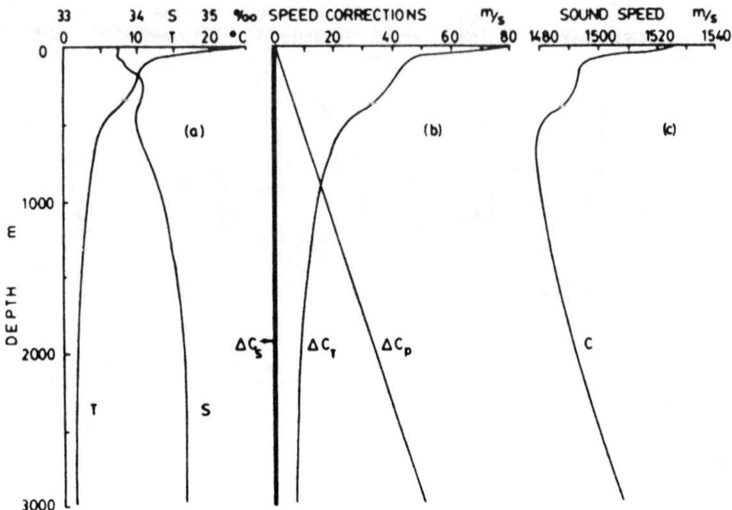

Figure A4–10. Derivation of the sound speed profile from temperature and depth dependence of sound speed.

Source: George L. Pickard and William J. Emery, *Descriptive Physical Oceanography,* 4th enl. ed. (New York: Pergamon Publishing, 1984), fig. 3.2, p. 23.

that in figure A4–10, part c is obtained. As figure A4–10, part b shows, the upper part of the sound speed profile is principally governed by the rapidly decreasing temperature with depth, while the lower part is governed by the effect of increasing depth. The result is that the sound speed reaches a minimum at around 1,000 meters, below which there is an approximately linear increase in sound speed to the bottom. This basic sound speed profile exists throughout the low and midlatitudes of the North Atlantic and North Pacific oceans. There may be local variations of this basic profile due to the intrusion by cold or warm currents, but these variations are limited in extent.

The layer of minimum sound speed becomes shallower with higher latitudes due to the fact that with less incoming solar radiation, the main thermocline does not penetrate to as great a depth. In the arctic regions where the temperature is relatively constant over the entire depth, the sound speed profile is completely governed by the steady increase in sound speed with depth so that the layer of minimum sound speed is at or near the surface. This has a profound effect on acoustic propagation and therefore on ASW operations in the Arctic because the undersurface of the ice is repeatedly encountered by upward refraction as the sound progresses outward in range.

The Deep Sound Channel

The depth plane of minimum sound velocity is called the axis of the sound velocity profile. The axis is associated with a very important acoustical effect:

as sound passes through the layers of changing speed above and below the axis, it is refracted according to Snell's Law, and since the axis is by definition the layer with the lowest speed, sound on either side of the axis is always refracted toward the axis. Sound ray paths from a nondirectional source can be plotted using equation A4.3. In figure A4–11, the source (*S*) is fixed at a depth of 600 meters, and four outgoing rays are shown marked *A, B, C,* and *D.* The rays in the figure appear to be much steeper in shape than they actually are due to the difference in the horizontal and vertical scales. These plots are called ray diagrams, and they are crucial pieces of information for real-time ASW tactical decision making. Many US ASW platforms have computers that can make ray traces from inputs of the sound speed profile and source depth.

The sound emitted from source *S* radiates in all directions. Each ray that emerges from *S* has a specific value of the quantity

$$G = \frac{C_0}{\cos\theta_0} \tag{A4.5}$$

where C_0 is the speed of sound at the depth of the source and θ_0 is the initial angle of the ray relative to horizontal. From equation A4.3, *G* is constant along any one ray. It immediately follows that the initially horizontal ray marked *B* in figure A4–11 must remain horizontal. Upward rays like *A* refract downward, while downward rays like *C* and *D* travel downward until they are refracted or reflected upward and, like *A,* pass through the axis. The ray paths oscillate around the axis with a short loop above and a long loop below the axis. As a result, some of this sound energy is trapped into oscillating around the axis. The layer within which the sound is trapped is called the deep sound channel.[13] Sound trapped in the sound channel propagates much greater distances than untrapped, uniformly spreading sound because it does not hit the surface or bottom, where sound is scattered and absorbed.

Not all the energy from the source is trapped by the sound channel. Upward rays significantly steeper than *A* are reflected both at the surface and at the bottom and may not oscillate around the axis in as well-behaved a manner as the rays shown. Downward rays like *D* may similarly reflect off the bottom if they are steep enough. Boundary reflections generally involve scattering and energy loss so that reflected rays are attenuated more rapidly than purely refracted rays. In addition, there may be energy loss out of the sound channel due to scattering from nonhomogeneities in the water itself.

Convergence Zones and Shadow Zones

The refractive characteristics of the sound channel create a complex lens effect by which sound rays are focused and defocused at regular intervals from a point source. Consider the point source at *S* in figure A4–11. Near the source, rays are emitted radially in all directions. Two rays, such as *C* and the one immediately above it, separate with increasing distance from the source. Since

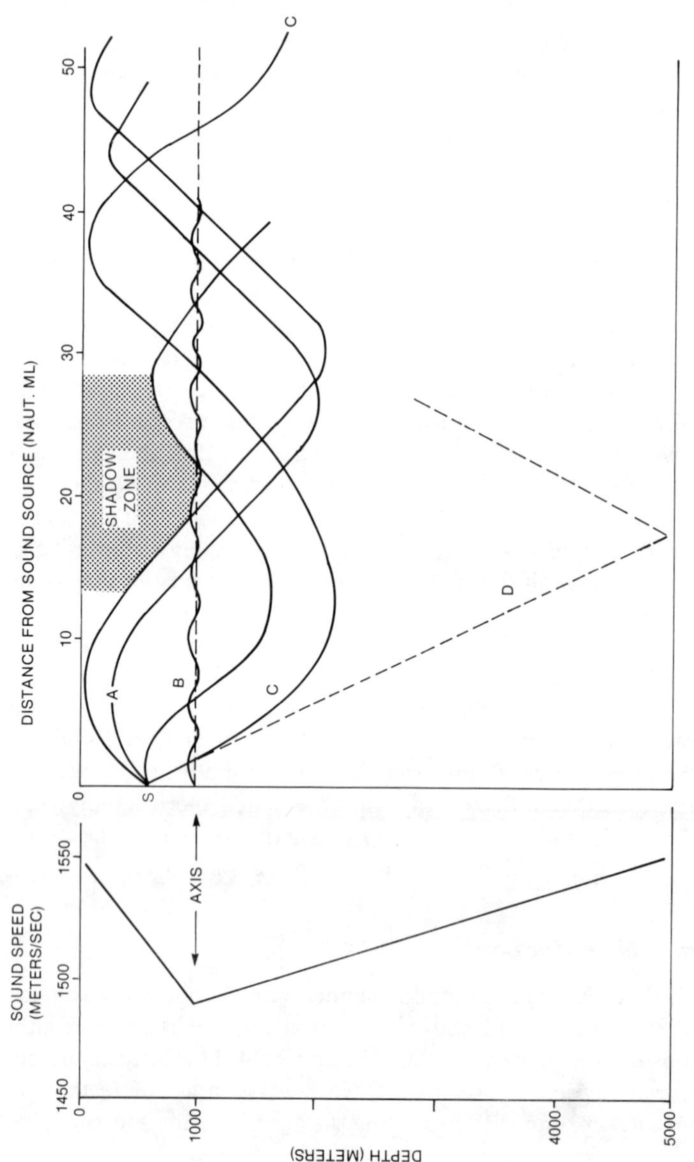

Figure A4–11. Ray diagram associated with a hypothetical sound speed profile.

a ray by definition is a path parallel to the direction of energy flow, then all the energy between two rays must remain between those two rays. The distance between the two rays at any point as they travel along is therefore an inverse measure of the sound intensity at that point, where intensity is defined in equation A4.2. In figure A4–11, the sound intensity in the vicinity of the path of ray *C* is a minimum at 15 nm from the source. At greater distances the rays reconverge until they actually meet at about 33 nm. The observed intensity in the vicinity of this convergence zone is significantly higher than it is along the path closer to the source. The ray theory breaks down at the points of ray crossings, or caustics, since an infinite intensity is predicted, which is of course physically impossible. Modified acoustic theories can be used to predict intensity near caustics. In the North Atlantic and North Pacific oceans, convergence zone spacing is typically about 33 nautical miles, and the zone itself is a few miles wide.[14] The convergence zones appear at multiples of the first convergence zone range—that is, at 33 nm, 66 nm, and 99 nm—while the widths of the zones themselves broaden with increasing range from the source. Beyond the third convergence zone, the amplification of the source sound is not usually very significant, since the energy is spread out and the zone is made diffuse by scattering and diffraction.

Ray theory also predicts zones that receive absolutely no sound from a point source in the sound channel. The shaded shadow zone in figure A4–11 indicates an area that is completely missed by rays emitted at point source *S*. According to ray theory, an observation taken within this shadow zone would show zero intensity. Some sound, however, does make its way into and out of the shadow zone from scattering at the boundaries and by diffraction off particles in the water. From a tactical point of view, the rays that are reflected off the bottom can be quite useful for detecting nearby submarines hiding in the shadow zone. In fact, submarines are seldom detected within shadow zones except via bottom bounce ray paths.[15] This is one of the main reasons for the deployment of spherical sonars common to US submarines, which can form receiving beams in the vertical as well as the horizontal. The shadow zone is clearly an important phenomenon in defensive and offensive undersea warfare tactics, and like the convergence zone, it can be predicted by shipboard ray-tracing computers, given sufficient information on the sound speed profile.

Conditions for the Existence of the Deep Sound Channel, Convergence Zones, and Shadow Zones

The deep sound channel in the ocean has an upper and lower bound that is determined by the ray that makes the largest vertical excursion between the crest of the upper loop and the trough of the lower loop. Equation A4.5 states that along a given ray the sound speed must be equal at the crest and the trough. There is generally a pair of depths where the sound speed is equal, one above and one below the axis of the deep sound channel. Figure A4–12 illustrates the three cases that can arise in the sound channel.

Case I: Sound Channel over the Entire Depth. In figure A4–12, part a, the sound speed at the surface just equals the sound speed at the bottom, so that the widest ray path just crests at the surface and troughs at the bottom, and a sound source or receiver is within the sound channel at any depth.

Case II: Bottom-limited Channel. In figure A4–12, part b, the water is not deep enough to allow the sound speed below the axis to rise to the value at the surface, so the bottom of the sound channel is cut off. The sound speed at the bottom is matched at *A,* however, so a sound channel exists but does not extend above the depth at *A*. A receiver above *A* will not benefit from the long-range transmission characteristics of the channel. In shallow water the relative importance of reflected rays is therefore greater.

Case III: Water Depth Greater Than Sound Channel Depth. Figure A4–12, part c, shows a case in which the water depth is below the turning depth

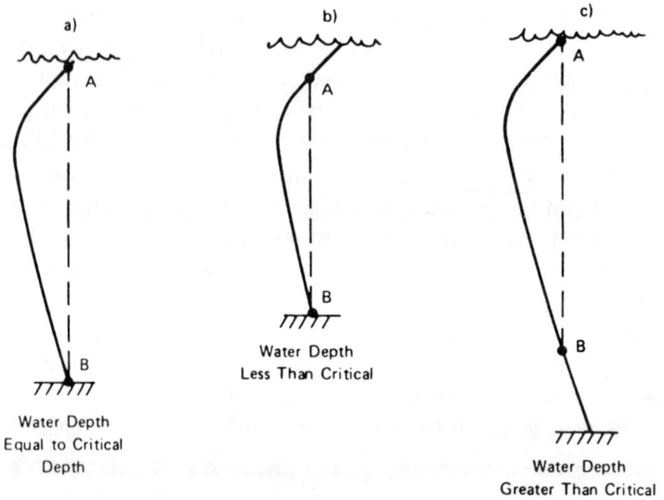

Figure A4–12. Velocity profile and the critical depth.

Note: In a) the water depth equals the critical depth and the entire water column forms the Deep Sound Channel. In b) and c) sound sources or receivers shallower than A in b) and deeper than B in c) would lie beyond the deep sound channel. Condition c) is required for the formation of a convergence zone.

Source: Robert J. Urick, *Sound Propagation in the Sea* (Los Altos, CA: Peninsula Publishing, 1982), p. 7-3.

of the deepest refracted ray. A receiver at the bottom is therefore outside the sound channel and is partially uncoupled from long-range acoustic transmission. The optimum placement of SOSUS and other long-range fixed acoustic receivers depends largely on good sound channel coupling, so these arrays are not placed in water that is too deep.

A useful concept that arises out of these cases is that with adequate water depth there is always a depth below the sound channel axis at which the sound speed equals the maximum value of the sound speed above the axis. The maximum sound speed above the axis is usually found at the surface and is determined approximately by the surface temperature. Below the axis, the sound speed increases linearly with depth. The depth below the axis at which the sound speed equals the sound speed at the surface is called the critical depth. In case I, the water depth equals the critical depth. In case II, the water depth is shallower than the critical depth. In case III, the water depth is greater than the critical depth.

In order better to understand the ASW environment, it is helpful to be able to predict whether convergence zones are present. Convergence zone reception depends on the presence of a sound channel. A sound channel exists when the vertical temperature distribution causes a well-defined sound speed minimum, a condition usually met at low and middle latitudes up to about 55 degrees north. Additional conditions for the existence of convergence zones are: (1) the sound source must lie in the sound channel, and (2) the water depth must exceed the critical depth by 1,200–1,800 feet in order that deep refracted rays may turn around and be brought into convergence.[16]

Predicting the existence and character of convergence zones is largely a matter of predicting the critical depth in relation to the water depth. This is simplified by the fact that the sound speed profile below the axis is very similar throughout the world. The surface temperature determines the surface sound speed and therefore the depth below the axis at which sound speed is equal—that is, the critical depth. A convergence zone prediction curve is shown in figure A4–13, on which is plotted a curve for predicting the existence of convergence zones (solid) and a curve for predicting convergence zone range (dashed). These curves apply to near-surface sources in the North Atlantic and North Pacific. The bottom scale indicates the surface water temperature. Convergence zones exist in water of a given depth and surface temperature if the point on the graph lies to the left of the solid line. The dashed line is used to find the convergence zone range on the right-hand scale, which corresponds to the surface temperature. Since the solid line approximates the curve of critical depth versus surface temperature, figure A4–13 can be used to predict roughly, given only the surface temperature, the maximum depth at which a bottom-mounted receiver will pick up distant acoustic signals from the sound channel. Because of seasonal changes in temperature, it follows that a given area may have a convergence zone in one season (winter) but not in another (summer).

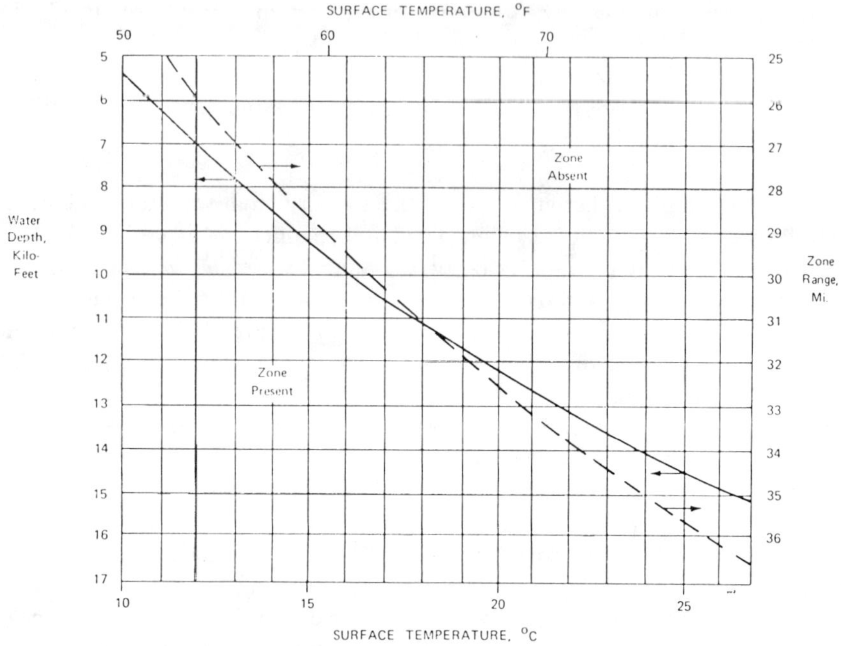

Figure A4–13. Convergence zone prediction curves.

Note: Water depth and surface temperature determine the presence or absence of a convergence zone (solid curve, left-hand scale). Dashed curve and right-hand scale give the zone range. For near-surface sources in the North Atlantic and North Pacific Oceans.

Source: Robert J. Urick, *Sound Propagation in the Sea* (Los Altos, CA: Peninsula Publishing, 1982), p. 8–10.

Thus seasonal effects are in many areas important for convergence zone propagation.

Reflection of Sound at the Surface and Bottom

Reflection and scattering of sound at the surface and bottom boundaries is a less efficient mechanism for sound propagation than refraction, though it is important for shallow water and for short-range detection. Water is acoustically shallow if the bottom plays a large role in determining the transmission of sound—that is, if over the transmission path of interest, many bottom interactions occur. A very rough guide to when water is acoustically shallow is when the depth is the same order of magnitude as 10 acoustic wavelengths. Thus, the term "shallow water" in acoustics is a frequency-dependent phenomenon, although since most of the discussion here relates to low frequencies on the order of 100 Hz, shallow water is on the order of 600 feet or less. Figure A4–2 shows the areas of the world ocean that are less than 660 feet (200 meters) deep, and it is important to note that these include much of the Soviet Union's SSBN patrol areas. Sound intensity loss due to multiple reflections at the bottom is the limiting factor in long-range shallow water transmission.

The reflection of sound at an ocean boundary is a complex process that involves energy loss at the interface and scattering of the incident wave in all directions. The ocean floor may be covered with mud that permits sound to penetrate to significant depths in the mud before being reflected or refracted back out into the water. Scattering of an incident ray is illustrated in figure A4–14. A surface that is smooth relative to the wavelength of the incident

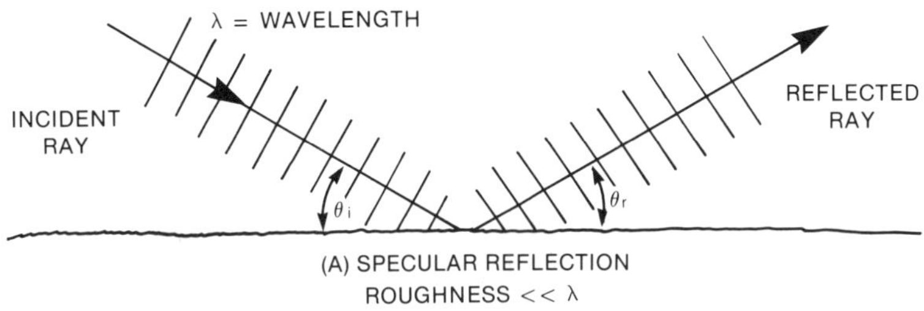

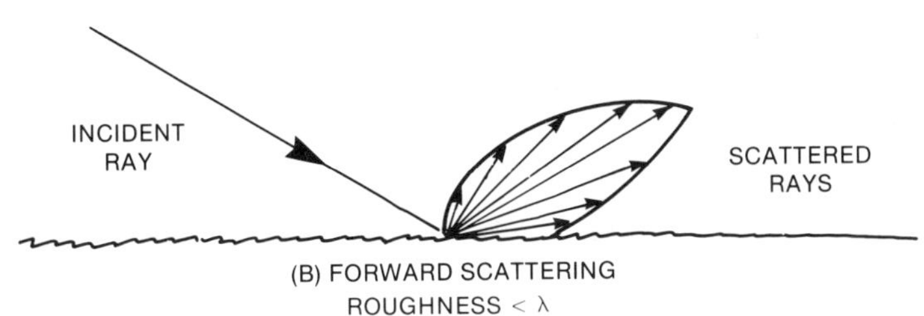

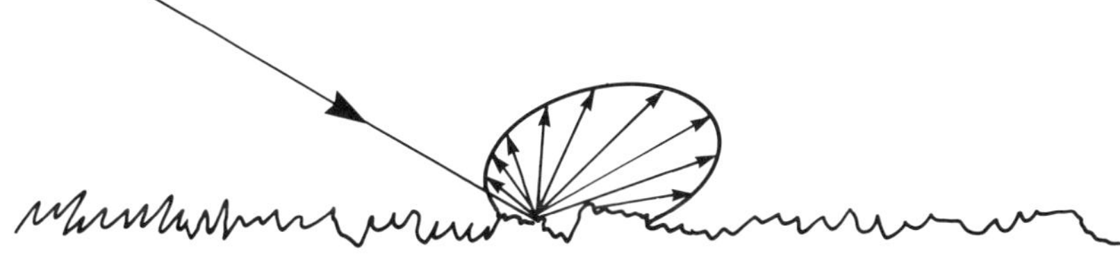

Figure A4–14. Reflection and scattering from the rough ocean bottom.

sound reflects with little or no scattering, and the angle of reflection θ_r is equal to the angle of incidence θ_i, as shown in figure A4–14. If the boundary roughness is increased, the incident sound is scattered around θ_r in a continuous distribution. Scattered sound is incoherent sound and cannot be detected by any form of coherent (for example, replica correlation) processing.[17] At the low frequencies important for long-range surveillance, the loss at the surface is negligible and the loss at the bottom is highly important in affecting propagation. Paths that are reflected at the surface, but do not strike the bottom—called refracted-surface reflected paths—are very effective for long-range propagation.

Notes

1. Albert W. Cox, *Sonar and Underwater Sound* (Lexington, Mass.: Lexington Books, 1974), p. 122.
2. When symmetric line arrays, such as the submarine-towed array system or the surface-towed TACTASS, are used there may also be a directional ambiguity, since such an array cannot distinguish one side from the other.
3. George L. Pickard and William J. Emery, *Descriptive Physical Oceanography* (Elmsford, N.Y.: Pergamon, 1982), pp. 5, 6.
4. F. P. Shepard, *The Earth beneath the Sea* (Baltimore: Johns Hopkins University Press, 1959).
5. Orr Kelly, "The Navy vs Soviet Subs-A Plus for US," *US News and World Report,* 13 November 1978, p. 79.
6. Pickard, *Descriptive Physical Oceanography,* p. 127.
7. Stanley M. Flatté et al., *Sound Transmission through a Fluctuating Ocean* (New York: Cambridge University Press, 1979), p. 61.
8. K. V. Mackenzie, "Effect of Sound Speed Equations on Critical Depths in the Ocean," *Journal of the Acoustical Society of America* 62(s1)s(19)A, 1977; *see* also Robert J. Urick, *Sound Propagation in the Sea* (Los Altos, Calif.: Peninsula Publishing, 1982), p. 4-6.
9. The term *middle latitude* refers to zones between about 30° and 55° north latitude; *high latitudes* are north of 55°; and *low latitudes* are south of 30°.
10. Pickard, *Descriptive Physical Oceanography,* p. 31.
11. Robert J. Urick, *Principles of Underwater Sound for Engineers* (New York: McGraw-Hill, 1975), p. 112. The diurnal temperature variation can reach 3-4° C in the upper 3 meters of the ocean, though it falls off rapidly with depth. The temperature gradient reaches a maximum in the afternoon, at which time sound transmission to the surface becomes weakest due to downward refraction. This "afternoon effect" can seriously impair hull-mounted sonar on surface ships but does not affect the performance of modern towed arrays and variable depth sonars.
12. Robert J. Urick, *Sound Propagation,* pp. 6-2.
13. The deep sound channel is sometimes called an acoustic waveguide, or the SOFAR (SOund Fixing and Ranging) channel.
14. In other oceans, the zones lie at different ranges because of differences in the sound speed profile. In the Mediterranean in the spring and autumn, for example, the first convergence zone lies at about 20 miles.
15. Robert J. Urick, personal communication.
16. Cox, *Sonar and Underwater Sound,* p. 25.
17. Urick, personal communication.

Appendix 5
Sonar and Sonar Arrays

Acoustic detection and localization of submarines employ both active and passive techniques. Active sonar involves generating a sound and then analyzing the echo reflected off the target. With passive sonar, the various sounds generated by the target submarine are detected directly. The following description of underwater sound emphasizes those phenomena important to passive detection, but many of the basic ideas are applicable to active systems. The purpose of this section is to introduce some quantitative models that provide insight into the acoustic detection of submarines.

Sonar and the Passive Sonar Equation

Underwater sound is a pressure wave that propagates energy from its source at the speed of sound, C. The unit of measurement of sound is its intensity, which is the amount of energy crossing a unit area in one second. The American National Standard for underwater sound intensity is 0.67×10^{-22} watts/cm^2, which is equivalent to the intensity of a plane pressure wave of 1 micropascal. Using this standard reference intensity, it is possible to describe all measured sound as a ratio of the measured intensity to the reference intensity. Instead of using the ratio directly, which can vary over many orders of magnitude, it is common practice to take ten times the logarithm of this ratio to be the sound level in "decibels," or dB. That is

$$\text{sound level (dB)} = 10 \log \left[\frac{I}{0.67 \times 10^{-22}} \right] \qquad \text{(A5.1)}$$

This definition of the decibel is expanded to include the ratio between any two sound intensities, I_1 and I_2, such that if

$$N = 10 \log \frac{I_2}{I_2} \qquad \text{(A5.2)}$$

I_1 and I_2 are said to differ by N dB.

Underwater sound is picked up by a hydrophone, which is simply an underwater microphone that converts pressure waves into an electric signal carrying the frequency and amplitude information of the acoustic signal. A hydrophone produces a very weak electrical signal, so amplifiers are used to boost the entire raw signal to a usable level. In the process of amplifying and digitizing this data, very low levels of electronic noise are introduced. The signal processor is where this amplified raw signal is analyzed to detect the submarine signature within the other noises. Finally, the analyzed signal is displayed in a form that makes it accessible to the sonar operator and commanding officer.

The factors that influence passive sonar detection at a given frequency can be associated with the equipment, the medium, and the target. These passive sonar parameters, which are defined as follows, generally depend on frequency.

1. *Equipment factors*
   a) *NL:* Self-noise level: The noise that is caused by the ship's own noise and electronics noise. Noise level is referred to a 1 micropascal plane wave and is usually given as the level in a 1 Hz band.
   b) *AG:* Receiving array gain: A measure of the angular resolution and improvement in signal-to-noise ratio of the sonar array. AG generally depends on the number of hydrophones in the sonar array, the array size and shape, and the frequency of the received sound.
   c) *DT:* Detection threshold: The level to which submarine signature must exceed noise in order to permit detection 50 percent (or any other percentage) of the time for a given probability of false alarms.
2. *Medium factors*
   a) *TL:* Transmission loss: The loss of sound intensity between the target submarine (at one yard) and the receiver.
   b) *NL:* Ambient noise level: Oceanic and man-made noise. Note that ambient and self-noise are lumped into the *NL* term.
3. *Target factors*
   a) *SL:* Source level: The intensity of the target submarine-generated sound, referred to a distance of 1 yard in the direction of the receiver, and referred to a 1 microPa plane wave in a 1 Hz band.

The equation that relates these quantities is called the passive sonar equation. It can be written as

$$SL + AG - TL - NL = DT \tag{A5.3}$$

This states that for a sonar system to make a detection, the source level (*SL*) and the noise-rejecting capacity of the directional array (*AG*) must be high enough to overcome the detrimental effects of transmission loss (TL) and noise (NL) so that the presence of the the signature is detectable. Figure A5-1 represents the various terms of the passive sonar equation. The following list gives the exact definitions of the terms. Each term will be discussed more thoroughly in the following sections.

Source level:

$$SL = 10 \log \left[\frac{\text{signature intensity 1 yard from source}}{\text{reference intensity}}\right]$$

Transmission loss:

$$TL = 10 \log \left[\frac{\text{signature intensity 1 yard from source}}{\text{signature intensity at receiver}}\right]$$

Detection threshold:

$$DT = 10 \log [\text{SNR for stated probabilities of detection and false alarm}]$$

Array gain:

$$AG = 10 \log \left[\frac{\text{SNR for array}}{\text{SNR for single hydrophone}}\right]$$

Transmission Loss

Sound intensity decreases with distance from the source due to three independent phenomena: the geometric spreading of energy, scattering, and the loss of energy through absorption.[1] In an unbounded ocean, the intensity of sound energy decreases proportionally to the square of the distance from the source. This spherical spreading model is accurate near the source, before the bottom and surface boundaries exert an influence. At distances of many times the water depth, waves begin to spread in a two-dimensional way because the spreading is confined, and the intensity drops off only as the first power of distance. This phenomenon is called cylindrical spreading.

The mechanisms for sound absorption by seawater are molecular in nature and occur as the water and its dissolved components are compressed and expanded due to the passage of the pressure wave. Viscous effects dissipate energy at very high frequencies, while the ionic relaxation of the magnesium sulfate and boric acid molecules in solution are primary mechanisms of energy dissipation at medium frequencies.[2] At very low frequencies energy is also lost as sound is scattered out of the deep sound channel.[3] Transmission loss due to

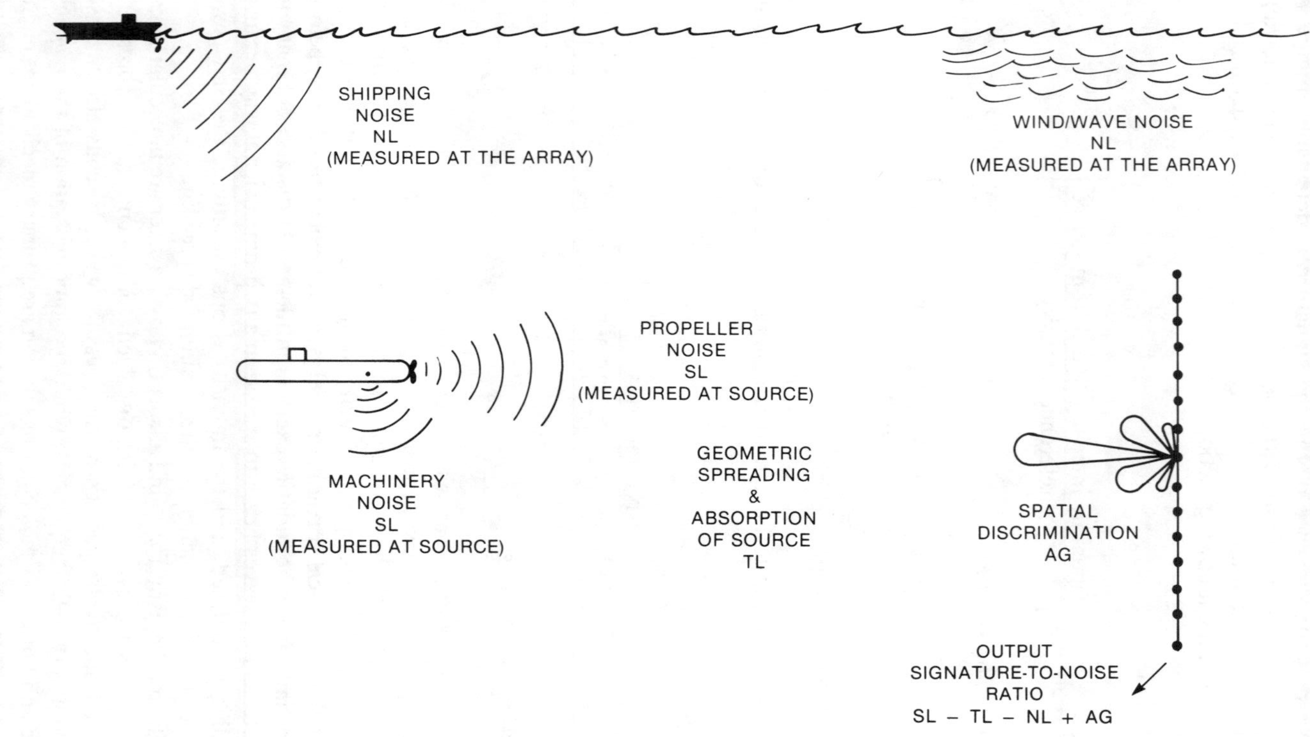

Figure A5–1. Schematic diagram of the passive sonar equation.

absorption is an exponential function of range, so in logarithmic decibel equations it appears as simply proportional to range. The transmission loss equation including spherical spreading and absorption is

$$TL = 10 \log R^n + \alpha R \times 10^{-3} \qquad \text{(A5.4)}$$

where R is in yards, α is the absorption coefficient (in dB per kiloyards) found from figure A5–2, and n is the geometric spreading factor, equal to 2 for spherical spreading and 1 for cylindrical spreading. The transition from spherical to cylindrical spreading depends upon propagation conditions but is of the order of a few miles in the deep ocean. Figure A5–3 shows attenuation versus frequency in the Pacific Ocean for very low frequencies.

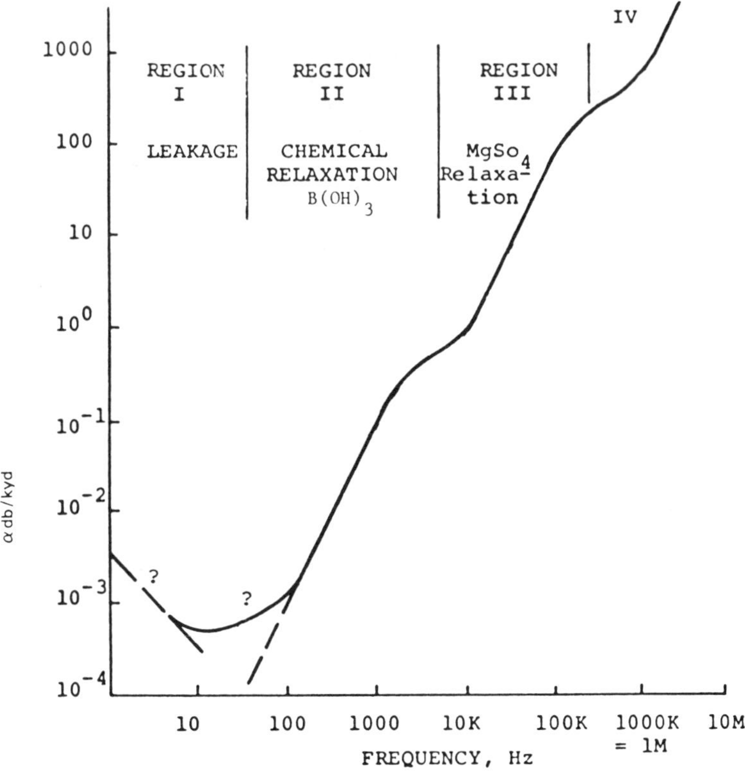

Figure A5–2. Sound attenuation coefficient as a function of frequency, showing the regions of different dominant processes.

Source: Robert J. Urick, *Sound Propagation in the Sea* (Los Altos, CA: Peninsula Publishing, 1982), p. 5–3.

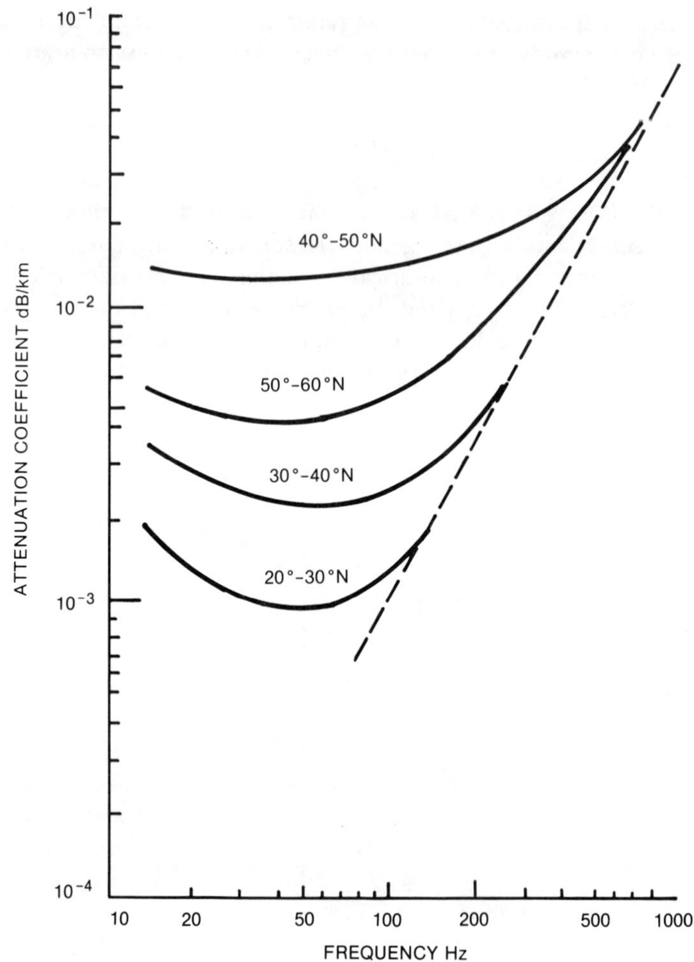

Figure A5–3. Low-frequency attenuation in the northeast Pacific Ocean, showing regional dependence.

Source: A. C. Kibblewhite et al., "Regional Dependence of Low Frequency Attenuation in the North Pacific Ocean," *Journal of the Acoustical Society of America* 61, May 1977, pp. 1169–1177.

Shallow water transmission loss is largely determined by the multiple reflections at the bottom and surface. The surface scatters sound while the bottom both absorbs and scatters.[4] The surface roughness due to waves determines the scattering pattern of reflected sound at a particular frequency. Surface waves that are much longer than the acoustic wavelength will reflect sound with little scattering. As the surface and acoustic wavelengths converge, the incident energy scatters over a wider angle. Both bottom roughness and material influence scattering and loss from that boundary. In addition, the thickness of the surface mixed layer and the sound speed profile are important since the profile determines how the sound is refracted and therefore influences the channeling of sound and the angle at which sound strikes the bottom. Predictions of transmission loss in shallow water are very approximate at best. Table A5–1 gives equations and coefficients for determining shallow water transmission loss based on a compilation of measurements. Figure A5–4 is a compilation of shallow water transmission loss measurements showing the wide range of measured data under nearly similar conditions of refraction (sound speed decreasing with depth) and frequency. Local bottom effects account for much of the observed variability.

Array Gain

The gain of an array of hydrophones is a measure of its ability to increase the ratio of submarine signature to background noise, and depends on its geometry and the characteristics of the signature and the noise. In this section some models for array gain are introduced, together with data that indicate fundamental limitations on array performance. A single hydrophone has very poor directional discrimination, which means that ambient noise arriving from all directions is received and masks the submarine signature that arrives from one direction. However, when the outputs of an array of several hydrophones are summed, the overall sensitivity, the directional capability, and the signal-to-noise ratio of the receiving system improve. Directionality may be illustrated by a polar plot of sensitivity versus angle, as in figure A5–5. In this figure, the sensitivity of the sonar array is plotted in decibels as the distance from the center. This sensitivity in decibels is referenced to the maximum sensitivity of the main lobe. The width of the main lobe is arbitrarily defined by the points at which the sensitivity drops 3 dB from the maximum sensitivity.

The performance of an array depends on the statistics of both signature and noise. If two signals are received by two hydrophones separated in space, one can calculate the correlation coefficient

$$p_{1-2} = \frac{\frac{1}{T}\int_0^T S_1(t)\,S_2(t)dt}{\left[\frac{1}{T}\int_0^T S_1^2(t)dt\right]^{\frac{1}{2}}\left[\frac{1}{T}\int_0^T S_2^2(t)dt\right]^{\frac{1}{2}}} \qquad \text{(A5.5)}$$

where $S_1(t)$ and $S_2(t)$ are the signals at the outputs of the two hydrophones. The term in the numerator is the time-average product of the two signals, which can be interpreted as a measure of how closely the two signals are

Table A5–1
Shallow water transmission loss equations and coefficients

Variables:

f	frequency (kilohertz)
H	ray skip distance (kiloyards)
D	water depth (feet)
L	mixed layer depth (feet)
α	absorption coefficient (dB/kiloyard)
k_L	boundary loss coefficient (near-field anomaly, dB)
a_T	shallow water attenuation (dB/bounce)
R	distance between source and receiver (kiloyards)
TL	transmission loss (dB)

I) Given sea state, bottom type, and frequency, determine a_T and k_L from the following tables.

Sea state	*0*		*1*		*2*		*3*		*4*		*5*	
f **(kHz)**	*Sand*	*Mud*	*Sand*	*Mud*	*Sand*	*Mud*	*Sand*	*Mud*	*Sand*	*Mud*	*Sand*	*Mud*
	a_T											
0.1	1.0	1.3	1.0	1.3	1.0	1.3	1.0	1.3	1.0	1.3	1.0	1.3
0.2	1.3	1.7	1.3	1.7	1.3	1.7	1.3	1.7	1.3	1.7	1.4	1.7
0.4	1.6	2.2	1.6	2.2	1.6	2.2	1.6	2.2	1.7	2.4	2.2	3.0
0.8	1.8	2.5	1.8	2.5	1.9	2.6	2.2	3.0	2.4	3.8	2.9	4.0
1.0	1.8	2.7	1.9	2.7	2.1	2.9	2.6	3.7	2.9	4.1	3.1	4.3
2.0	2.0	3.0	2.4	3.5	3.1	4.4	3.3	4.7	3.5	5.0	3.7	5.2
4.0	2.3	3.6	3.5	5.2	3.7	5.5	3.9	5.8	4.1	6.2	4.3	6.4
8.0	3.6	5.3	4.3	6.3	4.5	6.7	4.7	6.9	5.0	7.3	5.1	7.5
10.0	4.0	5.9	4.5	6.8	4.8	7.2	5.0	7.5	5.2	7.8	5.3	8.0

Sea state	*0*		*1*		*2*		*3*		*4*		*5*	
f **(kHz)**	*Sand*	*Mud*	*Sand*	*Mud*	*Sand*	*Mud*	*Sand*	*Mud*	*Sand*	*Mud*	*Sand*	*Mud*
	k_L											
0.1	7.0	6.2	7.0	6.2	7.0	6.2	7.0	6.2	7.0	6.2	7.0	6.2
0.2	6.2	6.1	6.2	6.1	6.2	6.1	6.2	6.1	6.2	6.0	6.2	6.0
0.4	6.1	5.8	6.1	5.8	6.1	5.8	6.1	5.8	6.1	5.8	4.7	4.6
0.8	6.0	5.7	6.0	5.6	5.9	5.6	5.3	5.0	4.3	5.9	3.9	3.0
1.0	6.0	5.6	5.9	5.5	5.7	5.3	4.6	4.2	4.1	3.7	3.8	3.4
2.0	5.8	5.4	5.3	4.9	4.2	3.8	3.8	3.4	3.5	3.1	3.1	2.8
4.0	5.7	5.1	3.9	3.5	3.6	3.1	3.2	2.8	2.9	2.4	2.6	2.2
8.0	4.3	3.8	3.3	2.8	2.9	2.5	2.6	2.2	2.3	1.9	2.1	1.7
10.0	3.9	3.4	3.1	2.6	2.7	2.2	2.4	2.0	2.2	1.7	2.0	1.6

II) Compute: $H = [1/8(D+L)]^{0.5}$

III) Find α from figures A5–2 or A5–3.

IV) Use the appropriate transmission loss equation:

If $R < H$ $\quad TL = 20 \log_{10}R + \alpha R + 60 - k_L$

If $H < R < 8H$ $\quad TL = 15 \log_{10}R + \alpha R + a_T(R/H - 1) + 5 \log_{10}H + 60 - k_L$

If $R > 8H$ $\quad TL = 10 \log_{10}R + \alpha R + a_T(R/H - 1) + 10 \log_{10}H + 64.5 - k_L$

V) Compute probable error of the estimate in dB from the following table:

	Frequency (Hz)			
Range, kyd	*112*	*446*	*1120*	*2820*
3	2	4	4	4
9	2	4	5	6
30	4	9	11	11
60	5	9	11	12
90	6	9	11	12

Source: H.W. Marsh and M. Schulkin, "Shallow-Water Transmission," *JASA* 34, 1962, pp. 863–864. Also, Robert J. Urick, *Principles of Underwater Sound for Engineers* (New York: McGraw-Hill, 1975), pp. 164–166.

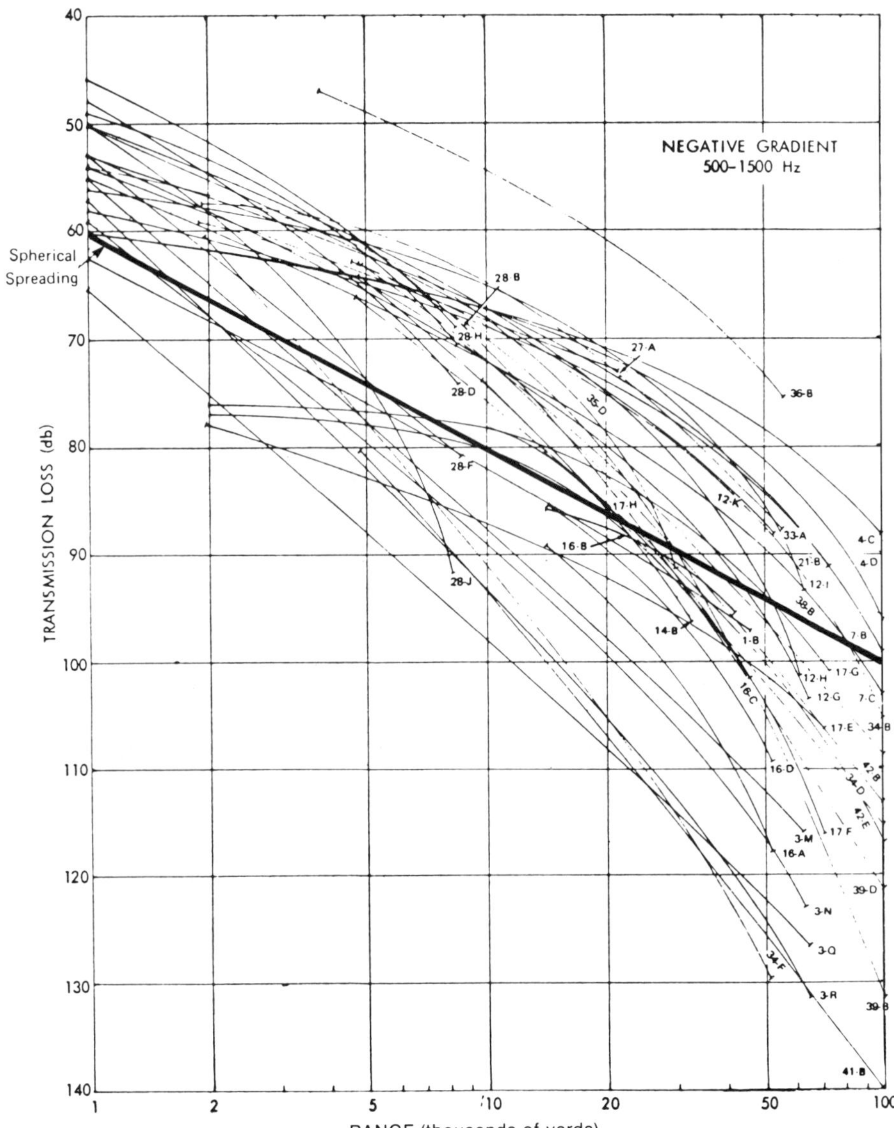

Figure A5–4. A compilation of shallow water transmission loss observations from the literature.

Source: Robert J. Urick, *Sound Propagation in the Sea* (Los Altos, CA: Peninsula Publishing, 1982), p. 9–2.

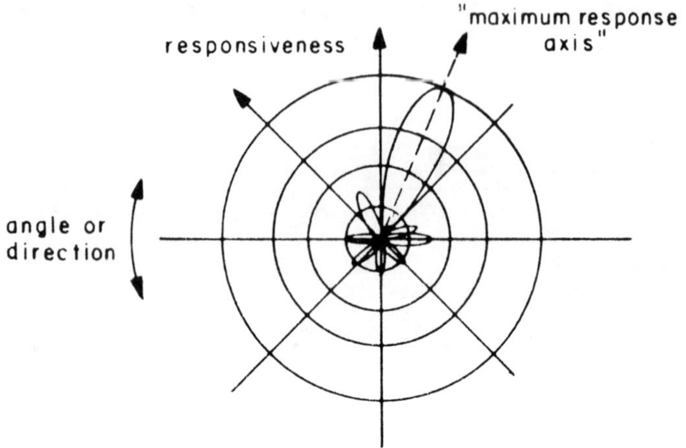

Figure A5–5. Directivity pattern of a sonar array.

Source: Randolph J. Steer, "Understanding Antisubmarine Warfare Technologies," in *Review of U.S. Military Research and Development 1984,* ed. Kosta Tsipis and Penny Janeway (New York: Pergamon-Brassey's, 1984), p. 165.

related, and the two terms in the denominator are normalizing factors. If the two signals are identical, the correlation coefficient equals unity, and the signals are said to be perfectly correlated. The correlation coefficient equals zero if the signals are random functions that have no statistical relation with each other. The correlation of two signals that are samples of sounds taken simultaneously but at different locations is spatial correlation. Temporal correlation is done with two signals taken at the same location but at slightly different times.

The ideal situation for detection in the presence of noise is a perfectly correlated target signature in uncorrelated noise, so that when the hydrophone outputs are summed, the signal intensity adds coherently and increases, and the noise intensity does not. In the case of an array of N hydrophones used to detect a perfectly correlated signal in uncorrelated noise, the array gain is

$$AG = 10 \log N \tag{A5.6}$$

In the ocean, however, the noise may be partially correlated and the signature not completely correlated, so the array gain will always be less than the prediction by equation A5.6.[5] It does not appear to be possible to predict array performance in an unfamiliar environment with much certainty, although there is a reasonable understanding of the factors that affect it. The following effects tend to degrade the array gain:

Noise coherence on submarine-mounted arrays: Submarine hulls vibrate due to mechanical and hydrodynamic forces. Coherent vibration of the hull is a coherent noise source and may seriously interfere with hull-mounted sonars. To the extent that this noise is correlated, it is impossible to remove from the signal without filtering, which then attenuates target signature.

Coherence of ambient noise: Narrowband low-frequency isotropic noise is not well correlated for hydrophone spacings equal to or greater than a half wavelength. To the extent that the noise at adjacent hydrophones is coherent, however, the array gain is decreased.

Decorrelation of the signal: The correlation coefficient between separated hydrophones falls off with distance at a rate that depends on the propagation multipaths and the directionality of the array. The correlation coefficient is small, generally beyond a hundred wavelengths, at low frequencies.

A simple, arbitrary measure of the correlation between separated hydrophones is given by the correlation distance, which is defined by the integral

$$r_0 = \int_0^\infty p(r)\, dr \tag{A5.7}$$

where $p(r)$ is the correlation coefficient as a function of separation, r. This can be applied to both signature and noise measurements. The correlation distance is generally regarded as the most important natural parameter involved in the design and performance of sonar arrays, but its magnitude depends greatly on propagation conditions.

The idealized case that yields a high narrowband array gain for detecting a signature in a noisy environment is the case of a perfectly correlated signal in noise that arrives with equal intensity from all directions—that is, isotropic noise. It can be shown that if a linear array contains hydrophones that are spaced at intervals of half the acoustic wavelength of interest, then equation A5.6 holds. The number of hydrophones, N, can be replaced by $2L/\lambda$, where L is the length of the array. It happens that this is the same result that is obtained for a linear continuous hydrophone, which is the limit approached by adding more and more discrete hydrophones at smaller and smaller spacings. However, an array in the idealized case of a correlated signal in isotropic noise does not perform quite as well as equation A5.6 when the wavelength associated with the frequency of interest is not an integer multiple of the hydrophone spacing. That is, in the idealized case, a particular hydrophone spacing "tunes" the array to receive optimally a discrete set of frequencies. Other frequencies will be received, but the array gain will be slightly lower than that given by equation A5.6[6]

Assume that in an idealized ocean the frequency that is to be detected is known. The array can be tuned for that frequency by using half-wavelength spacing, with the result that the gain of the array is proportional to the length of the array. In terms of submarine detection this means that if a new sonar was being designed to track a new submarine class that generated half as much noise as an older class, then simply doubling the length of the array (and expanding the computer to process the added inputs) would completely neutralize the acoustic advantage of the new submarine. Similarly, if the new class of submarine generates one-tenth the signature (which is plausible), the new array must be ten times as long. At some point, the costs and logistical constraints of increasing the length of arrays become prohibitive.

The most obvious logistical constraint on array size and placement is the geography of the oceans. Vertical arrays are of course limited by the depth of the oceans. Arrays are most effective if they lie at a depth near the axis of the deep sound channel, and since the only regions where the sea bottom intercepts the deep sound channel are on the continental slope, horizontal arrays can only be placed at the optimal depth where there is agreement with the adjacent landowner.[7] The most cursory glance at a map shows that the United States and its allies own most of the North Atlantic and North Pacific littoral, while the margin of the Arctic Ocean is about half Soviet and half NATO. However, long before geographical constraints on array length are encountered, financial and technical considerations arise.

The relation of processing cost to array size depends on the processing scheme. The most effective method of combining the hydrophones of an array to pick up a small signature in noise is simply to add the outputs of hydrophones.[8] However, each hydrophone output must be delayed (for beamforming), amplified, and summed (or alternatively, fast Fourier transformed), which means that the initial computational effort grows roughly proportionally to the number of elements in the array. In addition, beamforming requires a large number of connections, at least equal to the number of beams multiplied by the number of hydrophones,[9] and an equal number of delays or phase shifts to form the beams. In addition to these variable costs, there are large fixed costs for these surveillance arrays, which tend to ameliorate the average marginal cost of added array length. Hydrographic surveys, shore facilities, computer installations, and data transmitters are required and introduce costs that are quite independent of the length of the array. According to Prof. Ira Dyer of MIT, for the purpose of comparing new system designs (as opposed to expanding existing ones), the system cost tends to be roughly proportional to the number of hydrophones in the system.[10]

As an acoustic environment, the ocean is anything but ideal: low frequency ambient noise is not isotropic, it is concentrated near the horizontal, and signatures are not perfectly correlated over long distances. As a result, it is impossible to obtain consistently gains as high as equation A5.6 would predict for a given array. Spatial correlation is degraded over long propagation distances by the multiple paths along which sound can travel. In deep water with a deep sound channel, many of these paths are a combination of refractions through the channel, and reflections at the surface. The so-called refracted-surface-reflected (RSR) paths pass through many nonhomogeneous layers of water and are reflected from a time-varying ocean surface. As a result, narrowband signatures are slightly broadened (in frequency) and decorrelated. Bottom scattering further decorrelates the sound field, and in shallow water, where propagation involves many bottom bounces, the sound field is very complex and dependent on local bathymetry and bottom acoustic characteristics.

The basic principle that governs the relationship between array size and array gain is that the longer the length over which the sound field of the signature is correlated, the greater the gain, all other things being equal. In the ocean, correlation decays with hydrophone separation, and this decay is often modeled as exponential or linear. In the exponential model, the representative correlation length is taken as the distance at which the correlation coefficient falls to $1/e$, which equals 0.37, and the linear model uses the distance at which the correlation falls to 0.5. It has been established that arrays realize gain up to the point that the array length equals twice the correlation length, and beyond that there is no increase in array gain.[11] If the correlation length of a particular frequency was known in a particular area and set of circumstances, then the limiting size of an array could be estimated, from which one could infer the limitation on the array gain of the passive sonar performance equation. In general, it is impossible to predict correlation lengths independent of local conditions, and the estimate made here is only an approximate guide.

Table A5-2 is a summary of data on correlation length measurements from a recently declassified survey report. There are two main groups of data—horizontal and vertical—corresponding to the two principal means of deploying arrays: bottom cables and tethered buoys. Much of the data was generated by two experimental systems near Bermuda, a vertical array called Trident in 14,000 feet of water, and an array that apparently had both horizontal and vertical components called Artemis, which lay on a slope at depths extending between 2,000 and 4,000 feet, that is, near the deep sound channel axis. The experiments were mostly performed in deep water where the propagation paths were refracted or RSR, and the signals were detected with narrowband processing.

The results are expressed as coherence length normalized by acoustic wavelength. Measures of coherence length in horizontal arrays appear to fall mainly in the range of 10–110 wavelengths (six experiments, including two in

Table A5–2
Summary of coherence length data

Year of Publication	r_0 (feet)	r_0/λ	frequency (Hz)	Form of Signal	$T_{avg.}$ (sec.)	Source Depth (feet)	Receiver Depth (feet)	Source-Receiver Range (nm)	Comments
Horizontal arrays:									
1958	"Hundreds of miles"	1,000s	30	CW	?	Shallow	Axis	"Hundreds of miles"	SOSUS line array on bottom
1967	"Several hundred miles"	1,000s	100, 178 400	PRN Pulses	1.28	Shallow	Shallow	240 to 360	
1962	>2,000	>110	270	?	5.0	On bottom	On bottom	700	
1974	>4,000	40	<50	?	9.0	300	1,650	185	3 Hz bandwidth
1968	>4,000	>320	400	Pulse	360.0	?	2,000 to 4,000	19	Artemis, a hydrophone field on the bottom at deep sound channel axis near Bermuda
1974	2,000	51	125	CW	3,000.0	Shallow	10,900	to 380	Horizontal transverse orientation
1968	1,300	106	400	Pulse	?	1,200	2,000 to 4,000	270	Artemis
1971	290–490	30	300 to 500	Explosion	Shot duration	215	215	4	Horizontal transverse orientation, bandwidth = 200 Hz, shallow water

1971	54–70	10	700 to 900	Explosion	Shot duration	215	215	4	(same as above)
Vertical arrays:									
1969	48	7	750	CW	0.0016	9,500	14,000	24	Trident vertical array near Bermuda
1969	>300	>49	800	Pulse	0.005	9,500	14,000	24	Trident
1968	1,600	131	400	Pulse	360.0	?	2,000 to 4,000	19	Artemis
1974	<500	<13	125	CW	3,000.0	Shallow	40,000	to 380	
1968	700	57	400	Pulse	?	1,200	2,000 to 4,000	270	Artemis
1965	2,000	163	400	Pulse	?	?	to 4,000		
Orientation Unknown:									
1971	300	22	367	CW	840.0	?	2,000–4,000	700	Artemis
1971	1,000	74	367	CW	105.0	?	2,000–4,000	700	Artemis

Source: R. J. Urick, "Signal Coherence in the Sea and the Gain of a Receiving Array: An Overview of Theory and Measurements," Naval Ordnance Laboratory Tech. Rept. 74–195 (Silver Spring, Md: Naval Ordnance Lab, 1974).

Notes:
PRN = Pseudo random noise
CW = Continuous wave

shallow water), with two references to early experiments that yielded virtually unlimited coherence lengths, and little in between. The earliest available experimental data was published in 1958 and was based upon data from two isolated SOSUS arrays that were "able to determine the track of a moving frequency-stable source from the differing doppler frequencies on the widely separated arrays."[12] It is not clear why the data is clustered in this way, although part of the explanation is the different criteria used by different investigators to determine when two signals are correlated. The SOSUS experiments seemed to use Doppler shift to track the target, and perhaps the description of "coherence" used by those experimenters referred to comparing the two signals for frequency shift. Also, it is not clear which data is for coherence between two points and which is for coherence over the length of an array. It is very much more difficult to obtain consistent, long-term coherence over the entire length of an array.

The vertical array results show correlation lengths that vary from 7 to 163 wavelengths, though in any given situation "horizontally separated hydrophones are always more coherent than vertically separated hydrophones the same distance apart."[13] Experiments indicate that this difference is typically a factor of between two and four. There are also two experiments from the Artemis array for which no information is given on the orientation of the array, and the correlation lengths are given as 22 and 74 wavelengths. It appears that vertical correlation lengths occupy the same order of magnitude as horizontal but are generally lower.

The foregoing review suggests that the extremely high correlation lengths given by the two early experiments are very exceptional and probably arise from special experimental circumstances and particular definitions of correlation. The overwhelming mass of data suggests that correlation lengths lie between 10 and 150 wavelengths. The correlation length is lower for shallow water, higher frequencies,[14] longer averaging times, and wider frequency processing bandwidths.[15] Another summary of sonar signal processing states that "typical measures of coherence distances (i.e., for the wavefronts of a plane wave) are 10 to 100 wavelengths for horizontal separations and less than 10 wavelengths for vertical separations."[16] Therefore it seems reasonable to take a figure of 150 wavelengths as the practical maximum correlation length for sonar arrays in the ocean. This yields a maximum useful array length of 300 wavelengths. At 50 Hz this is about 9 kilometers, and at 400 Hz the maximum array is about 1 kilometer long.

In order to estimate the maximum gain associated with the largest practical array, a model of array gain for partially coherent signatures is needed. Two such models will be used, one that assumes half-wavelength spacing of hydrophones and exponential decay of signature coherence in an incoherent noise field, and one modeled on a linear decay of signature coherence in a partially coherent noise field.

Using the exponential model, the array gain for a 300 wavelength, 600 hydrophone array is about 25 dB for both conventional (filter, square, integrate) and optimal processing systems.[17]

This result is unrealistically high, however, because the influence of a partially coherent noise field is not included. The extremely limited experimental data on ambient noise coherence suggest that low-frequency shipping noise may be coherent over spacings of one-half to two wavelengths.[18] To introduce the effect of noise correlation on array gain, a model has been derived that assumes a linear decay of coherence for both signature and noise. For ratios of signature coherence length to noise coherence length much greater than one, it can be shown that the array gain is proportional to that ratio.[19] For the maximum array length of 300 wavelengths, the array gain in the presence of noise with a coherence length (coherence equal to 0.5) over one-half wavelength is 23 dB, while the array gain in the presence of noise with a coherence length of 1.5 wavelengths is 18 dB.

One experiment completed in the late 1970s by the Naval Research Laboratory "observed the largest physical broadside apertures yet reported over which the received signal was coherent." The maximum correlation length of a 15 Hz continuous wave signal corresponded to an aperture of 14 km at a range of 1600 km.[20] The acoustic wavelength of the signal was 100 meters, the ratio of aperture length to acoustic wavelength was 140, and the maximum possible array gain from such an aperture was therefore 21.5 dB. "The measured array gain for this aperture was 1.2 dB less than the maximum possible,"[21] or about 20 dB.

These models, and the data on array performance, suggest that the maximum gain that can be expected at low frequencies from an array in deep water is about 20 dB, and that partially correlated noise arriving from the direction of the target can drastically reduce this figure. In shallow water, where signature correlation lengths are smaller, maximum array gain should also be smaller. From the data in table A5–2, the correlation lengths are about one-tenth of what they are in deep water, so the gains that would be expected are on the order of 10 dB. An important tactical implication of this is that in areas where Soviet SSBNs patrol, such as relatively shallow waters and under ice (where repeated reflections off the ice ridges create many multipaths), sonar systems suffer an inevitable degradation of array gain and therefore of detection capability. These estimates of array gain are not intended to be generally applicable and are used only to provide an upper limit for assessing sonar system capability at low frequencies.

Beam Steering

Array gain is closely related to the directionality of arrays. One of the chief advantages of an array over an individual omnidirectional hydrophone is that the array can listen preferentially in a particular direction. In fact, "array gain" can be interpreted as the ability of an array to be insensitive to sound arriving from all directions other than a single selected direction. Sound arriving from this direction is received with the normal sensitivity of the individual hydrophones. The hydrophones of an array are usually attenuated in some pattern across the array to modify the directional characteristics, that is, the sensitivity pattern of the array. This process is called shading. The entire sensitivity pattern can be steered to any angle by introducing electronic time delays in the individual hydrophone outputs. Consider the wavefronts arriving at an angle to the two-element linear array shown in figure A5–6. If the outputs of the two

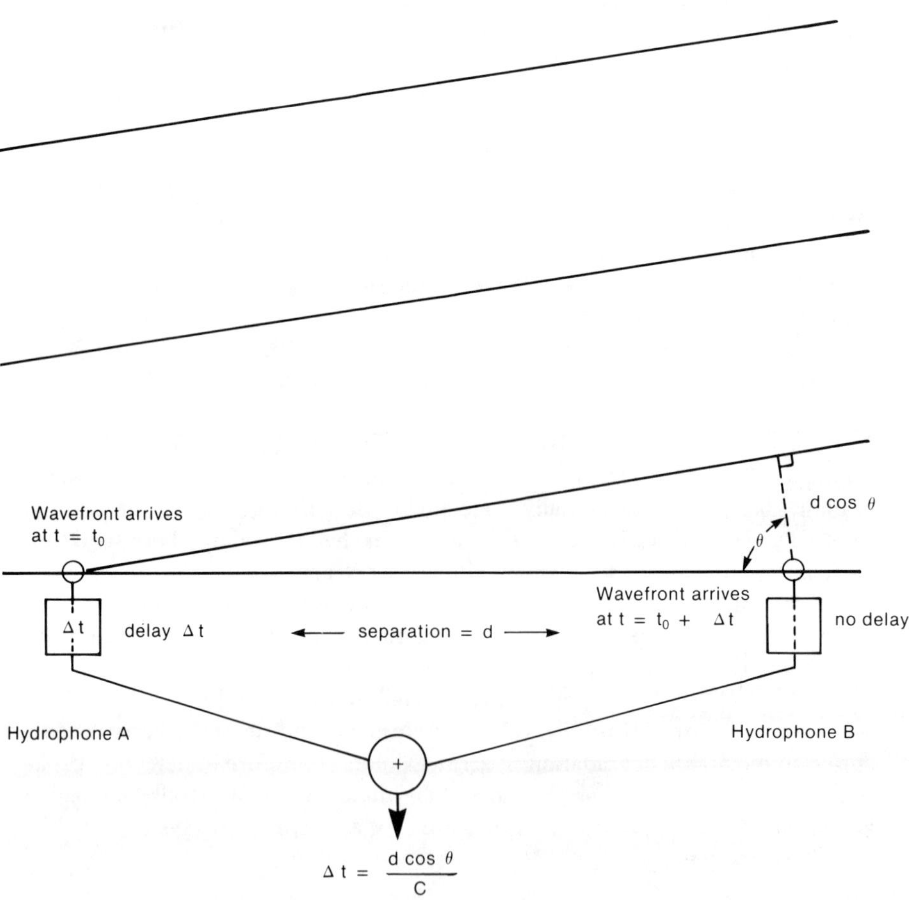

Figure A5–6. Using time delays to steer the sensitivity beam of a passive sonar array.

hydrophones are compared without any delay, the output from A is a time-shifted version of the output from B, with the signal at A leading (in time) the signal at B by $(d \cos \theta)/C$. If the signal from A were delayed by this amount of time, then the two signals would be in phase. The sum of two correlated signals is a maximum when the two signals are in phase, so that introducing a specific time delay is equivalent to selecting a particular direction to which the array will have the greatest sensitivity. The variation of array sensitivity with angle is called the beam pattern. Thus, without physically moving the array, the beam pattern shown in figure A5–5 can be rotated to any angle. An unsteered linear array yields the broadside beam pattern, so called because the main lobe is perpendicular to the array itself. Steering the array basically rotates the broadside beam pattern.

The shape of the main lobe of a linear array varies with steering angle as is shown in figure A5–7. The half-power angular width of the beam given is also in that figure, which is based upon a linear point array with half-wavelength hydrophone spacing. In addition, the noise is assumed to be isotropic, and the signal is assumed to be perfectly correlated. Since neither of these assumptions holds for long-range passive detection, figure A5–7 always underpredicts the beamwidth in the real ocean, though it can be used to make preliminary estimates of beamwidth for sonar arrays. The beamwidth broadside to the longest practical array (about 300 wavelengths) is about 0.2 degree and the beamwidth at 30 degrees (60 degrees away from broadside) is 0.3 degree, according to figure A5–7.

Localization Errors of Passive Arrays

In order to determine the location of a sound source, at least two lines of bearing to the target must be obtained from two known points. If the array is mobile, this involves some complications, since in the time it takes to move the array, the target may also move.

A simple model for localization from two arrays is shown in figure A5–8. Two arrays are fixed on a baseline, which is the vertical axis of a grid. The arrays are both a distance H from the horizontal axis or centerline between the two arrays. Since the target can be anywhere within the main beam of the passive arrays, there is an area of uncertainty within which the target is likely to be located. This area of uncertainty depends on the precision with which the beam can be steered, the beamwidth, and the location of the target.

Figures A5–9 and A5–10 show the areas of localization uncertainty assuming arrays that can be steered continuously through any angle, and which have a broadside beamwidth of about 2–3 degrees, which is on the order of the main beamwidth of a practical array at low frequency.[22] The figures have been drawn so that the length scale is arbitrarily normalized to the distance from the

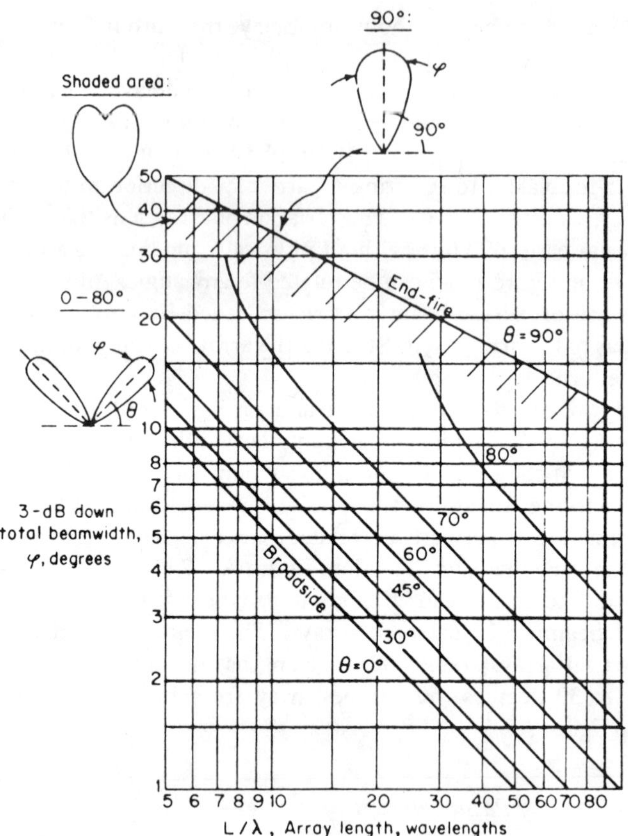

Figure A5–7. Beam pattern and angular width of main beam of an array as a function of steering angle, frequency, and array length.

Note: Hydrophones are separated by half the acoustic wavelength.

Source: R. S. Elliot, "Beamwidth and Directivity of Large Scanning Arrays," *Microwave Journal* (Dec. 1963). Reproduced from Robert J. Urick, *Principles of Underwater Sound,* rev. ed. (New York: McGraw-Hill, 1975), fig. 3.11, p. 53.

centerline to the array. The diamond-shaped figures are the areas of uncertainty surrounding a target detected in the center. Figure A5–9 is for targets near the arrays, and figure A5–10 is for targets far from the arrays.

The geometry of the arrays is intended to approximate two fixed surveillance arrays along a coastline or along a chokepoint. For example, if an array off Iceland and an array off the Faeroe Islands are used to localize targets in the Norwegian Sea, then the appropriate scaling for figures A5–9 and A5–10 is to

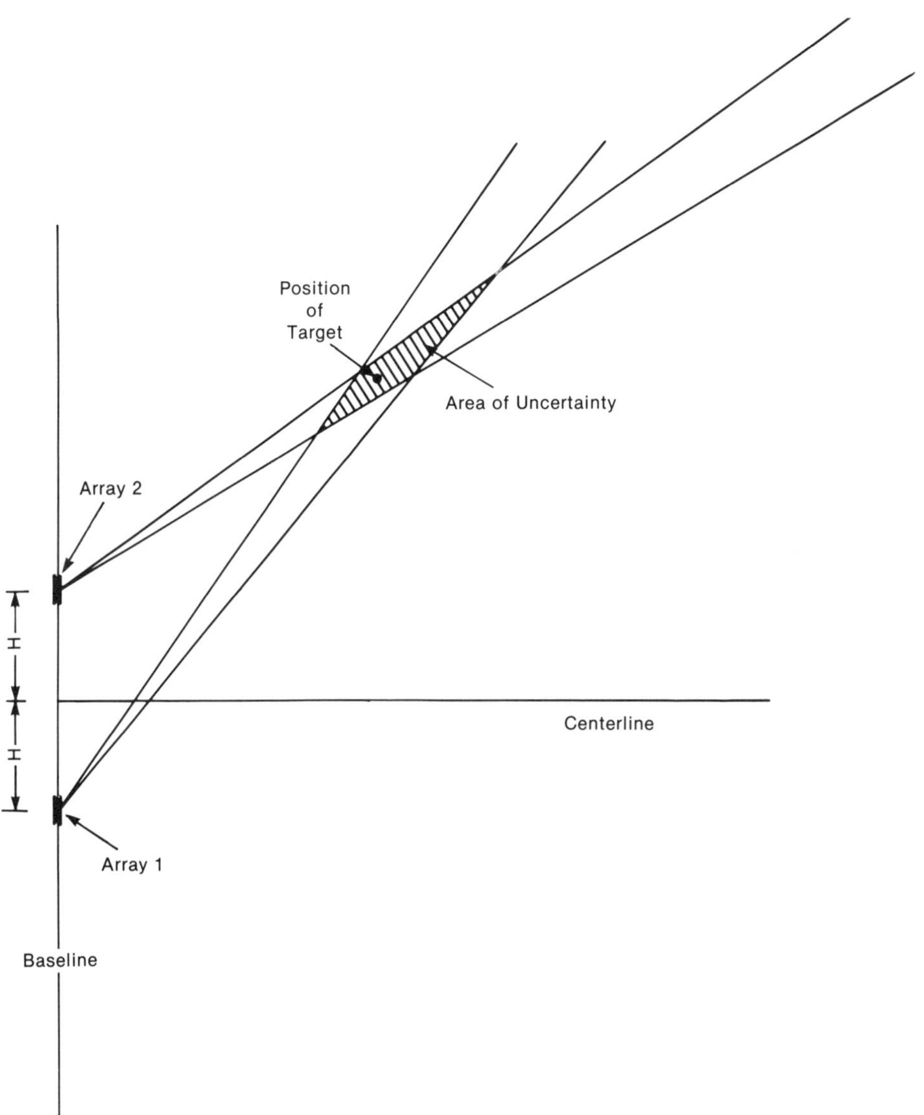

Figure A5–8. Schematic diagram of localization error from sensors with finite beamwidth.

set the distance between the arrays as the distance between Iceland and the Faeroes, 240 nautical miles, so that H is 120 nautical miles. The centerline runs midway between the two islands and northeast toward the Barents Sea. According to figure A5–9, a target at 120 miles northeast of the Iceland-Faeroes gap (that is, on the centerline) can be localized to within a 14-mile diameter circle. A target in the northern part of the Norwegian Sea, 600 miles northeast of the arrays (still on the centerline), can be localized to within an ellipse 120 miles by 50 miles. Targets off the centerline are difficult to localize at long ranges, as figure A5–10 suggests, and the triangulation yields a very long area of uncertainty.

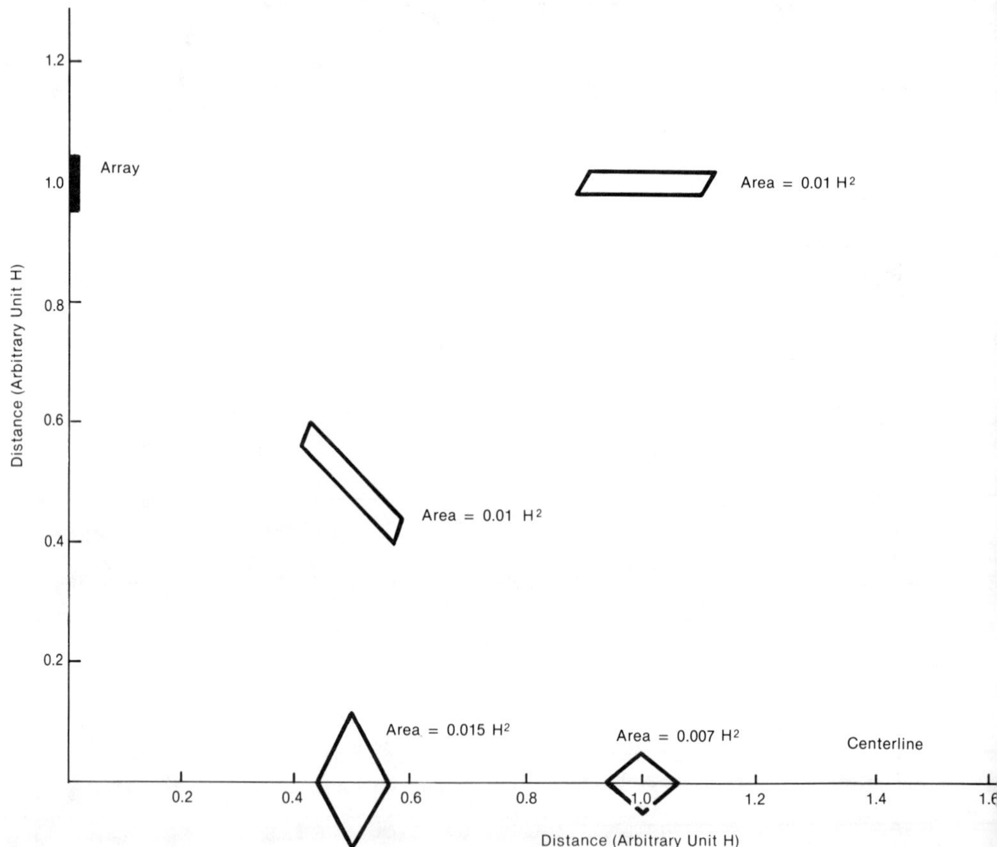

Figure A5–9. Localization error for two sonar arrays with 2–3 degree beamwidth: Nearfi

Note: Target distance on the order of array separation.

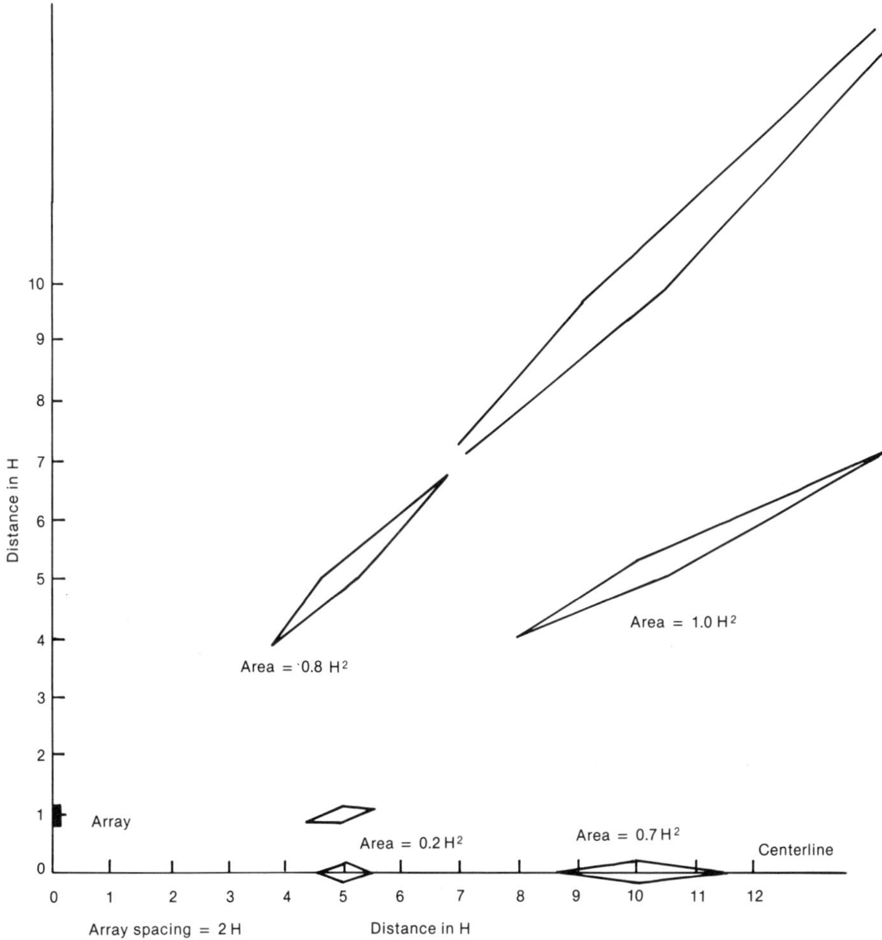

Figure A5–10. Localization error for two sonar arrays with 2–3 degree beamwidth: Farfield.

Note: Target distance much greater than array separation.

Notes

1. Scattering will be ignored in this discussion but can be an extremely important factor in active sonar performance.

2. Robert J. Urick, *Sound Propagation in the Sea* (Los Altos, Calif.: Peninsula Publishing, 1982), p. 5-3.

3. A. C. Kibblewhite et al., "Regional Dependence of Low Frequency Attenuation in the North Pacific Ocean," *Journal of the Acoustical Society of America* 61:5, May 1977, pp. 1169–1177.

4. Urick, *Sound Propagation,* chaps. 10, 11.

5. A somewhat more realistic model of the array gain has been derived by this author, assuming a linear variation of signature coherence with distance across the array. The result is that the array gain is approximately equal to the ratio of the signature coherence length and the noise coherence length.

6. For element spacings that are many times the wavelength of interest, deviations from equation A5.6 become very small, even when the spacing is not an integral of the half-wavelength. Thus, an array of just two widely spaced hydrophones has the widest frequency response, although its gain is at best a factor of 2 or 3 dB.

7. Arrays can also in principle be placed on seamounts, although the shore link becomes a major cable-laying project.

8. J. L. Brown and R. O. Rowlands, "Design and Directional Arrays," *JASA* 31, 1959, p. 1638.

9. Arthur Baggeroer, "Sonar Signal Processing," in *Applications of Digital Signal Processing,* ed. A. V. Oppenheim (New York: Prentice-Hall, 1978), pp. 331–437.

10. Prof. Ira Dyer, Dept. of Ocean Engineering, MIT, *Principles and Applications of Underwater Sound,* Lecture notes for course 13.851.

11. Robert Urick, *Signal Coherence in the Sea and the Gain of a Receiving Array: An Overview of Theory and Measurements* (White Oak, Md: Naval Ordnance Laboratory), NOLTR 74–195, 4 November 1974, Declassified December 1980.

12. Ibid.

13. Ibid., p. 8.

14. The frequency dependence is not completely normalized by expressing correlation as a multiple of wavelength.

15. Urick, *Signal Coherence.*

16. Baggeroer, "Sonar Signal Processing," p. 350.

17. Henry Cox, "Line Array Performance When Signal Coherence Is Spatially Dependent," *JASA* 54:6, 1973, p. 1743.

18. E. M. Arase and T. Arase, "Correlation of Ambient Sea Noise," *JASA* 40:1, 1966, p. 205; Robert J. Urick, *Ambient Noise in the Ocean,* NAVSEA, 1984, pp. 6–11; and Urick, *Sound Propagation,* p. 13-9.

19. The constant of proportionality is 0.67, or –2 dB.

20. R. M. Fitzgerald, A. N. Guthrie, and J. D. Shaffer, "Transverse Coherence of Low-Frequency Acoustic Signals," *Report of Naval Research Lab Progress* (Washington, DC: Naval Research Laboratory), May 1978, p. 1. The aperture was synthesized by towing a shallow sound source past a stationary receiver suspended in the axis of the deep sound channel.

21. Ibid.

22. The much narrower beamwidths associated with the ideal arrays discussed above would yield much smaller areas of uncertainty.

Appendix 6
Radiated Sound from Submarines and Ambient Noise in the Ocean

Passive methods of detecting and identifying submarines rely on the sound energy emitted by the submarine to the water. The spectrum of this sound depends both on the design of the submarine and on its mode of operation. Although sound data from modern submarines is highly classified, it is necessary to make some estimates in order to solve for the detection ranges of modern sonars.

The sea is filled with sound sources that are detected in passive sonar systems. The frequency spectrum and directionality of ambient noise are important parameters in determining the detection capability of a passive sonar system. The sources of ambient noise are shipping, wind, waves, undersea organisms, rain, and ice. In order to predict the total ambient noise in a particular region, the component spectra are estimated and then summed.

Characteristics and Origins of Submarine-generated Sound

No useful mechanical process can take place without generating some vibration and therefore some noise. A machine that produces usable mechanical energy also produces uncontrollable vibration due to imbalance and imperfect parts. In addition, electrical and fluid machinery can vibrate and generate sound.

Noise from submarines can be grouped into four categories according to its origin:

1. Machinery noise generated by machine vibration within the hull
2. Propeller noise generated by cavitation on the moving propeller blades
3. Propeller noise generated by the fluctuating thrust force as the propeller blades rotate through the asymmetric wake
4. Hydrodynamic noise generated by turbulent flow past the surface of the submarine

Machinery Noise

Machinery noise originates as the vibration of parts within the submarine. This vibration is coupled to the sea via the mountings of the machinery to the hull and the hull itself. Machine vibration is generated by the following processes: (1) rotating masses, such as shafts, motor armatures, turbines that are unbalanced, or reciprocating machinery, such as pistons; (2) repetitive discontinuities, such as gear teeth, armature slots, and turbine blades, and (3) cavitation and turbulence in pumps, pipes, valves, and condenser discharges.

Machinery noise is the dominant source of noise at low speeds, that is, before propeller cavitation sets in. The spectrum of machinery noise is generally in the form of a line spectrum at frequencies below 1,000 Hz. For instance, figure A6–1 shows the noise spectrum of a typical turbine generator. This machine emits a very strong discrete frequency, or tone, at the frequency of the turbine rotor, in this case 160 Hz. Other strong tones are emitted at 320 Hz and 360 Hz. Also shown is a sound spectrum from a World War II submarine.

The strongest potential sources of machinery noise are the gear-turbine unit and the main circulation pumps in the primary loop of the reactor cooling system. Vibration mounts are used to isolate acoustically machinery from the hull.[1] Vibration mounts can be as simple as rubber feet under a small machine or as complex as entire racks for large machines. The turbines, reduction gears, and other main propulsion and generating machines are mounted on such a suspended rack in British and US nuclear submarines. Flexible connectors are used to isolate propeller shafts and pipes that connect shock-mounted machinery to the hull and are therefore possible paths for machinery vibration to reach the hull.[2] Noise in the air within a submarine is damped by absorbing foam around the inside of the hull. Noise-reducing measures generally increase the amount of space required for shock-mounted machinery and absorbing material, and this in turn increases the size of the submarine.

Special methods of reducing the noise of reduction gears and of the circulating pumps have been explored by the US Navy. Turbine-electric drive (which is described in appendix 1) is quieter than gear-turbine drive because there are no high-speed reduction gears between the turbine and the propeller shaft. The turbine drives a quiet electric generator, which produces electricity. This electricity is used to drive a low-speed, high-torque motor, which can in turn drive the propeller with a minimum of gear reduction. The *Tullibee* (SSN-597) and *Glennard P. Lipscomb* (SSN-685) are the earliest US submarines to have turbine-electric drive systems.

The main circulating pumps can be eliminated by allowing the buoyant force of the hot reactor water to drive up through a heat exchanger and displace the cooler water there. This heat-driven or natural circulation requires no noisy pumps. The power output of a reactor determines how fast the cooling water must circulate in order to keep the core from overheating. The drawback to natural circulation is that it does not respond immediately to a sudden change

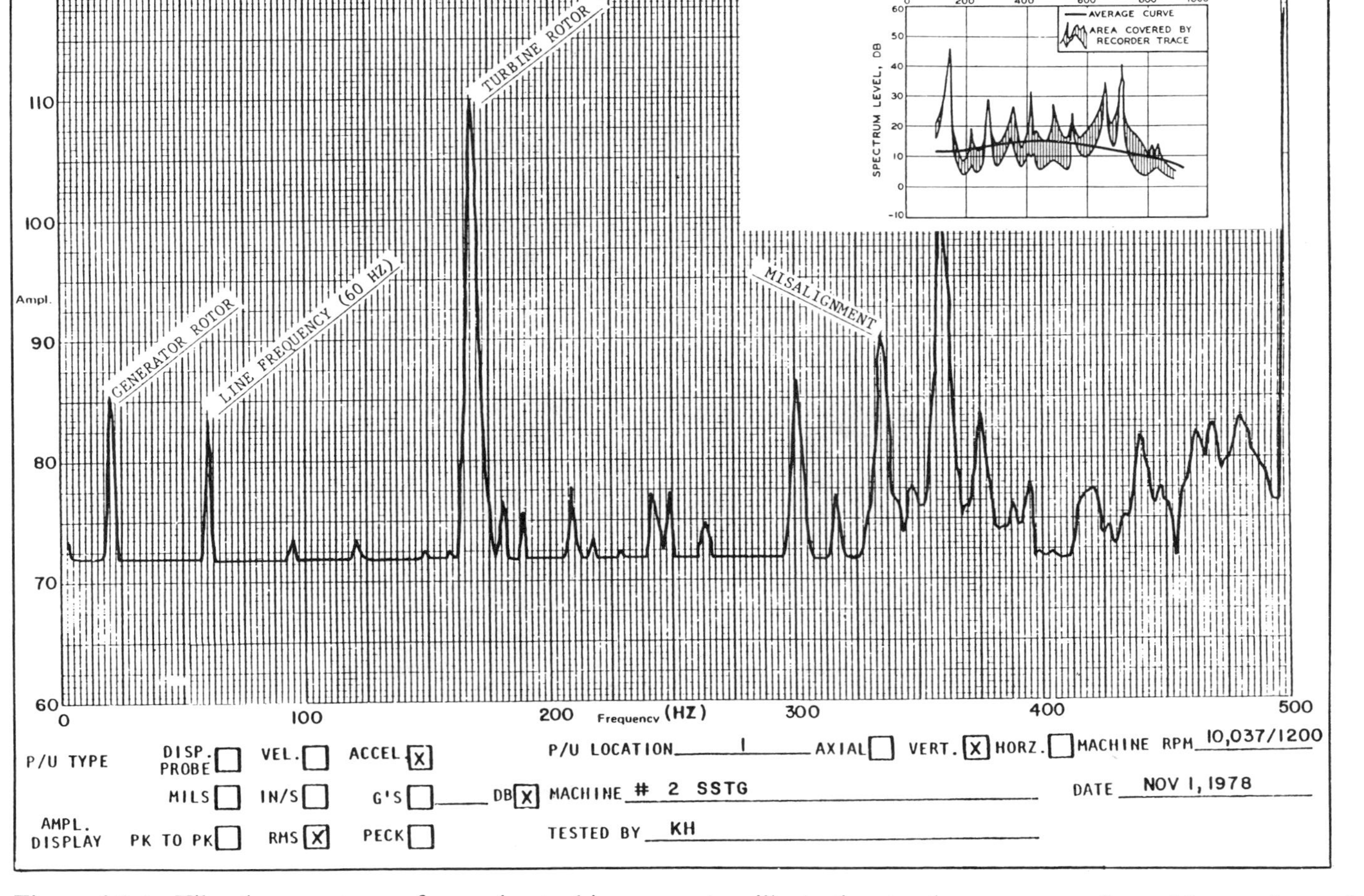

Figure A6–1. Vibration spectrum of a marine turbine generator, illustrating tonal components. *Inset:* Measured sound spectrum of a World War II submarine.

Source: Michael J. Schwaebe, "Machinery Vibration Analysis as a Planning Tool for Ships in a Five-Year Maintenance Cycle," *Naval Engineers Journal* (Feb. 1980), pp. 51–56. *Inset:* Carl Eckart, ed. *Principles and Applications of Underwater Sound* (Washington, DC: Naval Materiel Command, 1968), p. 242.

in core temperature, so the reactor power could not be increased quickly if the submarine needed to sprint, for example. However, pumps can be installed in the cooling loop that can be turned on to provide high flow rates in emergencies. The first US natural circulating reactor, the S5G, was put on only one submarine, the *Narwhal* (SSN-671).[3] The next vessel designed to use this type of system was the Ohio class missile submarine, and this fact partially explains the extraordinarily low radiated noise levels of that class.

Fluid machinery noise is the noise generated by turbulent flow through pipes and in the reactor core itself. This kind of noise occurs in the primary, secondary, and seawater cooling loops of the submarine.

Some machinery noise, such as propeller shaft noise, varies with submarine operations. On the other hand, essential machinery must continue to operate under all conditions. Two such systems are the cooling systems for the reactor core and the life support systems, including the noisy fans and blowers of the air recirculating system. Eliminating the primary cooling pumps, which are probably difficult to isolate,[4] reduces the vibrations reaching the hull, and covering the inside of the hull with sound-absorbing materials reduces the transmission of vibrations from the air to the hull.[5]

Propeller Cavitation Noise

Cavitation occurs when a decrease in local fluid pressure drops so far below the ambient pressure that the water vaporizes and many small cavities are formed. The bubbles then expand until they reach their maximum size.[6] As soon as the bubbles enter a region of higher pressure, they suddenly collapse creating sharp sound pulses.

Propellers work by producing very low pressure on the forward-facing side of the blade surface and high pressure on the back face. This creates a net force on the propeller in the forward direction. Propeller cavitation can occur on both faces (though usually on the forward "suction" face), the propeller hub, and the blade tips. Blade tip cavitation can occur at relatively low rotation rates, since the blade tips are the fastest-moving sections of the propeller. Of all types of cavitation, blade-surface cavitation on the forward (suction) face is the most noisy, and hub vortex cavitation the least.

Submarine propeller cavitation noise covers a very wide spectrum from around 20 Hz to 50,000 Hz. A theoretical cavitation spectrum model is shown in figure A6–2. The wideband character of this noise is due to the superposition of many short pulses generated by collapsing bubbles. Cavitation noise is modulated each time a blade moves through a disturbance in the wake. Submarines generally have two vertical and two horizontal stabilizers just forward of the propeller which introduce asymmetries in the wake. Each time a blade moves past a stabilizer, the cavitation fluctuates. This gives rise to cavitation noise peaks at frequencies equal to the rotation frequency of the shaft multiplied

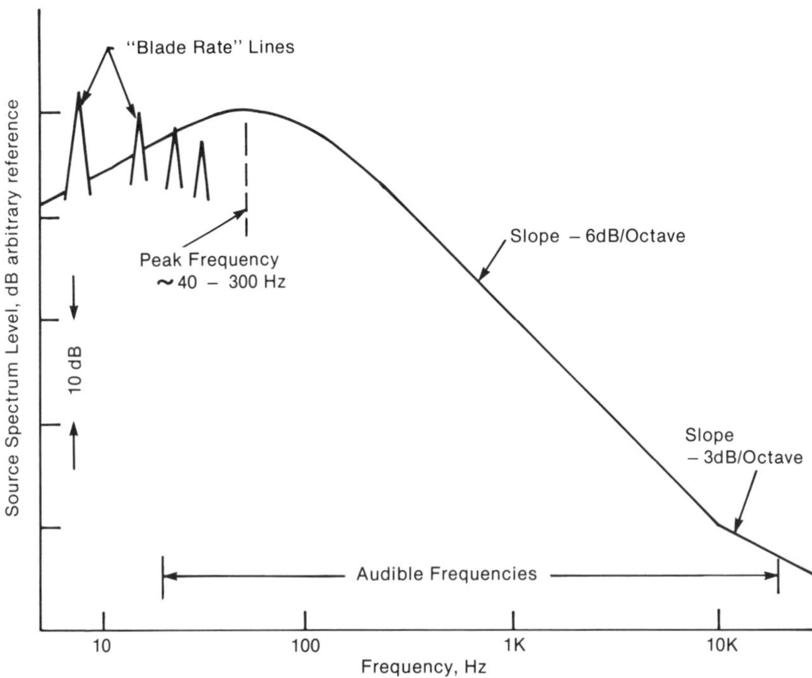

Figure A6–2. Typical propeller cavitation spectrum.

Source: Neal A. Brown, "Cavitation Noise Problems and Solutions," in *International Symposium on Shipboard Acoustics,* J.H. Janssen, ed. (New York: Elsevier, 1977), pp. 21–38.

by the number of propeller blades, and at integral multiples of that frequency, as shown in figure A6–2. Typical frequencies are very low, between 5 Hz and 40 Hz. These propeller cavitation tonals are most pronounced at speeds just high enough to start cavitation but not so high that cavitation becomes a steady, general roar,[7] and may be the most detectable component of modern quiet submarines operating at moderately high speeds at relatively shallow depths.

Figure A6–3 gives data on cavitation noise levels for World War II submarines. The high-frequency broadband propeller noise level is plotted as a function of the ratio of speed to hydrostatic pressure. There is a 10,000-fold increase (40 dB) in high-frequency noise with a speed increase of only 50 percent near the onset of cavitation. The influence of depth and propeller speed on propeller noise is illustrated in figure A6–4, again only for World War II submarines. It is clear that cavitation noise is strongly damped by increasing depth at speeds nearer the inception of cavitation. At higher speeds, cavitation noise cannot be completely suppressed, although modern submarines with larger, more slowly turning propellers are much less likely to cavitate than World War II submarines under the same speed and depth conditions.

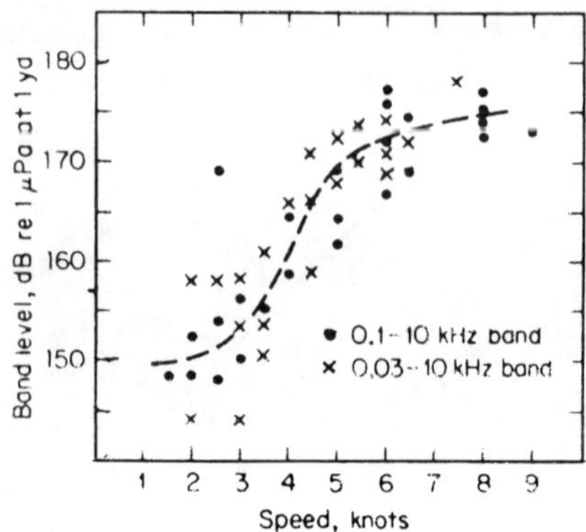

Figure A6–3. Noncavitation and cavitation noise from World War II submarines.

Source: Robert J. Urick, *Principles of Underwater Sound,* rev. ed. (New York: McGraw-Hill, 1975), fig. 10.7, p. 306.

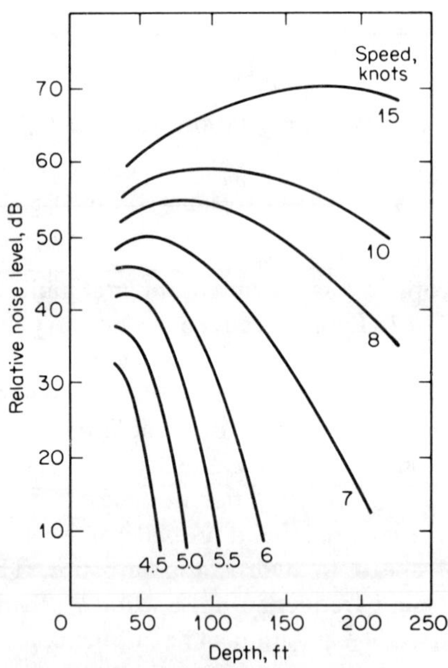

Figure A6–4. Effect of speed and depth on cavitation noise.

Source: Robert J. Urick, *Principles of Underwater Sound,* rev. ed. (New York: McGraw-Hill, 1975), fig. 10.9, p. 308.

Noncavitating Propeller Blade Tonals

The wake in the vicinity of a submarine propeller is disturbed by the appendages on the hull such as the sail, the stabilizers, rudders, and other fixtures. These disturbances cause fluctuations in the thrust developed by the propeller as it revolves. The fluctuating forces are periodic and occur at blade rate frequencies—that is, in integer multiples of the product of the rotation rate and the number of blades. US and Soviet submarines generally have five or seven blades, and the rotation rate of the propeller is on the order of one revolution per second at moderate speeds, so the blade rate is about 5–40 Hz.

It is important to distinguish between the cavitating and noncavitating blade tonals in two respects. Although the associated frequencies are the same, the propeller must at least be cavitating at the blade tips in order to produce the louder cavitating tonals. The noncavitating tonals, although much quieter, are always generated by a conventional propeller. This has led to consideration of placing propellers in tunnels from which this source of sound could not escape. Such designs would result in a jet-propelled submarine, and although turbulent jets produce sound, the turbulence is a much less efficient radiator of acoustic energy than is the fluctuating propeller thrust.[8]

The fraction of the propeller's mechanical energy that is converted into acoustic energy in the noncavitating blade tonals has been estimated to be between 10^{-10} and 10^{-8} for typical marine propellers.[9] For submarines the fraction may be lower since the wake of a submarine is more nearly symmetric than is the wake of a surface ship. Taking a range of 10^{-12}–10^{-10} for submarines, and using a figure of about 10^{7} watts (about 13,000 horsepower) for the mechanical power of a submarine propeller (20,000 hp is typical), the estimated acoustic radiated power is about 120–140 dB relative to one micropascal at one yard.

The chief of naval operations has suggested that the Soviet Victor III has sufficiently quiet machinery to force the US Navy to use instead the "blade rate" frequencies to detect it.[10] This suggests that at source levels between 120 dB and 140 dB, the blade rate tonals of noncavitating propellers begin to approach machinery noise in intensity. As submarines become quieter, there may be more design emphasis on ducted propellers for this reason.

Hydrodynamic noise is generated by fluid turbulence in the wake of the submarine and in the turbulent boundary layer. There are two mechanisms of sound generation by turbulence: (1) direct radiation of turbulent pressure fluctuations, and (2) radiation of sound from structures set in motion by the turbulence. The first of these is a weak sound source, and the second can be reduced in the structural design. Overall, hydrodynamic or turbulence noise is not considered to be nearly as important as machinery and propeller noise.[11]

Estimates of Submarine Source Levels

Information regarding the radiated noise spectra of submarines is highly classified, and estimates of submarine radiated noise levels can be made only within wide margins of uncertainty. The numbers presented here should be used only as indications of the order of magnitude of sound levels, and as indications of the change of relative sound levels over time and between classes. These estimates are assumed to refer to quiet patrol conditions, at speeds of 5 to 12 knots.

As figure A6–4 suggests, the noise generated by propeller cavitation varies enormously with depth and speed. It is possible that the next generation of US attack submarines will not fully cavitate at any speed, thanks to their large propellers and slow turning rates. It is certainly safe to assume that SSBNs do not cavitate when at patrol speed and depth. On the other hand, very fast attack submarines, such as the Soviet Alfa class, cavitate at speeds below their top speed (over 40 knots for the Alfa), probably at around 18 knots. The speed at which a submarine begins to cavitate is called the tactical speed. The propensity to cavitate may be decreased by increasing the blade area, increasing the number of blades, and decreasing the turning rate. It is difficult, however, to put low rpm/high torque reduction gears in the narrow stern end of small, fast submarines, since as rpm decreases, the size of the reduction gear increases.[12] In addition to propeller cavitation, it is possible that the hull itself may cavitate over 40 knots.[13]

In the theoretical spectrum for fully cavitating propellers shown in figure A6–2, the characteristic cavitating blade rate tones are indicated in terms of their relative magnitude. The spectrum can be described as having a maximum level at a frequency between 40 Hz and 300 Hz, and a decrease of 6 dB per octave (frequency doubling) at higher frequencies.[14] The peak frequency of measured submarine cavitation spectra is around 75 Hz.[15] According to data on World War II submarines, the total acoustic output of a fully cavitating spectrum is 175 dB. This corresponds to a peak spectrum level (1 Hz band) of 156 dB. The curve in figure A6–2 is probably a reasonable estimate of the noise spectrum of a modern, fully cavitating submarine near the surface, with the peak spectrum level around 154 dB re 1 micropascal at 1 yard.

While running on diesel at a transit speed of 15 knots, diesel-electric submarines generate spectrum levels around 160 dB at low frequencies, about the same as a small frigate.[16]

The estimates of total acoustic output or broadband source level of a variety of modern submarines are presented in figure A6–5, based upon many sources, which are given in the accompanying notes. Since data on total acoustic radiated power is very highly classified information, any estimates must be inferred and therefore must include a large degree of uncertainty. However, with the information available from unclassified sources, as well as some theoretical calculations, a reasonably clear picture of the trends in submarine source levels emerges. In general, the error on the estimates is plus or minus an order of magnitude.

Total acoustic output of a submarine is the integration of the radiated sound spectrum over all frequencies, so all spectral characteristics are lost in the estimates in figure A6–5. This simplification facilitates comparison between quiet submarines producing narrowband machinery noise and high-speed cavitating submarines, which produce broadband cavitation noise. Care must be taken when using these figures to estimate detection range in the passive sonar equation that all of the parameter estimates (such as ambient noise level and detection threshold) are consistently based upon the assumption of narrowband processing or broadband processing. Submarines operating below their tactical (that is, cavitating) speed produce most of their energy in a few narrow bands below 500 Hz, and narrowband processing is used to detect these signatures, whereas high-speed cavitating submarines generate broadband noise, which can be detected using broadband processing.

The estimates in figure A6–5 are associated with noise-minimizing operating practice at low speed, and it is assumed that when statements are given by reliable sources, they refer to total radiated sound levels at low speed. The so-called quiet speed of a submarine is the speed at which sensors can function with nearly maximum effectiveness. For most submarines the quiet speed is around 6–8 knots, perhaps as much as 10 for current US submarines.[17] "At high speeds US submarines have a major acoustic advantage" over Soviet ones,[18] probably due to a lower likelihood that US submarines will cavitate. The small Soviet Alfa class submarines "sound like big trucks going by at anything over 18 knots,"[19] although at lower speeds they might be significantly quieter.[20] Conversely, even the quietest of submarines, the Ohio class, can produce very high levels of sound if operated poorly.

There are two guidelines that can be used as upper and lower bounds when estimating submarine-radiated sound levels. The reasonable upper bound is the cavitation sound level that lies between 171 dB (1 watt) and 180 dB. Above 180 dB, broadband sound levels approach those associated with large surface ships. The lower limit is suggested by the size of the submarine. When source level is reduced to a sufficiently low value, the maximum detection range approaches the length scale of the submarine itself, and the very idea of acoustic detection loses its meaning. The practical lower limit of submarine noise level is 75–85 dB. It may be possible to achieve lower radiated sound levels in functional military submarines, but it is not worth the money, since there is no gain in military effectiveness.[21]

The historical trend in submarine quieting may be expected to follow the asymptotic "learning curve" that is so common in the long-term development of systems. These trends are shown in figure A6–6. Beginning with World War II vintage submarines, for which there are quantitative data on radiated sound, one can observe a very wide range of radiated sound levels, from about 135 dB

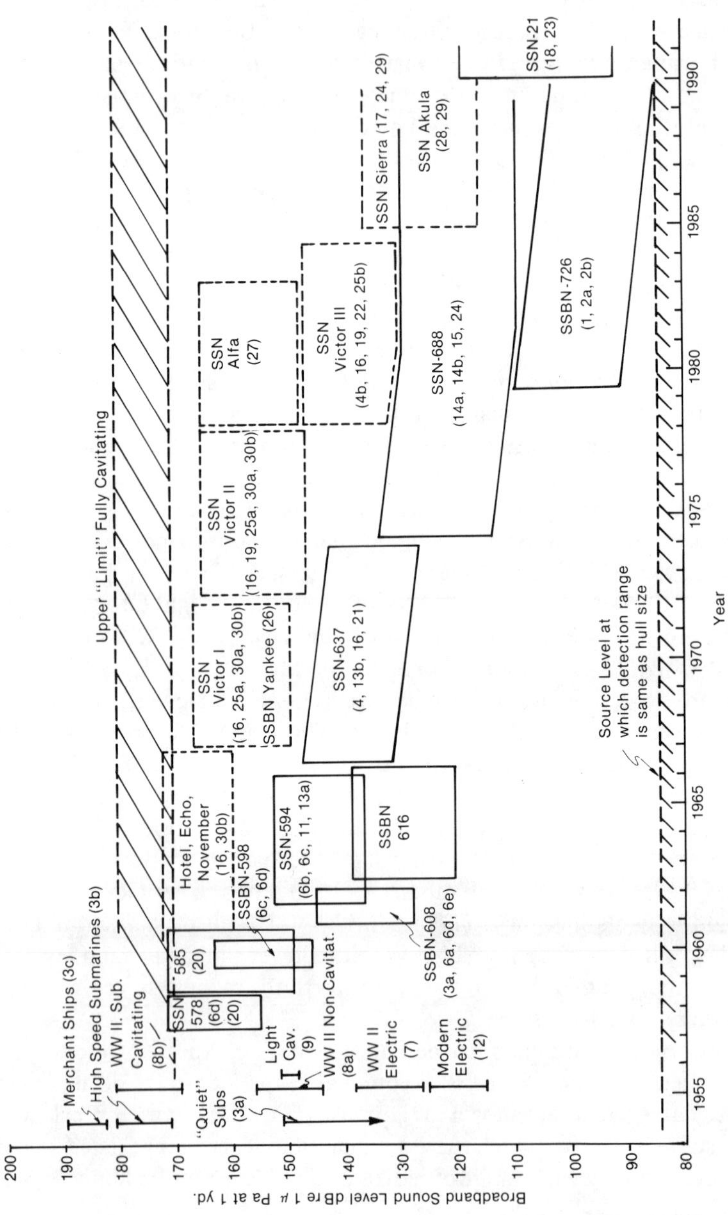

Figure A6–5. Estimated broadband acoustic sound level of US and Soviet submarines.

Notes on Figure A6–5

1. John Tierney, "The Invisible Force," *Science '83*, pp. 68–78: "We're getting to the point where two of these Tridents could pass within 1000 yards and not hear each other." This is a statement by "an executive that designs acoustic equipment for the Navy." Assuming spherical spreading loss of 60 dB, array gain of 20 dB, detection threshold of −16 dB, and ambient noise a quiet 66 dB, the source level is 90 dB. At higher ambient noise levels, the estimate of source level increases. A reasonable range for the source level estimate is 90–110 dB.

2. Adm. Frank Kelso, SASC, FY 1984, part 5, p. 2533:
   a. The Ohio is "probably the quietest submarine in the world."
   b. "Even with our sonar technology, we can only detect one of our [Ohio] submarines at [deleted] yards." This is a reasonably clear indication that the deleted figure was less than 10,000 yards, since that is about 5 nautical miles, and miles would be the natural unit to use. This corroborates the information in note 1 above.

3. Donald Ross, "Noise Sources, Radiation and Mitigation," in *Underwater Acoustics and Signal Processing*, Leif Bjørnø, ed. (Boston: D. Reidel, 1980), p. 3:
   a. A submarine at slow speed attempting to be quiet has a total acoustic output of less than 10 milliwatts. This is the same figure given by Dr. Richard Garwin in "Will Strategic Submarines Be Vulnerable?" *International Security*, Fall 1983, p. 60.
   b. Even at high speed submarine noise does not exceed a few watts.
   c. Merchant ships radiate 30 watts (186 dB).

4. Adm. James D. Watkins, HASC, FY 1984, part 4, p. 656:
   a. "We have been able to just about . . . stay . . . 8 to 10 years ahead of the Soviet Navy." (In reference to submarine technology, especially quieting.)
   b. "Our 637 class and the latest Victor class, the so-called Victor III, are comparable submarines, comparable in quietness and expected capability."

5. Gerald A. Cann, Principal Deputy Assistant Secretary of the Navy (Research, Engineering, and Systems), HAC, FY 1985, part 5, p. 204: "Those of us who are in the technical community had staked our reputations on the fact that when the Delta-class submarine went to sea in 1976 they were going to demonstrate a fundamental quieting program, and we had said that to the rest of the world and they did not do it and we lost a lot of credibility."

6. HASC, FY 1981, part 3, p. 253, Vice Adm. Charles H. Griffiths, Deputy Chief of Naval Operations, Submarine Warfare:
   a. "The 608 class . . . was the first built as an SSBN from the ground up . . . so they are deep diving, quiet submarines. Their engineering plants are on bed plates. They are very fine submarines."
   b. "The 608s are comparable to the 594 class . . . Essentially [the 608 class] are quiet ships, very quiet in comparison to the Soviet ships."
   c. "The 598s of course have hard mounted propulsion plants. They're comparable to pre-594 class submarines, such as the Skipjack [SSN-585] and noisy submarines."
   d. "The 598 and 608 class SSBNs are far better, for example, than the 578 class, of which there are four in operation right now . . . They're quieter platforms."
   e. "The five 608s are better than all the pre-594 class submarines."

7. Robert Urick, *Principles of Underwater Sound for Engineers* (New York: McGraw-Hill, 1975), p. 306, fig. 10.6:
   USS *Hake*
   Band: 20–500 Hz
   Total output: 131 dB re 1 micropascal at 1 yd (134 dB including 500–20,000 Hz)
   Speed: 90 rpm, 4.5 knots
   Depth: 55 feet
   Propeller: 8 feet diameter
   Operating conditions: Noncavitating, possibly on batteries

8. Urick, *Principles*, p. 306, fig. 10.7, "Many World War II Submarines":
   a. Noncavitating: 150 ± 6 dB, speed less than 2.5 knots.
   b. Cavitating: 175 ± 6 dB, speed greater than 7 knots.

9. Urick, *Principles*, p. 306, fig. 10.6:
   USS *Hoe*
   Band: 20–20,000 Hz
   Total output: 149 dB re 1 micropascal at 1 yd
   Speed: 170 rpm, 8.5 knots
   Depth: 300 feet
   Propeller: 8 feet diameter
   Operating conditions: Must be on battery at 300 feet, light cavitation at high ambient pressure

Notes on Figure A6–5 continued

10. Assume:
Ambient noise level = 65 dB
Array gain = 20 dB
Detection threshold = –16 dB

11. Norman Polmar, *Ships and Aircraft of the US Fleet,* 13th ed. (Annapolis: Naval Institute Press, 1983), p. 65: "These [594 class] submarines represented a radical development in submarine design with . . . a high degree of machinery quieting."

12. It is assumed that modern battery-powered conventional submarines are about 10 dB quieter than their World War II predecessors.

13. Adm. Nils Thunman, SASC, FY 1985, part 8, p. 4160:
a. The Permit (SSN-594) class "was a major step forward in submarine design, significantly quieter."
b. The Sturgeon (SSN-637) class "was a little bit better in quieting than the 594."

14. Adm. Nils Thunman, SASC, FY 1985, part 8, p. 4397:
a. "Diesel-electric submarines are quiet, but not as quiet as modern nuclear attack submarines at comparable speeds."
b. "Even on the battery today's diesels are more acoustically detectable than today's 688 class SSN" (p. 4399).

15. Adm. James D. Watkins, SASC, FY 1985, part 8, p. 3897: "The improved SSN-688s will have a clear advantage over any submarine or surface threat introduced by the Soviets in the next ten years, and should be highly effective against the Soviets for the rest of the century."

16. Adm. James D. Watkins, SASC, FY 1985, part 8, p. 3897: "While [the pre-688 class submarines] will be fully capable of opposing the 1960s [Hotel, Echo, November] and early 1970s vintage [Charlie I, Victor I and II, perhaps Yankee and Delta I SSBNs] submarines, they will be only marginally capable of opposing Soviet attack submarines introduced since the mid-70s [Victor III]." This reference seems to exclude the SSN-585 and 578 classes.

17. Adm. Nils Thunman, SASC, FY 1985, part 8, p. 4166: "We project [the Sierra, Mike, and converted Yankee SSN] to be extremely quiet submarines." Since the new designs are descendents of the Victor III, they should be at least as quiet.

18. Adm. Nils Thunman, SASC, FY 1985, part 8, p. 4167: The SSN-21 will be "several times quieter than today's 688 or the improved 688."

19. Adm. James D. Watkins, SASC, FY 1985, part 8, p. 3889: "We had misjudged the absolute sound and pressure levels of the Soviet Victor III. We had made an estimating error and found that they were quieter than we thought . . . We learned that they are very hard to find." The Victor III is the first Soviet SSN that has been considered "very hard to find," which implies that the Victor II is considerably louder. This may be the result of the Soviet Union's adopting the suspended machinery racks whose adoption in the West resulted in the major quieting improvement of the SSBN-608 and SSN-594 in 1961.

20. Norman Friedman, *Submarine Design and Development* (Annapolis: Naval Institute Press, 1984), p. 81: On the earliest US nuclear submarines (SSN-578 and SSN-585 classes, and earlier SSNs): "There was one surprise, nuclear machinery was quite noisy, so that early nuclear submarines could be detected passively at considerable distances, much like snorkellers."

21. Kosta Tsipis, "Underwater Acoustic Detection," in *The Future of the Sea-Based Deterrent,* ed. Kosta Tsipis et al. (Cambridge: MIT Press, 1973), p. 177: Nuclear submarines are said to emit "less than 10^{-3} watts," that is, less than 141 dB re 1 micropascal at 1 yard.

22. Adm. James D. Watkins, SASC, FY 1985, part 8, p. 3889: In reference to the Victor III: "We have put extra dollars into the low frequency end so we can go after the propeller blade rates and the other things we have to get on a quiet submarine." This hints that the Victor III has reached a level of machinery quieting that is as low as or lower than the sound emitted by the noncavitating rotating propeller at blade rate. The fundamental blade rate frequency is equal to the rotation rate times the number of blades—about 5–10 Hz. Blade rate harmonics can also be strong. These occur at integer multiples of the fundamental, so the fifth harmonic might be between 25 and 50 Hz.

According to acoustic theory, the conversion of mechanical power in the propeller to acoustic power is inefficient. An estimate by Donald Ross gives a conversion factor of 10^{-8}–10^{-10} for typical propellers. Perhaps submarine propellers in fairly uniform flows could be even quieter, with conversion factors of only 10^{-12}. However, the mechanical power of a submarine propeller is about 10^7 watts, so the radiated spectrum level of the blade rate tonal might be 10^{-5} to 10^{-3} watts, or 120–140 dB. (Source: Donald Ross, *The Mechanics of Underwater Noise* [Elmsford, N.Y.: Pergamon, 1976], p. 295.)

23. Gerald A. Cann, Principal Deputy Assistant Secretary of the Navy (Research, Engineering and Systems), HASC, FY 1986, part 3, p. 233: "I don't think that at the present time any of us have any conceptual idea of how to make a submarine quieter than the SSN-21 is going to be . . . I don't think we can make it quieter." Although this statement might be seen in the political context as an argument that the best conceivable technology will go into the SSN-21, the statement can also be interpreted to mean that the SSN-21 will be about as quiet as the SSBN-726 Ohio class.

24. Vice Adm. Lee Baggett, Jr., Director of Naval Warfare, SASC, FY 1986, part 8, p. 4373: "The SSN-688 class, the current SSN in the fleet, would be able to detect the Sierra at [deleted] in the Norwegian Sea, in that environment, and the Soviet detection range would be [deleted]. So the advantage is [deleted] . . . he gets quieter and decreases our ability to hear him first." This suggests that the Sierra is still louder than the current SSN-688. But it is quieter than the Victor III.

25. Gerald A. Cann, HASC, FY 1986, part 4, p. 783, 784:

a. "The Soviet Victor I and Victor II create [deleted] noise." This suggests that they have comparable noise levels.

b. "The Victor III is considerably quieter" [than the Victor I/II].

26. Adm. James D. Watkins, HAC, FY 1986, part 23, p. 913: In the context of a discussion of a simulated attack on a Yankee in the Eastern Pacific: "That is an older submarine, at about the 150 decibel level, which is easy to track."

27. Norman Polmar, *Guide to the Soviet Navy,* 3d ed. (Annapolis: Naval Institute Press), p. 105: "Acoustic data on the first Alfa SSNs indicated that the radiated noise levels at lesser speeds were generally similar to that of other Soviet SSNs, indicating a net improvement in view of the higher power of the Alfa reactor plant."

28. Adm. Kinnaird R. McKee, HAC, FY 1987, part 4:

a. "The Akula submarine represents . . . a significant breakthrough in performance" (p. 445).

b. "The Akula going to sea represents a substantial decrease in our advantage" (p. 451).

29. From figure A6–7, the Sierra and Akula should be 8 to 10 dB quieter than the Victor III since their surface displacement is about 1,000 tons greater.

30. US Navy, *CV Concept Study,* published around 1972–73, pp. B-2, B-16, B-17, table B-5.

a. The Soviet Navy's "new" nuclear submarines (Victor class is cited specifically), were believed to have "lower radiated noise levels (possibly equating to US Skipjack SSN-585 class SSNs) . . ."

b. "Table B-5: General Purpose Submarines Estimated Characteristics and Performance" (pp. B-16, B-17)

Type/Class	*At speed (knots) (low/high)*	*Noise Levels (LOFAR band)*
Echo I	6/13	60/72
Echo II	6/12	60/72
Charlie	5/14	55–60/65
November	7/15	60/72
Victor	5/14	55–60/65
Foxtrot, Whiskey	6 (snorkel)	60
	6 (battery)	45

It is assumed that these levels are given in dB, and are broadband low frequency sound levels. The reference intensity is not given, but the numerical values suggest that the common reference of 1 dyn/cm^2 was used. To convert to the new standard of 1 micropascal, add 100 dB to the values given above.

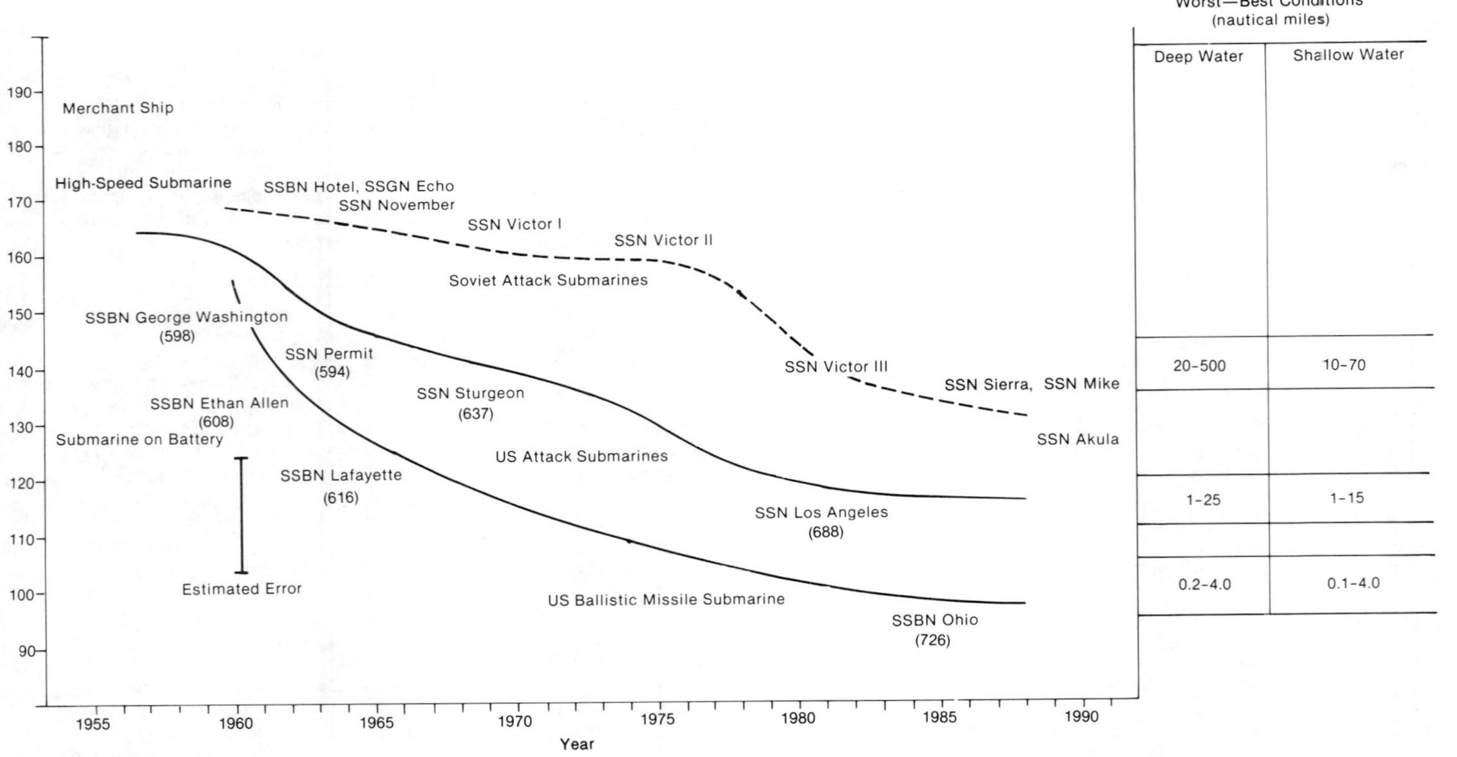

Figure A6–6. Estimate of US and Soviet submarine total radiated sound levels since 1958.

Note: Detection ranges associated with deep (greater than 4000 feet) and shallow (less than 1000 feet) water are given for a range of environmental conditions. At source levels below 90 dB, detection range approaches the length of the submarine.

for a submarine running on batteries, to 175 dB for a fully cavitating submarine probably running on diesel engines, a factor of 30,000 difference. Some intermediate sound levels have been observed, but these fall into a range that has been characterized by one knowledgeable author as "quiet" submarines and were associated with submarines either running on batteries or running at speeds below 2.5 knots. One can assume that the earliest nuclear submarine classes (SSN-575, 578, and 585) had sound levels between the upper bound and these moderately quiet World War II submarines. The most recent class of US missile submarine, the Ohio, has been attributed with sound levels so low that it cannot be heard beyond a few thousand yards. One reference claimed the maximum detection range was 1,000 yards, using the latest US sonar equipment. Assuming reasonable bounds on the sonar parameters, this implies total radiated sound levels between 90 dB and 115 dB, that is, on the order of one millionth of a watt. It is also noteworthy that the Ohio class submarine has approached sound levels so low that passive sonar is about as efficient a means of search as magnetic anomaly detection, in terms of detection range.

The remaining information on sound levels of current US and Soviet submarines is mostly relative information, and the estimates shown are consistent with this relative information. A few assumptions are implicit in the estimates: SSBNs are generally a bit quieter than SSNs of the same vintage; unless other data are available, successive classes introduce quieting of about 7 dB (a factor of five); submarine classes with long production runs get a bit quieter from submarine to submarine as better technologies become available. Some individual Soviet submarines are said to have become noticeably quieter just in the course of overhauls, so the assumption that production techniques can lower noise output seems reasonable.

There are a few notable features about figure A6–6. In 1961 the US built a propulsion system in which the noisiest parts rested on a "bed plate," which is a sound isolated platform inside the submarine. This system went into the SSBN-608 class and resulted in the first major reduction in radiated sound from nuclear submarines. British submarine designers introduced a similar system and probably had similar radiated noise levels. The general pattern of US submarine quieting appears to be an initial series of major improvements, followed by major improvements spaced more widely in time. Overall, the progression looks like what would be expected of a technological learning curve.

There is less data on Soviet submarines, though the pattern of their developments in quieting is apparent. The HEN (Hotel, Echo, November) classes are probably so loud that they would be very vulnerable in deep water while traveling at even moderate speeds. It is interesting to note the difference between the patterns of Soviet and US quieting. Improvements took place slowly and at a relatively constant rate between 1960 and 1978, when the HEN classes, the Victor I and II, the Yankee, and the early Delta classes were being constructed. The average rate of decrease was about 5–10 dB per decade. The lack of improvement was surprising at the time. Delta class SSBNs produced in the mid-1970s were projected by US officials to be considerably quieter than they actually turned out to be. Since one of the principal selling points of the SSN-688 program just a few years before was its capability against the projected "quiet" Soviet Delta SSBN, the news of the actual sound level of those vessels proved quite embarrassing to some officials.[22]

The first major improvement in submarine quieting (that is apparent) came with the introduction of the Victor III. The available evidence suggests that the Navy had predicted the Victor III would be noisier than it turned out to be. Given the magnitude of the improvement, the absence of previous improvements of that magnitude, and the US design experience, it can be hypothesized that the Victor III contains the first successful Soviet attempt at mounting main machinery on sound isolating rafts.

Projections of future submarine radiated sound levels are extremely uncertain, and virtually impossible with the limited data available in the unclassified realm. Some trends can be noted, however, that are likely to have important implications for naval operations and for the net assessment of Soviet and US naval capabilities. Submarines are likely to become quieter in the future, and the trend for the United States and the Soviet Union seems to be that radiated sound level is decreasing at a rate of about 10–15 dB per decade. By the late 1990s, the United States will have deployed the SSN-21 and the Ohio class SSBN, both of which probably approach the lower "limit" of quieting. This limit is not a physical limit but a cost-effectiveness limit. Since it is likely to be expensive to improve the acoustic design of these vessels, the US quieting curve may be flattening out. Soviet submarines are still much louder than the presumed lower limit, but it is important to remember that the Soviets traditionally have thought about quieting differently from the way the United States has, and that they have different cost-effectiveness criteria. At the current rate of quieting, by the mid-1990s the Soviet Union could be producing submarines with radiated sound levels about equal to those of the proposed SSN-21, though somewhat louder than the Ohio class submarines. Although for the next 10 years the United States is likely to maintain a substantial acoustic advantage over Soviet submarines on a fleetwide average basis, the newest Soviet submarines will become much more difficult to find.

As submarines become quieter, they tend to grow in size to accommodate the sound-isolating mounts, so that, along with the quieting trend, a trend toward larger submarines is expected. Figure A6–7 is a plot of estimated submarine-radiated sound levels versus surfaced displacement.

Surfaced displacement of a submarine is probably a reasonable estimate of the volume and weight allocated to achieving depth, speed, and signature reduction, whereas submerged displacement includes the displacement allocated to reserve buoyancy. Since Soviet submarines typically have a greater

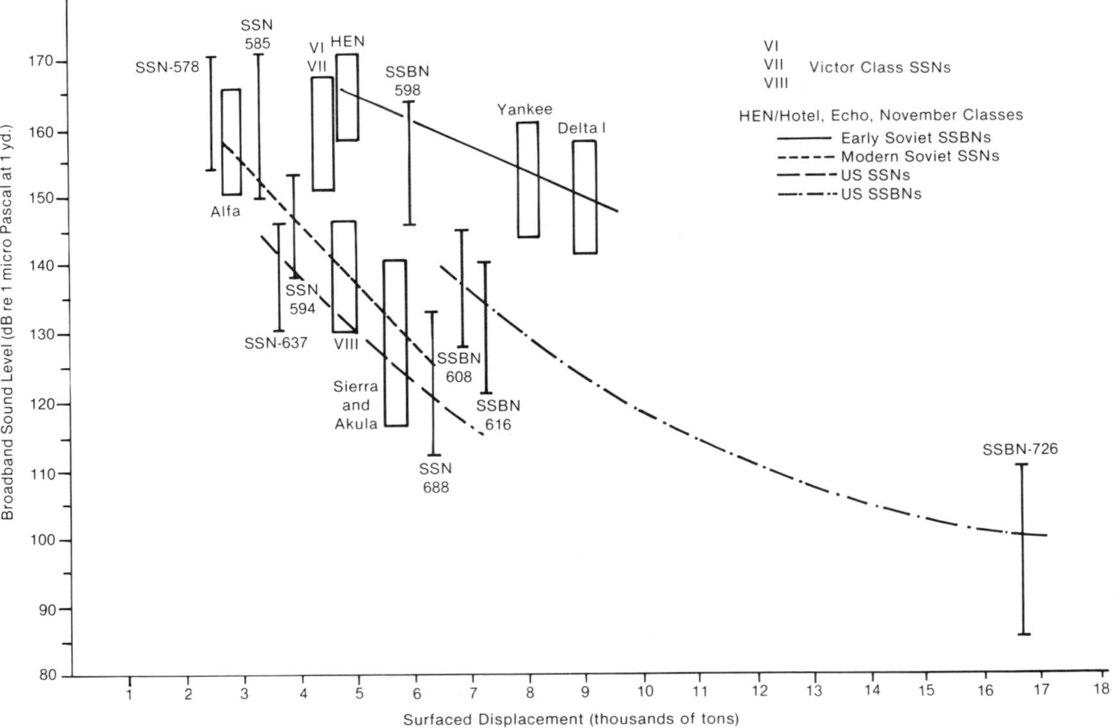

Figure A6–7. Broadband sound level versus surfaced displacement.

Note: Trend lines for different generations of quieting technology are identified.

reserve buoyancy than US submarines, using surfaced displacement eliminates the bias which would make Soviet vessels appear to have larger internal spaces.[23] Plotting the data in this way reveals some trends which are associated with the internal design. Older US and Soviet submarines do not show a strong trend of decreasing noise level with displacement. This is probably indicative of the fact that if little sound isolation is used in machinery mounting, the radiated sound level is relatively independent of size. US submarines built since 1962, and Soviet attack submarines built since 1979, show a strong trend of decreasing sound level for larger displacements.

US attack submarines of the SSN-594, SSN-637, and SSN-688 classes describe a trend line of relatively large decreases in radiated sound as displacement increases. The slope of this line is about 8 dB sound level reduction per 1,000 ton increase in displacement. Note that the two major classes of SSBNs built in the early and mid-1960s, the SSBN-608 and SSBN-616 classes, are relatively loud given their displacement, although in absolute terms the SSBN-616 class is relatively quiet. This probably reflects the fact that the size of an SSBN is primarily governed by the size of the missile, and that these designs are as large as they are not for quieting, but to fit the missile into a cylindrical pressure hull. One might think of the curve for US SSBNs as being the same as that of the SSNs, but shifted to the right by 2,000 tons.

US ballistic missile submarines of the SSBN-608, SSBN-616, and SSBN-726 classes describe another trend line that begins with a decrease in sound level of 8 dB per 1,000 tons, after which the trend seems to become less steep. This change may reflect the expected decreasing marginal returns to quieting effort, though it is difficult to interpret, since the displacement of the Ohio (SSBN-726) class submarine may have been driven by the size of the D-5 missile rather than by quieting requirements. The reader should also bear in mind that this data is very approximate.

Modern Soviet attack submarines of the Alfa, Victor III, and Sierra classes describe a trend line that is close to the line for US attack submarines, and perhaps higher. The Akula has the same displacement as Sierra, but a special note of concern in Navy testimony suggests that it is probably quieter. It is possible that the Akula is as quiet as the SSBN-616 class, or perhaps even as quiet as the early units of the SSN-688 class.

There are not many pieces of information regarding the noise levels of Soviet SSBNs, but the data released about the Yankee is some of the only absolute sound level data available. The trend shows the least decrease in noise level with displacement of any of the submarine types shown. The slope of the trend line is about 4 dB decrease per 1,000-ton increase in displacement.

Some general observations that can be drawn from this analysis follow:

1. In the early to mid-1970s, Soviet emphasis on quieting lagged behind that of the United States by 10–15 years. With the introduction of the Victor

III as the backbone of the Soviet attack submarine fleet, the lag in quieting has been reduced to about 8–10 years. Akula may eliminate the lag.

2. In terms of acoustic stealth, it is unlikely that the United States could improve upon the current Ohio class SSBN.
3. US attack submarines are generally about as quiet as Soviet attack submarines with about 750 tons' greater displacement. Given the uncertainty in the data, it is entirely possible that the trend lines are farther apart, or that they overlap.
4. At a given displacement, early US SSBNs are about 25 dB quieter than early Soviet SSBNs. There appears to be a great deal of potential for quieting Soviet SSBNs produced after the early Delta classes.

Ambient Noise

The noise level at a hydrophone array is the sum of all the noises in the water from distant sources, the noise generated by the platform carrying the hydrophone, and the electronic noise within the signal-processing devices. The platform noise is also called self-noise. If the hydrophone is mounted on the hull of a surface ship, the levels of self-noise are so high that the sonar range is limited by it. If the array is mounted on the ocean floor or towed far behind a submarine, the self-noise is negligible. Since the emphasis of this report is on long-range detection, I will not consider the short-range hull-mounted sonar and will assume that the only sources of noise are distant from the receiver. Electrical circuit noise is not significant for sonar except under extremely quiet ambient noise conditions.[24]

Sources of Ambient Noise

Of the many sources of underwater noise, some of the most significant are:

Distant surface shipping

Explosions from seismic testing

Oil rig drilling

Wind generated waves and whitecaps

Rain splashes on the ocean surface

Biological noises

Cracking in solid Arctic ice

Wind-driven collisions in broken ice

Shipping and drilling noise typically dominates in the sea at frequencies below 200 Hz, although in the deep sound channel, noise from high latitude winds may be significant. Wind/wave-generated noise dominates at frequencies above 200 Hz. Noise from heavy rainfall can dominate over wind noise, but heavy rainfall is intermittent and is generally not a significant noise source for long durations, whereas wind/wave noise can be persistent. Under the Arctic ice cap, the wind has a relatively small influence on noise levels, and there it can be extremely quiet if the ice is not cracking. On the other hand, when the air temperature is falling rapidly, thermal stress cracking in the ice can make the Arctic a relatively noisy area.[25] In the next few sections the most significant sources of underwater noise are discussed.

Shipping and Drilling Noise

Noise from surface ships and offshore drilling operations is lumped together because the sources are both (1) low frequency and (2) usually located on the continental shelf. For simplicity I will refer to this as simply shipping noise, though in some areas like the North Sea, drilling and pumping operations may well be the dominant noise source.

The noise level at any point in the ocean is the sum of all contributions from all the noise sources in the ocean within transmission range. The ambient noise level therefore depends not only on the number and intensity of the sources, but also on their geographic distribution and on the sound transmission characteristics of the ocean between the various sources and the point of interest.[26] Shipping is largely concentrated near the coasts. For example, consider some data on the average number of ships in 600 nm by 600 nm square areas of the North Atlantic Ocean. Near the East Coast of the United States the figure is about 22 ships, in the middle North Atlantic there are 6 or 7 ships per 360,000 square nautical miles, and off the coast of West Africa and France, the figure is about 25 ships. In the Greenland–Iceland–United Kingdom area there may be only a single ship in a 600 nm by 600 nm area.[27] However, the noise levels between Scotland and Iceland may well be high because of the large number of drilling rigs in the nearby North Sea.

The structure of the ocean basins provides a mechanism for broadcasting the coastal shipping noise into the deep ocean. The relatively steep continental slope acts as a kind of megaphone that projects noise off the continental shelf by reflecting it outward horizontally so that it travels to long ranges via the deep sound channel. Measurements of individual ship noise in deep water indicate that at great depths the received noise may increase 6–10 dB as the ship approaches the coast.[28] Because the highest shipping density is near the coast, it is likely that coastal shipping and drilling noise is a dominant low-frequency noise source even at long ranges from the coasts. The high noise levels and poor propagation also make the continental shelf and slope waters good acoustic hiding places for submarines.

Shipping noise data is given in table A6–1. This table gives noise spectrum levels in a 1 Hz band. The numbers are presented in decibels relative to the intensity of sound from a 1 micropascal plane wave. The information is based on recent estimates by Ross.[29] Noise level is given for deep water as a function of shipping concentration. "Remote" areas include those remote from shipping or protected from long-range sound, such as the South Pacific and southern Indian Ocean.[30] In the southern oceans, the shipping density is often so low that shipping noise is effectively absent or is dominated by wind noise. "Heavy" shipping noise levels occur near large, busy harbors or near major shipping lanes. Between these two extremes are "moderate" and "light" shipping levels. According to an expert on shipping noise, most of the North Atlantic and North Pacific are described as "moderate" and the densest shipping areas are described as "heavy."[31] Since the total noise power increases with the logarithm of the number of ships, predicted noise levels are not very sensitive to numbers of ships.

I have used this data on shipping noise for predicting noise in ocean areas that are relatively shallow, although the shipping noise data was intended to be used only for deep water. Transmission loss from a source to a measurement point is higher in shallow than in deep water. Therefore, the data presented in table A6–1 tends to overpredict noise levels in shallow water. One way to compensate crudely for this is simply to underestimate the shallow water shipping concentrations. I have used the "light" shipping data for moderate shipping in shallow water, and "moderate" for heavy.

Low-Frequency Noise Variability and Directionality

Ambient noise at low frequencies may vary by 10 dB in the course of a day.[32] The variations in noise level can be correlated with changes in local shipping

Table A6–1
Ambient noise levels due to shipping and drilling
(values in dB re 1 micropascal in 1 Hz band)

Shipping	*Frequency (Hz)*			
Activity	*10–40*	*40–100*	*100–200*	*200–300*[a]
Remote	67	70	62	55
Light	73	75	67	60
Moderate	83	85	73	66
Heavy	90	94	80	74

Source: Donald Ross, *The Mechanics of Underwater Noise* (Elmsford, N.Y.: Pergamon, 1976), p. 281.

[a]Spectrum falls rapidly over 200 Hz. Most places in the Northern Hemisphere have at least light to moderate shipping noise, while harbors correspond to "heavy" traffic. Estimates from Robert Urick, *Ambient Noise in the Sea* (Washington, D.C.: Naval Sea Systems Command, 1984), average 2–4 dB lower than Ross.

density and routing, and with local wind speed. In general, however, noise levels are somewhat random, and the figures given in table A6–1 should be considered accurate only to about 10 dB.

The low-frequency noise less than 200 Hz in the deep ocean is very directional. Almost all the shipping (and other low-frequency) noise arrives at a deep receiver at an angle within 20 degrees of the horizontal. Thus, there is no way for sonar systems to shut out noise by listening at an optimum elevation angle, since the signature and the noise arrive in approximately the same elevation angle.[33] At frequencies between 200 Hz and 500 Hz, the noise arrives equally from all directions in the vertical. Above 800 Hz the ambient noise arrives mainly from angles within about 45 degrees of vertical. This shift in the directionality for high frequencies is due to the fact that high-frequency wind-generated noise at the nearby sea surface dominates high-frequency noise from distant shipping. When the winds are heavy, vertically arriving noise dominates distant, horizontally arriving noise for frequencies above 200 Hz. When winds are weak, vertically arriving noise does not dominate over horizontally arriving noise until frequencies over 600 Hz are reached.[34] Some benefit can be obtained from vertical array directionality when frequencies over 200 Hz are of interest. Even a 30 degree beamwidth in a vertical array, if steered horizontally, may eradicate two-thirds of the ambient noise from higher angles, yielding a 5 dB decrease in the ambient noise level (*NL*).

Wind-generated Noise

The generation of noise at the sea surface is a complex phenomenon that depends on the local wind speed, the local waves, and the angle between the wind and waves.[35] The best single parameter to correlate with high-frequency noise is wind speed.[36] Table A6–2 shows the wind-generated noise levels as a

Table A6–2
Ambient noise levels due to wind/waves
(values in dB re 1 micropascal in 1 Hz band)

Wind Speed (knots)	*Frequency (Hz)*						
	40–60	*60–100*	*100–200*	*200–500*	*500–1,000*	*1,000–2,000*	*2,000–5,000*
1–3	42	45	48	48	45	42	35
4–10	53	56	63	63	60	55	50
11–16	60	64	69	68	64	60	55
17–27	65	72	73	74	70	63	58
28–33[a]	73	77	77	76	73	65	60
34–40	74	78	78	77	74	68	61

Source: Gordon M. Wenz, "Acoustic Ambient Noise in the Ocean: Spectra and Sources," *JASA* 34:12, December 1962, pp. 1936–56; and Robert J. Urick, *Ambient Noise in the Sea* (Washington, D.C.: Naval Sea Systems Command, 1984), appendix.

[a]Above 28 knots, noise level is virtually independent of wind speed. at 40–100 Hz, Urick is 10 dB higher than Wenz; between 100 and 1,000 Hz, 4–5 dB higher; above 1,000 Hz, the same. Where there is disagreement, Urick is used.

function of wind speed and frequency, revealing that wind noise dominates at high frequencies. The variability of wind generated noise tends to decrease with high wind speed. At 5 knots, the standard deviation of the noise is 12 dB, while at 20 knots the standard deviation is only about 2 dB. The wind itself, however, may vary widely over the course of a day.[37]

High-frequency wind noise decreases with depth from the surface to about 2,000 feet.[38] The decrease in noise level is generally about 5 dB altogether. Most of the decrease occurs in moving below the seasonal thermocline (200–400 feet at midlatitudes). Low-frequency noise does not change significantly with depth. Sonar detection capability of submarine against submarine probably increases somewhat below the seasonal thermocline (around 400 feet) due to the lower noise levels, other factors being equal.

Analysis of ambient noise in the South Pacific, where there are relatively few ships, suggests that the persistent winds at high latitudes near Antarctica generate noise similar to that usually observed in the northern hemisphere.[39] At those high latitudes, the sound channel approaches the surface. Consequently, the noise is efficiently transmitted through the sound channel and arrives at middle latitudes at nearly horizontal angles, at intensities similar to those associated with light to moderate shipping.[40] If this analysis is accurate, the worldwide ambient noise level may be less dependent on shipping than previously thought.

Rain Noise

When raindrops strike the surface of the sea, they generate a sharp impulsive sound. Heavy rain can be so loud that it dominates the wind noise. In some areas of the oceans during particular seasons, rain is quite frequent. In circumstances where this may affect submarine detection, I have tried to estimate the contribution of rain-generated noise to the overall ambient noise level. Since heavy rainfall is something of an extreme event, rain noise is included only in the extreme case of the noisiest conditions. The estimates of rain noise are shown in table A6–3. Data is presented for moderate and heavy rainfall rates,

Table A6–3
Ambient noise due to rain
(values in dB re 1 micropascal in 1 Hz band)

Rain Intensity	*Frequency (Hz)*					
	40–100	*100–200*	*200–500*	*500–1,000*	*1,000–2,000*	*2,000–5,000*
Moderate	60[a]	65	65	65	70	65
Heavy[b]	70	75	75	75	75	70

Source: Robert J. Urick, *Principles of Underwater Sound for Engineers* (New York: McGraw-Hill, 1975), pp. 196, 197.

[a]Scatter in the data is about 10 dB.

[b]Heavy rain is used in calculating worst detection conditions.

heavy rainfall being used in estimating the worst conditions for acoustic detection.

Ambient Noise under the Arctic Ice

Noise under the Arctic ice is extremely variable. It depends on the following factors:[41]

1. Rising air temperature—low noise
2. Rapidly falling air temperature—high noise
3. Continuous ice cover to shore—low noise
4. Broken ice at the edge of the ice pack with wind blowing onto the ice—high noise
5. Wind over non-continuous ice cover—high noise
6. Wind over continuous ice cover—low noise

It seems nearly impossible to predict the noise levels under the ice. Instead, I have taken a compilation of Arctic noise spectra measured over a long period under many different conditions and have used estimates of the 10 percent highest noise levels, the 10 percent lowest noise levels, and the "average" noise levels from all sources. This is consistent with the approach adopted later of trying to predict the worst, best, and average detection conditions. Table A6–4 gives the high, low, and average noise levels as a function of frequency. These figures should be used only in regions that are covered by ice and not in the zones near the edge of the ice pack.[42]

Table A6–4
Ambient noise levels under ice
(values in dB re 1 micropascal in 1 Hz band)

Percentage of Observations Exceeded	*Frequency (Hz)*						
	10–40	*40–100*	*100–200*	*200–500*	*500–1,000*	*1,000–2,000*	*2,000–5,000*
High: 10%	82	75	68	68	68	62	55
Avg.: 50%	68	62	55	55	55	50	45
Low: 90%	55	47	40	40	40	35	30

Source: Robert J. Urick, *Principles of Underwater Sound for Engineers* (New York: McGraw-Hill, 1975), p. 201. Also, Yie-Ming Chen, "*Underwater Acoustic Ambient Noise in the Arctic*" (Master's thesis, MIT, 1982), p. 22. Data is mostly from the Beaufort Basin and the Canada Deep.

Note: To estimate noise levels at the ice edge, add 5 dB to the sound level that is predicted under the same wind conditions in open water. This level applies 30 nm to both sides of ice edge.

The zone between the edge of the continuous Arctic ice pack and the ice-free water can be many tens of miles wide, though the zone in which the broken ice is highly concentrated may only be a mile or two wide. This concentrated broken ice nearest the solid pack is constantly colliding as it is driven by wind and waves. The highest noise levels occur within 30 miles on both sides of this dense, broken-ice zone. The noise levels in this 60-mile-wide swath are 5 dB higher than the noise levels under open water for the same wind speed. Therefore, when an ice edge is present, the highest probable noise levels are found by taking the highest probable wind levels, computing the noise associated with that wind speed, and adding 5 dB. Directly beneath a sharp ice edge, noise levels at low frequencies are often 10 dB greater than those associated with the same wind speed over open water.[43]

Underice noise and transmission loss is a significant area of underwater research. A large part of the Soviet SSBN force patrols near or even under the ice in the Arctic Ocean, the Sea of Okhotsk, and the Bering Sea. The only ASW weapons that can be used effectively under ice are submarine-launched torpedoes. Acoustic homing torpedoes use passive and active sonar to seek targets, and so they must be capable of distinguishing submarine signatures (or echo returns) from ambient noise.

Notes

1. See appendix 1, "The Design of Submarines."
2. V. M. Bukalov and A. A. Narusbayev, *Atomic-Powered Submarine Design* (Leningrad: Shipbuilding Publishing House, 1964), p. 226.
3. *Jane's Fighting Ships 1982/83*, p. 602.
4. This is due to the fact that the pipes must handle very high pressures and therefore cannot have flexible sound isolation sections, and to the fact that they must seal with the heavy reactor pressure vessel, which may be difficult to isolate from the hull.
5. Sound energy in air is very poorly coupled to the hull to begin with.
6. M. Strasberg, "Propeller Cavitation Noise after 35 Years of Study," *Noise and Fluids Engineering*, ed. Robert Hickling (Proceedings of the 1977 winter annual meeting of the American Society of Mechanical Engineers, New York: A.S.M.E., 1978), pp. 89–99.
7. Robert J. Urick, *Principles of Underwater Sound for Engineers* (New York: McGraw-Hill, 1975) p. 308.
8. Donald Ross, *The Mechanics of Underwater Noise* (Elmsford, N.Y.: Pergamon, 1976), chap. 3, 9.
9. Ibid., p. 295.
10. Adm. James D. Watkins, SASC, FY 1985, part 8, p. 3889.
11. Urick, *Principles*, p. 309.

12. Capt. Harry E. Jackson, USN, unpublished notes for summer course on submarine design, MIT, 1974.

13. W. F. Hunter, "An Introduction to Acoustic Exploration" in *Underwater Acoustics*, ed. R. W. B. Stephens (New York: Wiley-Interscience, 1970), pp. 91–127.

14. Neal A. Brown, "Cavitation Noise Problems and Solutions," in *International Symposium on Shipboard Acoustics*, ed. J. H. Hanssen (New York: Elsevier, 1977), pp. 21–38.

15. Urick, *Principles*, fig. 10.19, p. 319.

16. Ibid., fig. 10.19, p. 319, and table 10.2, p. 314.

17. HAC, FY 1986, part 2, p. 918, 919. The SSN-21 is claimed to have "two and a half times the acoustic speed" of current US SSNs, that is, "in excess of 20 knots."

18. SASC, FY 1986, part 8, p. 4350.

19. HAC, FY 1986, part 2, p. 926.

20. It is not clear which source of noise dominates at that speed, cavitation or machinery noise. If the Alfa has machinery on sound-isolated rafts, it would have to clamp that machinery to the hull at higher speeds, which would couple more noise to the sea. However, it seems unlikely that the Alfa contains much space for sound-isolating mounts.

21. This is not absolutely true, since under extremely quiet conditions, such as a windless day with constant temperature and a solid, shore-fast ice cover, remote from ships or marine sources of noise, extremely faint sounds may be detectable at some distance. In perfectly calm open water, however, the level of ambient noise at all frequencies of interest is at least 20 dB higher than it is under the most quiet underice conditions.

22. See the notes accompanying figure A6–5.

23. K. J. Moore, "Submarine Design and Development," *Submarine Review*, October 1984, pp. 96–103.

24. Urick, *Principles*, p. 328.

25. Ibid., p. 200.

26. Gordon M. Wenz, "Acoustic Ambient Noise in the Ocean: Spectra and Sources," *Journal of the Acoustical Society of America* (hereafter *JASA*) 34:12, December 1962, pp. 1936–1956.

27. I. Dyer, "Statistics of Distant Shipping Noise," *JASA* 53:2, 1973, pp. 564–570.

28. Ross, *Underwater Noise*, p. 283.

29. Ibid., p. 281.

30. Ibid., p. 280.

31. Donald Ross, personal communication.

32. R. W. Bannister, R. N. Denha, and K. M. Githrie, "Variability of Low Frequency Ambient Noise," *JASA* 65:5, May 1979.

33. E. H. Axelrod, B. A. Schoomer, and W. A. Von Winkle, "Vertical Directionality of Ambient Noise in the Deep Ocean at a Site Near Bermuda," *JASA* 37:January 1965, pp. 77–83.

34. Ibid.

35. Wenz, "Acoustic Ambient Noise."

36. Urick, *Principles,* p. 186.

37. Bannister, Denha, and Githrie, "Variability."

38. Urick, *Principles,* pp. 198, 199.

39. R. W. Bannister, "Deep Sound Channel Noise from High Latitude Winds," *JASA* 79, January 1986, pp. 41–48.

40. Ibid.

41. V. V. Bogorodskii, and A. V. Gusev, "Under-Ice Noise in the Ocean," *Soviet Physics Acoustics* 14:2, October–December 1968, pp. 127–133.

42. Urick, *Principles,* fig. 7.20.

43. O. I. Diachok, "Recent Advances in Arctic Hydroacoustics," *Naval Research Reviews* 29:5, May 1976, pp. 48–63.

Appendix 7
Detection of Submarine Signatures in Noise

A passive sonar system receives fluctuating ambient noise constantly. When a submarine is present in the beam, the input to the sonar system is expected to be higher than it would be if the submarine sounds or signature were not present. At the end of all the sonar processing, a decision must be made as to whether or not the signal contains signature plus noise or noise alone. In order to make such a determination, one must know the level of ambient noise in the ocean and the self-noise at the frequency and in the direction of interest, and then set a threshold just above that noise level. An acoustic level that exceeds the threshold is in all likelihood due to the presence of an anomalous source—such as a submarine—superimposed on the noise. The final detection decision usually remains with a human, although the information displayed by the signal processor is usually in the form of many independent threshold responses at individual frequencies over time in one direction, or responses at a single frequency in many directions over time. The human operator is the final phase of integration and is a crucial component in the signal processing scheme.

Figure A7–1 shows the possible responses of a sonar/decisionmaker system to the actual states. The erroneous states—false alarm and missed target—may have heavy penalties associated with them. Consider an attack submarine searching for SSBNs. A false alarm can lead to an unnecessary action that may alert the SSBN and put the attacker in danger. Since the main offensive and defensive strategies of submarines are based on remaining undetected, false alarms are very costly. For this reason, the false alarm probability is kept small. In addition, the probability of a missed target should be kept small also. These two probabilities are dependent, however, and decreasing the false alarm probability also decreases the probability of correctly detecting a submarine that is present. A basic trade-off is made between gaining greater sensitivity and avoiding false alarms.

The basic signal processing scheme is shown in Figure A7–2. Assume that a submarine is present and is making sounds in a typical set of narrow bands.

Decision \ Actual State	Target Present	Target Absent
"Target Present"	Correct Decision P_{det}	False Alarm P_{fa}
"Target Absent"	Missed Target $1 - P_{det}$	Correct Decision $1 - P_{fa}$

Figure A7–1. Possible states of a sonar detection/decision system.

An array that is steered toward that submarine picks up the signature, $s(t)$, and some noise, $n(t)$. The total signal out of the array is given by

$$u(t) = s(t) + n(t) \tag{A7.1}$$

This signal (signature plus noise) can be described in the frequency domain by its spectrum.

A hypothetical spectrum is shown in figure A7–3. The signature shows up as four narrowband spikes (for example, due to the submarine turbine) that are imbedded in broadband ambient noise. The excess signal power in those spikes, that is, the integral over the signature band, is small relative to the total noise power, which is the integral over the entire noise band. The signature-to-noise ratio can be improved significantly if the entire signal is passed through a filter that allows only the signature frequencies to pass. Of course, some noise in those passbands gets through, but the total noise power is greatly reduced.

Narrowband processing is particularly important in long-range ASW passive detection since the signature of a quiet submarine consists of low-frequency narrowband sounds. Low frequencies travel the longest distances in deep water because they are subject to the lowest levels of absorption, and the distribution of these narrowband sounds in frequency provides clues to the type of submarine and its speed. Equally important, however, is the fact that a narrowband signature that is narrowband filtered stands out much better against the noise. The narrower the filter width, the more noise is eliminated, until the filter bandwidth is equal to the width of the signature line.

The signal given in equation A7.1 is fed into a series of narrowband filters that divide the entire frequency range into separate bands, which are processed

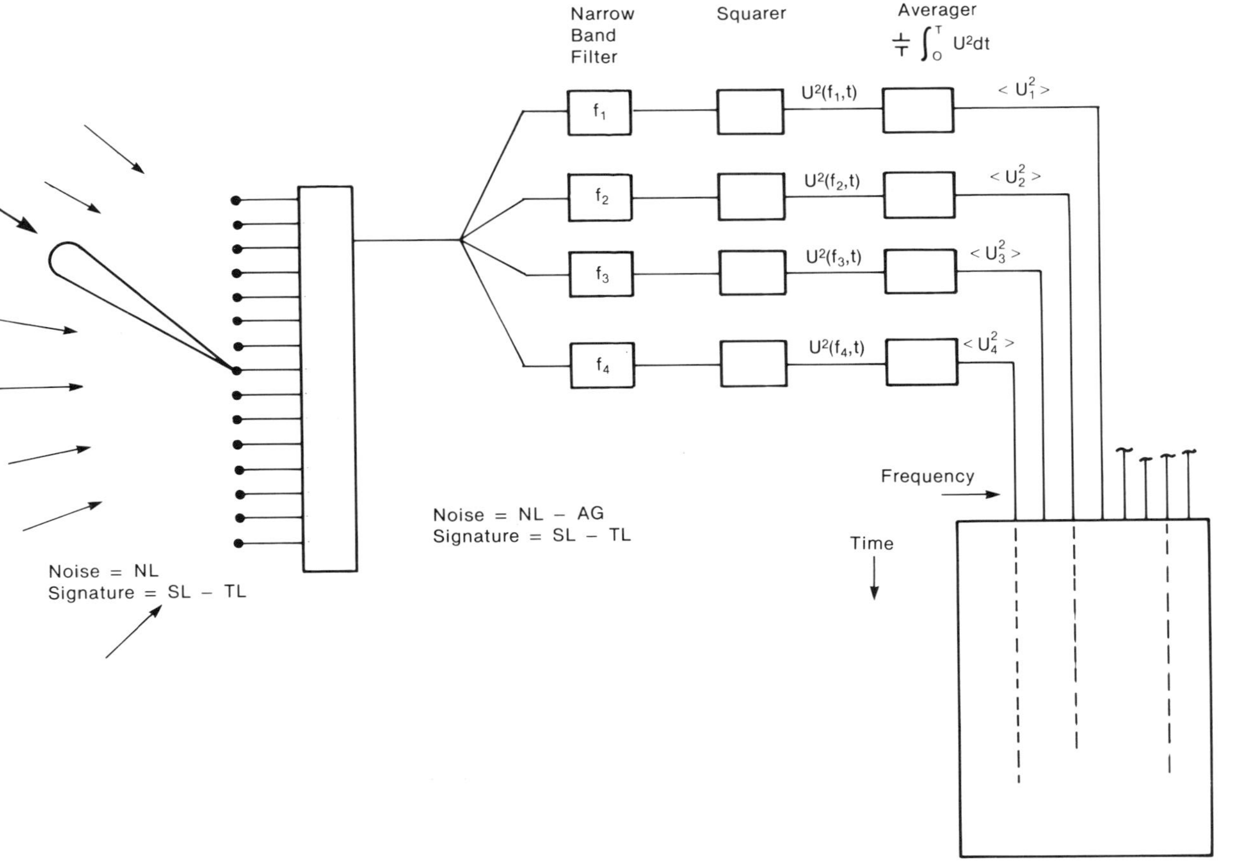

Figure A7-2. Sonar signal processing.

Note: In the ocean at the array, signature level is SL–TL, and ambient noise is NL. The array discriminates against noise, so that after the array, signature is still approximately SL–TL, but noise level is NL–AG. The total signal is frequency analyzed to determine the power contained in each frequency. Successive samples of the spectrum are shown on a visual display, resulting in a time history of the spectral estimates.

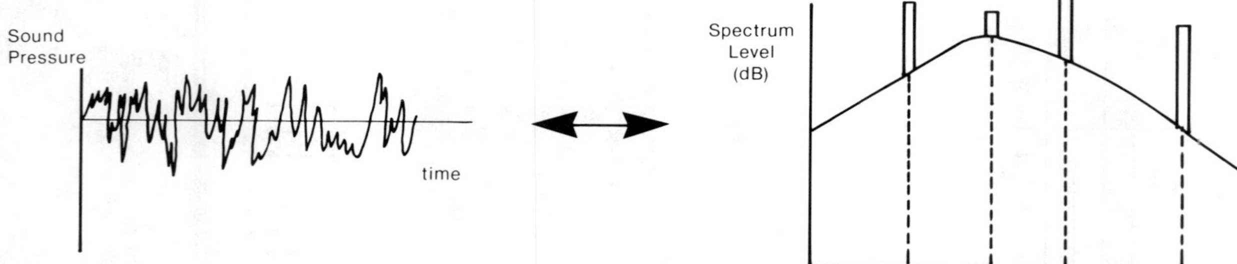

Figure A7–3. Frequency analysis of a total signal, showing broadband ambient noise and narrowband signature "tonals."

separately, as in figure A7–2.[1] Each filtered sample of the signal is then squared and averaged to give

$$\psi_u^2\ (f_c, B) = \frac{1}{BT} \int_0^T u^2\ (t, f_c, B)\ dt \tag{A7.2}$$

This is the signal power per Hz in the band of width B centered at frequency f_c. Time averaging evens out the fluctuations of the random signal. In theory, the longer the time averaging, the better is the estimate of the true signal power. Typical averaging times for passive acoustic detection are on the order of a few seconds to a few minutes.

If the signature and noise power levels are separated out of equation A7.2, they are

$$\psi_u^2 = \psi_s^2 + \psi_n^2$$

or simply

$$\tilde{U} = \tilde{S} + \tilde{N} \tag{A7.3}$$

Where $\tilde{S}$ is the average signature power per Hz and $\tilde{N}$ is the average noise power per Hz in a band. For a bandwidth of B hertz, the total noise power is $\tilde{N}B$.

The detection system must distinguish between the case when the signal power contains only noise and when it contains noise plus signature. This is represented in figure A7–4. In figure A7–4 the noise level is shown as a mean

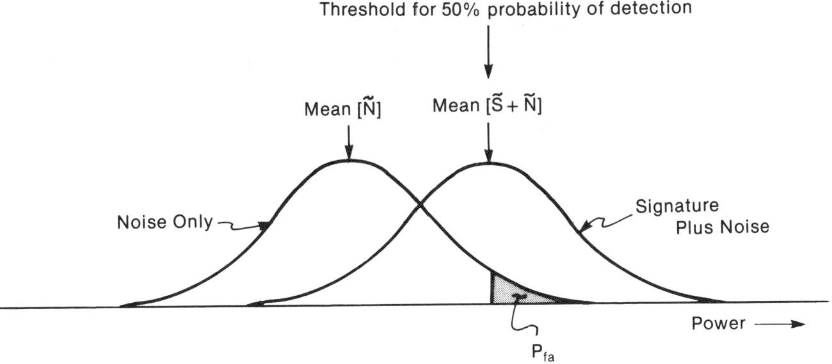

Figure A7–4. Probability distributions of noise only and signature plus noise in a given frequency band.

Note: If the threshold is set at the mean of the signature plus noise distribution, the p_{det} is by definition 0.5 and the p_{fa} is given by the shaded portion, which is the probability that the threshold is exceeded by noise only.

noise power with some random distribution. The probability distribution indicates the likelihood of the processor's estimating the noise to be at a given level. The more spread in the probability distribution, the greater is the expected difference between the estimate of the noise level and the true noise level as represented by the mean. The probability distribution of the noise itself is assumed to Gaussian, so the distribution of the noise power estimate is described by the chi-square distribution. The spread of this distribution is measured by its variance, which is given by

$$\sigma_N^2 = \frac{(\tilde{N}B)^2}{BT} \tag{A7.4}$$

When a submarine signature is present, the mean total signal level is given by

$$\tilde{S} + \tilde{N}B \tag{A7.5}$$

The variance of this level is

$$\sigma_{N+S}^2 = \frac{\tilde{N}^2 B}{T} + \frac{2\tilde{S}\tilde{N}}{T} \tag{A7.6}$$

where T is the averaging time. It is important to remember when using this detection theory that under some practical conditions, particularly under Arctic ice, the distribution of ambient noise fluctuations is not Gaussian, and this theory does not apply.

Now consider a detector that must determine whether or not a signature is present. The detector compares the incoming signal plus noise power to a predetermined threshold based on P_{det} and P_{fa}. If the signal plus noise exceeds the threshold, a detection is made. If the signal is less than the threshold, there is no detection. Suppose that the sonar must detect submarine signatures at a given level, $\tilde{S}$, 50 percent of the time that they are present. The threshold must be set at the mean signal level for signature plus noise as shown in figure A7–4, since there is a 50 percent chance that the signal will exceed this level. In order to increase the probability of detection for the same signature level, the threshold must be lowered.

The threshold level also determines the probability of a false alarm. In figure A7–4 the 50 percent detection threshold yields a false alarm probability that is represented by the shaded portion of the noise curve. This shaded area is the probability that the signal power will exceed the threshold when noise alone is present, giving a false alarm. The sonar operator must always trade between greater detection probability and a higher false alarm rate. The choice of threshold is therefore based on the expected cost of a false alarm and the expected benefit of a correct detection.

The threshold can be defined without considering the signature level if the maximum false alarm rate is specified. In this case the threshold is given by

$$K = \tilde{N}B + d\sigma_N \tag{A7.7}$$

where d is the threshold setting in the number of standard deviations above the mean noise level, and K is the absolute value of the threshold level. In this case, the signature that can be detected 50 percent of the time is

$$\tilde{S}_{50} = d\sigma_N \tag{A7.8}$$

Using equation A7.4, the signature-to-noise ratio for 50 percent detection is expressed in decibels.

$$(\tilde{S}_{50}/\tilde{N})\text{ dB} = \underbrace{5 \log_{10} B - 5 \log_{10} T}_{\text{Processor Sensitivity}} + 10 \log_{10} d \tag{A7.9}$$

This minimum detectable signal-to-noise ratio can be computed using figures A7–5 and A7–6. Enter figure A7–5 with the averaging time and the filter bandwidth and read the "processor sensitivity," as shown in equation A7.9. Also read the bandwidth-time product, BT. With the BT product and the false alarm probability, enter figure A7–6 to find the quantity $D = 10 \log d$. In actual sonar systems the minimum detectable SNR is a few dB greater than the result given by this procedure.[2]

Estimates of Sonar Detection Threshold

One can estimate the minimum detectable signature, or detection threshold, for sonar systems. The high level of security surrounding sonar system capabilities precludes any kind of definitive or precise estimates of detection threshold. However, starting with the basic model just described and identifying limitations imposed by the ocean medium, one can make estimates that are comparable in uncertainty to the uncertainty of the other terms in the sonar equation. Since the probability of detection and the probability of false alarm are system variables and can to some extent be varied at will, it is useful to examine the sensitivity of detection threshold to those parameters.

Among the many effects of random ocean acoustic transmission, there is a limit imposed on the minimum filter bandwidth and a limit imposed on the maximum integration time of the processing system. A pure tone of infinitesimally narrow bandwidth tends to be smeared over a finite band during propagation, and to integrate all the energy from the source, a wider bandwidth must be used, that introduces more of the broadband ambient noise.

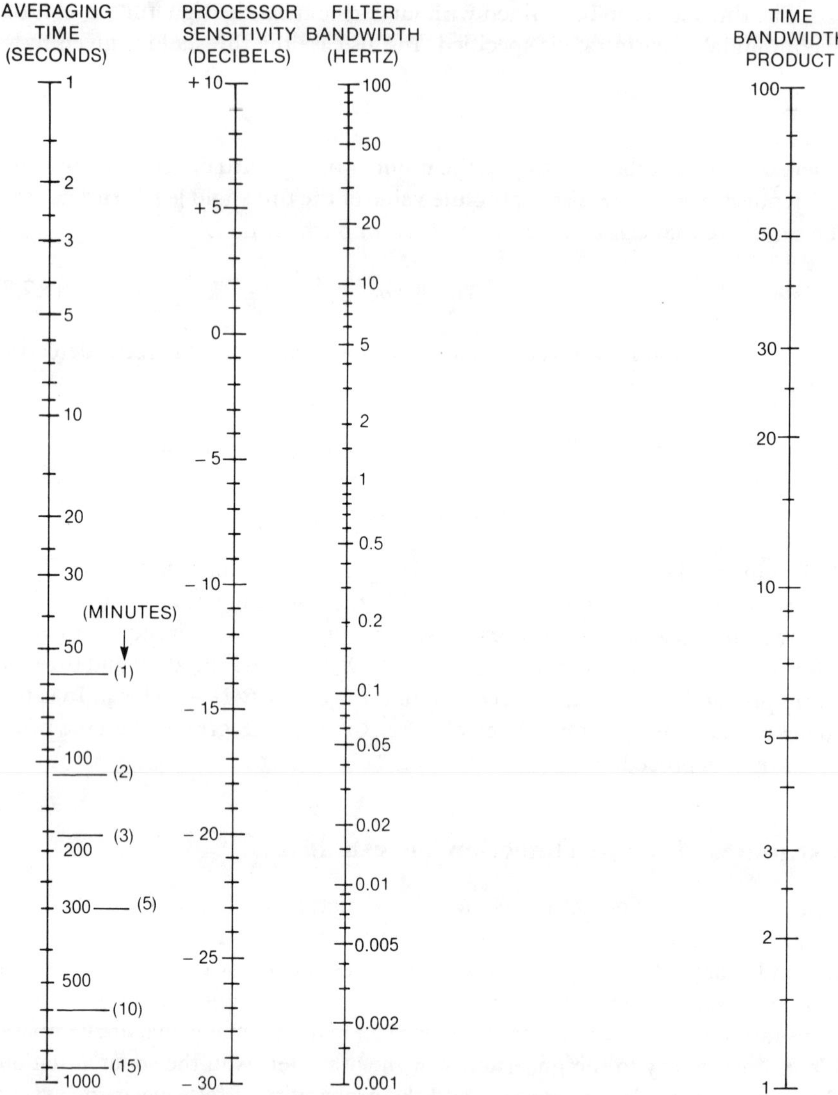

Figure A7–5. Nomograph for detecting processor sensitivity.

Source: C. Nicholas Pryor, *Calculation of the Minimum Detectable Signal for Practical Spectrum Analyzers* (Naval Ordnance Lab. Tech. Rept. 71–92, 1971).

The mechanism for this frequency spreading seems to be the interaction (through reflection or refraction) of sound with oceanic fluctuations such as surface waves and internal waves. A narrowband signal reflected off the moving surface will be Doppler shifted by the wave motion. There are up-Doppler and

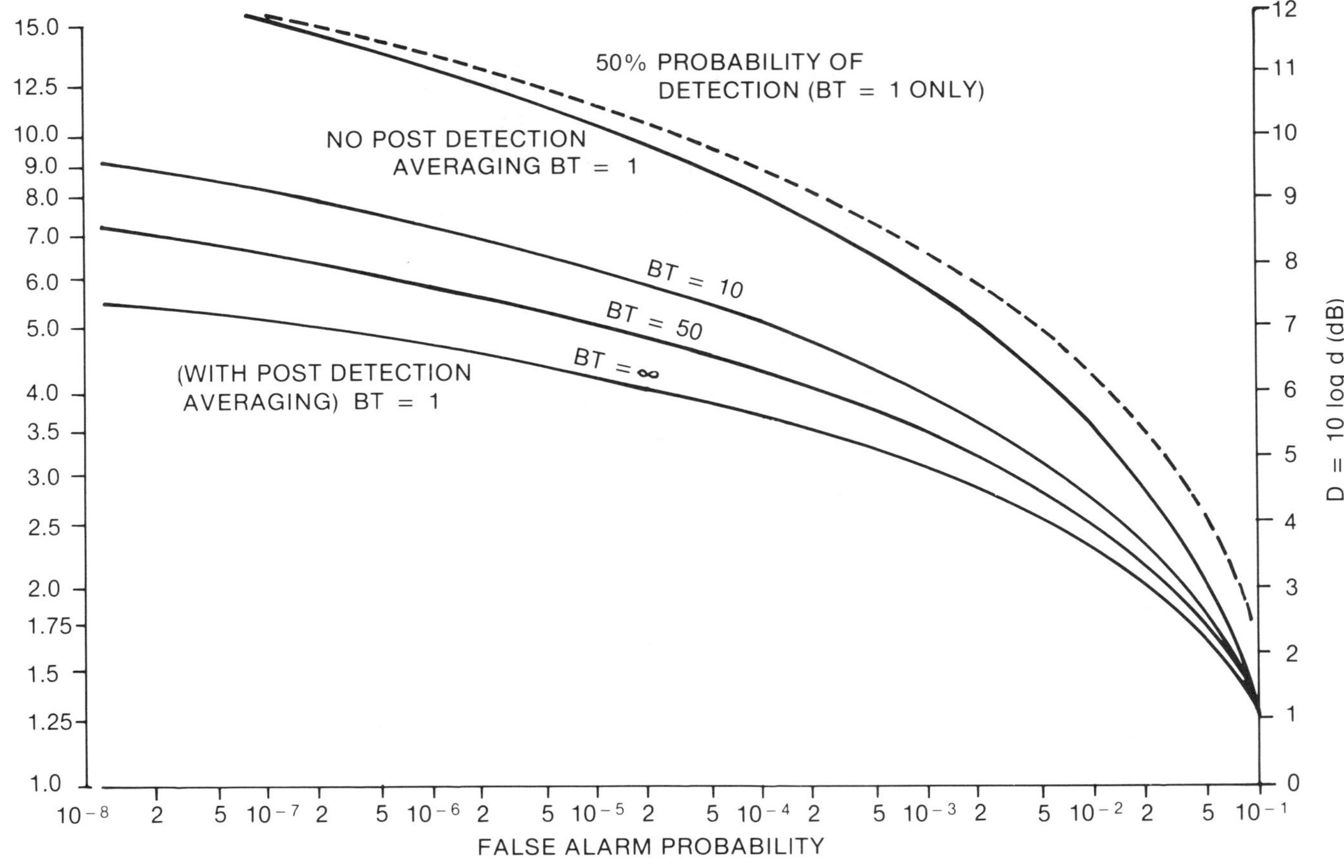

Figure A7–6. Threshold detector level versus false alarm probability.

Source: C. Nicholas Pryor, *Calculation of the Minimum Detectable Signal for Practical Spectrum Analyzers* (Naval Ord nance Lab. Tech. Rept. 71–92, 1971).

down-Doppler shifts that give rise to two sidebands around the center frequency. In the Arctic, frequency spreading effects may not be as severe, since the ice eliminates wave motion.

The shift from the center frequency is approximately equal to the peak in the surface wave spectrum, typically 0.3–0.1 Hz for low and high sea states, respectively. Direct measurements showed the spread to be always less than 1 Hz.[3] This type of spreading would tend to affect refracted surface-reflected sound. Transmissions that do not reflect off the surface are subject to smaller frequency spreading through interactions with lower-frequency fluctuations such as internal waves and currents. Typical bandwidths in the deep ocean are of the order of 0.01 Hz.[4] Currents can cause frequency shifts also; for example, a 0.5 knot current can shift 400 Hz sound by as much as 0.1 Hz when the current is different at the source and receiver.

The sensitivity of detection threshold to filter bandwidth can be seen in figures A7–5 and A7–6. For example, with a 60-second averaging time, if the bandwidth is reduced from 1 Hz to 0.1 Hz, the processor sensitivity is reduced by 5 dB. However, the concomitant decrease in the BT product from 60 to 6 drives the threshold detector level (figure A7–6) up about 1.5 dB, for a net decrease of 3.5 dB in the detection threshold for the same detection and false alarm probabilities.

Another limitation on narrowband processing is the degradation of array gain with increasing integration time. For example, an experiment with the Artemis horizontal receiving array in which a 550 Hz signal was detected at a range of 32.3 miles yielded a correlation length ($\rho = 0.50$) of 7,700 feet for 32 seconds integration time and 5,500 feet for 64 seconds integration time. At 1 Hz bandwidth, the 1.5 dB drop in detection threshold due to longer integration time was canceled by a 1.4 dB drop on the array gain.[5] In another experiment, the gain of a 920-foot array against ambient noise in the detection of a 367 Hz signal 700 miles away dropped from about 4 dB at 105 seconds to 1.4 dB at 840 seconds integration time.[6] The signals were processed in 2 Hz bands, and the 4.5 dB decrease in detection threshold is largely neutralized by a 2.6 dB decrease in array gain.

Still another effect is the wandering of the frequency line component at the source due to fluctuations in machinery speed and changes in the course/speed of the vessel. This has the effect of broadening the width of a line component.

The net effect of these interdependent constraints is to impose sharply diminishing returns to increasing frequency resolution and longer averaging times. The scant evidence available suggests that the minimum practical bandwidth is between 0.01 Hz (under favorable conditions) and 1 Hz. The averaging time appears to be limited to a very few minutes or less, with the lower bound being determined by the reciprocal of the bandwidth.

Experiments in the 800–1,600 Hz band suggest that processing gain—that term in the detection threshold model (equation A7.9) that lowers DT as

(5 log *T*)—is in fact virtually insensitive to increased averaging times between 0.5 and 120 seconds in the nonstationary noise that is characteristic of the ocean.[7] This would suggest that using the detection threshold model presented here overestimates the absolute magnitude of the detection threshold, that is, it overestimates sonar system capability in ocean noise.

Using an integration time of 1,000 seconds, which is longer than the typical 400-second long-term average used in modern sonars,[8] and a bandwidth of 0.05 Hz, which is very narrow, figure A7–5 gives a *BT* product of 50, which is reasonable for processor systems, and an "ideal" processor sensitivity of about -22 dB. A reasonable false alarm rate is 10^{-5},[9] so the threshold detector level, *D*, is about 7 dB. The "ideal" detection threshold is therefore about -15 dB. The adjustment of this figure for "real" effects such as nonideal filters raises this figure a few dB more,[10] although for this analysis I will not attempt to estimate this small correction.

The final large term in the estimate of detection threshold is the effect of the specified probability of detection. The parameter *d* is found in figure A7–6 as the threshold detector ratio, while d' approximately equals (p_{det} - 0.5) for p_{det} between 0.1 and 0.9. In order to see more clearly the effect of varying the probabilities of detection and false alarm, figure A7–7 was calculated based on a *BT* product of 50. It is clear that detection threshold is relatively insensitive to p_{fa} for values smaller than 10^{-4} and slightly more sensitive to p_{det} over ranges of that parameter from 0.1 to 0.9. For example, the increase in detection threshold due to increasing the probability of detection from 0.5 to 0.9 is 2 dB. The probability of detection is typically set at 0.5 and detection threshold calculated on that basis.

The model presented here is based on an entirely automated detection system that integrates all the information over the averaging time and makes a single threshold response. Actual sonar displays provide the operator with many responses, each of which may only be integrated over a few seconds, but each response is recorded on a visual display that provides a time history of the responses. An advantage of this method is that during periods when the signature fades and the signature-to-noise ratio drops, the visual display clearly indicates it, and when the signature comes back, it is visually apparent that it is caused by the same target. The long-term integration of these fades tends to result in poor processing gains for integration periods of tens to hundreds of seconds.[11] These visual displays make use of the powerful pattern recognition characteristics in humans to overcome the short-term variability of ambient noise and transmission. Using many short period integrations also helps avoid the deleterious effects of long-term signature incoherence on array gain. In return, there is a price to be paid by using these time history displays rather than integrating all the information electronically. However, a theoretical analysis has shown that the detection threshold is raised by only 2 dB when the display is used, a result that is also said to apply to human operators.[12] Therefore, the model described herein should be applicable to actual sonar systems.

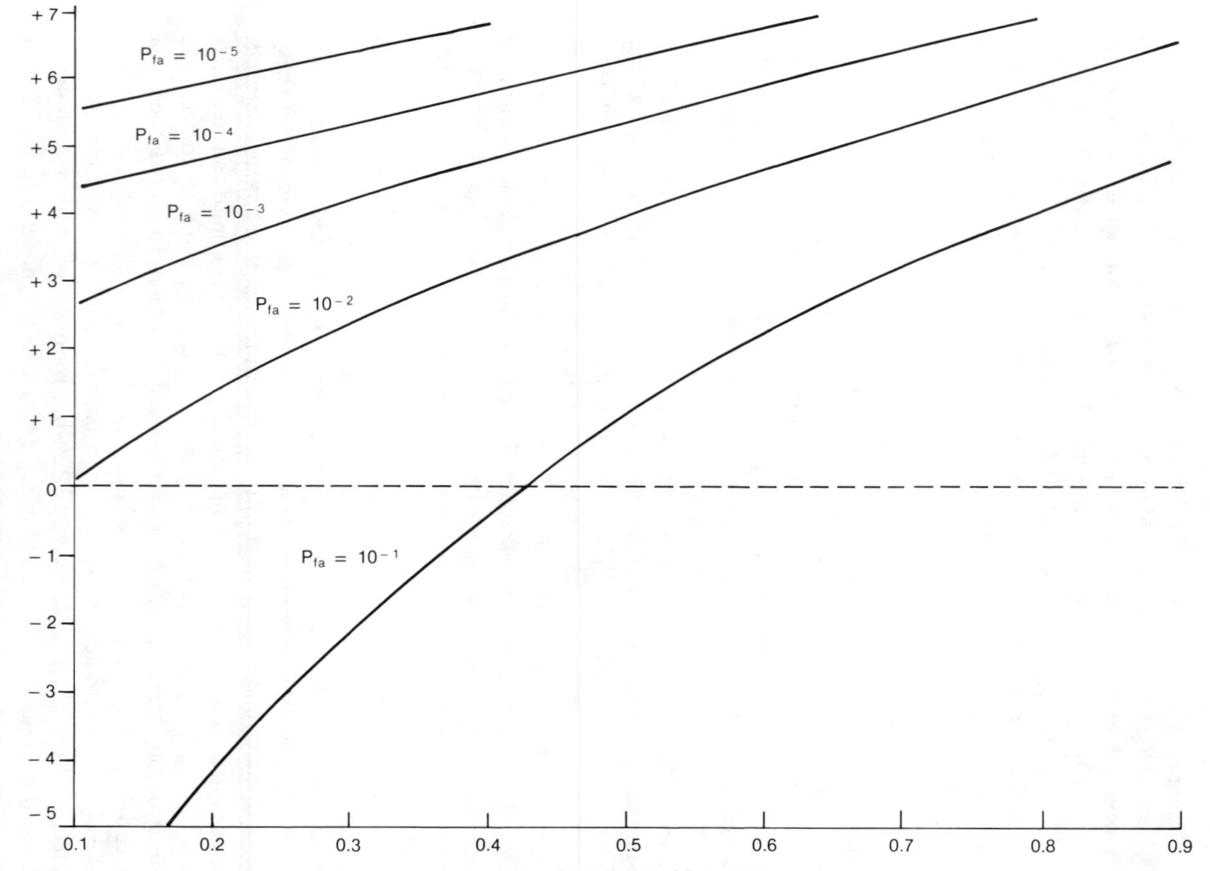

Figure A7–7. Adjustment to processor sensitivity for specific values of p_{det} and values of p_{fa} for *BT* of 50.

The maximum attainable detection threshold appears to be about –16 dB under favorable circumstances. In arriving at this estimate, several effects that would degrade processor performance by a few dB have been ignored, such as loss due to nonideal filters, to signal clipping, and to the display format. It is believed that the errors introduced by ignoring these factors is probably small in comparison to the uncertainties introduced by lack of knowledge of operator capabilities and peculiarities in the environment, such as non-Gaussian distribution of noise.

Detection Probability and Range to Target

The relationship between signal processing and sonar detection range is given by the passive sonar equation, with all quantities in decibels

$$(SL - NL + AG) - DT = TL \qquad \text{(A7.10)}$$

where

SL = source level
TL = transmission loss from source to the detecting sonar
NL = noise level
AG = array gain
DT = detection threshold

The detection threshold can be also defined as the minimum detectable signature-to-noise ratio in equation A7.9. If defined in this way the sonar equation can be interpreted as a sonar range equation. The quantity in parentheses in equation A7.10 is fixed for a given sonar system, target, and location. Transmission loss, however, increases with range. The allowable transmission loss, usually called the figure of merit, is the maximum allowable transmission loss for the assumed probabilities of detection and false alarm implied in the detection threshold.

Detection threshold (for a fixed p_{fa}) decreases with p_{det} according to figure A7-7. According to equation A7.10, the figure of merit (range) increases as the detection threshold (p_{det}) decreases. In other words, a given target can be detected at longer range but with a lower probability of detection. Thus the concept of range itself is a probabilistic notion. Take for example, a loud source generating 160 dB (re 1 micropascal at 1 yd per Hz) of low-frequency sound in the North Pacific. If the noise level is 80 dB and the array gain 15 dB, then a detection threshold of –15 dB should permit that sound to be detected at 380 miles 50 percent of the time, with a p_{fa} of 10^{-5}. If the target is to be detected 90 percent of the time, the detection threshold increases to –13 dB, and the detection range drops 55 miles to 325 miles.[13]

Notes

1. In practice, the processing is not done exactly this way, since it requires such a large number of filters. For analytical purposes, however, figure A7–2 is a sufficiently accurate model.

2. G. Nicholas Pryor, "Calculation of the Minimum Detectable Signal for Practical Spectrum Analyzers" (Silver Spring, Md: Naval Ordnance Laboratory, now Naval Surface Weapons Center), NOLTR 71-92, 1972; Richard B. Gilchrist, "Practical Limits of Time Processing," in *Signal Processing,* Proceedings of the NATO Advanced Study Institute (London: Academic Press, 1973), pp. 357–362.

3. William I. Roderick and Benjamin F. Cron, "Frequency Spectra of Forward Scattered Sound from the Ocean Surface," *Journal of the Acoustical Society of America* 48:3, 1970, pp. 759–766.

4. Arthur B. Baggeroer, "Sonar Signal Processing," in *Applications of Digital Signal Processing,* ed. A. V. Oppenheim (New York: Prentice-Hall, 1978), p. 350.

5. Data from Robert J. Urick, personal communication.

6. Bowen E. Parkins and George R. Fox, "Measurement of the Coherence and Fading of Long Range Acoustic Signals," *IEEE Transactions on Audio and Electroacoustics* AU-19:2, June 1971.

7. W. S. Hodgkiss and V. C. Anderson, "Detection of Sinusoids in Ocean Acoustic Background Noise," *JASA* 67:1, January 1980, pp. 214–219.

8. R. B. Delisle and J. T. Kroenert, "An Analytical Model for the Detection Performance of Multiple Channel Time History Display Formats," *JASA* 73:6, June 1983, pp. 2065–2070.

9. Ibid.

10. Pryor, "Calculation of Minimum Detectable Signal," and Gilchrist, "Practical Limits."

11. Hodgkiss and Anderson, "Detection of Sinusoids."

12. Delisle and Kroenert, "An Analytical Model."

13. Figure A8–21 is used to demonstrate the relationship between range and transmission loss in the example.

Appendix 8
Submarine Detection in the Arctic Ocean and Northern Seas

The ocean areas north of the Arctic Circle are strategically important because they are the most secure deployment areas for Soviet ballistic missile submarines. The southern part of the continental United States is about 4,200 nautical miles (nm) from the Barents Sea (see figure A8–1). This means that almost the entire continental United States is within range of Soviet Delta class submarines operating in the Soviet Arctic. The largest body of water in this region is the Arctic Ocean. Adjacent to the Arctic are several smaller seas, including the Barents and Kara seas off the northwestern coast of the USSR; the Chukchi, Beaufort, Lincoln, and Greenland seas off North America; and the Norwegian Sea off the Scandinavian peninsula (figure A8–2). I will refer generally to the seas north of the Greenland-Iceland-United Kingdom gap as "the Arctic," whereas the Arctic Ocean itself is called by that name.

Climate and Oceanography

The northern USSR near the Barents Sea is above the Arctic Circle, but the climate is moderated by the warm coastal North Cape current, which hugs the coast of Norway and the Kola peninsula and is one of the northernmost termini of the Gulf Stream. The yearly average temperature is approximately freezing, and the precipitation reaches 54 centimeters in the Kola region.[1] Most of the days are completely overcast, and at Murmansk, high winds (and therefore very low wind-chill temperatures) are common.

Wind is an important environmental factor in naval operations because of direct effects on surface ships and aircraft, as well as indirect effects such as wave generation and underwater ambient noise. Coupled with low temperatures, it can cause ice to form on ships' superstructures. Carrier operations can be inhibited or halted, as they were during a major exercise in the North Pacific during 1983. Wind speeds from 50 to 70 knots completely prevented flights from small deck carriers and limited operations from even the USS *Enterprise*.[2] In the shallow Barents Sea, local ambient acoustic conditions are often dominated by wind-generated noise.

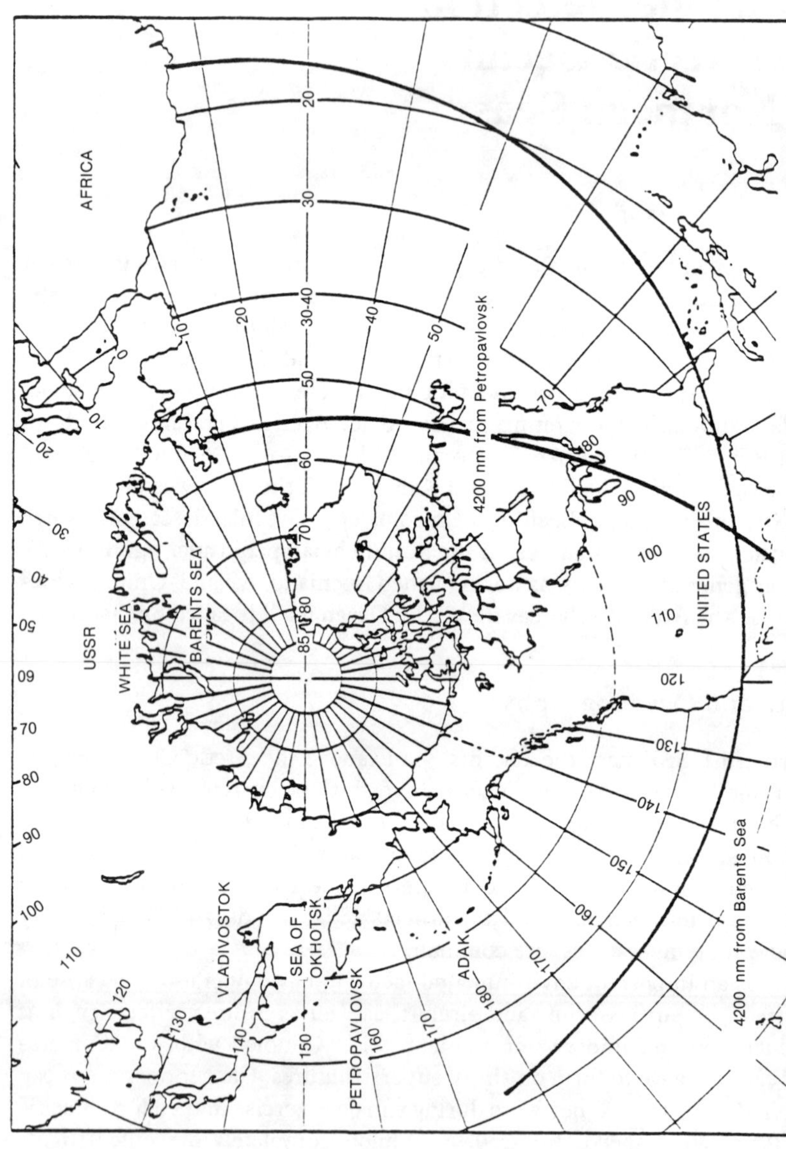

Figure A8–1. Maximum coverage of 4,200-nm-range submarine-launched missiles fired from Soviet SSBN deployment areas.

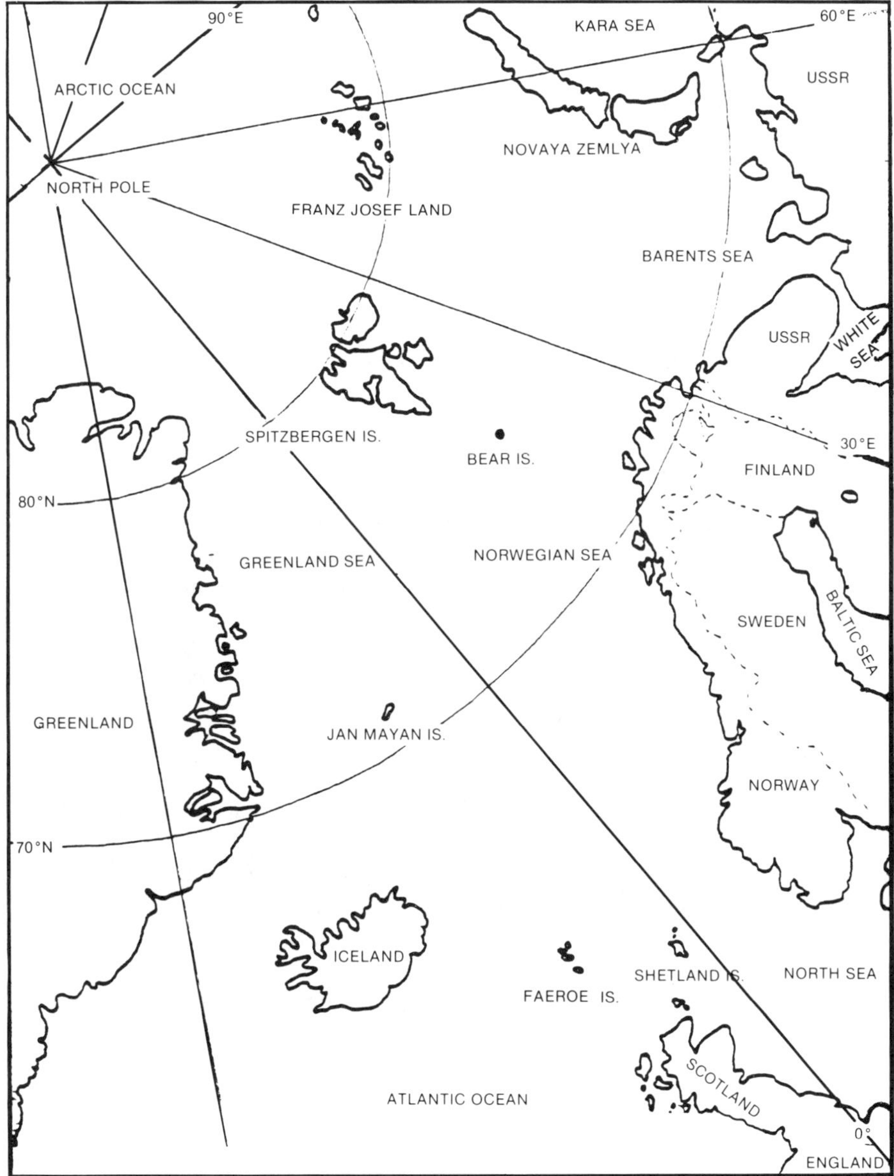

Figure A8–2. Location map of the Eurasian Arctic and adjoining seas.

Tables A8–1 and A8–2 give the percentage of time winds have been observed at various velocities. Data is available for most of the Arctic based on many observations over many years. The seas in the vicinity of the GIUK gap have some of the highest average winds of any place in the entire Arctic region.

Cloud cover restricts photographic and infrared surveillance, especially from satellites, and is therefore an important meteorological variable in non-acoustic ASW. The sky cover is reported in terms of the percentage of sky that is covered by clouds at any altitude. Tables A8–3 and A8–4 give the percentage of time that various amounts of cloud cover are observed. During the summer over the waters of the GIUK gap, for instance, the sky is almost completely covered 80 percent of the time.[3] Precipitation data is given as the percentage of all observations that report precipitation in any form, and then the percentage of precipitation observations that report snow.

Ocean Circulation and Water Characteristics

The mean circulation of the Arctic Ocean surface water is characterized by slow westward drift, forming a clockwise gyre (*see* figures A8–3, A4–5). The surface currents averaged over a year range from 1 nm/day near the northern coast of Alaska to 2 nm/day near the Barents and Greenland seas. Over short periods of time, however, these surface currents are extremely variable. Major inflows to the Arctic Ocean are from the Greenland and Norwegian seas (83 percent of the total) and the Bering Strait (16 percent of the total). Major outflows are the East Greenland current (76 percent) and via the Canadian archipelago (23 percent).[4]

The Kara and Barents seas exhibit a general counterclockwise circulation. Since there is a large amount of river runoff entering these marginal seas, the coastal currents can be expected to vary according to the volume rate of runoff, which is highest during the spring thaw. In the Barents Sea, relatively warm, saline Atlantic water intrudes upon the colder, less saline Arctic water and instead of mixing homogeneously, forms a complex irregular density structure,[5] which may complicate the local sound transmission characteristics. Occasionally, strong winds may modify the currents for short periods of time and intermix the water to a considerable depth. In the central regions of the Barents Sea the currents are weak and variable.[6]

The Norwegian and Greenland seas exhibit counterclockwise circulation, with strong permanent currents at the boundaries—typically 0.5–0.9 knots—and weak variable ones in the central regions.[7]

The subsurface currents in the Arctic Ocean are somewhat different from the surface currents there. The water found at depths greater than 600 feet flows in from the Greenland Sea, follows a counterclockwise route around the North Pole (the opposite of the surface current), and merges with a clockwise gyre in the Beaufort Sea north of Alaska. There is very little information on subsurface currents in the Barents and Kara seas. Wind and the complex bathymetry may result in local variations of the general circulation pattern there.

Table A8–1
Arctic wind speed percentage distribution, winter (February)

	Wind Speed (knots)				
Area	*0–3*	*4–10*	*11–16*	*17–27*	*>28*
Kara Sea	17	41	22	17	3
North Barents Sea	14	40	5	21	20
South Barents Sea	6	24	21	29	20
Arctic Ocean	3	45	22	20	10
Greenland Sea	8	22	15	28	27
Norwegian Sea	3	19	16	34	28

Source: Oceanographic Atlas of the Polar Seas, part 2, *Arctic* (NAVOCEANO pub. no. 705, 1970).

Table A8–2
Arctic wind speed percentage distribution, summer (August)

	Wind Speed (knots)				
Area	*0–3*	*4–10*	*11–16*	*17–27*	*>28*
Kara Sea	20	43	19	16	2
North Barents Sea	23	32	19	18	8
South Barents Sea	20	43	18	19	2
Arctic Ocean[a]	13	57	25	5	0
Greenland Sea	14	36	13	24	11
Norwegian Sea	11	29	20	27	13

Source: Oceanographic Atlas of the Polar Seas, part 2, *Arctic* (NAVOCEANO pub. no. 705, 1970).
[a]Data on the central Arctic are relatively sparse.

Table A8–3
Percentage occurrence of Arctic cloudiness and precipitation, winter (January)

	Cloud Cover (percentage)				
	Clear	*0–25*	*25–50*	*50–75*	*75–100*
Barents Sea:	5	5	6	23	61
Precipitation occurs 30 percent of the time. Of this, 80–90 percent is snow.					
Norwegian-Greenland Sea:	4	7	9	18	62
In the Greenland-Iceland-United Kingdom area, precipitation occurs 25 percent of the time. Of this, 20 percent is snow near the United Kingdom and 80 percent is snow near Greenland.					

Source: Oceanographic Atlas of the Polar Seas, part 2, *Arctic* (NAVOCEANO pub. no. 705, 1970).

Table A8–4
Percentage occurrence of Arctic cloudiness and precipitation, summer (July)

	Cloud Cover (percentage)				
	Clear	*0–25*	*25–50*	*50–75*	*75–100*
Barents Sea:	4	8	10	18	60
Precipitation occurs 20 percent of the time. All of this is rain. Sky is at least 25 percent cloudy 8 days out of 10.					
Norwegian-Greenland Sea:	2	3	4	10	81
Precipitation occurs 20 percent of the time. All of this is rain. Sky is at least 25 percent cloudy 9 days out of 10.					

Source: Oceanographic Atlas of the Polar Seas, part 2, *Arctic* (NAVOCEANO pub. no. 705, 1970).

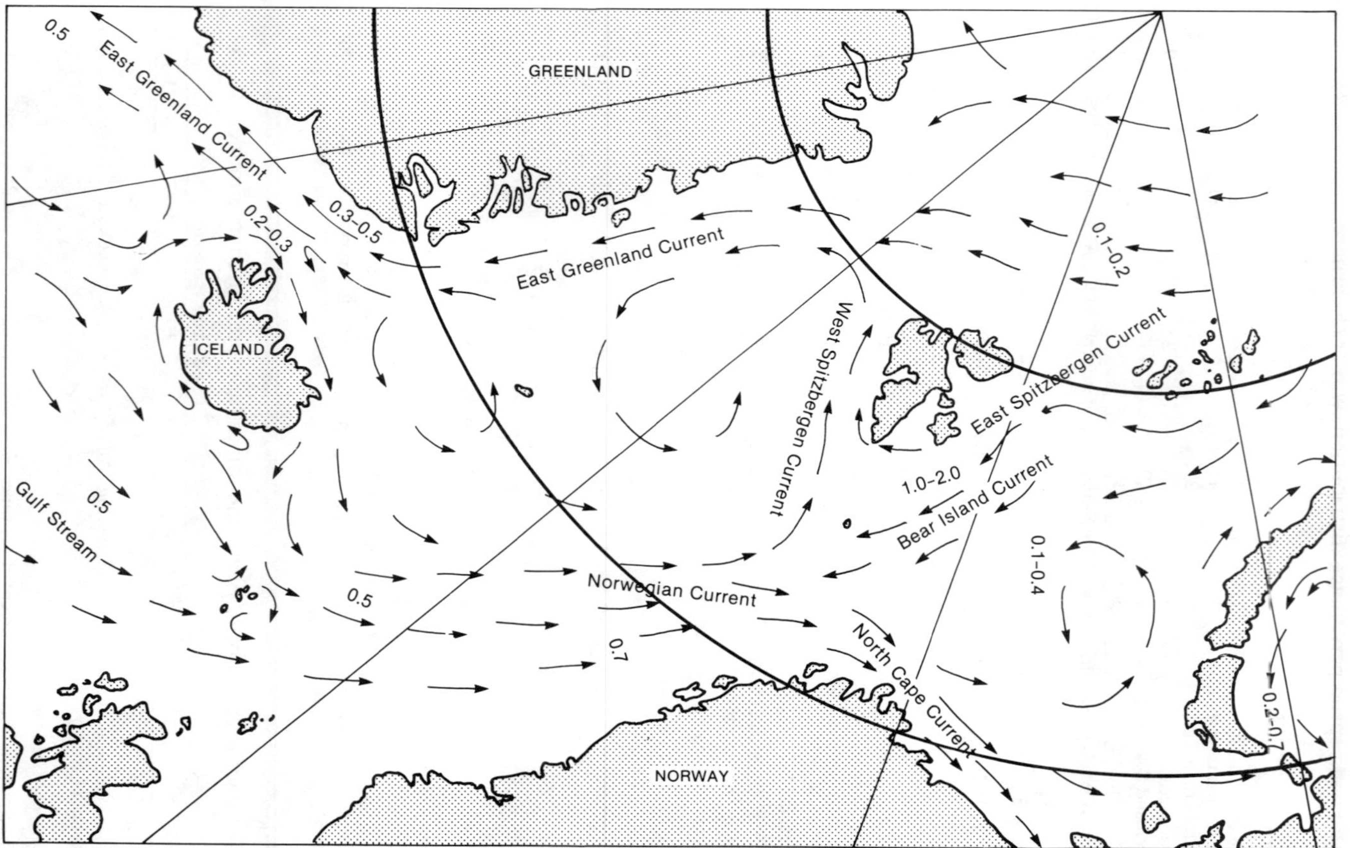

Figure A8–3. Average surface currents in the Norwegian, Greenland, and Barents seas.

Source: Surface Currents: Norwegian and Barents Seas (NAVOCEANO, 1978); *Oceanographic Atlas of the Polar Seas,* part 2, *Arctic* (NAVOCEANO pub. no. 705, 1970).

From October through June the temperature pattern in the Barents and Norwegian seas—figures A8–4 and A8–5—is strongly marked by a tongue of warm Gulf Stream water along the Norwegian coast, resulting in year-round temperatures of at least 42 degrees Fahrenheit off the North Cape of Norway and above freezing off the Kola peninsula. This is responsible for the ice-free conditions at the main Soviet naval complexes near Murmansk.

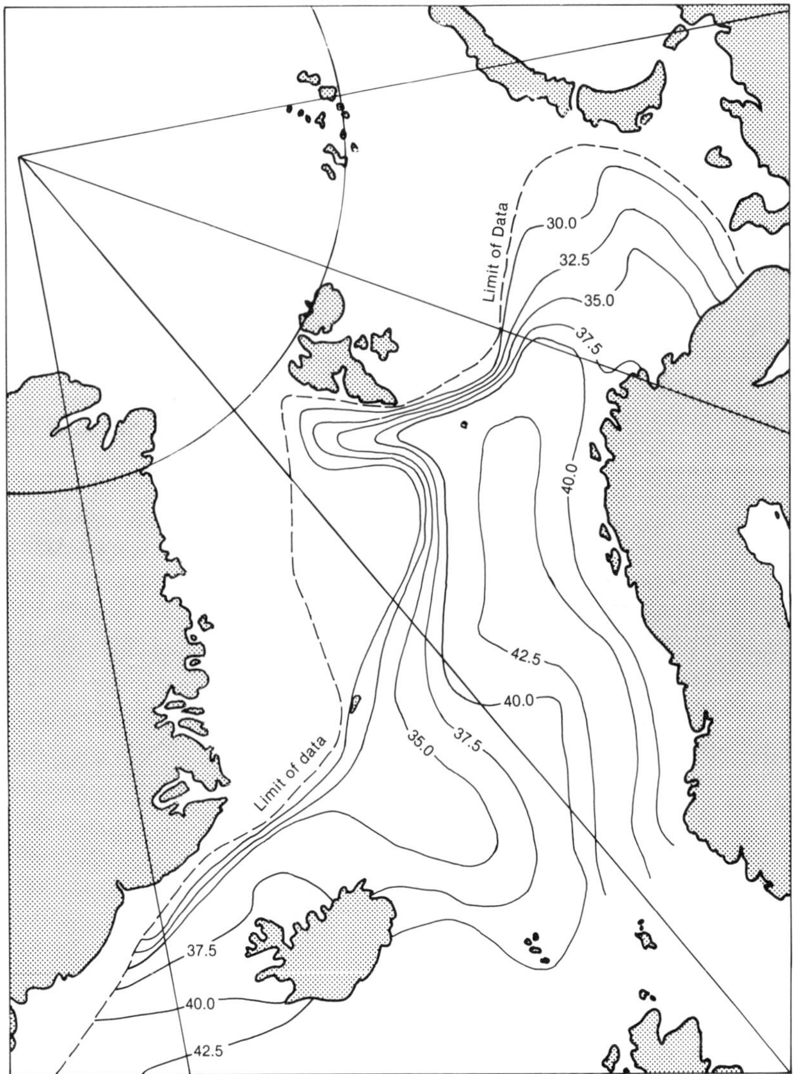

Figure A8–4. Surface water temperature in the Norwegian, Greenland, and Barents seas, degrees Fahrenheit: Winter.

Source: Oceanographic Atlas of the Polar Seas, part 2, *Arctic* (NAVOCEANO pub. no. 705, 1970).

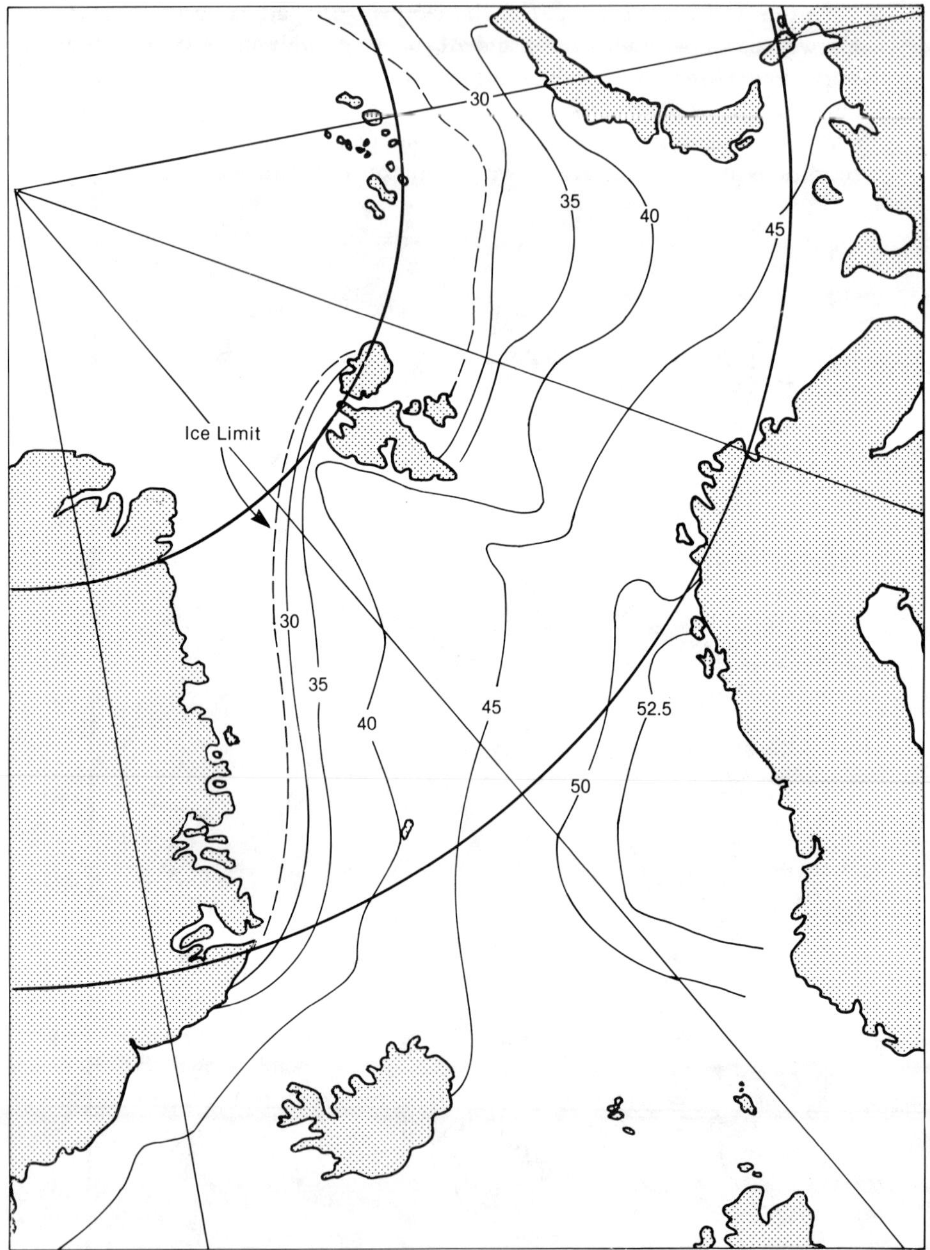

Figure A8-5. Surface water temperature in the Norwegian, Greenland, and Barents seas, degrees Fahrenheit: Summer.

Source: Oceanographic Atlas of the Polar Seas, part 2, *Arctic* (NAVOCEANO pub. no. 705, 1970).

Salinity is the weight percent of salt dissolved in the ocean. The warm Atlantic water is relatively saline, 35 parts per thousand, while the marginal seas adjoining the USSR are typically 34 ppt at the surface, and may drop to 32 ppt nearer the coast because of the large amount of fresh water inflow from river runoff. At greater depths there is much less variation in salinity, and the average throughout the Barents Sea is about 34.5 ppt at 300 feet. Variations in salinity of this magnitude do not have an appreciable effect on sonar and sound transmission properties, but salinity variations near the coasts may be important.

The vertical density structure in the Barents and northern Norwegian seas is of interest because the characteristics of the internal wave field are governed by it. Of particular interest is that submarine detection schemes using internal wave phenomena have been discussed in the US and Soviet literature. Typical density gradients in the summertime (August, September) Barents Sea are 0.002 grams/cm^3/50 meters in the upper 50 meters, below which density is virtually constant. In the northern Norwegian Sea between Norway and Spitzbergen, gradients are less than half the Barents Sea values. Typical density values are 1.027 gm/cm^3.[8] In the shallow Kara Sea (300–600 feet deep), gradients may exceed 0.014 gm/cm^3/50 meters.[9]

Another physical property of interest in submarine communications and nonacoustic detection technology is the transparency of the water. The standard measure is the depth at which a 30 cm white (Secchi) disk disappears from view. In the White Sea, this depth is 15–30 feet; in the southern Barents Sea, 30–60 feet; in the northern Barents, 60–90 feet; and in the Norwegian Sea, 30–60 feet.[10] In general, waters closer to the coast tend to be more opaque than waters farther out to sea.

Ice

Figures A8–6 and A8–7 are maps of ice showing the area of essentially solid ice in the central Arctic. The lines marked 0.5 and 0.1 are the lines of 50 percent and 10 percent coverage, respectively. It is important to note that these maps are based on the averages of many years' observations, and that the ice distribution in any given year may deviate greatly from the average.

The blanket of ice that covers the Arctic Ocean and its adjacent seas varies considerably in extent from season to season and from year to year. The polar ice cap is not a solid sheet; stretches of open water called polynyas are present throughout the ice pack in all seasons, though in the summer these areas of open water can occupy up to 20 percent of the surface area.

There are two basic kinds of ice: pack ice, which has accumulated over many years, and winter or annual ice, which is formed over a single winter season.[11] Pack ice tends to be more rough on its upper and lower surfaces than annual ice and has different acoustic properties. The average thickness of polar ice in the Arctic is normally about 10–13 feet by the end of winter, decreasing to

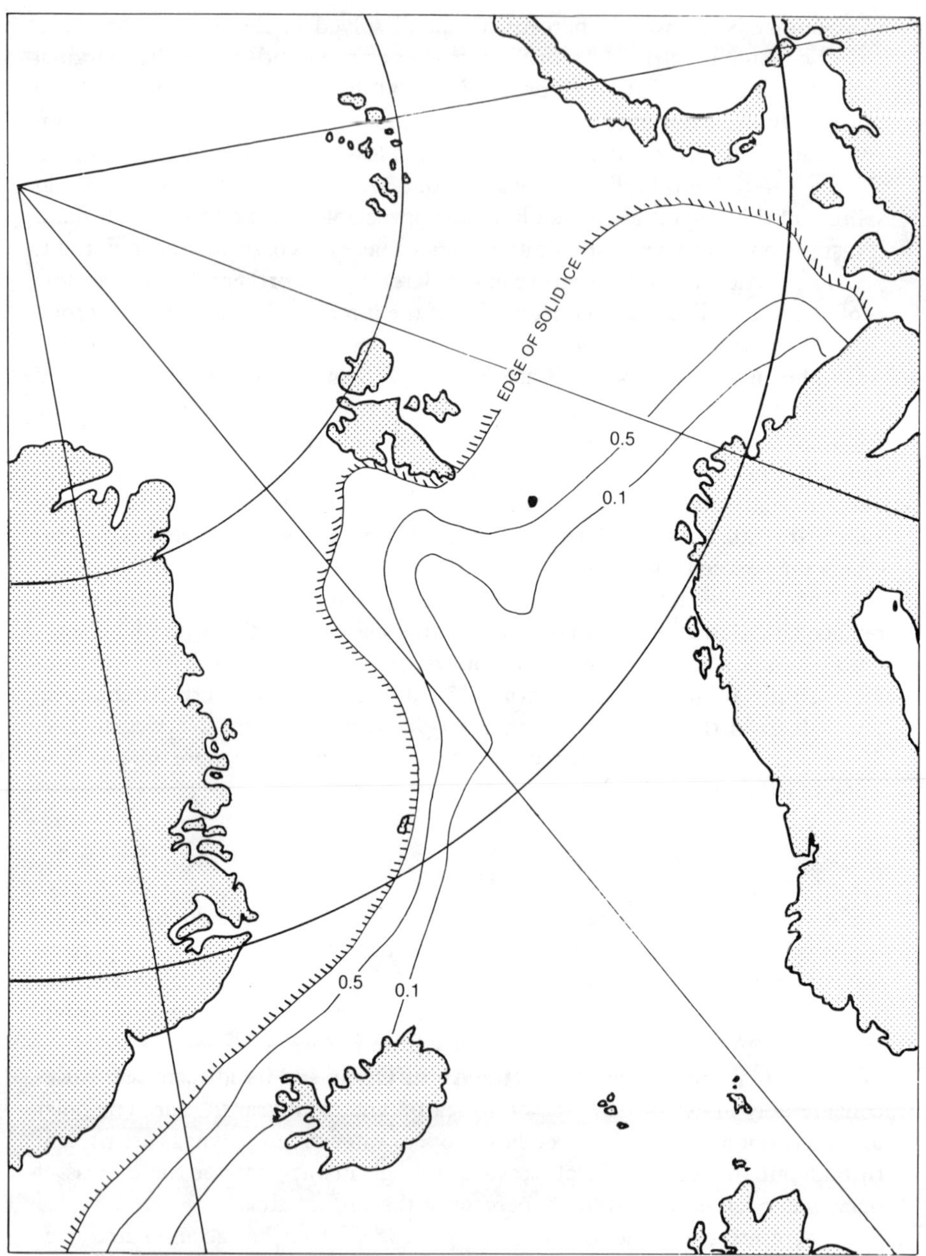

Figure A8–6. Arctic ice concentration and extent: Winter.

Source: Oceanographic Atlas of the Polar Seas, part 2, *Arctic* (NAVOCEANO pub. no. 705, 1970).

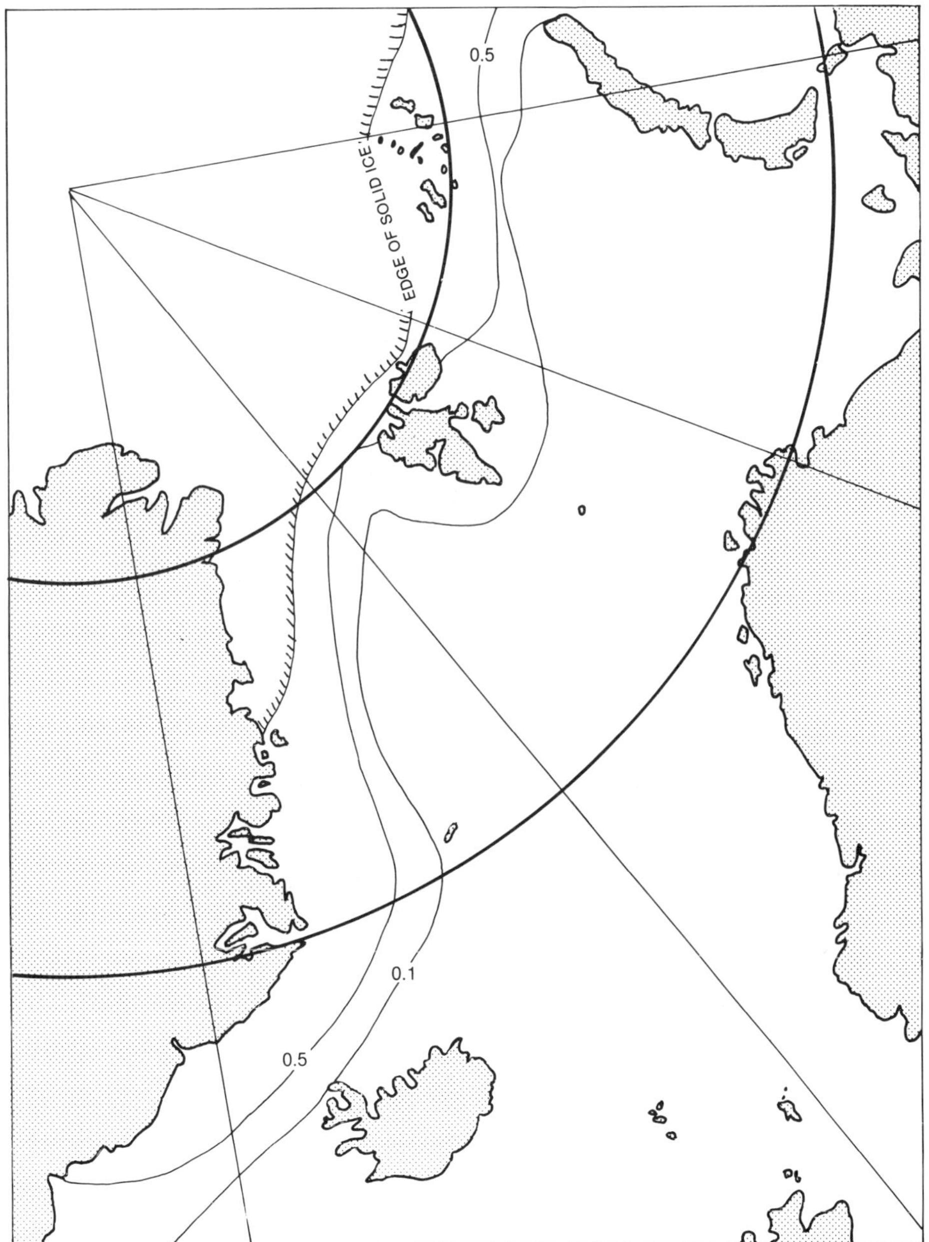

Figure A8–7. Arctic ice concentration and extent: Summer.

Source: Oceanographic Atlas of the Polar Seas, part 2, *Arctic* (NAVOCEANO pub. no. 705, 1970).

about 6–10 feet by the end of summer.[12] The ice does not usually cover the entire surface, even in winter, and polynyas are almost always present, though in the winter they may contain relatively thin annual ice. Typical maximum annual ice thicknesses are 6–8 feet. The ice surface underwater may be fairly smooth or very irregular, depending upon the degree of ridge formation due to winds and distant storms. During both winter and summer, underwater ice ridges may reach depths of 40–60 feet, and in places may exceed 100 feet.[13]

Most of the data on the statistical distribution of ice leads or polynyas is obtained from upward-looking sonars on submarines. One such study in the western Eurasian basin, north of Greenland,[14] found that in October leads covered 1–5 percent of the surface. In the marginal sea ice zone and in the zone immediately north of Greenland, 10–20 percent of the surface was occupied by leads. The average distance between polynyas in the M'Clure Strait and the Beaufort Sea shelf north of Alaska was measured in the summer and winter by two US submarines.[15] Polynyas 100 meters wide were encountered along the submarines' tracks every 2 kilometers in summer and every 15 kilometers in winter. Polynyas 200 meters wide (wide enough for a submarine to surface in) were encountered every 4 kilometers in summer and every 25 kilometers in winter. Thus a submarine traveling at a speed of 5 knots would encounter a polynya that was large enough to surface in once every three hours, on the average.

The Soviet marginal sea ice contains many openings throughout the year. From satellite imagery, it was determined that during the autumn and winter, "large areas of low ice concentrations, as low as 70 percent, occurred in the Chukchi, East Siberian, Bering, Laptev, and Kara Seas."[16] These areas would provide ample opportunities to use submarine communication systems, or to break through the ice in order to launch weapons.

The Norwegian and North Cape currents keep the coasts of Norway and the Kola peninsula free of ice in all months, except for the ice formed in some of the fjords. Ice is probably no hindrance to navigation within about 400 nm of the western Norwegian coast and 150 nm of the northern Norwegian coast during the winter.[17]

In the Barents Sea the ice reaches its greatest southern extent in March and April. Rapid melting takes place from May to August, after which the process rapidly reverses and freezing begins again. In winter the bays and gulfs of the eastern Barents Sea become icebound, and deeper portions of the sea are partially covered with drift ice, but it never freezes over completely.[18]

Freezing in the White Sea probably starts as early as October in the deep bays, such as at Archangel, and usually forms a continuous strip of ice along all the coasts by December. The White Sea drift ice reaches its greatest concentration in February and March. At Archangel there is solid or broken ice from early November to early May.[19] A 160-mile-long path from Severodvinsk and Archangel through the White Sea to the Barents Sea must be kept open with icebreakers for at least three months per year.

Although the Barents Sea is navigable year round, the combination of high winds, high seas, and low temperatures can cause severe ice accumulation on ships' decks and superstructures. Ice formation on the decks of surface ships is caused by the rapid freezing of sea spray, which can accumulate at a rate of over 2 tons an hour. Superstructure icing has been responsible for sinking 170-foot trawlers.[20] During February the probability of encountering some superstructure icing in the central Barents Sea is over 50 percent, and the probability of heavy icing is about 10 percent. Icing is somewhat less likely in the Norwegian Sea during this period.[21] Superstructure icing can impede the operation of surface ships, particularly frigates and smaller vessels.

General Bathymetry

The central Arctic Ocean (figure A8–8) is a basin about 12,000 feet deep. The basin is divided in half by the 6,000-foot-high Lomonosov ridge running from the Laptev Sea to Greenland. Submarine operations in the central Arctic Ocean are therefore unrestricted from below, as they are in the marginal seas. Moving from the North Pole toward the USSR, the bottom slopes upward very suddenly just north of Franz Josef Land to a broad continental margin with an average depth of about 800 feet. Bathymetry of the White Sea is shown in figure A8–9.

The sea floor to the west of the Barents Sea drops off into the basin of the Greenland and Norwegian seas between Spitzbergen, Bear Island, and Norway. The depth in the basin between Greenland, Iceland, Scandinavia, and Spitzbergen is about 9,000 feet.

There is an underwater ridge from Greenland to Iceland and from Iceland to the Faeroe Islands, which is a natural barrier to currents and underwater sound passing between the North Atlantic Ocean and the Norwegian and Greenland seas. Figures A8–10 and A8–11 show a cross section of the bottom in this area, along with winter and summer temperatures over depth. The shallow water restricts submarine operations over part of the GIUK gap. Of course this ridge provides the ideal setting for SOSUS arrays, since it intersects the axis of the deep sound channel.

Whales

The number of large whales (longer than 40 feet) in the Arctic, or anywhere in the world, is not very well known. Much of the data is from ship sightings, and therefore a bias enters the data since more sightings are taken in well-traveled shipping lanes. The number of whale catches is an important source of data, but again the observations tend to take place where the ships go. Another bias is introduced by the fact that whale counts depend very much on the whales' behavior, which is not well known. A typical counting problem is trying to determine if the whale sighted four times is the same one or four different ones

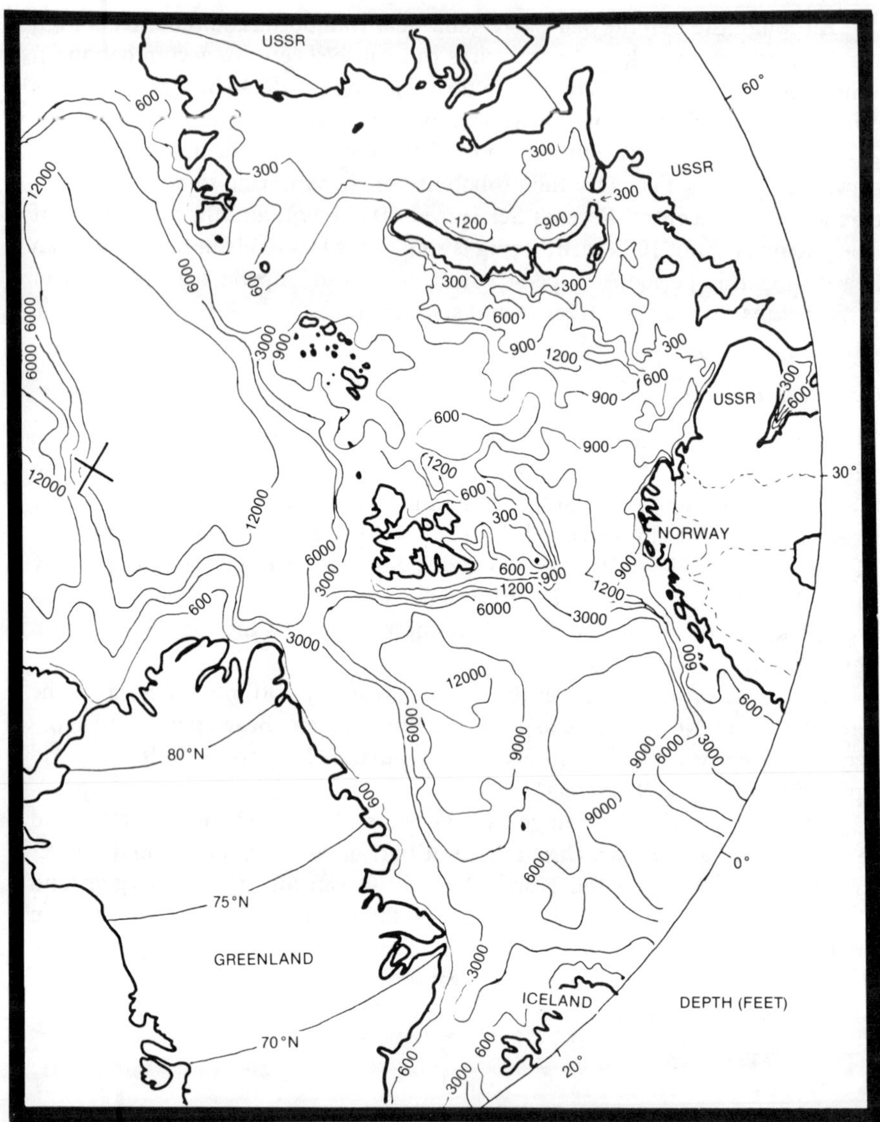

Figure A8–8. General bathymetry in the Eurasian Arctic and adjoining seas.

Source: Oceanographic Atlas of the Polar Seas, part 2, *Arctic* (NAVOCEANO pub. no. 705, 1970).

each surfacing once. Table A8–5 gives some rough estimates of numbers of whales per thousand square miles in various Arctic areas. The lengths of certain large species are also given.

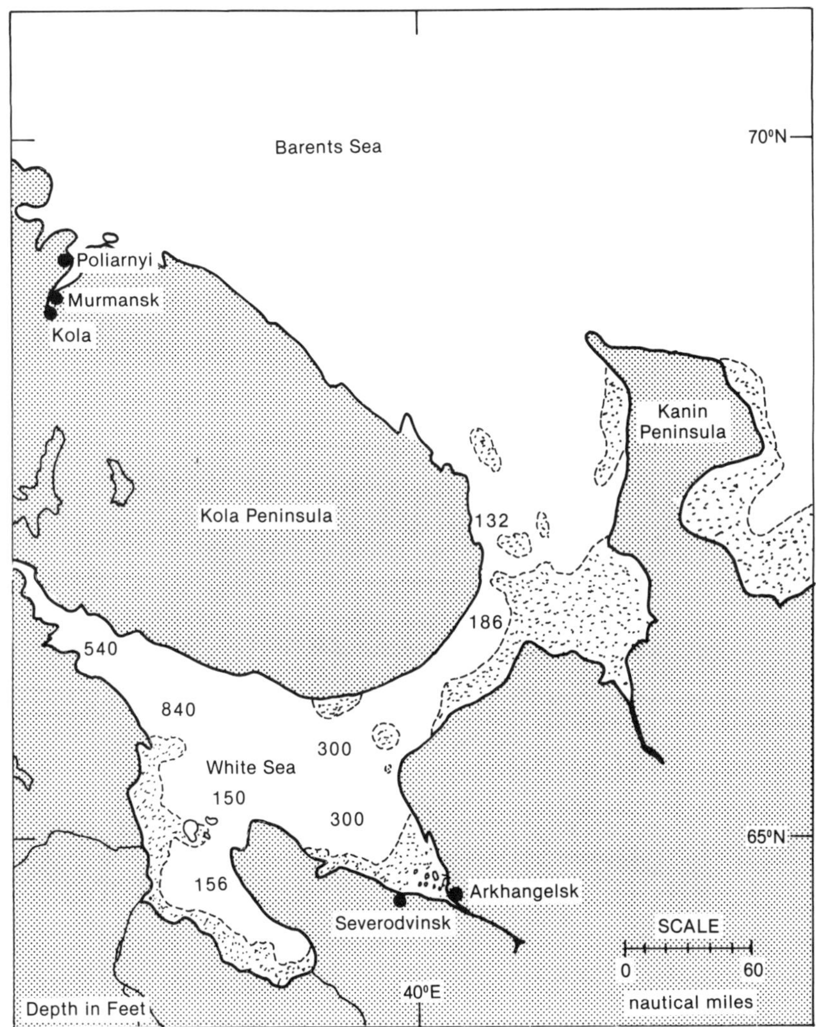

Figure A8-9. Bathymetry of the White Sea.

Note: Shaded areas are less than 60 feet deep.

Data on the presence of whales longer than 40 feet in the Arctic and adjacent seas is limited to the areas free of ice. In general, the largest concentration of whales is in the warm currents off Norway. Between March and August there are over 20 large whales per 1,000 square nautical miles there. In addition, there is a relatively large number of whales in the waters of the GIUK gap. Typical numbers in the North Atlantic range from 6 to 20 whales per 1,000

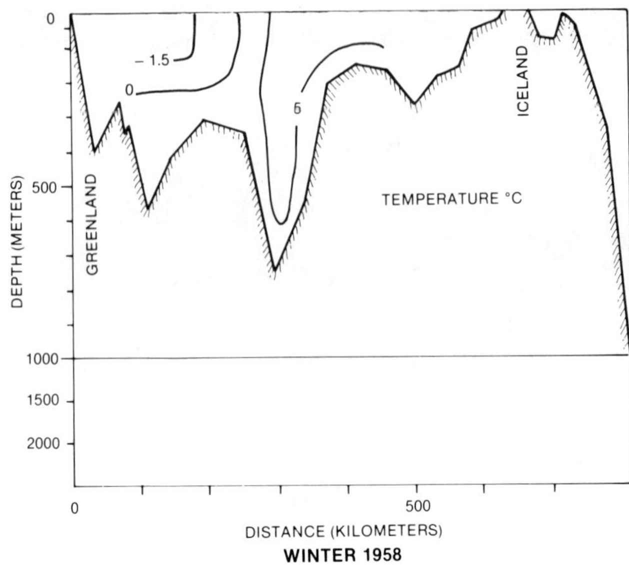

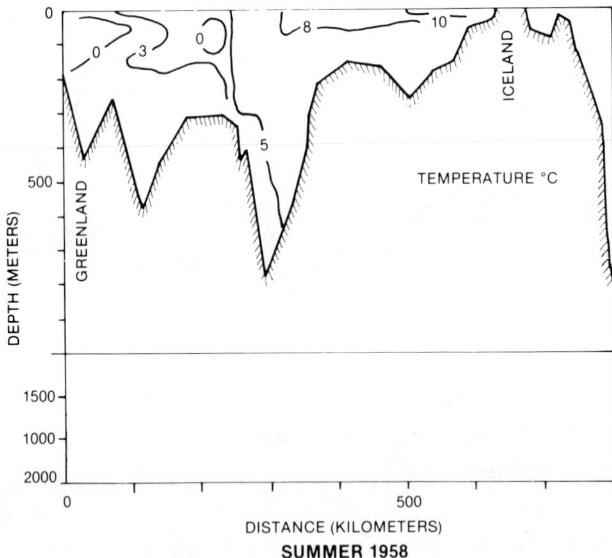

Figure A8–10. Cross section of bathymetry and temperature from Greenland to Iceland: Summer and Winter.

Source: Atlas of the Hydrography of the Northern North Atlantic Ocean, compiled by G. Dietrich, Conseil International pour l'Exploration de la Mer, Service Hydrographique, Denmark, 1969.

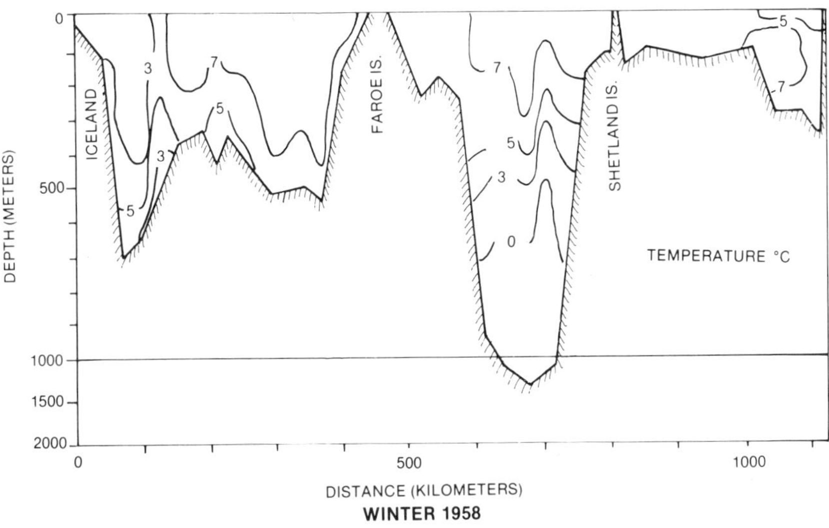

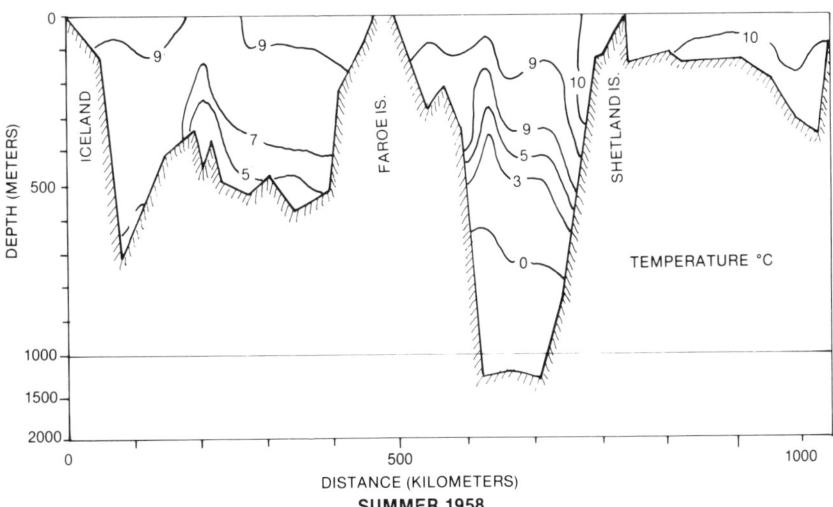

Figure A8-11. Cross section of bathymetry and temperature from Iceland to the Shetland Islands: Summer and Winter.

Source: Atlas of the Hydrography of the Northern North Atlantic Ocean, compiled by G. Dietrich, Conseil International pour l'Exploration de la Mer, Service Hydrographique, Denmark, 1969.

nm², with densities of up to 36 per 1,000 nm² reported off Nova Scotia.[22] It is interesting to note that many of the areas near the Soviet Union in which Soviet

Table A8–5
Population density of large whales in the Arctic
(per 1,000 nm²)

	December	*June*
Kara Sea	<1	3
South Barents and Norwegian Seas	9	24
Greenland Sea	<1	10
Large Whales	Size (feet)	
Sperm	44–50	
Fin	58–60	
Sei	39–40	
Blue	65–77	
Humpback	33–44	
Northern black right	50	
Black right	50	
Greenland right	50	

Sources: Oceanographic Atlas of the Polar Seas, part 2, *Arctic* (NAVOCEANO pub. no. 705, 1970); N. A. Mackintosh, *The Stocks of Whales* (Bath, England: Coward and Garrish, Ltd., 1965).

missile submarines patrol or in which US attack submarines operate also happen to be relatively active whaling grounds.[23]

Acoustic Oceanography of the Arctic Ocean and Adjacent Seas

Ambient Noise

Because ambient noise level is a function of random meteorological variables, it is itself a random variable. The scarcity and uncertainty of the available data does not justify an overly precise analysis, however, and in order to make some estimates, I have adopted the approach of calculating upper and lower bounds on detection capability. In the context of submarine detection, ambient noise degrades the capability of a given system, so it is assumed here that the noise levels that are the 25 percent highest levels expected constitute a reasonable worst case for detection.[24] Similarly, the 25 percent lowest noise levels are a reasonable best case for detection. Average noise levels can also be computed, but of course they give no information in themselves about the variability of ambient noise due to meteorological variability and variability of ship traffic.

The high and low noise spectra in a given ocean area for a given season are computed by the following method:

1. From the wind data of tables A8–1 and A8–2 compute the wind speed that is exceeded 25 percent of the time (high) and 75 percent of the time (low).

2. For each of these wind speeds, go to table A6–2 in appendix 6 and compute the wind noise spectra.
3. Choose the appropriate shipping noise spectrum from table A6–1, taking into consideration water depth, distance from major shipping routes, and season.
4. Compute the probability of rain from tables A8–3 and A8–4. If it is greater than 15 percent, include a "heavy rain noise" component spectrum to the high noise estimate only from table A6–3. If rain occurs less than 15 percent of the time, it is considered too extreme an event to be included in even the high noise estimate.
5. Determine the ice conditions. If the ice pack is continuous over the entire ocean area, then use the underice ambient noise spectra in table A6–4, with the 10 percent quietest and 10 percent noisiest spectra corresponding to the low and high noise estimates, respectively. If the ice pack partly covers a particular area, the worst case for detection is under the ice edge. At the ice edge, the noise levels generated by wind and breaking ice are assumed to be 5 dB higher than the noise levels generated by wind alone. The high estimate of wind noise is therefore increased by 5 dB. The low noise estimates ignore the presence of the ice altogether as the best detection condition is taken to be open water. It should be noted that the statistics available in the unclassified literature for noise under continuous ice cover are presented in terms of 10 percent extremes rather than 25 percent extremes as in the rest of the analysis. This inconsistency is unfortunate, and predictions of detection range under conditions involving continuous ice cover must be considered somewhat more extreme than the predictions under other conditions.
6. When all the component spectra have been estimated, they are summed within frequency bands. The levels are summed assuming the noise is uncorrelated.

One of the important assumptions underlying the method described above is that the extreme conditions of the individual noise components are assumed to occur at the same time. This is consistent with the "worst-case/best-case" approach but has the disadvantage of ignoring the correlation between the various phenomena that make noise. For example, shipping noise tends to decrease in very rough weather because fewer ships are apt to be at sea. Fortunately for this analysis, in the severest of storm conditions, wind, wave, and rain noise tends to dominate shipping noise through most of the spectrum in any case, so the result is insensitive to the shipping assumption. In addition, the meteorological variables of wind, waves, and rain tend to be correlated also. Obtaining statistical correlations between all the variables would be a refinement but probably would not be worth the effort since the rest of the data is so approximate to begin with.

Predicting Acoustic Noise in the Northern Region

Ambient noise in the Arctic is a function of the surface wind speed, ice conditions, shipping, and transmission loss. Summer and winter data are given so as to present the extremes of seasonal variations in the relevant variables. Where monthly data is available, the extreme month is taken to represent the season. July or August usually represents summer, and February or March represents winter. The entire area is divided into four zones, the Norwegian-Greenland Sea, the northern Barents Sea, the southern Barents Sea, and the Arctic Ocean.

The statistical distribution of wind speeds for most of the Arctic and northern seas is given in tables A8–1 and A8–2. For each region, these tables give the percent of observations that fall within wind speed ranges. From this data, one can estimate the percentage of time that the wind exceeds any particular speed. Conversely, one can estimate the wind speed that is exceeded a given percent of the time. Since noise increases with wind speed, high wind speeds make it harder to detect submarines. The worst conditions for submarine detection arise when the winds are highest in a given zone, and the best conditions occur when winds are lowest. I have chosen to represent the highest winds by the speed that is exceeded 25 percent of the time. Similarly, the lowest winds are represented by the speed that is exceeded 75 percent of the time. I use the 25 percent highest and lowest winds since they represent reasonable extremes. At greater extremes, say the 5 percent highest winds, the data and statistics are less reliable.

Wind-generated noise levels are estimated from these wind speeds. These noise levels represent the highest and lowest noise conditions in each zone for each season. When ice is present, the noise levels are modified in one of two ways. If the ice pack is solid, the wind noise levels are ignored and the Arctic ice pack noise levels are used from table A6–2 in appendix 6. If the edge of the ice pack is within the zone, the high noise levels are increased by 5 dB to represent the noisiest conditions, which are near the ice edge. The low noise levels are not increased and therefore represent the noise levels away from the ice edge under open water.

Rain noise is included in the ambient noise if at least 15 percent of the observations of a particular zone measure rain. In order to estimate the worst case for detection, noise levels associated with heavy rain are used. Since rain is usually not present, low noise estimates do not include any rain noise. Rain noise is estimated using table A6–3.

Given all the components of ambient noise, the final step is to add them. The sum of incoherent noise from two noise sources is simply the sum of intensities of each source. Decibels cannot be added directly, because decibels are the logarithm of the intensity. A simpler, approximate rule for decibel addition is sufficient for these calculations. Suppose there are two sound levels, in decibels, that are to be summed, M and N, to obtain a total T. The following table shows the approximate relationship between the three terms.

$N-M$ (dB)	T (dB)
0	$N+3$
1	$N+3$
2	$N+2$
3	$N+2$
4–9	$N+1$
>9	$N+0$

For example, if one noise level of 80 dB is added to a level of 75 dB, the total noise level is $80+1=81$ dB. If 80 dB is added to 81 dB the total is 84 dB.

Transmission Loss

The acoustic transmission properties of the deep Arctic Ocean are influenced heavily by the steady increase of sound speed with depth. The plane of minimum sound speed lies at or near the surface because the minimum temperature is at the surface. Acoustic rays are therefore always refracted upward, and then reflected downward at the sea surface as shown in figure A8–12. The

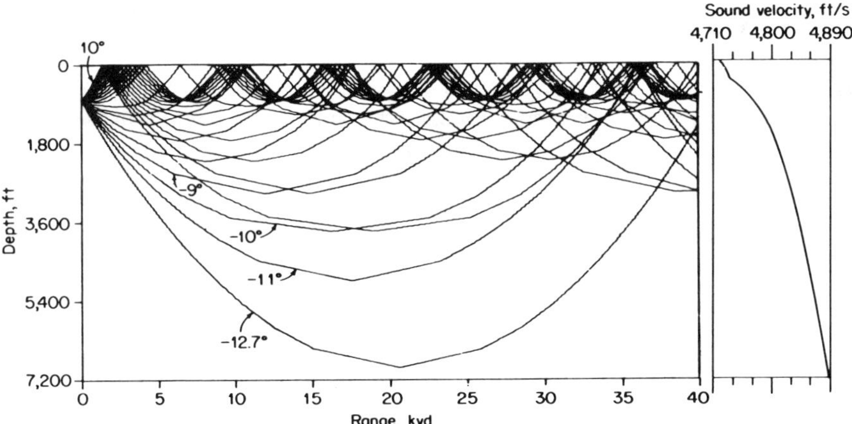

Figure A8–12. Typical sound speed profile and ray diagram in the central Arctic.

Source: Robert J. Urick, *Principles of Underwater Sound,* rev. ed. (New York: McGraw-Hill, 1975), fig. 6.18, p. 158.

long-range propagation of frequencies lower than 10 Hz is limited because these long acoustic waves are not easily trapped inside the waveguide, which is basically half of a deep sound channel. Frequencies greater than 30 Hz are attenuated due to reflection loss from the underice surface.

Figure A8–13 shows the transmission loss under ice in the central Arctic as a function of distance for different frequencies. At a range of 5–10 miles, surface ducting improves the transmission of all frequencies over free-field transmission. At 50 miles, frequencies lower than 150 Hz are transmitted with greater efficiency by the surface duct while frequencies greater than 300 Hz are attenuated due to absorption in the ice. At 500 miles all frequencies above 30 Hz are severely damped by the ice.

Transmission loss curves are either calculated or culled from observations for each area according to water depth, temperature structure, wave conditions, and ice conditions.

Ice-covered versus Ice-free Waters: A Summary

Relative to open water acoustics, underice acoustics may be characterized in the following ways:

Transmission: Better than free-field transmission (spherical spreading) at low frequencies and short ranges, due to surface ducting. Worse than deep sound channel transmission at high frequencies and long ranges, due to the scattering of sound off the ice and the inefficiency of half-channel transmission.

Ambient noise: Lower under a continuous ice cover with slowly rising temperatures and low wind speeds. Higher under a noncontinuous cover or in falling temperatures, which cause cracking in pack ice.

Surface scattering: Higher because of the ice. This also should lead to the generation of multiple paths, which tend to degrade array gain against noise.

Volume scattering: Lower due to upward refraction at all depths.

Convergence zones: Much weaker or nonexistent, due to scattering at the surface. If they exist, these convergence zones are formed by the deep sound channel.

Acoustic Detection in the Southern Barents Sea

The Barents Sea lacks a clear geographic feature between its northern and southern parts; rather, it is oceanography that suggests treating these regions

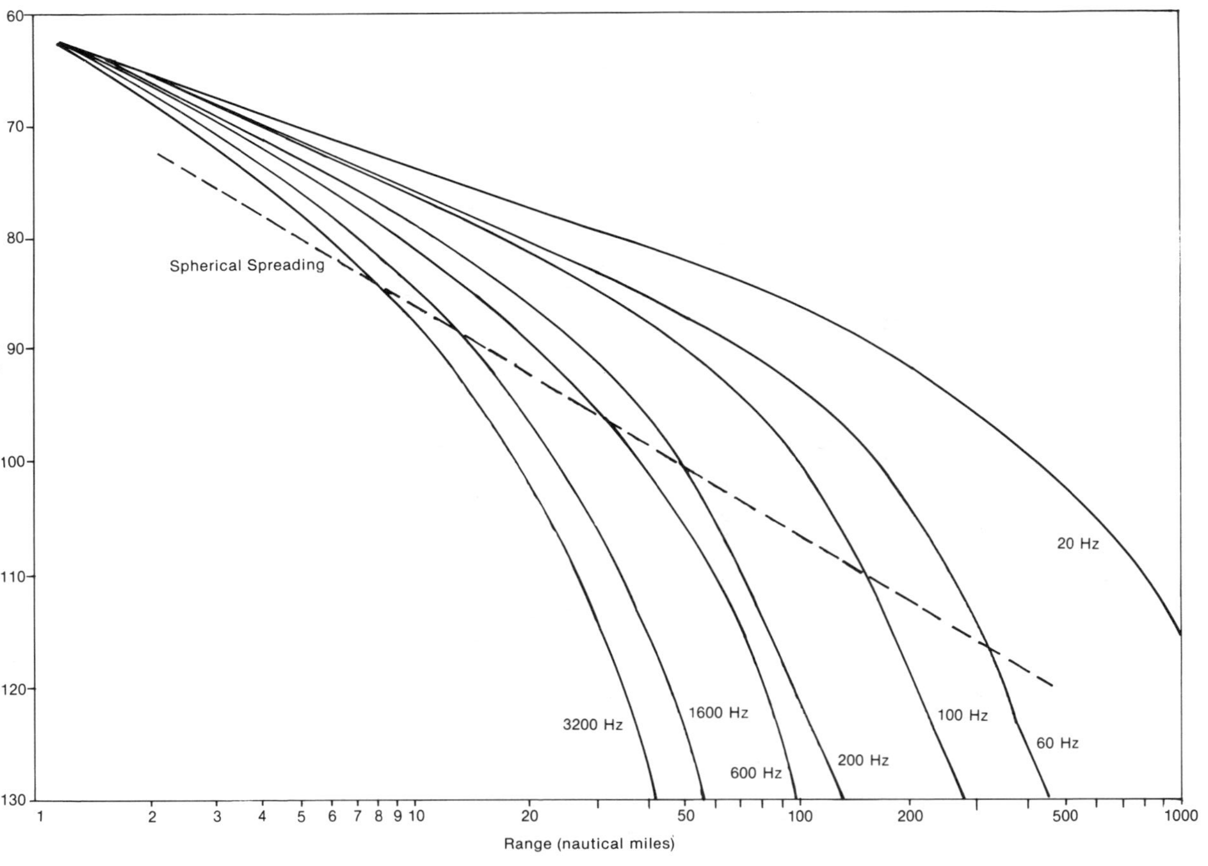

Figure A8–13. Transmission loss as a function of range in the central Arctic.

Source: Data from Robert J. Urick, *Sound Propagation in the Sea* (Los Altos, CA: Peninsula Publishing, 1982), p. 7–18.

Note: Standard errors in the curves are 6–9 dB.

separately. The warm North Cape (or Murman) current, which keeps the southern part of the Barents Sea free of consolidated ice, is the most significant feature. Its counterpart in the northern Barents is the cold Bear Island current, which flows from the Arctic Ocean and keeps the temperature there at or below 30 degrees Fahrenheit (−11° C). In the winter, the edge of the consolidated ice pack runs from the southern tip of Spitzbergen southeastward to the middle of Novaya Zemlya, leaving a gap of about 400 miles between the Kola peninsula and the edge of the ice pack. However, it is important to note that ice concentrations of more than 50 percent are typically found only 150 miles off the coast. Such ice concentrations can severely restrict ship operations, particularly for smaller vessels. For example, in 50–90 percent ice cover, where the ice is between 1 and 4 feet thick, only larger, specially reinforced vessels can operate, and then at restricted speeds. If the ice thickness exceeds 4 feet, only icebreakers can penetrate.[25] Ice concentrations up to 10 percent can be expected within 75 miles of the coast. This means that surface naval operations in the wintertime Barents Sea are heavily channeled into a relatively narrow swath off the Soviet and Norwegian coasts.

Diesel-electric submarine (SS) operations would be similarly restricted. Although SSs can avoid the ice when submerged and running on batteries, using a snorkel while underway beneath unconsolidated ice would be quite risky. In order to run the diesel engines, these submarines would probably have to stop or surface. Of course, they would be in grave danger beneath pack ice. Nuclear submarines, on the other hand, would not be severely restricted by the presence of ice.

The northern Barents Sea, when covered by the polar ice pack, is a very different environment for naval operations from that of the southern Barents. In the summertime, the pack ice retreats northward. Typically, the edge of the summer pack runs between the northern tip of Spitzbergen and Franz Josef Land, about 600 miles from the coast, and the sea area accessible to surface ships is much larger, virtually all of the Barents Sea.

Acoustically, the Barents Sea is relatively shallow water at low frequencies. The depth varies between about 600 and 1,200 feet in a complex bathymetry, and the bottom sediments are highly variable within this relatively small area. Sediment types, which have a major impact on shallow water transmission, can change from mud to gravel to sand within less than 100 miles.[26] This variability of depth and bottom type makes low-frequency acoustic transmission quite unpredictable in the Barents Sea. It should be noted that the transmission loss curve used to calculate detection range in the ice-free Barents Sea is from a compilation of many different observations and can provide at best a very rough guide for illustrative purposes. Convergence and shadow zones do not exist in the Barents Sea under any conditions.

The transmission loss curves when smooth annual ice cover is present are shown in figure A8–14. They are drawn from a measurement of transmission in

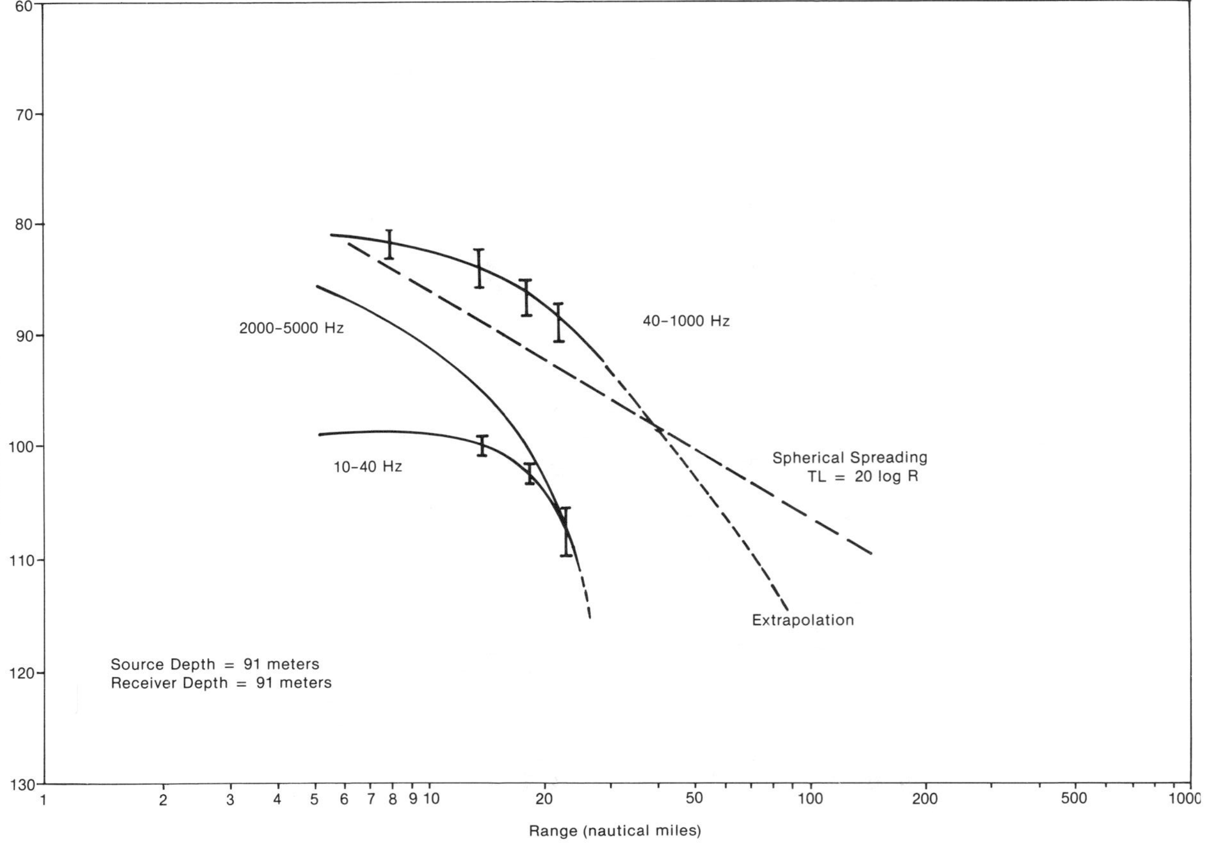

Figure A8-14. Transmission loss as a function of range in 600 to 900 feet of water under smooth annual ice, Parry Channel (Canadian Arctic).

Source: Data from Ronald Verrall, "Acoustic Transmission Losses and Ambient Noise in Parry Channel," in *The Question of Sound from Icebreaker Operations,* ed. N. Merle Peterson (British Columbia: Western Ecological Services, Ltd., Arctic Pilot Project, Petro-Canada, 1981), figure 4, pp. 220-231.

depths of 600–900 feet with the receiver and source at about 300 feet, typical of submarine operating depths.[27] The data is from the Parry Channel, the main east-west route through the Canadian Arctic archipelago. The ice cover conditions occur throughout the Central Barents Sea, near the coast of Novaya Zemlya and in the White Sea during the winter. The water is about 300–600 feet deep in these areas, and so transmission loss is expected to be higher than the curves used to calculate the detection range in figure A8–14. When using any curves in specific shallow water conditions, it should be remembered that they can provide only a rough guide to conditions elsewhere and should be considered single samples of a random function.

Winter

During the winter in the southern Barents Sea, the surface temperature ranges from 42° F (5.6° C) off the North Cape of Norway to 30° F (–1.1° C) at the edge of the ice pack. The extent of the ice pack has already been mentioned, but it is useful to remember that in addition to the Barents Sea, the White Sea is choked with ice through much of the winter. Ice begins to form in deep bays such as Archangel in October, and the sea is completely frozen by February, opening again in April. The major Soviet naval activity in the White Sea is the construction of submarines, particularly ballistic missile and cruise missile types, at Severodvinsk,[28] and the constrained access to the White Sea during the winter would not be a short term handicap to the Soviet Navy in wartime. The principal naval ports are in the vicinity of Murmansk, where the water temperature is typically 35° F (1.6° C) in winter. The wind speed over the Barents Sea exceeds 30 knots 25 percent of the time, and the predominant wind direction is out of the northeast to southeast. Cloud cover exceeds 75 percent about 6 days out of 10, and precipitation, almost always snow, occurs 3 days out of 10.

Best-Case Detection. The best case for acoustic detection occurs when the ice cover is consolidated under constant or slowly rising air temperature. Data from a five-year study by the Naval Oceanographic Office suggests that as one moves from the ice edge under the ice, noise levels decrease from a maximum at the ice edge to a lower level at a range of about 30 miles from the edge. Traveling farther beneath the ice does not seem to alter the noise level. At frequencies near 100 Hz, the underice noise levels 30 miles from the ice edge are about the same or a few dB lower than the wind noise level at the open ocean, whereas at higher frequencies, the noise levels are typically 5 dB lower.[29] The wind noise spectrum corresponding to a 10-knot wind is therefore adjusted downward to account for the presence of ice in the margins of the Barents Sea. Shipping traffic is assumed to be light for the best case of detection, and the maximum shipping noise level is 75 dB, which occurs in the 40–100 Hz band.

The total ambient noise spectrum, which is the incoherent power sum of the wind, ice, and shipping component, is completely governed by the shipping noise up to 100 Hz and is a function of wind, ice, and shipping between 100 and 1,000 Hz.

The "equipment factor" in the passive sonar equation (array gain minus detection threshold) is adversely affected by the acoustic effects of shallow water. Multiple reflections off the moving sea surface tend to spread narrow-band acoustic energy over bands up to 1 Hz. This raises the detection threshold for passive detection and also limits the coherent integration time—an important active sonar parameter—to about 0.5 second.[30] In the best detection case, I have assumed no degradation from the nominal maximum figure of -16 dB, although this assumption is probably too low, even if it is consistent with the best case assumption for detection. The array gain is assumed to suffer a 5 dB degradation from the nominal maximum of 20 dB. This assumption is somewhat heuristic in that it is the expected behavior, but there is very little data to back it. Some shallow water tests at 2,400 Hz reveal horizontal coherence lengths on the order of 15 acoustic wavelengths—a factor of 10 below the maximum expected coherence length in deep water.[31] Theoretical analysis of horizontal wind noise coherence in shallow water suggests that the noise coherence is strongly dependent on the transmission loss of the channel.[32] Given the spatial variability of the Barents Sea, it seems that a heuristic approach is the limit of predictive ability. It should be apparent by this point, however, that an error of 7 dB (a factor of 5) in the estimates of other sonar parameters is typical, so a similar imprecision in the array gain is certainly consistent.

The ambient noise spectrum has now been determined by summing the component spectra, and the array gain and detection threshold have been estimated. Using this information in the passive sonar equation, the figure of merit (allowable transmission loss) has been calculated for sources of various strengths and various frequencies. Detection range is then related to the FOM by transmission loss curves. Detection ranges in the best-case condition are shown in figure A8–15 as the upper end of the bars.

An important phenomenon that is not shown clearly in this figure is the dependence of transmission loss on frequency. As figure A8–13 shows, the transmission loss below 40 Hz and above 2,000 Hz exhibits a sharp increase beyond about 10 miles, corresponding to an FOM at 100. This means that as the figure of merit rises beyond this point, very little increase in detection range beyond 25 miles is realized. Since the frequencies assumed in these calculations are between 40 and 1,000 Hz, this cutoff does not come into play. Some degradation of transmission loss in the 500–1,000 Hz range is assumed, however, and the calculated FOMs show the typical behavior of increasing with frequency, leading to an increase in the expected detection range from 40 to 300 Hz. In the 500–1,000 Hz band, even though the FOM increases (it is about 10 dB higher than it is in the 200–300 Hz band), the detection range actually

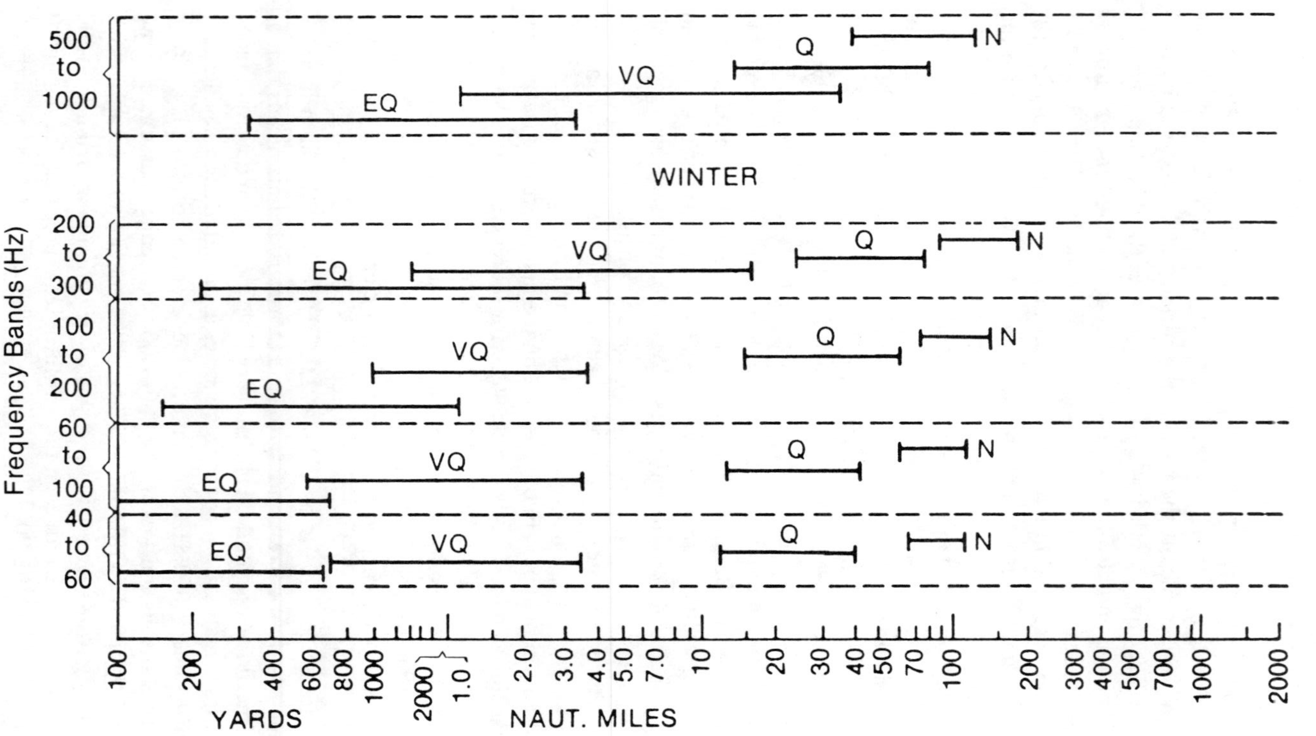
Frequency Bands (Hz)
500 to 1000
Q
N
VQ
EQ
WINTER
200 to 300
100 to 200
60 to 100
40 to 60
100
200
400
600
800
1000
2000
1.0
2.0
3.0
4.0
5.0
7.0
10
20
30
40
50
70
100
200
300
400
500
700
1000
2000
YARDS
NAUT. MILES

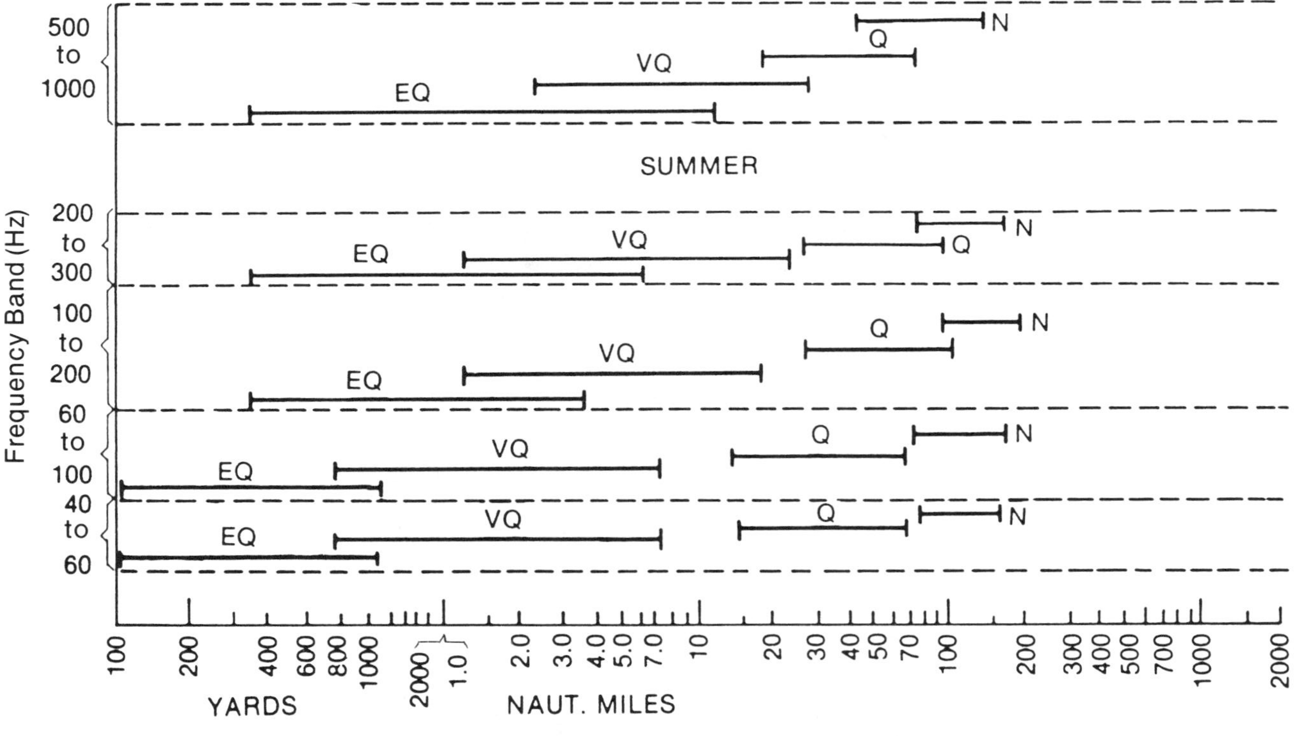

Figure A8–15. Estimated detection range of narrowband signals in the southern Barents Sea in conditions unfavorable (lower limit) and favorable (upper limit) to detection.

Note: Transmission loss data from figure A8–14 is used. Source levels (dB re 1 micropa at 1 yd., 1 Hz band) are 100 dB (extremely quiet—EQ), 115 dB (very quiet—VQ), 140 dB (quiet—Q), and 160 dB (noisy—N). Signal processing parameters set at $p_{det} = 0.5$, $p_{fa} = 10^{-5}$.

decreases due to the increase in transmission loss. The combination of the steadily increasing FOM and the increase of transmission loss with frequency results in a frequency band that is, in a sense, the optimum for detection. If all the sound radiated by a source is emitted in a single 1-Hz-wide tone, this tone may be detected at the greatest distance if it is in the optimum band, in this case 200–300 Hz. It should be noted that the optimum detection band for very quiet sources is higher, due to the lower sensitivity of transmission loss to frequency at short detection ranges.

Under the best detection conditions, very quiet sources can be detected at relatively long ranges, on the order of 30 miles. This is a result of the extremely low noise levels that are attainable beneath a solid cover of ice. Although these are the most favorable conditions for detection, they would not be expected to last for long periods of time.

Worst-Case Detection. The worst case for detecting submarines is when they are situated directly beneath the ice edge during a storm. The collisions of the broken ice at the edge of the pack ice generate enough noise to raise the ambient noise level 5–8 dB above that generated by equivalent wind conditions over open water.[33] Under special conditions, such as a very compact ice edge, noise levels may be 10 dB higher than those found in open water.[34] Noise levels drop slowly as one moves in either direction away from the ice edge, but there is a zone of about 30 miles to both sides of the edge within which the ambient noise level exceeds the open ocean level by at least 5 dB. This 60-mile-wide zone is a good acoustic hiding place for an evasive submarine since it is a region where the ambient noise is a maximum, and it is also an area that is inaccessible to surface ships and to air-launched detection devices.

The worst detection conditions are assumed to occur under the ice edge. Wind speeds above 30 knots occur 25 percent of the time, generating a spectral peak of at least 77 dB. Shipping is assumed to be moderate, although in wartime, with many ships at sea, the level could be higher. The total ambient noise spectrum is dominated by shipping noise only between 40 and 60 Hz. In the 60–100 Hz band, both shipping and wind/ice contribute, and above 100 Hz, the wind/ice noise dominates. As a consequence, ambient noise characteristics throughout most of the spectrum are relatively insensitive to the shipping noise level.[35]

The array gain (*AG*) is assumed to be 15 dB, which is the same value used in the best detection case. The detection threshold (*DT*) is raised 4 dB from the best case to −12 dB. The assumptions regarding the sonar system parameters are likely to be optimistic from the standpoint of detection, and the total system parameter in the sonar equation (*AG* − *DT*) may be far lower than the value of 27 assigned here. The data on shallow water coherence suggests array gains as low as 10 dB, and the tonal spreading associated with the forward scattering off the sea surface may limit practical narrowband processing to bandwidths greater than 0.5 Hz. Averaging times of less than a minute yield detection thresholds greater than -10 dB, and this does not include adjustments for nonideal filters, and so on. Values of $AG - DT$ of 15 dB are probably closer to what is practically attainable in these adverse ocean conditions. The more optimistic estimate of 27 dB represents a bias toward future advances in system capabilities.

Detection range is obtained from the transmission loss curves of figure A8–16. Since no convergence zones are present, the actual transmission loss in the Barents Sea should increase steadily, as shown in the figure. The low-frequency curve (100–200 Hz) is derived from the Marsh and Schulkin semi-empirical expressions.[36] The probable error in the transmission loss curve is about 6 dB for lower frequencies and 9 dB for frequencies between 400 and 1,000 Hz. The low-frequency curve fits the data from Verrall in the Canadian Arctic within the expected error. Note that at very low frequencies (20–40 Hz), the Verrall data exhibit poor transmission and a virtual cutoff at 25 miles.[37] In other words, beyond 25 miles, the transmission loss increases extremely quickly with distance. At frequencies of about 400 Hz, the Marsh and Schulkin expressions indicate some dependence on sea state. Since the worst detection conditions assume a high wind speed, the sea state 5 curve (corresponding to 27 knot winds) is used for high frequencies. At frequencies between 100 and 400 Hz, interpolation is used.

The figure of merit obtained for the worst case of detection is typically 15 dB below that obtained for the best case at low frequencies, and 29 dB lower at high frequencies. Detection range against extremely quiet and very quiet submarines is less than 1 mile at all frequencies. Quiet and noisy sources can be heard at the longest ranges if the source lies in the 200–300 Hz band. At higher frequencies, even though the FOM increases, the absorption losses begin rapidly to increase transmission loss. At frequencies above 400 Hz, there is a cutoff at about 50 miles range, to the extent that every additional dB in the FOM increases the detection range only by 2 percent—that is, about a mile. Extremely quiet and quiet sources are not as severely attenuated by absorption processes at shorter detection range, and so the steady increase in FOM with frequency leads to a steady increase in detection range with frequency.

Summer

In summer, which may include part of June through September, the region of open water expands as the ice retreats northward. The occasional iceberg carved from glaciers on Novaya Zemlya, Franz Josef Land, or Spitzbergen may be present, but in general all but the most northern part of the Barents Sea is ice free. There is no very clear pattern of dominant wind direction during the summer. The wave climate can be described in two ways: local wind-generated "seas," which tend to have periods of less than 5 or 6 seconds, and longer

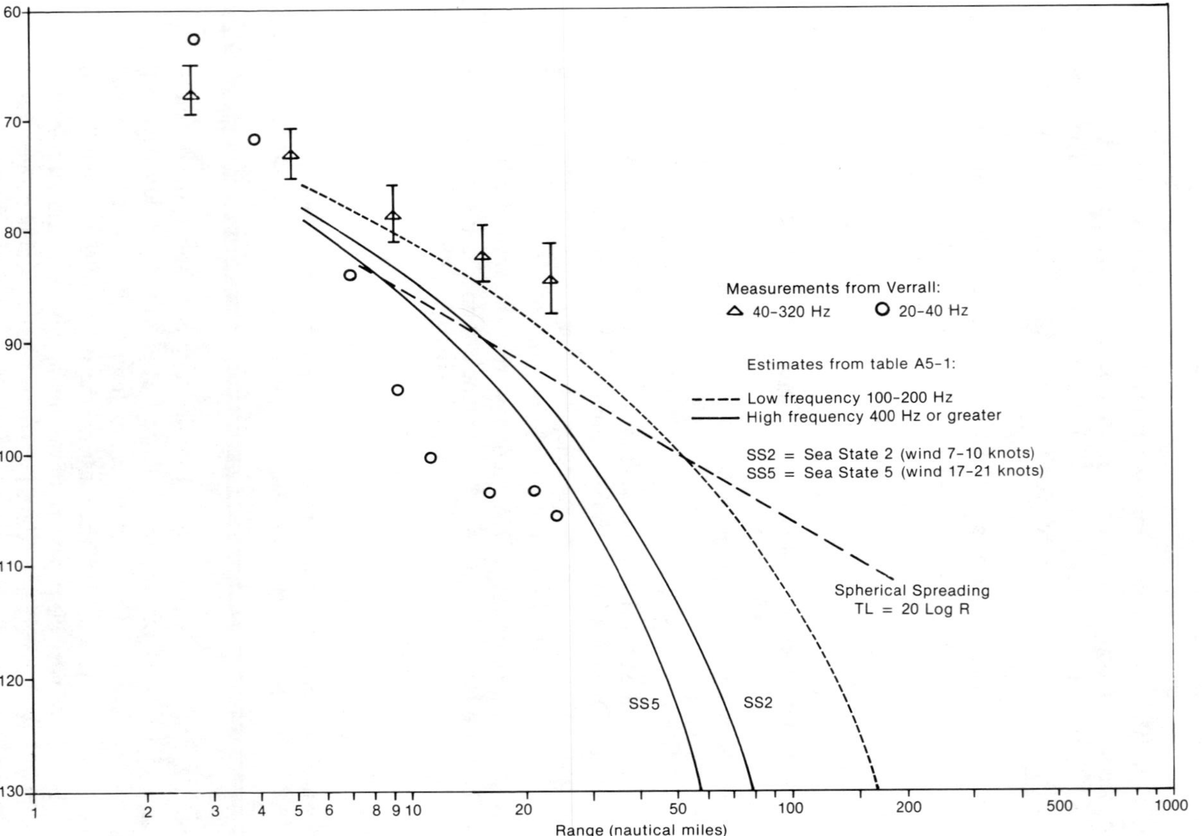

Figure A8–16. Transmission loss as a function of range in ice-free water 900 feet deep, Parry Channel.

Source: Data from Ronald Verrall, "Acoustic Transmission Losses and Ambient Noise in Parry Channel," in *The Question of Sound from Icebreaker Operations,* ed. N. Merle Peterson (British Columbia: Western Ecological Services, Ltd., Arctic Pilot Project, Petro-Canada, 1981), figure 6, pp. 220–231.

period "swell," usually generated at distant points and therefore less dependent on local weather conditions. Seas exceed 5 feet in height, and swell exceeds 12 feet about 1 day out of 10, on average.[38] Precipitation, always rain, occurs 1 day out of 5 and can unexpectedly degrade detection capability because of the noise that it generates as it strikes the sea surface. The cloud cover in summer is similar to that of wintertime, with 75 percent or greater coverage 60 percent of the time. Surface water temperatures range from 50° F (10° C) near the coast to freezing at the ice edge.

Worst-Case Detection. Wind speeds in the summer exceed 17 knots 25 percent of the time (compared to 30 knots in winter), generating peak noise spectral levels of 71 dB from 100–300 Hz. Since rain occurs 20 percent of the time, a worst-case assumption is that a heavy rain is falling. Detailed statistics on the distribution of rain intensity are not readily available, so the extreme condition of heavy rainfall is used to represent the worst case. Clearly, the occurrence of heavy rainfall is less likely than the occurrence of *any* precipitation and may be expected less than 10 percent of the time. Heavy rain generates ambient noise levels up to 75 dB over a broad spectrum from 100–1,000 Hz. Shipping density is assumed to be moderate.

The ambient noise spectrum is dominated by shipping noise below 100 Hz and by rain noise above that frequency, with wind-generated noise not making a noticeable contribution. Therefore, the results at higher frequencies are sensitive to the assumption that it is raining. For example, in the 500–1,000 Hz band, if no rain is falling, the expected ambient noise level drops 10 dB.

The transmission characteristics of the Barents Sea are represented by the curves in figure A8–16, with worst-case conditions at frequencies above 400 Hz represented by the sea state 5 curve. The shallow depths inhibit formation of convergence zones or shadow zones. Effects of shallow water on the array gain and detection threshold are included by choosing values of 15 and -12 dB for these parameters, respectively.

Detection range against extremely and very quiet sources increases steadily with frequency, since absorption losses do not accumulate over the short detection ranges. Sources above 140 dB can be detected best if they emit in the 100–200 Hz band. At higher frequencies, absorption in the ocean raises the transmission loss to the point that it counteracts the higher FOM. Sensitivity of range to a change in the FOM varies from 10 percent per dB (quiet source, 100–200 Hz) to 2 percent per dB (noisy source, 500–1,000 Hz).

Best-Case Detection. Wind speeds are less than or equal to 4 knots 25 percent of the time and generate ambient noise spectra with peaks less than 56 dB. Shipping density is assumed to be light, although the shipping noise levels under these conditions would be directional. An array in the northern part of the Barents Sea listening northward would detect a lower shipping noise component than would one in the south listening southward toward Murmansk. Much of the directional variability of shipping noise is eliminated, however, due to the poor long-range transmission characteristics of the shallow water. At distances in excess of 200 miles from main shipping concentrations, much of the ambient shipping noise will have been attenuated. Finally, under the best conditions for detection, there is no rain. Total ambient noise is dominated by shipping noise except at 500–1,000 Hz, where the shipping noise spectrum drops off more rapidly than the wind noise spectrum. Thus, the results are sensitive to the assumptions made about shipping noise levels.

Maximum detection ranges against very quiet sources exceed 20 miles in the 500–1,000 Hz band. Detection range against noisy sources may reach 150 miles in the optimum band of 100–200 Hz. It is instructive to compare the area within which such targets can be detected with the total area in which they operate. In this case, the quiet source can be detected within a 1,250-square-mile area, and the noise source can be detected within a 70,700-square-mile radius. The area of the Barents Sea is about 390,000 nm^2, so the very quiet (115 dB) source and the noisy (160 dB) source "occupy" 0.3 percent and 18 percent of the available space, respectively.

Acoustic Detection in the Northern Barents Sea

In summer, the ice-covered portion of the northern Barents Sea is a relatively narrow area between Spitzbergen and Franz Josef Land, the southern extent defined by the edge of the ice pack, and the northern extent defined by the sudden increase in depth that occurs just north of Franz Josef Land, where the continental shelf drops off into the 12,000-foot-deep Eurasian basin of the Arctic Ocean. In summer, this region may be only 150 miles wide, but it has acoustic properties that make it very distinct from the deep Arctic to the north and the ice-free parts of the Barents Sea to the south. The general conclusions of this section apply to the neighboring Kara Sea also.

The bathymetry of the northern Barents Sea is very irregular, and depths range from 600 to 1,200 feet, as in the south. The many small islands of the Franz Josef Land and Severnaya Zemlya (in the Kara Sea) island groups are surrounded by shallower waters. Even in August, these islands are partially surrounded by ice, and navigation through them is treacherous. It has been suggested that evasive submarines could simply sail into these islands and shake off trailing vessels; however, such an action would be laden with risks.

Winter

During the winter, the northern Barents and Kara seas are covered with pack ice, at 80–100 percent concentration. The ambient noise levels are therefore drawn from the observations under many conditions in the Arctic. Transmission loss is assumed to be governed by the curve in figure A8–14 for frequencies between 40 and 1,000 Hz. This curve is based on observations in the Canadian Arctic at depths from 600 to 900 feet. Another set of curves based on observations in 1,300-foot-deep water is given in figure A8–17, and in parts of the Barents Sea there are few large areas of 1,300-foot-deep water.

Worst-Case Detection. The 10 percent highest values of ambient noise under the ice occur when there are high winds and the air temperature is dropping rapidly. Peak spectrum levels of 75 dB occur in the 40–100 Hz band. Array gain is set at 12 dB, 4 dB down from its presumed maximum. Because the estimate of Arctic ambient noises have relatively flat spectra over the 100–1,000 Hz band, the figure of merit estimates in that range are constant, and variations in detection range are due entirely to frequency dependence of transmission loss.

Transmission loss in shallow, ice-covered water is a function of the water depth, the bathymetry, sediment characteristics, and ice characteristics. The last of these is difficult to predict but can be very influential. Ice formed within the current season may have a very smooth undersurface, provided no storms have disrupted it and formed ice ridges. Propagation under ice is significantly improved if there are no ridges from which the surface-reflected sound can scatter and diffuse. For example, in a particular 600–900-foot-deep channel, over a 22-mile range, measured transmission loss under shore-fast annual ice exceeded open water transmission loss by only 5 dB at 40–320 Hz and by 7 dB at 300–600 Hz.[39] Higher frequencies are much more strongly attenuated by the presence of even smooth annual ice. The effect of decreasing water depth is further to increase transmission loss under ice. Transmission loss at 22 miles in the 40–1,000 Hz band is about 10 dB greater in water 450 feet deep than it is in water 600–900 feet deep, both covered by shore-fast annual ice.[40] In some cases, the adverse effects of increased ice roughness can outweigh the salutary effects of greater depth on sound propagation. Measurements in 1,300-foot-water covered by rough pack ice (many seasons old) show that transmission loss can be considerably greater than in 600–900-foot-water that is covered by annual ice.[41]

In order to examine the effects of ice structure on detection range, two sets of transmission loss curves were used. Figure A8–14 corresponds to 600–900-foot depths under annual ice, and figure A8–17 corresponds to 1,300-foot-deep water under pack ice. Using the same figures of merit, two different sets of range estimates, A8–18 and A8–19 have been made for the northern Barents Sea in winter and are derived from figures A8–14 and A8–17, respectively.

Estimates of detection range under the worst conditions vary from 2 to 19 miles for very quiet sources, and from 67 to 90 miles for noisy sources, depending on the transmission loss curves used. The transmission loss under pack ice is greater due to the roughness of the ice, and the detection range estimates are

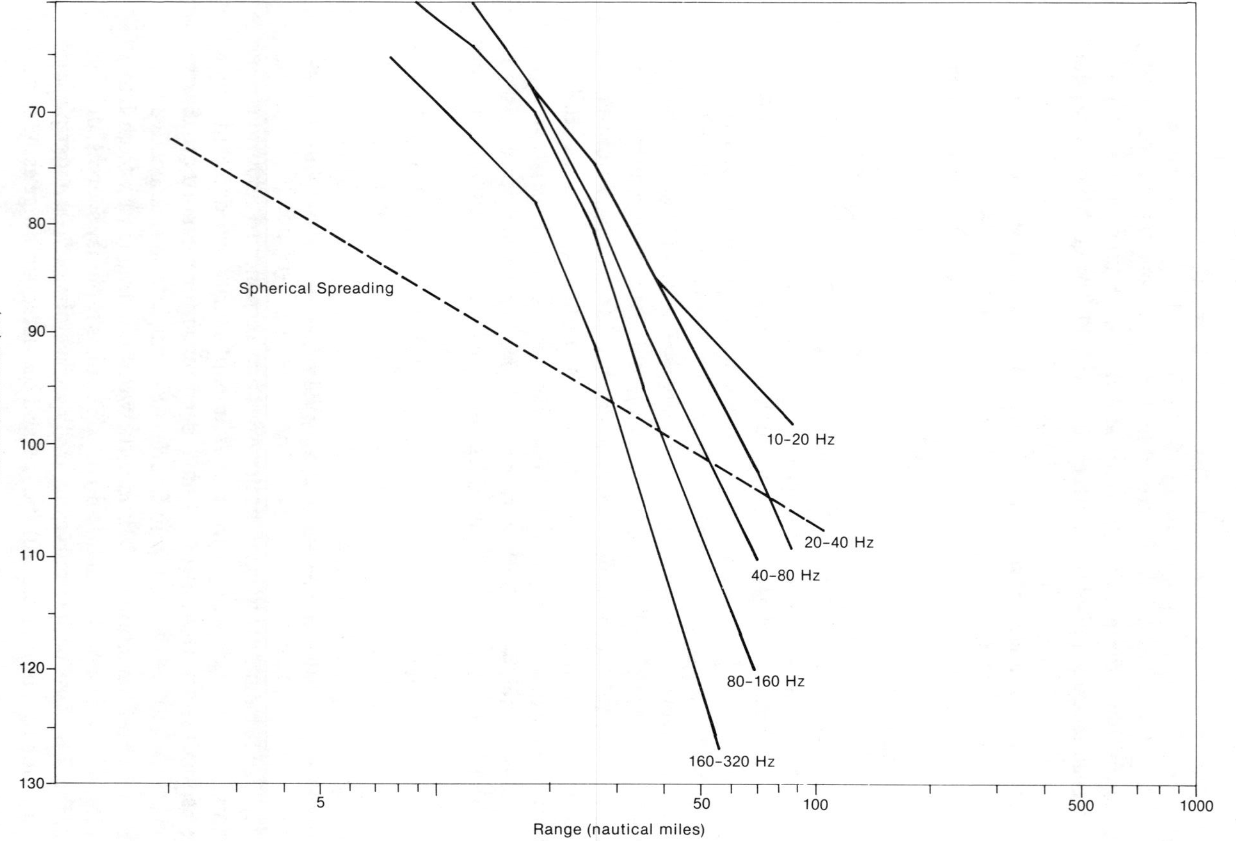

Figure A8–17. Transmission loss as a function of range in 1,300 feet of water covered by pack ice in the Parry Channel.

Source: Data from Ronald Verrall, "Acoustic Transmission Losses and Ambient Noise in Parry Channel," in *The Question of Sound from Icebreaker Operations*, ed. N. Merle Peterson (British Columbia: Western Ecological Services, Ltd., Arctic Pilot Project, Petro-Canada,

lower for noisy sources detected at long ranges. On the other hand, short-range detection of very quiet sources is better in the deeper water of the pack ice case. The reader should bear in mind that these estimates are valid only for the specific conditions under which the data was gathered. Those calculations should be viewed as one representative case, not as a general prediction.

Best Detection Conditions. The 10 percent lowest ambient noise levels under ice have a peak spectral level of only 47 dB in the 40–100 Hz band, almost 30 dB lower than the 10 percent highest levels. These very quiet levels would be found under shore-fast ice in slowly rising temperatures. Array gain is taken to be 20 dB and detection threshold -16, their presumed maximum values. These are certainly optimistic values, since shallow water is known to have deleterious effects on signal coherence and therefore on array gain. The impact on detection threshold is not clear, since the underice ambient noise statistics may deviate from the Gaussian distribution assumed in actually calculating that parameter.

Detection range against very quiet submarines varies with frequency from 19 to 70 miles, and against noisy submarines from 50 to 200 miles, in the conditions of 600–900-foot-deep water under smooth annual ice, shown in figure A8–18. Under rough ice and 1,300 feet of water, the ranges are similar: 25–60 miles for very quiet sources, and 50–150 miles for noisy sources as shown in figure A8–19. It is interesting to note that in the smooth ice case, range increases with frequency, and in the rough ice case, range decreases with frequency. This is a result of the strong attenuating effect of ice roughness on high frequency noise.

Summer

In the summer months the ice pack is at its northern limit and the northern Barents Sea is largely open water. The retreat of the ice pack opens the northern sea transportation route from the Barents Sea across the northern coast of the Soviet Union to the Bering Strait. The wind does not have a strongly dominant direction. Rain falls one day out of five on the average, and the cloud cover exceeds 75 percent three days out of five.

Worst-Case Detection. Wind speeds exceed 17 knots 25 percent of the time, with associated ambient noise peak levels of 71 dB. The presence of the edge of the ice pack provides an acoustic hiding zone for evasive submarines, and noise levels are typically 5 dB above the open water levels in a swath 30 miles wide centered on the ice edge. Rain falls 20 percent of the time, and though heavy rainfall is less frequent, it is adopted as the standard for the worst detection case. Shipping noise is based on light shipping density. The shipping routes from the Barents Sea to the Bering Strait would lie well to the south of the ice

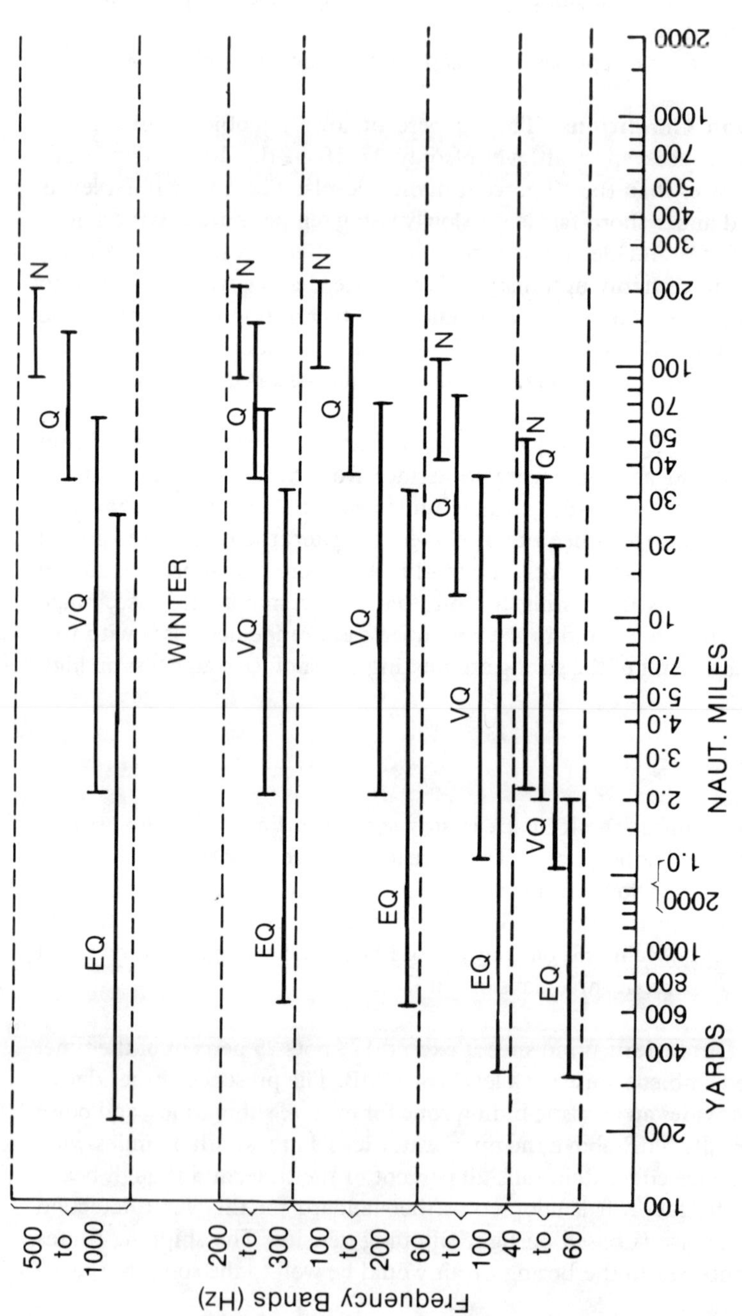
Frequency Bands (Hz)
500 to 1000
200 to 300
100 to 200
60 to 100
40 to 60
WINTER
N
Q
VQ
EQ
YARDS
100
200
400
600
800
1000
2000 } 1.0
2.0
3.0
4.0
5.0
7.0
10
20
30
40
50
70
100
200
300
400
500
700
1000
2000
NAUT. MILES

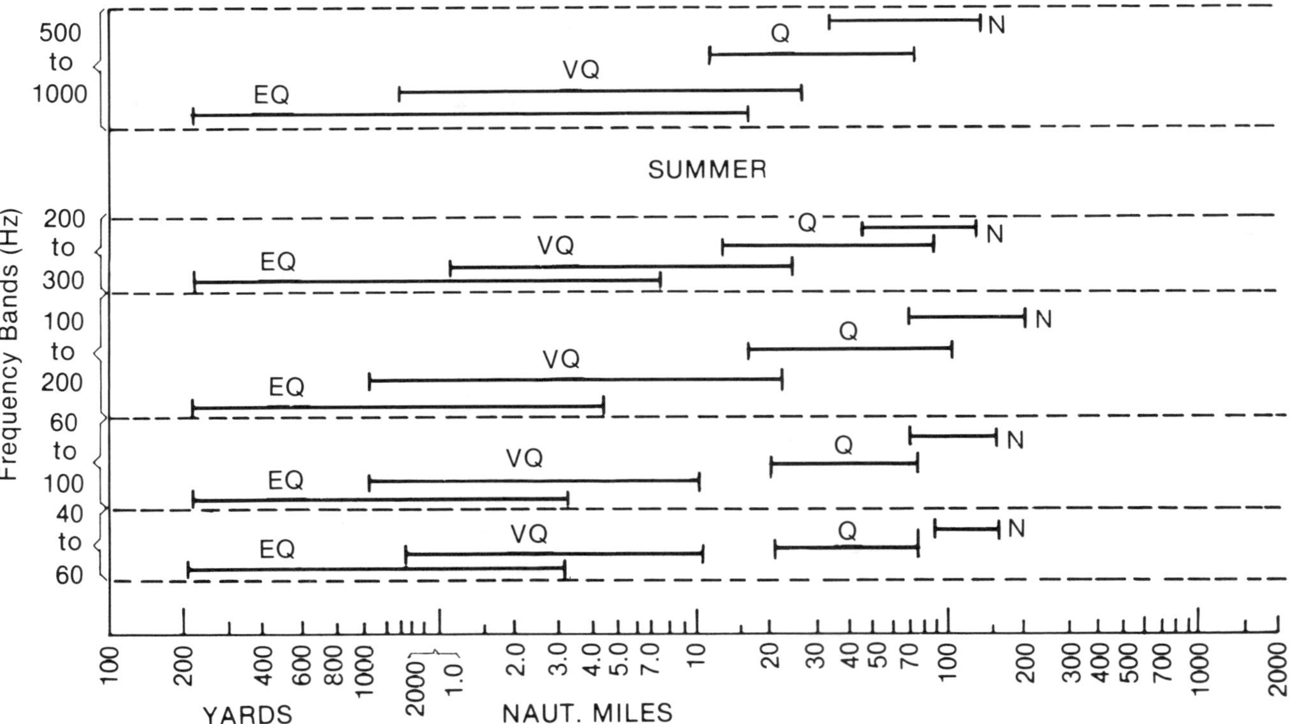

Figure A8–18. Estimated detection range of narrowband signals in the northern Barents Sea in conditions unfavorable (lower limit) and favorable (upper limit) to detection.

Note: Transmission loss data from figure A8–14 is used. Transmission loss based on figure A8–14. Source levels (dB re 1 micropa at 1 yd., 1 Hz band) are 100 dB (extremely quiet—EQ), 115 dB (very quiet—VQ), 140 dB (quiet—Q), and 160 dB (noisy—N). Signal processing parameters set at $p_{det} = 0.5$, $p_{fa} = 10^{-5}$.

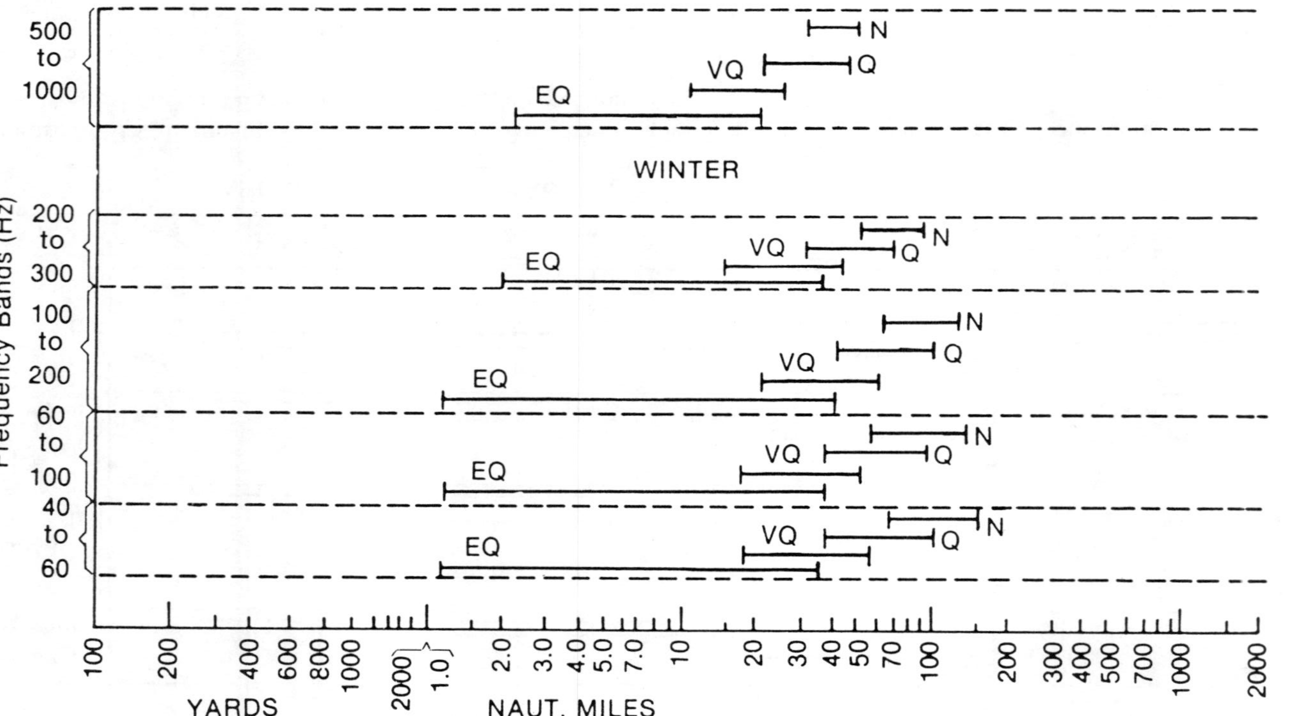

Figure A8–19. Estimated detection range of narrowband signals in the northern Barents Sea in conditions unfavorable (lower limit) and favorable (upper limit) to detection.

Note: Transmission loss data from figure A8–17 is used. Transmission loss based on figure A8–17. Source levels (dB re 1 micropa at 1 yd., 1 Hz band) are 100 dB (extremely quiet—EQ), 115 dB (very quiet—VQ), 140 dB (quiet—Q), and 160 dB (noisy—N). Signal processing parameters set at $p_{det} = 0.5$, $p_{fa} = 10^{-5}$.

edge. Because the transmission characteristics are poor in the Barents Sea, shipping noise is shielded at such ranges. The shipping noise data, being derived more from open ocean noise levels, does not include the screening effect. Therefore, "moderate" shipping densities generate a lower ambient noise level in shallow water than in deep water at long distances. The total ambient noise spectrum is dominated by shipping in the 40–100 Hz band and by wind, rain, and ice at higher frequencies. Peak levels reach 79 dB in the 100–300 Hz band. With higher levels of the shipping noise component the peak of the total ambient noise spectrum would increase in level and shift to lower frequencies. Array gain is assumed to be 12 dB, and detection threshold -12 dB.

The detection ranges under these conditions extend from 1,500 yards against very quiet sources to 78 miles against noisy sources, as shown in figure A8–18. The optimum frequencies for detecting quiet and noisy sources are in the lowest band—40–60 Hz. This is largely due to the fact that under the ambient noise assumptions, the wind and rain noise components dominate the total spectrum, and they peak at higher frequencies, making the lower frequencies better for detection. In the best detection conditions, shipping noise dominates the assumed spectrum, which therefore peaks at low frequencies. In this case the optimum detection frequency is 100–200 Hz.

Best-Case Detection. Wind speeds are less than or equal to 3 knots 25 percent of the time, generating peak spectrum levels of 54 dB. This is 50 times more quiet than the sea under a 17-knot wind. Shipping noise is assumed to be at the levels asociated with "remote" shipping. The assumption of "remote" shipping noise levels is based upon the shielding effect of the shallow water with its high transmission loss, as well as on the absence of surface ships from the northern reaches of the Barents Sea. The best oceanographic conditions for detection of submarines is assumed to be open water, since this has better transmission properties than shallow, ice-covered waters, and low wind-noise levels obtain. Furthermore, the region of solid ice cover in the northern Barents Sea is very limited in extent and is more closely related to the Arctic Ocean. Shipping noise, even with the assumption of "remote" shipping, dominates ambient noise at 40–100 Hz and strongly influences the total spectrum at higher frequencies. Array gain and detection threshold are set at the values of 20 dB and -16 dB, respectively.

Detection range against extremely quiet sources may exceed 16 miles at high frequencies, as shown in figure A8–18. It is interesting to note that while the figure of merit increases 40 dB—a factor of 10,000—between the extremely quiet and the noisy source, the maximum detection range increases only by a factor of 12, to 190 miles.

Acoustic Detection in the Central Arctic Ocean

The central Arctic basin (that is, the region within the ring of marginal seas) is actually two smaller basins divided by the Lomonosov ridge. Closer to the USSR is the Eurasian basin, which is 12,000 feet deep over most of its extent. On the other side of the ridge is the Canadian basin, about 9,000 feet deep on the average. The Lomonosov ridge itself is typically less than 6,000 feet deep, although there are few very shallow areas there. In general, the Arctic basin is acoustically deep water, and the primary determinant of acoustic transmission properties there is the minimum sound speed at the surface, which refracts all sound upwards onto the undersurface of the ice. The relative importance of underice reflection versus bottom reflection is much greater in the Arctic than it is in the Barents Sea. Therefore, most of the spatial variability in transmission in the Arctic is associated with changes in the roughness of the underice surface.[42]

The best propagation in the Arctic occurs in the 15–30 Hz band, approximately. Lower frequencies are not effectively trapped in the sound channel, and higher frequencies suffer rapid attenuation from multiple surface reflections.[43] Figure A8–13 shows transmission loss as a function of range and frequency based on a large number of tests in the Arctic. The standard errors associated with these curves are plus or minus 7–9 dB in the 60–800 Hz band and plus or minus 6 dB at higher and lower frequencies.

Ambient noise in the Arctic has been measured under a variety of oceanographical and meteorological conditions. Observations have been made in the Beaufort basin, which adjoins the Canadian basin and should be representative of the central Arctic. The dominant noise source under most conditions is ice ridge formation, with ice-cracking and ridging noise levels being significantly lower. In summer, the elastic properties of the warmer ice are less robust such that cracking and ridging are less intense than in winter.[44] Because the ridge formation, or ice-buckling mechanism, is responsible for most of the underice noise, it is correlated, to a fair degree, with wind and not correlated with temperature changes, as is shore-fast ice. Ridge formation is not completely correlated with local wind conditions, however, and there are processes involved that are not well understood.

The ambient noise levels in the Eurasian basin between the North Pole and the Soviet Union reach a minimum in July and a maximum in January. The low, mean, and high noise levels (levels that noise is less than or equal to 5 percent, 50 percent, and 95 percent of the time) at a depth of 100 feet illustrate the variability with season and frequency. In July, the low, mean, and high levels at 40 Hz are 57 dB, 65 dB, and 73 dB, while at 500 Hz the noise levels are 33 dB, 41 dB, and 49 dB. In January the noise levels at 40 Hz are about 13 dB higher than their summertime values: 69.5 dB, 77.5 dB, and 86 dB, and similarly, the noise levels at 500 Hz are about 13 dB higher than their summertime values: 45.5 dB, 53.5 dB, and 61.5 dB.[45]

The results shown in figure A8–20 suggest that the relative variability in detection range in the Arctic can be as large as in the deep ocean at lower latitudes. The structure and behavior of the ice cover—its thickness, roughness,

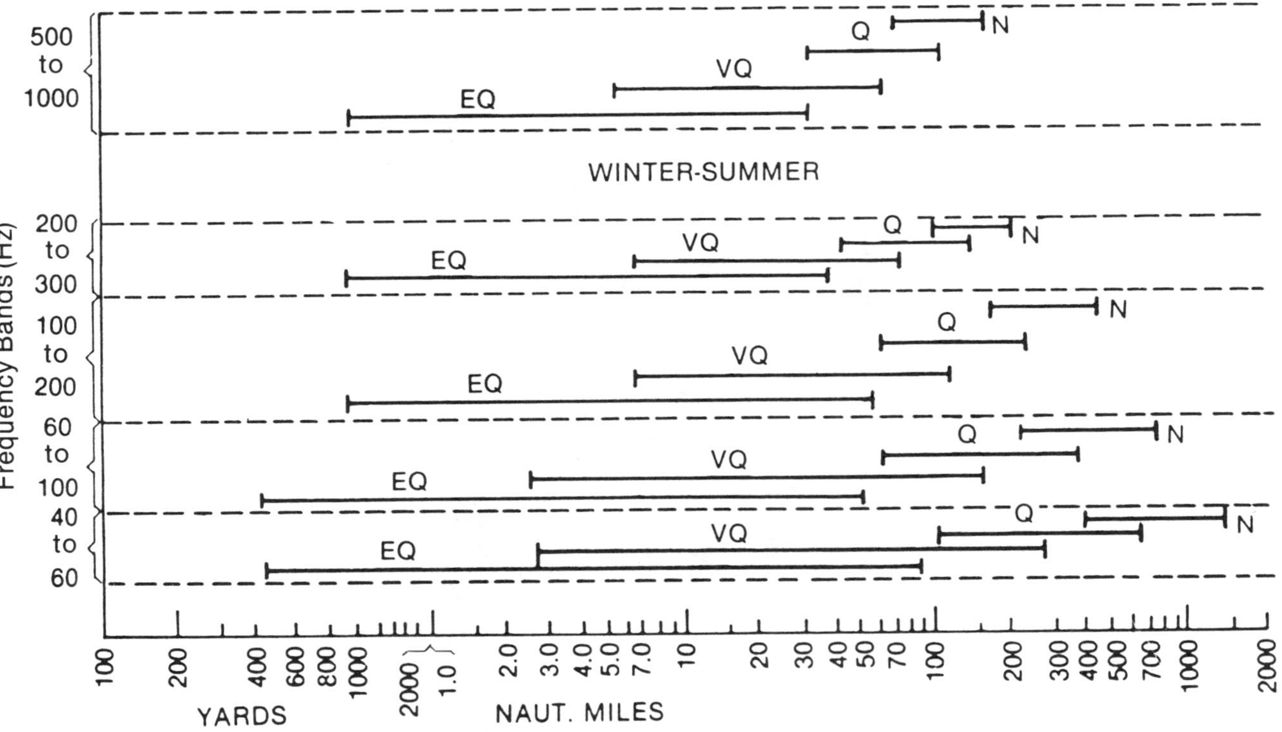

Figure A8–20. Estimated detection range of narrowband signals in the central Arctic Ocean in conditions unfavorable (lower limit) and favorable (upper limit) to detection.

Note: Source levels (dB re 1 micropa at 1 yd., 1 Hz band) are 100 dB (extremely quiet—EQ), 115 dB (very quiet—VQ), 140 dB (quiet—Q), and 160 dB (noisy—N).

coverage, and sounds—have as much if not more impact on detection range than meteorological conditions. It is therefore likely that detection conditions remain more stable in the Arctic than they do in the open ocean over short periods of time on the order of a few days. The apparently high variability of detection range in figure A8–20 is partially an artifact of the 10 and 90 percent extremes used in calculating the ambient noise condition.

At its very quietest and with a relatively smooth ice cover, the central Arctic can be one of the most difficult places for submarines to hide. The ambient noise levels are far below the lowest levels in the open ocean, and at frequencies between 40 and 1,000 Hz, sound is transmitted very effectively. Tones of only 100 dB may be detected at 20–80 miles under the most favorable circumstances. However, very low frequency tonals, such as blade rate frequencies, suffer much greater loss because of the basic structure of the Arctic waveguide. In general the optimum frequency band for transmission is between 20 and 100 Hz, the lower bound being quite sharply defined by the low-frequency cutoff of the channel, while the upper bound is more gradual.

Acoustic Detection in the Norwegian Sea

The Norwegian and Greenland seas are the only major links between the North Atlantic and the Arctic and are surrounded by NATO territories. The depth of the Norwegian-Greenland basin is 6,000–9,000 feet, and there is a sizeable portion of the Greenland Sea that exceeds 12,000 feet. The contiguous sea areas—the Arctic Ocean, Barents Sea, and North Atlantic—are to some degree separated from the Norwegian-Greenland basin by relatively shallow ridges. Between the Arctic Ocean and the Greenland Sea, the depth is about 3,000 feet, while the ridge in the GIUK gap is mostly about 1,600 feet deep. The deep sound channel of the Norwegian Sea is, therefore, strongly decoupled from the North Atlantic deep sound channel.

The surface currents follow a generally counterclockwise motion, with two smaller counterclockwise gyres, one north of Iceland and the other south of Spitzbergen, as shown in figure A8–3. Along the eastern side is the warm Norwegian current, which moves northward along the coast toward the Barents Sea. This is an offshoot of the Gulf Stream, and its relatively high temperatures keep the entire Norwegian Sea free of consolidated ice throughout the year. Typical average speeds of the Norwegian current are 0.5–0.7 knots. On the western side of the basin is the cold East Greenland current, which flows from the Arctic between Greenland and Spitzbergen. Besides carrying ice floes and icebergs from the north, this cold current keeps the western edge of the Greenland Sea covered with consolidated ice throughout the year. The ice-covered portion of the Greenland Sea is more like the central Arctic than it is like the northern Barents Sea, owing to the Greenland Sea's depth. Therefore, there is no separate analysis of acoustic detection in that region, and the reader is referred to the section on the central Arctic.

Winter

The sea surface temperature in the Norwegian Sea is between 38° and 43° F (6.1° C) and rapidly drops below freezing as one moves westward toward the Greenland Sea ice pack. At those temperatures, the portions of the Norwegian Sea that are 6,000–9,000 feet deep should exhibit convergence zone (and associated shadow zone) behavior, with spacings of 26–29 miles. Since the conditions are only marginally favorable to convergence zone transmission, it is probable that the convergence zone gain is less than one would find in the Atlantic. In addition, a significant portion of the eastern Norwegian Sea is shallower than 3,000 feet, and convergence zone propagation should not exist there.

The wave climate in the Norwegian Sea can be severe during the winter. Seas (steeper, locally generated waves) greater than 5 feet high are encountered more than 50 percent of the time throughout most of the Norwegian Sea. This is comparable to the wave statistics in the North Atlantic. In the GIUK, particularly southwest of Iceland, 5-foot seas are observed more frequently, as much as 70 percent of the time. Swell exceeding 12 feet occurs 10–20 percent of the time in the GIUK gap southwest of Iceland. Although these wave conditions do not inhibit submarine operations, smaller antisubmarine ships such as destroyers and frigates are adversely affected.[46] Superstructure icing can also degrade the performance of smaller combatant ships, and the likelihood of heavy icing is about 5 percent in the northern Norwegian Sea and in the vicinity of the Greenland Sea ice pack. The likelihood of some ice forming (not necessarily heavy accumulations) may exceed 50 percent near Spitzbergen. In the GIUK gap, superstructure icing is rare.[47]

The Greenland Sea ice pack covers the western third of the entire Norwegian-Greenland basin with consolidated ice. The concentration of broken drift ice drops to 10 percent within 100 miles of the edge of the pack. This leaves a corridor of virtually ice-free water about 500–600 miles wide in the central and southern Norwegian Sea. Off the northern coast of Norway, significant ice concentrations may approach within 100 miles of shore.

Cloud cover in the Norwegian Sea exceeds 75 percent of the sky about 6 days out of 10 and the sky is 50 percent or more *clear* only 2 days out of 10. Precipitation is observed 1 day out of 4 in the GIUK gap. The form of precipitation depends largely on the sea surface temperature, and the variation is quite dramatic; near the United Kingdom, 20 percent of the precipitation falls as snow and 80 percent as rain, and near Greenland, under the influence of the cold east Greenland current, 80 percent falls as snow and 20 percent as rain.

The bottom material in the Norwegian and Greenland seas is primarily mud, and the variation of bottom sediment type does not appear to be as great as it is in the Barents Sea. There is a belt of seismic activity throughout the Greenland Sea, with most of the historical events registering 5.3–5.9 in magnitude on the Richter scale. This activity is expected to contribute sporadically to the ambient noise below 100 Hz for short periods, with a peak around 10 Hz.[48] As of the mid-1950s, about 60 earthquakes had been recorded in this area.[49] Large whales are found in larger densities in the Norwegian Sea than anywhere in the Arctic region.

Worst-Case Detection. Wind speeds exceed 28 knots 25 percent of the time, generating ambient noise with spectral peaks of 75 dB in the 60–300 Hz band. Moderate shipping density is used to obtain the shipping noise level. Noise from human activities such as shipping and drilling for or pumping oil should vary with location and direction. For example, a sonar in the northern portion of the Norwegian Sea aimed toward quiescent ice should detect a considerably lower noise level than a sensor in the south aimed in the direction of the North Sea oil fields. Sound is transmitted more effectively in the Norwegian Sea than in the Barents Sea, and the "screening" effect that shallow water has on distant shipping noise is weaker. Rain is expected to occur about 15 percent of the time in the eastern Norwegian Sea, and the heavy rainfall spectrum is imposed in the worst case for detection.

The estimated ambient noise spectrum peaks in the 60–100 Hz band at a level of 86 dB, dominated by shipping noise. Above 100 Hz, rain and wind noises dominate the spectrum. The array gain is 20 dB, and the detection threshold −12 dB.

Transmission loss data for the Norwegian Sea were not available, and curves based on typical absorption measurements have been calculated and are shown in figure A8–21. At frequencies below 100 Hz, the attenuation coefficient is assumed to be 0.05 dB/km (0.09 dB/nm), which is the figure for the subarctic Pacific. The actual transmission loss in the Norwegian Sea is expected to be greater due to stronger influence of the bottom. The result is that detection range is likely to be overpredicted.[50] On the other hand, convergence zone detection is not accounted for, and sources that are predicted to be detectable at a few miles may be detected in the first or even second convergence zone, 26 or 52 miles out. Convergence zones are not expected to affect the estimate beyond the third zone, at 80 miles.

Detection range against a very quiet source is about 2 miles, when detected at frequencies higher than 500 Hz, as shown in figure A8–22. Against quiet and noisy sources, the detection range is 75 and 1,000 miles, respectively, in the 100–200 Hz range. Assuming a higher absorption rate in that band, 0.015 dB/km (.029 dB/nm), the predicted ranges are 62 and 440 miles.

Best-Case Detection. Wind speeds are less than 13 knots 25 percent of the time, and shipping noise is based on remote shipping. Rain is not present. The

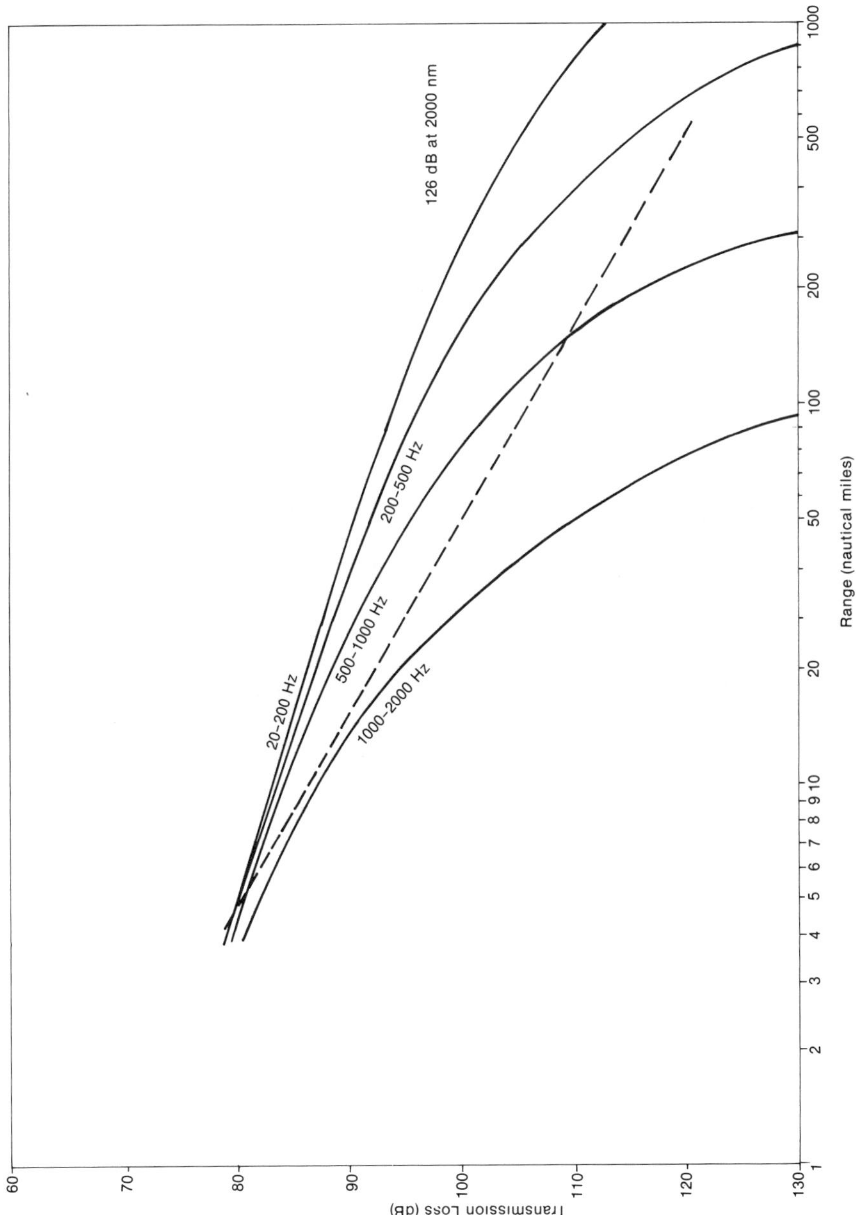

Figure A8–21. Transmission loss in deep water.

Source: Data on attenuation coefficient in subarctic Pacific from Kibblewhite et al., "Regional Dependence of Low Frequency Attenuation in the North Pacific Ocean," *Journal of the Acoustical Society of America* 61, no. 5 (May 1977), pp. 1169–1177.

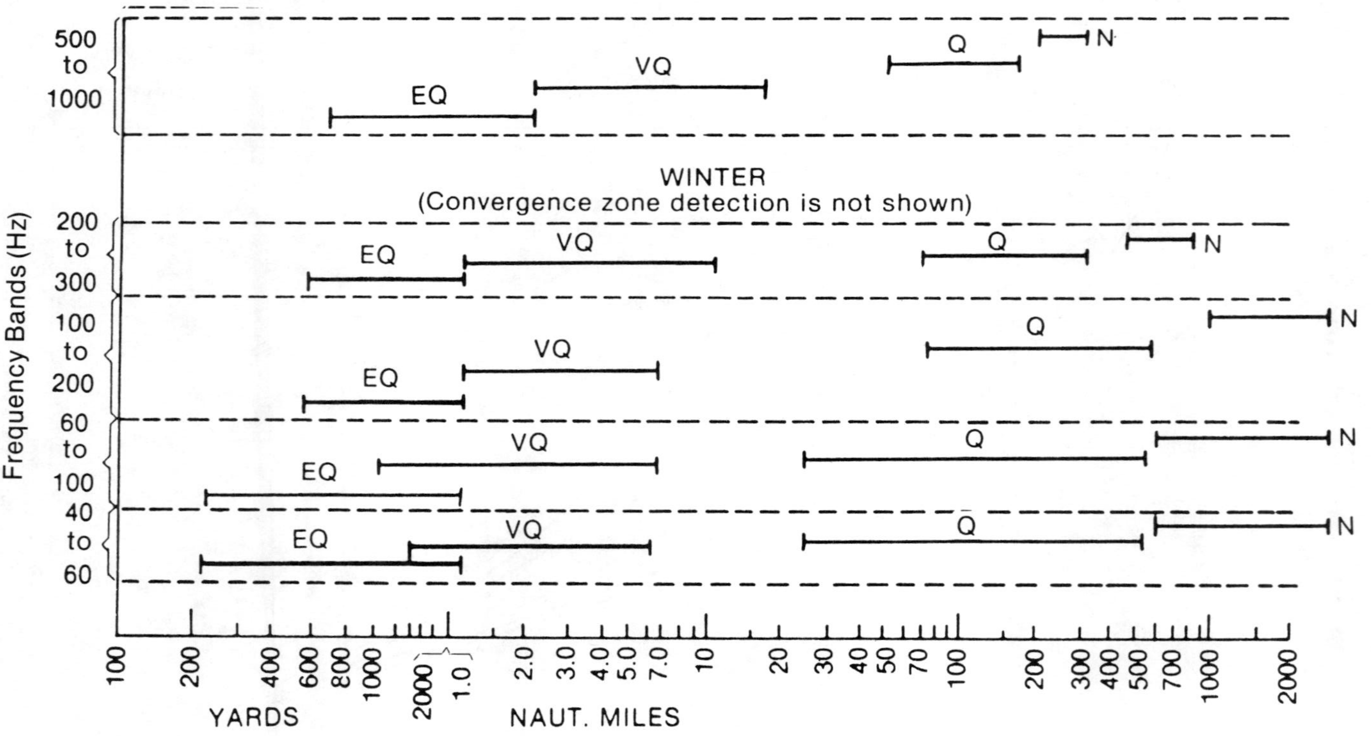
WINTER
(Convergence zone detection is not shown)
Frequency Bands (Hz)
500 to 1000
200 to 300
100 to 200
60 to 100
40 to 60
EQ
VQ
Q
N
100
200
400
600
800
1000
2000
1.0
2.0
3.0
4.0
5.0
7.0
10
20
30
40
50
70
100
200
300
400
500
700
1000
2000
YARDS
NAUT. MILES

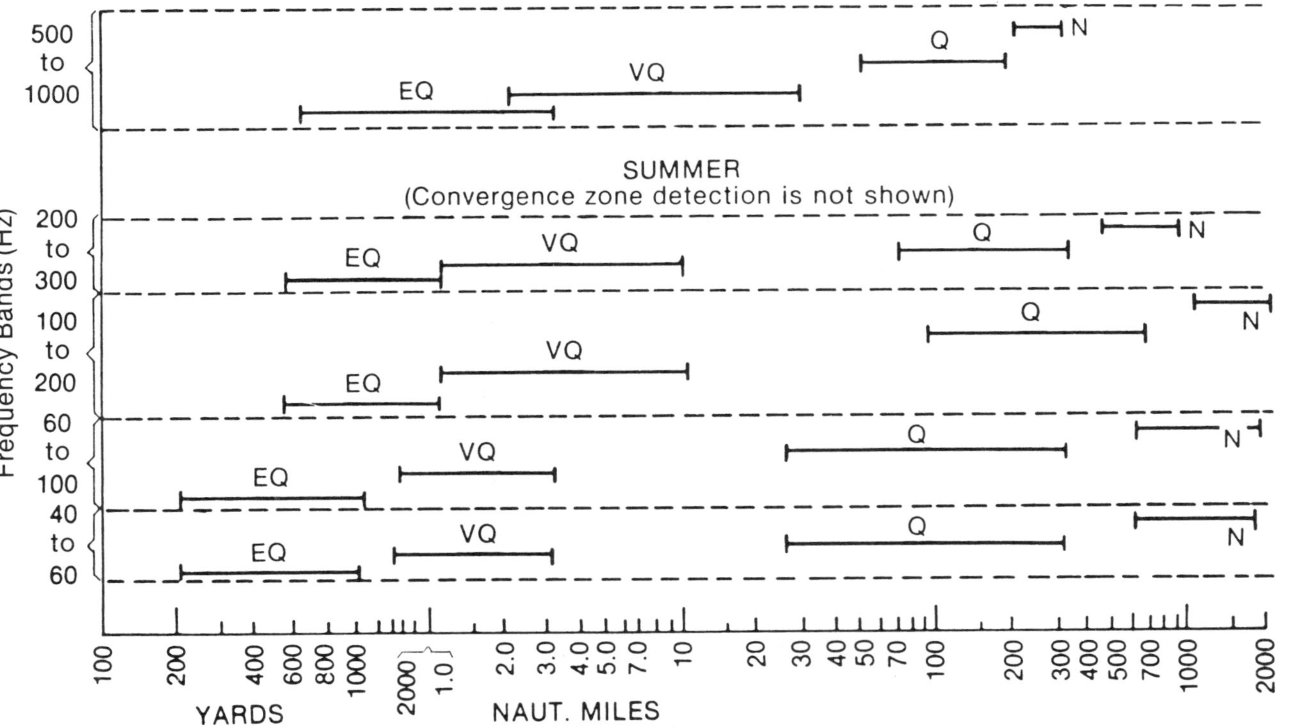

Figure A8–22. Estimated detection range of narrowband signals in the Norwegian Sea in conditions unfavorable (lower limit) and favorable (upper limit) to detection.

Note: Transmission loss data from figure A8–21. Source levels (dB re 1 micropa at 1 yd., 1 Hz band) are 100 dB (extremely quiet—EQ), 115 dB (very quiet—VQ), 140 dB (quiet—Q), and 160 dB (noisy—N). Signal processing parameters set at $p_{det} = 0.5$, $p_{fa} = 10^{-5}$.

ambient noise spectrum is dominated by shipping noise below 100 Hz and wind noise above, with a peak of 71 dB in the 60–100 Hz band.

Under these conditions, very quiet sources may be detected at ranges exceeding 16 miles at high frequencies, and noise sources can be detected at low frequencies throughout the entire basin. Basing the low-frequency transmission loss on an absorption rate of 0.028 dB/nm, quiet sources may be detected at 270 miles, and noisy sources at about 800 miles, still on the scale of the Norwegian Sea itself.

Summer

Under the influence of sea surface temperatures from 35° to 53° F, (1.6° to 11.7° C) the ice pack in the Greenland Sea retreats westward and northward toward Greenland and the Arctic, leaving most of the Norwegian-Greenland basin ice free. Winds generally come from the east and are stronger in the northern part of the Norwegian Sea. The cloud cover is unusually dense, amounting to 75 percent or greater coverage 8 days out of 10. Superstructure icing is only a threat near the ice pack and in the far north, and even then is rare. The wave climate is considerably milder than it is in winter: 12-foot swell is observed less than 10 percent of the time, and seas higher than 5 feet are observed 10 to 20 percent of the time. Conditions in the GIUK gap, however, are somewhat more intimidating. Whales are found in greatest numbers within a few hundred miles of the Norwegian coast, where they may number 24 per 1,000 nm^2. In the western Norwegian Sea and in the Greenland Sea, there are typically 9 whales per 1,000 nm^2. Rain falls 20 percent of the time.

The warmer surface temperatures require greater water depth for the formation of convergence zones. Convergence zones are expected to exist through much of the Norwegian Sea, but in general the conditions are not as favorable as they are in winter, and many areas that exhibit convergence zone behavior in winter may not in summer.

Worst-Case Detection. Wind speeds exceed 22 knots 25 percent of the time, and moderate shipping levels are assumed. In addition, heavy rain is assumed to be falling. The ambient noise spectrum is dominated by shipping noise below 100 Hz and by rain/wind noise above that frequency. Array gain is 20 dB, detection threshold -12 dB.

Detection range is similar to that of winter conditions, owing to the similarity in wind, rain, and shipping assumptions. However, the higher surface temperatures in the summer may alter the transmission characteristics; in particular, the sound channel is more nearly depth limited, and bottom losses may well be higher. Detection range against a quiet source is 90 miles, and against a noisy source, over 1,000 miles. Using the higher absorption loss (0.028 dB/nm) yields 74 nm and 460 nm, respectively.

Best-Case Detection. Wind speeds are less than 7 knots 25 percent of the time and shipping is assumed to be light. No rain is falling. Array gain is 20 dB, detection threshold -16 dB.

Extremely quiet sources (100 dB) may be detected at 3 miles at high frequencies. Detection range against quiet sources may be 670 miles (320 miles if the absorption is 0.028 dB/nm). As in the wintertime case, noisy sources may be detectable basin-wide.

Acoustic Detection: General Conclusions and Tactical Considerations

Passive detection range is a key tactical parameter in submarine warfare. It determines the rate at which targets can be found in a random search, the range at which a covert trail can be maintained, and the distance at which an attacker can begin to set up a fire control solution for a weapon launch.

Two system parameters must be given in order to define detection range unambiguously: probability of detection and probability of false alarm, both associated with detection threshold. In these calculations, the probability of detection was set at 0.5, and the probability of false alarm was set at 10^{-5}. One must be precise about the conditions that must be satisfied in order to claim a "detection." For example, sound transmission often occurs in surges and fades, and a signature detected occasionally in a surge may not be a sufficiently reliable contact on which to take action.

There is an important distinction between a detection and a classification. The former requires only that some sound energy that is recognizable as coming from a ship be detected. By performing narrowband processing on many frequencies over a wide band, the detection system will find the source spectral component with the highest signature-to-noise ratio. However, that single tonal may not yield sufficient tactical information, and the searcher may have to close on the target in order to obtain more information about the source spectrum. Consider an example set in the southern Barents Sea, under generally poor conditions for detection. A hypothetical target source spectrum contains three 1-Hz-wide tonals: 50 Hz, 80 Hz, and 150 Hz, each of which is 140 dB re 1 micropascal at 1 yard. This corresponds to a moderately quiet submarine. The 150 Hz tone can be detected at 22 miles, but in order to detect all three, the range must be reduced to 12 miles. Thus the criterion for detection depends on how much spectral information is required. Classification of the target via its spectral composition is sometimes considered a second phase of ASW operations after detection, but there is no clear division between the two. The amount of information required to classify a target depends on the spectrum itself and on the degree of classification required to make a tactical decision.

The latter is closely related to the rules of engagement that govern the general operations of the individual attack submarine. If the SSN is operating alone, in a geographic area from which all friendly forces are known or presumed to be absent, then the rule of engagement might be to destroy anything, subject only to the commander's assessment of the value of the target and the risk to the SSN. In this case, relatively little information about the target spectra may be needed. If the rule is to destroy only submarines, and only those of a particular class, then the amount of information needed may be considerably greater. In terms of detection, this may well mean that the range at which a legitimate target can be classified and distinguished from a decoy or from a friendly submarine may be considerably less than the initial detection range against that target. Of course, if the target is itself listening for hostile vessels, then the possibility exists that the target may counterdetect (but not classify) the searcher at the closer range. In general, it might be expected that the level of information obtained at closer range would come in the following order:

Ship type and operating condition: This would be based on blade rate tonals or main turbine or gear tonals. This would also indicate speed.

Nationality and class: This would depend on machinery noises particular to that class; for example, particular combinations of motor and pump sounds would be associated with the cooling system.

Particular unit: Although it would probably never be necessary to determine this, it would depend on the particular distribution of harmonics and secondary vibrations or propeller singing. Except for the latter, these sounds are generally much lower than the fundamental tonals.

In order to launch a weapon, an attack submarine may well have to approach target closer than the initial detection range. For example, the maximum range of the US Mk 48 ASW torpedo is about 25 miles (although the effective range is about half that), and assuming that a modern US submarine can obtain nearly maximum array and processor gains, under many conditions, tonals above 145 dB can be detected at this range or beyond. Moreover, the distance between a searcher and a target may have to be closed in order to determine the actual range to the target. Passive ranging accuracy increases at shorter ranges. Against louder targets, therefore, fire control and weapon range will limit the standoff range under many circumstances. Against quiet sources (total acoustic output on the order of 140 dB or less) local conditions will determine whether the target can be detected inside or outside weapon range. Against very quiet sources (115 dB) detection range will under most circumstances be less than weapon range, and against extremely quiet sources (100 dB) detection range is always less (usually by a considerable amount) than weapon range.

Counterdetection, that is, detection of the searcher by the target, may be an important tactical consideration. Consider a case in which a searcher detecting a target has a figure of merit of 100 dB, and the target has a FOM against the searcher of 85 dB. The differential would be due to higher source level of the target and less effective sonar systems on the target. Using a typical transmission loss curve in deep water at 300 Hz, this means the detection range of the searcher against the target is about 150 miles, but the target may detect the searcher only at 15 miles. As the searcher moves within weapon range, the second, and perhaps first convergence zones (at 60 and 30 miles) surrounding the searcher will pass over the target, boosting the received signal there by as much as 15 dB, and therefore eliminating (albeit for a short period of time) the acoustic advantage of the searcher and permitting a brief counterdetection by the target. Although such a convergence zone gain would only last for a few minutes due to the narrowness of the zones, it would allow sufficient integration time to make a detection and sufficient information to take countermeasures.

The directionality of low-frequency noise also complicates tactics. Consider a searcher detecting a target in the North Pacific, with the two submarines on a north-south line, the target to the north of the searcher. Data from the region northeast of Hawaii[51] indicates that an array pointed north, toward the shipping route between North America and Japan, detects a 10 dB higher noise level than an array pointed south. This gives the target a "free" 10 dB advantage over what it would have in isotropic noise.[52]

One could not list all the tactical situations that are possible, but this small sample should point up a main conclusion: the complexity and variability of the acoustic environment governs much of submarine and antisubmarine warfare tactics, and a key determinant of the system capability is the expertise and level of training of the officers and crews. Although the analysis detection capability is based on signature-to-noise ratios and decibels, the probability of detecting a particular source in the ocean also depends heavily on how well the detection gear is used, how alert the sonar operator is, how quiet the search platform is, and so forth.

The following sections contain some generalizations about passive detection based on the analysis. These can be categorized as deterministic statements, such as: detection range against loud targets is less in shallow water than in deep water; or as statements about inherent uncertainties in detection range due to uncertainties in the physical environment. Both types of generalization have important implications for tactics, on the level of the single engagement and at the level of an entire campaign. The focus in this study is on strategic submarine security, and since only the Soviet missile submarines are likely to be vulnerable to attrition, the campaign of interest is that of US attack submarines against Soviet SSBNs and the forces defending them. However, these conclusions are stated in general terms and have wider applicability.

Deterministic Results: General Trends

The figure of merit determines the amount of transmission loss that can be permitted and still allow detection to occur, and it therefore determines the range. Since the predicted FOM can change according to the assumptions made about ambient noise, source level, and sonar system parameters, it is helpful to begin with an analysis of the sensitivity of predicted range to change in the FOM. Essentially, this is the first derivative of the transmission loss curve, with transmission loss as the independent variable. In order to eliminate the specific range dependency of the result, the derivative is divided by range. This gives the percentage change in detection range for a 1 dB change in the FOM, at a specified range. The values are given in table A8-6.

The sensitivity of detection range to a 1 dB change in FOM tends, in all cases, to have a maximum at relatively short range—on the order of 10 miles—and then to decrease steadily with increasing range. At long range, the transmission loss exhibits an effective cutoff, which for purposes of this study is defined as the range where a 1 dB increase in FOM increases range by 2 percent or less. The maximum sensitivity at short range is typically a 10–20 percent increase in range with a 1 dB increase in FOM. It is useful to examine some of the general results under different circumstances.

Shallow water, with and without ice, has a strong cutoff between 10 and 25 miles for very low frequencies below 30 Hz and for high frequencies above 2,000 Hz. In the 40–1,000 Hz band, the sensitivity at 2 miles is about 10 percent per decibel, and at 10 miles 12–16 percent per decibel. Beyond 50 miles, transmission loss begins to increase more rapidly.

In the central Arctic, the cutoff range steadily decreases with frequency above 20 Hz, from over 1,000 nm at that frequency to 50 miles at 1,600 Hz. In addition, the maximum sensitivity at short range decreases with frequency from 21 percent per decibel at 20 Hz to 10 percent per decibel at 1,600 Hz.

In moderately deep water such as the Norwegian Sea and in deep water such as the North Pacific, detection range is most sensitive to change in the FOM. In the 20–500 Hz band, detection range will vary by 25 percent per decibel at 10 miles range. Even at longer ranges, in the lower part of that band, the sensitivity is 20 percent per decibel. For example, at 100 miles, a 3 dB change in the FOM changes the detection range by 60 miles! In practice, convergence zone phenomena would govern the maximum detection range to a large extent.

A direct result of the decrease in relative sensitivity with range is that the relative uncertainty in detection range against noisy targets is considerably less than it is against extremely quiet targets. In some cases, the difference between worst-case and best-case detection range against a noisy target is only a factor of 2, and against an extremely quiet target, a factor of 20. Of course in absolute terms the uncertainty in the first case is hundreds of miles, and in the second,

Table A8–6
Relative change in detection range due to a 1 dB change in the figure of merit

Shallow Ice-covered Waters (figure A8–14)	*Range (nm)*						
	2	*10*	*50*	*100*	*200*	*500*	*1,000*
10–40 Hz	cutoff at 25 miles						
40–1,000 Hz	0.08	0.16	0.05				
Shallow Open Water (figure A8–16)	*Range (nm)*						
	2	*10*	*50*	*100*	*200*	*500*	*1,000*
100–200 Hz	0.10	0.12	0.07	0.04			
>400 Hz	0.10	0.08	0.02				
Central Arctic Pack Ice (figure A8–13)	*Range (nm)*						
	2	*10*	*50*	*100*	*200*	*500*	*1,000*
20 Hz	0.18	0.21	0.19	0.14	0.11	0.07	0.04
100 Hz	0.18	0.15	0.09	0.05	0.03		
600 Hz	0.13	0.09	0.04	0.02			
1,600 Hz	0.10	0.07	0.02				
Deep Open Water (figure A8–21)	*Range (nm)*						
	2	*10*	*50*	*100*	*200*	*500*	*1,000*
20–200 Hz	0.18	0.27	0.23	0.19	0.16	0.11	0.07
200–500 Hz	0.18	0.25	0.18	0.14	0.10	0.05	0.03
500–1,000 Hz	0.16	0.18	0.11	0.07	0.04		

only a few miles. Detection range against louder targets often reaches into the cutoff region of transmission and is therefore relatively insensitive to the FOM.

The US Navy, prompted by its frustrating experience with trying to detect the low-level machinery noise of the Soviet Victor III, is putting increased emphasis on detecting lower-frequency sounds, such as propeller blade noise.[53] The acoustic frequency range of the blade-rate tonal at non- or minimally cavitating conditions would be on the order of 5–50 Hz. These frequencies propagate very well in deep waters such as the Norwegian Sea, the Atlantic, and the Pacific. In shallow water, however, there is some evidence that very low frequencies are attenuated more rapidly. Efforts to detect the blade-rate tonals of the Victor III would be much more difficult in the Barents Sea, the Arctic marginal seas, and the Sea of Okhotsk, precisely those areas where US submarines would have to hunt Soviet SSBNs.

As we have seen, there is usually an optimum frequency at which detection range is a maximum for a source of a given spectrum level. It is important to distinguish between three basic "optimum" frequencies. The frequency at which transmission loss is minimized is one kind of optimum. It has been shown that over relatively homogeneous shallow water channels, the minimum-loss frequency varies (roughly linearly) from about 100 Hz in 600 feet of water down to 30 Hz in 1,200 feet of water.[54] When ambient noise is included, then the criterion for optimality is maximum signature-to-noise ratio at a receiver, and the optimum frequency for long-range detection tends to be shifted up in frequency to the 100–300 Hz band in shallow and deep water, mostly due to the concentration of shipping noise at lower frequencies. However, this is not a realistic criterion yet because the distribution of source energy with frequency is not included. At this point, one can go no further since source spectra from modern submarines are highly classified. The best that can be done is to use typical machinery spectra, such as the turbine generator spectrum shown in figure A6–1 in appendix 6 to infer the general frequency range of tonals. The relative amplitudes of the tonals measured directly from machinery do *not* necessarily indicate the relative amplitudes of the tonals transmitted to the water, since the machine sits on racks and on vibration mounts that filter the spectrum prior to its transmission to the sea. Even without the source spectra, one can see from the estimates of detection range that the frequency at which detection range is maximized does not change by much more than a factor of three when environmental and system parameters are used. In practical applications, knowledge of the optimum frequency for long-range detection may not matter too much since sonar displays typically show (for a single beam) an entire set of adjacent narrowband responses for frequencies over wideband, the so-called waterfall display. The sonar operator therefore sees the true optimum frequency when a source is first detected.

Short-range detection against extremely quiet and very quiet sources is unlike longer-range detection in that the optimum frequency based on transmission loss and ambient noise is at high frequencies, often above 1,000 Hz. This is true because at short ranges (less than 15 miles), sound absorption is not a strong effect (except at very high frequencies) while ambient noise usually drops rapidly at higher frequencies. This results in relatively high signature-to-noise ratios at these higher frequencies and therefore in longer detection range. When ambient noise does not fall off quickly at higher frequencies, as is true under rain noises, higher frequencies are less conducive to detection. The importance of high-frequency narrowband detection probably applies only to the quietest submarine classes, such as the Ohio and perhaps the improved SSN-688 class. For example, a 115 dB source in the Pacific Ocean can be detected approximately 10 times as far at 1,000 Hz as it can be at 40 Hz. This would be an important concern for SSBN security.

Inherent Uncertainty in the Results

Sources of uncertainty in an estimate of acoustic detection range are related to ambient noise, transmission loss, and source level. More definite would be the system parameters, array gain and detection threshold, though as we have seen, variable noise statistics and coherence characteristics may introduce uncertainty even there. There are methods of reducing the uncertainties, such as averaging the detection response of a sonar over a long period to eliminate noise surges and signature fades.

The typical uncertainty found here is about plus or minus 12 dB, but it appears that most of this uncertainty is a result of a lack of information about the state of the ocean. In an actual tactical situation, the level of uncertainty is probably less because real-time methods of determining the ambient conditions are available. In advanced planning, however, considerable uncertainty would have to be built into predictions.

Another type of uncertainty is related to human activities. Noise levels may change radically in wartime over what they are measured to be in peacetime. For example, in the Soviet Arctic, from July through December, over 3 million tons of shipping annually pass from Murmansk through the southern Barents Sea into the Kara Sea via Proliv Karskiye Vorota south of Novaya Zemlya, and on into the major river systems of Siberia.[55] This might well become a strategically important wartime sea route for the transport of material between the western and eastern Soviet Union, and shipping noise levels would increase. In the shallow marginal seas, the routing of such ships would be a critical factor in local noise levels, due to the screening effect. In addition, noisemakers in the form of broadband maskers or narrowband simulators might significantly alter the acoustic environment in local areas.

Narrowband signature transmission under ice can be very stable,[56] and underice noise can be relatively low in the absence of cracking and ridge formation. Standard error in the Arctic transmission loss data used in this study ranges from 6 to 9 dB, but given the recent surge of interest in the Arctic, that uncertainty is likely to decrease. Ice ridging, thought to be the dominant noise source in the central Arctic ice[57] depends on local and remote meteorological conditions and on the strength of the ice.

Notes

1. Paul E. Lydolph, *Climates of the Soviet Union* (New York: Elsevier, 1977).
2. Adm. James D. Watkins, SASC, FY 1985, part 8, p. 3888.
3. J. M. Meserve, *US Navy Marine Climatic Atlas of the World,* vol. 1, *North Atlantic* (Washington, DC: US Office of Naval Operations, 1955), NAVAER 50-1C-528.
4. Yie-Ming Chen, "Underwater Acoustic Ambient Noise in the Arctic" (Master's thesis, MIT, 1982), p. 33.
5. *Oceanographic Atlas of the Polar Seas,* part 2, *Arctic* (NAVOCEANO, pub. no. 705, 1970), p. 3.

6. Ibid., pp. 3–7.
7. Ibid., p. 7.
8. Ibid., p. 40.
9. Ibid., p. 39.
10. Ibid., p. 44.
11. Ibid., p. 45.
12. Ibid.
13. Ibid.
14. Peter Wadhams, "Sea-ice Topography of the Arctic Ocean in the Region 70 degrees West to 25 degrees East," *Phil. Trans. Roy. Soc. London* srs A, vol. 302, 1981, pp. 45–85.
15. Peter Wadhams, "Arctic Sea Ice Morphology and Its Measurement," in *Arctic Technology and Policy,* ed. Ira Dyer and Chryssostomos Chryssostomidis (New York: Hemisphere Publishing, 1984), pp. 179–195.
16. W. J. Campbell et al., "Arctic Sea Ice Variations from Time Lapse Passive Microwave Imagery," *Boundary Layer Meteorology* 18, 1980, pp. 99–106.
17. *Oceanographic Atlas,* part 2, *Arctic,* p. 46.
18. Ibid.
19. Ibid.
20. Ibid., p. 49.
21. Ibid., p. 91.
22. *MX Missile Basing* (Washington, DC: Office of Technology Assessment, 1981), p. 185.
23. N. A. Mackintosh, *The Stocks of Whales* (Bath, England: Coward and Garrish, Ltd., 1965), pp. 58, 83, 96.
24. The choice of confidence interval is arbitrary. Upper and lower 5 percent bounds are more common, but are not justified in this analysis for lack of information in the "tails" of the distributions.
25. Capt. Karl F. Poehlman, USN, *Marine Geography of the Sea of Okhotsk* (Washington, DC: US Navy Hydrographic Office Pub. no. 578, 1965), p. 40.
26. *Oceanographic Atlas of the Polar Seas,* part 2, *Arctic,* p. 115.
27. Ronald Verrall, "Acoustic Transmission Losses and Ambient Noise in Parry Channel," in *The Question of Sound from Icebreaker Operations,* ed. N. Merle Peterson (British Columbia: Western Ecological Services Ltd., Arctic Pilot Project, Petro-Canada, 1981), pp. 220–231.
28. Norman Polmar, *Guide to the Soviet Navy,* 3rd ed. (Annapolis: Naval Institute Press, 1983), p. 401.
29. O. I. Diachok, "Recent Advances in Arctic Hydroacoustics," *Naval Research Reviews* 29:5, May 1976, pp. 48–63.
30. R. S. Thomas, J. C. Moldon, and J. M. Moss, "Shallow Water Acoustics Related to Signal Processing," in *Signal Processing,* ed. J. W. R. Griffiths, P. L. Stocklin, and C. Van Schooneveld, Proceedings of the NATO Advanced Study Institute (London: Academic Press, 1973), pp. 281–298.
31. Ibid., p. 286.
32. W. A. Kuperman and F. Ingenito, "Spatial Correlation of Surface-generated Noise in a Stratified Ocean," *Journal of The American Acoustical Society* 67, June 1980, pp. 1988–1998.

33. Diachok, "Recent Advances," pp. 50, 51.

34. Ibid., p. 52.

35. The reader will recall that in the best detection conditions (low wind speed), shipping noise was at least a major component throughout the entire spectrum.

36. H. W. Marsh and M. Schulkin, "Shallow Water Transmission," *JASA* 34, 1962, p. 863.

37. Verrall, "Acoustic Transmission Losses," pp. 220–231.

38. *Oceanographic Atlas of the Polar Seas,* part 2, *Arctic,* pp. 101, 106.

39. Verrall, "Acoustic Transmission Losses," fig. 4, 6.

40. Ibid., fig. 4, 5. In both cases the source and receiver depths were at 300 feet, typical of submarine operation depths.

41. Ibid., fig. 4, 7.

42. Robert J. Urick, *Sound Propagation in the Sea* (Los Altos, Calif.: Peninsula Publishing, 1982), pp. 7–16.

43. Urick, *Principles,* p. 156.

44. Beau M. Buck, Polar Research Lab, Inc., personal communication, November 1986.

45. Ibid.

46. Susan L. Bales, "Designing Ships to the Natural Environment," *Naval Engineers Journal,* March 1983, pp. 31–40.

47. *Oceanographic Atlas of the Polar Seas,* part 2, *Arctic,* p. 91.

48. Gordon Wenz, "Acoustic Ambient Noise in the Ocean," *JASA* 34:12, December 1962, pp. 1936–1956.

49. *Oceanographic Atlas of the Polar Seas,* part 2, *Arctic,* p. 116.

50. Comparison with observations at 2,000 Hz show good agreement. *Naval Operations Analysis* (Annapolis: Naval Institute Press, 1977), p. 183.

51. R. A. Wagstaff and J. W. Aitkenhead, "Horizontal Directionality of Ambient Noise in the SOFAR Channel in the Northeast Pacific Ocean," *JASA* 26, 1976, p. 279.

52. If towed arrays are used by both sides, this effect is reduced or eliminated, since the arrays pull in noise from both sides and average it.

53. Adm. James D. Watkins, SASC, FY 1985, part 8, p. 3889.

54. F. B. Jensen and W. A. Kuperman, "Optimum Frequency of Propagation in Shallow Water Environments," *JASA* 73:3, March 1983, pp. 813–819.

55. *Times Atlas of the Oceans,* ed. Alistair Couper (New York: Van Nostrand-Reinhold, 1983).

56. Peter N. Mikhalevsky, "Characteristics of CW Signals Propagated under the Ice in the Arctic," *JASA* 70:6, December 1981, pp. 1717–1722.

57. Robert S. Pritchard, "Arctic Ocean Background Noise Caused by Ridging of Sea Ice," *JASA* 75:2, February 1984, pp. 419–427.

Glossary

Active sonar: a system that detects underwater objects by emitting a pulse of sound and receiving the sound reflected off them. Active sonar can determine the range to object by measuring the travel time of the sound pulse.

Ambient noise: the total of all oceanic noise from human activities and natural causes.

Array gain: the increase in signal-to-noise ratio of sound detected by a sonar system due to the directionality of the receiving array.

Backscattering: the process by which light or sound is returned back from an interaction with many small particles or from a rough surface.

Beamwidth: the angle within which the sensitivity of a sonar array is maximum. Usually the angle is defined by the points at which the sensitivity falls to half its maximum value.

Bernoulli hump: a deflection of the water surface directly above a shallow, rapidly moving submarine.

Bioluminescence: light generated by living organisms.

Bottom bounce: a mode of active or passive sonar detection in which the sound is reflected off the bottom at least once in its path between the receiver and the target.

Broadband: pertaining to a signal which is distributed over a wide, continuous frequency band.

Brunt-Väisälä Period (frequency): the natural period (or frequency) of oscillation of a parcel of water in a vertical density gradient.

Cavitation: the formation of gas bubbles on an underwater surface, such as a propeller, due to a local drop in pressure.

Convergence zone: a zone ringing a shallow underwater sound source within which the intensity of the sound is anomalously high due to the focussing of sound rays in the deep sound channel. Convergence zones typically exist in deep water with heated surface layers, and occur at intervals of 25–35 miles from the source.

Decibel (dB): ten times the logarithm (base ten) of a ratio. The decibel is a convenient notation for ratios that vary over several orders of magnitude.

Deep sound channel (SOFAR channel): an ocean acoustic phenomenon created by maximum sound speed at the surface due to high temperatures, and maximum sound speed at great depths due to high pressures. Because sound tends to refract toward lower sound speeds, it will oscillate around the axis of minimum sound speed at a depth on the order of 3,000 feet.

Detection threshold: a signal-to-noise ratio at which a sound will be detected in noise with a given probability of false alarm and probability of detection.

Displacement: the volume of water displaced by a ship, or the weight of that volume of seawater. There are several definitions of displacement:

normal surface displacement: the volume (or equivalent weight of seawater) of the submarine when completely ready, carrying all necessary stores, trim ballast, and crew members. Equal to the constant buoyant volume of the submarine. Does not include the volume of the free-flooding areas.

submerged displacement: normal displacement plus the volume (or equivalent weight of seawater) in the main ballast tanks. Does not include the volume of the free-flooding areas.

full submerged displacement: submerged displacement plus the volume (or equivalent weight of seawater) in the free-flooding areas.

Dunking sonar: an active sonar system in which small transducers are lowered by cable into the water from a helicopter or surface ship.

Fast fourier transform (FFT): a method of computing the fourier transform of a signal. In signal processing the FFT is often used to compute the energy spectrum of a signal.

Figure of merit (FOM): a measure of the amount of transmission loss that will yield a detection by a passive sonar, given the probabilities of detection and false alarm and other system and environmental parameters.

Gaussian statistics: the so-called "normal" statistical distribution in the sample of a random variable. The distribution of a random variable is often assumed to be gaussian if it is itself the sum of a large number of other random variables of unknown distribution.

Hertz: one cycle per second.

Hydrophone: an underwater microphone used in sonar systems to convert acoustic pressure fluctuations into electrical signals.

Indiscretion rate: the fraction of its total operating time that a diesel-electric submarine must reveal its presence by running diesel engines.

Internal wave: an oscillation of the layers of varying density in the ocean.

Isotropic noise: noise which has the same intensity and statistics in all directions.

Jamming: the use of acoustic signals to disrupt the opponent's sonar. Counters to passive sonar include broadband jamming using continuous or impulsive generation of ambient noise to mask submarine noise. False targets may be created by submarine noise simulators. Active sonars may also be jammed by repeat-back devices that return the sonar pulse in a way that makes the target appear farther away than it actually is.

Kelvin wave: the surface wave pattern created by a moving vessel.

LIDAR: a system for locating objects by illuminating them with a pulse of laser light and measuring the travel time of the light reflected or scattered back to a receiver.

Marginal sea (ice zone): the region in the Arctic, particularly off the coast of the Soviet Union, defined by relatively shallow water and the periodic presence of sea ice.

Narrowband: pertaining to a signal which is confined to a set of very narrow (on the order of one Hz or less) frequency bands.

Noise level: the level of ambient noise measured at the sonar array, usually given in dB relative to 1 microPascal in a 1 Hz band.

Passive sonar: a system that detects underwater objects by listening for sounds that are emitted by them. Most passive sonars determine only the direction to a target from a single point.

Source level: the total sound spectrum radiated by a submarine, usually given in dB relative to 1 microPascal at a distance of 1 yard in a 1 Hz band.

Spherical spreading: the uniform geometric spreading of a sound wave in unbounded space, characterized by a loss of intensity as a function of the square of the distance.

SSBN: nuclear powered ballistic missile submarine, literally "submersible ship, ballistic, nuclear." **SSB** is a nonnuclear powered ballistic missile submarine.

SSGN: nuclear powered cruise missile submarine. **SSG** is a nonnuclear powered cruise missile submarine.

SSN: nuclear powered attack submarine. **SS** is a nonnuclear powered attack submarine.

Thermocline: a layer of the ocean in which there is a significant temperature change over depth.

Total radiated sound: the total intensity of sound radiated by a source at all frequencies.

Transmission loss: the ratio of signal intensity measured at a given distance to the intensity measured one yard from the source.

Index

About the Author

Tom Stefanick is currently at the House Armed Services Committee under the Science, Arms Control, and National Security Fellowship awarded by the American Association for the Advancement of Science (AAAS). He was formerly Research Associate for Naval Policy at the Federation of American Scientists in Washington, D.C. He has written on naval matters for several publications, including *Arms Control Today* and the *Christian Science Monitor*. Previously he worked on superpower naval policies at the Institute for Defense and Disarmament Studies in Massachusetts. He holds bachelor's and master's degrees from the Massachusetts Institute of Technology in the areas of coastal oceanography and systems analysis, and has participated in experimental work at the Woods Hole Oceanographic Institution.

About the Institute

Randall Forsberg
Executive Director
Institute for Defense & Disarmament Studies

The Institute for Defense and Disarmament Studies approaches the problem of arms reductions differently from many other organizations. The Institute's work is based on the view that until *the risk of conventional war* is greatly reduced, it will probably continue to prove impossible to make deep cuts in nuclear arms.

The role of most nuclear weapons has always been to deter conventional war. By posing a risk of escalation from a conventional war to a nuclear war, nuclear weapons make the big powers avoid conventional war with each other. Military planners believe that deep cuts in nuclear arms would increase the risk of a conventional war between East and West, which would be terrible in itself and could lead to nuclear war. This view has blocked nuclear reductions for 30 years.

The Institute's staff analyze long-term trends and project future developments that show the need to reduce the risk of conventional war and suggest safe ways to do so. The Institute conducts three kinds of research not performed elsewhere. First, researchers compile comprehensive, detailed, regularly updated data on world military forces, government arms control talks, and nongovernmental peace efforts. The World Weapon Database, covering all major weapons produced since 1945, compiles all data published in major sources. The monthly *Arms Control Reporter* gives a day-by-day chronology of the positions of all countries in all 35 ongoing arms control talks. The annual *Peace Resource Book* surveys all US national and local peace groups (5,700 groups) and recent literature on war and peace (1,000 publications since 1980).

Second, the weapon and arms control databases make it possible for Institute researchers to correct misleading views of Soviet and Western military strengths, to demonstrate that the role of most nuclear weapons has always been to deter conventional war, and to study the uses of conventional force that create pressure to perpetuate nuclear deterrence of conventional war. The weapon and arms control data also permit Institute scholars to project world nuclear and conventional forces 10–20 years in the future; to assess the impact of proposed arms control measures on future forces; and to show that most government proposals, if implemented, would not reverse the arms race.

Finally, Institute staff members will develop long-term global military policy alternatives that lead to greatly reduced nuclear and conventional arms and military spending. These illustrative policy alternatives should stimulate many scholars, analysts, and activists to explore their own variations and ultimately create an environment in which gradual steps toward fundamental change are possible.

The results of the Institute's work appear not only in forms intended for professional scholars, but also in forms intended for journalists, educators, and the concerned layperson. In 1987, for example, the Institute will publish the first edition of *World Military Forces and Alternatives,* a 100-page illustrated survey. Since March 1985 the Institute has published a popular newsletter, *Defense and Disarmament News,* which combines news and analysis on the peace movement, arms control talks, and the military. A list of other publications follows.

IDDS Publications

Books, Periodicals, and Reference Works

Peace Resource Book 1986. E. Bernstein et al. Cambridge, Mass.: Ballinger Publishing Co., 1985. 425pp. $14.95 paper. Out of print.

Soviet Missiles. B. Wright. Lexington, Mass.: Lexington Books, 1986. World Weapon Database, vol. 1.

Soviet Military Aircraft. N. Crawford. Lexington, Mass.: Lexington Books, forthcoming 1987. World Weapon Database, vol. 2.

Strategic Antisubmarine Warfare and Naval Strategy. T. Stefanick. Lexington, Mass.: Lexington Books, 1987. 416pp. $49.00 (tent.).

Defense & Disarmament News. Bimonthly coverage of the military, arms control, and the peace movement. C. Conetta, ed. Annual subscription $25.

Arms Control Reporter. Monthly looseleaf chronology of negotiations, proposals, and treaties. C. Hardenbergh, ed. From January 1982. Annual subscription $295 ($310 overseas); sample issue $5 ($10 overseas). Reduced rates for students and local peace groups.

Index of Soviet and Chinese Military Affairs in Annual US Defense Department Reports 1969–1983. B. Wright. 1983. 74pp. $6.

Reprints

"Parallel Cuts in Nuclear and Conventional Forces." R. Forsberg. *Bulletin of the Atomic Scientists,* August 1985. 4pp. $.50.

"A Bilateral Freeze as an Arms Control Objective." R. Forsberg. Testimony before the Committee on Foreign Affairs, US House of Representatives, 21 June 1984. 3pp. $.50.

"The Freeze and Beyond: Confining the Military to Defense as a Route to Disarmament." R. Forsberg. *World Policy* 1:2, 1984. 36pp. 1–99 copies, $1 each; $35 per hundred.

"Women and Military Policy-Making." R. Forsberg. *Barnard Alumnae Magazine,* Winter 1984. 3pp. $.50.

"Verification: No Obstacle to Arms Control." K. Pieragostini. *Arms Control Today* 13:5, June 1983. 4pp. $.50.

"What About a Nuclear Freeze?" R. Forsberg. *Social Education* 47:7, November–December 1983. Based on testimony before the Committee on Foreign Affairs, US House of Representatives, 17 February 1983. 2pp. $.50.

"Stalin's Postwar Army Reappraised." M. Evangelista. *International Security* 7:3, Winter 1982–83. 28pp. $2.

"RECOVERing Verification." K. Pieragostini. *Arms Control Today* 12:11, December 1982. 2pp. $.50.

"A Bilateral Nuclear-Weapon Freeze." R. Forsberg. *Scientific American* 247:5, November 1982. 10pp. $.50.

" 'START' Proposal Invites a Continued Arms Race." R. Forsberg. Hearings before the Subcommittee on International Security and Scientific Affairs, US House of Representatives, 11 May 1982. 12pp. $1.

"Information on Present Nuclear Arsenals." [R. Forsberg] in *Nuclear Weapons: Report of the UN Secretary General.* Brookline, Mass.: Autumn Press, 1981. 2 pp. $.50.

"Soviet Civil Defense." M. Evangelista. *PSR Newsletter* 2:1, Summer 1981. 1p. $.50.

"Military R&D: A Worldwide Institution?" R. Forsberg. *Proceedings of the American Philosophical Society* 124:4, August 1980. 5pp. $.50.

Call to Halt the Nuclear Arms Race. [R. Forsberg, 1980.] Rev. 1982. 4pp. $.50.

Unless otherwise indicated, order from: IDDS, 2001 Beacon St., Brookline, Massachusetts 02146. 617/734-4216.